# Introduction

WRITERS HAVE BEEN PUTTING THEIR thoughts on paper for centuries. In the beginning, every copy of every book was handwritten. After the printing press was invented in the 1400s, publishers could produce books in larger quantities. Books became more widely available, but only the educated classes of society knew how to read. So books weren't huge sellers at the time.

As the centuries progressed, and individuals in all walks of life became educated, books became more and more popular.

At the same time, new technologies made it easier and cheaper to mass-produce books. First, it was the printing press. (In the United States, the first books were printed in the 1600s.) Later, writers started using typewriters and word processers. When desktop publishing was invented in the mid-1980s, anyone with a computer could suddenly

***Opposite*: For hundreds of years, readers have been thrilled, frightened, educated, and entertained by the books they read. The form that books take may change through the centuries, but as long as there are writers, there will be books and people who read them.**

design and produce books. Today, we have digital, Internet, and e-book technology.

With the invention of e-readers in the late 1990s, many people predicted the end of the book business as we knew it. **Devotees** of hardcovers and paperbacks feared the end of libraries and bookstores.

In previous generations, **technophobes** feared radio would be the death of the newspaper, TV would kill the movie industry, and the Internet would spell the end of television. None of these have come to pass just yet—nor has the death of the "real" book.

Over the centuries, books have helped little children fall asleep at night. They have kept soldiers sane on battlefields during wartime. And they have helped commuters pass the hours on trains, buses, and airplanes.

Books have reflected the politics, society, and culture in which we live. Printed stories have thrilled, entertained, educated, and frightened readers for generations. In one form or another, they will continue to do so. As long as there are books, there will be readers.

And as long as there are readers, there will also be best-seller lists to tell readers what other readers are reading.

Early twentieth-century best-seller lists simply tallied the top-selling books in local bookstores. Now, they also include online sales. Books that reach the top spots on best-seller lists become must-reads of the day. They are the books people talk about. They are often the books that are made into movies. And occasionally (hint: Harry Potter), they change the direction of cultural trends of the time.

ONE

# 1950s: Happy at Home, Safe from the Enemy Abroad

IN THE 1950S, AMERICAN SOCIETY SUFFERED what some might call an identity crisis.

On one hand was a sense of optimism. World War II (1939–1945) was over—and the good guys had won! After a decade of darkness, families had been reunited, and life had returned to normal. Men who fought overseas returned to their jobs. Women who worked during the war returned to homemaking. Couples raised large families, bought new cars, and moved to the suburbs.

A fabulous new invention—the television—changed the way Americans viewed their world. By the end of the decade, almost every home had one. TV sets bombarded viewers with advertisements for all the luxurious things they could now afford to buy.

The 1950s were a time of prosperity, renewal, and a return to the American Dream. Bubbling beneath the nation's optimism, though, was a new fear. World War II may have ended, but the Cold War had just begun. The Cold War wasn't an actual battle. It was mostly a power struggle between the **capitalist** United States and the **communist** Soviet Union.

Many American citizens feared that communists were out to destroy their peaceful existence. The possibility of nuclear war also threatened the American Dream. The US and the USSR each had atomic weapons capable of wiping the other off the map.

These conflicting realities of American life were reflected in the best-selling books of the decade.

## HAPPY AT HOME

When *Betty Crocker's Picture Cook Book* topped nonfiction best-seller lists in 1950, it marked the start of a homey trend in literature. It wasn't the first time a cookbook had reached best-seller status. That honor went to the *Boston Cooking School Cook Book*, which cracked annual top-ten book lists from 1924 to 1926. It would be a quarter century before another guide to cookery—Betty Crocker's—made the cut.

For the next thirteen years, books related to home and family were all the rage. And not just cookbooks. Gardening, decorating, and handyman how-tos sold like hotcakes, as did guides to improving your golf game, building a dream home, and raising children. Etiquette, advice, and flower-arranging handbooks also made best-seller lists.

Faith and religion, which figured prominently in the lives of mid-century Americans, also appeared on the wholesome reading lists of the 1950s. Inspirational books written by, and about, religious figures were popular through the decade.

One of the most noteworthy books of this genre was *The Power of Positive Thinking*. Written by Reverend Norman Vincent Peale in 1952, the book blended the author's interest in modern psychology with his biblical beliefs. His work

Many nonfiction books of the 1950s reflected the post-war American Dream—the happy family living in the suburbs, led by a working dad and a homemaker mother. Books about cooking, gardening, raising children, and building a dream home dominated best-seller lists of the day.

clearly touched a nerve with Americans and readers around the world. When it was first released, the book spent three and a half years on the *New York Times* (*NYT*) Best Seller List, inspiring more than five million readers to have faith in life—and in themselves. It has since been translated into fifteen languages and remains in print today, more than sixty years after it first hit bookshelves.

## THE BIBLE OF BEST SELLERS

Today, the *NYT* Best Sellers List is considered the most important best-book register in the country. It is not the only one—many newspapers and websites offer similar listings. Nor was it the first.

The first American best-seller list was published in New York in 1895. It was called the *Bookman*, and it ran monthly until 1918. In 1912, *Publishers Weekly* launched its weekly best-seller list, which continues today.

The *NYT* first published its list of top titles in 1931. By the 1950s, the *NYT* list had become more important to **mainstream** readers than was the *Publishers Weekly* list, which is geared to industry insiders.

The two lists are usually similar. Differences occur because of the way each organization does its calculations—and those methods are trade secrets!

## THE BIRTH OF BOND

At the same time American readers were learning how to improve life at home, the so-called red menace of communism was never far from mind. (*The Red Menace* was the name of a 1949 anticommunist Hollywood movie. It wasn't a particularly popular film, but the name stuck.)

The world needed a hero. Enter James Bond. Created by British author Ian Fleming, "Bond—James Bond" made his fictional debut in a novel called *Casino Royale*. It was released in Britain in 1953, reaching American soil a year later.

In this tale of good versus evil, the good guy was Bond, a British secret agent with close ties to the CIA in the United States. The force of evil in this case was the Russian secret service. Of course, Bond wins the day, but not before falling

*Because of Winn-Dixie* (2000) is a book about a scruffy stray dog who adopts a girl at a grocery store. It was the first novel written by Philadelphia author Kate DiCamillo, and it won many awards upon its release. DiCamillo has written more than a dozen books since then, featuring such creatures as a mouse, a squirrel, a tiger, and a pig.

Another famous pig got her start in 2000. Olivia now stars in eleven books, all written and illustrated by Connecticut native Ian Falconer. The books have been translated into more than a dozen languages.

Two troublemakers, a mean principal, and a lot of potty humor add up to Captain Underpants, a book series that began in 1997. There are now twelve of these super-silly books in print.

## DECADE IN REVIEW

In the twenty-first century, new technologies dramatically changed the ways publishers created and distributed their products and how booklovers bought and read their favorite authors. Book content has also undergone a shift in this century.

The usual genres—horror, mystery, romance, thriller, and fantasy—are still best sellers, but unconventional main characters have stepped into the limelight.

For example, the main character in *Middlesex* is intersex. That means the person's gender isn't obvious, from an anatomical point of view. Detroit native Jeffrey Eugenides wrote the Pulitzer Prize–winning book in 2002, nine years after releasing his celebrated first book, *The Virgin Suicides*.

In 2002, Alice Sebold wrote *The Lovely Bones*. The main character in this book is unconventional in that she is dead.

A year later, Mark Haddon's *The Curious Incident of the Dog in the Night-Time* focused on an autistic boy. These progressive characters reflect a society that is dramatically more inclusive and open minded than it has been in days gone by.

Like generations past, readers of today turn to books to learn about the world around them, to make sense of that world, and to be entertained. A century ago, Americans had few options but the written word for those purposes. Now, they have TV, movies, websites, and social media to help them discover new ideas and put them in context. These new technologies may have opened minds, broadened horizons, and widened eyes, but it doesn't mean books have taken a backseat. It just means there are now new ways to engage with life's real and imagined stories.

As long as there are writers with thoughts to share, books will be part of our culture. Be they paperbacks, audiobooks, e-books, or a format yet to be discovered, books will find readers, and readers will always find new and wonderful words to savor.

# Notes

## CHAPTER ONE

p. 12, "Forty years later, it was named 'the best spy novel of all time' …": David Denby, "Which is the best John Le Carré novel?" *The New Yorker*, August 6, 2014, http://www.newyorker.com/culture/cultural-comment/best-le-carre-novel.

p. 15, "I have seen the best minds of my generation destroyed by madness, starving, hysterical, naked …": Allen Ginsberg, *Howl and Other Poems*, San Francisco: City Lights Books, 1956, 9.

p. 18, "J. R. R. Tolkien released what has become the second best-selling …": Whytoread, "10 Best Selling Books of All Time," http://whytoread.com/best-selling-books-of-all-time.

## CHAPTER TWO

p. 34, "Bradbury … considered himself a fantasy writer.": Carl Pettit, "10 Things You Didn't Know About Ray Bradbury," The FW website, http://thefw.com/things-you-didnt-know-about-ray-bradbury.

## CHAPTER THREE

p. 53, "Greed … is good.": Stanley Weiser and Oliver Stone, *Wall Street*. http://www.imdb.com/title/tt0094291/quotes.

p. 63, "With sales topping six hundred million copies, she is the …": Wordables, "Top 10 Bestselling Authors of All Time," http://wordables.com/top-10-bestselling-authors-of-all-time.

## CHAPTER SIX

p. 88, "as a role … young women.": Tim Walker. "Suzanne Collins' Hunger Games trilogy speaks to a generation of teenage readers like no other literary creation - but what's the big message?" *Independent*. November 22, 2013. http://www.independent.co.uk/arts-entertainment/films/features/suzanne-collins-hunger-games-trilogy-speaks-to-a-generation-of-teenage-readers-like-no-other-8958113.html.

p. 88, "the lines … this story.": Ibid.

# Glossary

**authorized** Granted permission.

**capitalist** Describing an economic system in which private companies (not governments) create and supply products; a free-market system.

**charismatic** Possessing an ability to influence others because of a charming personality.

**civil disobedience** Nonviolent protest against government to demand change.

**communist** A person or group of people who support the idea that the government should control goods and services.

**court-martial** To be tried in a military court for breaking military law.

**demographic** A segment of the population defined by particular characteristics.

**devotee** A fan, an admirer.

**double agent** A spy who works for both sides during a conflict.

**espionage** Using spies to gather information on an enemy.

**international trade** The exchange of money, goods, or services between countries.

**mainstream** The dominant trend in literature, fashion, art, or public opinion.

**pen name** A made-up name used by a writer instead of his or her real name.

**physiological** Relating to the body and its systems.

**plight** A bad or difficult situation.

**prestigious** Respected, admired, important.

**prodigal** A person who is wasteful, extravagant, or reckless when it comes to spending money

**reincarnation** A belief that someone or something is reborn after death.

**revolutionize** To change something dramatically.

**sage** A wise person.

**segregation** The enforced separation of groups of people, usually by race or religion.

**surrealism** A blending of unnatural, irrational, and fantastical ideas or images.

**technophobe** Someone who fears technology.

# Further Information

## BOOKS

Beidler, Peter G. *A Reader's Companion to J. D. Salinger's* The Catcher in the Rye. Seattle: Coffeetown Press, 2011.

Davis, Scott. *Female Force: Best Sellers; A Graphic Novel Biography Featuring JK Rowling, Stephenie Meyer, Anne Rice, and Charlaine Harris*. Vancouver, WA: Bluewater Productions, 2011.

Helgason, Jon, Sara Kärrholm, and Ann Steiner eds. *Hype: Bestsellers and Literary Culture*. Lund, Sweden: Nordic Academic Press, 2014.

Martin, William P. *A Lifetime of Fiction: The 500 Most Recommended Reads for Ages 2 to 102*. Plymouth, UK: Rowman and Littlefield Publishers, 2014.

Robb, Brian J. *A Brief Guide to the Hunger Games*. London, UK: Constable & Robinson Ltd., 2014.

## FILMS

*Dead Poets Society*. Touchstone Pictures, 1989.

*Finding Forrester*. Columbia Pictures, 2000.

*Stranger Than Fiction*. Sony Pictures, 2006.

## WEBSITES

The *Guardian* Children's Book Site
www.theguardian.com/childrens-books-site
The *Guardian* Children's Book Site is an international venue with articles, quizzes, and book-related facts for young readers. Individuals and families can also share book tips, start book discussions, and ask questions of authors.

The *New York Times* Best Seller List
www.nytimes.com/best-sellers-books
The *NYT* Best Sellers List website is the place to start to find out which books are hot sellers today. Look under the "Children's" heading for all the middle school and YA recommendations.

Teenreads
Kidsreads
www.teenreads.com
www.kidsreads.com
For anything and everything book-related for youth, teenreads.com and kidsreads.com are go-to websites. Both are part of the Book Report Network and offer book reviews, author interviews, contests, blogs, and suggested reading lists. Teenreads focuses on YA literature, while Kidsreads provides info for kids aged two to eighteen.

# Bibliography

Daniel, Clifton, and John W. Kirshon, eds. *20th Century Day by Day*. London, UK: DK Publishing, 1999.

Duden, Jane. *Timelines: 1960s*. New York: Crestwood House, 1989.

Epstein, Dan. *20th Century Pop Culture*. London, UK: Carleton Books, 1999.

Houle, David. *Entering the Shift Age*. Naperville, IL: Sourcebooks Inc., 2012

Sharman, Margaret. *Take Ten Years: 1950s*. London, UK: Evans Brothers Limited, 1996.

# Index

Page numbers in **boldface** are illustrations. Entries in **boldface** are glossary terms.

Adams, Richard, 42
*Alexander and the Terrible, Horrible, No Good, Very Bad Day*, 50
*All Creatures Great and Small*, 94
*All the President's Men*, 45
Alphabet series, 90
Andrews, V. C., 48
Angelou, Maya, 26
*Animalia*, 68
Archer, Jeffrey, 64
*Are You There God? It's Me, Margaret*, 48, **49**
*Art of Racing in the Rain, The*, 94
audiobooks, 62
Auel, Jean M., 64
**authorized**, 11
autobiographies, 25–26, 59–61

Baby-Sitters Club series, 68
Bach, Richard, 42
Baldacci, David, 90
Baldwin, James, 24
Banks, Lynne Reid, 68
Barker, Clive, 48
Barrett, Judi, 50
Base, Graeme, 68
*Batman: The Dark Knight Returns*, 66
Beat generation, 15–18, **16**, 31, 33
*Because of Winn-Dixie*, 98
*Be Here Now*, 39, **40**
*Bell Jar, The*, 28
Berenstain Bears series, 66, **67**, 68
biographies, 27, 41, 55, 59–61
Blume, Judy, 48, **49**, 50
Boynton, Sandra, 68
Bradbury, Ray, 34
Bridget Jones books, 72–74, **73**
*Bridge to Terabithia*, 50
Bridwell, Norman, 36
*Brief History of Time, A*, 61
Brown, Dan, 89–90, **89**
Burroughs, William S., 33
*Bury My Heart at Wounded Knee*, 43
Bush, George W., 91, 93
Bushnell, Candace, 73

*Caine Mutiny, The*, 19

**capitalist**, 8, 15
Captain Underpants series, 98
Carle, Eric, 36
Carson, Rachel, 36
*Catcher in the Rye, The*, 13–14, **14**
*Catch-22*, 30
**charismatic**, 21
*Charlotte's Web*, 19, 35
"chick lit," 72–74, **73**
children's books, 18–19, 35–36, 48, 50, 66, 68, 82–84, 86–88, 95, 98
Chronicles of Narnia, The, 18, 79
**civil disobedience**, 23
Clancy, Tom, 12, 64, 69, 74, 90
*Clan of the Cave Bear, The*, 64
Clarke, Arthur C., 32–34
*Cloudy with a Chance of Meatballs*, 50
Cold War, 8, 12–13, 22, 71
Collins, Jackie, 63
Collins, Suzanne, 87–88
**communism**, 8, 10, 12–13
*Contract with God, and Other Tenement Stories, A*, 66
cookbooks, 8, 55–56
Cornwell, Patricia, 78, 90
*Cosmos*, 61
**court-martial**, 19
Crichton, Michael, 80, **81**
*Curious Incident of the Dog in the Night-Time, The*, 99

Dahl, Roald, 50
*Da Vinci Code, The*, 89, **89**
**demographic**, 71
*Devil Wears Prada, The*, 74
**devotee**, 6, 17
*Dewey: The Small-Town Library Cat Who Touched the World*, 95
*Diary of a Mad Housewife*, 28
Diary of a Wimpy Kid series, 95
DiCamillo, Kate, 98
diet books, 55–56, 58, 69
Discworld series, 79
Donaldson, Julia, 84
Dork Diaries series, 95
**double agent**, 11
Dr. Seuss, 19, 35, 48, 83, 86
Dune series, 33

Earth's Children series, 64
Earthsea series, 79
Eastman, P. D., 36
*East of Eden*, 19
Eisner, Will, 66
*Electric Kool-Aid Acid Test, The*, 31
Ellison, Ralph, 24
e-readers, 6, 96, **97**
**espionage**, 12
Eugenides, Jeffrey, 98
Evanovich, Janet, 90
*Exorcist, The*, 46

Falconer, Ian, 98
*Female Eunuch, The*, 28
*Feminine Mystique, The*, 28, **29**
Fielding, Helen, 72–73, **73**
Fionavar Tapestry series, 79
Fleming, Ian, 10–12, **11**
Flynn, Gillian, 91
Fonda, Jane, 56, **57**
Friedan, Betty, 28, **29**
*From Here to Eternity*, 19
*Fun Home*, 66

Gardner, Erle Stanley, 77

in love with a beautiful **double agent**, who can't live with her life of deceit, so she commits suicide. But that's another story.

Over the next decade, Fleming would write eleven more Bond novels and two short story collections. After he died in 1964, nine other authors wrote a total of thirty-six more **authorized** Bond books and story collections. The most recent, *Trigger Mortis*, by Anthony Horowitz, was released on September 8, 2015, on what would have been Ian Fleming's 107th birthday. It contains never-before-published material written by Fleming.

*Casino Royale*, written by Ian Fleming, was the first James Bond book. Released in Britain in 1953 and in the United States a year later, the book launched the spy thriller genre.

In the 1950s and early 1960s, Fleming and other British authors dominated the spy thriller genre. In 1963, John le Carré, who was a *real* British intelligence agent at the time, wrote *The Spy Who Came In from the Cold*. Forty years later, it was named "the best spy novel of all time" by *Publishers Weekly*, a magazine for publishers, librarians, and booksellers.

Le Carré, whose work remains popular today, has written a total of twenty-three novels. Most are about international **espionage**, and most relate to the Cold War. The author's real name is David Cornwell. Because he was a spy when he started writing—and because he wrote about real-life spy stuff—he had to write under a **pen name.** After he became famous as le Carré, there was no going back to his real name!

While writers from the United Kingdom dominated the Cold War spy genre, a few American authors are known for their early work in the field.

A year after James Bond debuted in the United States, American author Edward S. Aarons introduced CIA agent Sam Durell in *Assignment to Disaster*. Over the next twenty years, Aarons wrote forty-eight more Durell books, each with the word "Assignment" in the title.

In Aarons's early books, the hero battled communists. As the series progressed and the Cold War's influence faded, Agent Durell took his evil-bashing mission to other exotic locales, including the Middle East, Africa, and Hawaii. Collectively, the Assignment spy series has sold twenty-three million copies.

In the 1970s and 1980s, two American writers—Robert Ludlum and Tom Clancy—became the new kings of the Cold War thriller. Many of these authors' books are still in print, and many have been turned into Hollywood blockbusters—for example, *The Bourne Identity* (2002), *The Bourne Supremacy* (2004), and *The Bourne Ultimatum* (2007).

Today, spy novels continue to sell well, but after the Cold War ended in the early 1990s, communists were no longer the bad guys in the books. Now, evildoers with other political agendas are the targets of fictitious secret agents.

## TEENAGE ANGST

In keeping with the return to the American Dream in the 1950s, a number of TV shows of the day portrayed the perfect American family: a stay-at-home mom, a tough-but-fair dad who goes off to work every day, and two or three kids who get into trouble now and then. Popular shows like *Leave It to Beaver, Father Knows Best,* and *The Adventures of Ozzie and Harriet* followed this formula.

As the decade progressed, though, it became clear that the perfect American family, as seen on TV, was a bit of a myth. The kids, in particular, were getting restless.

Many of the children born during the postwar baby boom were now young teenagers. They had money to spend, rock and roll music to dance to, and bad boy actors James Dean and Marlon Brando to idolize. Then there was the rebel to end all rebels—Elvis "The Pelvis" Presley—shaking things up all over.

The American Dream may have been a happy ideal, but the old-school rules of conduct that came with it were becoming a drag for the youth of the day. Books with rebellious young characters started making an appearance.

The first of the decade, and the most famous novel in this genre, was *The Catcher in the Rye*. American author J. D. Salinger wrote it in 1951. It tells the story of sixteen-year-old misfit Holden Caulfield, who gets kicked out of prep school and takes off to New York City. There, the disillusioned teen encounters all kinds of characters in his quest to protect himself from the "phoniness" of adulthood.

***The Catcher in the Rye*, written by J. D. Salinger in 1951, is among the most famous books reflecting the teenage angst that began creeping into American culture in the 1950s. It is required reading for many high-school students.**

*The Catcher in the Rye* earned mixed reviews when it was first published. Still, it spent twenty-nine weeks on the *NYT* Best Sellers List at the time. In the years since then, the classic novel has sold more than sixty-five million copies, making it one of the top ten best-selling books in history.

Four years after *Catcher* hit bookstores, *Lord of the Flies*, by English writer William Golding, made its debut. In this book, a group of what we would now call "tween" boys are stranded on a desert island. The boys attempt to create a civilized society to govern themselves but end up descending into a state of savagery. It is a book about lost innocence that gives humanity a bad name. The boys are caught between

youth and adulthood, rules and rebellion—the same place teenagers in the 1950s found themselves.

Similarly, John Knowles's *A Separate Peace* is the story of a teenager trying to find his sense of identity in a time of strict conformity. Published in 1959, the book focuses on the relationship of two teenagers—Gene and Finny—in the 1940s. The two are best friends and roommates at boarding school. Gene is a predictable rule follower; Finny is a free spirit who pushes Gene to let loose. Jealousy, an accident, and a mock trial lead to tragedy. Fifteen years later, Gene returns to the school, where he reflects on his youthful experience, finally making the transition into adulthood.

## MEET THE BEATS

"I have seen the best minds of my generation destroyed by madness, starving, hysterical, naked …" So began a 1955 poem called "Howl" by New York writer Allen Ginsberg. And so began a small but culture-shifting movement called the Beat generation.

The half-dozen men considered the founders of the Beat movement met in 1944 in New York City. They bonded over their need for nonconformity and self-expression, and their rage against capitalism. They were also known for their use of mind-altering drugs and "free love." The name "Beat" stemmed from being "beaten down" by society or being in a state of "beatitude," meaning supreme happiness.

For the next decade, the Beat writers toiled away, rejecting mainstream values, living transient lives, and meditating (and self-medicating) to achieve higher consciousness.

At the heart of this band of outsiders were Ginsberg and Jack Kerouac. In 1955, Ginsberg performed "Howl" for the first time at a San Francisco art gallery. (He had written the poem to be read aloud.) A few months later, the poem was

published in a book called *Howl and Other Poems*, and polite society was shocked. The language! The dirty references! In "Howl," Ginsberg exposed the underbelly of American life.

*Howl* was so offensive to some that, in March 1957, the manager of the bookstore that first sold it was arrested, as was the book's publisher. At their obscenity trial in October of that year, though, the judge declared the work's social value took priority over its perceived vulgarity. The bookseller and publisher were cleared of all charges. The trial earned so much publicity that, after it ended, *Howl and Other Poems* sold like hotcakes.

The stir it created brought so much attention to Ginsberg that he and the other Beat poets became famous.

**Allen Ginsberg (*left*) and Jack Kerouac (*right*) are considered the founders of the Beat movement. Their writing was shocking to mainstream society in the 1950s because it addressed subjects that weren't typically discussed in polite society.**

## IS THAT A BOOK IN YOUR POCKET?

The paperback book (as opposed to the hardcover book) was invented in Britain in 1935. Paperbacks were cheap to produce, inexpensive to buy, lightweight, and small enough to fit in a pocket.

"Pocket books," as they were also called, were first sold in the United States in 1939. They were an instant hit with readers.

For the next decade, the only paperbacks that existed were reprints of existing hardcover books. In 1950, though, American publisher Fawcett Publications tried something new. It began producing *original* fiction in paperback. Critics said the move would destroy the whole publishing industry. Instead, it **revolutionized** the book biz. Within six months, Fawcett sold more than nine million copies of original paperback fiction. Westerns, thrillers, and romance novels sold particularly well in this new format.

In 1960, sales of paperbacks surpassed hardcover sales for the first time. Today, largely because of a significant price difference between the two formats, paperbacks continue to outsell hardcovers.

Meanwhile, in 1951, while living in New York City, Kerouac wrote *On the Road*. It took six years for him to find a publisher willing to print the book about a pair of pals roaming America, trying to find meaning.

Like Ginsberg's work, *On the Road* featured content some would consider obscene. The publisher who finally agreed to print it insisted Kerouac tone it down. When *On the Road* was released in the summer of 1957, it became a must-read for everyone.

Soon, the devotees of the Beat writers and their ideals became known as Beatniks. By the early 1960s, though, the

## LORD OF THE LIBRARY

In the mid-1950s, English author J. R. R. Tolkien released what has become the second-best-selling book in history (after *A Tale of Two Cities*, published in 1859 by Charles Dickens).

The Lord of the Rings, a three-volume fantasy, was released over a period of a year—from July 1954 to October 1955. It launched the modern fantasy genre and has sold more than 150 million copies in thirty-eight languages around the world.

The three volumes are *The Fellowship of the Ring, The Two Towers,* and *The Return of the King*. In short, the story is about a hobbit who has a ring that must be destroyed to keep it out of enemy hands.

The themes in this good-versus-evil epic have been studied, discussed, and debated for the past sixty years. Some say it is about racial inequality or the middle class versus the working class. Others point to themes of religion and transformation. Whatever the deeper meaning, The Lord of the Rings is simply a good read.

fame of the Beat writers faded—but the ideals they embraced lived on in the years to come.

## FOR THE KIDS

The 1950s were great years for children who loved to read. Many classic kids' books that are still popular today were written all those years ago.

*The Lion, the Witch and the Wardrobe* (1950) was the first of seven books in the series titled The Chronicles of Narnia by C. S. Lewis. In the series, four siblings enter a magical world through an old wardrobe in a professor's house. *The Lion, the Witch and the Wardrobe* is one of the top-selling English-language children's books of all time.

*Charlotte's Web* (1952), E. B. White's tale of the friendship between a pig named Wilbur and a spider named Charlotte, is another of the best-selling kids' books of all times. More than fifty million copies have been sold. The story has been made into at least two films, a stage play, and a video game.

*The Cat in the Hat* (1957), a book about a couple of kids, a crazy cat, and a rainy day, has sold more copies than any other Dr. Seuss book. He wrote a total of ten books between 1950 and 1959. You've probably heard of some of the others—*Horton Hears a Who!* (1954), *How the Grinch Stole Christmas!* (1957), and *The Cat in the Hat Comes Back* (1958).

## DECADE IN REVIEW

After World War II, the United States did its best to return to the baseball-and-apple-pie, all-American values of the past. But there was no going back to a simpler time. Not all women were happy homemakers. Young people craved change. And the fear of evil outsiders overshadowed everything.

Book trends of the decade captured these opposing themes. A number of best-selling books also foreshadowed the *internal* strife the country was about to face.

*From Here to Eternity* (1951) by James Jones is about a soldier who sticks to his guns despite abuse from his commanding officer. In *The Caine Mutiny* (1951), two seamen take control of their ship when their commanding officer fails to do so. They save the ship but are **court-martialed** for refusing to follow orders. John Steinbeck's *East of Eden* (1952) follows two generations of good and evil within a family.

All three of these books are now considered classics. They pointed to the enemy within. What nobody knew at the time was that these internal rumblings of discontent were about to boil over into full-on cultural chaos.

TWO

# 1960s: A Decade of Distrust and Disagreement

DESPITE THE RESTLESSNESS SIMMERING below the surface of the late 1950s, the following decade opened with a sense of optimism. In 1960, handsome, **charismatic** John F. Kennedy became the youngest person to be elected president in US history. His beautiful wife set fashion trends of the day, and his two children, and their pets and ponies, completed the picture-perfect American family.

Civil rights leader Martin Luther King Jr. had a dream, the Beatles took America by storm, and everyone was doing the Twist. The government passed the Civil Rights Act, women were granted equal pay for equal work (at least in theory), and Americans walked on the moon.

**_Opposite_: President John F. Kennedy, his wife Jacqueline, and their children Caroline and John Jr. were seen as the perfect American family. When JFK was elected president in 1960, it sparked an optimistic era for the United States.**

Before long, though, the state of the union was anything but rosy. In 1963, JFK was assassinated. Five years later, his brother, Senator Robert F. Kennedy of New York, was murdered, as was Martin Luther King Jr. Also during the 1960s, the United States joined the war in Vietnam, the Cold War persisted, and the threat of nuclear war loomed.

By the middle of the decade, Americans had had enough. Antiwar protests, civil rights marches, and race riots pitted Americans against each other, and their government.

**US national guardsmen face protesters during a July 1967 race riot in Newark, New Jersey.**

The 1960s was a time of turmoil, social revolution, and **civil disobedience**. Americans—particularly young Americans—refused to accept the path their country was following. They launched what became known as the "counterculture" movement, separating themselves from mainstream society and its ideals.

Hippies, flower children, and peaceniks lobbied for love, peace, and equality for all. "Make love not war" was their rallying cry, the "summer of love" (1967) their time to shine, and Woodstock (1969) their promised land.

Young people in the 1960s created a peace-love-antiwar counterculture to separate themselves from the mainstream society of the day and the direction it was heading.

The 1960s was a decade of growing pains for a young nation—ten conflicted, life-changing, and downright weird years. The literature of the day was equally conflicted, life-changing, and often downright weird.

## US VERSUS THEM

Racial inequality was a hot topic in the 1950s. It exploded the following decade. Literature by African-American writers mirrored this movement.

**Segregation** in schools was outlawed in 1954. Segregation on interstate public transit was banned a year later. That meant African Americans were legally allowed to attend "white" schools and use "white" transportation. Not everyone in the country was happy about these changes.

In the 1960s, civil rights leaders called for equality for all. Many people opposed their efforts—even after the Civil Rights Act passed in 1964. Ultimately, this black-versus-white struggle led to boycotts, protests, race riots, and even murders across the nation.

One of the first writers to raise awareness of racism in America was Mississippi-born Richard Wright. He was a teenager when he wrote his first stories. His later, more influential works—*Native Son* (1940), *Black Boy* (1945), and *The Outsider* (1953)—were unforgiving in their portrayal of the struggles of African Americans in the early twentieth century. Wright's books are credited with changing the course of race relations in the United States.

In 1952, author Ralph Ellison penned *The Invisible Man,* a book often found on lists of all-time best novels. Like Wright, Ellison addressed social and political inequalities facing twentieth-century African Americans. Influential author James Baldwin did the same. His *Go Tell It on the Mountain* (1953) was about growing up in Harlem.

These 1950s books were among the first to shine a light on the injustices facing Americans of color. But it was during the 1960s that books relating to racial inequality and civil rights moved into the mainstream.

Martin Luther King Jr. wrote *Why We Can't Wait* in 1963. Another civil rights icon, Malcolm X, wrote his autobiography

Civil rights leader Martin Luther King Jr. wrote *Why We Can't Wait* in 1963. It was one of many books that thrust racial inequality and the civil rights movement into the limelight during the 1960s.

two years later. Academics wrote volumes about the **plight** of African Americans.

The 1960s was also a time when white writers began addressing the problems faced by their non-white neighbors. In 1960, Harper Lee published the book considered by many to be the greatest novel ever written. *To Kill a Mockingbird* tells the story of a white lawyer defending an African-American man falsely accused of rape. Even though the book was set in the 1930s, its portrayal of us-versus-them hostility and racial injustice clearly reflected the turbulent 1960s. *To Kill a Mockingbird* won a Pulitzer Prize in 1961 and was made into a celebrated film a year later.

Another significant book about the African-American experience came out in 1969. In *I Know Why the Caged Bird Sings,* writer Maya Angelou documented her life, from age three to seventeen. She recounted being abandoned as a child, later becoming a victim of racism, rape, violence, and homelessness. Rather than remaining a victim, though, young Angelou turned to literature and reading to find her voice. She earned a scholarship to study in San Francisco. By the end of *Caged Bird,* Angelou was no longer a scared, powerless child who felt worthless. She exited the book a dignified, strong young woman who believed in herself and her abilities.

*I Know Why the Caged Bird Sings* is groundbreaking because it was one of the first books written by an African-American *woman* documenting her own experiences in her own voice. It combined the struggles of race with the struggles of being a woman in a man's world, two of the key cultural battlegrounds of the decade.

## The Beginning and End of an Era

In 1956, then–Massachusetts senator John F. Kennedy published a book called *Profiles in Courage*. It was a collection of short biographies of United States senators throughout history. Three weeks after the book came out, it landed on the *NYT* Best Seller List. A year later, it earned a Pulitzer Prize, one of the most **prestigious** literary honors in the nation. It was later revealed that one of Kennedy's speechwriters mostly wrote the book. It is now considered a collaboration between the two men.

After JFK became president in 1960, sales of *Profiles* soared. But it was only after he was killed in 1963 that it reached the number-one spot on national best-seller lists.

Kennedy's assassination was one of the most devastating events in American history, and it created a mini-trend in the literature of the day. In 1964, five of the top-ten best sellers of the year, including *Profiles in Courage*, were related to Kennedy, his life, and his death.

For the following three years, JFK-connected titles were among the nation's top sellers. New books about the Kennedy assassination, and the conspiracy theories surrounding it, are still being written today.

## THE WRITES OF WOMEN

In the early 1960s, polite society expected women to get married and look after their husbands, homes, and children. Women who worked outside the home were typically teachers, nurses, and secretaries. The ones who managed to break into male-dominated careers were paid less than their male counterparts. The assumption was that women would get married, have babies, and quit—and their husbands would look after them, so they didn't need much money. The myth was that all women were content with this way of life.

In 1963, author and activist Betty Friedan cried foul. Her book, *The Feminine Mystique,* exposed a culture of unhappiness and frustration among unfulfilled housewives. She encouraged women to move beyond home and husband, if that's what they truly wanted. With that, *The Feminine Mystique* launched a fight for women's equality along the lines of the civil rights movement.

Feminist writings had been slim during the past three decades. Friedan's work opened the floodgates. In the 1960s, as American women demanded equality, dozens of authors wrote about the female experience.

Sylvia Plath's *The Bell Jar* (1963) is part fiction, part memoir—and fully tragic. It deals with crushing mental illness and the impact of society's expectations on the lives of women. Plath killed herself just after her book was released.

In 1967, novelist Sue Kaufman wrote *Diary of a Mad Housewife,* a fictional account of the frustrations facing a bored, unhappy, mistreated 1960s housewife. In 1970, Germaine Greer wrote *The Female Eunuch,* the first and most famous of her ten feminist books. In it, she challenged the second-rate role of women and questioned the culture that kept them there. Journalist and activist Gloria Steinem also began speaking

**Feminist writer Betty Friedan (*far right*) joins women's rights advocates Susan B. Anthony II (*far left*), Bella Abzug (*wearing red sash*), and Peggy Kokernot (*wearing yellow shorts*) in a demonstration. Friedan's book, *The Feminine Mystique*, is credited with launching the women's movement in the 1960s.**

out through her writing during this decade. Ultimately, she co-founded the feminist magazine *Ms.* in 1972.

Since then, books about women's health, sexuality, politics, and identity have continued to flow freely. Some of the best-known American feminist writers include Hillary Clinton, Naomi Wolf, Susan Faludi, Eve Ensler, bell hooks, and Erica Jong.

## Between a Rock and a Hard Place

You might have heard the phrase "catch-22." It means that Thing A can't happen until Thing B happens. But Thing A has to happen *before* Thing B can occur. For example, you can't get a job without work experience, but you can't get work experience without a job. That's a catch-22.

*Catch-22* is also the title of a famous book, written by New Yorker Joseph Heller in 1961. The story centers on a US Air Force flyer who begins to believe everyone around him is insane.

The catch-22 situation the flyer encounters is this: if you are crazy, you are unfit to fly dangerous missions; but if you apply to be excused from flying a dangerous mission, you are clearly sane enough to recognize the risks involved. Therefore, you're *not* crazy, and you are cleared to fly. So … either you're crazy enough to fly, or you're *not* crazy—and you have to fly.

*Catch-22* is a satire of war that initially earned mixed reviews. Over the years, though, the book has sold more than ten million copies worldwide and is considered one of the greatest and most influential English-language books ever written.

## Turn On, Tune In, Drop Out

It's no secret that drug use was a big part of the psychedelic 1960s. Some of the iconic literature of the decade was, in fact, drug induced. Some of the writing was inspired. Much of it was just plain weird.

Timothy Leary was a psychologist and university professor in the 1960s. He conducted experiments with hallucinogenic drugs. His famous phrase, "Turn on, tune in, drop out," became

a mantra for the counterculture movement. Over the years, Leary wrote many books about his drug experiments—including *The Psychedelic Experience* (1964, which he co-wrote) and *The Politics of Ecstasy* (1968). His experiments later got him fired from his job and jailed on many occasions.

Through Beat poets Allen Ginsberg and Jack Kerouac, Leary met fellow druggie Ken Kesey. In the late 1950s, Kesey had participated in government-run medical tests involving psychedelic drugs. At the same time, he'd worked a night shift at a San Francisco–area mental health hospital. The two activities, taken together, inspired Kesey to write *One Flew Over the Cuckoo's Nest* (1962). This novel, about rebellion against conformity, is set in a mental institution. It is considered one of the most important books about mental health of all time.

Kesey got to know Leary after publishing *Cuckoo's Nest*. With his new friend, Kesey continued experimenting with drugs. In 1964, he and some friends took a trip across America in an old school bus—while high on drugs.

Another writer, Tom Wolfe, wrote about this cross-country bus tour in a book called *The Electric Kool-Aid Acid Test* (1968). Wolfe was not a drug user, nor was he on the bus, but through his book, he took readers inside an authentic hippie experience.

The book also launched a new style of writing, a blend of nonfiction and creativity that came to be known as new journalism.

## GENRE BENDING

You can't think about the 1960s without thinking about weird science fiction.

The golden age of sci-fi had flowed through the 1930s, 1940s, and 1950s. Three authors dominated the genre

during those years—Isaac Asimov, Arthur C. Clarke, and Robert A. Heinlein. Their work was classic sci-fi, with a focus on future worlds, faraway galaxies, and mysterious undersea colonies. Spaceships, robots, and technologically advanced gizmos also figured in the works of this era. The science fiction of the day concerned itself largely with ... well ... science. Story and character development weren't necessarily focal points of the stories. Science was the star.

Robert A. Heinlein's *Stranger in a Strange Land*, published in 1961, is an example of the so-called new wave of science fiction. This genre focused more on the weird and dysfunctional world in which we live than on outer space, rocket ships, and robots.

With the social and cultural upheaval of the 1960s, though, came an upheaval in the genre. Beat writer William S. Burroughs is credited with launching the genre's transition in 1959 with *Naked Lunch*. The book (which was banned in a number of US cities for its "obscenity") wasn't classic science fiction. It had no rocket ships or aliens. Instead, it was a sort of social science fiction. It explored such things as genetic and cultural engineering, weird (but not faraway) societies, and giant bugs, blobs, and other drug-induced alien beings.

With that, sci-fi took a twist. The new wave sci-fi of the 1960s shifted its focus from technology to psychology, from science to **surrealism**. The writers of the older generation continued penning novels, but they, too, changed their styles. Like other writers of the day, their work became more literary and addressed the ills of current culture. Through their work, they questioned the weird and dysfunctional world in which they lived.

Heinlein's *Stranger in a Strange Land* (1961), for example, is about a man raised on Mars by Martians. The poor fellow lands on Earth and must cope with life on this complex planet. Five years later, Heinlein published *The Moon is a Harsh Mistress*. It dealt with social revolution, racial integration, and freedom for the individual. Sound familiar? This was exactly what Americans were fighting for at the time.

In the mid-1960s, Frank Herbert launched his Dune series. Set in the far future in a land far away, the surreal series dealt with politics, religion, environmentalism, gender roles, and emotion. While technology was certainly part of the story, the focus of the series was on society and relationships.

In 1968, Clarke released *2001: A Space Odyssey*, which clearly contained elements of space and technology. But it was about so much more. It looked at evolution, the dangers

## Ahead of His Time

Ray Bradbury made his debut as a sci-fi writer during the genre's golden age, with short story collections and his first novel, *The Martian Chronicles* (1950). Unlike the other golden age writers, his work was never about hard science. Most of his work, including *Martian,* was about contemporary society, with an emphasis on odd or alien characters in current times.

By the time he died at age ninety-one, Bradbury had written eleven novels and hundreds of short stories, plays, TV scripts, and even kids' stories. In addition to *Martian*, his most celebrated works are *The Illustrated Man* (1951), *Fahrenheit 451* (1953), and *Something Wicked This Way Comes* (1962). A number of his stories were adapted for a TV series in the mid-1980s.

Although Bradbury is considered one of the greatest sci-fi writers of the twentieth century, he said he never wrote science fiction. He considered himself a fantasy writer.

of technology, and the threat of nuclear war—which still loomed over America at the time.

By the end of the 1960s, the new wave of sci-fi had already waned. But in its wake, mainstream books had made a clear shift from "hard" to "soft" science fiction. That means the genre had shifted its focus from the *physical* sciences—chemistry, physics, astronomy—to the *social* sciences—psychology, political science, anthropology.

It was around this time, too, that writers such as Ursula K. Le Guin began to blend fantasy worlds with science fiction in ways that paved the way for the likes of *The Hunger Games* in the not-so-distant future.

## FOR THE KIDS

Dr. Seuss once again hopped to the top of children's book sales in the 1960s. He produced eleven books during the decade, including *One Fish, Two Fish, Red Fish, Blue Fish* (1960), *Green Eggs and Ham* (1960), and *Hop on Pop* (1965). But he wasn't the only kids' author to leave his mark on the decade.

Richard Scarry wrote and illustrated his first few children's books in the 1950s. His productivity skyrocketed during the 1960s, when he created 30 new books. Some of his best-known 1960s titles are *Best Word Book Ever* (1964), *Best Mother Goose Ever* (1964), and *Best Storybook Ever* (1967). Before he died in 1994, Scarry wrote and illustrated 130 more books!

Susan Eloise Hinton wrote her first—and most successful—novel when she was still a teenager. *The Outsiders*, published in 1967, is the second-highest selling *paperback* youth book of all time (after *Charlotte's Web*). This story of rival gangs is also one of the most controversial books for young people ever published. Some schools banned it because it featured gang violence, teenage smoking, and drinking. Other schools considered it an important part of their curriculum. Hinton has written four more young adult novels, two children's books, and two books for adults.

Brooklyn-born Maurice Sendak was primarily a children's book illustrator until 1963, when he wrote (and illustrated) *Where the Wild Things Are*. Many industry insiders consider it the top picture book of all time. Another of Sendak's books, *In the Night Kitchen* (1970), has been banned in some places because it features pictures of a little boy running around naked. In total, Sendak wrote twenty books and illustrated about ninety others before his death in 2012.

*The Very Hungry Caterpillar* (Eric Carle, 1969), *Are You My Mother?* (P. D. Eastman, 1960), and *Clifford the Big Red Dog* (Norman Bridwell, 1963) are also products of the 1960s.

## DECADE IN REVIEW

The 1960s was one of the most turbulent times in American history. It was a decade of disagreement. Young people, in particular, challenged the status quo. They said no to war and yes to love. Long-haired men and short-skirted women stood up to "the man," the powers that be.

This social and cultural revolution showed up in the books of the time. Some were weird; others were wise—just like the trends of the day.

This was the decade of *A Clockwork Orange* (1962) by Anthony Burgess. The book is about good and evil choices connected with free will. It is bursting with extreme teen violence, mental illness, and drug use. Still, it remains a classic in the angry-young-man genre.

*Rosemary's Baby* also falls into the decade's weird category. Written by Ira Levin in 1967, this hot-selling horror novel is about a young woman who gives birth to Satan's child. Believe it or not, it's also a satire about the quest for the perfect home, career, and all-American family.

In the wise category of best-selling 1960s books was Rachel Carson's *Silent Spring* (1962). It was the first to warn the world about chemicals that were killing the planet. While the book didn't launch a literary trend, it did launch the general public's concern for the environment. Within a decade of the book's release, some pesticides had been banned, and the world celebrated its first Earth Day.

Environmental awareness was one of many seeds planted in the 1960s that were to blossom in the coming decade.

# THREE

## 1970s:
# A Colorful New Age for the Nation

THE LIFE-SHIFTING SOCIAL UPHEAVAL OF the 1960s couldn't help but spill over into the early 1970s. In the first years of the decade, university students across the nation staged massive anti–Vietnam War protests. Tens of thousands of people demonstrated in Washington, DC. The peace sign was everywhere, a silent symbol of protest.

The early 1970s were also a time of economic trouble, sparked by an international energy crisis. Gasoline was rationed, and for the first time, the world realized that oil and gas supplies could run dry one day. It also proved that corporate progress was hurting the natural environment.

In 1973, the US finally pulled out of the war in Vietnam, and the nation's mood began to shift. Americans celebrated the end of the conflict. A few years later, in 1976, they celebrated their country's two-hundredth birthday. Citizens also celebrated newfound personal freedoms that stemmed from struggles of the 1960s.

Women entered the workforce in record numbers. African Americans became stars of film and TV. The gay community began to "come out" into the limelight.

**In the late 1960s and early 1970s, thousands of people protested the Vietnam War. Here, in a gesture of peace, a young man places flowers in the barrels of soldiers' rifles.**

Subjects that had formerly been taboo—love, sex, divorce, death—became topics of mainstream conversation and culture.

The late 1970s were colorful years. Tie-dyed clothing, yellow smiley faces, and rainbow-colored polyester pantsuits were in. Disco was all the rage on the dance floor.

By the end of the decade, technological advances had produced pocket calculators, the Sony Walkman, and microwave ovens. The 1970s also gave us our first computers, video games, and mobile phones. The world was expanding, and the possibilities seemed endless.

At the same time, Americans began looking inward. After banding together to fight the ills of the world during the 1960s, they started to see themselves as individuals. Because of this trend, author Tom Wolfe labeled the 1970s "the me decade." And readers by the millions turned to New Age literature to help them "find" themselves.

## THE AGE OF AQUARIUS

In the early 1970s, the hippie movement faded, and a new subculture emerged. Individuals sought inner peace, enlightenment, and spiritual guidance. Many looked to alternative religions and philosophies to understand their places in the world. This inner quest of the masses launched the New Age movement, sometimes called the Age of Aquarius. A number of books and authors are credited with bringing this movement to the mainstream.

A spiritual leader named Ram Dass is considered one of the founding fathers of the trend. His real name was Richard Alpert, and he had experimented with hallucinogenic drugs with Timothy Leary in the 1960s. The two men co-wrote the best-selling book *The Psychedelic Experience*. Like Leary, Alpert was fired from Harvard University for drug-related reasons. In the late 1960s, he traveled to India to study with Eastern spiritual leaders. He changed his name to Ram Dass, returned to the United States, and founded a number of organizations dedicated to education and spiritual health.

He also wrote a number of top-selling books about spiritual growth. *Be Here Now* (1971) is his best known, but he penned five others during the decade. Ram Dass has recently published four new books, including two sequels to his early best seller.

Another writer who contributed to the rise of New Age interest was astrologer Linda Goodman. In 1968, her *Sun Signs*

Spiritual leader Ram Dass's book *Be Here Now* is one of the books that launched a New Age trend in literature.

was the first astrology book ever to reach *NYT* Best Seller List status. A decade later, her book *Love Signs* (1978) was equally popular. She wrote two more best-selling astrology books before her death in 1995.

Past lives, future lives, and spirit lives also fascinated the public during the 1970s. The idea of **reincarnation** had first grabbed America's attention in 1956. That year, a book about a woman's past life spent weeks on the best-seller lists—until it was found to be fake. At that point, *The Search for Bridey Murphy*, by Morey Bernstein, quickly faded from the public eye.

In the 1960s, a book about psychic Edgar Cayce moved into the spotlight. Cayce believed in life after death—and his followers believed he had the ability to see beyond this earthly world. A biography called *Edgar Cayce: The Sleeping Prophet* (by Jess Stearn) was a huge hit in 1967.

Three years later, actress Shirley MacLaine published her first book—about her life and her quest for spiritual enlightenment. *Don't Fall Off the Mountain* was the first of a half-dozen New Age books she wrote. She was famous, so her writing made headlines. Over the years, her work got progressively more "out there." She wrote about her experiences with reincarnation, UFOs, communicating with dead people, and meditation. In the 1980s, MacLaine was considered a **sage** by some, a joke by others.

Authors like Ram Dass, Linda Goodman, and Shirley MacLaine inspired so many writers that New Age became a new genre of literature. Bookstores dedicated to these alternative writings sprang up throughout the 1970s. Topics to be discovered on their shelves included everything from angels and drum circles to vegetarianism and time travel.

These alternative subjects definitely contributed to the colorful reputation—and literature—of the decade. New Age books continue to sell well today.

## ABOUT A BIRD

Who could have predicted that a book about a bird would become one of the top-selling books of all time? Richard Bach wrote *Jonathan Livingston Seagull* in 1970. It spent almost a year on best-seller lists, and has since sold more than forty-four million copies around the world.

*Jonathan Livingston Seagull* was one of the earliest books in the New Age genre—and it wasn't actually about a bird. It was about an individual's quest for self-discovery and purpose. The main character of the book just happened to be a seagull.

Similarly, *Watership Down* (1972) by Richard Adams wasn't about bunnies. The book stars a rabbit with ESP (extrasensory perception), who has a vision that all the rabbits are in danger. He and the small band of bunnies who believe him take off to find a safe new place to live.

The little hoppers dodge their share of troubles as they struggle to break free of the mainstream bunny world. Eventually, they find independence and safety. In the end, one of the bunnies leaves his body behind and travels into a new realm with a spirit guide by his side.

Like *Jonathan Livingston Seagull*, *Watership Down* has deep themes. Both books are about following your heart and believing in yourself, even when the world around you says you're wrong to do so.

## NEW VOICES

As the 1970s dawned, so did a new awareness of Native American culture. This was partly related to Americans' newfound need to explore different forms of spirituality. It was also because a new generation of Native Americans had come of age and had begun speaking out—through high-profile protests and through the written word.

In 1969, N. Scott Momaday earned the Pulitzer Prize for his 1968 novel *House Made of Dawn*, a story about growing up as an outsider in America. Some consider it the book that launched mainstream interest in Native American literature.

Beginning in 1970, a book titled *Bury My Heart at Wounded Knee* spent more than a year on best-seller lists across the nation. It presented a harsh history of the abuse faced by Native Americans at the hands of the United States government. The book remains in print today and has sold millions of copies in seventeen languages.

Surprisingly, that book was written by a white man named Dee Brown. But a flood of books written by Native Americans also burst onto the literary scene at the time. These volumes did not necessarily reach best-seller status, but they were historically significant in that they presented a new perspective about the lives of Native Americans.

Writers of the day, including Leslie Marmon Silko, Vine Deloria Jr., and James Welch, paved the way for a later wave of Native American authors. Today, Louise Erdrich, Sherman Alexie, and Gerald Vizenor are among the best-known contemporary Native American writers and poets.

## S-E-X

As women became more liberated—and Americans, in general, began openly discussing formerly forbidden topics—it's no surprise that the talk of the nation turned to sex.

It all started with the feminists of the 1960s. In 1962, bookstores couldn't keep Helen Gurley Brown's new book on the shelves. *Sex and the Single Girl* sold two million copies in its first three weeks on the market. The book spent more than a year on American best-seller lists and was published in twenty-eight other countries.

In 1966, researchers William Masters and Virginia Johnson released a scientific book about human sexuality. The **physiological** focus of *Human Sexual Response* didn't deter readers. The book was an instant hit and was translated into dozens of languages around the world.

After that, the sexual revolution was born. The number of best-selling books on the subject soared through the 1970s. *The Joy of Sex, The Sensuous Woman, The Sensuous Man, Any Woman Can!*, and *Everything You Wanted to Know about Sex but Were Afraid to Ask* were just a few of the top-selling nonfiction books of the decade. Each one immediately sold millions of copies.

Today, adult readers and writers barely blink an eye when it comes to exploring sexuality. But in the 1970s, open communication on the subject was controversial.

## DON'T READ THESE BOOKS AT BEDTIME

In the 1970s, the Vietnam War ended, the threat of nuclear destruction waned, and longtime enemies—the United States and the USSR—began working together on an international space program. For the first time in years, Americans had nothing to fear.

## TRICKY DICKY

In 1974, President Richard Nixon resigned from office, in the wake of the Watergate scandal. The problems for "Tricky Dicky," as he came to be known, had started two years earlier.

In 1972, during the presidential campaign, a number of Nixon's staffers broke into offices at the Watergate Hotel in Washington, DC. Their goal was to plant bugs, or hidden microphones, to gather information from the Democrats—Nixon's competition. Nixon was said to have known about the break-ins, but he resigned the presidency before the issue came to trial. Like the assassination of John F. Kennedy a decade earlier, this incident set off a mini-trend in the best-selling books of the day.

The *Washington Post* reporters who investigated the story (Carl Bernstein and Bob Woodward) published two books on the subject—*All the President's Men* (1974) and *The Final Days* (1976). Each book spent six months on best-seller lists. With another writer, Woodward published a third, related book in 1979. It was called *The Brethren: Inside the Supreme Court*. It, too, was a national best seller.

At least six more books about Nixon and Watergate topped best-seller lists in the 1970s. The former president's own book, *RN: The Memoirs of Richard Nixon* (1978) spent eleven weeks on the best-seller lists, although it never reached the number-one position.

One of the oddest books about Nixon was a slim volume called *The Poetry of Richard Milhous Nixon* by Jack S. Margolis. Printed in 1974, it was a collection of poems created by stringing together phrases heard on the audio recordings that proved Nixon was involved in Watergate. This book never reached best-seller status, and it is long out of print.

Weirdly, some scholars believe this may be one of the reasons the 1970s spawned a rash of horror novels. Perhaps readers missed the adrenaline rush of *real* conflict. Perhaps they needed to keep themselves on their toes, to be reminded that the world was not necessarily as calm as it appeared. Or perhaps it was a way of (safely) living on the edge.

Whatever the reasons, horror novels burst onto the scene in the 1970s. It started with *The Exorcist* by William P. Blatty in 1971, continued with Peter Benchley's *Jaws* in 1974, and included *The Amityville Horror*, published by Jay Anson in 1977. As if to prove America's love of horror, all three of those books became blockbuster movies within a year or two of publication.

The 1970s was also the decade readers met a man from Maine named Stephen King. His first novel, *Carrie*, hit bookstores in 1974—and King has been freaking us out ever since. By 1980, he'd written seven more scary novels. In the 1980s, King wrote another fifteen books, including *Cujo* (1981), *Christine* (1983), *It* (1986), and *Misery* (1987). Over the years, he has penned more than fifty novels. Almost every one has been an instant best seller, and many have been turned into equally popular films. In total, King's books have sold more than 350 million copies around the globe.

But Stephen King wasn't the only author in the creepiness category to take off in the 1970s. Anne Rice published her first novel in 1976. *Interview with the Vampire* was the first in her eleven-book vampire series.

The creator of the super-sinister Hannibal Lecter is another product of the 1970s. Thomas Harris's first book, *Black Sunday* (1975), wasn't too creepy—it was a crime thriller. Six years later, though, in *Red Dragon*, he introduced readers to the most evil of all evil villains. In 1988, Harris released his most famous work, *Silence of the Lambs*. He wrote two

In the 1970s, readers first met the master of horror, Stephen King. Since his first novel, *Carrie*, was published in 1974, King has written another fifty-plus books. Almost every one of them is an instant best seller.

more Hannibal Lecter books during the next two decades. All five of the reclusive author's books have been made into Hollywood films.

V. C. Andrews also made her debut in the 1970s with *Flowers in the Attic*, the first in a five-part series. Andrews died in 1986, having published ten so-called gothic horror novels. But you may still see her name in bookstores. After Andrews died, her estate hired another writer, Andrew Neiderman, to continue writing under her name. He has written at least seventy-five books as V. C. Andrews.

Today, horror novels are as popular as ever. Stephen King is still ... well ... the king of the genre. Other longtime writers, including Dean Koontz and Clive Barker, remain masters of the creepy category, while a few up-and-comers are now making names for themselves. Some horror hit masters to watch for today include Justin Cronin (author of the Passage trilogy), Jack Ketchum, B. E. Ellis, and Chuck Palahniuk.

Writing under the pen name Joe Hill, Joseph Hillstrom King is another author beginning to make his mark on the horror scene. How could he not? His dad is none other than Stephen King.

## FOR THE KIDS

Dr. Seuss continued to influence young minds in the 1970s. He published eleven more books that decade. Most significantly, perhaps, was *The Lorax* (1971), which addressed environmental concerns facing the world. The 1970s was also the decade we heard from other notable children's authors.

Judy Blume wrote her first book in 1969, but the 1970s were the years her books landed on best-seller lists. *Are You There God? It's Me, Margaret* (1970) was about the struggles of a girl of mixed heritage going through puberty. A year later, Blume wrote *Then Again, Maybe I Won't* about a boy going

Kids' writer Judy Blume first landed on best-seller lists in 1970 with *Are You There God? It's Me, Margaret*. In this and future books, she addressed tough issues that young people face every day.

through puberty. In *Tales of a Fourth Grade Nothing* (1972), Blume dealt with sibling rivalry and the death of a pet. In subsequent books, she tackled bullying, body image, racism, and divorce—many of the issues being addressed in adult books of the day.

Roald Dahl was a Welsh writer whose work has been celebrated through the decades. In the 1960s, he brought us *James and the Giant Peach* (1961) and *Charlie and the Chocolate Factory* (1964). In the 1970s, he wrote *Fantastic Mr. Fox* (1970) and *Danny, the Champion of the World* (1975). In the 1980s, Dahl came up with *Matilda* (1988) and *The BFG* (1982), which stands for "Big Friendly Giant."

Chicago writer Shel Silverstein first grabbed kids' attention with his 1964 book *The Giving Tree*. He came to fame again in 1974 with *Where the Sidewalk Ends*, a big book of illustrated poetry that addressed many of the issues kids dealt with every day. He penned another six kids' books before he died in 1999.

Other memorable kids' books from the 1970s include *Alexander and the Terrible, Horrible, No Good, Very Bad Day* (Judith Viorst, 1972); *Jacob Two-Two Meets the Hooded Fang* (Mordecai Richler, 1975); *Bridge to Terabithia* (Katherine Paterson, 1977); and *Cloudy with a Chance of Meatballs* (Judi Barrett, 1978).

## DECADE IN REVIEW

As the "me decade" wound down, Americans continued exploring their innermost feelings. Self-help and pop psychology books began creeping onto best-seller lists. Writers including Dr. Wayne W. Dyer and Gail Sheehy taught Americans to be the best they could be. Dyer's *Your Erroneous Zones* (1976) is one of the top-selling self-help books ever, with thirty-five million copies sold. His next book, *Pulling Your Own Strings* (1978) spent six months on best-seller lists. Sheehy's *Passages*

(1976) spent more than a year on the *NYT* Best Seller List when it first came out. Since the 1970s, books in the how-to-live-a-better-life category have never left best-sellers lists.

Another pop culture phenomenon that began in the 1970s was the TV miniseries. Usually based on books, these multi-part shows would run for several weeks. The first in North America was 1974's *The National Dream,* based on a book of the same name by Canadian writer Pierre Berton. Next up was *QB VII,* based on a novel by American author Leon Uris.

In 1977, though, the miniseries took on blockbuster status when Alex Haley's 1976 nonfiction work *Roots* hit the small screen. *Roots,* the book, certainly sold well when it first came out, but after the miniseries aired, it, too, achieved blockbuster status. A history of Haley's family, from its roots in slavery through to the 1970s, the book is considered among the most important American works of the twentieth century.

Like *Roots,* a number of other 1970s novels also focused on generations of family history. This need to look inward, and backward, continued as the country moved forward into the 1980s.

# FOUR

## 1980s: Fit, Flashy, and Fabulous

THE COLORFUL TONE OF THE LATE 1970S faded at the dawn of the 1980s. The first few years of the new decade were bleak. Inflation and unemployment rates skyrocketed. Incomes plunged. Poverty levels and homelessness reached new heights.

Then a new, conservative president—Ronald Reagan—took office in 1981. He believed **international trade** was the answer to the nation's financial crisis. This allowed corporate America to flourish, and by the middle of the decade, the economy had turned around.

After that, Americans witnessed the rise of the yuppie class—young, urban professionals who had money and flaunted it with designer clothes, flashy cars, and lavish homes. The movie *Wall Street* (1987) told Americans that "greed ... is good." The American Dream was suddenly all about money, money, money. In some circles, the 1980s became known as "the greed decade" because of this hunger for material goods.

***Opposite*: The rise of the "yuppie"—the young, urban professional—was reflected in the movies and books of the 1980s. Image was everything during this decade of decadence.**

Popular TV shows of the 1980s, such as *Dallas, Dynasty,* and *Falcon Crest,* portrayed this culture of wealth. The big hair, huge shoulder pads, heavy makeup, business suits, and poufy gowns worn by the women on these shows became the costume of the day.

But you had to do more than dress the part to be taken seriously in the cash culture of the 1980s. You also had to be physically fit. Workout videos and exercise books were huge sellers during those years. For the first time since the 1960s, cookbooks made their way back to the best-seller lists. This time, though, the cookbooks were mostly *diet* cookbooks.

The best-selling fiction of the decade also portrayed the bigness of the time, with epic tales of wealth and romance. Readers also indulged their curiosity about how the other half lived. Biographies and memoirs documenting the lives of the rich and famous were hot sellers throughout the decade.

In the 1980s, Americans wanted it all—health, wealth, and happiness—and they wanted it now. And they turned to best-selling books to help them achieve it.

## BODY BEAUTIFUL

It wasn't as if Americans didn't care about their health and appearance before the 1980s. But this was the decade when image became everything.

Diet books had started to appear in the 1970s. The first, and among the most famous of the day, was *Dr. Atkins Diet Revolution* in 1972. It spent a year at the top of best-seller lists. But it was in 1979 that the trend toward cutting calories truly took off. That year, *The Pritkin Program for Diet and Exercise* and *The Complete Scarsdale Medical Diet* were two of

***Opposite*: Michael Douglas played high-finance executive Gordon Gekko in the 1987 movie *Wall Street*, considered one of the defining films of the "greed decade."**

the top-ten best sellers of the year. The Pritkin book spent a few weeks longer on best-seller lists, but the Scarsdale Diet was more famous. That's because a jilted lover murdered one of the book's authors, Dr. Herman Tarnower, in March 1980. There's nothing like a scandal to put a book back into the spotlight—and back on best-seller lists!

By then, the rush was on. Books that told Americans what, and how, to eat flooded the market. Millions of readers tried *The Beverly Hills Diet* (1981), *Craig Claiborne's Gourmet Diet* (1981), *Dr. Berger's Immune Power Diet* (1985), and *The Rotation Diet* (1986) during the decade. They learned how to *Eat to Win* (1984). They discovered *The 8-Week Cholesterol Cure* (1988). And they found the secret to *Life Extension: Adding Years to Your Life and Life to Your Years* (1982).

Weight Watchers, a diet program founded in the 1960s by New York homemaker Jean Nidetch, produced seven best-selling cookbooks during the 1980s.

Celebrities also jumped on the looking-good bandwagon. Fitness guru Richard Simmons published his *Never-Say-Diet Book* (1980) and his *Never-Say-Diet Cookbook* (1982). Both were best sellers, as were workout books by famous actors Jane Fonda and Victoria Principal.

*Jane Fonda's Workout* is considered by many to be the video that launched the fitness craze of the 1980s. Millions of fans plugged the workout into their VCRs and sweated it out with Jane. Over the years, Fonda has churned out a total of twenty-three workout videos, many of which have been rereleased on DVD for twenty-first century fitness buffs.

On the heels of her first best-selling workout video, the actor and activist released *Jane Fonda's Workout Book* (1981). It spent almost two years on the *NYT* Best Seller List before being bumped off by Principal's first book, *The Body Principal* (1983). That one only spent three months on best-seller lists,

*Jane Fonda's Workout* is said to have launched the fitness craze of the 1980s. *Jane Fonda's Workout Book* spent almost two years on the *New York Times* Best Sellers List.

**Donald Trump was a model of the rich-and-famous lifestyle in the 1980s. His book *Trump: The Art of the Deal* mixed autobiography with advice on how to get rich, and it spent months on best-seller lists of the day.**

readers insights into his world. It spent almost a year on best-seller lists.

Toward the end of the big-haired 1980s, the public's interest started to shift from merely the rich, to the rich and famous.

Biographies and autobiographies were in vogue. Among those whose lives appeared on paper were director

Woody Allen, newscaster Andy Rooney, and legendary sportscaster Howard Cosell. Books by and about actors, comedians, and musicians also began flooding the market. Michael Jackson, Roseanne Barr, and Carol Burnett wrote top-selling autobiographies. Controversial biographer Kitty Kelley spilled about Elizabeth Taylor and Frank Sinatra. Every celeb wanted in on the literary act—and Americans wanted to know what made the stars tick.

## The Science of Book Sales

Science books might seem like a tough sell to the general public. But two such books defied that belief and sold millions and millions of copies in the 1980s.

When astronomer Carl Sagan's *Cosmos* was published in 1980, it spent seventy weeks on the *NYT* Best Seller list. That made it the best-selling science book in history. The book was designed to make science simple, so the average reader could understand it.

A companion book to a thirteen-part TV series, *Cosmos* looked at the history of inner and outer space through astronomy, genetics, philosophy, biochemistry, and even the study of extraterrestrial life.

A few years later, another scientist's work knocked *Cosmos* out of the record books. *A Brief History of Time*, by physicist Stephen Hawking, spent 112 weeks on the *NYT* Best Seller List after its 1988 release. That record has yet to be broken by another science book.

In *A Brief History of Time*, Hawking wrote about such things as gravity, black holes, and the origin of the universe—and he did it in such a way that non-scientists could relate to it. It has sold more than ten million copies around the world.

## TALKING BOOKS

Until the 1930s, the only way to read a book was to scan words on a page. In 1934, though, a pair of organizations for the visually impaired launched a "talking book" program. The first recordings were done on small discs that had to be played on a specific machine.

Twenty years later, thanks to the invention of LP records, talking books became more popular. A number of record companies began producing and selling them—mostly to schools and libraries. These recordings were still produced with visually impaired people in mind.

After the invention of the cassette tape in 1963, audiobooks began to appeal to the general public. By the late 1970s, many cars had built-in cassette players. Audiobooks made for perfect entertainment on long drives!

The industry continued to expand until 1986, when it exploded. That year, audiobook publishers banded together to form an association to promote their wares. At the same time, mainstream publishers began producing audio versions of their popular books. Most bookstores started carrying audiobooks. By the end of the decade, the audiobook business was worth about $200 million a year. Five years later, it earned eight times that.

CDs took over from cassettes in the early years of the twenty-first century—and the audiobook industry continues to grow. Today, people listen to their "talking books" on digital media players, connected car platforms, and online.

## IN LOVE WITH LOVE

The undisputed star of the 1980s fiction scene was New Yorker Danielle Steel. She had written a few books in the previous decade, but her name stormed best-seller lists in the 1980s. Like the nonfiction books of the time, Steel's fiction focused on the lives of the wealthy.

The books, which fell into the romance category, mostly followed a formula—rich family gets into a pickle because of blackmail, murder, an affair, suicide, war, disability ... you get the idea. Relationships are strained. Then everything gets sorted out.

Steel wrote nineteen novels during the 1980s. In total, she has penned about one hundred, almost every one a best seller. With sales topping six hundred million copies, she is the fourth-best-selling author of all time—after William Shakespeare, British mystery writer Agatha Christie, and fellow romance writer Barbara Cartland.

Danielle Steel wasn't the only writer of rich-and-famous romances to reach celebrity status during the 1980s. Judith Krantz made the best-seller lists with *Scruples* in 1978. She followed up with *Princess Daisy* (1980) and four others by 1990.

In the 1980s, Jackie Collins wrote some of her most famous—and most scandalous—novels, including *Hollywood Wives* (1983).

In addition to romance novels, other popular writers of the decade wrote romantic and historical epics—stories that followed families and relationships through the generations.

Colleen McCullough was one such writer. She bounced back and forth between romance and epic during her career. *An Indecent Obsession* (1981), for example, fell into the romance

category, while her most famous work, *The Thorn Birds* (1977), blended romance *and* epic.

Chicago native Jean M. Auel set her first novel, *The Clan of the Cave Bear* (1980), in prehistoric times. It was an instant hit, and the first book in a series called Earth's Children. By 1990, there were four Earth's Children novels, each selling multimillions of copies. The series, which now totals six books, follows the life and loves of a single character. It's epic in that it spans six novels, even though it only covers twenty-six years in the woman's life.

British writer Jeffrey Archer has written in many genres during his career, but it was the multigenerational epic category that brought him to prominence in the 1980s. He followed his best-selling first book, *Kane and Abel* (1979), with *The* ***Prodigal*** *Daughter* (1982) and several more best sellers.

In addition to the epic and romance authors of the day, writers Stephen King, Robert Ludlum, Ken Follett, Tom Clancy, and John le Carré continued to dominate best-seller lists.

## DRAWING ON HISTORY

It wasn't a new genre, but the graphic novel became legit in the 1980s. In the early twentieth century, kids read comic books. The magazine-style publications mostly focused on superheroes, cowboys, detectives, and adventurers. In the mid-1950s, parents became concerned that comic book content had become too graphic. Inappropriate language was creeping in. This led to a Comics Code that required language and content to be more wholesome.

Most comic books in the 1960s and 1970s were for kids, with cartoony characters and silly storylines. At the same time, though, an underground comic industry continued. By the late 1970s, specialty shops started popping up to

# AUTHOR UNDER ATTACK

In 1988, novelist Salman Rushdie wrote a book called *The Satanic Verses*. It wasn't his first novel, nor would it be his last. But it was the one that almost got him killed.

As soon as the book came out, people of the Muslim faith began protesting. They said the book was disrespectful to the Prophet Muhammad. Within months, fourteen countries with large Muslim populations had banned the book. At the same time, protestors publicly burned copies and set fire to bookstores that carried the novel.

In early 1989, the leader of Iran called for the death of the book's author. He said any Muslim who saw Rushdie was to kill him.

Meanwhile, book sales skyrocketed because of the publicity over the controversy. *The Satanic Verses* spent about six months on best-seller lists, then faded away.

For the next nine years, Rushdie lived in hiding in Britain, under police protection. While he was never harmed, others connected to the book were. Two translators and a publisher were victims of assassination attempts. One translator was murdered.

In 1998, the government of Iran said it no longer supported the killing of Rushdie. The writer came out of hiding.

**Salman Rushdie's 1988 novel, *The Satanic Verses*, prompted protests by people of the Muslim faith.**

sell those comics—and the underground industry became more mainstream.

The shift from comics to the "graphic novel" happened in 1978, with the publication of *A Contract with God, and Other Tenement Stories* by Will Eisner.

Like words-only novels, graphic novels are complete books. They just happen to have illustrations that tell part of the story. Comic books, on the other hand, tend to tell very short stories, or they tell a single story over many issues of a publication.

The year 1986 marked a turning point for graphic novels, when three of the most famous, and most significant, were published—*Watchmen* by Alan Moore and Dave Gibbons; *Maus: A Survivor's Tale* by Art Spiegelman; and *Batman: The Dark Knight Returns* by Frank Miller. All three appeared on the *NYT* Best Sellers List.

Since then, the popularity of graphic novels has skyrocketed. Today, there are graphic novels for everyone—adults and kids of all ages and interests. Bookstores dedicate whole sections to graphic novels.

Some of the best-respected include *Ghost World* (Daniel Clowes, 1997); *Jimmy Corrigan, the Smartest Kid on Earth* (Chris Ware, 2000); *Persepolis* (Marjane Satrapi, 2000); and *Fun Home* (Alison Bechdel, 2006).

## FOR THE KIDS

In 1987, children first asked *Where's Waldo?* (In Britain, children searched for Wally.) Since then, British illustrator Martin Handford has drawn six more Waldo books. Waldo has been translated into more than thirty languages. The 1980s also introduced kids to more well-known books and authors.

Stan and Jan Berenstain produced more than sixty Berenstain Bears books during the 1980s. In total, the couple

Authors Stan and Jan Berenstain brought to life Papa Bear, Mama Bear, Brother Bear, and Sister Bear for generations of readers to enjoy. Later, in the early 2000s, Honey Bear joined the family.

produced more than three hundred books about the famous grizzly bear family.

Sandra Boynton wrote and illustrated her first book, *Hippos Go Berserk!*, in 1977, but the popularity of her cartoony characters soared in the 1980s. Six of her books are on the *Publishers Weekly* list of best-selling children's books of the twentieth century. Four of those six are products of the 1980s, including *Moo, Baa, La La La!* (1980) and *The Going to Bed Book* (1982).

One of the most loved books printed in the 1980s was Robert Munsch's *Love You Forever* (1986). It wasn't his first book—that honor goes to 1977's *Mud Puddle*. But *Love You Forever* is definitely the top-seller of his fifty-plus titles.

Other famous kids' books from this decade include *Animalia* (1986) by Graeme Base, *The Polar Express* (1985) by Chris Van Allsburg, and *The Indian in the Cupboard* (1980) by Lynne Reid Banks. Ann Martin's Baby-Sitters Club series also got its start during this decade, as did the Choose Your Own Adventure series.

## DECADE IN REVIEW

The 1980s started on a low—and ended on a low. In the final year of the decade, the stock market suffered its greatest one-day loss in history. A lot of wealthy people lost a lot of money. It was an ironic ending to the "greed decade."

Throughout the 1980s, Americans had focused on their health, their appearance, and their money. These were the years of Madonna, the Material Girl, and Michael Jackson, the King of Pop. The decade brought us MTV, CDs, and a new thing called the World Wide Web.

As Americans moved into the 1990s, they had more entertainment options than ever before—video games, blockbuster movies, and music videos.

It was the last decade in which the general public looked to literature to make sense of life. Instead, people increasingly turned to their TVs for that.

That's not to say people no longer read books. What it meant, though, was that public interest became more varied. Nonfiction book trends—those that had focused on single themes, such as diet and exercise—ended with the 1980s.

As readers moved into the next decade, their nonfiction interests became more scattered. But when it came to fiction, they remained loyal to writers they already knew and loved. Every book published by the likes of King, Ludlum, Steel, and Clancy became an instant best seller.

The TV series *Friends* celebrated the gen X lifestyle. The six main characters were single, independent, and considered each other family. Here, Phoebe (played by Lisa Kudrow) and Rachel (Jennifer Aniston) raise a glass with Monica (Courteney Cox).

# FIVE

## 1990s: Independent, Inclusive, and Open-Minded

AFTER THE STOCK MARKET CRASH OF 1989, the 1990s opened on a low note. Major corporations laid off tens of thousands of workers, and studies showed that millions of children lived in poverty. Once again, Americans had to tighten their belts.

On the upside, after more than four decades of tension, the United States and the Soviet Union made peace. The Cold War was finally over. That meant the United States was now the world's only superpower.

By the middle of the decade, Bill Clinton had become the first "baby boomer" president, shining a youthful, liberal glow across the nation. The economy had recovered; the nation was once again prosperous, and single, urban, independent twenty- and thirty-somethings had become the dominant **demographic** of the day.

TV shows like *Friends* and *Seinfeld* idealized the single life, in which friends were now family and children were not (yet) part of the picture. Canadian writer Douglas Coupland called this group of educated, active young adults "generation X."

Gen Xers are typically tolerant, inclusive, and focused on fairness. It may be no surprise, then, that the 1990s saw a shift in certain cultural and political attitudes. Americans lobbied for gay rights and called for an end to discrimination against people with disabilities. Violence against women, teen sexuality, and AIDS became subjects of open discussion.

Interestingly, though, the best-selling books of the 1990s didn't necessarily reflect the goings-on of the nation during this period.

## SISTERS IN SINGLETON

A literary trend that *did* follow the social shifts of the 1990s was the rise of a genre known as "chick lit." That's literature for chicks, or young women. Leading the way in this new best-selling direction was Bridget Jones and her now-famous diary.

Quirky Bridget was a member of the growing class of urban, independent, single young adults in the UK and the United States. Created by British writer Helen Fielding in 1996, Bridget was a thirty-something singleton looking for love in all the wrong places. She worried about her weight, her smoking and drinking habits, and her career.

*Bridget Jones's Diary* may not have appeared on American best-seller lists when it first came out, but it definitely launched a trend—on both sides of the Atlantic.

Chick lit was a genre written *by* young women, *for* young women. Readers related to characters struggling to find their ways in the world. Chick lit dealt with dating, workplace troubles, best friends, and reality. It was lighthearted easy reading, witty, and sometimes downright silly. It allowed young women to laugh at themselves and bond with each other over the heroines' familiar antics.

In 1999, Fielding published a sequel, *Bridget Jones: The Edge of Reason*. Together, the pair of Bridget books have sold more than fifteen million copies worldwide.

A year after *Bridget Jones's Diary* landed in bookstores, a writer for the *New York Observer* named Candace Bushnell published a collection of her columns in a book titled *Sex and the City*. The stories followed a quartet of besties as they looked for love, shopped for shoes, and lived the good life in New York City.

British author Helen Fielding launched the chick-lit craze in 1996 with *Bridget Jones's Diary*. Here, she is pictured at a 1999 launch for the second book in the series, *Bridget Jones: The Edge of Reason*.

Two years later, Philadelphian Melissa Banks published *The Girls' Guide to Hunting and Fishing*. Her collection of connected short stories spent about three months on the *NYT* Best Sellers List.

Following quickly on the heels of *Bridget*, *Sex and the City*, and *Girls' Guide*, chick lit books took off. There was *The Temp*, about a twenty-something who takes temporary jobs (Serena Mackesy, 1999); *The Nanny Diaries* (Emma McLaughlin and Nicola Kraus, 2002); and *The Devil Wears Prada* (Lauren Weisberger, 2003).

British writer Sophie Kinsella gave us *Confessions of a Shopaholic* in 2001. She followed with eight more Shopaholic novels that tracked the shopaholic as she got married, went on an extended honeymoon, and had a baby.

The boom in chick lit lasted about ten years. It's still a popular genre, but not nearly as trendy as it was in the late 1990s and early 2000s. And it's not cool to call it "chick lit" any more. Some writers feel the term now stands for "fluff," and they don't want their works labeled as such.

Some current writers of women's fiction worth reading include Anna Maxted, Marian Keyes, and Jane Green.

## DOCTORS AND LAWYERS

The best-selling novelists of previous decades—Stephen King, Danielle Steel, Robert Ludlum, Tom Clancy, and Anne Rice—continued to top best-seller lists in the 1990s. But a newcomer to the literary scene outsold every one of them during this decade.

A young lawyer named John Grisham wrote his first book in the late 1980s. It was called *A Time to Kill*, and the first twenty-eight publishers he approached rejected it. Finally, a small New York publisher agreed to take a chance on the unknown writer.

## Men Are from Mars

In the 1990s, one particular nonfiction book, written by a man, could almost be counted as part of the women's lit craze. The author was John Gray, and the book was *Men Are from Mars, Women Are from Venus*. It came out in 1993 and spent the next four years on national best-seller lists.

Gray's theory was that most relationship problems stem from the fact that men and women come from different planets. Not literally. That's a metaphor meaning that the two genders think, communicate, and relate to each other in different ways. For example, he said, women want to talk about problems; men want to solve them. These opposing goals might lead to conflict.

*Men Are from Mars* was a hit as a how-to book—as in how to understand the opposite sex. As popular as it was among readers, psychologists and academics criticized Gray for reinforcing male-female stereotypes.

Still, Gray managed to sell millions of copies, and write sixteen *Mars-Venus* spin-off books in the following fifteen years. The original book is still in print.

When the book was released in 1989, nobody noticed. Right after he finished writing *A Time to Kill*, Grisham started on his next book, *The Firm*. When it came out two years later, everybody noticed! By this time, *Law and Order* was one of the top TV shows of the time—and readers craved legal drama as much as TV audiences did.

*The Firm*, a legal thriller, spent almost a year on the *NYT* Best Sellers List. Weirdly, it never reached the number one position. But *The Pelican Brief*, Grisham's next book, *debuted*

Twenty-eight publishers rejected John Grisham's first book, *A Time to Kill*, before he found one willing to take a risk on an unknown writer. After Grisham became a best-selling author, *A Time to Kill* went on to sell more than fifteen million copies. Here, Grisham (*right*) and playwright Rupert Holmes meet at the world premiere of the stage adaption of the book.

at number one in 1992 and became the best-selling adult book of the entire decade.

Grisham's *The Client* (1993) debuted at number one, as did *The Chamber* in 1994, as did *The Rainmaker* in 1995, as did … well, you get the idea.

By the end of the decade, Grisham had sold almost sixty-one million copies of the ten legal thrillers he'd written to date—including his first book, *A Time To Kill*. It was picked up and reissued by a major publisher after Grisham had become a household name.

Since the 1990s, Grisham has written twenty more best-selling novels, including five that have nothing to do with the law or lawyers. His sales now tally more than three hundred million books in forty languages.

Grisham may be the most successful author in the legal suspense genre, but he certainly wasn't the first. As long as there have been lawyers with pens, there have been books about the courtroom. In the 1930s, lawyer Erle Stanley Gardner created one of the most famous fictitious courtroom lawyers of all time—Perry Mason. By the time he died in 1970, Gardner had written more than eighty Perry Mason novels, along with dozens of other books and hundreds of short stories.

Other famous courtroom thrillers include *Anatomy of a Murder* (1958) by John D. Voelker, *To Kill a Mockingbird* (1960) by Harper Lee, and *QB VII* (1970) by Leon Uris.

Other than those few, the genre didn't make a significant splash until the late 1980s, when Chicago lawyer Scott Turow first put pen to paper. His first book, *Presumed Innocent* (1987), spent about eleven months on the *NYT* Best Sellers list and is credited with kickstarting the public's love of legal thrillers. Like Grisham, Turow was a staple on best-seller lists through the 1990s. He continues to write today.

As the 1990s progressed, more and more crime dramas took to the TV airwaves. At the same time, a pair of medical shows—*ER* and *Chicago Hope*—also rose to most-watched status. Suddenly, readers craved books that blended the two types of story—crime and medical science. Enter writer Patricia Cornwell and her fictitious medical examiner Dr. Kay Scarpetta. The Miami-born author first introduced the coroner character in *Postmortem* in 1990. At the time, the author worked as a computer analyst in a medical examiner's office.

*Postmortem,* a thriller about crime and forensic science, earned five mystery writer awards. But it wasn't until the third Kay Scarpetta book, *All That Remains* (1992), that Cornwell landed on national best-seller lists. Her fifth book, *The Body Farm,* went to number one in 1994. Most of the books she's written since then have reached the same milestone. Cornwell has written about thirty novels in total, most starring Dr. Kay Scarpetta. Her total sales have topped one hundred million copies.

Real-life forensic scientist Kathy Reichs earned comparisons to Cornwell when she burst onto the literary scene in the late-1990s. In her first book, *Déjà Dead* (1997), Reichs introduced readers to Dr. Temperance Brennan, a character based on the author herself. There are now eighteen best-selling books in the series, and the TV show *Bones* is based on Reichs's books.

Since Cornwell and Reichs launched their books, forensics and CSI (crime scene investigation) have become hot topics for writers. James Patterson's fifteen-part Women's Murder Club series, for example, features a team of crime-solving friends, one of whom is a medical examiner. British writer Colin Cotterill has written ten best-selling novels starring Dr. Siri Paiboun, a coroner in Laos. And M. R. Hall, a former

lawyer in Wales, has released six novels and one novella, or short novel, featuring British coroner Jenny Cooper.

## FANTASTIC FANTASY

You can't talk about the 1990s without mentioning fantasy. It was the decade the genre made its mark. Think Game of Thrones and Harry Potter.

There is no question that J. R. R. Tolkien and C. S. Lewis were the founding fathers of modern fantasy books. Their Lord of the Rings and Chronicles of Narnia, first published in the 1950s, remain among the top-ten best-selling books of all time.

In the 1960s, Ursula K. Le Guin's Earthsea series solidified fantasy as a legitimate genre. A decade later, Terry Brooks penned *The Sword of Shannara* (1977). It was the first fantasy novel to instantly land on the *NYT* Best Sellers List. With that, the genre catapulted into the limelight. Ultimately, Brooks would write another thirty books in the Shannara series, one of the top-selling book collections of all time.

Brooks's success paved the way for an explosion of fantasy titles in the 1980s and 1990s. Among the best series launched during that time were: Discworld (Terry Pratchett, 1983); The Fionavar Tapestry (Guy Gavriel Kay, 1984); Memory, Sorrow, and Thorn (Tad Williams, 1988); and The Wheel of Time (Robert Jordan, 1990).

The most famous fantasy series to come out of the 1990s began with a book called *Game of Thrones* (1996) by George R. R. Martin. It was the first book in his Song of Ice and Fire series, and it earned rave reviews from critics when it came out. But it didn't make best-seller lists at the time. The next two installments did, although they didn't reach the number-one position. The first book in the series to achieve

## FROM *JURASSIC PARK* TO THE *ER*

The 1990s were big years for author Michael Crichton. First, he wrote *Jurassic Park*, a novel about a scientist who clones dinosaurs for an amusement park. The book came out in 1990 and spent thirty-six weeks on the *NYT* Best Sellers List. Three years later, it was a blockbuster movie.

Crichton, who had written sixteen novels before *Jurassic Park*, released five more best sellers before the end of the 1990s. Another six of his books were made into movies during the decade, with a seventh produced in 2003.

Two of the top-ten best-selling books of the 1990s were Crichton's—*Jurassic Park* and *Rising Sun* (1992). In total, he sold 27.4 million books in that ten-year period.

As if that wasn't enough fame and fortune for the writer, he was also the executive producer of the top-rated TV medical drama *ER*. Crichton had come up with the idea and written a screenplay for the show in 1974. It went nowhere, and he got distracted with other projects.

After he and director Steven Spielberg worked together on the film version of *Jurassic Park*, they turned their attention to Crichton's twenty-year-old script, which was adapted from a film into a television series. *ER* first aired in 1994. It was an instant hit and ran for fourteen years.

**In 1990, Michael Crichton's book *Jurassic Park* spent nine months on best-seller lists. Three years later, it was made into a blockbuster movie starring Sam Neill and youngsters Joseph Mazzello and Ariana Richards.**

that honor was *A Feast for Crows* (2005). The following volume, *A Dance with Dragons,* debuted in the top spot. That was in 2011, a few months after the TV adaptation, *Game of Thrones,* had taken to the airwaves. At the same time, the original book, *Game of Thrones,* (finally) reached best-seller status.

Fans are anxiously awaiting the next book in Martin's Song of Ice and Fire series. It will be called *The Winds of Winter.* But it's a guessing game as to when it will be published. As of 2016, the best guess is that it will hit bookstores sometime before 2018.

## FOR THE KIDS

When it comes to kids' books in the 1990s, two words stand out: Harry Potter.

J. K. Rowling's first book about the boy wizard came out in 1997. It was called *Harry Potter and the Philosopher's Stone,* and it has become the fifth top-selling book of all time. In the United States, the book was released as *Harry Potter and the Sorcerer's Stone.* All seven of the Harry Potter books are among the top-twenty best-selling *individual* books in history. And the seven-book collection is the top-selling book *series* of all time. More than 450 million Harry Potter books have been read around the world.

It's interesting to note that the second-best-selling book series in history was also a product of the 1990s—and it was also written for kids. R. L. Stine's Goosebumps collection takes that honor, with more than 350 million books sold. Stine wrote sixty-two of the kids' horror novellas from 1992 to 1995.

A third top-selling children's series also started during the 1990s. The first book in Lemony Snicket's A Series of Unfortunate Events came out in 1999. (Lemony's real name is Daniel Handler.) *The Bad Beginning* introduced readers

Lemony Snicket's A Series of Unfortunate Events, a thirteen-part series, is one of the top-selling children's book series of all times. Lemony Snicket's All the Wrong Questions is a prequel series launched in 2012 with this book, *Who Could That Be at This Hour?*

to three orphans who go to live with nasty Count Olaf, who then tries to steal their inheritance. The thirteen-book series wrapped in 2006 with *The End*.

Believe it or not, Dr. Seuss's name was still on best-seller lists in the 1990s. By then, he'd been writing children's books for more than half a century. *Oh, the Places You'll Go!* (1990) was the last book he published before he died in 1991.

Facebook and Twitter, texting and Wikipedia—all of these are innovations that exploded during the 2000s.

For the book business, this shifting technology has changed how authors research books, how publishers sell books, and how readers buy books. It has even changed how we *read* books.

Before we talk about technology, though, let's talk more about Harry Potter.

## YA, YA, YA

Harry Potter changed everything. From 1998 to 2000, J. K. Rowling's books about the boy wizard dominated best-seller lists.

Sure, there had been kids' books on best-seller lists in the past. For example: *A Tree Grows in Brooklyn* (Betty Smith) spent four months atop the *NYT* Best Sellers List in 1944; *Watership Down* (Richard Adams) took top spot for two months in 1974; and Dr. Seuss's *Oh The Places You'll Go!* led the list for a few weeks in 1990.

But Harry Potter didn't just *appear* on best-seller lists. He *ruled* them. For two years, the first three Potter books lived on those lists. Adult readers began making waves. They objected to the fact that kids' books were knocking adult titles off best-seller lists. In 2000, with *Harry Potter and the Goblet of Fire* about to be released—and likely to take up another precious position on the best-books roster—editors at the *NYT* made a decision.

In July 2000, they created a Children's Best Sellers List. At first, it was a monthly tally of top kids' and teens' titles. A decade later, though, the once-a-month list was no longer enough. By then, young adult, or YA, fiction had become the hottest-selling genre in the literary world.

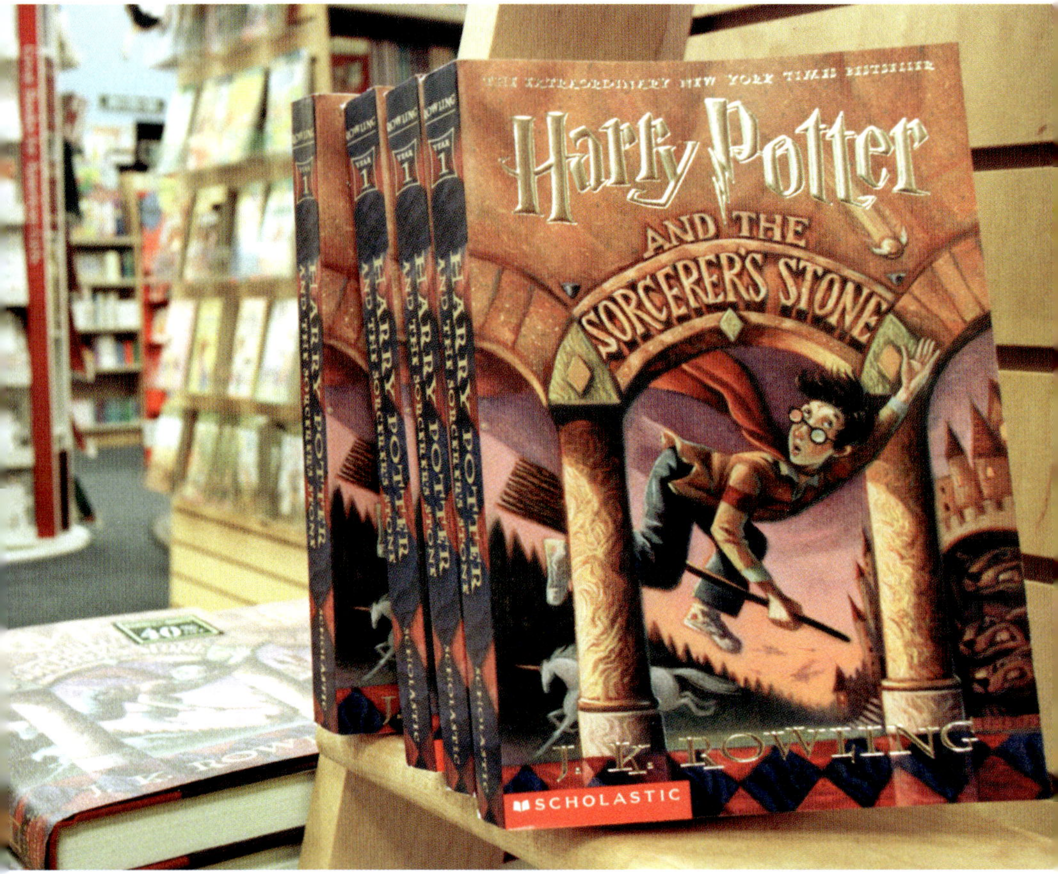


**This is the book that changed everything in kids' literature. *Harry Potter and the Sorcerer's Stone*, the first in the seven-part Harry Potter series, was released in 1997.**

It had started with Harry Potter and continued with Stephenie Meyer's four-book Twilight series, which debuted in 2005. In 2008, the year of the final Twilight book, Suzanne Collins launched The Hunger Games. Young readers also loved Sara Shepard and her Pretty Little Liars, The Maze Runner (James Dashner), and Percy Jackson & the Olympians (Rick Riordan).

## MAY THE ODDS BE EVER IN YOUR FAVOR

In 2008, readers were first introduced to heroine Katniss Everdeen in the adventure novel *The Hunger Games*. Set in the futuristic country of Panem, the Hunger Games is an annual event that pits twenty-four tributes from twelve districts against one another in a battle to the death. As the story unfolds in *Catching Fire* (2009) and *Mockingjay* (2010), Katniss leads a rebellion to overthrow the evil Capitol. With her guts and grit, the character was recognized as "a role model for a new generation of young women."

Series author Suzanne Collins was inspired to write her best-selling trilogy from real-life events. After channel surfing one evening between a reality TV contest and news coverage of the war in Iraq, she recalled how "the lines began to blur in this very unsettling way, and I thought of this story." And what a story it was—after the first book hit store shelves, fans were hooked. Millions of copies of each title have been devoured by readers, and the entire series has been adapted for the big screen, with Collins's help writing the screenplays.

A monthly list couldn't keep up with the wave of new YA titles and authors. So, in 2011, the Children's Best Sellers List became a weekly *NYT* feature.

A year later, the list was still overflowing, so the editors further divided the children's list into two—one for middle-grade readers (ages eight to twelve) and one for YA readers (ages thirteen to eighteen).

Since then, the number of youth books being published has continued to explode. The *NYT* Children's Best Sellers Lists have been *further* divided. There are now eight weekly kids' lists, ranging from picture books, to middle-grade hardcover, to YA e-books, to series for all ages.

## CODE BROWN

After Harry Potter moved off adult best-seller lists in the 2000s, a new book moved in and took over. *The Da Vinci Code* (2003), by Dan Brown, is the story of a university professor who solves a murder by decoding symbols. Critics said it was badly written and historically inaccurate—but readers didn't care. The book spent more than three years on best-seller lists when it first came out, and it is now among the top-ten best-selling books ever published.

Brown's next novel, *The Lost Symbol*, debuted at number one on the *NYT* list in 2009, but didn't do as well as the previous book. It moved off the best-books list after just six months, as did the British writer's next book, *Inferno* (2013). *The Da Vinci Code* became a blockbuster movie in 2006, and a film version of *Inferno* was released in 2016.

*The Da Vinci Code*, by Dan Brown, spent more than three years on best-seller lists after its 2003 release. The book opens with a murder in the Louvre, a famous art museum in Paris, seen here in the background.

## A New Generation

In the mid-1970s, California author Maxine Hong Kingston became one of the first writers to document the Asian-American experience in the United States. Her first two books, *Woman Warrior* (1976) and *China Men* (1980), paved the way for other Asian Americans to share their stories.

In 1989, Amy Tan wrote *The Joy Luck Club*, about a group of Chinese-born mothers and their American-born daughters. It spent six months on the *NYT* Best Sellers List.

Other than these two writers, Asian Americans weren't well-represented in the mainstream literary world—at least not until the turn of this century. The early 2000s could be considered a breakthrough period for authors of Asian and South Asian descent.

In 2000, Jhumpa Lahiri won the Pulitzer Prize for her first book, *Interpreter of Maladies* (released in 1999). A decade later, her story collection *Unaccustomed Earth* (2008) reached number one on the

**Khaled Hosseini is one of a number of authors of Asian and South Asian descent who burst onto best-seller lists in the twenty-first century. Each of Hosseini's three novels has sold millions of copies in the United States.**

*NYT* Best Sellers List. Her latest book, *The Lowland* (2013), was another chart topper.

Khaled Hosseini was born in Afghanistan and moved to California as a teenager. He burst onto best-seller lists in 2003 with *The Kite Runner*. His next two books, *A Thousand Splendid Suns* (2007) and *And the Mountains Echoed* (2013) also earned rave reviews.

Another Asian-American name often found on best-seller lists is Lisa See. Among her best-known novels are *Flower Net* (1997), *Snow Flower and the Secret Fan* (2005), and *Dreams of Joy* (2011).

Other Asian-American writers to watch for today include Chang-Rae Lee, Anchee Min, Chitra Banerjee Divakaruni, and Daniyal Mueenuddin.

on best-seller lists during this period. Former presidents Jimmy Carter and Bill Clinton wrote hot sellers of their own. Even more recent presidents like George W. Bush and Barack Obama put their thoughts to paper. It was a time of unprecedented fascination with political and presidential writings and memoirs.

Even presidents' families and running mates got into the publishing game during the first decade of the twenty-first century. Former First Lady Laura Bush, JFK's brother Edward Kennedy, former vice-president Dick Cheney, former vice-presidential candidate Sarah Palin, and presidential hopeful Mitt Romney all penned top-selling volumes.

Not all the writings were positive, though. Book after book criticized president George W. Bush's handling of 9/11, his decision to invade Iraq, and his way of governing in general. As soon as Obama became president, he and his administration became the targets of at least half a dozen *NYT* top best sellers.

The passion for all things presidential hasn't ended, but it tapered off around 2013.

## OUR BEST FRIENDS

Readers have always loved animal stories. Think *Moby Dick* (Herman Melville, 1851), *Black Beauty* (Anna Sewell, 1877), *The Jungle Book* (Rudyard Kipling, 1894), and *The Call of the Wild* (Jack London, 1903).

More recently, British veterinarian James Herriot became a best-selling author on this side of the Atlantic with his first book, *All Creatures Great and Small*. It landed in America in 1972. Herriot, who based his stories on his real-life veterinary work, dominated the adult animal book category through the 1970s and 1980s.

British novelist and jockey Dick Francis also broke into the American market during this time. His crime stories centered on horses and the horseracing world. He wrote almost fifty novels before he died in 2010.

Other that these, and a few dog-training guides, there haven't been a ton of best-selling animal titles for adults—until now. Since 2000, books about dogs and cats (and a number of other critters) have been unleashed!

It may be that baby boomers (those born in the years following World War II) are now empty nesters. Their kids have grown up and moved out, so their focus has turned to their pets. Whatever the reason, animal books for adults are massively popular these days. In 2001, we read about a horse called *Seabiscuit* (Laura Hillenbrand). In 2005, the dog story *Marley and Me* (John Grogan) topped best-seller lists. *The Art of Racing in the Rain*, a novel written from a dog's point of view (by Garth Stein) was a must-read in 2008. A doggie road trip story, *Travels with Casey* (Benoit Denizet-Lewis), was a hit among readers in 2014.

Toward the end of the first decade of the twenty-first century, cats started to take over best-seller lists. It started with Dewey, a cat who lived in a library in Iowa. In 2008, author (and library director) Vicki Myron wrote *Dewey: The Small-Town Library Cat Who Touched the World*. Dewey had already gone to kitty heaven by then, but his life story took him to the top of the *NYT* Best Sellers List.

Then there was *Homer's Odyssey* (Gwen Cooper, 2009) about a blind kitty, *A Street Cat Named Bob* (James Bowen, 2012), and the comic *How To Tell If Your Cat Is Trying to Kill You* (Matthew Inman, 2012).

Animal books have become so popular that, in September 2014, the *NYT* began publishing a monthly list of best-selling animal books. Birds, elephants, a donkey, and even an octopus have been the subject of books on that list ever since.

## FOR THE KIDS

Two diaries, a dog, a pig, and an underdressed superhero are among the best-selling kids' books released so far in the twenty-first century.

Before Diary of a Wimpy Kid was a book series, it was an online journal created by cartoonist Jeff Kinney. Every day, beginning in 2004, a fictitious middle-school boy named Greg (the wimpy kid of the title) posted his thoughts online. When the first Wimpy Kid book was published in 2007, it was an instant best seller. There are now ten books in the series.

Another diary series, The Dork Diaries, premiered in 2009. This series also numbers ten books. Like the Wimpy Kid series, this one is also written and drawn by a grownup—Rachel Renee Russell. The difference is that the Dork series is the diary of a middle-school girl. And in the case of the Dork, the author's daughters help her write and illustrate the books.

## E-BOOKS, IBOOKS, AND KINDLE

In recent years, a new way of reading has overtaken every part of the book biz.

The first hints of the techno-change to come happened in 1998. That's when the first e-readers were invented. But they had limited storage space and battery life, so they didn't catch on.

A decade later came the Kindle, launched by online superstore Amazon in 2007. This time, thanks to an aggressive marketing campaign and a low price, sales of the e-reading device soared.

Within a few years of Kindle came the Kobo, the Nook, and the iPad, with its collection of iBooks. At the same time, public libraries began lending e-books to their members, and major American publishers started producing e-versions of their titles.

Because of these advances, sales of e-readers and e-books skyrocketed between 2008 and 2010. By early 2011, Amazon reported that e-books were outselling print books for the first time. This shift in readers' habits meant publishers and authors lost money. Digital books sold at significantly lower prices than print books, and that translated into lower profits for everyone. In addition, e-book sales happened online. The sudden drop in traditional book sales forced many independent bookstores out of business.

By the end of 2011, it appeared that e-books were about to knock print books right off their shelves. And then, out of the blue, something changed. Sales of e-readers and e-books suddenly tapered off. The rush to own these bright new devices was over. Printed books became popular again. Today, hard-copy books account for two-thirds of annual book sales.

That doesn't mean e-books are set to fizzle out any time soon. What it does mean is that fans of the old-fashioned print book have spoken. They're not ready to let go. It also shows that there's room in the market for the virtual and the actual to live side by side.

***Opposite*: When e-readers took to the market in 2007, they sold so well that some publishers, booksellers, and readers predicted the end of the print book. E-reader sales have since tapered off, proving there is room in the book world for traditional and contemporary book formats.**

# Contents


INTRODUCTION 5

1. 1950s: HAPPY AT HOME, SAFE FROM THE ENEMY ABROAD 7

2. 1960s: A DECADE OF DISTRUST AND DISAGREEMENT 21

3. 1970s: A COLORFUL NEW AGE FOR THE NATION 37

4. 1980s: FIT, FLASHY, AND FABULOUS 53

5. 1990s: INDEPENDENT, INCLUSIVE, AND OPEN-MINDED 71

6. 2000s: NEW MILLENIUM, NEW VOICES, NEW TECHNOLOGY 85

NOTES 100

GLOSSARY 102

FURTHER INFORMATION 104

BIBLIOGRAPHY 106

INDEX 107

ABOUT THE AUTHOR 112

Published in 2017 by Cavendish Square Publishing, LLC
243 5th Avenue, Suite 136, New York, NY 10016



First Edition



Cataloging-in-Publication Data
Names: Dakers, Diane.
Title: American life and best sellers from the Catcher in the Rye to the Hunger Games / Diane Dakers.
Description: New York : Cavendish Square, 2017. | Series: Pop culture | Includes index.
Identifiers: ISBN 9781502619815 (library bound) | ISBN 9781502619822 (ebook)
Subjects: LCSH: American literature--20th century. | American literature--21st century. | Popular culture--United States--20th century |Popular culture--United States--21st century.
Classification: LCC PS509.U52 D37 2017 | DDC 810.8'006--dc23

Editorial Director: David McNamara
Editor: Kelly Spence
Copy Editor: Nathan Heidelberger
Art Director: Jeffrey Talbot
Designer: Jessica Nevins
Production Assistant: Karol Szymczuk
Photo Research: J8 Media

The photographs in this book are used by permission and through the courtesy of: MANDEL NGAN/AFP/Getty Images, cover background, Araya Diaz/WireImage/Getty Images, cover; Yellow Dog Productions/Digital Vision/Getty Images, 4; H. Armstrong Roberts/ClassicStock/Getty Images, 9; Ben Stansall/AFP/Getty Images, 11; MANDEL NGAN/AFP/Getty Images, 14; Walter Bibikow/Danita DelimontPhotography/Newscom, 16; John F. Kennedy Library/Archive Photos/Getty Images, 20; Mel Finkelstein/NY Daily News Archive /Getty Images, 22; Stanley Sherman/Express/Hulton Archive/Getty Images, 23; New York World-Telegram and the Sun staff photographer: Albertin, Walter, photographer./Library of Congress/File:Martin Luther King Jr NYWTS 4.jpg/Wikimedia Commons, 25; Steve Northup/The LIFE Images Collection/Getty Images, 29; DWD-Media/Alamy Stock Photo, 32; Everett Collection Historical/Alamy Stock Photo, 38; INTERFOTO/Alamy Stock Photo, 40; Kenzo Tribouillard/AFP/Getty Images, 47; Charles Knoblock/AP Images; 49; Eugene Gebhardt/The Image Bank/Getty Images, 52; 20th CENTURY FOX/Ronald Grant Archive Alamy Stock Photo, 54; Lynne Sutherland/Alamy Stock Photo, 57; Joe McNally/Hulton Archive/Getty Images, 60; Kaveh Kazemi/Hulton Archive/Getty Images, 65; Dan Loh/AP Images, 67; ZUMA Press¨Inc/Alamy Stock Photo, 70; Fred Duval/FilmMagic/Getty Images, 73; Jose Luis Magana/AP Images; 76; AF archive/Alamy Stock Photo, 81; © Greg Sorber/Albuquerque Journal/ZUMAPRESS.com, 83; by Alex Wong/Newsmakers/Getty Images, 87; Travel Pictures/Alamy Stock Photo, 89; Charles Sykes/Invision/AP Images, 92; shahfarshid/iStock/Thinkstock.com, 97.

Printed in the United States of America

POP CULTURE

# American Life and Best Sellers from The Catcher in the Rye to The Hunger Games

DIANE DAKERS

Cavendish Square
New York

*Ghost World*, 66
Gibbons, Dave, 66
Ginsberg, Allen, 15–17, **16**, 31
*Girls' Guide to Hunting and Fishing, The*, 74
*Giver, The*, 84
*Giving Tree, The*, 50
Golding, William, 14
*Gone Girl*, 91
Goodman, Linda, 39, 41
Goosebumps series, 82
Grafton, Sue, 90
graphic novels, 64, 66
Gray, John, 75
Grisham, John, 74–75, **76**, 77, 90
*Gruffalo, The*, 84
*Guess How Much I Love You*, 84

Haddon, Mark, 99
Handford, Martin, 66
Handler, Daniel, 82
Harris, Thomas, 46, 48
Harry Potter series, 6, 79, 82, 86–87, **87**, 89
Hawking, Stephen, 61
Heinlein, Robert A., 32–33, **32**
Heller, Joseph, 30
*Help, The*, 91
Herbert, Frank, 33
Herriot, James, 94
Hinton, Susan Eloise, 35
horror novels, 36, 46, 48, 82, 98
Hosseini, Khaled, **92**, 93
"Howl," 15–16
*Human Sexual Response*, 44
Hunger Games series, 34, 87–88

*I Know Why the Caged Bird Sings*, 26
*Indian in the Cupboard, The*, 68
**international trade**, 53
*Interview with the Vampire*, 46
*Invisible Man, The*, 24

*Jacob Two-Two Meets the Hooded Fang*, 50
James Bond series, 10–12, **11**
*Jimmy Corrigan, the Smartest Kid on Earth*, 66
*Jonathan Livingston Seagull*, 42
*Joy Luck Club, The*, 92
*Jurassic Park*, 80, **81**

Kay Scarpetta books, 78
Kennedy, John F., **20**, 21–22, 27, 45, 91
Kerouac, Jack, 15, **16**, 17, 31
Kesey, Ken, 31
King, Martin Luther, Jr., 21–22, 25, **25**
King, Stephen, 46, **47**, 48, 64, 69, 74, 90
Kingston, Maxine Hong, 92
Kinney, Jeff, 95
*Kite Runner, The*, 93
Koontz, Dean, 48, 90

Lahiri, Jhumpa, 92–93
Larsson, Stieg, 91
Leary, Timothy, 30–31, 39
le Carré, John, 12, 64
Le Guin, Ursula K., 34, 79
Lee, Harper, 26, 77
Lemony Snicket's A Series of Unfortunate Events, 82–83, **83**
Lewis, C. S., 18, 79

*Lord of the Flies*, 14
Lord of the Rings, 18, 79
*Lovely Bones, The*, 98
*Love You Forever*, 68
Lowry, Lois, 84
Ludlum, Robert, 12, 61, 69, 74

MacLaine, Shirley, 41
**mainstream**, 10, 15, **16**, 23, **23**, 25, 34, 38–39, 42–43, 62, 66, 92
Malcolm X, 25–26
*Marley and Me*, 94
Martin, George R. R., 79, 82
*Maus: A Survivor's Tale*, 66
Maze Runner series, 87
McBratney, Sam, 84
McCullough, Colleen, 63–64
memoirs, 28, 45, 55, 59, 93
Memory, Sorrow, and Thorn series, 79
*Men Are from Mars, Women Are from Venus*, 75
Meyer, Stephanie, 87
*Middlesex*, 98
Millennium series, 91
Miller, Frank, 66
Momaday, N. Scott, 43
Moore, Alan, 66
Munsch, Robert, 68

*Naked Lunch*, 33
*Nanny Diaries, The*, 74
Native Americans, 43
New Age movement, 39, **40**, 41–42
*New York Times*, 9–10, 14, 27, 41, 51, 56, **57**, 59, 61, 66, 74–75, 77, 79–80, 84, 86, 88–90, 92–93, 95
Nixon, Richard, 45

Obama, Barack, 91, 93
Olivia series, 98
*One Flew Over the Cuckoo's Nest*, 31
One Minute Manager series, 59
*On the Road*, 17
*Outsiders, The*, 35

paperback books, 17
Paterson, Katherine, 50
Patterson, James, 78, 90
Peale, Norman Vincent, 8–9
**pen name**, 12, 48
Percy Jackson & the Olympians series, 87
Perry Mason books, 77
*Persepolis*, 66
Pfister, Marcus, 84
**physiological**, 44
Plath, Sylvia, 28
**plight**, 26
*Polar Express, The*, 68
*Power of Positive Thinking, The*, 8–9
**prestigious**, 27
Pretty Little Liars series, 87
Principal, Victoria, 56, 58
**prodigal**, 64
*Publishers Weekly*, 10, 12, 68

*Rainbow Fish*, 84
Ram Dass, 39, **40**, 41
Reagan, Ronald, 53, 91
Reichs, Kathy, 78
**reincarnation**, 41
**revolutionize**, 17
Rice, Anne, 46, 74
Richler, Mordecai, 50
romance novels, 17, 55, 63–64, 91, 98

*Roots*, 51
*Rosemary's Baby*, 36
Rowling, J. K., 82, 86
Rushdie, Salman, 65
Russell, Rachel Renee, 95

Sagan, Carl, 61
**sage**, 41
Salinger, J. D., 13–14, **14**
*Satanic Verses, The*, 65
Scarry, Richard, 35
Scheffler, Axel, 84
science fiction, 31–34, **32**
*Seabiscuit*, 94
See, Lisa, 93
**segregation**, 24
Sendak, Maurice, 35
*Separate Peace, A*, 15
September 11 attacks, 85, 91
*Sex and the City*, 73
*Sex and the Single Girl*, 44
Shannara series, 79
Sheehy, Gail, 50–51
Shepard, Sara, 87
Shopaholic series, 74
*Silence of the Lambs*, 46
*Silent Spring*, 36
Silverstein, Shel, 50
Simmons, Richard, 56
Song of Ice and Fire series, 79, 82
Sparks, Nicholas, 91
Spiegelman, Art, 66
*Spy Who Came In from the Cold, The*, 12
Steel, Danielle, 63, 69, 74, 90
Steinbeck, John, 19
Steinem, Gloria, 28–29
Stine, R. L., 82
*Stranger in a Strange Land*, **32**, 33
**surrealism**, 33

Tan, Amy, 92
**technophobe**, 6
*Temp, The*, 74
Temperance Brennan books, 78
*To Kill a Mockingbird*, 26, 77
Tolkien, J. R. R., 18, 79
*Travels with Casey*, 94
Trump, Donald, 59–60, **60**
*Tuesdays with Morrie*, 84
Turow, Scott, 77
Twilight series, 87
*2001: A Space Odyssey*, 33–34

Van Allsburg, Chris, 68
Vietnam War, 22, 37, **38**, 44
Viorst, Judith, 50

*Watchmen*, 66
*Watership Down*, 42, 86
Wheel of Time series, 79
*Where's Waldo?*, 66
*Where the Sidewalk Ends*, 50
*Where the Wild Things Are*, 35
Wolfe, Tom, 31, 39
Women's Murder Club series, 78
World War II, 7, 19, 94
Wright, Richard, 24

# About the Author

DIANE DAKERS was born and raised in Toronto, Ontario, and now makes her home on Canada's West Coast. Diane has been a newspaper, magazine, television, and radio journalist since 1991. She has written three novels and fifteen nonfiction books for middle school and young adult readers.

# MAGNIFICENT OBSESSION

## The Outrageous History of Film Buffs, Collectors, Scholars, and Fanatics

**Anthony Slide**

UNIVERSITY PRESS OF MISSISSIPPI • JACKSON

www.upress.state.ms.us

Designed by Peter D. Halverson

The University Press of Mississippi is a member of the Association of American University Presses.


Manufactured in the United States of America

First printing 2018
∞

Library of Congress Cataloging-in-Publication Data

Names: Slide, Anthony, author.
Title: Magnificent obsession : the outrageous history of film buffs, collectors, scholars, and fanatics / Anthony Slide.
Description: Jackson : University Press of Mississippi, 2018 | Includes bibliographical references and index. |
Identifiers: LCCN 2017035688 (print) | LCCN 2017042952 (ebook) | ISBN 9781496815989 (epub single) | ISBN 9781496815996 (epub institutional) | ISBN 9781496816009 ( pdf single) | ISBN 9781496816016 (pdf institutional) | ISBN 9781496810533 (hardcover : alk. paper)
Subjects: LCSH: Motion picture audiences. | Fans (Persons) | Motion pictures—Collectors and collecting. | Motion pictures—Study and teaching.
Classification: LCC PN1995.9.A8 (ebook) | LCC PN1995.9.A8 S57 2018 (print) | DDC 302.23/43—dc23
LC record available at https://lccn.loc.gov/2017035688

British Library Cataloging-in-Publication Data available

Here's to you, please. Gravediggers, buzzards, scavengers!
That's what you are! Dealing with dead and old stuff.
Here's to you. All of you.

—Erich von Stroheim drinking a toast to the staff on a visit to the British Film Institute in the 1950s

# CONTENTS

Acknowledgments XI

Introduction 3

**Chapter 1.** Enter the Film Buff 21

**Chapter 2.** Fan Clubs and Fan Mail 45

**Chapter 3.** Chaw Mank 61

**Chapter 4.** Film Buff Screenings 73

**Chapter 5.** David Bradley and Herb Graff and the Film Collector as Film Buff 95

**Chapter 6.** Film Buff Meets Film Scholar 111

**Chapter 7.** Publishing, Publications, and Bookstores for the Film Buff 130

**Chapter 8.** The Silent Movie Theatre 147

**Chapter 9.** Sex and the Film Buff 162

**Chapter 10.** Organized Film Buffs 173

**Chapter 11.** Joe Franklin 187

**Chapter 12.** Stalkers 195

**Chapter 13.** The Film Buff, the Internet, and the New Age 206

Notes 215

Bibliography 232

Index 239

# WARNING

This Book Contains Material That May Be Offensive to Film Buffs.
Discretion Is Advised.
Similarly, Because of Its Anecdotal Style,
Together with Some of the Author's Comments,
the Book May Well Offend Academics in the Film Community.

BECAUSE OF ITS SUBJECT MATTER, THIS BOOK WILL OUTRAGE A SMALL, inarticulate, but loudmouthed group of individuals, easily identifiable as today's film buffs. It is not intended for their pleasure, and obviously they will not believe anything to be found herein. Except perhaps heavily disguised, they, the living, will not find themselves in the pages of this book. What I have to say about them is too inflammatory for public consumption. I do write, and often with genuine affection, of many of the film buffs of the past, whom I knew and liked—and who, most importantly, were kind and helpful to me. I will remember them with pleasure as I grow old and I see their hobby diminished by their successor film buffs. I similarly expect that academics will find much to criticize here, in large because I dismiss the jargon in which they delight, and I write for a discerning audience of which I do not consider them a meaningful part. Much here is not as well documented as I would like or as academics would expect—not that I do not find a surprising number of academic texts often to lack accurate sources—and this is because I am relying on my memory of events and individuals, neither of which were committed to paper at the time.

It is the subject matter, in fact, that may not only antagonize but also confuse. While the basic story is that of the film buff, this volume also covers a wide range of supplemental and related issues, with which a film buff might be associated—from collecting autographs, film stills, and films themselves, to all the "small" industries that cater to their tastes (conventions, publications, etc.).

# ACKNOWLEDGMENTS

HOW DOES ONE ACKNOWLEDGE WHAT IS PERHAPS ALMOST A LIFETIME'S research, conducted not only in libraries and archives, but also, and more importantly, through interface with the subjects of this book, encountered through the years at "paper shows," conventions, and film screenings? Sadly, libel laws prevent my naming and discussing many of today's film buffs, and so the emphasis of this volume is primarily on the past and almost exclusively on American film buffs.

In researching this book, I have made extensive use of the holdings of the Margaret Herrick Library of the Academy of Motion Picture Arts and Sciences and the Cinematic Arts Library (what a pretentious title) at the University of Southern California. Special thanks at the latter, as always, to Ned Comstock and Steve Hanson.

Among individuals who have been willing to talk or communicate with me while knowing of my plans are Cliff Adam, Catherine Barbour, Rudy and Stacey Behlmer, Joan Cohen, Bill Dowson (Deanna Durbin Society), Sue Garland (Appreciating Jeanette MacDonald Club), Robert Gitt, Jere Guldin, Patricia King Hanson, Mike Hawks, John T. Hillman, Richard Koszarski, Marv Lachman, Richard Lamparski (a great resource), Steve Lewis, Bennett Lovett-Graff, Leonard Maltin, Howard Mandelbaum, Jeffrey Mantor (Larry Edmunds Bookshop), Marsha McCreadie, the late George J. Mitchell, James Robert Parish, Gary Rhodes, Andre Soares, Eric Spilker, Lea Whittington, and Valerie Yaros.

Special thanks to Ronald Bowers, Eleanor Knowles Dugan, Ed and Mary Maguire, Charles Shibuk, Romano Tozzi, and Jerry Vermilye, who were there. Without William J. Felchner, it would not have been possible to write the chapter on Chaw Mank. Thanks to Bambi Everson for sharing memories of her father, and Brad Franklin for his amazing help with the chapter on his father, Joe Franklin.

There is much that is personal and subjective here, and so I recall with affection those who are no longer with us but who will live on, I hope, in part through participation in this volume: DeWitt Bodeen, Bob Chatterton, John Dewar, William K. Everson, George Geltzer, Robert Giroux, Herb Graff, Henry Hart, Larry Lee Holland, John LeBold, Robin Little, Don Miller, Norman Miller, Charles Phillips Reilly, and, yes, even David Bradley.

At the University Press of Mississippi, I would like to thank director Craig W. Gill, project editor Valerie Jones, designer Pete Halverson, and copy editor Peter Tonguette (who confesses that perhaps he is a film buff).

The illustrations in the book are primarily from the author's collection, with others provided by Catherine Barbour, Mike Hawks, Richard Lamparski, Bennett Lovett-Graff, Jeffrey Mantor, Gary Rhodes, Jerry Vermilye, and Marc Wanamaker/Bison Archives.

# MAGNIFICENT OBSESSION

# INTRODUCTION

FILM—THE MOTION PICTURE, THE MOVIES, CALL IT WHAT YOU WILL—HAS been for more than a century the licit visual, and later vocal, drug of choice for the masses. It is the siren song for those seeking not simply entertainment or an escape from reality, but rather something to experience which does not cost too much and which gets one out of the house for a few hours. Simply put, the movies are there to entertain, and that they do very well, even if at times the purveyors of the medium do not fully understand what it is their audiences expect.

New movies attract the average man and woman, often in the twenty-first century much younger than they were a half-century earlier. To this group, an older film is one made a decade or so ago, and an older movie star is not Humphrey Bogart or James Cagney, but more likely Liam Neeson, Kevin Costner, or Russell Crowe. But there is a second, smaller, yet quite vocal group, and they are the ones to whom an "old" movie can have been made in the 1910s or the 1950s, though seldom little later, and they are the ones for whom most of the stars on whom they dote are no longer at Metro-Goldwyn-Mayer, which once boasted more stars than are in Heaven, but in a literal Heaven or its cinematic equivalent. They are the film buffs, to whom, as one writer put it, "moviegoing in America is a blood sport,"[1] and for whom the local multiplex shows nothing of interest. If they actually attend a film screening, it will be at an art house or the local museum with attendant movie auditorium. More likely, they will be found on a Saturday night, or any other night of the week for that matter, at home with the television tuned to Turner Classic Movies. They get their advice on what to watch not from Kenneth Turan in the *Los Angeles Times* or Anthony Lane in the *New Yorker*, but from Robert Osborne, hosting Turner Classic Movies and offering informative facts with which many a film buff will take issue or contradict.[2]

"Film buff" may be an informal noun, suggesting nothing more than someone who knows a lot about film, but a true film buff is anything but informal in his or her chosen semi-profession. And, yes, it is a profession in that it has generally taken over the film buff's life to the detriment of relationships and paying work. A film buff works to pay for his fixation, as much as a drug addict needs money for his fix, and a film buff's relationships are governed by similar obsessive feelings towards film. A film buff may be able to identify the presence of a microphone shadow down to the sprocket hole, but he is not someone who knows a lot about current motion pictures. Recent films are not part of a genuine film buff's world. The cinema for which he or she has a nostalgia is one from a bygone age, and the nostalgia is in no way based on the film buff's having lived through that era. A film buff may host an Academy Awards party, but the winners are of no particular interest. What is of more appeal is who from the past will be present at the ceremony; in 2014, it was Kim Novak and Sidney Poitier whom the film buff turned on the television to watch, not Bradley Cooper or Angelina Jolie. A film buff works for the honor that the title implies. He or she keeps careful records of films seen, even the locations at which they were seen, and is scrupulous in documenting any discrepancies in the running times between those on television or at the theatre and those reported in the *Film Daily Yearbook*.

Back in 1964, the legendary film buff, film collector, and film historian William K. Everson described the members of the Theodore Huff Memorial Film Society, a definition that would apply to all film buffs at least up through the birth of the twenty-first century:

> Film Society members are a dedicated bunch, but not always too easy to get along with. There are always the handful of self-appointed "authorities," and a few neurotics drawn to films of the past because they find the present untenable, and thus are able to retreat into memories of happier days. Fortunately, these are at a minimum, but the rest of us are a little opinionated and hard-to-take at times, and few of us are completely normal.[3]

The film buffs of whom Everson writes lived in a kinder, gentler time when film buffs were similarly kind and gentle, caring of other and anxious to share their knowledge. Yes, some might be eccentric, and some might be decidedly odd. But you could enjoy, be amused by their company. They were part of a noble breed of people who loved movies—even film professors back then, once upon a time, actually had an affection for their subject. How times have changed.

Compared to William K. Everson, Richard Lamparski, of *Whatever Became Of . . . ?* fame, never liked talking to fans or film buffs. They made him uncomfortable. And as he points out, "They don't really like the stars. They want to be these people. Envy. The ultimate deadly sin."[4] And might that be why today's film buffs use blog sites to criticize published writers and professionals? Nothing more than envy?

It has been suggested that the cultural identity of a fan is based on a commitment "to something seemingly unimportant and 'trivial' as a film or TV series."[5] Yet, no film buff would consider a film or TV series to which he was committed as "trivial." Just as this same author advises that "'cult' and 'fandom' are contested terms both inside and outside the Academy,"[6] so is the definition of a film buff equally contested, confused, and basically impossible for anyone to agree upon.

A film buff reads the *American Film Institute Catalog* not for the wealth of carefully researched documentation it provides, but rather in the hope of finding an error. Better yet, has the *Catalog* neglected a title? The delight in such a discovery is not diminished by the reality that the running time of the film is under the four-reel minimum for inclusion or that, despite production data being published in the trade papers, the film was never actually made. The latter is a feeble excuse as far as most film buffs are concerned; they would rather believe a seventy-year-old entry in the *Hollywood Reporter* or *Variety* than that "assembled" by the *Catalog* staff.

The running time for a film as published in the *American Film Institute Catalog* is based on a contemporary published source. But a film buff will reject such running times, preferring to sit and watch a film while keeping one eye on a stopwatch. The suggestion that there might be a slight variance in the speed at which a projector can run is an irrelevancy. Is the average film buff aware that films can be compressed in terms of length when aired on television? Does he not realize that for many years in the United Kingdom films have been aired on television at twenty-five, as opposed to twenty-four, frames per second, and that VHS tapes and DVDs recorded in Britain will be running at a faster speed?

A genuine film buff also keeps lists of every film he or she has seen, often with information as to location of the screening and perhaps a brief, as short as one-word, critical summary. Film buffs will boast of the films they have seen and can even come to the attention of a periodical during a slow news period. As early as the summer of 1955, *Look* magazine devoted five pages to a thirty-two-year-old Waco, Texas, sportswriter, George Raborn, who had seen 5,592 films since 1928 and paid $6,258.48 for the privilege. Raborn nominated *A Place in the Sun* as the greatest movie of all time. *Look* magazine obviously got the story from gossip columnist James Bacon, who had written of Raborn in his March 15, 1955, column.

Obviously impressed with his self-created fame, George Raborn decided to advance himself further with the self-publication of a sixty-four-page book, *How Hollywood Rates*, in which he provides his personal statistics on All-Time Super Stars, All-Time Best Actors and Actresses, 100 Best Movie Kisses, Most Disappointing Movies, Worst Performances—Men and Women, and Worst Movies, among other categories. In an age when self-publication was less commonplace than it is today, his volume represented quite an achievement. For the record, Clark Gable and Lana Turner top the list of All-Time Super Stars, and *White Pongo* (1945) is named Worst Movie of All Time. Raborn, who appears to have been unmarried (no surprise), dedicates the book to his mother, "who to me is more beautiful than Lana Turner and more talented than Bette Davis."

George Raborn may have published a book, but his fame as a film buff is as nothing compared to that of "Preview Henry," aka Henry Bone, whose death was marked with full-page tributes in both the *Hollywood Reporter* and *Daily Variety* on January 7, 1987, paid for by Columbia, M-G-M/UA, Paramount, Twentieth Century-Fox, Universal, Walt Disney, and Warner Bros. A victim of autism, an illness perhaps affecting more film buffs than might be diagnosed as sufferers, Henry was a familiar presence at film previews and film premiers, with his trademark baseball cap on top of his balding head, bony features, diminutive size, sports shirt, and string tie. As reported in the *Los Angeles Times* (January 7, 1987), "He was a lonely figure who spent his days caring for his mother and the remainder of his time catching buses from his Hollywood home to the sites of his favored previews."

It all started in 1954, when Henry was given a free ticket to a sneak preview of the Lucille Ball–Desi Arnaz vehicle (no pun intended), *The Long, Long Trailer*. Discovering how previews worked, Henry went to just about every one of them, and he also gained some work as an extra. He would read the trade papers at a Hollywood newsstand, and soon became a regular and welcome presence at the screenings. Publicists discovered that what Henry liked would be a box-office success, and Henry became a good luck charm. In 1976, he was the guest of honor at the premiere of *Train Ride to Hollywood*, and presented with a lifetime theatre pass by comedian Jack Oakie. Despite the honor, *Train Ride to Hollywood* did not make it to his list of favorite films, which was topped by *The Sound of Music*.

In 1980, he and his mother were the victims of a home invasion, with thieves taking his memorabilia, and leaving the two tied up. The couple were not found for five days, and the ordeal led to the eighty-year-old mother dying, and Henry's spending six weeks in hospital. As evidence of just how much of a good luck charm was Henry, during his hospitalization, Michael Cimino's *Heaven's Gate* opened, and became arguably the most unappreciated film in Hollywood history. Henry Bone died on January 3, 1987, with his age estimated to be in the late fifties.

In 1923, a ten-year-old in Meade, Kansas, Madeleine Fayette, began collecting fan magazines. When storage became a problem, she decided to clip the photographs and captions from the fan magazines, discarding the remaining pages—a tragedy as any film buff or, for that matter, anyone interested in film history will agree. The clipped photographs, along with whatever film stills she might acquire, were pasted into scrapbooks, one volume per star. The accumulated pages were sold off in 1978 at $2.50 a page, with the exception of the 1,034 pages devoted to Joan Crawford (with which Fayette refused to part). Some were sold at discount, including Cybill Shepherd: "I don't know why I even wasted the glue on people like her or Zsa Zsa Gabor."[7]

Asked by *Los Angeles Times* staff writer Burt Prelutsky if she regretted the thousands of hours she had spent in compiling her scrapbooks, Madeleine Fayette responded, "Honey, during the '40s and early '50s, I hardly spent any time on them. It was during that period that I had two disastrous marriages. Believe me, all things considered, I would have been a lot better off staying home and cutting out the pictures."[8] At least Fayette enjoyed a couple of relationships, which is probably two more than most film buffs have ever achieved.

Among the most impressive of film buff-collected, scrapbook-pasted clippings are those of Constance McCormick, whose mother was fan magazine writer Constance Palmer and father was character actor Lucien Littlefield. She began clipping fan magazines in 1934, and later all manner of periodicals and newspapers, indexing and scrapbooking by subject. In 1966, she decided to donate the collection to the Academy of Motion Picture Arts and Sciences, but on arrival at its then-Melrose Avenue location was horrified as the boxes were taken away from her, loaded onto carts, and whisked into storage. Connie wanted her scrapbooks to be living entities, changed her mind, and donated the collection on November 2, 1966 (her fortieth birthday) to the Cinematic Arts Library at the University of Southern California. Up until her death in 2014, she visited on a regular basis and constantly added to the collection, by then identified by all as "a search engine name Connie."

Madeleine Fayette and Constance McCormick are interesting examples of female film buffs, and not simply because they are female. Rather, like so many young girls, they compiled scrapbooks, a hobby that most grew out of while still teenagers. Young ladies moved on, rejected a childish hobby, and they were replaced by male film buffs, who found the joy of magazine and newspaper clippings and their content as adults, when they should have known better. Madeleine Fayette and Constance McCormick continued with their hobby as adult and female keepers, not of the flame, but of the scrapbook.

There is at least one entire family which might be designated film buffs. They are the Gents of Milford Haven in Wales, who promoted themselves as the Hollywood Musical Family, corresponded with similar enthusiasts throughout the world, and were the proud possessors of more than 2,000 photographs of Jane Powell, displayed in fifty albums.[9]

Of course, it should be acknowledged that one did not need to be either a film buff or young to be an obsessive moviegoer. In 1974, ninety-one-year-old Paul Morgan, who had emigrated from Yugoslavia in 1905 and had worked in the Detroit auto industry, was identified as having spent a total of 9,125 days at his local movie theatre in Miami, Florida, during the previous twenty-five years. Morgan would watch the same film as many as four times in two days and considered the time well spent, not to mention a worthwhile use of his income consisting of Social Security and earnings from the cleaning of rooms at the apartment house in which he lived.[10]

Similarly, film buffs can come from a variety of backgrounds. One very active autograph seeker of the 1970s and 1980s was a police officer, Lieutenant Luther Hathcock, living in Hickory, North Carolina. Elderly female former stars were impressed by his title—the thrill of having a police lieutenant write to them. Through correspondence and occasional telephone calls, he was able to amass eighteen albums of signed photographs and letters, which he shared not with fellow film buffs—somewhat unknown in his hometown—but with the residents of local senior citizen clubs. In return for his presence and the presence of his albums, Hathcock would ask that the audience send a card to African American character actor Stepin

Fetchit, at that time living alone and relatively forgotten in the Motion Picture Country House.

Film buffs usually pursue their hobby alone, rather than in packs, and seldom with family members. There is an exception in the twin brothers Austin and Howard Mutti-Mewse, who began corresponding with stars of the past at the age of twelve from their home in New Malden, Surrey, England. Their first letter was to Lillian Gish, an actress always willing to respond to correspondence from just about anybody, and her acknowledgment of them resulted in the Mutti-Mewse brothers writing up to thirty letters a week to former stars. The pair made their first trip to the United States in 1992; they met Ginger Rogers, James Stewart (who asked if their English schooling meant an ignorance of the American poets), and Frank Sinatra, who told them, "You're making me feel so young telling me about all those old people." After giving their parents' telephone number to Marlene Dietrich, she called them at 3 a.m., and as the telephone was in the parents' bedroom, they talked with her while they slept on.[11] In 2014, at the age of forty-one, and married, the brothers published a collection of their autographed photographs and correspondence under the title of *I Used to Be in Pictures: An Untold Story of Hollywood*.[12]

An obsession can be a dangerous thing, and so it most certainly is with some film buffs. To such film buffs, theft is not a crime. When a film buff sees a particularly desirable item in a library, his first thought is whether this is the best repository for such material. Would it not be better housed, and, more importantly, better loved in the film buff's home? If the answer is a resounding "yes," then the film buff will have no hesitation in purloining the treasure.

Perhaps the oddest, most obsessive film buff that Mike Hawks encountered at Larry Edmunds Bookstore was a fan of the 1935 film *The Black Room*, in which Boris Karloff plays two brothers, one good and one bad. The good brother has a paralyzed arm, which, defying any physical possibility, appears to be attached across his chest.[13] One day, Hawks and colleague Pete Bateman were standing at the stills counter at the old store, approached by a central corridor, hemmed in by books:

> I look down the corridor and slowly coming towards us is this guy who looks about twenty, with an older woman, and he's like this [puts arm across chest]. Fuck. I'm thinking there's only one possibility. He wants *The Black Room*. He is standing at the counter, and, sure enough, he wants to

> see the file on *The Black Room*. And, of course, he's only using one arm, and I'm thinking, "When is he going to drop the illusion, the game he's playing here." He's found a couple of stills and he's using only one arm. When is he going to put the arm down? He goes up to the front desk, and finally when he has to pay, the arm comes down.[14]

Unnatural death is not unknown in the film buff community. At least one prominent film buff, Brooklyn-based John Cocchi, who according to the Internet Movie Database "was reputed [*sic*] for his encyclopedic knowledge of old Hollywood films," was well-known in the community, in particular for his ability to identify obscure cast members in equally obscure "B" movies.[15] Seventy-four years old, and depressed at what he had perhaps realized was a meaningless life, Cocchi was last seen outside his home on April 16, 2014. His body was found in the waters off Sandy Hook, New Jersey, on June 16, an apparent suicide.

F. "Froggy" Gwynplaine MacIntyre was not as highly regarded as a film buff as Cocchi, but he did have some reputation as an eccentric writer of science fiction, fantasy, and horror stories and novels. Much of MacIntyre's life appears to have been a fantasy of his own making, including the claim that he was a Scottish orphan brought up in Australia, and had three wives and two children. He adopted the name "Gwynplaine" after the character in Victor Hugo's novel *The Man Who Laughs* and the 1928 film of the same name, whose mouth has been carved into a permanent, horrific smile. MacIntyre was notorious for claiming to have found and viewed "lost" films, antagonizing fellow film buffs with his statements and critical commentary published on the Internet Movie Database (IMDb).

He has been described by the *New York Times* as "a huge gentle fellow . . . an enigmatic, eccentric loner,"[16] more precisely a visual and mental mess. One individual who might question the *Times* description is neighbor Helene Lapointe, whom MacIntyre allegedly stripped naked, duct-taped to a chair, and sprayed with black paint. On June 25, 2010, MacIntyre set afire the Bensonhurst, New York, apartment, where he had lived for twenty-five years, destroying himself and all his belongings. His body remained unclaimed.

Barry Brown was a good-looking, young actor, whose most successful role was opposite Cybill Shepherd in *Daisy Miller* (1974). He was also a film buff, obsessed with the collection of data on the births and deaths of actors, primarily obscure ones. Brown was a frequent visitor to the Margaret Herrick Library of the Academy of Motion Picture Arts and Sciences, discussing his work and showing off a gun with which he seemed as fixated as

Marian Marsh with Boris Karloff as the bad brother pretending to be the good brother with the paralyzed arm in *The Black Room* (1935).

with his research; as this writer can testify, the gun was not exactly a welcome guest in the library. It was with that gun that Barry Brown ended his life on June 25, 1978, at the age of twenty-seven.[17]

There have been quite a few highly eccentric film collectors, but none more so perhaps than Alois "Al" Detlaff (1921–2005), whose main claim to fame is that he owned the only surviving print of the 1910 one-reel version of Edison's *Frankenstein*. Not only did he own the print in its original 35mm nitrate format, but he refused to allow anyone to view it outside of his presence and he would carry the print with him by plane, train, or car to a screening destination, including the Pordenone Film Festival in Italy in 2003. He was generally eccentrically attired, often referred to as Old Father Time, and his film collection was equally eccentrically housed, for the most part lying around his Cudahy, Wisconsin, home on the floor and with no protective covering.

In 1986, Robert Wise, president of the Academy of Motion Picture Arts and Sciences, invited Detlaff to Los Angeles in an abortive attempt to

Barry Brown.

allow the Academy to preserve *Frankenstein*. Detlaff did permit Wise to see the film, unwinding it on a conference table, and he did persuade the famed editor-director to allow him to be photographed with Wise's Oscar. Thenceforth, Detlaff would sign copies of the photograph, "Academy Award winner Al Detlaff." His body was found by the police, perhaps a month after he had died, decomposing on the floor—along with his films.

Susan and Christopher Edwards were a middle-aged, lower-middle-class British couple, obsessed with the collection of movie memorabilia, for which they paid over-the-top prices. With limited personal funds, the obvious way to finance their favorite leisure-time occupation was to seek money from Susan's elderly parents. In reality, the demand was somewhat less than a voluntary one, as in 1998 the couple murdered the parents, burying their bodies in the back garden of the home in Mansfield in the North of England. When police finally uncovered the crime in 2012, the pair escaped to the continent, trying any means to raise money except one; they held onto the movie memorabilia. More than $24,000 had been invested in the collection, including $5,000 for a signed photograph of Gary Cooper, worth, in reality, little more than a few hundred dollars. When that memorabilia was eventually sold in compliance with the Proceeds of Crime Act in 2014, it was valued at a mere $5,000.

The tale of Susan and Christopher Edwards is a cautionary one, a warning to film buffs that crime really does not pay.

Crime may not pay, but the devotion of film buffs can be beneficial to a star, as Charles Bronson discovered in February 1999, when a retired chemist in Kentucky, named Audrey Jean Knauer, died, at the age of fifty-five, and in a subsequently contested, handwritten will left her entire estate of around $300,000 to the actor, with the proviso that anything he did not want be given to the Louisville Public Library.

The death of a film buff might not evoke any interest, or for that matter sympathy, from the film industry. But the industry did at one time worry how the death of a star might affect the fans and the buffs. While there had been earlier deaths of film stars, the first such occurrence to cause concern came in 1920, when Robert Harron, a young man who had been discovered by D. W. Griffith and on screen since 1907, died of a self-inflicted gunshot wound on September 5. Harron had recently signed a contract with Metro and completed his first film there, *Coincidence*. The studio was nonplussed as to how to handle the situation; it waited almost a year before timidly releasing the production and without any fanfare or acknowledgment of its star. How different it was a few years later, when Rudolph Valentino died on August 23, 1926. There was mass mourning and what can only be described as mass celebration of his passing, with one of the song hits of the year being "There's a New Star in Heaven Tonight" by J. Keirn Brennan, Jimmy McHugh, and Irving Mills. Dedicated to Valentino, it begins with the lyrics:

> Stars may come and stars may go up there in that starry space.
> There's a new star in heaven tonight that will never fade from our sight.

With his film work in decline, it might be argued that the best career move Valentino could have made was to die. It has certainly paid off through the years, with lasting fame endorsed and encouraged by the film buffs.

Robert Harron (center) in *Coincidence* (1920).

In view of the sexual identity of so many film buffs, it is not surprising that much of the interest in Valentino is governed by the issue of whether or not he was gay. Similar interest concerns Robert Harron, perhaps more so in recent years than at the time, despite one aged film buff, who was alive when the actor died, telling me that rumor had it that he was "buggered to death" by Griffith.

Who are these film buffs? They are to be found in every town and city in the United States, somehow attracted to each other by an obsession rather than a hobby. Where did they originate? How old is this strange phenomenon?

Questions abound, many, if not all of which, will be answered in the following pages. When did portions of the movie audience cease to be merely viewers and become buffs? Why did film buffs decide to collect autographs, and when did those movie star autographs became more valuable than those of some American presidents? When did the film buff become fixated with collecting not just autographs but also film stills, lobby cards, posters, and the like? When did dealers first develop to service these needs? When did art museums begin to promote screenings of films supposedly for those interested in the art of the motion picture but in reality for a growing film buff audience? At what stage did the industry realize the potential of such screenings for promotional purposes? For decades, the industry denigrated film buffs, refusing to cooperate with their drug-like need for memorabilia of the past, and then came VHS tapes, laserdiscs and DVDs, and suddenly film buffs were a group to be cherished or at the least exploited.

Does the film buff wish to be a part of the film industry? There are certainly film buffs gainfully employed there, often in a menial capacity, but film buffs seldom seek a position of importance—with the possible exception of a handful of directors, including Joe Dante, John Landis, Martin Scorsese, and Quentin Tarantino[18]—and books such as *Careers for Film Buffs*, by Jaq Greenspan, and *Cool Careers without College for Film and Television Buffs*, by Katie Haegle, both of which advocate industry careers, misunderstand the nature of the film buff.[19]

What is the relationship of the film buff, with his or her (generally his) passion, to the passionless academics who study and write, often in unreadable fashion on film in its many guises? Whatever else one may call film buffs, they are passionate for their medium of choice and love. The same cannot be said of the film academic. There is no intense excitement here in approach to the subject, only a cold-blooded interest in the money and the fame that may be generated. Certainly, as will be discussed later, there have been and presumably will continue to be some film academics who disgrace their profession by actually loving the subject they teach, and there are even some who may well be classified as film buffs. Thanks to the advent of the DVD, and with so much content readily available, colleges and universities have no need of 16mm prints to screen for their students, but less than a couple of decades ago, there were a number of film collectors, little more than film buffs, who were hired as film professors not on the basis of their academic credentials but on the number of 16mm film prints they could provide to their employer.

Psychologist Samuel Heckman had warned in 1920 that "the movies are . . . a make-believe world in which the characters are not real, mere shadows on the screen. Evidence, however [suggests] that to many young people . . . the world of the movies is not less real than life itself; the emotions and responses of the young to the fevered life of the screen are much the same as those in actual life."[20]

What Heckman wrote almost a century ago is applicable today, not to young people but to film buffs in any age group. They inhabit a world in which real life seldom intrudes, a world dominated by movies of the past, films from a different age. Indeed, theirs is a different world from that in which the rest of us live and try to survive.

As early as 1921, Dr. A. T. Poffenberger concluded that many adult movie fans were "morons" with the mental age of an eleven-year-old. He posited that "undeveloped" moviegoers were incapable of distinguishing between film and reality, much as do many film buffs today. "They constitute a real danger, since their physical age, which may be from fifteen years up, places them in a position to act upon suggestions more readily than the child."[21] Those who have suffered attack at the blog sites frequented by film buffs would agree.

In 1928, the fan magazine *Photoplay* approached psychiatrist Dr. Louis E. Bisch to consider whether the motion picture audience was comprised of morons. As *Photoplay* editor James R. Quirk explained, "Every day, from all sides, people throw mud at the moving picture audiences. They call them morons. If these millions of movie fans are morons, then, by far and large, the majority who compose the general public are morons too."[22] After careful study, Dr. Bisch concluded that the American public is not a "bunch of morons." His reasoning was that

> even persons whose intellect is far above the average like the movies and attend them regularly.
>
> But these people—sensible people—do not take the movies too seriously.
>
> They don't attend pictures to be edified.
>
> They don't want to be instructed.
>
> They don't seek uplift.
>
> No, people crowd the picture houses because they want to be entertained![23]

The non-morons comprising the audience could walk out before the film was over, they could comprehend that others in the audience might react differently than they did. They did not adopt the attitude that anyone who did not agree with their point of view was a moron.

And so the vast majority of those attending a film screening are normal people. But consider the attitude of the film buff in relation to the above reasons for identifying the audience as non-moronic. Such film buffs cannot be categorized as tolerant or as uninterested in taking the film too seriously. "Are We Morons?" asked *Photoplay*. And the answer is a definitive "yes" if we are film buffs.

The modern film buff has evolved in much the same way as the human has evolved from the ape, but perhaps without the same level of sophistication or the same notion of cleanliness and good health. Back in the 1990s, I recall talking with film historian Rudy Behlmer at a "paper show," at which film buffs and others bought and sold their memorabilia. Rudy had asked me to point out a particular film buff whom he wished to meet, and I identified him as the one with bad teeth. Rudy stared at the assembled crowd and responded, "But they all have bad teeth." And such it was and such it is.

Owners of memorabilia stores in Los Angeles would routinely call one another when a film buff with money came into the shop, alerting their colleagues that the individual might be on his way to their outlets. Asked what the prospective client looked like, the answer was always the same: "You'll know him when you see him."

There are those who resemble *Dracula*'s Renfield on a bad day. There is the prevalent smell of bad odor, the physical deformities. One New York-based collector would salivate so much over the photographs he was contemplating that a dry crust of saliva would form around his mouth. The same collector wore glasses attached to his ears with rubber bands, and, yes, worked the graveyard shift at the post office.

While it might be easy, and cruel, to dismiss most film buffs as the unwashed and quite definitely the unloved, there is an emotion here, often tempestuous in nature, that is deserving of respect and in need of nurturing. Without film buffs, many films of another age might well die or at least disappear from public view. Certainly, there will always be an audience for *Gone with the Wind* or *The Wizard of Oz*, but there will be less of an audience for the silent version of the latter, starring Larry Semon, or a 1930s drama with a Civil War theme such as *Of Human Hearts*. It is not without credulity that film archivists have designated non-major studio films, without fame and without apparent copyright claimants, as "orphan films." Nobody loves these films except for the film buff, and, sadly, not even a small majority of such film buffs.

Where would we be without the film buff? To whom could the "forgotten" screen personalities of the past look for recognition and a modicum of appreciation? Without the film buff, a Hollywood has-been would have absolute claim to such a title, but, thanks to the film buff, there are really no has-beens in today's film industry. Everyone has at least a handful of film buffs who adore and appreciate them. Truth be told, the film buffs don't buy film books and don't nurture the authors who scrupulously research and write such volumes. To them, the written word is an irrelevancy. Film is a visual medium, and the film buff likes that visual aspect as represented by the photographic still, the poster, and the lobby card. When actress Janet Gaynor's home was on fire, her husband Cedric Gibbons told her to grab the most valuable items she had. She rescued her film stills. There are few film buffs who would disagree with her decision.

As Erich von Stroheim had it, the film buffs deal with the dead and the old stuff. But in so doing they keep the past—not always the greatest part of the past and certainly not the immediate past, but they keep their concept of the past—alive. Von Stroheim does not hold perhaps major interest to them, no more than do John Ford or Jean Renoir, but the past for the film buff lies in the films of directors like William Beaudine or Reginald LeBorg—individuals who were never likely to be recognized as great filmmakers but who were mainstays of the industry.

There were former stars or, more correctly, featured players, who enjoyed the adulation that the film buffs proffered. Mae Clarke, who had appeared as Dr. Frankenstein's intended bride in the original *Frankenstein* and who, uncredited on screen, was the recipient of half a grapefruit in the face from James Cagney in *Public Enemy*, ended her years as a resident at the Motion Picture Country House. Each day, she would be seated in a dining room ostentatiously reading her fan mail in front of her fellow and sister residents who could not have cared less. She was sitting by herself at a table previously occupied by Mary Astor, a genuine star who had little time for fans and film buffs, and who refused to eat her meals at a table shared with other residents. At her demise, Mae Clarke donned the mantle of leading lady of the Motion Picture Country House and requisitioned Mary Astor's table.

Exemplifying the determined and often blinkered attitude of the film buff is the issue of the two Mrs. Roscoe "Fatty" Arbuckles. It was the first, Minta Durfee (whom Arbuckle married in 1908 and divorced in 1923), who had the attention of the film buffs, attending conventions and screenings and accepting appropriate adulation. When she eventually moved into the Motion Picture Country House, she spent her last days in the hospital there, still visited by her adoring buffs. Sitting with her, as a nurse-volunteer, was a woman ignored by the visitors. It was a curious experience, as that woman, Addie McPhail, once told me, to hear Minta Durfee addressed as "Mrs. Arbuckle," while she, Addie McPhail, as the widow, had actually been the last Mrs. Roscoe "Fatty" Arbuckle.

For every former star and leading player promoting a fan base there are those with little or no interest in the attention of film buffs. When she died in March 1991, Vilma Banky, glamorous Samuel Goldwyn star of the 1920s, felt herself forgotten, and had directed her lawyer that there be no report of her demise. Banky claimed that nobody had visited her house in many years, a spurious claim in that surely there were such routine visitors as the mailman, the gardener, or even the man from the Department of Water and Power to read the meter. She did not wish for recognition as her former self but never hid it. In the 1980s, a former RKO executive and his wife were eating an al fresco lunch at the Farmers Market in Los Angeles, and an elderly lady asked if she might sit at their table. In conversation, the RKO executive told her of his former position. "I worked for Goldwyn," the lady responded. "Were you a secretary?" he asked. "No, I was an actress named Vilma Banky." Luckily for Miss Banky, the executive was also a film buff and happy to acknowledge her fame and prominence.[24]

At least Vilma Banky identified herself, unlike Corinne Griffith, one of the most beautiful of silent stars, who during very messy divorce proceedings on May 5, 1966, took the witness stand in court and denied she was who she was. She also maintained that she was not seventy-one years old but only fifty-one and that she had been Corinne Griffith's stand-in in the early 1930s, that the real Corinne Griffith had died in Mexico, and that she was her on-screen replacement. Despite former silent stars Betty Blythe and Claire Windsor being called to identify her as the real Corinne Griffith, the substitute Corinne Griffith persisted in her claim. Luckily for film buffs, the substitute Corinne Griffith was still happy to sign autographs, not as the silent star she claimed not to be but as Corinne Griffith, the author of half-a-dozen books published from the 1950s through the 1970s.[25]

Until her death in 1990, Greta Garbo was the most prized of former stars for film buffs in terms of actual personal interaction (however slight). Many a film buff would approach the reclusive star as she walked the streets of Manhattan, generally wearing large sunglasses and a scarf, asking if she could tell them the time or the way to the Metropolitan Museum of Art. One elderly film buff worked in the fur department at New York's B. Altman department store on Fifth Avenue. When Garbo came in one day, inquiring about the storage of her furs for the summer months, the enthusiastic salesman drew up a lengthy agreement which he asked her to sign. The agreement remained his prized possession until sold many years later for $1,000.[26]

Somewhat less responsive to a film buff's ardor was Sylvia Sidney. Eric Sherman, whom Leonard Maltin remembers as a "wonderful character with a wild mop of hair,"[27] was a regular at the Theodore Huff Memorial Film Society. By day, he worked at the arts and crafts supply store of Arthur Brown & Brother. When Sylvia Sidney walked in one day, Sherman's first

Sylvia Sidney grudgingly signs autographs for fans in the 1930s.

words were, "Oh Miss Sidney, I just saw you in *Confessions of a Co-Ed* [1931]," to which the actress's response was, "Are you out of your fucking mind?"

Stars might recognize the value of the fans when at the height of their fame, but at its demise, found the attention irritating. The most famous of responses to fans was from dramatic and talented silent screen star Norma Talmadge, who was approached by a group of autograph collectors as she left the Vendome Restaurant in West Hollywood after lunch in October 1933. "Run along kiddies," she told them, "I don't need you now!"[28]

## Chapter One

# ENTER THE FILM BUFF

HOW DID IT ALL BEGIN? WHAT THEATRE AUDIENCE IN THE DAYS OF THE nickelodeon gave birth to the bona fide fan or buff? The term "buff" predates the motion picture by more than fifty years, originating in New York as early as 1820. Volunteer firefighters in the city wore buff-colored coats, and "buff" came into use to describe those who would follow the firemen and enjoy the experience of watching a fire and, in time, enthusiasts of all types. Enjoyment of a fire—whether caused by an accident or arson—suggests a level of maniacal fever, of which many film buffs might be accused. However, for more than half of the twentieth century, there was no linkage of "film" and "buff." Although there might have been many descriptive terms in use for decades in reference to film buffs, they were never actually identified as such.

A number of terms developed to describe a fixation with the motion picture itself, including, rather obviously, "cinemania," "filmania," and "flickeritis." Those fixated individuals were "movie-nuts," "cinemaddicts," "cinementhusiasts," "movie-ites," or simply "flicker fans." Autograph collectors were identified as "autografans," while male film enthusiasts briefly were identified as "reel boys."[1] Above all, they were autodidacts, self-taught in that there were no colleges or universities offering film courses to the first film buffs, and when such courses did materialize, they were generally beyond the means, both financially and intellectually, of an average film buff.

Just as there is no confirmed origin for the term "film buff," or equally "movie buff," so there is no precise definition. As of 2014, even Wikipedia had not posted an article using that exact term. WikiHow offers an eight-step program on becoming a film buff, which basically requires purchase of a film guide by Roger Ebert or Leonard Maltin, the viewing of lots of films, and the acquisition of DVDs from the cheapest sources available. There is no reference to such obvious film buff requirements as keeping lists, acquiring movie memorabilia, and attending film conventions, as well as deploring all remakes, approving of all silent films, and preferring black-and-white over color, unless such color happens to be in the form of an original Technicolor print from the 1930s or 1940s. A film buff can be many things to many people, and therein lies the problem of definition. Even the first usage is undocumented, with *Collins English Dictionary* suggesting that it dates back no further than the 1990s. But then the dictionary also defines a film buff as being a "connoisseur," and that is something very much in doubt.

With ease, academics can provide such definitions as: "Fandom is a sociocultural phenomenon largely associated with modern capitalist societies, electronic media, mass culture and public performance."[2]

Others might have some difficulty with such a ready-made comment. Film buffs would equally be nonplussed, undoubtedly wondering what the academic was talking about. "You talkin' to me?" in the words of Paul Schrader/Robert De Niro. Or, to quote Ozzy Osbourne, "You looking at me?"

Print-wise, it would seem that "film buff" was seldom, if ever, used prior to the first half of the twentieth century. The earliest documented use of the term in any major newspaper is in the November 21, 1960, issue of the *New York Times*, in a piece about John Hampton, owner of the Silent Movie Theatre in Los Angeles.[3] In December 1968, film critic Renata Adler asked in the *New York Times* if she was writing for the "film buff."[4] In the *Los Angeles Times*, the earliest reference to a film buff occurs on December 23, 1969, when film critic Charles Champlin (revered in the industry for seldom if ever reviewing a film he did not like) offered his selection of current film books, and managed to reference both "film buffs" and "film nuts" in the same piece.[5] Presumably, the terms are interchangeable.

It was the Japanese who first came up with an appropriate phrase applicable to all film buffs: "otaku." Basically, while it does not translate as such, it means someone who stays at home all the time and has no life. Initially, highly negative, otaku has become in recent years more acceptable, with a considerable number of Japanese, particularly those obsessing about anime and manga, self-identifying as otaku. (Because serial killer Tsutomu Kiyazaki had supposedly been influenced by anime and horror films, he was identified in 1990 as "The Otaku Murderer.")

Perhaps the first individual in the film industry to recognize the existence of film buffs, or at the least the rabidity of fans, was pioneer Carl Laemmle. Prior to his creation of Universal Pictures, Laemmle had founded in 1909 the Independent Moving Picture Company of America or IMP. That same year, he was able to lure leading lady Florence Lawrence away

Florence Lawrence.

from the American Biograph Company, where she had been recognized by filmgoers as a major star but remained unheralded and unidentified by order of her producers. Lawrence had been billed simply as "The Biograph Girl," and Laemmle obviously did not wish to promote a rival company by using the same name. Instead, he mounted a publicity campaign claiming that Lawrence had been killed in an accident in St. Louis. Once the story had been picked up by the trade papers, Laemmle denounced it as false, a lie planted in the press by his rivals in an effort to destroy the reputation of his new star. Florence Lawrence was now recognized in her own right and her own name by the fans and the buffs. The cult of personality had been acknowledged by the film community.

To Carl Laemmle must also go credit for catering to film buffs and film fans with the introduction of the studio tour, which originated at Universal Studios in 1915. Visitors were able to watch filming from the vantage point of bleacher seats built above the dressing room, with the price of admission also including a box lunch. The coming of sound made visiting the sets impractical, and it was discontinued until June 1964, when the current Universal Studio Tours came into being.

They may not have been described as film buffs, but as early as 1911, the trade paper *Moving Picture World* revealed that there were obsessive fans with many of the same traits found in film buffs of a more recent vintage. These early film buffs could identify the studio responsible for a specific one-reel short subject without viewing the credit title. "The easiest to tell, I think, is the Biograph," reported the unidentified writer. "Now a Kalem is easy to tell by the outdoor setting." A French-produced Pathé film was identifiable in comparison with a French-produced film from Gaumont. The same writer, in very film buff-like fashion, complained that *Among the Japanese* should have been titled *Among the Japanese in Chicago* or *Orientals Tramping around the Studio*. He continued, "The number of critical and sharpeyed fans is increasing every day and they [the producers] should know enough to know that pictures of Japan should be taken in Japan."[6]

Also in 1911, the *Moving Picture World* and another trade paper, the *New York Dramatic Mirror*, began weekly columns in which an in-house authority—Frank Woods, writing as "The Spectator," at the *Mirror*—answered questions from filmgoers. The questions generally addressed the identity of an actress or an actor, and both trade papers made it clear that no information on the personal lives of the players would be revealed. As the *Moving Picture World* made readers prissily aware, "Inquiry as to the private affairs of photoplays will not be answered. This includes the question as to whether or not they are married."[7]

As early as the first "Letters and Questions" column in the *New York Dramatic Mirror*, on July 5, 1911, Frank Woods displayed a certain flippant quality in his replies. When "A Lonesome Old Bachelor" in Philadelphia wrote of Mabel Normand's being "a lovable, sweet girl, with two great, large eyes and a wonderful personality," Woods responded, "Really Old Bach [*sic*] ought to get married. It's a pity to waste such honest worship on screen girls."[8]

Woods is also surprised at the naiveté of his readers. When one in Brooklyn asks as to the identity of "the colored mother" in Vitagraph's *Easter Babies*, he answers, "Good gracious! No, she isn't colored; she's white."[9]

An argument might be made that the appearance of these columns was evidence of the existence of the earliest film buffs, but, of course, truth be told, film buffs would not be asking questions, they would be answering them. It was America's first fan magazine, *Motion Picture Story Magazine*, which began actively catering to film buffs, when in July 1912, it announced, "We shall try to reserve a few pages each month for expressions of appreciation from our readers." The age of the opinionated film buff had arrived, and *Motion Picture Story Magazine* was quick to acknowledge the worth of the film buff's opinion when it added that readers were free to send letters, "for which no pay is expected."[10]

The earliest known individual who can accurately be described as a film buff is Richard Hoffman, who was born in Manhattan on June 20, 1901, presumably to a fairly affluent, middle-class family. He was an ardent moviegoer, beginning as early as 1913, while living on Staten Island with his mother, Laura, and his stepfather, Basil Scott, and he continued his obsession after a move in the summer of 1914 to the Germantown suburb of Philadelphia, visiting not only theatres in that city but also making regular trips to New York movie houses.

Richard Hoffman was a collector, interested not only in the obvious items, such as fan magazines, easily available to moviegoers, but also trade journals and house organs, and other exhibitor-oriented publications, together with film stills. What sets him apart and definitely "brands" Hoffman as a film buff is the handwritten record that he kept of all the films that he had seen. He divided a loose-leaf binder into sections by distributor, recording the title of the film, the stars, the production company, and the number of reels. He had, as Richard Koszarski has noted, a "methodical approach to his passion."[11] Hoffman's extant collection ends in January 1917, and no one will ever know if the "passion" continued into his adult life.

Richard Koszarski, who has undertaken extensive research into the collection, concludes that

> his collecting had nothing to do with *participating* in the new medium but instead allowed him to capture some record of the magic he discovered while sitting in those motion picture theaters. Hoffman's spiritual

> descendants today are less likely to be found in film schools than at movie "paper shows" and memorabilia auctions—activities that, if my experience is any guide, tend to be completely dominated by males.[12]

The collection survives, pretty much intact, thanks to a childhood friend, William R. Bogert Jr., who donated it to the Museum of the Moving Image in Astoria, New York, in 1984, having acquired it after Hoffman's death, the date of which is unknown, but was apparently a suicide.[13] Many film buffs today would surely wish that their collections might survive, and, more importantly, be archived and studied like Richard Hoffman's.

In 1916, the eminent psychologist Hugo Munsterberg published *The Photoplay: A Psychological Study*, in which he warned, apropos the motion picture and its audience, of "the trivializing influence of a steady contact with things which are not worth knowing."[14] Munsterberg was undoubtedly unaware of the existence of film buffs, but his comment would seem directed towards them. "An intellectually trained spectator" was what the motion picture needed, not the typical film buff audience.

Also in 1916, a critical year it would appear for recognition of the film buff, Anna Steese Richardson wrote in *McClure's* magazine of a disease sweeping the United States and which she identified as "filmitis." "The germs of infection lurk in every moving picture theatre," she wrote,[15] describing not so much an enthusiasm for the motion picture as an ego crisis affecting many in the audience who felt they could deliver a better performance than those actors on screen and that it was time for them to make the trip to Hollywood and find immediate employment in the industry.

At least one scholar has pointed out that "disease soon became a popular metaphor for fandom, one that was repeated endlessly in the press. Overtaken by the movie bug, fans allegedly lost control of their senses."[16]

In September 1926, this mass hysteria culminated in the funeral of Rudolph Valentino, seemingly more popular in death than in life. *Merton of the Movies* (1924) and *Movie Crazy* (1932) told in comic form of young men obsessed with an acting career in Hollywood, with the first based on a popular 1922 novel by Harry Leon Wilson, in turn based on an earlier *Saturday Evening Post* serialization.

Anna Steese Richardson was a former editor of the *Woman's Home Companion*, founder of the Better Babies Bureau, and for most of her long and active life heavily involved in women's issues. She recognized that the primary audience for motion pictures during the industry's formative years was female, and her article on "filmitis" is obviously addressed to a feminine

Guy Madison is so anxious to read his fan mail that he does not even have time to put on a shirt.

audience. She was not alone. Fan magazine publishers acknowledged that their readership was female, despite an early attempt to encourage more of a mixed subscription list. In determining an early female enthusiasm for the motion picture, there is a need to recognize that such enthusiasm did not identify itself as manic or buff-ish.

There can be little argument that autographs by stars for fans have changed drastically in the last one hundred years. In the 1910s, a star might sign a photograph to a fan with the sentiment, "Most Sincerely," and, generally from a male actor, "Cordially." The photograph might be a head-and-shoulders shot but it is not unusual for it to be full-body with severe, modest attire. Typical of the formality of the times is a 1917 letter to a fan from George Walsh, which reads in part, "it is gratifying to know that I have staunch friends who express themselves so sincerely as you."[17] Today, someone like Channing Tatum signs a photograph of himself at the minimum stripped to the waist and often further exposed, endorsing it with the words, "All My Love."

In the past, Anna May Wong, obviously, would sign off with "Orientally Yours." After publishing his autobiography, *Two Reels and a Crank*, the co-founder of the Vitagraph Company of America, Albert E. Smith, would sign, "Vitagraphically Yours," although there is no record that he used that sentiment during the period during which his company was in existence. Alice Lake, a Metro star of the early 1920s, would sign her fan mail with the greeting, "Oceans of Good Cheer from A Lake." Character actor Hugh Herbert's catchphrase was "woo hoo," and he would use that phrase to sign off his fan letters.

In 1916, not surprisingly Bessie Love (born Juanita Horton) signed off a letter to a fan "lovingly," telling her admirer from Des Moines, Iowa, that "after weeks of hard work on a picture, it is nice to know that it was a success." For fear that the fan might not realize just how hard it was to act on screen, she continued, "Our work is very trying some times. Emotional acting is not easy."[18]

There were stars partial to a particular color for their signature; Ginger Rogers in her prime would always use green ink. In semi-retirement, Rogers became more suspicious of "fans" writing for autographs, suspecting that her signature was being sold (it was), and so she actually kept a card file on those film buffs requesting an autograph, and once a name was in the file, no more signatures were forthcoming.

Some stars were not content with a mere signature; Liberace would add a piano or a candelabra or both to his signature, while Arthur Lake would often add below his signature a very pleasing sketch of himself as Dagwood in the "Blondie" film series.

Clark Gable explained in 1934 that he would always sign at the top of a sheet of paper or page in an autograph album, with a line drawn above his signature. He had discovered that a fellow actor had been confronted with an IOU, the amount involved being written above his name, signed for an autograph collector.

The location in which to find a potential autograph varies, being sometimes as mundane as the local supermarket. In Studio City, where I live, I have seen everyone from Ralph Bellamy and Estelle Winwood to Charlton Heston and Marlon Brando shopping at my local Hughes store. Lee Graham grimly reported in 1970 that with fewer stars active, "Autograph Hunters now stand outside the unemployment office and fill their books with big name stars."[19]

Film buffs, it must be noted, are not that dishonest, but certainly they are aggressive enough to force an actor or actress to sign their name on numerous photographs or index cards, with the intent to sell the surplus or at the least exchange with another film buff. The value of the signature was/is determined by the willingness of the star to provide an autograph. Lillian Gish was most amenable, and would often sit for an hour or more after her one-woman show signing autographs, as well as answering all fan mail (with the help of manager James Frasher). Her signature is relatively inexpensive today. Surprisingly, Louise Brooks in old age would often write abusive letters to fans, and yet her autograph and those letters sell to film buffs in the many hundreds of dollars. A star's autograph might show up in an unlikely location.

Decades ago, in Rochester, New York, where Louise Brooks lived in old age and died, I was chatting with a librarian from the Rochester Public Library. He told me that Brooks had been banned from the library because she would deface books. Such books were subsequently deaccessioned, and lucky buyers at a library sale might be able to acquire for a few dollars volumes with inflammatory Louise Brooks commentary. One such book owned by the librarian was Lita Grey Chaplin's 1966 autobiography of her life with Chaplin, which now contained additional and explicit commentary on the comedian's sex life and genital size, disagreeing with Lita Grey's assessment.

Astonishingly, a few stars made an effort to help somewhat overly aggressive buffs. One wrote to actress Ann Harding complaining that an oversize photograph he had sent for her to sign had been returned damaged. "I am sorry that the photograph you sent was creased at the corners—and along my nose!" replied Harding.

> May I suggest that if you have a collection of photographs of this size, that you wish to be autographed, you would best lay in a supply of tougher backing for them? I took the trouble to measure the enclosed photograph, which is 10 x 13 . . . a dimension I am not familiar with. 11 x 14, yes, but I am a bit curious as to where and how you acquired this ancient artifact![20]

Concurrent with a newfound enthusiasm for film-related autographs was a similar interest in film-related photographs or similar types of memorabilia. In the 1910s, *Photoplay* would sell "art prints" of stars, from which its

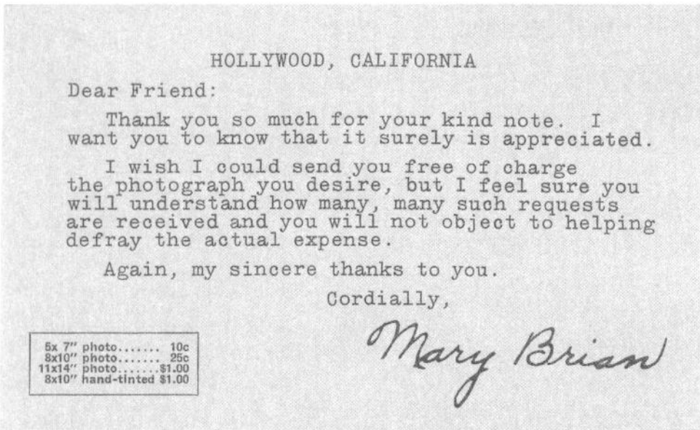

HOLLYWOOD, CALIFORNIA

Dear Friend:

Thank you so much for your kind note. I want you to know that it surely is appreciated.

I wish I could send you free of charge the photograph you desire, but I feel sure you will understand how many, many such requests are received and you will not object to helping defray the actual expense.

Again, my sincere thanks to you.

Cordially,

Mary Brian

5x 7" photo....... 10c
8x10" photo....... 25c
11x14" photo.......$1.00
8x10" hand-tinted $1.00

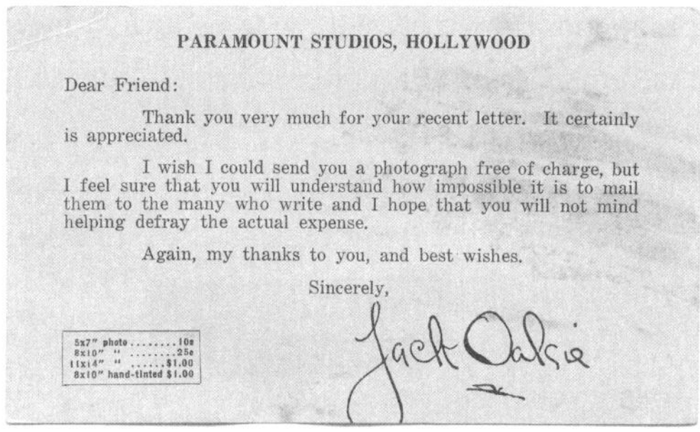

PARAMOUNT STUDIOS, HOLLYWOOD

Dear Friend:

Thank you very much for your recent letter. It certainly is appreciated.

I wish I could send you a photograph free of charge, but I feel sure that you will understand how impossible it is to mail them to the many who write and I hope that you will not mind helping defray the actual expense.

Again, my thanks to you, and best wishes.

Sincerely,

Jack Oakie

5x7" photo........10c
8x10" " ........25c
11x14" " ......$1.00
8x10" hand-tinted $1.00

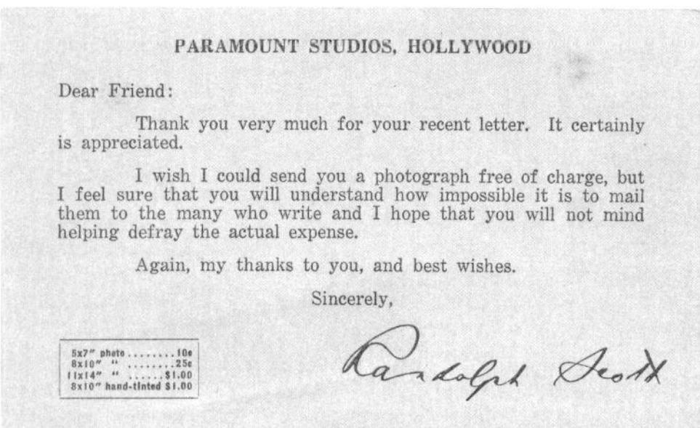

PARAMOUNT STUDIOS, HOLLYWOOD

Dear Friend:

Thank you very much for your recent letter. It certainly is appreciated.

I wish I could send you a photograph free of charge, but I feel sure that you will understand how impossible it is to mail them to the many who write and I hope that you will not mind helping defray the actual expense.

Again, my thanks to you, and best wishes.

Sincerely,

Randolph Scott

5x7" photo........10c
8x10" " ........25c
11x14" " ......$1.00
8x10" hand-tinted $1.00

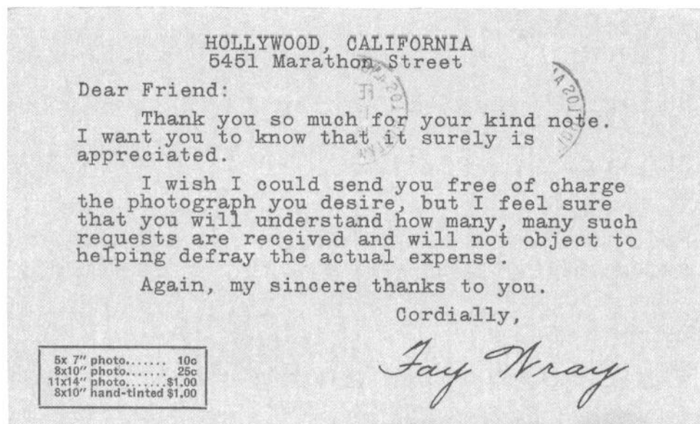

HOLLYWOOD, CALIFORNIA
5451 Marathon Street

Dear Friend:

Thank you so much for your kind note. I want you to know that it surely is appreciated.

I wish I could send you free of charge the photograph you desire, but I feel sure that you will understand how many, many such requests are received and will not object to helping defray the actual expense.

Again, my sincere thanks to you.

Cordially,

Fay Wray

5x 7" photo....... 10c
8x10" photo....... 25c
11x14" photo.......$1.00
8x10" hand-tinted $1.00

cover illustrations were made, at a cost of 25¢ each. For the same amount, the Movie Photo Co. of Virginville, Pennsylvania, offered twelve sepia photographs of "film favorites." For 25¢, the Wyanoak Publishing Co. in New York sold 11 x 14-inch photographs directly or through your local theatre. At least into the 1920s, Wyanoak also printed lobby cards, under the heading of "Gelatine Photo Lobby Displays," but these were intended for theatre use rather than individual sale, although it is certain that many film fans and buffs surreptitiously removed the cards from the theatre lobbies. Richard Hoffman's collection includes material from Wyanoak.

By the 1920s, studios were sending out to fans 5 x 7-inch photographs of their contract players, generally with facsimile signatures. In 1922, a theatre owner in Greensburg, Pennsylvania, purchased 1,500 still photographs of Rudolph Valentino to give as souvenirs to audience members for *The Sheik*.[21]

Some stars were reduced almost to begging for money from fans. In 1923, a request for a photograph, signed or otherwise, from that same Rudolph Valentino, resulted in the following response:

> I should be happy to send you my picture, but I am forced to ask the customary charge of 35¢ which barely covers the cost of picture, mailing expenses, etc. I wish I were in a position to send my picture free of charge, but since I left Famous Players-Lasky I have not received any salary nor am

> I in a position to earn any money as they obtained an injunction against me in the New York courts.[22]

By the late 1920s, it was commonplace for fans writing to their favorite players to receive a response similar to that sent out by Paramount leading lady Mary Brian:

> Thank you so much for your kind note. I want you to know that it surely is appreciated.
>
> I wish I could send you free of charge the photograph you desire, but I feel sure you will understand how many, many such requests are received and you will not object to helping defray the actual expenses.

Below was a price list: 10¢ for a 5 x 7-inch photograph, 25¢ for an 8 x 10, $1 for an 11 x 14 or an 8 x 10 hand-tinted.

What the actress or actor does not indicate in such generic mail is the importance attached to that "kind note." In 1928, Paramount had considered releasing Mary Brian from her contract, but after discovering that she received as much fan mail as did Bebe Daniels, and that the bulk of such mail was from students and women wanting to mother her, it was decided to promote her to the ranks of featured players with the potential for stardom.[23]

It was pointed out that it cost Clara Bow, or rather her studio, Paramount, $2,550 a month to answer her fan mail, the cost of a very expensive automobile. Postage alone cost $750. "The feeling prevails," wrote *Photoplay* in 1928, that "if the public realized the expense of answering fan mail, more money would be forthcoming with photo requests."[24]

Perhaps. Certainly, a year later, studios and their contract players were no longer responding to fan mail that was not accompanied with money. "After being carefully counted, as an indication of the star's popularity, all other letters are destroyed."[25]

Some photographs were given away as premiums. For example, in the late 1920s, the Jacobsen Publishing Co., Inc., of New York offered a set of twenty-four, with the purchase of various facial soaps or lotions. The initial group consisted of Richard Arlen, Vilma Banky, Richard Barthelmess, Ronald Colman, Gary Cooper, Dolores Costello, Joan Crawford, Marion Davies, Richard Dix, Charles Farrell, Janet Gaynor, John Gilbert, William Haines, Norman Kerry, Laura La Plante, Conrad Nagel, Marion Nixon, Mary Nolan, Charles "Buddy" Rogers, Lewis Stone, Gloria Swanson, Estelle Taylor, Florence Vidor, and Claire Windsor.

From the 1930s onwards, film buffs and others were able to acquire 5 x 7-inch colored lithographic reproductions of photographs of their favorite stars, modestly priced at 25¢ each per set of twenty-five, from Screen Art Studios based in Chicago. "Wouldn't you like to have a complete set of the Popular Stars?" asked an advertising flyer from the company.

> To get acquainted with them, to be able to recognize them when you see them on the screen, to be able to win Movie Contests or make up a Scrap Book, you'd be surprised how much you will enjoy looking thru it in your spare moments and what more brilliant children, beautiful talented women and handsome men pictures could you possess?

It was a surprisingly eclectic group that Screen Arts Studios had on offer, including such relatively obscure performers as Edith Fellows, John McGuire, June Travis, Marjorie Weaver, and Eleanore Whitney. All producers were represented with each photograph boasting a printed signature and the name of the contract studio. The photographs were sold through small, thumbnail advertisements in fan magazines and specialist periodicals such as *Boys' Life*.

In the United Kingdom, a number of fan magazines—*Cinema Chat*, *Film Weekly*, *Picture Show*, and *Pictures and the Picturegoer*—would make postcard-size photographs of stars available to their readership. However, both the American and the British efforts at catering to the film fans and buffs was nothing compared to what was happening in Germany.

Here, the movie postcard market was dominated by one company, Ross Verlag, whose releases, generally on cream-colored stock, were of the highest quality, and included both German and other nationalities—for example, the company released a reported 589 postcards of Garbo[26]—with the emphasis on portraits, but also including scene stills. Four-fifths of the postcard was taken up with the photograph, while the remaining one-fifth had the name of the player, the Ross Verlag name, and the identity of the studio, with copyright.

The company was founded in Berlin in 1918 by Heinrich Ross (1870–1957) and published all manner of photographs, before introducing its most popular film-related line in 1924, in the tradition of the earlier company Film Sterne. Many of the early Ross Verlag photographs were the work of Alexander Binder (1888–1929), after whose death Atelier Binder continued to supply film star photographs to Ross Verlag through 1937. That year marked the end of Heinrich Ross's involvement in his company, although he had

One of the many Ross Verlag postcards available of Garbo.

earlier lost control as the Nazis came to power and forced Jews such as Ross to relinquish ownership of their businesses. The Ross Verlag name continued to be used until 1941, when the company became Film Foto Verlag.

Heinrich Ross's escape from Germany is not without interest. He was one of the passengers in May 1939 on the fateful trip of the SS *St. Louis* from Hamburg to Cuba, where the ship's Jewish passengers were scheduled to land. Cuba refused entry, and the ship next sailed for the United States, where again the Jewish passengers were refused permission to land. The ship returned to Europe, where its passengers found themselves assigned to various countries, the majority of which were to fall to the Nazis with the result that many of those of the SS *St. Louis* eventually were transported to concentration camps. Heinrich Ross was lucky in that he was one of the small group who went to England; from there, in 1942, he left for the United States, where he died.

In all, more than 40,000 different postcards were issued by Ross Verlag, and just as in the 1920s and 1930s, these postcards are today eagerly sought after by film buffs. The Ross Verlag named remains triumphantly to the fore in terms of photographic quality and collectability.[27]

Both British and German cigarette manufacturers issued cards on all manner of subjects contained in each pack of cigarettes, with the first such cards dating back to the 1870s, and the first featuring actors and actresses (from the stage) in the 1890s. Those devoted to film stars would boast a color or "colorized" photograph on the front with a brief biographical sketch on the reverse. Each set could be mounted in a book, available on demand once the collector had the complete run of the cards. There is no definitive record of just now many of these cards were issued. John Player & Sons (a division of the Imperial Tobacco Company) issued the first series of its film star cards in 1934, with the third series released in 1938. W. D. and H. O. Wills issued its first series of "Famous Film Stars" in 1933, but they were in black-and-white or sepia and not in color. Cards were not limited to cigarette manufacturers, with, for example, the British chocolate maker A. J. Caley & Sons issuing a series of film star cards in 1930.

William K. Everson recalled that about one series in twelve was devoted to the movies:

> The cigarette cards relied on stamina and chance. One had to watch for an adult to throw away the empty cigarette carton in the street and then pounce, hoping it would still contain the card. Usually it did, since smokers themselves seemed to have little interest in collecting. Some of the cards were truly beautiful, all shapes and sizes and themes—though it was frustrating to want only movie cards and constantly to salvage Kings and Queens or Wild Life![28]

Aside from non-relatives, parents would also purchase the cigarettes, giving the cards to their children, who would in turn encourage the adults to smoke and thus indulge their collecting hobby. The cards and albums are no longer collected by children but by films buffs, willing not only to acquire complete sets but also individual cards, which sell on eBay for a few dollars apiece.

Like most film-related hobbies, the participants of the past remain anonymous. According to Margaret Farrand Thorp in her 1946 study, *America at the Movies*, the first known collector of movie stills was one Henry Pierson. As his collection grew and he acquired more duplicate copies, he would sell or give these to friends, who subsequently became collectors. When his collection became unmanageable, Pierson decided to concentrate on stills relating to Academy Award winners, eventually boasting a collection of 1,200, which Thorp declares is "probably the largest private collection in the country."[29] The claim seems highly unlikely in view of the collection of Theodore Huff, numbering in the tens of thousands, donated on his death to the International Museum of Photography at George Eastman House, or that of Hollywood-based Paul Ballard, whose collection was given to the Margaret Herrick Library of the Academy of Motion Picture Arts and Sciences.[30]

What did collectors look for in a still photograph? According to David Dietz, photoplay editor of the *Cleveland Leader*, interviewed in 1919, it was the same as what exhibitors and newspaper editors wanted: "A still must appeal; it must tell some interesting fragment of the story; but most of all it must make the person who looks at it have a strong desire to see the production."[31]

Some film buffs preferred to take their own, original photographs, rather than rely on the studio output. In the pre-digital, pre-selfie age, Gary Boas, a fifteen-year-old schoolboy from Lancaster, Pennsylvania, would beg his mother, and later his boyfriend, to drive him to New York, where he would hang around at stage doors, in hotel lobbies, and outside restaurants, hoping to catch a glimpse of a star—or, much preferred, an aging character actor—and photograph them, often posing himself in the shot. Robert Goulet has the honor of being Boas's first photographic model. Eventually, Boas finished up with a reported 100,000 images, from which he made a selection for his 2000 book, *Starstruck: Photographs from a Fan*. In that Boas is a film buff, an eccentric, one critic perceptively noticed that in the shots he shares with the stars, it is the latter who seem to belong to the everyday world and "the ordinary-looking fellow in street clothes" who appears to inhabit a different universe:

> Like pornography, Boas' impersonal images ultimately focus on the act rather than the person—in this case, the act of being famous. Instead of

> penetrating beneath the star's social mask, then, or insinuating an aura of psychological insight, these pictures do something more concrete: They nakedly lay out the choreographed gestures with which the famous greet their adoring and intrusive public.[32]

Gary Boas was not the only amateur photographer in the 1970s actively seeking out movie stars. In Los Angeles, there were Jon Virzi and later Marty Jackson, whose photographs of stars past their prime graced many of the pages in the *Whatever Became of . . . ?* books from Richard Lamparski. "Each one had their own neurotic stories," comments Lamparski.[33] Jon Virzi would photograph celebrities and also collect autographs on index cards, often requesting multiple signings, hanging out at "in" restaurants and hotels. For a while he worked at the post office in the change of address department, thus obtaining access to latest addresses of the stars. Virzi might often be found in the company of a lady known as "Whispering Suzy," because she never spoke above a whisper.

Also in Los Angeles was Roger Karnbad, determined to have a professional career as a celebrity photographer. I first came across Roger when I was programming tributes at the Academy of Motion Picture Arts and Sciences in the 1970s, and he asked if it was OK to come into the theatre and photograph the various on-stage conversations. I didn't think anything of it, and was happy to grant permission, in all my naiveté not realizing that perhaps one needed some type of credentials. Years later, Roger told me that I was, in part, responsible for his career, as he moved on from Academy tributes to celebrity tributes, conventions, and general paparazzi activities.

Film buffs who heavily prize still photographs would not agree with a critic's 1936 comment that "still-photographs of films and plays which invariably hang outside the doors of cinema halls and theatres are possibly the worst form of advertisement the entertainment to be had within could be given. It is rather as if we took a chord from a new orchestral piece and played it by itself in order to demonstrate the piece's excellence."[34]

It was the exhibitors who were generally the source for the still collector's archive. As was hypothesized by the *Hollywood Reporter* in 1939, "exhibitors secure their stocks from distributors who have no immediate or further use of growing files and are glad to dispose of them at cut-prices."[35]

It was revealed that studios actually sold still photographs to the players for 10¢ apiece. There was concern that these same still photographs, obviously struck from the original negatives, were being offered for sale at "bargain prices," with production stills selling at six for 25¢.

The primary source not only for still photographs but also posters, lobby cards, and trailers (for film collectors) was National Screen Service, which had distribution centers across the United States, with the main warehouse in Kansas City. Its function was to provide exhibitors, on behalf of the studios, with promotional materials, but in that such items had a limited lifespan based on the number of weeks or months a film was in distribution, the "paper" that it generated would be discarded, eagerly to be acquired by buffs and others. The true buff or collector would perhaps sneer at still photographs from National Screen Service in that the image was captioned below with information as to the film, stars, etc., and was at least one generation removed from the still photographs sent out for publicity purposes by the studios.

Many collectors relied on "moles" within National Screen Service. One veteran film collector in Hickory, North Carolina, was "Moon" Mullins, who combined a hobby of collecting and displaying Native American artifacts with collecting and screening 35mm and 16mm films. Each week, the "mole" at National Screen Service would bring Mullins stacks of posters and paper bags full of 35mm trailers.

National Screen Service had been established in 1919, and by 1940, it had become the service agency for Paramount and RKO. By the end of the decade, it had taken over production and distribution of theatrical advertising matter for all the major studios.

Many a film buff would rather have a still photograph from a film than the pleasure of viewing the actual film. Film buffs are hard-pressed to determine what is important as evidenced by an Indian billionaire with whom I was discussing some years ago the sad situation of his country's films not being adequately preserved. The billionaire's response was that he had only limited funds available and would rather devote his energy and his money to acquiring and preserving the posters for such films. The films themselves had less intrinsic worth than the posters promoting them.

William K. Everson has also voiced a similar theme, noting that there is something wrong when the price asked for a poster can buy ten or twenty 16mm prints. However, proving that he is very much a film buff at heart, Everson told of being offered $10,000 by a dealer for his one-sheet *King Kong* poster. He had purchased it for 25¢ and faced a moral dilemma as to whether to sell or not. Eventually, he agreed to exchange the poster for a 16mm print of a rare film worth a few hundred dollars; "on paper, thousands of dollars had changed hands, yet in actual fact my initial 25¢ was the only hard cash involved."[36]

There have been a number of retail outlets marketing film stills to buffs and others, most notably in Los Angeles, Eddie Brandt's Saturday Matinee in North Hollywood, Backlot Books in West Hollywood, and Larry Edmunds Bookstore in Hollywood, with perhaps the best known name in the field being Movie Star News of New York, although others might argue in support of Mark Ricci's Memory Shop or Jerry Ohlinger.

Eddie Brandt (1920–2011) was assuredly a film buff, with a major interest in "B" Westerns. The store, which eventually became known as Eddie Brandt's Saturday Matinee, opened in 1967, and was first located on a small corner at Victory and Lankershim in North Hollywood, next to a Mexican bar. It was primarily a secondhand store, selling used furniture, books, and the like, and a small quantity of movie memorabilia. Gradually, Eddie Brandt began adding more and more movie stills to his holdings, beginning with the photographic holdings of the *Los Angeles Herald-Examiner* after it closed. In the summer of 1973, he hired his first full-time employee, Mike Hawks, who had earlier been working there on Saturdays for credit rather than cash.

Mike Hawks (born 1950) is a very open, friendly, relaxed, and easygoing individual with something of an unusual past in that most of his work experience was as a sales person at Robinson's Department Store in downtown Los Angeles. Nothing unusual in that except that, prior to working at Robinson's, he had simply walked out of the army after two weeks of basic training in Fort Lewis, Washington. "I decided that the army and I were not going to get along," he explains.[37] After two years and nine months, living at the Alexandria Hotel in downtown Los Angeles and working in sales, he was arrested for desertion. He was looking at five years in Leavenworth Prison, but thanks to the military's losing the paperwork and failing to bring him to trial within ninety days, he was summarily released after five months.

To a large extent, Mike Hawks was the face of Eddie Brandt's Saturday Matinee, the guy behind the counter who serviced every request for stills with equanimity. While he sold the stills, Eddie Brandt acquired them. One source was a security guard at Metro-Goldwyn-Mayer named Ken Hollywood, who removed tens of thousands of M-G-M and Goldwyn photographs from the studio lot. "He would bring in those boxes with about 400, 500 photos per box. He would not go through them. It was x amount of dollars per box. You might find something from *Eskimo*, with nobody in it, or Greta Garbo, and everything in between. You couldn't really pick it out. It was pot luck." Mike Hawks recalls the guys who brought in piles of Mary Pickford stills, all assumed to have been stolen, and another guy who brought in key books for Warner Bros. and First National films from the silent and early sound era, which were split between Eddie Brandt and Larry Edmunds Bookstore. In the 1970s, the American Film Institute approached Eddie Brandt and sold him a large quantity of surplus or duplicate still photographs. I can recall witnessing an entertainment reporter from the *Los Angeles Times* visiting the store with many hundreds of photographs from the newspaper archives on loan for copying, obviously without the newspaper's consent.

Through Mike's years at Eddie Brandt's, there were many strange customers, of whom perhaps the weirdest was a middle-aged individual who would come in with a binder of clippings and purchase photographs of male child stars, from Jackie Coogan through Bobby Driscoll.

> Finally, I can't stand it any longer. That's when he says to me, "You know I'm doing this because I'm all these people." He's Jackie Coogan, he's Alfalfa [of "Our Gang"], he's Scotty Beckett, he's Dickie Moore. He's not one of the black kids. In a thirty-year timeframe, that's him. [Pointing to the binder of clippings, he explains] "These are cases when I went to court, trying to get residual checks for performances." Every case, they're thrown out of court. Then comes the topper, when he asked for the file on Mark Hamill. I said, "Wait a minute, you're all these other guys, the twenties into the fifties. You're in *Star Wars*? How is this possible?" *Star Wars* he says was made at the beginning of the sound era. There was a major preview for all of the heads of the studios, they were so amazed at what they saw, they paid to have the film withhold because it would have destroyed all of what they were doing. So they held it back 'til 1977.

Mike Hawks remained at Eddie Brandt's for ten years, until he was fired in the summer of 1973. Hawks blames his firing on Eddie Brandt's mounting and unrelenting paranoia, which had led to his earlier firing of another employee, who had worked there for seven years. Mike had worked Saturdays, the shop was closed Sundays and Mondays, and when he showed up on Tuesday, the doors were locked. He was given two weeks' pay and allowed to retrieve a toothbrush and tube of toothpaste from the toilet, under Eddie Brandt's supervision.

"Usually, he and I got along," recalls Mike, who never took an actual vacation during his ten years at the store. He acknowledges the pay was fair, and also notes that he was paid a weekly bonus, based on sales, that after ten years amounted to $30,000 a year.

Eddie Brandt claimed that he had let Mike Hawks go because he wanted to bring in his kids to run the store. "They're going to work, because if they don't work, they're not going to stay at the house any more. Drafted into the Brandt Army." After Mike's departure, the emphasis at the store was on videotape rentals, consisting in large part of movies which Eddie Brandt had taped himself off the air. Eventually, the shop had some 72,000 titles and was a treasure trove not only for film buffs but also for industry executives in search of an elusive title unavailable from any other source.[38] It was always claimed that the film industry turned a blind eye to his questionable activities in taping and renting out the tapes without copyright clearance because it needed access to Brandt's collection.

Backlot Books—which despite its title was basically a source for still photographs, often piled in the hundreds and thousands, unsorted in large boxes—was founded in 1972 by Doug Hart. Presumably, he adopted the name because he was for forty years an employee of Warner Bros., and acquired much of the material he sold at the shop from its backlot. Hart always insisted that the studio had no use for the photographs, scripts, posters, etc., and that he had permission to remove the materials from the lot. His shop, open only on weekends, was situated in a small garage behind a flower shop and beauty salon on Sunset Boulevard.

After Hart's death in 1999, the company was acquired by a former employee, Sabin Gray, and relocated to a storefront on Hollywood Boulevard, immediately west of Vine Street. In 2004, Gray partnered with Jack Condon, and two years later, the latter became sole owner, changing the company to an Internet outlet. (In 2007, Condon was inducted into the Guinness Book of World Records as owner of the largest collection of memorabilia relating to the television series *Charlie's Angels.*)

In New York, film buffs might try and cajole Mark Ricci (1926–1992)[39] of the Memory Shop, located at 100 Fourth Avenue, to wander deep into his three-story establishment, filled with both stills and posters, as well as a reported 100,000 comic books. In 1975, Ricci acquired the stock of a long-forgotten New York stills dealer named Henry Kier, whose Kier's Celebrity Photos was initially located at Sixth Avenue and West Forty-Fourth Street, prior to moving to West Fortieth Street and Fifth Avenue. Thin and white-haired, with a deeply lined red face and what was described as a "Fieldsian veined nose," Kier is remembered by Leonard Maltin for telling his customers that "a scene still is 25¢ but a portrait still is 50¢."[40] When a scene still the customer wanted was located, Kier would then insist it was a portrait still because it featured only one actor in the shot.

Ricci, who resembled actor Eli Wallach, actually hired somebody simply to watch the customers and make sure they were not stealing his inventory. He "always reminded me of Pancho Villa in more ways than one," recalled Leonard Maltin,[41] in that Ricci resembled a stereotypical Mexican bandit and would often take advantage of customers. Poster collector Mike Kaplan, who is also a publicist and producer, talked of finding two-thirds of a three-sheet poster for Errol Flynn's *The Dawn Patrol* (1938) in the Memory Shop. After he had acquired it, he advertised for the missing third and found it with a collector in New Jersey who had earlier purchased it from the Memory Shop.[42]

A reporter for the *Village Voice* followed one film buff to the Memory Shop in 1975, and wrote,

> Mark Ricci, the owner and manager, is a big guy with a ready laugh and an eye for a hot still. He tries to be cynical; but you can see he's caught up in the cinema effect. "They all come in here looking for crazy things. One guy says I got to have a picture of Tab Hunter in a bathing suit. But the bathing suit's got to be green with a red stripe down the side. I had it. Can you believe it? I had it . . . Another guy only wants pictures of Elizabeth Taylor, on horseback. Not just *National Velvet*. . . . Who knows what his hangup could be?"[43]

Jerry Vermilye recalls,

> Mark Ricci was a very complex and enigmatic individual. I got to know him over a period of years, and through my good friend Allan Turner (a lifelong stills collector) was allowed to browse for photos in a place where most of his customers were never allowed. My "co-authorship" of the Elizabeth Taylor book [*The Films of Elizabeth Taylor*] was a bit of a sham. Ricci had already established a book-author relationship with Citadel Press, getting his name on previous volumes he had nothing to do with editorially. I had only authored one previous volume for a small publisher when Mark proposed we collaborate on *The Films of Elizabeth Taylor* for Citadel, which we did—or rather I did. His participation was only a few stills (I had most of which we needed) and the contract. After that, I worked on my own with other Citadel titles.[44]

The *Films of* . . . series at Citadel Press existed very much thanks to Mark Ricci, even if generally his contribution was limited to providing illustrations, regardless of what a book's credit might suggest. Ricci brought in Dion

The 1954 edition of the Movie Star News catalog.

McGregor (1922–1994) as one of the credited authors of *The Films of Greta Garbo* (1984). McGregor was a would-be songwriter (working in 1953 with former Metro-Goldwyn-Mayer leading man, Carleton Carpenter), a witty man, a film buff, and an individual whose biggest claim to fame was that he talked in his sleep; his comments and stories were recorded in an album and accompanying book titled *The Dream World of Dion McGregor (He Talks in His Sleep)*, released in 1964.[45] The book's cover was the work of Edward Gorey, a film buff who was a fairly regular visitor to William K. Everson's Saturday night screenings. Gorey and Carleton Carpenter have something in common in that both at various times took on Dion McGregor, who had no money and no fixed abode, as a roommate.

Dion McGregor boasted a large collection of film stills, apparently purloined from various archives and libraries, until he was apprehended and banned by the Lincoln Center Library for the Performing Arts. He was also something of a bitchy, gay wit, referring to fellow film buffs in feminine form; for example, Douglas Whitney was always called Dame May Whitney.

A somewhat strange and truncated description of Mark Ricci is provided by Joe Franklin: "He has a reputation of being a necrophiliac for a long time. I don't know if we want to get into that. He was a very peculiar guy, but we shared a great love of memorabilia. I don't think he ever got married. He wore a toupee."[46]

Joe Franklin had wanted to purchase the contents of the Memory Shop, but after Mark Ricci's death, his stock was taken over by Jerry Ohlinger, who had been in business since 1978, initially on New York's West Third Street. He closed the business, by then located on Thirty-Fifth Street, in January 2016, a victim of the Internet and a monthly rent of $9,000. As the *New Yorker* commented,

> This is unfortunate, because a computer screen will never provide the physical, sensory experience you get when you step into Ohlinger's. An obsessively organized clutter of movie posters and postcards, stacks of DVDs, and boxes full of eight-by-seventeen poster reproductions, the small front of the store is walled by towering shelves packed with shopworn three-ring binders, all strapped with duct tape and hand-labelled in Magic Marker with the names of the movie stars contained within. The space smells of Jerry's cigar and the musty vanilla aroma of old paper slowly decaying.[47]

Movie Star News was founded by Brooklyn-born Irving Klaw (1910–1966), in association with his younger sister, Paula. In 1938, Klaw opened a used bookstore at 209 East Fourteenth Street in Manhattan, with Paula serving as his assistant. Legend has it that Klaw noticed a teenage girl ripping a photograph of Clark Gable from the pages of one of the books, and came to the realization that similar individuals might be interested in actually purchasing film stills and publicity photographs. A year later, Klaw moved across Fourteenth Street, to 212, and there he established Irving Klaw's Pin-Up Photos, with the emphasis on studio-produced pin-up publicity shots of stars such as Dorothy Lamour and Betty Grable. In time, the name was changed to Movie Star News, and Klaw was selling both modern and historical film stills, dating back to 1915, with the emphasis on the productions of Paramount, the key still books of which he had at some point acquired from the New York office. This writer can attest to how truly amazing it was to visit Movie Star News and pull original bound key books of Paramount stills, arranged by film title, and to remove whatever one desired or had the money to purchase.

Expanding into other areas, discussed elsewhere in this book, Irving Klaw and Movie Star News continued to operate, with the store remaining open following Klaw's death. In the 1980s, Movie Star News was the victim of a rent increase and forced to move to 134 West Eighteenth Street. In 2012, it was acquired by Las Vegas-based Entertainment Collectibles,[48] which, according to the *New York Daily News* (July 30, 2012) handed over 100 file cabinets and 300 cartons of photographs and memorabilia to Guernsey's. In turn, the latter auctioned off the collection in April of the following year.

Chapter Two

# FAN CLUBS AND FAN MAIL

"WHEN A FAN WRITES A LETTER," EXPLAINED A MAGAZINE EDITOR IN 1950, "he is enraptured and wants only the joy of expressing his emotions. He is especially prone to hopeless love, gnawing frustrations and a variety of illnesses and strange symptoms."[1]

An argument might well be made that fan clubs and fan publications that are contemporary with a star's immediate fame are not necessarily the province of the film buff but rather the film fan. It has been claimed by academics that film fans "lacked what normal spectators possessed: the maturity and intelligence to separate the screen and life. . . . Fans . . . were the ultimate victims of the modern mass media: seduced by the cinema's powerful illusion of reality, they swooned over actors, wasted hours on fan activities, and mimicked what they saw in films, all with harmful consequences."[2]

Yes, indeed, but the behavior assigned above to fans might equally apply to film buffs, particularly the lack of maturity and intelligence. At the same time, a film buff is more likely to become obsessed with a celebrity after his or her prime, often after the star's death. Publications honoring most film performers are published concurrent with that individual's mainstream popularity on screen; they are intended as much for the average or typical moviegoer of the period as for the most enthusiastic of fans. They are neither directed at, or of primary interest to, the film buff. Or at least, they are not while they are contemporary; once the star and the publication are long past their "sell by" dates, then both the publication and star have a new appeal—to the film buff.

Given the choice of two players about which to obsess, the film buff will choose the secondary one. During the late silent era, there were two sisters on screen, Alberta and Adamae Vaughn.[3] Alberta was the better-known of the two, but it was Adamae with whom the film buff would be corresponding, thrilled to receive a response as sad perhaps as his obsession:

Unruly fans outside London's Ritz Hotel in 1920, trying to reach Mary Pickford and Douglas Fairbanks.

> You don't know how glad I was to receive your letter asking for a picture. I never expect to be as popular as Alberta or have as many friends, but I know that Alberta's friends are my friends or you never would have written the lovely letter as Alberta asked you. So thank you for being so kind. . . .
>
> When you write the Answer Man in care of *Motion Picture Magazine*, 175 Duffield Street, Brooklyn, N.Y., about Alberta, you are helping to keep her on the top—aren't you? Would you mind giving me a little boost, too, by asking a question about me—just any question?[4]

During Hollywood's so-called "golden age," the studios welcomed fan mail as an instrument to measure a contract star's success. One 1928 fan magazine[5] provides a very detailed record of the number of fan letters per month received by various stars:

Clara Bow—33,727
Billie Dove—31,128
Helene and Dolores Costello—25,000
Charles "Buddy" Rogers—19,618
Mary Pickford—14,000
Dolores Del Rio—15,000
Richard Dix—12,002
May McAvoy—12,000
Harold Lloyd—12,000
Mary Brian—11,000
Bebe Daniels—10,980
Janet Gaynor—10,000
Charles Farrell—10,000
Esther Ralston—8,000
Rin Tin Tin—8,000
Louise Fazenda—8,000
Richard Barthelmess—7,349
Victor McLaglen—6,000
John Gilbert—6,000
Gary Cooper—5,852
Charlie Chaplin—5,600
Marion Davies—5,500
Louise Brooks—5,021
Norma Shearer—5,000
Ramon Novarro—4,800
Joan Crawford—4,000
William Haines—4,000
Mary Astor—2,642
Reginald Denny—2,300
Douglas Fairbanks Sr.—2,000
Corinne Griffith—1,982
Jack Mulhall—1,781
Lon Chaney—1,241
Conrad Nagel—500
Emil Jannings—680
Polly Moran—300

The members of "Our Gang" received, as a group, some 10,000 fan letters a month, with African American Farina (Allen Clayton Hoskins Jr.) receiving the most; Joe Cobb, "the fat kid," coming in second; and Pete the Dog third.

It might be interesting to compare this scorecard with a similar one produced by today's film buffs. Of course, no such record exists, but based on prices realized for autographs, modern books and articles on the subject, and popularity with modern audience, the top player would be Louise Brooks, followed by Clara Bow and Lon Chaney. Bow is the only one in the top echelon who has retained, and perhaps enhanced her appeal, with Dove, the Costello sisters, and Charles "Buddy" Rogers evincing little modern interest. Mary Pickford does not rate highly, and is surpassed in popularity by her one-time husband, Douglas Fairbanks Sr., way down on the 1928 listing.

It is perhaps ominous as to the powerful influence of the film buffs of America that at a November 1993 auction, a signed photograph of Larry, Curly, and Moe of the Three Stooges sold for $1,820, while a signed group photograph of presidents Nixon, Ford, and Carter sold for $275.[6] In December 2016, RR Auctions (Boston) sold a signed 1938 photograph of the Three Stooges for $8,467.20.

The various fan clubs gave rise to "umbrella" organizations, such as the Movie Club Guild, founded in Chicago by Adolphe Becker in 1933, with which were affiliated fan clubs for Dolores Del Rio, Billie Dove, Ruth Roland, Barbara Stanwyck, Gloria Stuart, and others. In the 1920s, the Moving Picture Club of America, Inc., was organized "For the Fans By the Fans," and had its own publication, *Star Dust Magazine*.[7]

There were fans such as E. M. Orowitz, who obviously considered himself as important as any star, and founded the EMO Movie Fan Club in 1933, which published *The Movie Fan* and which, within three years, had a membership of 40,000. As were later film buffs, members of EMO were vigilant in pointing out discrepancies between studio publicity and reality, be it as innocuous as proving that George Raft was four inches shorter than his Paramount publicity claimed. "The Official EMO Movie Club Star Album" was available to members, who were encouraged to collect 8 x 10-inch, linen-textured photographs of their favorite stars (of which there were more than 200 available as of 1938) for inclusion therein.

Of all the stars, perhaps Joan Crawford was the most considerate of her fans. Her fan club was established in September 1931 and, as of World War II, it was considered one of the largest in existence, with membership extending not only across the United States but also to the British Isles, Australia, and South Africa. Members received an autographed photograph of the star, six issues a year of *The Crawford News*, and other privileges. The president, Marian Dommer, can certainly be considered both a fan and a film buff and, obviously, had quite a high standing in the film community, so

Sorting the fan mail at M-G-M in the late 1930s.

much so that in 1937, when Metro-Goldwyn-Mayer released Crawford's latest film, *Mannequin*, it used a photograph and a quote from Dommer in its advertising.[8]

Gossip columnist Jimmie Fiddler noted that in 1933 Joan Crawford was "possibly THE biggest star now, and gets a terrific lot of mail—more than 20,000 letters every month. Do you realize how many letters 20,000 are? The task of answering is impossible; I want to tell you that I am amazed that she even finds time to autograph her photos, which she personally attends to."[9]

Joan Crawford, a star who always appreciated her fans.

One film buff who benefitted from Crawford's affection for her fans was Isidore "Dore" Freeman. Legend has it that while working as a Western Union messenger awaiting arrival of Crawford's train at New York's Grand Central Station, he was concerned that the star was unable to answer questions thrown at her by reporters regarding her divorce from Douglas Fairbanks Jr. and her impending marriage to Franchot Tone. "Tell them, time will tell, Joan," he yelled. She did, and a few days later she delivered a gold watch to him, inscribed, "Time will tell. Love, Joan Crawford."

Thus began a fan worship that lasted until Crawford's death, with Freeman's collecting a reported 23,000 photographs of his heroine and her finding him a job in the publicity department at M-G-M. Freeman died a bachelor, alone except for his two dogs named after Crawford's adopted children, Christopher and Christina.[10]

Even in retirement, Joan Crawford would not fail to respond to a letter from a fan or film buff. As Associated Press columnist Bob Thomas recalled, she was equally generous of her time with journalists: "The most prolific of movie stars was Joan Crawford. She was constantly in touch with reporters, using either Western Union or her own stationary."[11]

Knowing Crawford's penchant for hard work, one might assume she actually typed all the letters herself. Certainly, she could type, but she relied on long-time secretary Betty Barker (1916–2012), who in later years lived in West Hollywood while Crawford resided in New York. Barker would type the replies and mail them to New York, where Crawford would sign and mail them. One has a wonderful image of Crawford, delicately applying her tongue to each of the envelopes, providing a rare opportunity surely for film buffs to acquire not only a signature but also the star's DNA.

Rudolph Valentino's appeal was as great outside of the United States as here. Three days after his death, a Londoner named Peggy Scott committed suicide, leaving a note stating, "I am only a lonely butterfly made for sunshine and I cannot stand loneliness and shadow. With his death, my last bit of courage has flown."[12]

In that the Rudolph Valentino Memorial Guild by its very name did not come into existence until after its hero's death, it is at once both unusual and unique for the number of years in which it flourished. It was founded in London, early in 1927, by Mercia Stanhope, who claimed to have known the star personally. As she explained,

> While he lived we were diffident about fighting for him, lest it embarrass him, but now we can defend him as we wish, and the Valentino Memorial Guild has put itself into the position of champion. The larger it becomes, the more powerful will it become, and I ask every man and woman who loved and loves Rudolph Valentino, be they persons in private life or film stars—we are all equal in our affection for him—to write to me and join so that the Guild may become such a band of fellowship as has never been known before, and Rudy's name live forever.

The Guild need not have worried that Valentino's name live on, for it most assuredly did, not least through the annual memorial event in his honor, held at what is now the Hollywood Forever Cemetery, where he is interred.[13] Similarly, the Guild lived on into the 1980s, although never expanding much beyond the twenty or so members it had in 1927.

The survival of the Guild was in large part thanks to Leslie Flint, a direct voice medium (who had frequent contact with the star), and who lived with his male partner in the basement flat at 140 Westbourne Terrace in the Paddington Station area of London.[14] That house, a Grade II-listed building from the 1840s, was designed by Isambard Kingdon Brunel, and it holds a special place in my life.

While still a teenager in the 1960s, I had joined the Valentino Memorial Guild, attending its monthly meetings, at which a Valentino film was screened, and members were treated to afternoon tea and appropriate delicacies. There were two sisters, Cis and Roz Crawford, whose enthusiasm for Valentino dated back to the 1920s and who were quite raucous. They typified the age group of the membership, aside from myself, who must have been prematurely old, and which included two who had published books on Valentino, Alan Arnold (*Valentino*, London: Hutchinson, 1952) and Lynn Russell (*The Voice of Valentino, through Leslie Flint*, London: Regency Press, 1965).

The members of the Valentino Memorial Guild in those later years were film buffs, but of a somewhat unique variety, being prim and proper in their way but letting their communal hair down on a Sunday afternoon as they remembered with affection, and with all the social niceties in place, their hero who had died decades earlier.

Holding the Guild together and worshipped by the members almost as much as Valentino was Leslie Flint, a somewhat controversial medium and quite definitely an egotist, as evidenced by the larger-than-life-size painting that hung over the fireplace of himself in Valentino's costume for *Monsieur Beaucaire*. I owe a lot to Leslie, and much as it may be easy to ridicule spiritualism and his lifestyle, I am very much aware that in the late 1960s, when I had nowhere to live in London, he made available to me a fully furnished second floor flat at 140 Westbourne Terrace.

What a house that was, and film buffs if they knew about it should be making pilgrimages to the building. On the ground floor lived the owner, an elderly lady who had grown up as a member of the British Raj in India and been taken care of by a native servant whose daughter was Merle Oberon. Above me lived an antique dealer named Michael Hall, who had once been an actor, playing Myrna Loy's son in *The Best Years of Our Life*. From that building, in 1968, Paul O'Dell and I launched *The Silent Picture*, the first serious quarterly devoted to the art and history of the silent film.

The Ramon Novarro Fan Club's date of founding is unrecorded. I came across it in the 1960s, when it was run by its secretary, Audrey Homan. She had been active in the theatre as wardrobe mistress for the Ram Gopal Ballet Company and was an accomplished artist. She had transformed her kitchen into a treetop eyrie in an Amazonian rain forest, with the skillful application of paint and brush.[15] Novarro was always kindly disposed towards his fans, despite the small number of members of the club. At meetings, which were few and far between, there would be a telephone call from the former star, and on his birthday, he would be treated to a rendition of "Happy Birthday"

The most loyal of Valentino's fans was Ditra Flame (1905–1984), known as "The Lady in Black," who visited the star's crypt on each anniversary of his death through 1955.

from those same fans. As a reward for her faithful devotion, in October 1963, Audrey Homan was invited to visit Novarro in Los Angeles, and at that time she presented him with a bedspread embroidered by members of the club, with its center inscribed, "A Tribute to Ramon Novarro Star of the Silver Screen from the R.N.F.C."

One affluent and celebrated member of the Ramon Novarro Fan Club was John Lanchbery, composer and at that time conductor of the Royal Ballet Company, Covent Garden. He would host meetings at his home in Chelsea, and they were quite elegant affairs. John was a gay man, who had

In January 1954, Ramon Novarro hosted a dinner at London's Savoy Hotel for members of his fan club. From left to right: Mrs. Mary Greenhill, Miss Margaret Neville, Miss Audrey Homan, and Mrs. Molly Sutcliffe.

also been invited to stay with Novarro, and on his return, he told me of his plans to invite the star to London, and, also, somewhat controversially, to persuade a couple of the male dancers with the Royal Ballet to provide the star with sexual comfort.

It was not to be. Novarro was murdered at his home by two male hustlers on October 30, 1968. John's primary concern was the impact that the gay-related murder would have on the lady fans, who knew nothing of their hero's sex life. He need not have worried. To a woman, the members of the club declared the more sordid aspects of the reports of Novarro's death to be nothing more than rumor and innuendo.

Through me, and through 140 Westbourne Terrace, the Ramon Novarro Fan Club and the Valentino Memorial Guild share a link. I had invited the members of the Ramon Novarro Fan Club over one afternoon to view an interview with Novarro, conducted by Philip Jenkinson.[16] Unfortunately, my 16mm projector failed to work, but Leslie Flint and the Valentino Memorial Guild came to the rescue, inviting Club members to watch the film on a screen normally reserved for Valentino's work, and later serving afternoon tea. It was all very civilized and very British.

A similar comment cannot be made as to the infighting that broke out among Jeanette MacDonald fans.

Fan club members tended to be teachers and clerks, and also predominantly what used to be described as "spinsters," and so it was with the International Jeanette MacDonald Fan Club, headed out of Topeka, Kansas, by fourth-grade schoolteacher Clara Rhodes, president since 1954, and her partner and vice president Tessa Williams, identified as a lyric soprano. The two ladies would host the annual Jeanette MacDonald Clan Clave in Los Angeles, with honored guest, MacDonald's husband, Gene Raymond.

Sharon Rich founded the Mac/Eddy Club in 1977 as the first to honor both MacDonald and Eddy, and set up the first website for both stars in 1996, pointing out, "The constant bickering and animosity between the original Nelson Eddy and Jeanette MacDonald clubs proved to be detrimental to the stars during their lifetime. Generously, the Mac/Eddy Club allows its members to 'love' either star but insists that they show respect to both."

The history of the early Jeanette MacDonald and Nelson Eddy fans clubs is complicated, but happily has been documented by Philip Castanza, author of *The Complete Films of Jeanette MacDonald and Nelson Eddy*. The first Jeanette MacDonald Fan Club was also founded in New York in honor of her first costar, Maurice Chevalier, in 1930; by 1934, it had become the Original Jeanette MacDonald Fan Club, and eventually disbanded in 1965. The second fan club, the International Jeanette MacDonald Fan Club, was founded in 1938 by Mary Miller. From that year through 1985, the club published what is certainly the longest-running of all fan club publications, *The Golden Comet*. On the distaff side was the Nelson Eddy Music Club, founded in 1935 and disbanded in 1967.[17]

The two clubs were basically at war, with members recording the number of close-ups each respective star received in each new film, and noting the amount of time given on screen to each star's singing.

The war between MacDonald and Eddy fans while the two were still making films was as nothing compared to the war that broke out between Clara Rhodes and her fan club and Sharon Rich and her organization. In her 1994 book, *Sweethearts*, Rich maintained that MacDonald and Eddy were secret lovers, and would have married had not their studio, Metro-Goldwyn-Mayer, been opposed to the idea. The marriage between MacDonald and actor Gene Raymond was a sham, and as Sharon Rich made very clear after Raymond's 1998 death, the actor was a closeted homosexual. As one reporter had it, the book was "a lurid expose of the secret love affair between the two—complete with suicide attempts, illegitimate pregnancies and marriages to others—that lasted for nearly three decades."[18]

There were accusations that Gene Raymond paid for the International Jeanette MacDonald's Clan Claves, which, if true, is hardly a crime. Certainly, on the one occasion I was invited to a Clan Clave, I found Raymond a most pleasant and amusing gentleman, and I am sure he would have been delightful and appealing to members of either sex. Perhaps what most offended the older members of the International Jeanette MacDonald Fan Club was that they viewed the club as their family, they shared their reminiscences, their collections, their devotion to the star with other like-minded individuals. Sharon Rich came along and, rather like a spoiled child, was determined to drag the family into the twenty-first century, to tell them a few home truths that simply they did not want to believe—and, in reality, were unwilling to believe under any circumstances.

As a report in the *Los Angeles Times* once noted, "In some quarters, death is not a downer."[19] Certainly, not as far as Jeanette MacDonald and Nelson Eddy and their fans are concerned.

Clara Rhodes left instructions that the Jeanette MacDonald International Fan Club should cease to exist with her death on August 15, 2011. Her wishes were respected, but on February 15, 2012, a new fan club, in the tradition of the one established by Clara Rhodes, came into being in Los Angeles. The Appreciating Jeanette MacDonald Club was created by Sue Garland, who had been associated with the earlier club since 1975. It says much for Sue Garland's devotion to the cause that she operates the club without Internet access, without email, and with an unlisted telephone number.[20]

A slightly less acrimonious argument than that between Clara Rhodes and Sharon Rich broke out between members of two fan organizations associated with another, and far more delightful, musical star of the 1930s and later, Deanna Durbin. Her primary fan club was the Deanna Durbin Devotees, founded in 1937 by a fingerprint expert with the US Department of Justice. It was not the largest fan club in the United States, but it claimed to be the most devoted. It merged with an earlier club, founded in 1936, by four teenagers, Marguerite Slancy, Mary Blockwell, Ann Inman, and Marian Jentz, publisher of *Deanna's Diary*. In 1938, the Deanna Durbin Devotees became embroiled in a dispute with the We-Love-Deanna-Durbin-Club at Harvard University, founded by a group of students as an "association of admirers and lovers of Deanna Durbin at Harvard." There was no fee charged to join, but the club required that members must view every one of the star's films at least three times and dream of her at least four nights in succession. It dismissed the Deanna Durbin Devotees as "not serious enough for us."[21]

At least both organizations were magnanimous in their goal that the Canadian-born Deanna Durbin be constitutionally declared queen of the United States.

The later reincarnation of the Deanna Durbin Devotees was headquartered in England, which already had a queen and so had dropped the earlier demand. It continues to publish a quarterly newsletter, holds an annual convention, and since 2010 has hosted an Internet blog, "The Amazing Deanna Durbin."

The club, which had its first meeting in London in 1982, was honored with the full support of Durbin, who had been noted for many years as reclusive and unsympathetic to fans. When she died in April 2013, it was the Deanna Durbin Devotees who were first told the news by her son.

There is little question as to the identity of Judy Garland's number one fan, and he is Wayne Martin (1912–1993), affectionately known as "Uncle Wayne, a circumspect gay man described as "kind but cranky, wise but childlike, savvy but ridiculous."[22] It is a description that might be applied to many fans and to many film buffs. Born in Iowa, Wayne Martin came to Hollywood, with his siblings, in 1934, and became a devoted Jean Harlow fan. When she died in 1937, he changed his affiliation and devotion to Judy Garland, meeting and obtaining her autograph that year. Martin would collect memorabilia, meet the star whenever possible, attend premieres of her films, and write on a regular basis to M-G-M's publicity department. The studio recognized him as a serious Judy Garland fan, and began to invite him to press screenings of her films.

He worked occasionally as an extra—recognizable, apparently as one of the peasants, in Abbott and Costello's *Jack and the Beanstalk*—and by the 1950s, Uncle Wayne had become the "official" Judy Garland fan. As he became older, he went into decline, rather like his idol, and he was forced to sell off much of his memorabilia along with recordings he had made of his telephone conversations with Garland. Just as Joan Crawford had sent a studio publicist to check on a fan magazine writer from whom she had not heard recently, so in 1966 did Garland send two policemen to Martin's home. "Miss Garland sent us . . . She couldn't reach you by telephone and wanted to make sure you were all right."[23]

In more recent years, and with a larger membership, film buffs have supported the Count Dracula Society and the International Wizard of Oz Club. The former, which should not be confused with the British-based

Dr. Donald Reed (center).

Dracula Society, was founded in 1962 by Dr. Donald A. Reed, for the furtherance of "the serious study of horror films and gothic literature," and by 1977, it boasted more than 500 members, and was presenting the Ann Radcliffe Awards. It evolved into the Academy of Science Fiction, Fantasy and Horror Films, founded in 1972, and which presents the annual Saturn Awards. The International Wizard of Oz Club was founded by a thirteen-year-old schoolboy, Justin G. Schiller, in Michigan in 1957, and within two decades it claimed a membership of 1,500. Somewhat more prestigious than the Count Dracula Society, the International Wizard of Oz Club honors its namesake in both the mediums of film and literature, and publishes two journals, *The Baum Bugle* and *Oziana*. Other similar organizations include one dedicated to Dean Martin, which held its eighteenth convention in 2014 in Steubenville, Ohio, the singer's birthplace, and the Lucille Ball Comedy Festival, located in Jamestown, New York, and hosted by the Lucille Ball-Desi Arnaz Museum & Center for Comedy.

Surviving still are the Jimmy Stewart Museum in Indiana, Pennsylvania; the Ava Gardner Museum, supported by Ava Advocates, in Smithfield, North Carolina; and the Mario Lanza Institute and Museum in Philadelphia.

Not that those organizing fan clubs while a star was in his or her prime cannot be obsessive. "Very simple people were sometimes driven crazy by

Mary Lou Van Ness, responsible for the fan mail at Paramount in the 1940s, assists Mary Jane Saunders in answering the first batch of her fan mail. Saunders made her screen debut in *Sorrowful Jones* (1949).

stardom," wrote Richard Schickel.[24] Take, for example, Constance Riquier of Cleveland, Ohio, who became fascinated with Constance and Norma Talmadge while still a teenager, and in the early 1920s established a fan club in honor of the latter. As she explained it, she waited until she graduated high school and then exclaimed, "Well, that's over . . . Now I can give *all* my time to the fan club."[25]

As president of the Norma Talmadge Fan Club, Riquier organized promotion throughout Cleveland and Columbus, persuaded Talmadge (whom she never met) to be honorary secretary, and signed up other stars, including Charles Ray, Norma Shearer, Ruth Roland, and Dorothy Dalton, to be members of the club, which by 1924 boasted in excess of 500 members.

The club gave its members a purpose in life, and, more importantly, as far as Talmadge and her studio were concerned, provided a free publicity outlet. Typical of communications from the star to her club is this telegram dated October 16, 1924: "Greetings to Cleveland branch Norma Talmadge Club. I hope that your chapter will obtain as much pleasure from seeing *The Only Woman* as I did in making it. You all have my sincerest good wishes in your altruistic endeavors to be of real help in your community."[26]

Just as fans might belong to more than one club, so could they be fickle in their infatuation. Some fans might indeed live up to Richard Schickel's "individual celebrity dreams, our favorite lusts and fugitive longing, our fantasy relationships, whatever their emotional tone, with this or that famous person."

But then there are other fans or buffs. Robert Cushman (1946–2009), who for thirty-seven years headed the photographic archives of the Margaret Herrick Library of the Academy of Motion Picture Arts and Sciences, and was obsessive in his devotion to Mary Pickford, was said to have an equally large number of photographs of Judy Garland available to replace those of Pickford on his wall should his liking change. A little old retired lady would come into Eddie Brandt's on a regular basis, exclusively purchasing photographs of Tyrone Power. One day she came in and announced that she was no longer interested in Tyrone Power; she had started to collect photographs of an inanimate object, lighthouses. As Mike Hawks recalls, "She stopped coming back because we could never find any photographs of lighthouses."[27]

The story is told of 159 members of the Chicago branch of the Jane Withers Fan Club arriving at her studio, Twentieth Century-Fox, and being denied access. When Warner Bros. heard of this, the company invited the fans over to its lot, and, as a result, the Jane Withers Fan Club-Chicago branch offered to rename itself in honor of a Warner Bros. child star.[28]

In her later years, her career over, Jane Withers was one of the most avid of film buffs, collecting just about anything that was Hollywood-related, in particular costumes. Her plans to create a museum—just like that conceived of by Debbie Reynolds—came to nothing, but she did endear herself to films buffs with her willingness to appear at almost any function, no matter how trivial, to sign endless autographs and speak in almost childlike fashion and with childlike enthusiasm, often beginning sentences with, "Gosh, golly."

## Chapter Three

# CHAW MANK

THE FIRST MAJOR FILM BUFF TO BE RECOGNIZED AS SUCH, AS WELL AS THE first to realize that his interest could generate an income and a modicum of fame for himself, was a young man from Staunton, Illinois, named Chaw Mank. Today, he is forgotten, and yet his influence in the field of the fan club was substantial, and he also co-wrote one of the first biographies to recognize the appeal of a famous name coupled with the suggestion of relatively undiscussed (at the time) sexual practices, a book that became a film by Ken Russell, a director who found most types of sexual encounters of interest.

Charles Otto William Menk Jr. was born on September 30, 1902, the son of Charles Menk and Clydetta (Rasor) Menk, and lived his entire life in a small, white frame house at 226 East Mill Street, with his widowed mother, and, until her marriage, his sister Gloria, who gave him the name "Chaw," or more precisely "chaw-chaw," as she was unable to pronounce "Charles." He never married, and after his coal-mining father's death when Chaw was fifteen, he took upon himself the task of raising his sister. The first money he earned was as an organist at the Labor Temple Theatre on Wood Street in Staunton, providing musical accompaniment for silent films there, proudly noting that he could already play 500 songs from memory.

He claimed to have founded his first fan club, and perhaps the first in the world devoted to a film star, at the age of seven. It was called the Movie Fans Friendship Club (MFFC) and was dedicated to Mary Pickford. The actress supposedly never forgot Chaw Mank, and would send him a Christmas card every year until her death in 1979. In the early 1920s, he maintained he met Rudolph Valentino, at a live appearance at the Orpheum Theatre, St. Louis. Menk (now Mank) established his second fan club in honor of the actor, and helped set up an organization of fan clubs devoted to the star.[1]

It was through Valentino's interest, and the fact that he supposedly looked like Wallace Reid, that Chaw Mank was invited to Hollywood in 1923 to make a screen test, or so he claimed.[2] Mank similarly asserted that he had

Chaw Mank.

also met William Powell in St. Louis—date unknown—and the star had also suggested a Hollywood screen test.[3]

Whatever the truth or fantasy in regard to Chaw Mank's acting career, there is no question that he became a unique enabler of movie-related fan clubs, honoring both the living and the dead. For Chaw Mank, who claimed to be psychic and even published *Chaw Mank's Psychic Diary of the* Stars,[4] death was a minor inconvenience when it came to honoring a movie star.

He operated twenty-five "Lest We Forget" clubs, honoring everyone from James Dean to Marilyn Monroe, with the Elvis Presley Memorial Fan Club having the largest membership.

During the Depression, Mank turned his attention to music, at which he was proficient both as a performer (pianist, organist, or conductor) and composer. He gave piano lessons to local children, taught dance at Scott Air Force Base, was pianist with the Fred Weidner Orchestra, and had an eight-man orchestra, the Blue Ribbon Dance Band, which for ten years played the Coliseum Ballroom in Benld, Illinois, billed as the largest ballroom between St. Louis and Chicago, and opened in 1924. It was Mank's proud boast that he and his band played as far away from his home state as Wisconsin.

As early as 1926, Chaw Mank was recruiting stars as honorary presidents of his Movie Fans Friendship Club. Richard Dix's secretary wrote that her boss would "be glad to send photographs free of charge to fans who write for them," and that he would also provide Mank with any number of framed photographs for his personal use.[5] Carmel Myers's secretary wrote that the actress accepted an honorary presidency with pleasure, and was forwarding a scarf of her favorite color worn in her latest film, *The Understanding Heart*, as a prize for an unidentified competition being conducted by Mank.[6]

In 1927, Mank began publication of *The Movie Fans' News*, intended to keep fans informed as to what their favorite stars were doing. It was typical of all of Chaw Mank's fan publications in that it was small in size, small in terms of the number of pages, printed on flimsy paper, and had a relatively cheap look to it. In the 1930s, most of Mank's publications were no more than four pages in length and all connected to his Movie Fans Friendship Club.

Typical is *The Cesar Romero News*, presented by the Official Cesar Romero Friendship/Personality/Stamp Club. The issue for April–May–June 1937, whose numbering suggests that the first issue was published the previous year, contains a tribute to Cesar Romero by Donald P. Holt, a listing of new members of the club, and a lengthy column by Chaw Mank titled "Real News." Much of the column is concerned with promoting individuals offering help for a small fee: Olive Scott Stainsby has a new book out on *How to Write Poems*, available for 60¢; A. S. Draper will rewrite any poems or material you send him; and members are urged to purchase *Hollywood Low Down* magazine for a mere 20¢.

Cesar Romero's own contribution to his newsletter is one paragraph in length and tells of his latest film appearance in *She's Dangerous*, and his current project, *Wee Willie Winkie*, with Shirley Temple. Romero is also offering rare poses of himself, available from Chaw Mank, at 15¢ each or two for 25¢.

Almost identical in format is the Robert Taylor Friendship Club newsletter, dated April–May–June 1939 (the first issue), again featuring a tribute by Donald P. Holt, together with a separate tribute to Bob and Barbara Taylor, in recognition of Taylor's marriage to Barbara Stanwyck. Presumably, Stanwyck did not have her own friendship club, and was worthy of recognition only as Mrs. Taylor.

Chaw Mank's fan clubs recognized the talent of their subjects. Thus, there was the John Boles Golden Voice Club, extant at least from 1939 through 1941. Each issue of the club's newsletter features a suitably groveling letter from the singer-actor. In May–August 1940, he thanks Chaw Mank for "the beautiful handkerchiefs" and "the time and thought that you put into the preparing and choosing of my scrap-book." By January–March 1941, the members are bemoaning the "great injustice" that has been done to their star by Hollywood in that he is no longer wanted on screen and is forced to tour South America.

John Boles might not have died until 1969, but perhaps in recognition that his Hollywood career is over, he is featured extensively in the July–August–September 1940, and the first issue of the "Lest We Forget" Club newsletter, designed "to Serve and Please 'Shut-Ins' Everywhere, may God Bless us all." Curiously, the club lists a bunch of honorary presidents, all of whom are (perhaps appropriately) dead, and include Valentino, Barbara Lamarr, Milton Sills, John Gilbert, and Ruth Roland.

The various newsletters titled *The Movie Fans Friendship Club News* all boasted one purpose: "We stand for 'Boosting' not 'Knocking.'" The Winter 1935–36 issue features a lengthy list of stars, with the heading "Boost," and among their number are both major (Joan Crawford, Jean Harlow, Norma Shearer, and Shirley Temple) and minor (definitely in the majority, and including Ben Bard, Johnny Downs, Bodil Rosing, and Peggy Shannon).[7] Chaw Mank published his own message to his readership, "The stars give to the fans so much sincere pleasure and joy—that it is such a joy and happiness to boost these names. Upon the lips of millions of fans these names shall again be discussed for 1936."

Later, probably in the 1940s, Mank published a small, twenty-eight-page booklet, titled *Of Praises We Sing*, with tributes by various fans to Dick Powell, Marie Wilson, Wayne Morris, Bing Crosby, and others. A similar booklet, titled *We Salute*, was published during World War II, honoring Minna Gombell (a Chaw Mank favorite) and Vaughn De Leath. It consisted primarily of poems by the publisher, and the titles—"Broken Hearted Cowboy," "You're As Sweet as a Big Bunch of Violets," and "Buckaroo

Chaw Mank (standing second from left) with members of the Fan Club Guild en route to Hollywood in August 1935.

Lullaby"—are indicative of the quality of the pieces. In the early 1950s, Mank authored and published a twenty-four-page booklet, *Perfumed Shamrock*, dedicated to Maureen O'Hara.

Hollywood celebrities were urged to join the Movie Fans Friendship Club, which claimed a membership of 5,000. Each was expected to pay dues of 53¢ a year. A typical application is from Doris Nolan, perhaps best remembered as Katharine Hepburn's sister in *Holiday*. She gives her name, her address (Universal Studios), her date of birth (July 14, 1916), and encloses one dollar.[8]

Unquestionably, Hollywood players showered Mank with gifts. Minna Gombell sent him a tie[9] and a book by Norman Vincent Peale. Rosalind Russell sent him a fountain pen. She had wanted to gift him "a unique incense burner," but was unable to find one in Los Angeles (though she promised to seek one in San Francisco when she was next there).[10] Apparently, in the late 1930s, Mank was collecting incense burners, and claimed to have been given a couple from Humphrey Bogart and James Stewart.

MEMBERSHIP CARD

THIS IS TO CERTIFY THAT

Chaw Mank

IS A MEMBER OF

THE LON McCALLISTER FAN CLUB

August, 1952
DUES EXPIRE

HONORARY PRESIDENT

Chaw Mank's membership card for the Lon McCallister Fan Club.

Some in Hollywood were repulsed by Chaw Mank. Spencer Tracy's secretary advised Mank that he already had a couple of fan clubs and was planning a long vacation. "Because of the above, and because he belongs to a good many clubs, he does not feel that he has the time to devote to any others at present."[11] Anna Neagle's secretary explained, "Miss Neagle does not have any fan clubs in England, and in view of this fact, does not care to have any started in this country." She did, however, send Mank a personally autographed photograph.[12]

Sometimes it was a relative assigned to explain the situation to Mank. Veda Ann Borg is a name for film buffs to conjure with, rather than serious scholars of film who might be unaware of her work. Despite not being a star and working at Republic at the time, she left it to her mother to write in 1941, "We are interested in your work & appreciate your writing—but things have never been solid enough to warrant fan clubs and such."[13]

However, for all the stars who were not exactly overwhelmed with gratitude at Chaw Mank's efforts on their behalf, there were lesser players, particularly character people, who appreciated him. Typical is Albert Conti, who had worked with Valentino in *The Eagle* (1925) and D. W. Griffith in *Lady of the Pavements* (1929). Acknowledging in 1932 that "conditions in pictures are, pardon me, lousy at the moment," he promised that he would send Christmas cards to all fans directed to him by Mank. He continued,

> I have not worked for 2 solid months. Can you blame me if I get depressed and blue and start to get shaky in my self-confidence? Thank God I am getting a hold of myself and, believe it or not, your letter helped me a great deal! Thanks old pal and I hope that sometime in the future I will be able to show you my gratefulness! Not only talk about it![14]

Danish-born character actress Bodil Rosing had formed her own club in Hollywood, with a newsletter titled *Bodil and Her Friends*, and in 1933, she turned to Chaw Mank for advice. "It takes clever exploitation to put over a fan club for a character actress but I guess we can do it, what you say?!"[15]

While there can be no doubt as to Chaw Mank's devotion to and obsession with his multitude of stars—he never, for example, tried to sell any of the gifts given to him during his lifetime—there were ugly questions raised as to the monies the fan clubs might be generating. It was not a large amount, certainly not enough to justify a move from Staunton, Illinois, but during the 1930s, it guaranteed that Chaw Mank would not go hungry.

Paramount, in particular, was suspicious of Chaw Mank's activities. When Rochelle Hudson, a Fox contract player, had the notion of a fan club associated with Chaw Mank, a publicist at the studio, who had previously been at Paramount, fought against the idea. Harmony Hayes, fan mail editor at *Hollywood Magazine*, explained to Mank, "I find that most people consider you have too many clubs already and therefore are unwilling to join with you—makes it look on the surface like a racket."[16]

Joe Penner, a prominent comedian on radio—known for the catchphrase "Wanna buy a duck?"—appears to have been happy to subsidize Mank's work. In February 1937, his secretary sent a check for $15 to cover in full any expenses incurred in publication of the March issue of *The Movie Fans Friendship Club News*, in his honor. He also arranged for RKO to send material from its publicity department, and included a number of items for use, including one "about Joe building a home at Holmby Hills, one of the beauty spots of Southern California, which will have, among other things, a miniature baseball diamond and a barnyard kennel for his police dog, 'Coco.'"[17]

In 1938, Mank published "A New Star Shines in Heaven," with words by himself and music by Luther A. Clark. The song was dedicated to Jean Harlow, and the lyrics are well worth quoting, at least in part,

> I know you're there, both lovely and fair,
> Changed into a star overnight.
> I wish you well, where'er you dwell,
> Jean Harlow, so lovely and bright.

In return for having his photograph included on the sheet music cover, and, more importantly, the dedication, "In Reverence and Gratitude Joe Penner," the comedian paid Mank $15 and also selected the words in the dedication, or more precisely, his secretary did.[18]

Chaw Mank's original composition dedicated to the memory of Jean Harlow, "A New Star Shines in Heaven."

"A New Star Shines in Heaven" is a reminder that when he was not working his entrepreneurial skills as a marketer of fan clubs, Chaw Mank was equally busy in the musical field. Aside from his Blue Ribbon Band, he also had the Blue Ribbon recording label, with the band surviving until 1978 and ending its activities only because of Mank's ill health. Among the songs he wrote, for publication by the Blue Ribbon Music Co., were "The Flying Fortress" (1944), dedicated to Gene Autry, "When I Dream about the Wabash" (1945), "The Grandpappy Polka" (1947), "The Illinois Waltz" (1948), and "Atom Bomb Heart" (1955), described as "a Cold War ditty." He claimed to have paid $35 to take the Liberace piano playing plan, but was so good that not only did he get his money back, but Liberace sent him a money clip with $5 as a Christmas gift.

Certainly, Chaw Mank kept abreast of the times. In January–February–March 1943, he published the first issue of *The Voice*, dedicated to Frank Sinatra, very similar in content to the John Boles Golden Voice Club newsletter, except that the subject of the publication is not particularly discussed, with a tribute piece devoted to Hedy Lamarr and a photograph of Minna Gombell, identified as "A Star of Stars."

He wrote to everyone, and received a surprising number of replies. He wrote to Ronald Reagan in the 1950s, and was a member of his fan club. "I'm a Democrat, but I voted for him," he told a local reporter. "I'd never do it again."[19] Generally, Mank kept in contact with the film community and its fans through correspondence, sending and receiving as many as 10,000 letters a year,[20] and spending more than $4,500 annually on postage, but he did make occasional trips to Hollywood and, more frequently, to Nashville.

Among the many small books or booklets that Mank published in the 1950s was one titled *My Favorite Prayers*. He planned to update it in the 1980s, asking the cinema's current batch of teenage stars to contribute: "I didn't get one answer. I don't think they pray. Ninety percent of them, I would say, are atheists."[21]

Fame, notoriety, and financial success came late in life for Chaw Mank, but come it did, when in 1966 McFadden-Bartell published *Valentino*. As Mank's coauthor, Brad Steiger, recalls,

> Chaw contacted me and said that he had been the head of the Valentino fan club and had Rudy's personal scrapbook and other memorabilia. My agent said that sounded like a potential book, and I went to visit Chaw and discuss the subject with him.

> The kids were fascinated with the house in which the downstairs rooms were so cluttered with books and magazines that the only way to move about was to follow the pathways Chaw had made between massive piles of mags, newspapers, and other collectibles of the stars.
>
> As you surmised, I wrote the book, Chaw provided the research. My aunt, who lived in Chicago, had starred in a number of Broadway productions and had known Rudy and had attended his funeral was also a big help. . . .
>
> When deadline time grew near, McFadden-Bartell flew me out from my college teaching job in Iowa and put me up in the Iroquois Hotel where an occasional editor would visit me and go over the pages I hammered out on my 1923 Underwood.
>
> Chaw would check in from time to time and provide additional details. He seemed to know an incredible network of fans and movie buffs who claimed to know who would provide some more information.[22]

*Valentino* has everything both a film buff and a casual reader might desire in a biography of a Hollywood legend. At times, it reads as nothing more than a somewhat pedantic study of a life and career. At other times, it is positively lurid and titillating as Valentino is invited to a male-only evening at a club, with pool and convenient private rooms known as the Torch. Here the great lover is introduced to male-male sex thanks to an overweight, unidentified director:

> The man's eyes widened with lust, and his tongue extended itself to sponge dry lips, sweep back into a grinning mouth. His [Valentino's] thin shanks began to quiver in anticipation.
>
> "Pretty boy," the director said, daubs of saliva flecking his lips, "get yourself down on your knees."[23]

The biography came to the attention of British director Ken Russell, who cast Rudolf Nureyev in the lead, with a supporting cast including Michelle Phillips, Leslie Caron, and Carol Kane, for a screen adaptation, released in 1981. The film was neither a critical nor a commercial success, but "Chaw seemed transported to paradise. The ultimate show biz and movie buff now able to see his name at the beginning of every showing: Based on a book by Brad Steiger and Chaw Mank."[24]

Chaw Mank continued with little regard for fame and fortune, living in the same house, playing a piano with broken keys, and, in later years,

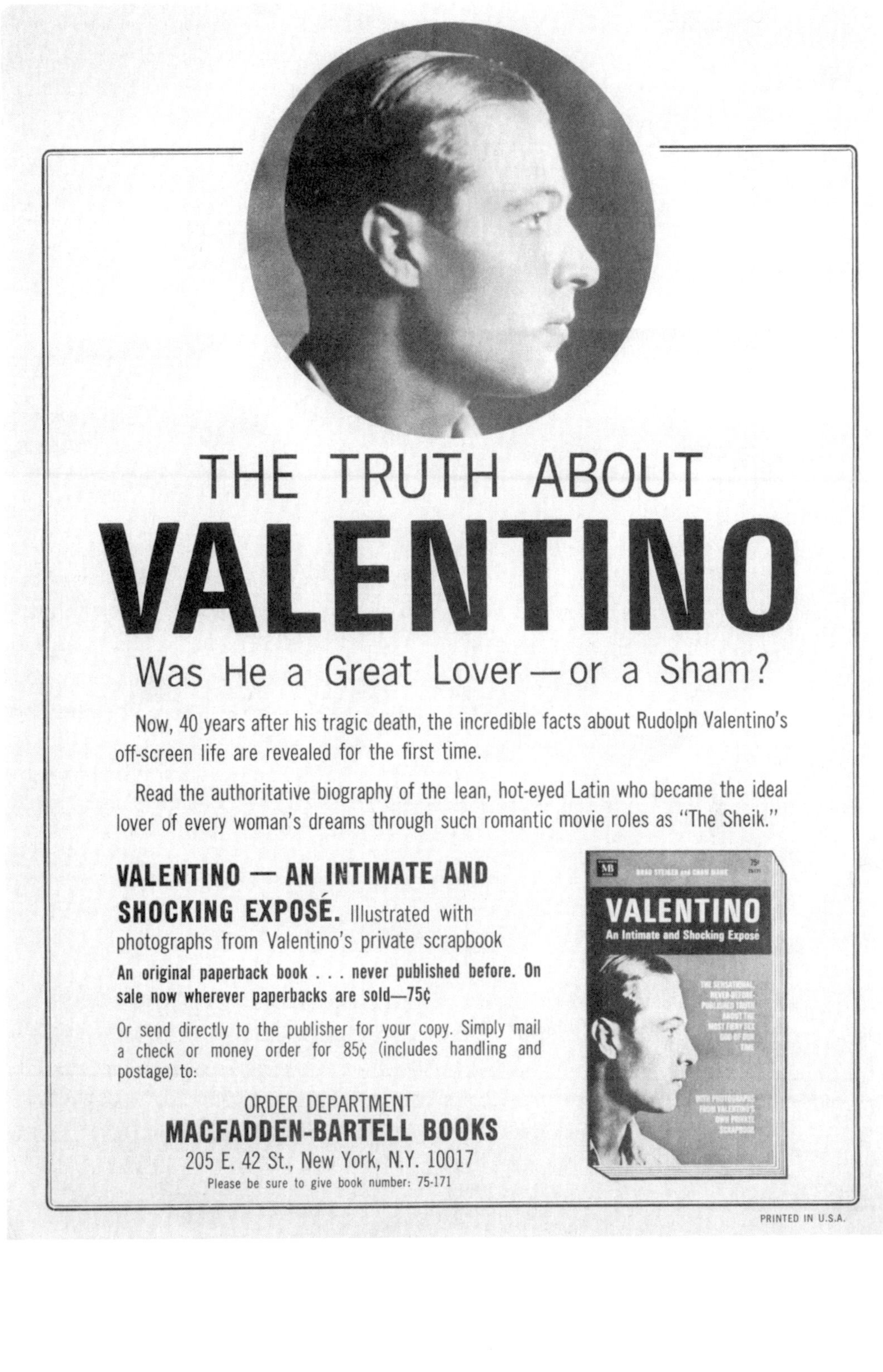
THE TRUTH ABOUT
VALENTINO
Was He a Great Lover—or a Sham?
Now, 40 years after his tragic death, the incredible facts about Rudolph Valentino's off-screen life are revealed for the first time.
Read the authoritative biography of the lean, hot-eyed Latin who became the ideal lover of every woman's dreams through such romantic movie roles as "The Sheik."
VALENTINO — AN INTIMATE AND SHOCKING EXPOSÉ. Illustrated with photographs from Valentino's private scrapbook
An original paperback book . . . never published before. On sale now wherever paperbacks are sold—75¢
Or send directly to the publisher for your copy. Simply mail a check or money order for 85¢ (includes handling and postage) to:
ORDER DEPARTMENT
MACFADDEN-BARTELL BOOKS
205 E. 42 St., New York, N.Y. 10017
Please be sure to give book number: 75-171
VALENTINO
An Intimate and Shocking Exposé
PRINTED IN U.S.A.

contributing a column, "You Ask—I'll Tell," to the *Benld Enterprise* as well as a column titled "The Fans Club House" to *Classic Film Collector*, beginning in 1982. The latter contains such fascinating news items as "Miss Betty Joyce Forber, Cornfield, Ohio, likes cactus flowers and Burt Reynolds."[25]

"The World's Champion Movie Fan," as he was known, died of cancer at the Staunton Community Memorial Hospital on April 14, 1985. His sister disposed of his collection.

## Chapter Four

# FILM BUFF SCREENINGS

AS ONE ACADEMIC HAS NOTED, PUBLIC SCREENINGS IN MUSEUMS HAVE helped raise films "from ephemeral entertainment to enduring cultural monument."[1] The statement might also be applied to film buffs who did their part in that elevation by their passionate attendance at such screenings.

Repertory seasons of older films arguably began in the late 1910s when, concurrent with the May 1919 premiere of *Broken Blossoms*, D. W. Griffith organized a retrospective season of his films at New York's George M. Cohan Theatre. The season gave the director an opportunity to "revise" some of his earlier films and also to screen two "new" films, *The Mother and the Law* and *The Fall of Babylon*, taken from his 1916 masterwork, *Intolerance*. The latter was revived at New York's 55th Street Playhouse in November 1933, with the director present.

In the fall of 1935, the Museum of Modern Art (MOMA) established a film department, under the leadership of British-born librarian and critic Iris Barry. The initial impetus was the collection and preservation of motion pictures, but the museum quickly established a screening program, firstly at the Museum of Natural History and later, in 1939, at the new Museum of Modern Art Building at 11 West Fifty-Third Street. The screenings became the focal point for gatherings of New York film buffs, continuing as such for decades.

A level of decorum was demanded not so much by the museum as by the buffs, who would often find their attention distracted from the screen by ordinary visitors who had paid an admission fee that also included free access to the auditorium. In anguish, one buff, Barnett G. Braverman who was later to jostle for position with Seymour Stern as D. W. Griffith's biographer, wrote to the *New York Times* (July 9, 1939), using his birth name of B. G. Braver-Mann: "I can hardly recall a single occasion on which the audience did not indulge either in loud and prolonged talking or in inexcusably boorish and raucous laughter throughout the showing."

One individual with strong opinions as to the behavior of the museum's audience in the 1930s was Theodore Huff, who had worked at MOMA from 1935 to 1940. Discharged from the museum as part of a budget-cutting campaign, he wrote a lengthy letter to D. W. Griffith, suggesting the filmmaker should remove his films and papers from the museum because of the pro-communist attitudes of Iris Barry and others, including assistant Jay Leyda:

> The vast majority of the audiences who attend the film shows consist of pseudo-intellectual sophisticates, whose only interest in silent films is one of cynical curiosity, and local Communists, who come for the express purpose of jeering at anything and everything that does not agree with their prescribed theories and dogmas. The Museum's daily film shows are held at an extremely inconvenient hour—4:00 P.M., and except for an occasional Saturday or Sunday, it is possible to count on the fingers of one hand the people who come because they love the old films or because they have a genuine and scholarly interest in your work.
>
> This was clearly seen during the Spring and Summer of 1939, when five of your pictures were exhibited. The Communist element was particularly mean spirited in going out of its way to mock and laugh at your work.[2] The officials of the Library, John Abbott and Iris Barry, not only made no attempt to educate this new public (which the Library has always proclaimed as one of its chief purposes), but, on the contrary. They had a stock-in-trade of apologies and excuses for any and every demonstration that occurred in the auditorium, and took the view that this was "the audience's privilege."[3]

During his tenure with MOMA, Theodore Huff had been responsible for arranging musical accompaniment for the screenings there of silent films. He, or rather his name, was to play a prominent role later in the New York film buff screening scene.

By the 1960s and 1970s, a pattern had emerged at the museum's screenings, with the front row taken over by the hardcore film buffs. They knew their place—and their place was as close to the screen as possible. Such film buffs even had their designated seats in the front row. One of the front-row brigade was a little old lady, remembered only as Celia, while another lady, here and at the Huff Society screenings, would become so engrossed in the film that she would talk back to the screen. Edward Maguire took it upon himself to distribute schedules of all film buff-related New York screenings. He even hosted such screenings at his home, with his wife, Mary, providing a Christmas Day meal for those with nowhere else to go (which was probably most of the film buffs). Ed Maguire would always sit in the front row, on and across the aisle from the auditorium's central seating area. Charles Shibuk tells me that he would sit in the same seat in the theatre's penultimate row, keeping an "aesthetic distance" from Maguire.[4]

Interestingly, Charles Shibuk explains that he has some very good reasons to distance himself from film buffs:

> I had a stable home environment.
>
> I dressed neatly and shaved every day.
>
> I was a college graduate. I minored in English and classics, and majored in motion pictures.[5]

I can attest that Ed and Mary Maguire, a delightful couple, are generous in sharing memories with me, recalling forensic pathologist Dr. Bob Kalish, sitting in the front row at MOMA, often resting with his head in his hands, and Ida Belaney, who was a big fan of Tom Mix; she was also a fan of Adolf Hitler, applauding whenever he happened to appear on screen.

The film buffs at the Museum of Modern Art are perhaps somewhat eccentric but at heart decent, hard-working folks. One has less sympathy and respect for the five New Yorkers appearing in the 2003 German/American documentary, *Cinemania*. They are impassioned, obsessed, and obviously quite egotistical in agreeing to appear as themselves onscreen. Included in their number is Roberta Hill, who is banned from many New York theatres and who was known to get into fights with ticket collectors who would tear too much off her ticket stub, and Jack Angstreich, who has no interest in life outside of his moviegoing and would only make love to Rita Hayworth if it could be done in black-and-white.[6]

Theodore Huff (1905–1953), real named Edmund Huff, is more deserving of recognition as a pioneering film historian than a film buff, although he did display some buffish traits, such as spending most of his life living with his mother and collecting still photographs and other types of movie memorabilia. Seymour Stern hypothesized to film collector David Bradley that Huff's early death was the result of his never having had sex with a woman, an unnatural way of life.[7] He was the "arbiter supreme of film fact," and could be obsessive in compiling lists of factual errors, such as those occurring in Lewis Jacobs's *The Rise of the American Film: A Critical History* (New York: Harcourt Brace, 1939). Huff had not only worked for the Museum of Modern Art, but also the Library of Congress, where he was instrumental in the rediscovery of the paper print collection. He was also a filmmaker, and author of the first, serious study of Charlie Chaplin, published by a relatively minor New York house, Henry Schuman, in 1951. As the New York Public Library's Gerald D. McDonald commented,

> Ted Huff had the scholar's regard for truth and accuracy. "When you make a statement," he used to say, "you have to be careful or you will repeat the same old errors." . . . He recognized the distortions of film history that result from personal vanity and publicity releases, and he readily spotted the canards that are copied and copied from unreliable "authorities."[8]

But, as McDonald continued, as you and he looked over some still photographs, placing each in its proper niche in film history, "the old collector would have come forward and he would have said: 'How would you like to trade them for some Ruth Rolands?'"[9]

It is Theodore Huff who has given his name to a legendary New York screening group, whose membership comprised both film buffs and film historians, together with quite a few genuine eccentrics (who probably fall into the film buff category). One who had no problem with being a buff was a gentleman named Bert Gray (1924–1978), noted for his thick spectacles and gray complexion (presumably the result of too much time spent inside watching films). If Gray cackled three times during a screening, it was a sign he approved of the movie being shown. Gray, who boasted of having seen more than 20,000 films, argued, "Please call us buffs. Calling us freaks and nuts makes it sound strange and I love going to the movies and I don't see anything strange about it."[10]

Gray liked to identified by his film buff colleagues as "Doctor Gray" or "Professor Gray," and could certainly have made a name for himself with the academic community, having once delivered a well-received lecture on the significance of rocks in Western films.

The most famous of attendees at Huff Society screenings was Calvin Beck, founder and publisher from 1962 to 1975 of *Castle of Frankenstein*, which has claim to being the only nationwide publication with serious coverage of "B" movies, as well as horror films from all eras. However, it is not for *Castle of Frankenstein* that Beck is remembered, but rather as the possible inspiration for Robert Bloch's Norman Bates in *Psycho*. Beck was nothing like Tony Perkins, it must be noted; he wore glasses, was fat, greasy-looking, with unattractive black hair and a moustache, and generally unhealthy in appearance. Whether Beck was the model for Norman Bates has never been fully determined, but as one film buff noted, he was "a good representative of that type."[11]

Beck also had a mother, who would never leave his side. Her husband had suffered a stroke, after which he was banished to an upstairs bedroom and never seen again. She was described as "extremely possessive and controlling, and quite mad." She would not permit Beck to have any close relationships with men or women. One film buff recalls that whenever Beck had to visit the bathroom at a screening, his mother would escort him to the door, and then stand guard outside, refusing to allow others to enter.

There were also some nonhuman members of the Huff audience, such as a monkey, whose owner brought it in, hidden inside his windbreaker. The animal was allowed to stay as it paid attention to the screen, and was, one suspected, better behaved than some of the regular attendees and appreciated the films more.

However, it must be acknowledged, as Leonard Maltin has pointed out,

> There was more knowledge in that room—there was more collective knowledge about film history than in any library. Everyone had a specialty. Most people there were experts in some specific area. . . . Bill exposed us to stuff we would never have seen anywhere else or by any other means or through any other means. It was amazing. It was wonderful. It was slightly surreal.[12]

> It's not that the people at the Huff were gay, interested only in same-sex relationships. Many of them were asexual. Old movies were their passion. That was where they sublimated all of their feelings.[13]

The Theodore Huff Memorial Film Society was founded in 1952 by a group of friends, Herman G. Weinberg, William K. Everson, George Geltzer, D. W. Griffith biographer Seymour Stern, filmmaker Robert Youngson, Charles L. Turner,[14] Paramount publicist Bill Kenly,[15] and Huff himself, with the informal title of the Film Circle, and meeting usually on a Friday every two weeks. (Weinberg objected to the name, claiming it sounded like a sewing circle.[16]) Everyone involved had some connection to the film industry, to prints, and to a rental-free 35mm screening room. Initially, the screenings were held at Film Counselors, 500 Fifth Avenue, with the first film on screen there being David Bradley's version of *Julius Caesar*, starring Charlton Heston, and with the director present. Everson was sometimes able to borrow the New Yorker Theatre for Sunday morning screenings of 35mm films, which he was somehow able to smuggle out of Lloyd's Film Storage.

When the latter was no longer available, and with Huff's death, the group formalized as the Theodore Huff Memorial Film Society, and membership expanded. A committee decided the films to be screened, and various individuals took care of different functions, including program notes and music. There was a brief "hiccup" in the society's operation as a result of its being sued over the screening of the Hedy Lamarr vehicle, *Ecstasy* (1933), without permission of the copyright owner. As Lieutenant Colonel George J. Mitchell recalled,

> I had gotten a print of *Ecstasy*, and I bought it quite legally in France from a place there called the Film Office. I think I paid $150 for it, which was a hell of a lot of money at that time. Everson borrowed this print from me for his film society. I thought nothing of it, and I didn't think there would be any problem. But apparently a man by the name of Samuel Cummins had the rights to *Ecstasy*, which he guarded zealously. Everson ran the film at the Theodore Huff Film Society, Everson publicized it, and Cummins came down on them like Grant did on Richmond. I was stationed at the Presidio [San Francisco] at the time and I was getting these frantic calls from Everson. If they'll surrender the print to him [Cummins], everything will be fine. If I'd used my head at the time, I should have said, "So let him sue me." I was a major in the army. I'd gotten the thing quite legally. He's going to sue me for it? I could have laughed at him. But I'd just gotten to know these fellows, so I said, "OK." That was an example of what Bill Everson could get you into.[17]

The Theodore Huff Memorial Film Society returned to its former glory, and indeed expanded and flourished, with screenings in a hall in the vicinity of New York's Union Square. Screenings increased from once a month to as many as once a week. The mission always was to screen "rare" films that were not necessarily great and certainly not film classics but contributed to the understanding of film history. "Better by far to dig up some unknown films by Robert Florey or Walter Forde and fill in a few gaps instead of adding further cement to existing pedestals."[18] The reference to British director Walter Forde is indicative of the considerable number of features that were screened from Everson's native land.

As Everson described it, "we operate in a kind of no man's land of legality—many of the films we show we have permission to show, others we don't."[19] Adding to the mystique was the society's refusal to generate publicity as to its screenings or the location. "The Huff members don't want just anyone coming to their screenings."[20]

In its early years, the Theodore Huff Memorial Society had operated with a committee, consisting of Edward Gorey, Dorothy Lovell, and Everson. Lovell would provide sketches to enhance the program notes, and the society also sponsored research projects; for example, Charles Shibuk compiled the first two in what was intended to be a series of mimeographed works consisting of *An Index to the Films of William Wyler* and *An Index to the Films of Lewis Milestone*. "Possibly I did that stuff just to prove I could do it," comments Shibuk. "Printing cost nothing. I got the paper at work and at least seventy-five copies were printed initially, more later." He continues,

> When I first knew Bill, I was in his office and he asked me if I'd like to see a very short film. I said, "Yes." It was *The Flower Fairy*. I liked it very much and said so. Bill asked me if I'd like to write a few words about it and I did. Bill liked what I did and printed it on the Huff notes for this film. Later, I did notes for *White Shadows in the South Seas* without seeing the film. . . . I did a few more later, *Phantom of the Opera*, *Nosferatu*, *Dr. Jekyll and Mr. Hyde* (1932), and [Fritz] Lang's *Destiny*. Why I did them I'll never know.[21]

With the passing years, the society ceased to be run on democratic principles, and, apparently, in October 1953, it became a benign dictatorship, with William K. Everson operating a one-man operation. There was no right of appeal against the screening of any film, and while Everson had no objection to members' requesting a specific film, the question was somewhat moot in that Everson was limited to films he had available.

Everson would send out a mailing announcing Huff Society screenings over a three-month period. He would address the envelopes himself, sometimes with help from Charles Shibuk, using little bits of paper on which he had the names and addresses of members. Postage was paid by Everson. After a while, Shibuk suggested that to make life easier, Everson ask members to provide stamped and addressed envelopes. "He said 'It wouldn't work' (considering the mental caliber of too many of the members). One member sent envelopes to Bill, but they were addressed to Bill. . . . Another member, a small part actor with a large ego, told Bill that he thought Bill would miss him and send him a schedule anyway. Bill said he only worked from the envelopes he had and never mind about Bill's missing him, 'Look what films *you* missed.'"[22]

Anthony Slide, Leonard Maltin, and William K. Everson.

Everson's screenings were not limited to the Theodore Huff Memorial Society. He also presented screenings as part of his teaching assignments at the New School [for Social Research] and he also hosted Saturday night film showings at his home, initially in a hotel room and then at his apartment on West Seventy-Ninth Street until circa 1994, when he became ill.[23] I had the good fortune to attend occasionally when I was in New York, and my fellow and sister attendees were a curious bunch, not given to social intercourse before or after the films. When college professor, and film buff, Arthur Lennig (more about him later) was present, the atmosphere was decidedly more convivial. The apartment was not exactly the cleanest in New York, and the bathroom was to be avoided. I recall on one occasion that a guest had brought a cake. It was placed on a table next to the screen, and during the movie, it was somewhat alarming to watch a very large cockroach creep up the leg of the table and enjoy feasting on the cake. Cockroach or not, I am sure Everson would have enjoyed the cake, in that his diet would often consist more of cake, ice cream, pie with custard, and chocolates than of salad and fresh fish.

Arthur Lennig recalled one Saturday night screening, attended by a gentleman identified as Everson's oldest American friend:

> I remember being convulsed with laughter when Ed Connor—one of the faithful at Everson's Saturday night screenings—sat with me through my first viewing of my beloved Lugosi's *Chandu on the Magic Isle*, which Everson screened at my request. Connor not only knew every line, but made outrageous comments about the action. Whenever Lugosi was in a dire situation, he would, by telepathy, ask the all-powerful and all-knowing Yogi for help, and Yogi's reply invariably would be, more or less, "You figure it out, my son." Connor was the most jovial of guests, a welcome contrast to some who sat grim-faced through both tragedy and comedy. Who could forget Connor's joyous hoop of derision when George O'Brien—in one of his Westerns—would take off his shirt to show off his muscles."[24]

Ed Connor was an inveterate punster, and Leonard Maltin recalls one of his best efforts,

> I found Sara Allgood.
> I liked Gerald Mohr.
> But I found Edna Best.[25]

William K. Everson (1929–1996) was a legendary film collector and film historian, who was extraordinarily generous in terms of his collection and of his knowledge. He was a buff who became a historian. Born in England, he had no university education and entered the film industry while still a teenager, working for Renown Pictures and as a cinema manager. He immigrated to the United States in 1950, and began his career here as a publicist in New York with Monogram Pictures. He was also active working for producer Paul Killiam (who is most deserving of more attention) on the *Movie Museum* and *Silents Please* series. Eventually, his film collection was of such size and scope that it provided him with an academic career, as he taught film history at the School of Visual Arts (1964–1984) and New York University (1972–1996).[26] His obsessive and compulsive collecting instincts paid off well. Along the way, Everson wrote a number of film books, all popular at the time, but some of which now appear somewhat dated and almost a waste of Everson's talent. The two most important volumes are, unquestionably, *The American Movie* (New York: Oxford University Press, 1978) and *The Westerns: From Silents to the Seventies* (New York: Orion Press, 1962), coauthored with George N. Fenin.

There was certainly something mythical about Everson, and there are many stories that have added to the legend. Certainly it is true that he named his son Griffith (now a computer wiz in New York) after the director whom he so admired. And equally certain is that it is sometimes difficult to separate fiction from reality. Perhaps the most famous story concerning Everson, reported in Kevin Brownlow's *The Parade's Gone By* and on Wikipedia, is that when he planned to screen a print of the 1926 version of *Ben-Hur*,[27] Metro-Goldwyn-Mayer alerted the FBI, he was charged with an unidentified crime and it was only through the intervention of Lillian Gish that he was saved from a jail term.

What nonsense! Surely only a film buff would accept this story? A fellow collector, George J. Mitchell, had access to the FBI files because of his position in military intelligence. The reality is that two FBI agents were in the audience when the film was screened. They questioned Everson in regard to the print, asked him to turn it over to them, and asked that he provide them information as to its source. Everson complied, apologized, and the FBI agents reported that he was naïve in his belief that he had the right to screen the print and that there was no need for any further action. There was no charge, no trial, and no intervention on the witness stand by Lillian Gish. As Mitchell pointed out, "The upshot of it is Everson is a dangerous man to let have a picture that you don't want other people to know you have."[28]

One William K. Everson story that is apparently true was told by his friend, fellow film collector Herb Graff. He, Everson, and others were traveling by car. Everson had fallen asleep, but was awakened when a fellow passenger mentioned *King Kong*. Everson was somewhat irritated to discover that the reference was of no particular interest. When Herb Graff asked him why he was upset, his friend responded, "I wish you hadn't woken me. I was dreaming that I was screening *The Spider* with Edmund Lowe [at that time assumed to be a 'lost' film]."

Asked how it was, Everson responded, in true Everson fashion, "Wonderful picture—terrible print."[29]

On another occasion, Everson was asked what heaven would be, and he responded that it would consist of all 35mm nitrate tinted and toned prints. "And what of hell?" He responded, in typical English fashion, "No projector."[30]

Apart from the legendary stories, there is also the tale of a family man, little recorded or acknowledged. Everson's daughter, Bambi, was named by her mother after American dancer and choreographer Bambi Linn. Her second name is Elizabeth, after Everson's much-loved silent star, Betty Bronson, and her Aunt Betty. If she had been a boy, her father planned to call her

Wolfgang, and, if he had been allowed to name her, he would have chosen Constance, after Constance Bennett or Constance Moore. Bambi writes,

> Happy to talk about growing up in that cramped, wonderful and dangerous apartment.
>
> I adored my dad. We had some issues during my teenage and early adult phases, but it worked itself out by the time he was a grandpa. He was a wonderful grandfather!! My daughter Sarah had a very unique relationship with him. I am sorry he didn't get to see her grow up.
>
> The house . . . well you know what it looked like . . . absolute craziness.
>
> But the redeeming factor was that it was filled with films you couldn't see anywhere else.
>
> So I had great birthday parties.
>
> Except for my 8th one when my dad decided to run *The Biscuit Eater*! Every single kid left in tears!![31]
>
> Halloween parties were the best.
>
> As a kid I showed *Dead of Night, Abbott and Costello Meet Frankenstein, Freaks* and *Night of the Demon.*
>
> But I know I didn't live like other people.
>
> His hoard was legendary and the state of the house mostly an embarrassment but people never strayed from the living room, and the coolness factor outweighed the mess for most teenagers.
>
> My dad enjoyed things other than movies.
>
> Sundays we would go to the Central Park lake and collect tadpoles. He loved country walks in England although he never missed the opportunity to make a film reference. He loved amusement parks.[32]

There can be little question that the legend of William K. Everson will continue, and I do not doubt or argue with his status in the Parthenon of film scholars, historians, collectors, and, yes, buffs. Everson once commented that only after thirty years of film viewings might a buff call himself a historian. Certainly, he reached that status. Further, he did it with a generosity of spirit, sharing his film collection with all, buff and scholar, without financial recompense and expectation of any reward. As Rick DeCroix has written, "He mastered film history the best way possible, by watching films. No doubt precisely because he was *not* an academic, William K. Everson fully understood how to present film to all people, making cinema an unusually thrilling place of discovery and rediscovery."[33]

What is perhaps depressing is that the young, Internet-obsessed film buffs of today do not fully grasp or understand Everson's importance in the exhibition and "recovery" of vast swathes of film history thanks to such screenings. Films are available today on DVDs, on Turner Classic Movies, on YouTube. Who needs a 16mm film collector such as William K. Everson?

In New York, film buffs organized their own regular screenings. One of the earliest documented groups was the Sutton Cinema Society, organized by actor and film collector John Griggs,[34] initially out of his apartment on Sutton Place, and then continuing with the name wherever he happened to be. Griggs was primarily a radio actor, heard on more than 5,000 programs (most notably Mutual's *The House of Mystery*, 1945–1949). He sold copies of many of the films in his collection through a company he called Griggs-Moviedrome, and after his death in 1967, the collection formed the basis for the Yale Film Study Center. Everyone has a good word to say about Griggs, but all note the tragedy of his alcoholism, which obviously affected his ability to obtain acting roles.

The price tag Yale paid for John Griggs film collection was determined by Herman G. Weinberg and Robert E. "Bob" Lee (1911–1992), who had known the actor/collector from the 1940s when they both worked, in very different capacities, at WOR-New York. Lee also was a film collector, and from 1939 to 1992, he had been operating the Essex Film Club out of his home in Nutley, New Jersey. The first film he screened was *Cimarron*, starring Irene Dunne and Richard Dix. Bob Lee was one of the few film collectors to have a moment of fame on television, when he appeared, in 1973, on the popular *To Tell the Truth*.

Circa 1963, actor Don Koll (a one-time president of the Catholic Actors Guild), who worked primarily in television commercials and as an extra, along with Eleanor Knowles founded Loew's 3rd Street film club in the former's Third Street/Second Avenue apartment. Eleanor Knowles recalls,

> He and I actually started it when somehow I came up with $50 and rented prints of *The Love Parade* and *Vagabond King* both with Jeanette and ran them here. I had a projector, but my mini apartment would barely have held six viewers. His floor plan allowed a dozen or more. His screenings became a weekly event. I remember well the night when Miles Kreuger phoned at 11:45 p.m. saying he was on his way over in a cab and don't anyone move. He arrived with the footage of Broadway musicals from 1930 on, shot from the audience by the kid who got a camera for his bar mitzvah or whatever the situation was.[35] We stayed until the sun came up, seeing

John Griggs with Carol Stone on stage in *Mackerel Skies* (January 1934).

> Marilyn Miller and Ethel Merman and all the immortals . . . Merman spotted him filming, shook her finger at him and smiled. . . . I know I went to work the next day, in no pain from the euphoria of that experience.[36]

One of the regular female attendees at Don Koll's apartment had been traumatized as a child by a film scene involving a man on a horse. She attended every one of Koll's screenings in the hope that she might see that scene again and delete it from her memory.[37]

Alan G. Barbour, who retired in 1996 as manager, Artists and Repertoire from BMG Video Club, and his wife, Catherine, hosted regular Friday evening events, with screenings in 16mm and the emphasis on "B" movies, Westerns, and serials. The group called itself the Serial Society of New York (SSONY).

Alan Barbour, the well-dressed film buff (courtesy of Catherine Barbour).

Joe Judice was an electrician and carpenter, a self-effacing individual, who built a theatre at a location on Fortieth Street, tapping into the building's electricity supply. It was widely identified as Joe's Place until the New York Police Department inadvertently raided the place, suspecting it as a screening facility for pornography, and Joe's Place officially became the Co-operative Film Society. Eventually, a rent increase forced Joe's Place to close, but not before John Cocchi had programmed such events as a screening of six "B" Westerns in one day, three in the afternoon and three in the evening, and Leonard Maltin had sponsored a number of evenings featuring seven or eight Hal Roach two-reel sound comedies thanks to his having access to the Roach library. There were also two notable Broadway theatres at which film buffs would hang out, the Thalia (from 1931 to 1987) at Ninety-Fifth Street and Dan Talbot's New Yorker Theatre (from 1960 to 1973) at Eighty-Eighth Street, as well as the Eighth Street Playhouse (which had opened in 1929 as the Film Guild Cinema, and closed in 1992). Another theatre, using its location as its name is Theatre 80 St. Marks 80, which, like many of the film buff screening facilities around New York, used 16mm projectors, with the added issue of back-projection only. It was opened as a revival house in 1971 by actor/singer Howard Otway, who persuaded some stars of the past (including Joan Crawford and Joan Bennett) to leave their handprints and footprints in the cement of the sidewalk outside the theatre. Wrote one journalist:

> Entering the theatre's lobby is like walking into something between a Cocteau and an Astaire-Rogers film set; at the theatre's impressively candlelit snack bar it's something of a letdown when you realize they're pushing the same old Three Musketeers, granola, and Pepsi.
>
> The cinema is touted as being "under the personal direction of Howard Otway," and this direction shows-the emphasis is on English-language features too obscure to be in other theatres. Great stars and directors at the beginnings of their careers can be caught here during the week; on weekends the theatre resorts to attempting to make money with bigger pictures (i.e., something the general public has heard of).[38]

Aside from Howard Otway, another prominent name associated with New York repertory theatres is real estate magnate Sid Geffen, who, in the 1970s, owned the Bleecker Street Cinema and leased the Carnegie Hall Cinema. Geffen also briefly at the end of the decade published the short-lived monthly *The Thousand Eyes Cinema Guide*, providing schedules for all repertory theatres in the city, and presumably intended for film buffs who did not have access to the ever-helpful Ed Maguire.

Jim Cronin warned students at Columbia University that "Carnegie Hall, for some reason, seems to attract one of the weirder audiences in the city—especially at the monthly silent-film-and-organ recitals. If you go, be careful. Those people aren't human."

All of these screening facilities kept alive what film critic Elliott Stein called FOOFS (or Friends of Old Films). It is a term that has somewhat fallen into disuse but was commonplace in the 1960s and 1970s to refer to obsessive filmgoers. The man responsible, Elliott Stein (1928–2012), was both a critic and a film buff, noted for enjoying a happy, if not apparently healthy, gay lifestyle. He lived part of his life in Paris, where he was a film critic for a number of English-language periodicals, and he boasted of having worked with Kenneth Anger on the creation of the latter's infamous exposé of the American film industry, *Hollywood Babylon*.

Kenneth Anger was always blunt in what he had to say or write, and it is curious that while *Hollywood Babylon* provoked massive bouts of anger from film buffs horrified at what he had to say about their favorite stars, today it is almost insipid when compared to the writings of David Bret in England or Darwin Porter in the US.

Obviously, there have been film buff screening groups across the United States that have not received the recognition they arguably deserve. In the 1960s and 1970s, Robert Wade "Bob" Chatterton (1918–1985) hosted screenings in what he described as the Parlour Cinema, located in his North Hollywood apartment. He would use a hand microphone to talk to an audience of about twenty, and tolerated no negative behavior. As Richard Lamparski recalled, "No talking once the projector began to roll and no comments that could be considered criticism or ridicule no matter what was on the screen."[39]

There were distinct rules during the screenings. It was OK to clap for the studio logo at the beginning of the film, the star's name in the opening credits, and the star's first appearance. After that, there was to be no more clapping until the end of the film—which sometimes could not come soon enough.

As to those in attendance, the best description comes from Richard Lamparski himself, who wrote that the regular members of the audience had "about them the blandness of manner and appearance one associates with clerical workers."[40]

Obviously here there is no comparison between film buff audiences in Los Angeles and their New York counterparts.

Bob Chatterton is an interesting character, who owned a large collection of 16mm film prints, and claimed to be second cousin of actress Ruth Chatterton (who was well represented in his collection). Born in Cleveland, Chatterton had come to Los Angeles in the 1940s, worked in the film industry as an extra, and became a close friend to Stan Laurel. Chatterton served as the official film archivist and historian for the Variety Arts Center in downtown Los Angeles, a club founded by Milt Larson, who was also responsible for the Magic Castle in Hollywood. It was Chatterton who, in November 1979, co-presented an event that film buffs and others will never forget, a group of live performances by the great British musical star, accompanied by a young and then-unknown Michael Feinstein, "Miss Jessie Matthews in Concert," at the Mayfair Music Hall in Santa Monica

He was also an underground filmmaker—and I believe he shot the 16mm footage of D. W. Griffith's memorial service at the Masonic Temple in Hollywood, often credited to others. Most notably, Chatterton made *Passion in a Seaside Slum* (1962), featuring Andy Warhol star Taylor Mead, and what are identified as "The Venice, California, Films" (1959–1962).

Bob Chatterton hosted what was pretentiously titled Robert Wade Chatterton's Memorable Film Society, which held Monday evening screenings from March 1 through April 26, 1948, at the International Recorder's Auditorium on Sunset Boulevard. The screenings were of major Hollywood films, with guest speakers, such as Jean Renoir introducing *The Southerner* and Fritz Lang introducing *Hangmen Also Die*. Chatterton was working at the time in cooperation with Raymond Rohauer, about whom most people would have little positive to say, who had created the Society of Cinema Arts, described as "a non-profit organization, entirely philanthropic in its purpose, devoted to preserving and presenting fine motion pictures of the past."[41] In 1950, Rohauer began film presentations at the still-extant Coronet Theatre at 366 North La Cienega Boulevard in West Hollywood, and continued there for some twelve years. While he did screen some older titles of appeal to film buffs, most of the programs were devoted to independent and experimental films and filmmakers. Later screenings, from 1960 to 1962, were held at the Riviera-Capri Theatre on Hollywood Boulevard.

An earlier exhibitor at the Coronet Theatre was film buff Paul Ballard. Under the umbrella title, the Ballard Film Society, he had first screened art and experimental films at his apartment in the historic Garden Court

Apartments on Hollywood Boulevard in 1945. From there, he moved his initial audience of twenty-five to the Coronet Theatre.

Film buffs were well served in Los Angeles in the 1970s and 1980s through screenings in two theatres, the Vagabond, on Wilshire Boulevard, close to McArthur Park, and the Tiffany, on Sunset Boulevard in West Hollywood. Both theatres were operated by Tommy Cooper, a film buff himself, who knew exactly what his fellow buffs would appreciate in film presentations, with 35mm screenings of rare films at a time when such films were not generally available, and when it was still possible to screen original 35mm nitrate prints (thanks to the beneficence of Bob Epstein, cofounder of the UCLA Film and Television Archive).

The Vagabond was a relatively small theatre, seating only 190, and had opened in 1926 as a legitimate house, the Masque Theatre. In 1950, it was converted into a movie theatre, and renamed the Vagabond, with Tommy Cooper's taking it over in the 1970s and operating it through 1985.[42] The Tiffany Theatre was a modern auditorium, which opened in 1966 with 400 seats, and was taken over in 1977 by Tommy Cooper, who ran the complex through 1983.

The Tiffany is actually best remembered not as a revival house but as the original location for the once-popular midnight screening of *The Rocky Horror Picture Show*, which began here in June 1977. While they are undoubtedly buffs, the audience for those midnight screenings, appearing in appropriate costumes worn by characters in the film and participating in what are perhaps the first sing-a-longs (years before similar presentations were made of *The Sound of Music*, *Grease*, and other features), are not exactly film buffs. Their buff experience is limited to one film only. The theatre proudly displayed the underpants worn by Barry Bostwick in the film, a 1981 gift from the actor. The Tiffany closed on March 13, 1983, after the final midnight screening of *The Rocky Horror Picture Show*.

Aside from the stars of *The Rocky Horror Picture Show*, the most famous movie star attraction to appear at the Tiffany—in July 1977—was Rita Hayworth, making one of her first public appearances following a court appearance involving her disability through mental illness and alcoholism. It was very obvious that something was wrong when the actress agreed to appear on the condition that she was given a new television, which was presented to her prior to her going on stage.

In Los Angeles, regular screenings for film buffs and others are today dominated by two organizations, the American Cinematheque (operating out of the Egyptian Theatre in Hollywood and the Aero Theatre in Santa

Filmex at the ABC Entertainment Center in Century City.

Monica) and the UCLA Film and Television Archive (with presentations at the Billy Wilder Theatre in the Hammer Museum). The latter was founded in 1981, with its first screenings six years later, and is a successor to the Los Angeles Film Exposition or Filmex annual festival held in Los Angeles at various locations from 1971 to 1983, and which was founded by domestic partners Gary Essert (1938–1992) and Gary Abrahams (1944–1992), both of whom died of AIDS. The two men were affable and dedicated film buffs, known collectively as "the Garys," who also had a reputation for cruising for potential sex partners the lines of attendees waiting to enter the screenings.

In an appreciation, *Los Angeles Times* longtime film critic Charles Champlin, noting "the cost of AIDS epidemic hasn't often seemed so clear, mournful," wrote in what might be considered a tribute to all film buffs of the period,

> There are millions who love the movies in a nice genteel way. Then there are those who love the movies with a passion bordering on obsession, and

Filmex founder, Gary Essert.

> whose devotion to film overshadows almost everything else in their lives.
>
> . . . .
>
> But the best kind of zealots are always in short supply, and we are losing them at a rate society can ill afford.[43]

Gary Essert had cofounded a high school film society in Oakland with his best friend, Ron Haver (1939–1993). It was Haver, after military service and work as a projectionist with the American Film Institute, who in 1972 created the permanent film program at the Los Angeles County Museum of Art (LACMA). At that time it was the preeminent screening facility for film buffs and others, carefully programmed by a man who was both a scholar and, as his assistant Joan Cohen remarks, "the ultimate film buff who made a career out of it."

> During his years at LACMA he programmed tributes to all of his heroes and managed to meet them all. One of his finest hours was during the Bette Davis tribute; he told no one that she was going to appear that night and after the first movie (*Dark Victory*) told the audience to stay in their seats for some rare footage. Instead, he lit two cigarettes and Bette walked across the stage, put one in her mouth and answered questions before the screening of *Now Voyager*. The audience went wild.[44]

Joan Cohen notes that university film societies were once breeding grounds for film buffs, identifying three: Stanford University and Todd McCarthy, the University of Wisconsin at Madison and Joseph McBride, and the University of Chicago and Myron Meisel.

> All three of these men were regulars during the glory days of LACMA's film department under Ron Haver. They all wrote program notes for me, were on my guest list nearly every weekend, and lived and breathed film. Also to a lesser extent, Joe Dante and Allan Arkush who became directors. Todd wrote the Howard Hawks book[45] and has been film critic for both *Variety* and *The Hollywood Reporter* for years. Joe [McBride] wrote books on Hawks and Frank Capra,[46] teaches film in San Francisco, and Myron, although he went to law school, helped restore Orson Welles's film *It's All True*.[47] These guys were film obsessed, had their heroes. I remember at one of LACMA's receptions, they had surrounded Sam Fuller and were begging him for stories. Somehow it rubbed me the wrong way, their idolatry, and I went over to Sam and asked him to show me baby pictures of his new daughter Samantha, which he proudly did (nothing like a new father even if he is a famous director). The boys glared at me for interrupting film talk from their hero but I was glad I did it.[48]

In 1981, Ron Haver began his mammoth restoration of the Judy Garland/George Cukor version of *A Star Is Born*, culminating in a 1983 re-premiere at Radio City Music Hall. The restoration was a triumph for film buffs both in terms of resurrection and exhibition. Indeed, the success of the restoration was due in part to a film buff and film collector named Merle Ray Harlin, who had worked as a film librarian at Warner Bros. and later at Columbia. From the former's trash bins, he took home the four-and-a-half-minute negative of Judy Garland's number "Lose That Long Face," which had been cut from the original release of *A Star Is Born*. Harlin also "saved" from Warner Bros. trash other footage, including *Mystery of the Wax*

Ron Haver on stage at the Los Angeles County Museum of Art.

*Museum* (1933), which was at that time considered a "lost" film. In August 1983, the Los Angeles District Attorney's office seized Harlin's film collection and charged him with possession of stolen property. It was the start of a bad period for film buffs who were also film collectors, persecuted by the Film Security Office of the Motion Picture Association of America.

Chapter Five

# DAVID BRADLEY AND HERB GRAFF AND THE FILM COLLECTOR AS FILM BUFF

MOST, IF NOT ALL, FILM COLLECTORS QUALIFY AS FILM BUFFS TO DIFFERING degrees of intensity. Just as film buffs are not new, neither is film collecting in any way a recent phenomenon. One of the earliest known film collections was that of Australian-born actor George "André" Beranger (1893–1973), whose silent career included appearances in films directed by D. W. Griffith and Ernst Lubitsch. He would often portray Frenchmen, but, in reality, his family was of German origin. Beranger collected 28mm films, released by the Pathé Company and intended for the home market (rather like 16mm films somewhat later). His collection was rich in one-reelers from American Biograph and, of course, Pathé, and in the 1920s he would show his films to fellow actors at the Hollywood Athletic Club. By 1927, Beranger had some 128 reels of 28mm film, and offered them for sale as a package for $3,500.[1] There were no takers, and the actor held onto the films until 1942, when he considered returning to Australia. He offered to sell the collection for $500 to cinematographer and amateur film historian Charles G. Clarke. The latter was not interested, but he did persuade the Academy of Motion Picture Arts and Sciences to acquire the collection, which eventually it did in 1947.

Beranger, who was gay, married for convenience's sake in the 1940s, but he and his wife lived in separate homes in Laguna Beach. Eventually, he became a recluse, and after his death it was several days before his body was discovered. Bodies undiscovered or unclaimed is an ongoing theme in the history of film buffs. Beranger is well deserving of rediscovery, not only as a pioneering Hollywood film collector but also someone who had a prominent role in *The Birth of a Nation*, and also worked on the film as an assistant to Griffith.

Actor and film collector André Beranger.

Other actors amassed film collections, including, most notably, John Griggs, Roddy McDowall, and Rock Hudson, and certainly Griggs and McDowall might be considered film buffs. Roddy loved entertaining former stars and supporting players. He was such a big fan of silent star, Viola Dana, that when I made a twenty-minute, 16mm film with her in 1990, he was more than happy to sign on as unpaid narrator. The actor always carried with him a copy of Deems Taylor's 1943 book, *A Pictorial History of the Movies*; he was determined to get every photograph on every page signed by the subject(s). When he met an actor or actress not represented in the book, Roddy would insert pages for them to sign. He was so proud of that self-made autograph book and would change from a rather aloof figure to a genuinely friendly and happy film buff when sharing it with others.

A celebrity film buff and film collector generally unacknowledged is J. D. Salinger, who would entertain guests with 16mm screenings. He was particularly fond of the films of Laurel and Hardy and also the Alfred Hitchcock British films, written by Charles Bennett.

William K. Everson was undoubtedly the best known of early film collectors, but he was not the first, and neither was he the most famous outside of film buff circles. Here, I provide both an objective and a personal look at two of Everson's colleagues, David Bradley and Herb Graff, whom I am quick to admit do not belong in the same chapter. In all probability, they would not be happy to be in the same room today. But I have assigned a single chapter to them because to me they represent the bad and the good of film collecting. Both were entertaining in their own right, one often at the expense of others, and both were avid film buffs with very different approaches to life.

Born in Chicago, David Shedd Bradley (1920–1997) was the son of a wealthy investor and banker, although he always claimed to be the illegitimate son of director/screenwriter Preston Sturges. He also liked to boast that he had attended a private school, the Todd School for Boys, from which Orson Welles had graduated in 1931. One critic, Marie Seton, wrote of Bradley's *Julius Caesar* that it "reminds me of Welles in his early days."[2]

David Bradley began making 16mm films in the mid-1930s, and while attending the Goodman Memorial Theatre Drama Department of the Art Institute of Chicago in 1941, he filmed a silent, 16mm version of *Peer Gynt*, featuring a seventeen-year-old high school student named Charlton Heston. Heston also stars, as Mark Antony, in a 16mm production of *Julius Caesar*, which Bradley directed in and around Chicago in 1950. Bradley played Brutus, and the title role was taken by Harold Tasker. *Julius Caesar* was photographed by Louis McMahon, whose name crops up later among New York film buffs. It is perhaps not surprising that Bradley, a gay man, should have Heston appear almost nude in an opening scene, looking as one Internet critic has it, "like Caesar's rent boy."[3] *Julius Caesar* was not Bradley's only attempt at a Shakespearian adaptation; in 1946, he had filmed *Macbeth*, with himself in the title role.

Thanks to *Julius Caesar*, Bradley came to the attention of Dore Schary and was offered a contract at M-G-M. Initially, he was treated as an intern at the studio, and it was not until 1952 that Bradley was given his first directorial assignment, *Talk about a Stranger*. At thirty-two, he was heralded as the studio's youngest director. *Talk about a Stranger* starred George Murphy, Nancy Reagan, and Billy Gray, as a young boy who arouses a town's suspicions regarding a mysterious stranger.

*Talk about a Stranger* was Bradley's first, and last, M-G-M film, with his blatant anti-Semitism persuading the studio to quietly cancel his contract.

A semi-nude Charlton Heston, as Mark Antony, in David Bradley's production of *Julius Caesar* (1950).

Bradley directed three other features elsewhere, *Dragstrip Riot* (1958), *12 to the Moon* (1960), and *The Madmen of Mandoras* (1963).[4] The last involved removal by a group of Nazis of Hitler's living head and its being hidden in South America for later resurrection. It was adapted, with the use of additional footage shot by UCLA film students, as the 1968 television movie, *They Saved Hitler's Brain*. The film acquired something of a cult status, being referenced a number of times on *The Simpsons* and in a handful of popular songs.

In October 1979, Ottawa, Canada, hosted the First World's Worst Film Festival, and the winner, not surprisingly, was *They Saved Hitler's Brain*. The morning of the announcement, my telephone rang, and there was an enthusiastic David Bradley, proudly announcing that he had directed the worst film of all time, a singular honor in which he rejoiced. He was truly delighted.

The use of UCLA students to film additional footage for *They Saved Hitler's Brain* is interesting in terms of Bradley's next career move—from film director to academic. He had been collecting 16mm films since the

David Bradley (left) with director King Vidor.

1930s, and he had amassed a collection of several thousand. These were ideal teaching tools as far as UCLA and other institutions were concerned. For the cost of hiring Bradley as a professor, the university also gained films for its classes, thus saving on rental costs. UCLA was not the only institution to embrace such a policy, and Bradley was not the only film collector who suddenly found himself in demand as a college professor despite the lack of any discernable academic qualifications.

It did not take long for Bradley to become embroiled in a fight with another, more distinguished UCLA academic, Dr. Howard Suber. Angry words were exchanged in person and also by Bradley in typed memoranda, referencing his being "the victim of a mean spirited and outrageous conspiracy,"[5] leading to his dismissal in the spring of 1973. Bradley's teaching did not end with the UCLA dismissal as he subsequently joined the part-time faculty at Santa Monica City College. In all probability, students actually enjoyed Bradley's teaching in comparison to Howard Suber's dry approach to film history. And, also in all probability, their enjoyment was enhanced by Bradley's outrageous behavior and failure to observe any decorum or recognition of how one should behave in polite society.

David Bradley was a large, bulky guy, with a loud, gruff voice, and an intimidating and bullying manner. He could be, and he was, frightening, although some have pointed out that he was also a coward who would back down if an opponent went on the attack. I had known him since the early 1970s, and I must confess that I would often feel nervous in his presence. For example, he had a passionate hatred for aging organist Chauncey Haines, who had apparently damaged one of Bradley's film prints that he had borrowed. On one occasion, while talking to me, Bradley grabbed the fingers of my right hand, telling me how he planned to end Haines's career by breaking each of his fingers. I was desperately telling Bradley, "Please let go of my fingers."

The threat of physical violence inflicted on those he hated was a David Bradley trait, never to the best of my knowledge actually acted upon. Bradley threatened violence on both Howard Suber and his wife, with the wife also to be the subject of a sexual attack. David Bradley was very much into gay SM. When I first met him, he had a lover named Tom Webster, who was obviously subjected to physical and sexual abuse. Webster was some years younger that Bradley, unemployed, a writer of unpublishable poetry, and mentally ill. There was one memorable Christmas party, at which Bob Hope's sister, Lee, was one of the guests. Tom dressed up as Santa Claus, and for some reason took a dislike to Ms. Hope, attacking her with the carving knife intended for use on the turkey. She was not hurt, but the whole evening took on a positively surreal quality. When Webster was seriously ill, confined to his bed, and close to death, Bradley would take guests into the bedroom, pull back the sheets exposing Webster's naked body, and comment, "Look at him, no damned use to anyone."

There were certain individuals for whom Bradley held a major hatred. For reasons unclear, but probably because of some problem with the city concerning his home on Crescent Height Boulevard, in the hills overlooking West Hollywood, he hated Los Angeles Mayor Tom Bradley, and would continually use the "N" word when describing him. I recall a party at Charles Higham's house, at which Bradley was ranting and raving about "Nigger Bradley," and actor Norman Lloyd and his wife, Peggy, were so offended that they had to leave. On another occasion, at a party again hosted by Charles Higham, Bradley suddenly began to attack and insult my partner, UCLA preservationist Robert Gitt, because UCLA was screening a film in which David had a proprietary interest. We were forced to leave, with Higham's apologizing but explaining he could do nothing as it was more important to keep David happy and have access to his film collection than worry about insulted guests.

Another subject of Bradley's hatred was not an individual but the entire Los Angeles Philharmonic, "the worst damn symphony orchestra in the world." He would play recordings of the philharmonic as loudly as possible, with the music bellowing over the canyon in front of his house, while all the while harshly denigrating it. His enthusiasm was for the Chicago Symphony Orchestra.

One film historian and fellow film collector who had utilized David Bradley for what was ultimately a good cause was Kevin Brownlow, who visited Bradley in 1964, stayed in his home, and was driven around by Bradley's companion as he interviewed various silent film people for what was to become *The Parade's Gone By*. Bradley also worked in an advisory capacity on Brownlow's *Hollywood* series. As the years passed, Bradley became increasingly obsessed with the notion that Kevin Brownlow had used him and provided little in return. Eventually, Bradley's anger exploded in the form of a twenty-five page letter, dated April 14, 1989, addressed to Kevin, and widely circulated to others.[6] Kevin Brownlow tried, without success, to pacify Bradley, writing, "You say that you never bothered to look at our Buster Keaton documentary. Why don't I return the compliment and not bother to read the document?"[7]

One tolerated David Bradley because of the size and scope of his film collection. He could boast of a complete run of 16mm prints covering the complete careers of many filmmakers, with the films stored not in alphabetical order but by director. Films were housed in metal cases inside shipping cases stored on shelves in the guest cottage and the garage. He was heavily involved in copying prints that he might borrow from other collectors, and he also routinely rented 16mm films from the Museum of Modern Art, quickly making 16mm negatives and prints at a local film lab, and returning the original copies to the museum. This went on for years. Bradley was no William K. Everson in that he seldom screened films for scholars or students. He would rent the films to colleges and universities, and he was also active for a number of years in renting 16mm prints to Raymond Rohauer for screenings at the Coronet Theatre. Rentals were recorded in a card index, indicating the borrower, the amount paid, and the dates involved.

The high spot of David Bradley's year, and that of a number of others as well, was the annual New Year's Day party, held in the late afternoon. He would invite to his home former silent players and other aging movie people, as well as various friends, including myself and Robert Gitt. All were expected to be appropriately respectful to David, and the gentlemen were all required to wear jackets and ties. Among celebrities present through the years were Madge Bellamy, Gregory Nava, Josef von Sternberg, his wife and son, Sam Jaffe and his wife, and Miliza Korjus.[8] In 1979, Robert Gitt and I

Mary Philbin "unmasks" David Bradley. An appropriate theme for one of Bradley's Christmas cards.

were instructed to bring silent leading lady Priscilla Bonner and her sister, Marjorie (widow of novelist Malcolm Lowry), and we tried to discourage them. David would have the names of selected guests pinned to the chairs, and those unrecognized would not be permitted to sit; Priscilla made it and Marjorie did not. The two women were eventually reduced to tears, and we had to take them home.

David, with the help of students, would film the party using a 16mm camera, and he would demand that guests repeat actions until he was satisfied. Thus, it was necessary to make several trips along the pathway to the front door, to take a glass of punch, pretend to drink it, return the contents of the glass to the punch bowl, and do it all again. I was not present, but on one memorable occasion he remade the unmasking scene from *The Phantom of the Opera*, with his sitting at the piano (substituting for an organ) and leading lady Mary Philbin's unmasking him and screaming in horror.

The parties would conclude with David's screening the edited footage from the previous year's event, and announcing, "He's dead" or "She's dead" as the guests appeared on screen. He would have a flashlight and when someone from the last year appeared who was also there this year, he would shine the flashlight in that person's face.

At Bradley's death, critic Todd McCarthy, who was also a regular guest and should have known better, described the footage as "likely the last celluloid documents of many of these figures."

There would be valet parking, but he would not hire a caterer, instead flying in his mother from Chicago to prepare the food, which was basically nothing more than sandwiches. One year, while he was screening the previous year's home movies and his mother was relaxing in the kitchen, there came the distant sound of her conversation with a friend. David became more and more agitated and suddenly yelled at the top of his voice, "If you don't stop talking I will come in there and smash your teeth down your fucking throat." His mother had little reason to tolerate or love her son, who telephoned me with the news of her death at the age of ninety-six in April 1987, announcing, "Mother's dead. I'm a millionaire."

After Tom Webster's death, David entered into a relationship with a minor actor/extra named Ken Du Main (1923–2001), who tried, unsuccessfully to control his partner. The two men, who were of approximately the same age, would dress in sailor suits, impersonating Laurel and Hardy in *Two Tars*, showing up so attired at events to which they were invited. Ken was obviously very much attached to David, and after his death he crashed his car on Crescent Heights Boulevard in what would appear to have been a suicide attempt.

After Bradley's death, I was hired to appraise the collection of films, papers, books, and periodicals, all of which were bequeathed to the Lilly Library at Indiana University. Some years earlier, back in 1986, he had made a donation of some of his papers to Northwestern University, and there was a suspicion that a somewhat confused Bradley had actually meant the remainder of his collection to go there. At one point, he had announced he was donating the films to the UCLA Film and Television Archive, but as his relationship with UCLA diminished, so did the potential for the donation. Much to everyone's surprise, not too long before his demise, David Bradley had sold all of his 16mm negatives to a fellow collector, Harold "Rusty" Casselton (1954–2007), who had succeeded his business partner and fellow film collector, Ted Larson, as director of film studies at Minnesota State University Moorhead.

The housekeeper at Bradley's house, after his death, whose name was Elizabeth, would often discard items before I had a chance to value and pack them. She did at least take care of the disposition of David's pornography collection from his bedroom, including dildos of various sizes. Perhaps also that collection should have gone to Indiana, home of the Kinsey Institute?

In retrospect, I wonder why anyone abided this horrible man. Yes, it could be entertaining to be around him, provided you were not on the receiving end of his temper. But he was crass, vulgar, and totally lacking in social graces, while oozing false sincerity when he was around the generally minor celebrities who came to his New Year's parties. Ultimately, it was the film collection. If one wanted access to those titles in an era before VHS tapes and DVDs, then you had to be nice to David Bradley.

Not only could one abide fellow film collector Herb Graff (1926–2000); one positively wallowed in his presence and in the stories—all true, unlike so many from film buffs—that he had to tell.

The *New Yorker* has published its share of profiles of film personalities both from in front and behind the camera. But on only one occasion, as far as I am aware, has the magazine published a profile of a gentleman who was both a film collector and a film buff, and that gentleman was Herb Graff. In a way, he was just as important as many a filmmaker. As Mel Gussow wrote in the *New York Times* (January 15, 2000) at Herb's death,

> Mr. Graff—always Herb, never Herbert—was not a critic or an author and he never expressed a desire to be a director, but he made a significant contribution to the art of movies. He knew more about them than most historians or archivists. For him, film was a passion and a valuable cultural heritage.

Herb was not physically attractive; he was not handsome and he tended to look rather scruffy, with an unkempt beard and the signs of baldness, but he was incredibly knowledgeable, intelligent, and witty. He was roughhewn, but he had savvy and a big heart. He could hold the attention of an audience not only of film buffs but all manner of types. He was a raconteur in the tradition of Mark Twain, Oscar Wilde, or even Stephen Fry, and yet, as do all true raconteurs, he had his own unique, individual style of delivery. One never ceased to be amazed at his circle of friends, which obviously included fellow film collectors and film buffs (in particular William K. Everson and Leonard Maltin), but his circle of close acquaintances was wide and varied. He was a self-made intellectual in a world of film buffs

Herb Graff (courtesy of Bennett Lovett-Graff).

and film collectors, and he was perfectly relaxed and sure of himself no matter his company.

When Herb heard that the then theatre critic for the *Herald Tribune*, Walter Kerr, was working on a study of silent comedy, titled *Silent* Clowns,[9] he contacted him and offered access to his collection. A friendship developed, and whenever Kerr's wife, Jean, was unable to accompany him to the press preview of a new play, Herb Graff would be invited to be his companion. The two men became such a familiar couple seated together on the aisle that a joke developed that Herb Graff was actually Jean Kerr, so seldom was she seen with her husband. Most importantly, because he was always to be seen in Walter Kerr's company, it was assumed that he must be somebody.

Once he invited me to be his guest at a meeting of the Dutch Treat Club in New York. I had never really believed that Herb actually knew those about whom he talked, but how wrong I was when I met up with Herb and discovered I was seated with some of his closest friends: Isaac Asimov,

Lowell Thomas, and 1930s crooner Lanny Ross (who off the bat had decided to bring me an autographed photograph—well, one does, of course). He was a frequent visitor at my and Robert Gitt's home in Los Angeles, arranging for us to screen various films, and always surprising us with guests who would show up on the doorstep, including, as I recall, Adolph Green[10] and composer Albert Hague.

One of the more interesting, if lesser known, individuals whom Herb would bring to the house was Lottie Da (real name Lottie Jo Meyers), a sex worker and one of the founders of COYOTE (Call Off Your Old Tired Ethics), which advocated the decriminalization of prostitution. Lottie was certainly an unusual film buff, if she can be so described; she organized the International Hookers Film Festival in San Francisco in March 1977 and was one of the guest speakers at the Second World Whores' Congress in Brussels in October 1986. Asked to explain the difference between a whore and a politician, she responded (perhaps not with total originality), "There are some things that a whore will not do for money."

Lottie and Herb had found each other when the former was working on a book, *Bad Girls of the Silver Screen*, which was intended as a scholarly discussion of the subject but eventually published (by Carroll and Graf in 1989) as little more than a picture book, coauthored with Jan Alexander. Herb would constantly complain that what Lottie wanted from him in terms of resources would require several hours of his time, whereas what she gave in return took only two minutes. On one memorable evening, Lottie arrived at the house and ran her car into the fence surrounding the property. The group went over to Herb's favorite Studio City restaurant, Jerry's Deli,[11] and after giving our order, Lottie and the waitress retired to the ladies' room to smoke a joint and have sex. Those were the days. . . .

Leonard Maltin first met Herb Graff at a screening of a 1937 Republic film, *The Wrong Road*, at the Huff Society. Richard Cromwell and Rochelle Hudson are on the run after the former is accused of a crime he has not committed. At the film's close, they are running through the woods and Hudson says, "I'm tired of running. . . . I want to be able to laugh again," at which point Lionel Atwill appears, declares Cromwell innocent and announces, "You kids can start laughing right now." As the lights came up, Maltin repeated the immortal last line, and a voice behind him responded, "I started laughing when I sold this print to Bill Everson." The voice belonged to Herb Graff and the two started talking.

On another occasion at the Huff, Herb appeared wearing an elegant top coat. When Leonard expressed his approval, Herb responded, "This cost me

*Top Hat*." He could have purchased either the coat or a print of *Top Hat*, but because it was cold he went for the coat. I suspect most film buffs would have selected differently.

It was Herb Graff who introduced Leonard Maltin to his future wife, Alice, at an evening extension course he was teaching at New York University, at which Leonard was a guest lecturer. Herb had taken her under his wing, but initially Alice found Maltin unfriendly. "She told Herb I was kind of cold. So I was either gay or I had a girlfriend already. I was not responsive."[12] The relationship improved after Herb again brought them together at a Huff screening at the School of Visual Arts of Maurice Tourneur's *The Whip* and Paul Bern's *Open All Night*. "So our first evening together was watching two silent films at the Theodore Huff Society. We pride ourselves as the only social conquest in the history of the Theodore Huff Society."[13]

The courtship was interrupted when Leonard had an engagement at the Zagreb Animation Festival, and Alice went out on a couple of dates with John Cocchi. But the couple met again at a Sons of the Desert banquet, and on their second date they talked very seriously about relationships and marriage. Six weeks later they were engaged. "John Cocchi never forgave either of us. John remained our friend, but he never really forgave me."[14]

It was Isaac Asimov who was the inspiration behind Herb's business card, which read simply, "Film Resource." Asimov had a similar card, reading, "Human Resource."

The film resource, and never was a truer description to be found, was born in Boston, the son of a rabbi, and he grew up in Brooklyn. Attending yeshiva for twelve years until he joined the navy in 1943, Herb would study Hebrew in the morning and English in the afternoon. At lunchtime, he would walk to the local movie house, the Miller Theatre, and look at the lobby cards and still photographs on display. In 1936, his uncle took him to see *Modern Times* at Loew's Premier, followed by two further screenings of the Chaplin classic elsewhere, and, later, his mother took him to a retrospective of Chaplin two-reel comedies at the Museum of Modern Art. "It stopped me from being a bum," recalled Herb. "Every time I went to the Museum was one less time I went to the poolroom."[15]

While still a teenager, Herb began collecting films, some from film exchanges and others from legitimate sources for heavily cut-down versions of Chaplin films and other productions, such as Castle Films. For his bar mitzvah, he had been given a projector, replaced by a better 16mm projector as a wedding present; what his wife, Anita, thought of the gift is not known, but eventually—in 1984—she asked him, the projector, and the film collection to leave their Brooklyn house, and Herb moved to a rented apartment on West Fifty-Seventh Street.[16] In the meantime, in 1947, Herb Graff began his career as a salesman in the New York garment industry, working for Charles Greenberg & Sons, manufacturer of Lucky Girl and Boy shirts.

Herb Graff kept his place of employment as a deep, dark secret to all but his closest friends. "He never broadcast the fact that he was a schmutter salesperson," says Leonard Maltin.

> Herb actually developed a second career as a film consultant, expert, and lecturer, but his boss, Charles Greenberg, had no tolerance for this. So Herb had to make up an array of excuses as to why he would come in late on certain mornings, leave early on certain evenings. He would only accept lecture dates that were a short distance away, that he could fly there and back the next morning, and still show up for work. He was a magnificent liar. He could lie at the drop of a hat, come up with wonderful answers to get out of situations
>
> He ordered a George M. Cohan lobby card from a dealer who never came through, never got an answer. So he wrote a letter to this guy, "Do you know why I ordered this particular lobby card? I want you to understand why I am so upset you haven't sent it. There is a little girl who lives on my block who's dying of cancer and her only interest in life is theatre history and George M. Cohan. It means the world to her that I will be able to give her this particular lobby card." The next day it was in his mailbox.
>
> My favorite story is a guy calls up out of the blue, says he's doing a term paper on the Ginger Rogers/Fred Astaire film and can he screen them in chronological order for him. Herb says, "I don't have those films, I only collect Westerns." It means this guy has to either call him a liar or there's no more conversation. [My wife] Alice and I use that as a catchphrase in our lives when we're trying to think of something to say to get out of something we say, "We only collect Westerns." To come up with an answer like that is so brilliant.[17]

It was not until 1983 that Herb Graff quit Charles Greenberg & Sons after visiting London and seeing one of the familiar blue plaques on a building, honoring Ivor Novello with the words, "Actor, Manager and Composer—1893–1951." He said,

> My God in Heaven, here's a man, he lived till he was fifty-eight years old, and he wrote plays, and he wrote films, and he had a full life. Here I am, past fifty, and if I were to die my tombstone would read "HERE LIES

HERB GRAFF. SOLD SHIRTS IN WHITE, PINK, BEIGE, AND BLUE, AND EVERY FIVE YEARS LILAC.[18]

Herb Graff, Leonard Maltin, and Gene Stavis decided to exploit their film collections under the collective name of Filmavens, a company which they formed in February 1982 and dissolved in 1987. Leonard Maltin's on-screen job at *Entertainment Tonight* was helpful in the trio's licensing footage to that program:

> *ET* or my boss was never entirely happy with it. They thought as I was working for them I should provide the footage for nothing. They were just annoyed because it felt like they were paying me more money when I was already working for them. I said, "This is not me. I'm a partner in a company."[19]

Gene Stavis (1943–2013) always had an air of affluence about him (somewhat marred when a meal with him would end with his credit card being declined), with an apartment overlooking New York's East River, in which he stored his 1,500 film prints, and a large, avuncular manner, matched by his equally large size. In fact, he had some of the physical and overwhelming charms of Henri Langlois, founder of the Cinémathèque Francaise, who was Stavis's mentor and for whom Stavis worked as titular head of the Cinémathèque's American arm in the 1970s. He had also worked for Janus Films and for an earlier, self-owned distribution company called Twelvetrees, after 1930s star Helen Twelvetrees.

Gene Stavis was also a gay man, who with two others, Frank O'Dowd and Steve Bie, founded Truth, Justice and the American Way, Inc., which produced the first gay-themed cable television show, *Emerald City*, seen from 1977 to 1979.

Herb Graff was a devoted member of the Society for Cinephiles and a regular attendee at its Cinecon conventions. In 1976, he hosted the Cinecon in New York, with invited guests Madge Evans, her husband-director Sidney Kingsley, and Myrna Loy. He had wanted to invited Gloria Swanson, but her list of requirements included a Bentley to pick her up; "We sent Myrna Loy a cab," recalled Herb.[20] Long before the Cinecon convention, Herb had been presenting film screenings in New York, the first in 1960 at the Manhattan Beach Jewish Center. As a result of this, he went on to host a series of film screenings for local PBS station, WNET, Channel 13. In 1972 and 1973, he accepted an invitation from New York University to present screenings at

Town Hall, which the university owned; twenty-five Saturday afternoon presentations in all.

It was not just Herb's film collection that was in demand, but the man himself, who had the verbal skill of a great comedian. For many years, he would be a featured guest at the Cinecon conventions in Hollywood, a stand-up comic, with a film buff-related style, perfect to work the crowd prior to the presentation of that year's awards, better than many a professional warm-up comedian. The problem was I do not believe that organizers of the event always appreciated just what they had in Herb Graff. His appearances at the dais began earlier and earlier until he was doing his "shtick" while the guests were still eating. As he once commented to me, he would be soon appearing before the guests entered the banqueting hall. It was too bad.

After retirement from the garment industry, Herb determined to work full-time somewhere where his knowledge, enthusiasm, and film collection would be appreciated. He was hired by Castle Hill Productions, which specialized in the distribution and restoration of classic and independent films.[21] "So a hobby that became an avocation then became a vocation."[22]

Through the years, Herb Graff remained as kindly and caring as always. Leonard Maltin identifies him as a surrogate father to John Cocchi in the way he looked after his fellow film buff. "And John needed looking after."[23] He was always very generous, often in odd ways. For example, when he visited the University of Wisconsin at Madison to view films in its Warner Bros. collection, he was told by a curator that the archive had a problem in obtaining plastic cores on which to store the films. When Herb returned to New York, he ordered a gross of cores and had them shipped to Wisconsin.

A stroke in 1991 slowed Herb down, but he continued to present his film programs while seated in a wheelchair, and never lost his enthusiasm. In 2015, Herb's sons, Bennett and Michael, presented his film collection to the Yale Film Archive.

Would that we have film buffs today with the honesty, integrity, passion, and the entertainment value of a Herb Graff. He was once asked to list his "favorite films," and responded, "Instead of 'favorite films' I think of what movies I'd want to see if I were stranded on a desert island. It's not the same thing. I might consider *Citizen Kane* a great movie, but I wouldn't want to see it over and over." The list was certainly an eclectic one: *City Lights, Our Hospitality*, any Paramount Marx Brothers film (before they had love stories), *Top Hat, Dodsworth, Counsellor-at-Law, Pinocchio, A New Leaf, Annie Hall*, and *My Favorite Year*.[24]

## Chapter Six

# FILM BUFF MEETS FILM SCHOLAR

WHEN THE PUBLICATION WAS AT THE HEIGHT OF ITS FAME, ONE WIT HAD it, in reference to the detailed filmographies accompanying each of its career articles, with accurate and definitive credit information, *Films in Review* knew the credits of everything but the value of nothing. It is an amusing comment, but not strictly accurate in that while *Films in Review* was very much a film buff publication (in the best and long-forgotten sense of the phrase), it was also a publication appealing to film scholars and students. And it numbered many well-known names among its contributors.

What set *Films in Review* apart from other motion picture publications of the period were the career articles and the meticulously compiled filmographies. The essays were erudite, compelling, and written as much by film scholars as by film buffs. It was the one publication in which the two could rub shoulders amicably; there was none of the academic jargon that makes academic film journals unreadable to far too many, and there was none of the relentlessly gushing pieces that make today's film buff publications so amateurish. Always fascinating were the letters, which filled many pages at the rear of the magazine and which were concerned as much with corrections to the filmographies as the provision of arcane facts of cinema history.

The periodical's origins go back to 1909, when the National Board of Censorship of Motion Pictures, Inc., which in 1916 became the National Board of Review of Motion Pictures, Inc., was founded in New York as a citizens' group to evaluate current motion pictures. "Passed by the National Board of Review" was a familiar phrase at the opening of most films of the silent era, but soon to a large extent, the board became irrelevant, and moved into other fields, selecting the ten best films of the year from 1920 onwards, and publishing various periodicals—*National Board of Review Magazine* (1926–1942), *New Movies* (1942–1949), and *Films in Review*—which has little connection with the earlier titles.

For its first seven issues, from February through October 1950, *Films in Review* was edited by John B. Turner (1904–1964),[1] but in November of that year, Henry Hart's name appeared on the journal's masthead as its editor. He was also treasurer of the National Board of Review. Certainly, Henry Hart is the most colorful character associated with *Films in Review* throughout its history, although with his conservative attire (business suit and tie), he would strongly repudiate the "colorful" description.

Henry Gideon Hart IV (1903–1990) was the scion of an aristocratic Philadelphia family, whose ancestor, John Hart, was a signatory of the Declaration of Independence. When his father died a bankrupt, Hart was forced to take work as a newspaper reporter with the *Philadelphia Record* and other publications. He also became a communist, and in the 1930s was secretary of the New York State Communist Party.

As did many others, he denounced the party after the signing of the 1940 Hitler-Stalin Nonaggression Pact, and from then on he was an avid anti-communist and ultra-conservative. Some have compared him to Whittaker Chambers, but a more apt comparison is with Seymour Stern, an eccentric and opinionated historian, and self-appointed D. W. Griffith biographer, who had been a communist until World War II, and who first contributed a piece to *Films in Review*, on "Griffith and Poe," in November 1951. Both men, like Saul/Paul on the Road to Damascus, experienced a conversion—not from Judaism to Christianity but from communism to conservatism. Once converted, they were every bit as determined as Paul to spread the new word to the masses, or at least, as far as Henry Hart was concerned, the readers of *Films in Review*.

Henry Hart published one novel, *The Great One: A Novel of American Life* (John Day Company, 1934)[2], set in Philadelphia and with a newspaper reporter hero, Bayard Stuart, modeled after Republican politician Boies Penrose, who coined the phrase, "Public office is the last refuge of a scoundrel." In it, according to Granville Hicks in *New Masses* (January 1, 1935), he portrayed "a member of the ruling class in such a way as both to make him a human being and to show his social role is a problem still to be resolved." Aside from literary aspirations, Henry Hart also had a strong interest in film and biography. He lobbied unsuccessfully to "author" what was loosely to be Lillian Gish's autobiography, *Life and Lillian Gish* (Macmillan, 1932), but the actress rejected him in favor of Albert Bigelow Paine. Hart never forgave Gish for this slight, and ensured she received no favorable publicity in *Films in Review*.

Listed alongside John B. Turner on the first masthead of *Films in Review* is editorial secretary Elspeth Burke Chapin. In 1952, she and Hart married, and he became stepfather to her four sons by a previous marriage, one of whom was folk singer-songwriter Harry Chapin. It was not a happy marriage, least of all for Harry Chapin, whose lifestyle Hart did not understand and to whom he was apparently both verbally and physically abusive. Returning to the office from lunch with a friend, he once commented ironically to a colleague, "Well, I'm not a very nice person."[3]

The marriage ended in divorce, but through it all, the strange lifestyle to which Hart was subjected by his wife and sons, and the fight to retain both his conservative philosophy and his conservative attire, the man continued to edit *Films in Review*, making it his life work and ultimately his memorial, a monument and source of information that is sadly neglected and forgotten today thanks to the power of Internet research and the amount of plagiarism from its pages in both books and articles.

For the first year of its life, *Films in Review* was serious, boasting well-known "names" but also slightly dull and with somewhat short articles. The first issue included pieces by Terry Ramsaye and Siegfried Kracauer (writing on Preston Sturges, of all people), who also contributed to the December 1950 edition, with a discussion of stage vs. screen acting. A symposium on "What I Look for in a Film," published in the March and April issues, included comments by Pearl S. Buck, Margaret Mead, Ferenc Molnar, William Saroyan, Tennessee Williams, and others. James Agee reviewed *Sunset Blvd.* in May–June 1950, Herman G. Weinberg made his first appearance in July–August, and other contributors that first year included Theodore Huff, Richard Griffith and Gilbert Seldes (September), and Hurd Hatfield and Ida Lupino (December). For the next couple of years or so, the same serious tone dominated, with essays by industry figures, including directors Clarence Brown and Lindsay Anderson (February 1951), Stanley Kramer (March 1951), Walt Disney (April 1951), George Sidney (June–July 1951), Dimitri Tiomkin (November 1951), Carl Th. Dreyer (January 1952 and April 1955), Richard Brooks (February 1952), Jean Renoir (March 1952), King Vidor and Paul Henreid (June–July 1952), Josef von Sternberg (October 1952), John Houseman (April 1953), and Cecil B. DeMille (March 1956).

In June 1958, Dudley Nichols wrote to *Films in Review*, with commentary on Lamar Trotti and *Mourning Becomes Electra*. In a reply, Henry Hart explains the raison d'etre for the journal:

> One of the reasons that prompt us to devote considerable time and energy to a magazine like this is to prevent the work of film-makers from being ephemeral. The population of people seriously interested in the movies as

> the most dynamic art of our day slowly increases. One of the prime purposes of FIR is to preserve for those who come after us the facts and the truths about movies up to now.[4]

The primary problem facing writers for *Films in Review* during Hart's tenure was that the editor had a fixation with rewriting every piece in his own style. As Charles L. Turner recalled,

> I wrote the two-part Victor Sjostrom obituary with help from Carl Dreyer and Ingmar Bergman and others. Henry Hart had this mania for rewriting almost every word. I had a terrible long distance bill because I was way out in the middle of the country shooting and arguing with him over the telephone about the cuts and changes he made in my piece. He rewrote my acknowledgments. What really bothered me was that he rewrote Carl Dreyer's letter. There had been a Scandinavian poem quoted in the article and he rewrote the poem to a different number of lines.... So I didn't write for him again because I couldn't direct pictures and fight with someone at a distance over my text. He was a nice guy and all, but he couldn't leave a line alone.... He just rewrote everybody.[5]

Another contributor, Rudy Behlmer notes,

> Yes, there were certain things that bothered me. On occasion he did put in certain things that were his opinion. He had very strong opinions. I said, "Henry, that's what you're saying, but it makes me look bad or I don't want that in print or I don't agree with you." I think he pretty much gave me my way. He was, for the most part, with me fair and understanding.[6]

In June–July 1963, Behlmer published an essay in *Films in Review* on "The Career of David O. Selznick." He recalls writing to the producer with some questions, Selznick's contacting Hart, "Who is this man?" and being invited to the Waldorf-Astoria Towers in New York to meet the legendary figure in film production:

> I sat there, and David was doing his memo bit, which I thought was swell. He had this guy there who was doing a transcript. Occasionally, he would say, "Let me tell you what actually happened." I went back to my hotel. The next morning, relatively early, there was a knock on the door, and here's the transcript of what we had been talking about.[7]

Behlmer reports that Selznick was "reasonably pleased" with the article, as apparently was son, Danny Selznick, and years later, Rudy Behlmer was given the opportunity to edit a seminal work on film history, *Memo from David O. Selznick* (first published in 1972).

The first of the career articles began to appear in 1953, with essays on Tod Browning and Lon Chaney. That same year, William K. Everson made his first appearance with an article on "Stock Shots." From April 1952 through February 1954, Herman G. Weinberg contributed a column designed for film buffs, albeit somewhat intellectual and sophisticated ones, with "Coffee, Brandy and Cigars: Things You Never Knew Till Now, and Got on Just as Well Without."

The film buffs heavily represented in the pages of *Films in Review* include DeWitt Bodeen, Ronald L. Bowers, Edward Connor (a church organist), Homer Dickens, George Geltzer, Jack Jacobs (who worked in a New York bookstore), Alvin H. Marill, Jack Edmund Nolan, Gene Ringgold, Robert C. Roman, Romano Tozzi, and Roi Uselton.

DeWitt Bodeen (1908–1988) was, in my opinion, the most important essayist to contribute to *Films in Review*. Generally, he wrote about stars, whom he had known many years previous, and always with affection but with a willingness to acknowledge whatever faults they might have. His filmographies were meticulous; they were, as he noted, "the spine of the article." The only star with whom he had an issue was Mary Miles Minter, who threatened to sue him if he wrote anything truthful about her; as a result, DeWitt wrote the October 1969 *Films in Review* essay on her under the name of Aydelott Ames. DeWitt's first contribution to *Films in Review* was a career article on Val Lewton in April 1963. It was appropriate tribute for DeWitt in that he had known Lewton since 1943, when the filmmaker became aware of his work in adapting *Jane Eyre* for the screen. For Lewton, DeWitt wrote *Cat People* (1942), arguably his most important work, *The Seventh Victim* (1943), and *The Curse of the Cat People* (1944).

Other important films followed, including *The Enchanted Cottage* (1945), *I Remember Mama* (1948), and *Mrs. Mike* (1949), and there was much television work in the 1950s. He came to write for *Films in Review* for a very odd reason. His last film, *Billy Budd* in 1960, was subject to dispute as to screen credit, and DeWitt finished up only with credit as the writer in Europe. In a desperate effort to gain further screenwriting assignments, he decided to contribute career articles to *Films in Review* in the hope that they and his name would come to the attention of producers. It didn't work out as DeWitt planned, but it did give us some of the best pieces to be found in the journal.[8]

DeWitt Bodeen.

Through it all, DeWitt displayed no bitterness at the downturn in his career. He was forced to rely on friends, such as actor Val Dufour, for invitations for lengthy stays at their homes, and when he was in Los Angeles, he would live at a small, rundown hotel in Beverly Hills, which did not even provide a telephone in his room. He researched primarily at the Margaret Herrick Library of the Academy of Motion Picture Arts and Sciences, kept no papers, and recorded his findings on index cards. DeWitt Bodeen's last years were spent at the Motion Picture Country House in Woodland Hills, California. There were a few film buffs, including Larry Lee Holland and

James Robert Parish, who visited him on a regular basis, but absent from their ranks are the loudmouthed, opinionated film buffs inhabiting today's Internet.

George H. Geltzer was a deaf-mute, living with his wife, Elaine, also a deaf-mute, in the Bronx, and a very fine, long-forgotten researcher into silent film.[9] Visits with him could be something of a strain in that all "conversation" took place in the form of handwritten notes passed backwards and forwards. I was taken to meet him by a film buff named Norman Miller, who was always attired in a suit and tie, was generally assumed to be a banker, and has been accurately described as "a true gentleman."[10] He was one of those who would always sit in the front row at the Museum of Modern Art screenings, equipped with a stopwatch with which he would time each film down to the second, along with a flashlight. There was always a crowd around him after the show to check if the museum's print was of the same length as the print reviewed many years earlier in *Film Daily*.

Gene Ringgold (1918–1985), who also used the named Kenneth G. Laurence,[11] authored a number of *Films of . . .* books for Citadel Press (including ones devoted to Maurice Chevalier, with DeWitt Bodeen; Bette Davis; Cecil B. DeMille, with DeWitt Bodeen; Rita Hayworth; Frank Sinatra, with Clifford McCarty). Legend has it that he was offered the editorship of *Films in Review* after Henry Hart retired, but on a visit to New York he was mugged and decided not to return to the city.

Jack Spears (1920–2012) was more film scholar than film buff, but he did contribute many important career articles to *Films in Review*, while holding down a professional position as executive director of the Tulsa County Medical Association from 1941 to 1985. He authored two books, *Hollywood: The Golden Era*, an anthology of his *Films in Review* articles, and *The Civil War on Screen*. I have only fond memories of my conversations and correspondence with him. I have less enthusiasm for Herbert G. Luft (1907–1992), an officious little man, who claimed to be both a film historian (with emphasis on filmmakers from Germany, where he was born) and a producer, as well as two-term president of the Hollywood Foreign Press Association.[12]

Alvin H. Marill (1934–2010) also was more a film historian than a film buff, authoring some twenty-four books on both film and television. His most important work is the five-volume *Movies Made for Television: 1964–2004* (2005), first published in a somewhat smaller format back in 1980. The first regular column in *Films in Review* devoted to films on television, beginning in April 1956, was compiled by Don Koll (1927–1983), a good-looking man of uncertain age, who was responsible possibly for the first book-length study (and a good one) of the "B" Western, titled *Hollywood Corral: A Stirring Nostalgic Tribute to the Sagebrush Sagas That Made Cinema History*, published in paperback in 1976, under the editorship of Leonard Maltin.[13] Maltin himself contributed an essay to *Films in Review* on the subject of Walt Disney's Films in October 1967.

Romano Tozzi wrote his first piece for *Films in Review* in 1955. In 1961, he was invited by Henry Hart to join the magazine as his assistant, a regular nine-to-five job which he held for more than five years until he accepted a better-paying position with *TV Guide*. Tozzi notes, "Although others found him difficult, Henry would always be fair and considerate to me. I do not regret my association with the magazine."[14]

The most famous, and certainly the most controversial, of all *Films in Review* columnists was Page Cook (1944–1993), who began writing on film music, under the heading of "Soundtrack," while still a teenager in November 1963. He was opinionated, rude, and outspoken in regard to the composers whom he liked or disliked—or, as one blogger had it, "prissy, effete, snobby and unbearable."[15] It is not difficult to understand why his polemical style should have appealed to editor Henry Hart, as Cook denounced Quincy Adams's score for *McKenna's Gold* as "inadequate noise," Nino Rota's work on *Satyricon* as "the most worthless 'score' of 1970, Michel Legrand's score for *Wuthering Heights* as "garbage," or Leslie Bricusse's songs for *Goodbye, Mr. Chips* as "tuneless globs . . . hideous gargle . . . so asinine it's incredible."

For reasons unclear, Page Cook was always vitriolic towards Henry Mancini. One would not have thought that a composer of Mancini's stature would care, but he did. As fellow *Films in Review* contributor Rudy Behlmer recalled, he was invited to the Mancini household for dinner. All went well until Rudy mentioned he wrote for *Films in Review*. Mancini became positively ice-like in his demeanor, and Rudy was "suddenly the bad guy." Apparently, Mancini purchased *Films in Review* each month to determine what Page Cook had to write about him.[16]

He was always entertaining, no more so when writing about recordings and composers that did not exist, which he did on a number of occasions. He was a film buff who knew his film music, no matter how much one might disagree with him, and he continued his column, as possibly the only music critic writing for a national periodical, with his column eventually ending with the March–April 1993 issue.

Page Cook's real name was, unbelievably, Charles Boyer, but he had no connection to the actor. He was a gay man who lived much of the time with his mother, who would grow frantic if it started to rain and he had left the apartment without his umbrella. He had no money and no permanent job. He was, as blogger Ron Pulliam noted, "virtually a pauper."[17] Pulliam further adds that Cook had a well-developed death wish, behind which somehow lurked his death from AIDS:

> Charles worshipped the idea of walking into heaven like Richard Burton and Jean Simmons in *The Robe*, backed by a blue-screen filled with clouds and a heavenly orchestra and choir, overseen by Alfred Newman and Ken Darby [who would sometimes send him money]. Unfortunately, I think Charles' own End Title sequence may not have been quite so melodic or well story-boarded and art-directed.[18]

Roi Uselton (1916–2007) was a frequent contributor.[19] In the January 1972 issue, he wrote what is the quintessential film buff piece, "Cooperative Scholarship," in which he took five pages pointing out the mistakes in the third edition of Leslie Halliwell's *The Filmgoer's Companion*.[20] Much of Uselton's writings were in the film buff mold, with articles on stars who died in airplanes, automobiles, and as suicides.

In February 1970, Robert A. Evans contributed the first of his annual chronicles of "The Marriages, Births and Deaths Among Film-Related Personalities." It was the earliest necrology devoted to those in the film industry, and paved the way for similar efforts by Bill H. Doyle, who for many years contributed a monthly "Obituaries" column to *Films in Review*; Eugene Michael Vazzana; and Harris M. Lentz III, whose annual *Obituaries in the Performing Arts* series has been published since the 1996 volume by McFarland.

(Aside from Doyle, the best known of necrologists is Dale Crawford, self-described as the "Death Maven." Not only did he obsessively collect data as to when a film personality died, but also he tracked down that individual's grave site long before such information was readily available on the Internet through sites such as findagrave.com.)

Jerry Vermilye was not only a contributor but also an assistant to Henry Hart, whom he describes as formidable. He recalls,

> For about a year in the mid-1960s I slaved away as his [Hart's] assistant, initially with the idea that he was looking for someone eventually to replace him as editor. But about 10 months as his "whipping boy" was enough, and I returned to work at a previous job with a great sigh of relief.[21]

Jerry Vermilye in 1972 (courtesy of Jerry Vermilye).

Later, Vermilye learned that Hart was looking for someone to groom as his successor, and telephoned, asking that the two might meet and talk about this:

> So he set up a lunch together at his favorite local tavern, and during the meal he brought up what he considered a serious issue . . . "Now Jerry, I know that you live with another man (I then had my one and only roommate) and that you're 34 and not married." (Big pause) "Do I have anything to worry about?" My demeanor remained calm as my brain raced, processing his outrageous query, thinking about his quirks and his biases, but I looked him square in the eye and said, "No Henry, you have nothing to worry about." The words "worry about" amused me no end. Did he think that were I gay I'd attempt to seduce him?[22]

There were few women to be found among *Films in Review*'s contributors. The most prominent, and the first to submit a career article, was Jeanne Stein, who wrote on Raymond Massey in the August–September 1963 issue, on Claude Rains in the November 1963 issue, and on Fay Bainter in the January 1965 issue. Jeanne Stein contributed a career article on Edward

Everett Horton to the first issue, January–February 1970, of the British journal *Focus on Film*. Edited by Allen Eyles, *Focus on Film*, which ceased publication in March 1981 after thirty-seven issues, was very much a more serious, scholarly version of *Films in Review*, with contributors including this author, DeWitt Bodeen, British film historian Jeffrey Richards, and even Louise Brooks.

In many ways, *Films in Review*, in the first twenty years or so of its life, was Henry Hart's publication. It reflected his conservative, reactionary politics. He was not only its editor, but he also rewrote articles to suit his style, and he wrote many of the reviews, not only in his own name but that of various females, whose identities it was claimed he had stolen from gravestones found in various New York area cemeteries. There is no accurate record of the pseudonyms that he used, but they probably include Prudence Ashford, Gwenneth Britt, Adelaide Comerford, Arlene Kramborg, Alice Canby Pearson, Elaine Rothschild, Eunice Sinkler, and Flavia Wharton. Curiously, what would on the surface appear to be an obvious fictitious character was actually a real person, one Tatiana Balkoff Drowne, whose full-time job was as a Russian translator.

Henry Hart's reviews were much concerned with assumed sexual improprieties and the like. In the Charles Laughton character in *Advise and Consent*, he identified "a degenerate vice."[23] Similarly, Lawrence of Arabia was "a sex degenerate whose vice debilitated his intellectual gifts."[24] He dismissed *The Balcony* as of interest to "only the neurotic and sexually perverted."[25] Writing as Gwenneth Britt, Hart was outraged by *Myra Breckinridge*, "This cinemation of Gore Vidal's novel about a male sex pervert who has himself transexualized is lower than any respectable studio has hitherto gone in chasing a buck." (An asterisk and accompanying footnote after the word "transexualized" explained this was "the fantasy of homosexuals that they can acquire the sexual organs, as well as the secondary sexual characteristics of the opposite sex."[26])

*Dr. Strangelove, or: How I Learned to Stop Worrying and Love the Bomb* was "twirpish twiddle." Of Katherine Anne Porter's *Ship of Fools*, he wrote, "The only cliché missing is a self-portrait of a childless lady-writer who thinks *every* living creature a fool."[27] Reviewing *The Loves of Isadore*, Hart opined that "Vanessa Redgrave resembles Isadore Duncan only in her insistence of having children out of wedlock."[28] Writing as Elaine Rothschild, he described *Carnal Knowledge* as "a badly directed jumble of four-letter immaturies; coital scenes; male nudity; Ann-Margaret's mammary glands; woman-libish soapera."[29] Hart described *The Silence* as "one of Bergman's sexploiters—a quickly and inexpensively made black-&-whiter depending on notoriety from scenes of coition (clothed) and masturbation (also clothed)."[30]

Under Henry Hart's editorship, *Films in Review* was no fan of directors such as Stanley Kubrick or Ingmar Bergman. As someone who proudly claimed to have seen the Laurence Olivier/Vivien Leigh vehicle, *That Hamilton Woman*, eighty-three times, Andrew Sarris might well be designated a film buff, but he had no time for Henry Hart's review policy, writing, "In the prayerful pages of *Films in Review*, such art-house deities as Resnais, Bergman, and Fellini are defiled as incompetent perverts with subversive intentions."[31]

Henry Hart was at his worst, or some may argue at his best, when, under the name of N. C. Chambers he reviewed the Academy Awards presentations, with an honesty that has not been matched since. From May 1958, the annual May edition of *Films in Review*, featuring N. C. Chambers with comments the first couple of years from his cynical wife, "Mrs. C.," was an issue not to be ignored. When he retired after the 1972 ceremony, he was sorely missed by many—and I for one would not object to his like reappearing to review the presentations today. Here are a few samples of his commentary:

1958—Gregory Peck "unbrushed and unshaven."[32]

1961—"Juliet Prowse and some things that looked like men hopped about."[33]

1962—"a caterwauler named Johnny Mathis." "Rosalind Russell, rather ridiculous in a shapeless evening gown and a band of the same material around her head."[34]

1963—Eddie Fisher's "delivery [of a medley of Academy Award songs of the past], like his voice, was second-rate." Rita Moreno was "devoid of any grace or charm." Of Ethel Merman, "I was surprised to note how little of her unabashed vulgarity came over the air and up from my tv screen. Since unabashed vulgarity is all Merman has, her medley [of Irving Berlin songs] was not a success." Laurence Olivier's "receding hair was undisguised."[35]

1964—Tuesday Weld was "a 30-year-old kook." Of Shirley MacLaine, "Her hair looked like a busby and her dress like Flatbush Avenue after the snow has gotten dirty." Rita Hayworth is described as "looking somewhat the worse for wear."[36]

1965—Of Merle Oberon, "The immobility of her heavily maquillaged face was downright frightening, as was the fear lurking in her heavily made-up eyes."[37]

1966—"Natalie Wood, looking like a Beatle with two blackened eyes."[38]

1967—"Vanessa Redgrave . . . wearing what looked like a sack, and with her hair in a mess."[39]

1968—Eva Marie Saint, "wearing an oversize flour sack."[40]

1969—Rosalind Russell "as tastelessly dressed as she usually is."[41]

1972—Of Debbie Reynolds, "Her make-up intended to protract her immaturity was a disfigurement." Tennessee Williams "came mincingly forward."[42]

While he was critical of many actresses of the past, he always welcomed Joan Crawford's presence on the show, and, of the newer performers, Angie Dickinson was a favorite.

N. C. Chambers's most famous insult was from 1970, when his commentary on Fred Astaire's appearance at that year's presentation was venal, referencing "the dyed, disfiguring wig," which "accentuated the *special* pathos aging has in a dancer."[43]

Fred Astaire responded with a lengthy letter, published in the August–September issue of the journal, writing, in part,

> one of your reviewers has overstepped his status with a grossly insulting commentary on me. . . . It is his deliberate attack, and effort to describe me as a decrepit old ham trying to hang on by a thread or something, that I resent vehemently. I will not tolerate this presumptuous, patronizing attitude. . . .
>
> Chambers attacked my appearance, my work, everything, to a shocking extent. . . .
>
> Mr. Chambers' reference to a "dyed wig" that disfigured me was most mystifying since I wore just exactly what I have always worn in my recent tv specials and pictures. I saw it on the monitor and it was completely ok. . . .[44]

As an example of how a well-documented incident can become distorted, one need search no further than the autobiography of much-disliked biographer Charles Higham. He recounts a meeting with Astaire, at which the dancer claimed the hair was his own, and was told by Higham that the piece had been written by Henry Hart under the pseudonym of Tatiana Balkoff Drowne.[45]

Henry Hart retired as editor of *Films in Review* with the February 1972 issue.[46] One of the last pieces that he wrote for the journal, in April 1977, was a tribute to Quincy Howe (1900–1977), who had been named president of the National Board of Review on January 1, 1942. Howe was succeeded as president by Robert Giroux, of the publishing house Farrar, Straus and Giroux, and who held the post from 1975 through 1982, and was honored with a special citation from the board in 1989. Giroux published a two-part career essay on Mack Sennett in *Films in Review*, December 1968 and January 1969, and is also the author of *A Deed of Death: The Story of the Unsolved Murder of Hollywood Director William Desmond Taylor* (Knopf, 1990).

Succeeding Hart as editor of *Films in Review* was Charles Phillips Reilly, an affable Irish-American who just happened to be Giroux's long-time domestic partner. At the time I knew both Reilly and Giroux, they gave no indication as to their relationship. A Catholic couple who had been together since World War II, including the years when Giroux was married, Reilly and Giroux were noticeably reticent, initially living in houses next to each other, and then moving to the same country home, to the same assisted-living facility, and then dying within months of each other. Giroux's biographer, Boris Kachka, is equally reserved in discussing the couple in *Hothouse*, which provides little documentation on Reilly and ignores Giroux's presidency of the National Board of Review. On September 6, 2008, the *New York Times* published a lengthy obituary of Robert Giroux, in which Reilly was not mentioned.

When in New York, I would have lunch with Reilly or lunch with Giroux, but never the two of them together. I recall a memorable early afternoon touring the Union Square area of New York, with Giroux's pointing out to me various film history-related locations, but Reilly did not join us.

The editorial address of *Films in Review* in its earlier years was 31 Union Square. During the reign of Charles Phillips Reilly, and presumably earlier as well as later, *Films in Review* operated out of the basement of a Manhattan apartment building at 210 East Sixty-Eighth Street. It was obviously the janitor's quarters, and was furnished with two desks, one for the editor and one for John Chapin, who took care of the daily business of running the publication (and was apparently no relation to Elspeth Chapin). There was also a couch, upon which were piled review copies of books, and Charles was always generous in inviting visitors to take what they wished, whether or not they intended to submit a review. Towards the end of Charles Phillip Reilly's tenure as editor, the two-man staff moved to a spare room in Chapin's rent-controlled apartment at 205 East Sixty-Sixth Street.

Charles Phillips Reilly's name had first appeared in the journal as a reviewer of *Bartleby* in March 1972, and *The Godfather* the following month. Unquestionably, *Films in Review* became a more welcoming publication under his editorship. In April 1977, I took over the "Films on 8 & 16" column, which had been started by Samuel A. Peeples in October 1965. The name

Charles Phillips Reilly (left), Blanche Sweet, and Robert Giroux celebrate the 1975 placing of a plaque at 11 East Fourteenth Street, New York, the site of the American Biograph Studios, where D. W. Griffith made his directorial debut. Blanche, who paid for the plaque, asked me to provide the wording, but few ever saw what comments I made in that within weeks of the unveiling, the plaque was stolen and never recovered.

was changed to "The Collecting Scene" in May 1981, and the column ended in April 1982. William K. Everson became a regular contributor. My mentor and coauthor, Edward Wagenknecht, contributed a handful of career studies. DeWitt Bodeen was more frequently to be found in the journal's pages. In October 1977, Barry Brown contributed a career article on Ben Turpin.

When Charles Phillips Reilly retired, Ronald Bowers was appointed editor. He was a good match for the magazine, having written a career article (on Vivien Leigh) as early as August–September 1965, contributed some fifty articles to the journal over a ten-year period, and started his own coverage of the Academy Awards in the May 1978 issue. Bowers began his editorship in February 1979, and his name last appears as editor in May 1981. He recalls,

> I had admired Henry Hart's erudition and what appeared to be his avuncular demeanor. When Reilly became editor he and I became friends—so I thought. But once he retired he became Mr. Hyde, joined by both Hart and Giroux. Some trio. I think Reilly regretted retiring—he was not happy and there was his drinking.... Their constant petty interference became impossible to deal with every week and I decided I needed a fresh start.
>
> I am pleased with a few things I accomplished while there—bringing the physical look of the magazine into the twentieth century, establishing the first two annual awards ceremonies—Myrna Loy and Gloria Swanson.

> So no regrets. The one thing this farm boy should have done the very first day on the job was to arrive not only carrying a Louis Vuitton briefcase, but also a shovel.[47]

The end was somewhat abrupt. He went out of the "office" for lunch, bidding farewell to John Chapin, longtime circulation manager (first acknowledged as such in January 1980), and never returned. "It was the end of the month and I was fed up with the subterfuge of both Giroux and Reilly, typed a one-sentence letter of resignation and left for a pleasant brunch alone!!!"[48] Charles Phillips Reilly briefly returned to edit the June–July 1981 issue, and was then followed, with the August–September 1981 issue, by Brendan Ward. I know nothing, and can find nothing on Ward's background, but he was ill-suited to be editor, with his penchant for using the slang language perpetuated in *Variety*, and his desire to leave his mark on *Films in Review* in little and big ways, such as moving the "Letters" column to the front of the periodical and heavily truncating it as well as introducing a "From the Editor" page in October 1982. Ward quit, unannounced, with the June–July 1983 edition.

After Brendan Ward's editorship, it was a pleasure to welcome Robin Little (died 2007), who had enjoyed a career as an editor with a major New York publisher. She lived in an apartment at 245 East Seventy-Second Street, apparently paid for by the National Board of Review and used to house all back issues of *Films in Review*. Robin was both good and bad for the magazine, with what was bad probably forced upon her by others. After readers had become used to the compact, pocket-size edition of *Films in Review*, a "completely new design" was introduced in February 1994, with the page size increased to 9 ½ x 7 inches. While the National Board of Review was still listed as publisher, in March 1994, the credit of Harry Pearson Jr.[49] for Pearson Publishing appeared. Pearson's name disappeared in January–February 1995, but in July–August of that year, the name of Roy Frumkes was listed as Robin Little's coeditor. With the somewhat snobbish first name of "Roi," Frumkes's name had first appeared in the journal in February 1968, with a review of *The Power*.

By November–December 1995, Roy Frumkes was the sole editor—"his brother [Lewis][50] bought him the magazine," states one insider[51]—and with the next issue *Films in Review* suddenly boasted the heading, "From Movie Theater to Home Theater," a phrase signifying nothing except that the periodical was no longer Henry Hart's great publication.

A new publisher, Then and There Media, was announced in July–August 1997, and then and there, *Films in Review* became an online publication in

HAPPY NEW YEAR
FROM
FILMS IN REVIEW'S
STAFF AND CONTRIBUTORS



(See page 44)

The January 1984 issue of *Films in Review* offers a page with photographs of staff and contributors: 1, Robin Little; 2, Marcia Magill; 3, William K. Everson; 4, DeWitt Bodeen; 5, Page Cook; 6, Michael Buckley; 7, John Gallagher; 8, Pat Anderson; 9, John Nangle; 10, Larry Lee Holland; 11, Herbert G. Luft; 12, Roy Frumkes; 13, Alvin H. Marill.

1997, but most former readers were beyond caring. The National Board of Review continues as an organization which presents annual awards in a few categories to those in the film industry. Again, it is difficult to comprehend why anyone should care outside of the winners, and even they must surely wonder what an award means from an organization whose membership is unknown in terms of size, intelligence, or locality.[52] I have yet to come across anyone who claims membership (except for Roy Frumkes).[53]

Aside from its own, venerable place in the history of film history, *Films in Review* can also be credited with serving as an example for two similar publications, aside from the aforementioned *Focus on Film*, which began during its life.

Alan G. Barbour (1933–2002) edited and published *Screen Facts* from 1963 to 1972, in collaboration with Larry Edmunds Bookstore. Among its contributors were such familiar names from *Films in Review* as DeWitt Bodeen, Edward Connor, William K. Everson, Gene Ringgold, and Alvin H. Marill. Born in Oakland, California, Alan Barbour attended Rutgers University; he met his wife, actress Jean Callovini, while stationed at Walter Reed Hospital in 1958, and the couple performed in many plays together, including their favorite, *The Enchanted Cottage*. He was a charter member of the Sons of the Desert,[54] an organization founded to celebrate Stan Laurel and Oliver Hardy, and whose members curiously do not fit the description of either "buff" or "fan." They are something unique and precious. As Barbour's wife recalls,

> When we married and came to live in New York City in 1960, he couldn't sell the idea of a book on films. And today the publishing world is covered with them and that is why he started *Screen Facts*. It gave the many film buffs we knew and wanted to write an opportunity as well as our artist friend Al Kilgore,[55] a terrific artist, to do some good covers of film stars.[56]

A bespectacled and conservatively attired individual, Barbour was a lover of all things that the phrase "Saturday matinee" brings to mind, most notably "B" Westerns and serials (which he saw for the first time in 1940 at the Broadway Theatre in Oakland, California).[57] He published a number of other periodical titles, little more than collections of illustrations,[58] and authored two volumes in the Pyramid Illustrated History of the Movies series, advertised as "made by film buffs, for film buffs, about film buffs," on Humphrey Bogart (1973) and John Wayne (1974).

Alan G. Barbour was also one of the individuals behind production of the four-part spoof silent serial, *Captain Celluloid vs. the Film Pirates* (1966), shot in New Jersey. Directed by a professional cinematographer, Louis McMahon (1919–2016), Robert Miller played the title role of Captain Celluloid, fighting Master Duper and the League of Film Pirates who copy old films to sell to collectors. William K. Everson, who came up with the idea, was featured as D. W. Hart.

*Film Fan Monthly* is generally associated with Leonard Maltin, but it was actually founded as a newsletter for 8mm and 16mm film collectors by Daryl A. Davy in July 1961. Fifteen-year-old Leonard Maltin took over in

1966, and continued publication through June 1975. He specialized in featuring character players and lesser-known performers rather than major stars, as did *Films in Review*. With the emphasis on career articles with filmographies, the style was very much in the *Films in Review* tradition, but perhaps a little more enthusiastic.

Certainly *Film Fan Monthly* was not above poking fun of its more conservative competitor. The April 1969 issue contains a fake career article written by Jerry Vermilye in the style of a *Films in Review* piece. Just as Henry Hart used female pseudonyms, the piece here is the work of "Adelaide Hartford." Just as *Films in Review* would generally subtitle the title of the career article, the piece on the nonexistent actress, Gladys Corbin is described as "Managed to Ennoble the Woman of Easy Virtue Despite an Unwillingness to Eschew Respectability." There is even more than a hint of Henry Hart's conservative bent, with a reference to "lavender leftists," while a photograph supposedly of Gladys Corbin is captioned, "Corbin's face was not unlike that of a woman's."

Back in the 1970s, I did have the good fortune to attend a few of the National Board of Review screenings in New York of new films, in the company of former silent star Blanche Sweet, who was a member of the board. The screenings were sponsored by the various distributors, and the National Board of Review was expected to share the screening facility with members of the Legion of Decency, equally an irrelevance by that time.

The members of the board attending those screenings were all conservatively dressed, of a certain age, and generally of a certain political persuasion that matched their attire, although there must have been a handful of liberals other than Blanche Sweet in the audience. "It seemed very much like a film-oriented country club for the very old and wealthy," recalled Jim Beaver,[59] who had written a number of pieces for *Films in Review* in its later years. At the end of the film, the members of the Legion of Decency were requested to retire, and the members of the National Board of Review were asked for their comments and opinion. To what end I do not know.

In a way, it was all very civilized. And of such civility was the makeup, the contributors, and the readership of *Films in Review* in what might be described as not the "golden age" of Hollywood but rather the "golden age" of the film buff.

Chapter Seven

# PUBLISHING, PUBLICATIONS, AND BOOKSTORES FOR THE FILM BUFF

THERE HAS LONG BEEN A NUMBER OF SUPPORTING INDUSTRIES CATERING to the film buff. What might be described as buffery, or at times perhaps buffoonery. Generally, publishers have found the film buff market disappointing in that if they have money available (and many do not), film buffs seem unwilling to spend it on the purchase of a book, no matter the subject matter.

Citadel Press made a valiant attempt to break into the film buff market in the 1960s and 1970s, with its *Films of . . .* series, devoted to stars from Charlie Chaplin to Joan Crawford, and as variant in quality as the authors involved. The format was always the same, with an introduction followed by a chronological listing of the relevant films, with credits, synopses, and a selection of contemporary critical comments. The publishing house was a subsidiary of Lyle Stuart, Inc., founded in the mid-1950s by the controversial publisher, Lyle Stuart (1926–2010),[1] after winning a libel suit against Walter Winchell. Despite the calm, sympathetic approach of the authors in the *Films of . . .* series, Lyle Stuart was anything but quiet and non-controversial, notorious for publication in 1970 of *The Anarchist Cookbook*, and for frequent clashes with various authorities over freedom of speech. "I'm a great believer in letting anybody publish the most outrageous, unpopular things there are," he once told the *Washington Post*, but such a policy did not really extend to the *Films of . . .* series, which concentrated only on the best-known of film personalities, even, for example, rejecting a volume on Deanna Durbin.

Citadel Press had been founded by Allan J. Wilson (1917–2011) in partnership with Morris Sorkin, and it was Wilson who was the film buff. After Lyle Stuart sold his company to Carol Publishing in 1989, Wilson continued with the new publisher, while Stuart founded Barricade Books, specializing in controversial, and saleable, titles. Eventually, well past retirement age, Wilson was let go by Carol Publishing. However, Lyle Stuart and his wife, Carole, were so fond of Wilson that they told him he would always have a desk at Barricade Books, and he would often make the bus trip from his home in New York to Barricade headquarters in Fort Lee, New Jersey. Carole Stuart recalled, "Lyle called Allan a bon vivant. He wore an ascot tie, smoked cigars and held open doors for ladies. Lyle said he reminded him of Franchot Tone. He was quite a gentleman."[2]

Founded in 1993, Arcadia Press is the largest publisher of paperback books on local history. Its pocket-size volumes are familiar to most readers, and it has produced more than its share of books to delight the film buff, documenting local movie theatres, including *The Chicago Movie Palaces of Balaban and Katz* (2006) and *Milwaukee Movie Theatres* (2010), and other film-related subjects such as *Silent-Era Filmmaking in Santa Barbara* (2007), *Old Tucson Studios* (2008), and *Location Filming in Los Angeles* (2010).

Currently, the major (and really the only successful) outlet of books for the film buff is BearManor Media, established in 2001 by Ben Ohmart. Ohmart's primary interest is American radio, and BearManor came into existence as a result of his self-publishing books on the subject, beginning in 2000 with *Walter Tetley: For Corn's Sake* (coauthored with Charles Stumpf). (For those unfamiliar with Walter Tetley, and you are in the millions, he was the star of the popular radio series of the 1940s and 1950s, *The Great Gildersleeve*.) "In the process of researching and interviewing celebrities," commented Ohmart in 2014, "I came across supporting players and forgotten actors who couldn't get their life stories published, or didn't know who to approach about being published. I published a few of these and business began to snowball. Now I'm close to my 700th title in print, with more coming out monthly."[3]

The company operates out of Ben Ohmart's home in Kyoto, Japan, with production editors and other freelance staffers based across the United States, and even in Europe. The publication address for individual books can change depending upon the individual supervising production, and while in the past, Ohmart would publish 1,000 copies of each title, the volumes are now released as print-on-demand.

"I'm afraid I have never aimed directly at the mainstream audience, because my own mind is like a film buff. I do like modern films, but I don't see a lot of greatness out there. And obviously there are too many versions of what great is."[4]

The earliest periodical really to be aimed at a film buff rather than a fan audience was *Hollywood Studio Magazine*, which began publication in May 1966 as the monthly *Studio Magazine*, renaming itself in July 1968. First edited and published for its entire life by Dorothy H. Denny, with the headquarters in the San Fernando Valley area of Los Angeles, the magazine initially had no logic to its content, with, for example, an article in the October 1966 issue devoted to Marco Muffler and Auto Safety Services Shop. Advertising predominated, and studio employees were promised free subscriptions. It was "for and about people in the industry," but in time, while it remained about people in the industry both past and present, its audience became predominantly the film buff.

By 1970, it was publishing articles on film buffs or film enthusiasts, such as Raymond Lee, who "chases movie history," while writing such photo-driven volumes as *Fit for the Chase: Cars and the Movies* (1969), *Not So Dumb: The Life and Times of the Animal Actors* (1970), *The Films of Mary Pickford* (1970), and *Gangsters and Hoodlums: The Underworld in the Cinema* (1971). Lee was actually one of the first to highlight the work of a studio photographer, not George Hurrell but Clarence Sinclair Bull, with *The Faces of Hollywood* (1969).[5]

*Hollywood Studio Magazine* also had its own gossip columnist in Lee Graham (1923–1992), with his "Man About Town" column, which continued from 1970 until the magazine's demise.[6] Joe Franklin wrote a spasmodic "Down Memory Lane" column from September 1988 through August 1989. By 1971, it was providing a service for "movie hobbyists," who were encouraged to tell other readers about their collections. Among the film buffs who were regular contributors were Patrick Brock (in the UK), Kirk Crivello, Jess L. Hoaglin, Doug McClelland, and Lou Valentino.

Articles were always lightweight, with no filmographies; typical was Tom Scalzo's piece on Wallace Reid, which informed readers that the subject was "the most popular star in early silent films . . . now almost completely forgotten."[7] The private lives of the featured players remained out of reach, and so as Robert Rosterman was "Looking Back: at Lon McCallister,"[8] he was not reaching far enough back so as to report on his homosexuality and his long-term relationship with fellow actor William Eythe.

There never seemed to be enough superlatives for featured subjects, ranging from "sensational" and "finest" to "gorgeous." Where it was difficult to find appropriate qualitative comment, editors and authors would resort to reference distinctive areas of a star's personality; Sylvia Sidney was "gutsy," Errol Flynn was a "handsome rebel," and Lloyd Nolan was "underrated."

The May 1983 issue of *Hollywood Studio Magazine*.

It was obvious the end was at hand when *Hollywood Studio Magazine* featured "Nude Stars!" on the cover of its January–February 1992 issue, with a photo spread amply featuring buttocks and breasts bared to the readership. It ceased publication in October of that year.

*Film Buff*'s title suggests its audience, but this monthly newsletter, in typed format, appears more geared towards film collectors than film buffs in general. Edited by Fred Muro, it was first published in 1971 by Baltimore-based Impact Promotion and Publishing, survived through the decade, and boasted a readership of 750.[9]

Much as *Film Buff* took on a highly accessible name without total regard to its content, so did the Film Buff in Toronto, Canada,[10] a video store that closed at the end of 2014 after almost two decades in operation, providing not just titles that film buffs would want but all manner of VHS tapes and later DVDs—a reported 35,000—from all periods and all countries, as well as an ice cream counter.

The two major publications for film buffs who were also film collectors were *Big Reel* and *Movie Collector's World*. The former, devoted to "the exciting world of film collector," was a monthly newspaper-style periodical from Empire Publishing. The articles were generally amateurish and worthless, but the reason for purchasing *Big Reel* was not the editorial content but rather the advertisements in which film collectors bought and sold films in both 16mm and 35mm formats. The head of the Film Security Office of the Motion Picture Association of America maintained that *Big Reel* was offering "more than $100,000 worth of copyrighted films per issue."[11] It was published from 1974 to 2013. *Movie Collector's World* was initially a monthly publication, later becoming biweekly, from Krause Publications and later Arena Publishing. First published in 1984, *Movie Collector's World* never had the same audience of film collecting zealots as did *Big Reel*, and in its later years, despite its title, it was more concerned with poster collecting. In 2012, it was acquired by *Classic Images*, which like *Big Reel* and *Movie Collector's World*, was published in tabloid newspaper format.

*Classic Images* owes its existence to a man named Samuel K. (Karl) Rubin (1918–2009), the owner of a furniture store in Indiana, Pennsylvania, coincidentally the birthplace of Jimmy Stewart. Sam Rubin was also a film collector, primarily of silent films, as well as being an amateur moviemaker, and he determined there was a need for film collectors to share their common interests through a newspaper, *8mm Collector*, the first issue of which was published on June 7, 1962. Cheaply typed and printed, the first four issues were irregular in size, until a standard tabloid format was adopted with the fifth issue, circulated apparently to some 6,000 potential subscribers thanks to utilizing the mailing list of Entertainment Films.

This first issue featured Kalton C. Lahue on its front page, with an article titled "Slide Bonanza." Kalton C. Lahue (died 1993) was one of the first to produce popular volumes on film history that were also valuable and reliable as reference sources. He was not specifically a film buff in that I am dubious that he cared fanatically about the subject, and, indeed, ceased writing on film in the 1970s, as he became diverted by the subject of photographic techniques and automobiles and their maintenance. Lahue's *Continued Next Week: History of the Moving Picture Serial* remains a crucial source on silent serials.[12]

*8mm Collector* consisted primarily of short articles, news items, occasional advertising, and reprints of newspaper stories. In issue no. 2, September 24, 1962, film dealer William Donnachie tells of how he came to the United States from his native Scotland in 1927, providing a rare glimpse into the personal life of a notorious film pirate. A book review section is introduced in issue no. 7, February 1964, by Palm Springs-based film collector and movie memorabilia seller Martin "Marty" Kearns. In that same issue, a very young Leonard Maltin introduced "Research Unlimited," offering to take on research, at no charge, for readers, and in issue no. 9, September 1964, he contributed a brief article on comedy pioneer Mack Sennett.

The periodical grew in size, first to more than twenty pages and then, within a couple of years, to over sixty. And who will forget "Dani's Doughnuts," a column supposedly hosted by Rubin's very young granddaughter, which began with issue no. 9, winter 1970, and continued for a few years.

*8mm Collector* became *Classic Film Collector* in the summer of 1966. Twelve years later, Rubin sold the publication to Blackhawk Films, which published it through the *Muscatine Journal*, a subsidiary of Lee Enterprises. Rubin retired as editor in 1988. Under the new management and editorship, *Classic Film Collector* became *Classic Film/Video Images* (later simplified to *Classic Images*), and in 1995, a sister publication, *Films of the Golden Age*, was introduced, publishing lengthy career pieces, generally lacking both the qualities of research and writing exemplified earlier by *Films in Review*.

Thanks to Sam Rubin and *8mm Collector*, the most popular of film buff conventions, the Cinecon,[13] came into existence. It was hosted by the Society for Cinephiles, Ltd., activated on January 1, 1965, with Tom Seller, who came up with the name, as the first president. The first convention was held at the newly constructed Holiday Inn in Indiana, Pennsylvania, over the 1965

Labor Day Weekend. It began on the Saturday, with a reception at Rubin's house, thirty-five people in attendance, and with film dealer/collector I. K. Meginnis as the guest speaker. William C. Beeler Jr. of Hamilton, Ohio, was elected president. Cinecon has continued ever since, at the same time of year, for a couple of decades alternating in various cities until 1990, when it took up permanent residence in Hollywood. In recent years, the convention was presented as if it was the personal fiefdom of Cinephiles' president, Bob Birchard (1950–2016), who selected films for screening not on the basis of their importance or artistic worth, but rather because he, personally, wanted to see them.

Cinecon attendees are generally referred to as "Cinegoons," and their devotion to their past leader, Birchard, was somewhat short-lived as one audience member at the 2016 convention pointed out to me. On the first day, the announcement of a tribute to Birchard was prominently placed in the center of the bulletin board. On the second day, it had moved to the bottom of the board in order to accommodate notices of items for sale. By the fourth day, it was still in the same location, but now crowded and partially covered by sales notices. That same attendee, who wishes to remain anonymous comments,

> If the "Tribute to Bob" at the Cinecon starts late and runs long, persons will clear out fast once it intrudes by even a minute into the supper hour. Not that Bob wouldn't do the same if the tribute had been for any of us. Moral of the story: Cinegoon love does not last long, particularly when food and making money are on the line.[14]

The most prominent part of the Cinecon was always the banquet, held on a Sunday evening and attended by various film celebrities of the past. As the years progressed, it became obvious there were fewer and fewer available, and the same tired, old faces (seldom if ever attached to the body of a star) prevailed. If evidence of the lack of respect film buffs actually have for these players of the past, whom presumably they idolize, one need look no further than the attire adopted by many. While a jacket and tie might seem obvious to anyone of intelligence or sophistication, film buffs would show up not only tieless, but wearing jeans, sneakers, and shirts that had not in recent memory seen a laundry.

The Cinephiles organized an English junket in March 1971, with presentations by this writer, Kevin Brownlow, and others. A semi-rival organization, the Cinefest, was held in Syracuse, New York, beginning in 1967, organized by Phil Serling (died 2002). In true film buff fashion, the website for the Cinecon, cinecon.org, provides a list of every film screened since 1965.

Just as *Big Reel* and *Movie Collector's World* provided film buff collectors with an outlet for individual film and video sales, so were there many companies specializing in the sale of 8mm and/or 16mm films for the collector market. The most prominent was Blackhawk Films, founded in 1945 by Kent D. Eastin (1909–1981), but there were many others, including Nick Fiorentino, I. K. Meginnis, Minot, Niles (the assets of which were sold in February 1982 to JEF Films), and Thunderbird. Murray Glass operated two companies, Glenn Photo, selling 16mm and later VHS tapes, and Em Gee Film Library, renting out the same.

Founded in 1978 by Jack Hardy, Phoenix-based Grapevine was initially involved in marketing silent film prints to collectors. It expanded into Beta and VHS and now DVDs, with the emphasis as much on rare sound films as those from the silent era. Noted for the high quality of its digital work for its DVD releases, all intended for the film buff market, is Los Angeles-based Flicker Alley, using the nickname given to Cecil Court, London's early film distribution center, prior to the establishment of Wardour Street. The company was founded in 2002 by Jeffery Masino.

The best-known of companies providing high-quality DVDs for the film buff market is Criterion, established in 1984, and later a part of the Voyager Company until the latter's dissolution in the late 1990s. The first releases from Criterion were *Citizen Kane* and *King Kong*, which introduced the concept of an audio commentary (by Ron Haver). The early releases were available on laserdisc, which was the film buff's medium of choice for home video presentations, with the quality being particularly high and the discs, resembling LPs looking very collectible and easily storable. In large part because of the high purchase price, laserdiscs never caught on with the general public, and they were superseded in the late 1990s by the DVD format. However, there is still a limited market for laserdiscs among film buffs and collectors, with some releases not available in any other format being highly desirable.

In addition to DVDs, today's film buffs could take advantage of two, now down to one, specialist basic cable channels, American Movie Classics (AMC) and Turner Classic Movies (TCM). AMC made its debut on October 1, 1984, screening classic films (as its name suggested), uncut and with no commercial interruptions. It consolidated its hold on its audience and its ability to access newly restored and preserved films with the introduction

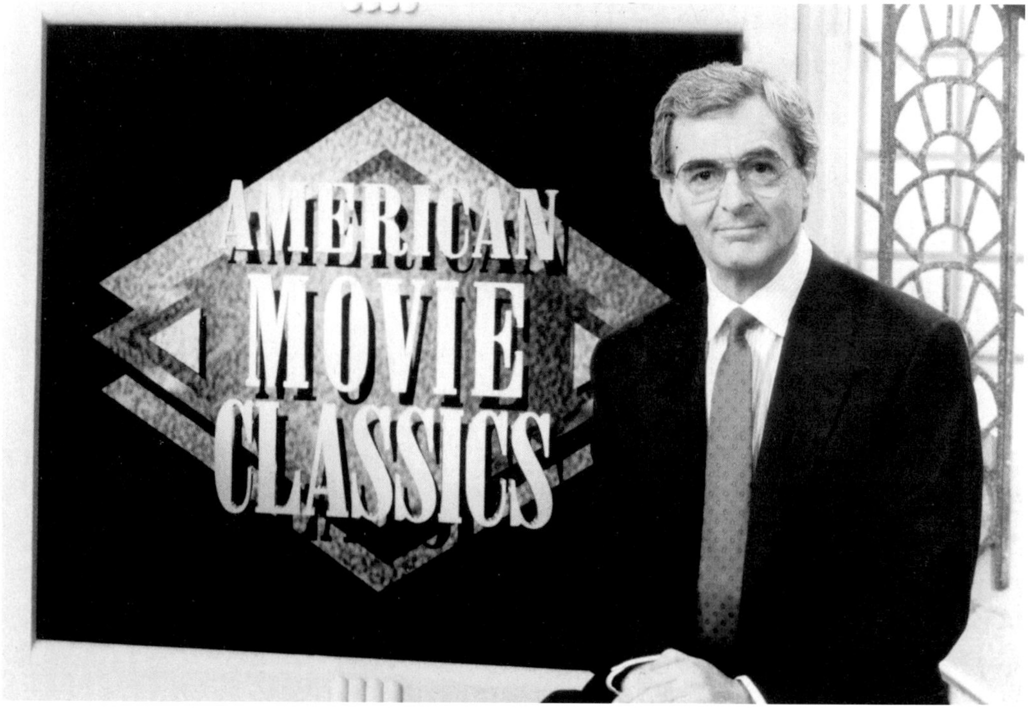


Bob Dorian.

of a Film Preservation Festival in December 1990. The face of AMC was actor Bob Dorian (born 1933), who parted company with AMC in 2000; he always had a kindly, semi-professorial manner, but never pretended that he was a film buff or that he had a thorough knowledge of film history. For five years in the 1990s, Dorian shared hosting chores with George Clooney's affable father, Nick (born 1934). The network changed its modus operandi in September 2002 with the introduction of commercial breaks, and within a couple of years had started airing original programming and turned its back on the original premise of presenting commercial-free, classic films.

Somehow, AMC never generated the love or support given by viewers in general and film buffs in particular to Turner Classic Movies (TCM), founded by billionaire Ted Turner, which made its debut on April 14, 1994. The first film to be aired was *Gone with the Wind*, proof positive if needed that Ted Turner not only owned that classic film but all others released by Metro-Goldwyn-Mayer, which he had acquired in 1986. Like AMC, Turner Classic Movies was, and remains, commercial free, and since its creation it has had only one full-time host, and that is former actor and well-informed and intelligent film buff/film historian Robert Osborne (1932–2017). As Bob Dorian explained, "The major difference between us is that Osborne is a film

Robert Osborne (1999).

historian. I'm hardly that. What I am is an actor and a fan. I love good films (and a lot of bad ones), and I know a lot of great stories."[15]

Lawrence O'Connell Edmunds (1906–1941) was a native of North Carolina, who came to Los Angeles and went to work for bookseller Stanley Rose. In 1938, he opened his own bookstore, Larry Edmunds, located at 1603 North Cahuenga Boulevard in Hollywood; it was not a movie bookstore, but it did attract a movie clientele. Edmunds had mental issues and put his head in the gas oven at his guest house apartment on North Beachwood Drive, killing himself. Supposedly he left a note reading, "If you think this is easy you're crazy."

The bookstore was left to his employee, Milt Luboviski, whose first wife, Florence, Larry Edmunds had later married, and it was Milt and his second wife, Git, who oversaw the change in the store to one specializing in film books and memorabilia. She and Milt moved the store in 1955 to 6658 Hollywood Boulevard, and, after Milt had left her, she moved it again in 1980 to 6644 Hollywood Boulevard.

Apparently, film books are not a major source of income for booksellers, and so Luboviski began selling pornography under the counter. He became friendly with Henry Miller, providing him with money and accommodation. In return, Miller began writing pornography, at one dollar a page, for Luboviski to sell to clients, including such industry luminaries as Joseph L. Mankiewicz, Billy Wilder, Frederick Hollander, and Henry Blanke. The stories were gathered together in a book that Miller titled *Opus Pistorum*, and in 1942, Luboviski typed up five copies, four to sell and one for his archives.[16] Luboviski recalled in later years for the *New York Times*, "In those days, the shop was not doing well and I supplemented our income by selling various items of pornography whenever it was possible to obtain."[17]

There are stories of Larry Edmunds Bookstore continuing to sell under-the-counter pornography for many years, certainly into the 1950s, but no one is willing to discuss this, either on or off the record. During the same period, the bookstore was a hangout for left-wingers, neo-communists, and communists working in the film industry.

In actuality, it was not Milt, but his wife Git who realized the potential for a bookstore specializing in film-related items. The concept arose when a retired motion picture publicist named Ted Taylor sold his collection to the store. However, as Milt explained it in 1978, taking full credit,

> The great novels are over with, they ended with the 1930s and 1940s. The bright young men today want to make great American film. My specialty was signed copies of Hemingway, Faulkner, Fitzgerald, but business was not so hot, we'd maybe sell one once every three months. So I branched out into the Hollywood movieland whatever books there were on film. When I started to specialize all the other book dealers thought I was insane. They said, "You can't specialize in an area if there aren't any books." I'd like to say

> now that I knew what I was doing, but I never thought it would explode the way it has. I can't keep track anymore, it's become overpowering.[18]

Early customers at Larry Edmunds recall that Milt would be standing in the store while Git would be upstairs on the mezzanine level. Communication would be in the form of shouted questions, answers, and comments to each other. Many years later, a similar and more confrontational style of communication was adopted by Milt's brother, Phil, and bookshop assistant Gwen Feldman. Often it constituted the most entertaining portion of a visit to Larry Edmunds Bookstore until Gwen left to join the staff of the Samuel French Bookstore on Sunset Boulevard.

In the 1960s and 1970s, Milt Luboviski worked out of Larry Edmunds as an appraiser primarily for tax purposes of entertainment memorabilia. A 1964 appraisal of Walter Wanger-owned memorabilia, not limited only to film items, was valued at $1 million. However, a number of his appraisals were controversial and rejected by the Internal Revenue Service, including one in 1973 for Jack Benny. Most notably, Luboviski's appraisal of the library of United Artists-owned films, donated to the Library of Congress, proved most contentious, with ultimately the film company losing its battle with the IRS. However, the amount of money that Luboviski earned from that one appraisal was sufficient to allow him to retire to France, to divorce Git, and eventually to remarry. Milton Luboviski died in the south of France on February 6, 2003, at the age of ninety.

Git Luboviski (died 2017) continued managing the store, working with Milt's two brothers, Din (Eugene) (1929– ?) and Phil (1923–2007). The same day that Mike Hawks was fired by Eddie Brandt, Git telephoned and offered him a job, which he accepted. It was almost a coming-home celebration in that he had purchased his first lobby card, for *Bonnie and Clyde*, from Larry Edmunds when he first started collecting them. After a three-month vacation, Mike joined the staff of four in October 1983. Initially, he handled mail-order sales and occasionally helped Pete Bateman (1957–2008) at the stills counter. When, after twenty-five years, Pete moved on in 2006, only to die of cancer, Mike took over the stills sales. As he recalls, 2006 was a pivotal year in the history of the store:

> Things were getting bad. And it's primarily because of the Internet. The Internet destroyed our shop along with a lot of other business. Everything's going wrong, everything's going downhill. Phil and Din are working less

Mike Hawks welcomes Mary Philbin to Larry Edmunds Bookstore in 1989 (courtesy of Mike Hawks).

> hours. Not that they don't deserve to work less, because they've been there a long time. They're already in their early eighties. They've had enough of the place. Git's already in Malibu hanging out.[19]

With both Din and Phil deceased, in 2007 Git decided it was time to retire, and she handed the store over to the current proprietor, Jeffrey Mantor, who had worked at the store for a number of years after leaving Book City across the street. Mantor is more a businessman than a buff, deeply committed to keeping Larry Edmunds Bookstore alive, and this despite the presence of a tattoo of Rita Hayworth on his left bicep and of Anita Ekberg in *La Dolce Vita* on his right.

Sadly, just as Hollywood Boulevard has changed, so has Larry Edmunds, with perhaps all of the once-rare stock depleted. It no longer stocks plays as it once did, leaving that to Samuel French. In its "golden" years, Larry Edmunds co-published Alan G. Barbour's *Screen Facts*, published voluminous catalogs of rare collectibles, and reprinted D. W. Griffith's 1916 tract, *The Rise and Fall of Free Speech in America*. A visit to Larry Edmunds today will not result in a casual meeting with fellow shoppers like Paul Schrader or François Truffaut. Those days will not return, much as older film buffs

The cover from one of the earliest of Larry Edmunds catalogs (courtesy of Jeffrey Mantor).

might wish otherwise. In part, the problem, or the fault if one will, lies with new film buffs overly attached to the Internet and unwilling to rise up from their computers and support a bookstore that once stood for everything in which a film buff believed.

There is no Paul Schrader and François Truffaut, and there is no Mike Hawks, who quit on September 15, 2014, unable to deal with the craziness of Hollywood Boulevard.

All manner of movie memorabilia, including books and most prominently still photographs (a claimed three million) could be found at Collectors Bookstore, initially located at 1717 North Wilcox Avenue, then located in the old Montmartre Café building on Hollywood Boulevard at Highland Avenue, and later in the Pantages Theatre Building on Hollywood Boulevard at Vine Street. The bookstore was opened in 1965 by Malcolm Willits and comic book collector Leonard Brown. Following Brown's retirement in 1983, Willits had been partnered with former employee Mark Willoughby.

Collectors Bookstore was noted for a generally unfriendly attitude towards customers. If you didn't purchase any still photographs after a couple of files had been pulled, in all likelihood you would not be allowed to look any longer. Mike Hawks recalls an encounter that a friend of his had with Mark Willoughby:

> The guy had a magazine with him, so, of course, they put it behind the counter because you could slip something into it. As you perhaps know, they could be really nasty. If they didn't like you, what you were wearing, the color of your underwear, forget it. You're going to have a hard time. So my friend is not finding anything, and Mark is mumbling under his breath. My friend is in a testy mood, he gets his magazine back, and at just the right moment, he slapped Mark across the face as hard as he could, and he just walked out the door.[20]

In part because of rent increases and competition on the Internet, Willits closed the shop to the public in 2002. The inventory was sold at auction by Profiles in History on December 12–14, 2008, with entire filing cabinets of still photographs on the auction block.

Collectors Bookstore was not the only Hollywood Boulevard shop noted for the attitude of its staff. Hollywood Book and Poster was operated from 1977 through 2015 by Eric Caidin.[21] Regular shoppers included a number from the film industry, such as J. J. Abrams, John Landis, and, of course, Quentin Tarantino. Presumably they were not faced by staff whose faces clearly said, "Don't mess with me, just don't."

There were other Hollywood Boulevard bookstores of interest to film buffs in the golden age of the 1970s: Cherokee (best remembered for its huge comic book holdings), Gilbert's Books (actually just off Hollywood Boulevard on Vine Street),[22] Book City (1973–2005), and Pickwick Books. The latter was basically an all-purpose store selling new books, although the third floor was devoted to used and remaindered titles. It was opened in May 1936 at 6743 Hollywood Boulevard by Louis Epstein (1901–1991), a Russian emigré who was a major figure in Los Angeles bookselling history; B. Dalton acquired the store in 1968, and it closed in 1995. Perhaps Pickwick appealed to film buffs since for many years it was managed by former child star Ted Donaldson (best known for the 1945 production of *A Tree Grows in Brooklyn*).

The New York equivalent of Larry Edmunds was Cinemabilia, whose owner, Ernest D. Burns, has often been described as "morose," although personally I always found him very pleasant and helpful. Burns was certainly somewhat eccentric, and treated his staff imperiously. The difference between the two stores was well summed up by Sol Chaneles: "The Hollywood

Ted Donaldson, seen here publicizing *Once upon a Time* (1944) with Cary Grant and Janet Blair, was the primary reason in later years for film buffs to visit Pickwick Books in Hollywood.

shop is more specialized in books about the movies and the New York City shop is more specialized in movie graphics."[23]

Founded in 1973, Cinemabilia was originally located on Cornelia Street, later moving to 10 West Thirteenth Street in the East Village. The store was a treasure trove of books, periodicals, and all manner of movie-related memorabilia, with a poster for Charlie Chaplin's *Limelight* looming overhead of the store's browsers. Both François Truffaut and Jean-Luc Godard were regular clients on each New York trip. According to the *New Yorker*, the former "bought a treasure trove of magazines and books there" in 1976.

Another visitor to the store in the early 1970s was film buff Ira M. Resnick, who purchased a lobby card from Katharine Hepburn's *Stage Door* for $50 and posters for *Love before Breakfast* and *The Awful Truth* for

$35 apiece. That was the beginning of a collection comprising some 2,000 vintage posters and 1,500 still photographs and lobby cards, which led to Resnick's publishing, through Abbeville Books, a coffee-table volume displaying some of his treasures, *Starstruck*, in 2010.

(Another film buff with a poster collection as impressive as that owned by Resnick is Mike Kaplan, now a resident of Idaho, who had worked in the film industry as a publicist and producer. In 2014, through Lagoon Press, he published *Gotta Dance!: The Art of the Dance Movie Poster*.)

*New York* magazine complained of "the off-hand, sometimes rude manner of the people who worked there,"[24] but perhaps its reporter was unaware with whom he was exactly dealing, for Cinemabilia was a legendary breeding ground for punk rockers. "Everyone who worked there was like a seminal figure in the punk rock movement," commented one chronicler of East Village life.[25] The manager was Terry Ork (died 2004), band manager and record producer of new wave/punk rock music in the mid-1970s. Punk music legend Richard Hell was in residence, along with Richard Lloyd and Robert Quine. It has been suggested that cinemabilia was essential to the East Village punk community.

Cinemabilia published catalogs as detailed and as magnificent as those from Larry Edmunds Bookstore. Just how many there were is in question in that only two volumes seem to survive, Volume IV (1972) and Volume VII (1980). Were there any more, or were Ernest Burns and Cinemabilia enjoying a private joke at the expense of those with a well-organized mindset. Cinemabilia also distributed Paul Scaramazza's privately published 1974 paperback anthology of reviews from *Photoplay* in the 1920s, *Ten Years in Paradise*, the first volume for which I wrote an introduction.

Cinemabilia closed in 1993, falling foul of the tax man, who always expects his share, even from film buffs.

Chapter Eight

# THE SILENT MOVIE THEATRE

THE SILENT MOVIE THEATRE HAS A HISTORY AS CONTROVERSIAL, LURID, and squalid as any silent film melodrama. It boasts a cast of characters who might equally be at home in such a silent film if dramas of that era actually included male prostitutes, drug addicts, pedophiles, copyright infringers, fantasists, and hit men. However, the reality is that the only well-known film to have a scene set at the Silent Movie Theatre is William Castle's 1959 horror film *The Tingler*, and it seems that perhaps the shots supposed to take place there were not really filmed in the theatre. The only shots recorded at the Silent Movie Theatre were audio rather than visual, and from a gun used to kill the then-owner.

It all began in either 1919 or 1920 when a nine-year-old boy in Oklahoma City went to his local movie house and saw an episode of the serial, *Elmo the Mighty*, starring Elmo Lincoln and Grace Cunard. "I never really outgrew the love for silent films I acquired during that period," reminisced John Hampton six decades later. "They were a separate and distinctive art form, and I was afraid that they would be forgotten and lost when talkies became popular."[1]

Born in Oklahoma City in 1910, Hampton, with his brother Gilbert, began presenting movie shows in his family's living room at the age of thirteen, using a 35mm Powers projector and films scavenged from the trash bins outside local movie houses, from film exchanges, and from the next door neighbor, Phil Isley, who was a local distributor. Isley's daughter, Phyllis, was also later to gain fame in Hollywood under the name of Jennifer Jones.

During the Depression of the 1930s, after an apprenticeship at local movie houses, Hampton acquired a 16mm projector and "old" 16mm prints, and toured small hamlets across Oklahoma presenting movie shows to communities that had no access to a theatre. Hampton also worked as a printer and at hand-painting movie posters for local exhibitors. In 1934, he married Dorothy Beatrice McBrayer (1914–2000).

An early photograph of John and Dorothy Hampton (courtesy of Marc Wanamaker/ Bison Archives).

In the late 1930s, John and Dorothy had decided to open a theatre devoted strictly to silent films in Oklahoma City, but it proved financially impossible, as did a proposed theatre in Miami. Instead, the couple moved to Los Angeles in 1940, obtained a bank loan, and purchased a lot at 611 North Fairfax Avenue in what was to become primarily a Jewish neighborhood in the city. Work on building the aesthetically unappealing 200-seat or so theatre began the following year, and on February 25, 1942, it opened its doors, identified not as the Silent Movie Theatre but simply with a sign reading "Silent Movies." The first presentation was Cecil B. DeMille's *King of Kings*, somewhat early for what became its usual Easter presentation around town. Admission was 5¢ for children and 10¢ for adults, and there were two identical programs a night, consisting of a feature film, serial, and selected short subjects, at 7:00 and 9:00 p.m.

John Hampton tried, without success, to rent 16mm prints from the Museum of Modern Art. As it was described by a writer in the early 1950s:

> He made a special trip to New York. He was told it would not be possible for him to use the Museum's films because his Silent Movies was neither an educational institution nor a not-for-profit film society and hence was classified as "commercial" by the Museum. Hampton offered to show the

> films free. The Museum said that would increase the prestige of his commercial undertaking. Compared with Silent Movies' low admission price and studied avoidance of competition with regular theatres, no film club is less commercial. Hampton is the only person in Los Angeles showing silent movies without the help of the Museum of Modern Art.[2]

Dorothy took charge of the box office and combined candy concession. Her husband took care of front-of-house advertising, operated the projector, and handled the playing of suitable musical accompaniment. Throughout his tenure, Hampton always utilized 78 rpm records and two turntables; there was never any live musical accompaniment. In addition to his presentation work, John Hampton also served as the janitor, sweeping inside and outside of the building.

During the war years, John Hampton apparently was registered as a conscientious objector. Information as to what happened during the period is confused and contradictory. One story has it that within months of opening, the theatre closed while Hampton was sent to a detention center, returning in 1946. This is patently untrue in that the *Los Angeles Times* published a story on the Hamptons and their theatre, very much open, in the spring of 1943. Another story has it that Hampton, as a conscientious objector, distributed subversive, antiwar literature, was arrested, and sentenced to five years' imprisonment, subsequently reduced to two.

The Hamptons probably lived only slightly above the poverty level, occupying a small apartment above the theatre. "They lived like packrats," said one friend, "It got to the point where you literally couldn't walk except along a narrow path they'd cleared out."[3] As Hampton explained,

> We try to avoid the academic approach of a museum. Our approach has always been to try to recreate the same sort of atmosphere that silent theaters had originally.
>
> We present the films in a dignified manner, without resorting to burlesque.
>
> It's a hobby actually. It's something we'll never get rich at but we make a living and we feel we're doing something that ought to be done.[4]

Unquestionably, the exhibition of silent films, from another era, appealed to the devoutly religious couple. They refused to open the theatre on a Sunday, and in 1943, promised audiences "Clean Pictures Always—Fun for the Family!"[5]

Although always known as the Silent Movie Theatre, the sign across the front of the building actually read "Old Time Movie," and at some point the last "e" disappeared. Hampton had no particular incentive to refurbish the sign, and so the Silent Movie Theatre remained, as far as passersby were concerned, "Old Time Movi."

The failure to replace the "e" is indicative of the impoverished circumstances under which the Hamptons ran the theatre. What money John Hampton had available was presumably spent in acquiring screening prints. He was to a large extent an amateur film archive, editing multiple prints together to create one good one, and using his bathtub as a makeshift processing tank. As he explained to Philip K. Scheuer, film critic of the *Los Angeles Times* (April 10, 1966), "I have put together a picture from as many as eight prints." For many decades, it was claimed that Hampton's print of the original release version of Lon Chaney's *The Phantom of the Opera* was the best in existence. Perhaps because of the hard times he and Dorothy had faced during the Depression, Hampton was cautious when it came to spending money; he did not take out insurance on the building and its contents, and he chose not to purchase health insurance for either himself or his wife.

The auditorium always showed signs of ill-care. The wooden seats were so uncomfortable that anyone in the know brought their own cushions.

Aside from some Douglas Fairbanks features, including *Robin Hood* (1922), D. W. Griffith's *Intolerance*, and Lon Chaney's *The Phantom of the Opera* and *The Hunchback of Notre Dame*, generally, the silent films presented by John Hampton were not major features, but rather program pictures and minor fare, including a number of Thomas H. Ince productions from the early 1920s, such as *Soul of the Beast* (1923) with Cullen Landis and Madge Bellamy, and Universal films, such as *The Home Maker* (1925), actually a very good production starring Alice Joyce and Clive Brook. Hampton would always advertise the film, using the name of its director and promoting it as "King Baggot's Masterpiece," a somewhat dubious claim but nonetheless an amusing one.

He was certainly unconcerned that any of the films might be deemed politically incorrect. Thus, for example, in June 1948, he screened *The Birth of a Nation*, and was proud that audiences lined up from the theatre, along Fairfax Avenue and as far north as Melrose Avenue. Later, another owner promised two screenings of *The Birth of a Nation*, the first in August 2000 and the second in August 2004. Each time, the screenings were canceled because that owner claimed he received personal threats and warnings that the theatre would be destroyed. The announcement and cancellation garnered

The Silent Movie Theatre in its early years (courtesy of Marc Wanamaker/Bison Archives).

much publicity in the *Los Angeles Times*, whose reporters apparently could not understand a publicity stunt when it was so patently obvious.

The film prints that John Hampton was acquiring were not limited to silent films, or, more precisely, to traditional silent films. In addition, Hampton had acquired a collection of films relating both to adult and to child pornography. If confronted as to his collection on the latter, he would explain that he was working for a private organization investigating child pornography and that it was necessary to examine all the relevant evidence. As one individual who did see Hampton at work commented, "But was it necessary to keep looking at those films?"[6]

The one child unmentioned by either John or Dorothy was a son, born in 1962, who was mentally retarded, and was to spend his entire life as a public ward in state-run mental hospitals.

By the 1960s, attendance at the Silent Movie Theatre was down, but the semi-empty theatre did attract the attention of a number of drug dealers and their clients, who found its empty back rows were ideally suited to a business unrelated to silent motion pictures. Whether John and Dorothy Hampton were aware of what was taking place is unknown, but they would presumably have welcomed the extra business, and certainly they did not participate in the profits made from the drug dealing. It should also be noted that Dorothy apparently had no knowledge of her husband's porno film collection.

Along with the drug dealers, the Silent Movie Theatre did attract a number of celebrities. Hampton would point out that Mae West would sometimes be in attendance, seated between her chauffeur and her bodyguard, and that Clara Bow was a frequent visitor, as were Roscoe "Fatty" Arbuckle's first wife, Minta Durfee, Alan Hale Jr., Will Rogers Jr., and John Drew Barrymore. Jetta Goudal decided to present a tribute to herself at the Silent Movie Theatre, programming two of her lesser features from the 1920s and providing her guests with valet parking. It was perhaps the only time such a service had been on offer at a theatre which did not even boast a parking lot.

The silent Movie Theatre also drew the attention of a less desirable entity in the corporate person of Paramount Pictures, which noticed that it had been screening its 1923 copyrighted film, *The Covered Wagon*, on a number of occasions, in March 1942, November 1948, and January 1952. With a planned remake in discussion, a Paramount attorney contacted Hampton on April 21, 1955, and advised him that any exhibition of his print of *The Covered Wagon* would constitute an infringement of Paramount's copyright. Hampton ignored Paramount's warning and exhibited the film in his theatre on April 27, 1955. Paramount sent him a telegram, again warning him and ordering him to desist from any further screenings. Again, Hampton ignored the notification from Paramount and continued to screen *The Covered Wagon* for the remainder of the week.

As a result, Paramount filed a complaint against John and Dorothy Hampton. At a non-jury trial, the Hamptons were found guilty, enjoined from exhibiting *The Covered Wagon* for profit without Paramount's consent, but no damages were awarded. In response, rather than letting the matter drop, the Hamptons filed an appeal, claiming, accurately, that on February 21, 1938, they had purchased the 16mm print from the Kodascope Library, which had acquired rights to the film through a 1927 agreement with Paramount. The Hamptons had been screening this print, along with other Paramount films acquired from the Kodascope Library not only at the Silent Movie Theatre, but also in road shows in Oklahoma. Ultimately, an appeals court ruled, in June 1960, that the agreement related to non-theatrical distribution and exhibition and not commercial exhibition as practiced by the Hamptons.[7]

Perhaps as a result of the lawsuit, John Hampton took it upon himself to remove the studio logos not only at the front of all the films he projected, but also from the end titles. Thus, an M-G-M feature would never begin with the roaring lion.

Hampton did, however, screen *The Covered Wagon* once more, this time in February 1962, with receipts from the screenings given to the Pacific State Hospital for the Mentally Retarded in Pomona, where the Hampton's son was a resident.

Some years after Hampton's death, *The Covered Wagon* was again at the Silent Movie Theatre, in May 2003, in the form of a 35mm print loaned by Paramount (which was presumably paid a fee). Introducing the film was veteran Paramount employee and occasional producer A. C. Lyles (1918–2013), a colorful character in that he claimed always to know just about everyone from the past, particularly those under contract to Paramount, and to have enjoyed a more illustrious career than in real life. A. [Andrew] C. [Craddock] Lyles was a true film buff, unconcerned about reality. He spoke as if he had been at Paramount at a time when its roster of stars included Gloria Swanson, Marlene Dietrich, and Pola Negri, when in truth his connection with Paramount dated back to 1928, when he worked at the company's Florida Theatre. It was not until 1937 that he joined the studio as an office boy. In later years, he would always claim to have been Adolph Zukor's office boy, ignoring the reality that Zukor was unlikely to have had his own personal office boy, and that the former Paramount head worked out of New York and not Los Angeles.

In later years, Lyles became a semi-official greeter at the studio, brought out whenever a prominent visitor was there. Towards the end of his life, Paramount kept him in the background, in all probability because of complaints of harassment from some of the female staff.[8]

Operating costs, plus illness, perhaps occasioned by Hampton's close proximity to nitrate film and to various developing and dying chemicals,[9] led to the Silent Movie Theatre's being closed in 1980. The official explanation was that the Hamptons had left Los Angeles to return to Oklahoma for the funeral of Dorothy's mother. The closure was announced as only temporary, with plans to reopen in April 1981, after refurbishment, repainting, and replacement of the outside sign. The Hamptons spent a couple of years in Oklahoma, and upon return to Los Angeles they again took up residence in the apartment above the theatre, which remained closed. The couple generated some income from renting clips from their films for use in documentaries and television commercials. In the summer of 1988, Hampton claimed in an Associated Press story that he was about to reopen the theatre.

John Hampton died in May 1990, and Dorothy, apparently suffering from Alzheimer's disease, moved next door, into the King Solomon Home for the Elderly. It was John Hampton's wish that the Silent Movie Theatre be sold—perhaps to the King Solomon Home for the Elderly—and that the money raised be used to pay not only for Dorothy's care but also that of the son about whom everyone appeared to have forgotten.[10] It was not to be thanks to one man, a fantasist, a charlatan, a fraud, who was praised by many, but who had apparently known John and Dorothy for many years and claimed to be regarded by them as nothing less than a son. His name was Laurence "Larry" Austin.

His biography was completely false, but it was one accepted by many in the Los Angeles media, by film buffs, and by those who should have had the intelligence to know better. He claimed that his father was Albert Austin, a British comedian who had worked in silent films and was a member of Charlie Chaplin's stock company, and that his mother was Cecil B. DeMille's personal tailor. In reality, his mother was a seamstress and his father a gardener, who despised his son for being gay. Austin was a student at Fairfax High School, across the street from the Silent Movie Theatre, and he became a regular visitor there, and certainly became close to the Hamptons. As one writer noted, "Larry was the son the couple didn't have,"[11] but, of course, the Hamptons did have a son.

Just as he was dishonest in terms of his background, so was Austin dishonest in real life. In 1972, he was sentenced to five years of probation for embezzlement of $6,000, and again in 1983, he was sentenced to two years in jail for embezzling $42,500.

Larry Austin was good at what he did, which was insinuating himself into the good graces of film buffs and, more importantly, Dorothy Hampton, who was persuaded not only to permit Austin to reopen the theatre in January 1991, but also signed over the property and its contents (valued at $2 million) to him in 1993. Under Austin, working with volunteers, the Silent Movie Theatre was certainly refurbished and improved in terms of ambience, seating, and projection. The sign above the theatre read again "Silent Movie." From 1992 through 2009, organist Bob Mitchell (1913–2009) performed at the Silent Movie Theatre on a regular basis. Austin would insist on personally introducing the film, proudly walking down the aisle to the front of the theatre to the strains of the "Pomp and Circumstance March" by Edward Elgar. Many in the audience cringed at such presentations, much as might have Sir Edward a century earlier. "The place was a sanctuary," said one of Larry's disciples, "and Larry was the high priest." Perhaps

Larry Austin (courtesy of Marc Wanamaker/Bison Archives).

most importantly, on a human level, Larry Austin brought back new life to Dorothy Hampton, escorting her as often as possible from her assisted-living facility to the Silent Movie Theatre, where she would take her place at the box office, selling tickets and candy. Austin and Dorothy were honored in April 1991 with the first Max Laemmle Award "for recognizing and promoting film as an art form."

Larry Austin was a con man, nothing more or nothing less. He was "a larger-than-life figure, with a flair for the dramatic. Thin and tall with a receding hairline, he projected a persona that was at once regal and comical."[12]

As indicated, Austin was not a physically attractive man, and relied on young, male prostitutes for sex. Apparently, a favorite "scene" for Austin was his wearing one of Dorothy's old dresses while performing a sexual act on the hired help.[13] Sometime in the summer of 1990, James Van Sickle visited the theatre, offering his services as a handyman, met Austin, and the two became lovers. Austin presumably knew something of Van Sickle's past, including a charge of attempted murder in Compton in 1988 and a jail sentence in Orange County in 1989 for selling drugs. Reporters Ron Russell and Victor Mejía point out,

> Austin wasn't the first older man Van Sickle had taken up with. In the summer of 1983, he moved into the Bel-Air estate of a real estate tycoon, ostensibly as a handyman but also as a lover provided with luxury accommodations and a handsome allowance, court records show. The affair didn't last. Two weeks before Christmas that year, he attacked his host with a hammer, tied him up, dragged him to the basement, and made off with several thousand dollars and the man's Mercedes. He went to jail after pleading guilty to assault with a deadly weapon.

One knowledgeable witness described the Austin-Van Sickle relationship as one of love-hate. In April 1996, Austin went to the police, accusing Van Sickle of assaulting and robbing him, but the next day the two were together at the theatre as if nothing had happened.

On January 17, 1977, the feature presentation at the Silent Movie Theatre was F. W. Murnau's 1927 classic, *Sunrise*, reportedly Larry Austin's favorite silent film. The supporting program included the Larry Semon comedy short, *School Days*. Generally, it was no laughing matter when Larry Semon was on screen, and it definitely was no laughing matter that night, when a member of the audience, later identified as nineteen-year-old Christian Rodriguez, walked out of the auditorium and up to the box office/candy counter. He drew a .357 revolver from his jacket and demanded, "Give me the money." Larry Austin handed over the takings, amounting to little more than $200, placed them in a white canvas bag, and handed the bag over to Rodriguez. The latter shot Austin in the face, then shot twenty-one-year-old Mary Giles, who was working at the concessions counter, in the chest, and finally shot Austin twice more also in the chest.

The gunman dropped the bag, ran through the auditorium, firing at the ceiling, and exited through the rear doors of the theatre. Organist Dean Mora stopped playing, and ran up the aisle into the lobby, while audience members either cowered in their seats or attempted to leave. James Van Sickle, acting as the theatre projectionist that evening, came out of the booth, and disappeared, leaving Mora to pull the plug for the projector from its socket and to turn on the house lights. Shortly thereafter, police from the Hollywood Division arrived, along with paramedics.

A firsthand account of what happened is provided by Valerie Yaros, the historian for the Screen Actors Guild, who was present that night with her boyfriend Russ:

At about 8:15 or 8:20 p.m., I notice someone take the aisle seat to my right—since my purse was on the floor between us—I turned to see who it was. I was not comforted. He was a young Latino who, although very clean and tidy, was dressed a little too suspiciously for my comfort. He wore a black driving/racing cap turned backwards and just slightly oversized black clothing. His actions were not at all suspicious, but he was very definitely out-of-place, and not the type of person who goes to this theatre . . . I surmised he'd wandered in off the street, found no one at the box office, and decided to come in and sit down.

It unsettled me since he was only one seat away, and my first thoughts honestly were "You're not getting my purse" . . . As the minutes ticked by *The Golf Bug* [a silent *Our Gang* short] was not getting any funnier. The young man still sat impassively watching the screen and, I thought to myself, that he was quite brave sitting through any of it. I hoped it wasn't his first exposure to silent films.

He sat for a total of around five minutes, and then abruptly got up and passed through the black curtain into the lobby behind us. My first thought was "don't like this sort of thing, eh?" but my second thought and feeling was of relief . . . I can relax again. I immediately rescued my purse.

Now the third short, *School Days*, was showing on the screen. Perhaps two minutes had passed and I'd entirely forgotten about my former seatmate.

BAM!!!!!! A pause of a second or two, then BAM!!!!!! BAM!!!!!! BAM!!!!!!

A commotion to my right—someone has run through the curtains separating the lobby from the audience, and has stumbled almost to the floor. It's my former seatmate. . . .

I don't know how to react to it . . . no great panic has broken out, and Larry Semon continues mugging across the screen . . . My seatmate stumbles down the aisle, trying to regain his balance and, when he is upright again, and running, raises his left arm into the air and fires a gun: BAM!!!!!! BAM!!!!!! . . . I hear no projectile and believe this has to be an act, and there are blanks in the gun. . . . The contrast between what is on screen with what is running down the aisle is grotesque.

Dean Mora, the organist, has stopped playing, and in a flash races up the left aisle into the lobby. The seconds pass, and he reappears . . . under a framed portrait of Lillian Gish announcing "Mister Austin has been shot."[14]

Based on a description from Mary Giles, police arrested Christian Rodriguez. Shortly thereafter, James Van Sickle was also arrested, and he was identified as being the orchestrator of the crime, paying Rodriguez $25,000 to kill Austin and a further $5,000 to kill Giles, in order to make it appear a robbery gone wrong. The two men went to trial on January 4, 1999; both were found guilty, sentenced to life imprisonment without the possibility of parole. The most heinous aspect of the crime was Van Sickle's wanting a totally innocent woman, Mary Giles, also to be killed in order to prevent the appearance of a targeted killing of his lover.

(There is another murder associated with the Silent Movie Theatre, which is generally overlooked, and that is of Harry Major, a film buff who helped Larry Austin clean up the theatre prior to its reopening. Harry Major was an openly gay man, a former and popular teacher at Hollywood High School, who had a bad habit of corresponding with often-violent prisoners, inviting them to stay with him upon their release on the understanding they have sex with him. One of those ex-cons, Scott Kralian, killed the eighty-two-year-old Harry Major on February 10, 2015. As another ex-con said of Major, "He had a dangerous habit that finally caught up with him.")[15]

Following Austin's murder, the first revelations as to his past began to come to light, but film buffs paid little attention, and their estimation of him remained high. The front of the Silent Movie Theatre became a shrine to his memory, with flowers, photographs, and testimonials. He was buried at Forest Lawn Memorial Park, Glendale, in January 1997, with a marker reading, "The Silent Master." It seemed as if nobody previously had acknowledged the art and history of the silent film—at least as far as the sycophantic film buffs were concerned. One critic wrote,

> For obvious reasons, Los Angeles has always attracted a huge number of silent-movie fans motivated by nostalgia, scholarship and love for an extinct but powerful art form. These fans have supported and come to depend on the Silent Movie's programming.[16]

The whole sorry story was published on a regular basis on the website "The Silents Majority: The Online Journal of Silent Film," an excellent, now-defunct site maintained by film buffs Diane MacIntyre and Spike Lewis.

In a handwritten will, Larry Austin left his estate to James Van Sickle, who could not inherit as a result of the murder conviction. A legal battle over the Silent Movie Theatre was about to ensue, with LAPD bunco detectives and the Los Angeles County Public Guardian's office claiming that Austin had defrauded Dorothy Hampton, who was perhaps suffering from Alzheimer's disease, when she gave the theatre to him on January 25, 1993. John Hampton's brother, Gilbert, maintained that the Public Guardian should protect the estate for Hampton's son, now a thirty-five-year-old retarded man in a state hospital. "We have no interest in receiving any money for ourselves," Gilbert Hampton told the *Hollywood Reporter* (April 3, 1997), "but to see that it goes toward taking care of my brother's son and his mother." Opposed were Larry Austin's relatives, from whom he was estranged. The Internal Revenue Service was also involved, claiming a financial interest in Austin's estate.

Aside from the theatre, also in dispute was a collection of 2,000 films, which were taken into the custodianship of the UCLA Film and Television Archive. Earlier, in the 1980s, John Hampton had been forced to sell a reported 1,000 films to billionaire David W. Packard in order to pay various medical expenses. Rumors abounded that Hampton, who generally owned two or more prints of many films in his collection, did not sell the best versions to Packard, retaining those for later use himself.

Eventually, the courts ruled that Austin did legitimately own the theatre and its assets, and his heirs went ahead with disposing of the building. The remaining films were sold at auction by Butterfield & Butterfield (now Bonhams) on May 23, 1999. It was, by all accounts, a most haphazard sale, with shorts sold in groups of as many as eighty-five and as few as eighteen. Feature films were similarly sold in groups, with no regard as to similarity of title. One lot of eleven titles included sound features, such as *Singin' in the Rain* and *Shall We Dance*, along with silent program pictures, such as *The Volga Boatman* and *The Marriage Circle*, and Harry Langdon's classic *Tramp, Tramp, Tramp*. The group sold for $1,300. Many buyers discovered missing reels from their features replaced with odd reels from other features, and there was general confusion as one purchaser attempted to marry a missing reel from his lot with a lot containing that missing reel sold to another. It was not Butterfield & Butterfield's finest hour.

Also on sale were still photographs, posters, and other memorabilia. John Hampton's collection of 3,700 78 rpm recordings sold, as a group, for $2,500.

Charles Lustman (born 1965) on the surface seems ideally suited to be the new owner of a theatre that has attracted so many unusual characters. He had, apparently, lived in Copenhagen for a number of years writing English-language songs for Danish performers, who must, presumably, have had a problem with mainstream English-language songs. He returned to the United States in 1999, tired of his Danish career, and settled in Santa Monica, California. In search of a falafel on Fairfax Avenue—as one does—he caught his first glimpse of the Silent Movie Theatre in a state of disrepair. Utilizing credit cards and with his mother's help, he purchased the building and its contents for $650,000, explaining to the *New York Times* (January 11, 2000),

> I have no idea what I'm doing, I'm just doing it. But Hollywood was built on the backs of these silent-movie pioneers, and it's something that I think needs to be appreciated. . . . I'm just some guy who doesn't know squat about silent movies who drove by and bought it on a whim.

If nothing else, Charles Lustman was a good publicist. He knew how to promote himself, boasting of how he had revived the Silent Movie Theatre and posing in a style that went out of fashion during the silent era, sometimes wearing the type of cap adopted by newsboys of the 1910s and 1920s. "Nobody's me. Nobody has my personality," he claimed.[17] Initially, Lustman insisted the theatre was haunted by the ghost of Larry Austin: "We had an American Indian ritual guy come here—a shaman. He was burning [sage] everywhere. He did the entire theater, every corner, for three hours. And then we put rose crystals down where Laurence was murdered. And we sat there and tried to cleanse the whole thing."[18]

The Silent Theatre reopened to the public, yet again, on Sunday, November 7, 1999, with Chaplin's *Modern Times*, followed by *The Jazz Singer* on November 9, and Mary Pickford's *My Best Girl* on November 10 and 11. In the first two months, it was obvious that Lustman was playing it safe, running well-known, popular silent features, such as *City Lights*, *The Kid*, *The Son of the Sheik*, *Steamboat Bill, Jr.*, and *The General.*

Dorothy Hampton was no longer at the box office and concession stand, although she did not die until January 2000, at the age of eighty-seven.

Generally, the film buffs turned against Lustman, claiming he was interested only in box-office returns and self-promotion, and that he and his personality might be better suited to running a nightclub. He introduced evenings of 3-D films, which were commercially successful, but which many argued were inappropriate to the theatre. Prior to the first such evening in 2000, Lustman walked into a display case, sustaining a black eye, and had one of his projectors cease functioning minutes prior to the screening. He was dealing with "the unhappy ghost of John Hampton," he explained to any reporter foolish enough to listen. He also hosted a tribute to Larry Austin in January 2000, screening *Sunrise*. There were outside bookings with the theatre's hosting weddings, wrap parties, and bar mitzvahs.

Ill health and declining box-office receipts resulted in Lustman's selling the theatre in the autumn of 2006 for a reported $2.9 million, to two brothers, Sammy and Dan Harkham, who operated it through their nonprofit organization, "the Cinefamily," and who changed the programming yet again. The concentration now was on esoteric new and old films, independent and avant-garde subjects, with an occasional silent feature. The Silent Movie Theatre now seated a comfortable 158 audience members, and also operated a small café on the premises. Admission was $10.

Sexual harassment allegations (which first surfaced in 2014) were made against Cinefamily executives in the summer of 2017, and the organization "temporarily" shuttered its operations at the theatre.

The Silent Movie Theatre remains into a new century, despite a checkered, controversial history and the suggestion that it is cursed. The only difference is perhaps that it is no longer a center for film buff activity in Los Angeles.

Chapter Nine

# SEX AND THE FILM BUFF

SO HERE IT IS, THE CHAPTER TO WHICH EVERY FILM BUFF (AND PROBABLY quite a few academics) have turned to first with mounting interest and excitement. Will it satisfy? Probably not. But then, most film buffs are used to that when it comes to matters of sex. I recall one female film buff, naming a couple of films buffs in Los Angeles, with whom she had been to bed, and complaining that all they thought about during the encounter was themselves. What did she expect?

When film buffs get together for sex, it is generally a matter of having a shared interest—aside from the actual sex. Herb Graff was once at a screening of a Kay Francis film at New York's New School and needed to visit the toilet. Hidden within a cubicle, he heard the entrance of two film buffs. Both were excited at the star's performance, with film buff number one telling of his Kay Francis collection. Film buff number two responded that he actually owned one of Kay Francis's dresses, adding, "If you come home with me for the night, I will let you try it on."

A shared hobby does not always lead to a shared personal life, as Mike Hawks recalls of a friend who

> had made contact with a fellow collector out of state who had similar interests, the same person that she collected. This guy moves to California. They become friends. She trusts him enough that when she's out of town for any length of time he's got a key to feed a pet. Then something happens. She comes home one night late, goes to bed, there's an earthquake. She's startled, gets up, turns on the light waiting for an aftershock. There isn't one. Because she gets back into bed, the bed starts to move, but there's nothing else moving in the apartment. This guy was under the bed, laying there, fully clothed. I guess he must have been waiting for her to come back home, fallen asleep, and while asleep moved around. So she orders the guy

> out of her place. The police arrive, and it turns out the guy was sitting in his car outside her building, waiting for who knows what. This is really nuts.[1]

One member of the Huff Society named Ariel Berlin tried unsuccessfully to persuade William K. Everson to invite him to Everson's "private" Saturday night screenings. Everson had the good sense to ignore Berlin's request. In July 2005, Berlin, who collected popular sheet music of the past, placed an advertisement with a telephone dating service, requesting a gay encounter. He was invited to an apartment in the East Village by a twenty-six-year-old man who suggested Berlin might enjoy "playing" with him and his five-year-old daughter. Berlin was met at the door by the man, dressed in female attire, and holding his daughter's hand. Berlin subsequently stripped and touched the child's vagina as the father watched.

The distraught film buff subsequently told his therapist what he had done, was arrested on July 29, 2005, and in September 2006, Berlin was sentenced to a five-year prison term.

Sex generally is not a topic of major interest among film buffs—except perhaps for ruminating as to whether a particular actor is gay. Leonard Maltin in reminiscing about Movie Star News wrote of talking to Paula Klaw: "We were talking to the sister—the sister—of Irving Klaw, fabled pornographer and purveyor of naughty photos. We were just interested in stills of Laurel & Hardy. We'd never heard of Bettie Page."[2]

Movie Star News might have represented the Holy Grail to movie buffs, but its proprietor, Irving Klaw, was a legend to those interested in soft-core adult photographs of women in various stages of undress and bondage. It was an area that Klaw catered to in the 1940s and 1950s to such an extent that he became synonymous with BDSM photographs, and yet it was not a field in which he had the slightest sexual interest. As two Internet writers have it,

> Irving Klaw holds a strange and yet central place in the history of heterosexual BDSM in the 20th century, in part because of the curious paradoxes in his life. He was a non-kinky person who produced and sold arguably more BDSM imagery than anyone before or since. He became a symbol for the cause of sexual freedom, and a martyr to anti-sex initiatives by the Federal Government, yet he was non-political, uninterested in activism and never intended to be a martyr for anything. Klaw was a businessman, motivated primarily by the ambition to earn money. And yet, somehow, in the course of a couple of decades, Irving Klaw created a small empire

EYEFUL
Glorifying the American Girl
PDC
ARE YOU BROAD-MINDED?
See page 24
BETTIE PAGE

around a vast range of kinky people, sex industry workers, and outside artists that profoundly influenced the world of kink as today's BDSMers know it.[3]

From 1947 onwards, the marketing of vintage movie stills became secondary to a mail-order business devoted to SM/fetish photographs, shot in a third-floor studio above Movie Star News. By the mid-1950s, Klaw claimed to be earning more than $1.5 million a year, in large part thanks to one featured lady, Bettie Page, who began working for him in 1952, and who "looked beautiful in bondage and looked beautiful putting other women in bondage. She gave spankings and received them. She looked great in fetish gear and even better in a leopard bikini."[4]

In January 1955, Bettie Page was featured as a *Playboy* centerfold, but within three years she had quit her original chosen profession, found God, and had a major breakdown, resulting in incarceration in a California mental institution. There is not necessarily a correlation between the last three. In the 1980s, there was a revival of interest in Bettie Page, she became the subject of a major 1997 biography, and the tragic events of her life became public knowledge. Bettie Page died in December 2008 at the age of eighty-five. Before her death, she was the subject of two feature films, *Bettie Page: Dark Angel* (2004) and *The Notorious Bettie Page* (2005), with Irving Klaw played in the first by Dukey Flyswatter (real name Michael David Sonye) and by Chris Bauer in the second.

Irving Klaw's activities had been the subject of FBI investigations as early as 1950. In 1955, a committee headed by Senator Estes Kefauver examined the connection between teenage vandalism and pornography, and accused Klaw of contributing to the delinquency of minors. In 1963, Klaw and his brother-in-law, Jack Kramer, were convicted of conspiracy to use the US mails for the distribution of pornography. Movie Star News continued, but Irving Klaw's days as a pioneer of BDSM/photographs were over. He died in 1966.

What Irving Klaw had on offer to his clients was very mild and offensive only in terms of political correctness and implied violence to women. What one writer for *Films in Review* had on offer was nothing less than hard-core pornography. The writer was Larry Lee Holland (1948–1986), who contributed a number of first-rate, well-researched pieces to the journal, including career articles on Francis X. Bushman (March 1978), Florence Lawrence (August–September 1980), Clifton Webb (April 1981), Lila Lee (November 1984), Mary MacLaren and Katherine MacDonald (April 1985), and Warner

Oland (June 1985). When he was not providing his services without charge to *Films in Review*, Larry Lee Holland, who resembled a surf boy with his blonde hair and tanned and muscular body, was providing enthusiasts of gay pornography with full access to his body, at least on film, in a number of hard-core porno efforts.

There is little written about Holland, who has sadly been forgotten both for his pornographic career and his prominent career articles in *Films in Review*. He was always affable and friendly, willing to share his research, and a regular visitor to the Margaret Herrick Library of the Academy of Motion Picture Arts and Sciences. His presence there did worry at least one female librarian, who noticed Larry's friendly assistance of a teenage boy, who was also a regular user of the library. I can well recall her expressing concern that the relationship was getting too close, and asking me if there was some action might be taken. There was none, and it was not necessary. Larry kept his two "lives" completely separate.

He did have a close friendship with an older gay man, DeWitt Bodeen, with whom he co-wrote a February 1979 piece in *Films in Review*, "Neptune's Daughter," on Annette Kellerman and Esther Williams (who portrayed her in a bio-film). DeWitt would sometimes stay with Larry and his partner, a very possessive, slightly older man, apparently a lawyer, and reported back on the wild parties that would take place, without, it might be noted, DeWitt's participation.

Rick Sandford (1963–1995) was not perhaps as well known among film buffs as Larry Lee Holland, but he was certainly one of them, as well as a porno star and something of a hustler.

Born in Denver, Colorado, he was passionate about motion pictures, as his journals indicate, and this intense fascination led to his coming in 1969 to Los Angeles, where he obtained work as an usher at Grauman's Chinese Theatre and found work as a researcher for Robert Osborne on his *50 Golden Years of Oscar: The Official History of the Academy of Motion Picture Arts and Sciences* and Ronald Haver's *David O. Selznick's Hollywood*. In true film buff fashion, he kept a list of every film he had seen.[5]

Rick Sandford was obviously willing to offer, although perhaps not sell, his body to interested gay parties within the film community, including (as I can testify) director Curtis Harrington. He became friendly with both Christopher Isherwood and his partner, Don Bachardy, consulting with the former as to his potential as a writer, and offering sexual favors. Don Bachardy provides a nude sketch of Rick Sandford in the 1983 book *October*. In *October*, Isherwood writes of Sandford,

Larry Lee Holland.

> Rick is an ardent student of films. He can talk for hours about the work of actors, directors, cameramen and art directors; he is equally intense in discussing his likes and dislikes. . . .
>
> Rick has recently produced a massive (448 pages) typewritten script which he has called *A Movie Compendium*. It lists the 2,160 films he has seen between January 1, 1963 and December 31, 1978.[6]

As an actor, Rick Sandford had worked primarily as an extra in some Hollywood films. He was more prominently featured, as Benjamin or Ben Barker, in a group of gay porno films, including *The Boys of San Francisco*

Rick Sandford.

(1981), *Rear Deliveries* (1982), and *A Night at Halsted's* (1982). His one and only major contribution to literature is the 2000 novel *Boys across the Street*, identified as by a gay porn star about a gay porn star. It was described by a reviewer in the *Chicago Tribune* (February 2, 2000) as "a flamboyant memorial to a brash but winning personality."

Rick Sandford has some recognition within the gay community. Sadly, the same cannot be said of Sam Frank, who has no recognition anywhere today, despite a highly fascinating and almost scurrilous double life as both a film buff and something very much else. Sam Frank's life was a lonely and tragic one. He had little money, could not drive, and was generally reduced to hitchhiking around Los Angeles from a North Hollywood apartment building, where he earned a small pittance as little more than a janitor. (Briefly, he came up in the world when I saw him working at Staples in Studio City, California.)

As a film buff, indeed as a human being, Sam Frank was a highly emotional man and not one to hide his feelings. His complaints in 1996 in regard to the US Postal Service failing to deliver mail to his North Hollywood apartment led to complaints to, and a subsequent story in, the *Los Angeles Times*. Again, he turned to the newspaper, when Groucho Marx died, writing in a letter published on August 30, 1977, "The news of Groucho's death made me so sad I cried. I never met the man, but I felt as though I had lost a close friend."

Groucho Marx may have been special, but no actor was more important to Sam Frank than Ronald Colman. He had obsessed about the star of *Lost Horizon* since 1965, and eventually in 1997, this fixation resulted in a somewhat staid, reference work, *Ronald Colman: A Bio Bibliography*. It was wrote Sam Frank in his introduction the culmination of "29 years of obsessive love and research."[7]

"Obsessive" is an adjective that barely describes Sam Frank's approach to anyone who might listen to him and might have the potential to be his friend. Patricia King Hanson, editor of the *American Film Institute Catalog*, never met Sam Frank, but she did commission him to write some essays for *Magill's Survey of Cinema*, which she was editing in the late 1970s. As a result, Frank would telephone her at home at all times of the day and night. He was at his worst after the death of his father, often telephoning Hanson at 2 or 3 a.m. In the end, her husband was forced to take the telephone calls and tell Sam Frank never to make contact again.

"The weird guy. He just was so bizarre, really bizarre," recalls Rudy Behlmer. "One time I went over to Pacific Pioneer Broadcasters and I had an appointment to look at some stuff. He walks in and he comes over and starts talking about something irrelevant. I'd say, 'Excuse me, I only have an hour-and-a-half.' Finally, I just got up and left. I got a call later from Pacific Pioneer Broadcasters saying they were awfully sorry."[8]

Joan Cohen was associate film programmer at the Los Angeles County Museum of Art, and remembers, "Sam Frank always wanted to write program notes and would call me and complain all the time about how badly he was treated by Ron Haver, Ron was a hack, etc. Sam tried to turn his love of film into a writing career but he was a very unpleasant person and put people off—still he was on the guest list."[9]

Ron Haver would come on stage to introduce the evening's film, a model of affability. There in the audience would be Sam Frank, raising his hand. Ron would stop, sigh, and ask with trepidation, "Yes, Sam?"

Leonard Maltin recalls,

> I was always accessible when I lived on the East Coast because I never had an unlisted number. One day I got a letter from this fellow, Sam Frank, in Los Angeles, the gist of which was that he was a big admirer of my *Movie Guide*, articles I'd written . . . He's even written about it in some local California newspapers. We're about the same age, so I appreciate your success all the more. Then, all of sudden, there's this sharp turn in the letter: Why shouldn't I too enjoy this success. It was this strange turn of tone from one of a fan letter, admirer, to someone who was openly jealous and borderline hostile.
>
> Well, it was my habit to answer every letter. Also he's reviewing my book somewhere, so it would be unwise to ignore him. I wrote back, said thank you very much for your kind words, and I wish you great success in your career. Then he wrote me again, and I did not feel obliged to answer his second letter. I didn't want to carry on a correspondence. Then he wrote me a third time, chastising me for not answering. So I wrote back again, and said please understand I don't have a secretary or an assistant and it's hard for me to keep up with mail. Then I started getting telephone calls from him. One time he called me, choking back tears, his father had died. Why would he choose to call me? I felt sorry for him. I tried to give him what consolation I could. Very odd. But "very odd" is how you would describe Sam Frank.
>
> When I got married, [my wife] Alice would usually pick up the phone and when she heard it was Sam Frank, she would say, "Oh, I'm so sorry, he's at a screening." Sometimes he would keep her on the phone for ten minutes. Then one time he called and said he was going to be visiting New York and looked forward to meeting us. She said, "Well, Sam, I think we're going to be traveling down to the Jersey shore that week." He said, "Well, I can take the train and come with you."
>
> Well, sure enough, a couple of weeks later, we were out in the afternoon and went back to our apartment building, which did not have a doorman. And on the bench inside was a letter from Sam Frank. He had gotten into the building. This is not a good feeling. I don't think he was a violent character, but still it was not comfortable that he had gotten into the building. Thank goodness we weren't home.

> He would have been pathetic if he was not so obnoxious. It's easy to say from a distance that he was sad, but he was so annoying so obnoxious, so off-putting that it was hard to feel sorry for him for long. He was one of the strangest people I ever met.[10]

Anyone who had any modern involvement with Ronald Colman and his films could expect to be approached by Sam Frank, often in highly emotional fashion. Robert Gitt's preservation/restoration work includes the Frank Capra-Ronald Colman version of *Lost Horizon*. He remembers a typical inappropriate Sam Frank moment: "He used to come to the UCLA screening, the Preservation Festival. I got there one time and he said, 'I just love to hear you speak. It's so wonderful. You don't know very much. And you don't speak very well. But you do it anyway.'"[11]

In addition to Ronald Colman, Sam Frank had an obsession with Vincent Price. Any event at which the actor was appearing would have Sam Frank in the audience, and Price became so familiar with him that he would yell at him to leave.

Sam Frank managed to bamboozle *Daily Variety*'s longtime editor, Tom Pryor, into hiring him—a big mistake. One day, one of the paper's staffers goes into the men's room, finds a billfold on the floor, picks it up, and opens it to find the identity of the owner. What he finds inside are checks for "Sam 'Hung Like a Stallion' Frank."[12] That marked the beginning of the end of Sam Frank's career at the trade paper.

In 1986, Sam Frank published *Sex in the Cinema*,[13] intended in part as a sequel to Parker Tyler's somewhat more intellectual volume, *A Pictorial History of Sex in the Cinema* (1974). It was dedicated to a small-time actress named Veronica Hart, whom Frank identified as "honey," and J. David Kiser, who "knows my guilty pleasures and understands them." Just what were those "guilty pleasures," Sam Frank does not reveal. However, he does note that the swinging sixties involved "the search for well-endowed men of any race by single and married women."[14]

It may be no more than a passing reference but it opens a door into the secret life of Sam Frank, otherwise known as "Jim Boyd." At some point probably in the 1970s, Jim Boyd (as we will now call him) founded the Hung Jury, otherwise known as the "big cock club," with membership limited to those with eight inches or longer. Members received mailers addressed to "Dear Hung Dude," and were encouraged to share their sexual activities with others. Membership was limited to heterosexual males, although one correspondent to the LPSG (the Large Penis Support Group, founded in

1999) suggested that Jim Boyd used the information to masturbate at 2 a.m. in his "run down Hollywood Apartment."[15]

Jim Boyd/Sam Frank would actually solicit membership among celebrities. A letter exists, with a row of erect penises along its bottom edge, suggesting to Stevie Nicks of Fleetwood Mac that he was well equipped to join the Hung Jury. Of course, Stevie Nicks is a woman.

The Hung Jury published an occasional offset-printed newsletter titled *Measuring Up*, and also had a Mistress of Measurement named Christine Carlisle (which may very well be a pseudonym). As she explained, "a gentleman must have at least eight inches. . . . I measure them and verify that."[16] Jim Boyd claimed eight inches, with five-and-a-half inches around.

He was, as LPSG member, thirteenbyseven wrote, "a short rotund Jewish social misfit." He was forty pounds overweight, five feet, four inches in height, wore unattractive spectacles, dressed poorly, and as British comedian/television presenter Jonathan Ross said of him and his group, if it wasn't for their size, they "wouldn't get anyone to go near them."[17]

Aside from appearing in a filmed documentary program with Jonathan Ross, Sam Frank was also booked for an American program with a disastrous result, as Leonard Maltin recalled,

> He agreed to be on a panel on one of those smarmy television talk shows that was being shot at CBS Television City. He arrived at CBS and was so nervous that he shit his pants. Things had to be done, some emergency procedure had to be taken in order to get him on the show and remove the odor from the hallways.[18]

Sam Frank died in the late 1990s, post-1997—I have been unable to determine the exact year—and was apparently in his mid-forties. He was a highly disturbed individual, always aggressive apparently because as a child he had been taught that was the only way to get attention.

## Chapter Ten

# ORGANIZED FILM BUFFS

A NUMBER OF FILM BUFFS HAVE TRIED, WITH LIMITED DEGREES OF SUCcess, to create their own film institution or film museum, often with high pretentions but low professionalism. After all, if a movie star can become president of the United States, then what boundaries cannot a film buff cross? It might be well-meaning and homey, such as the Rosemary Award Association, the creation of a former Washington, DC-based actor named Thomas Fulbright (1908–1981), generally referred to, outside of his hearing, as "Fruity Fulbright," for what must be obvious reasons. First presented in 1970 and continuing into the 1980s, the Rosemary Awards—"Rosemary" for "remembrance"—were intended to honor actresses from the silent and early sound eras. Tom Fulbright, a kindly man, would often call upon me to make the presentations, which generally took place in the individual's home without publicity. Indeed, the only silent star I can recall who insisted upon my arranging for the presentation to be at the least the subject of a news item in *Hollywood Studio Magazine* was Jetta Goudal.

New Yorker Miles Kreuger (born 1934) had been collecting all manner of memorabilia relating to the musical on stage and screen, and so, in 1972, incorporated himself as the Institute of the American Musical. On a whim almost, he relocated to Los Angeles. The highlight of Miles's holdings is the Ray Knight collection of 16mm "home movie" footage of New York musicals, shot through the years without permission. Being, as the *Los Angeles Times* (February 13, 2005) reported, "a raconteur of considerable charm," Kreuger is a film buff happy to share his archives and his knowledge with just about anyone.[1]

Only a block away from Grauman's Chinese Theatre on Hollywood Boulevard, in a former bank building, a film buff and collector named John LeBold (1939–2012) opened the Hollywood Museum (not the first to use that name but certainly the first actually to be a functioning museum). Here he displayed what was described as the "Hollywood Legends Collection," with items borrowed from Paramount, including costumes worn by Marlene Dietrich in *Shanghai Express* and Gloria Swanson in *Sunset Blvd.*[2] The museum survived, if not exactly flourished, for two years, from 1983 to 1985.

Aside from borrowing costumes from Paramount, it seems that LeBold also "borrowed" from others. In the 1970s, he had been hired as curator of the Debbie Reynolds Collection, and while there he had allegedly removed some 600 items from Warner Bros., leading to his arrest and charge of larceny in 1980.

With the true resilience of a film buff, John LeBold was undeterred, and moved himself and his collection to New England. He had the audacity to offer his collection for sale on eBay for $2.5 million, resulting in a March 2000 lawsuit by first Warner Bros. and then Debbie Reynolds. The current disposition of the "Hollywood Legends Collection" is unknown, although what is left, after the return of various items to their legitimate owners, is perhaps for sale.

After acquiring a considerable quantity of movie memorabilia, some of it rather worthless, Don Schneider (1923–2014) founded the Electric Theatre Movie Museum, Inc., in Los Angeles in 1979. His efforts at establishing the museum on a firm financial footing, or even with a building to house the collection, went nowhere, and in 1994, Schneider moved his operation to Owosso, Michigan, taking over an abandoned church on North Water Street, with the exhibits lacking any identifying labels, but open to the public for a donation of between $5 and $12. After his death, others began selling off the collection in February 2015 on eBay and elsewhere.

Somewhat more ambitious was Doug Wright, who put together a collection of equipment, posters, photographs, lobby cards, props, and some three-dimensional objects, and founded the Motion Picture Hall of Fame. He began collecting at the age of eleven in his native Pittsburgh. In Los Angeles, he always claimed to live a double life, working by day as a motion picture promoter and at night as a collector:

> If you work in the movie industry, there are two things that can bring the kiss of death. One is to let it be known that you have acting ambitious. If you do, then everybody thinks you are using your job only as a stepping-stone.
>
> The other is to be a known collector of motion picture artifacts. Then, if anything is missing, they think you took it.[3]

Like Don Schneider's dream, the Motion Picture Hall of Fame was to be established in Hollywood, but Wright was forced to cut back on his

In 1981, even François Truffaut was persuaded to accept an award from Doug Wright's Motion Picture Hall of Fame.

plans, and in June 1971, he opened the Old Time Movie Theatre and Motion Picture Hall of Fame in the converted banqueting room of the Saga Motel on South Harbor Boulevard, across the street from Disneyland in Anaheim, California. The space was divided between the museum and the forty-eight-seat screening facility with films projected in 16mm. Despite the location and lack of publicity, Wright did attract some surprising celebrities. I was present in March 1973, when he screened *King Kong* for its producer-director, Merian C. Cooper, and one of the film's special effects team, Marcel Delgado. The audience was minimal, and after the film was over, half a dozen of us, including Cooper, adjourned to a local coffee shop, where we were regaled with stories about the making of film, and where the waitress was impressed enough by the guests to ask Merian C. Cooper for his autograph.

The Old Time Movie Theatre and Motion Picture Hall of Fame closed later in the 1970s. Doug Wright continued with his main business, which was the promotion of local "paper" shows, usually at the Glendale Civic Auditorium.

Florida-based Ray and Sharon Courts were later the leading presenters of similar shows, which also featured celebrities selling their autographs. The first of the Courts' shows was held at the Beverly Garland Howard Johnson Hotel[4] in North Hollywood in June 1991, and there were also later shows in Chicago. The last show took place in October 2011, but the concept was revived by the Courts in September 2014 with the Celebrity Fan/Fest at the Burbank Marriott Hotel.

A fascinating glimpse into one of the shows in 2007 is provided by a reporter for the *Los Angeles Times*:

> From the moment fans started filing in, this is clearly about making money. It is an old school, cash box on the table, sure-we-can-break-a-hundred action. Most stars bring a helper to make change and take orders. Signs clearly spell out the deals, like specials on a deli blackboard: Pee Wee Herman (actor Paul Reubens) autographed photo: $30. Your item signed: $30. Your premium item (i.e. collectible figurine) signed: $40. Digital photo of you and Pee Wee: $40. The gathered stars pay the Courts nothing. Vendors pay for booth space, but for celebrities the day is 100% profit (an attractive selling point for enticing bigger names).[5]

Sally Struthers is there, with a fixed smile as she is ordered to sign in the lower corner of a photograph with a black sharpie, name only. An eBay rather than a Kodak moment. Adam West is happy to sign, but his manager refuses permission for the *Times* to photograph the *Batman* star. Even a star's demise does not prevent his or her presence in some form, as evidenced by tables devoted to memorabilia from the late Yvonne De Carlo and the late Don Adams.

The son-in-law of Ray and Sharon Courts is Packy Smith, a film buff closely associated with the Western genre, who honed his hobby, the collection of Westerns, into a business with the Nostalgia Merchant and Cumberland Video, as well as the founding of the Memphis Film Festival in 1972.

There are film buffs who have, with intelligence, turned their hobbies into careers within the industry. Among those active in the field who might be designated film buffs are Sam Sherman,[6] heavily involved as a producer and distributor in low-budget production, and the English-born brothers

Richard (1925–2011) and Alex Gordon (1922–2003), with the former working in New York as a distributor and the latter active in various capacities in Los Angeles. The most famous of Alex Gordon's activities, at least as far as film buffs are concerned, is the supposed preservation of hundreds of early Fox and Twentieth Century-Fox productions. In reality, the preservation work, if it can even be identified as such, was shoddy, and Gordon was more active in making 16mm prints of the studio library for various film collectors. The ultimate tragedy is that if a film was incomplete, Gordon would discard if after making a 16mm reversal print for his friend, William K. Everson. As a result, all that survived of a "lost" Frank Borzage film from 1929, *The River*, was Everson's print. At least, Everson was cooperative, and when I was with the American Film Institute in the early 1970s, I was able to arrange to have a 16mm negative made from that print for the Library of Congress. When Twentieth Century-Fox, in 1976, discovered what Alex Gordon had been up to, he was fired, escorted from the lot, and never allowed to return. Alex had organized the British Gene Autry fan club, and after being summarily dismissed by Twentieth Century-Fox, he joined the Gene Autry Organization.

Ronnie James was an Orange County, California, collector of television programming who turned his archive into a type of stock footage library. Jeff Joseph, another collector, founded SabuCat Productions as a stock footage library and was also involved in selling films through advertising in *Big Reel* and in the launching of a 3-D film festival in Los Angeles. Rick Mitchell (1946–2011), a foley editor, was a mine of information on the technical history of the cinema, which he shared with readers of *American Cinematographer*, *Films in Review*, and other publications.

New Yorker Eric Spilker (born 1939) also had a substantial film collection, specializing in Technicolor prints. He would also host Deanna Durbin sleepover parties for male films buffs. The audience would dress in night attire, while Deanna Durbin films played on screen to varying degrees of interest from the assembled company. Spilker's screening at his studio apartment would sometimes attract stars such as Kitty Carlisle, who showed up, dripping diamonds and furs, in a chauffeur-driven car, pleased to have the opportunity to see again a film she had made in the 1930s. In 1972, Spilker was able to negotiate a contract with Twentieth Century-Fox to reissue the 1943 Carmen Miranda film *The Gang's All Here*, and, perhaps equally importantly, was able to have Technicolor produce new dye-transfer prints. Best known for the phallic symbolism, involving gigantic bananas in the "The Lady with the Tutti-Frutti Hat" number, *The Gang's All Here* opened at New York's Murray Hill Theatre, and proved to be a highly successful reissue, so much so that Spilker negotiated with the Library of Congress to acquire a 35mm print of a public domain Barbara Stanwyck feature, *Lady of Burlesque*, and added that to the Spilker Film Company's library.

I do not believe that Marvin Paige (1927–2013) ever escorted Kitty Carlisle very much, if at all, but if not, she was surely one of the few stars and leading ladies of the past that he had not latched upon. It is difficult to describe or discuss Marvin, who was both liked and actively disliked in equal measure. He was not an attractive man, and there are certainly rumors circulating as to his casting methods, which unfortunately I have been unable to prove or disprove. Few will talk for the record.

Richard Lamparski, who first met Paige in 1955, when he was booking the radio show, *Lunch at Sardi's*, maintains that most people in the industry were aware of the casting couch on which Marvin Paige insisted good-looking, young actors perform. According to Lamparski, Shirley Temple always referred to Paige as "Uriah Heep."[7]

Marvin was a casting director, whose credits are sometimes in doubt, but who definitely cast ABC's *General Hospital* from 1980 to 2006, and was generally to be found escorting the soap opera's best known and aging matriarch, Anna Lee, around Los Angeles—in later years, in a wheelchair. He was a celebrity wrangler, providing elderly actresses, such as Anne Jeffreys, Joan Leslie, and Ann Rutherford to events, and keeping a close watch over them. The closest comparison is perhaps that of a pimp to his prostitutes, but with a little more (but not a great deal more) class. The celebrities of the past would always respond to Marvin's demands in large part, one suspects, because with his job as a casting director, they held out the hope that he might find them roles. Finally, Marvin was a resource for photographs and other research materials through his company, Motion Picture & Television Research Archive, housed in his San Fernando Valley home. Shortly after his death, there was a burglary at his home and many items in the collection were stolen, including the painting of Laura from the 1944 film of the same name. The bulk of the Marvin Paige collection was sold by auction house Profiles in History in June 2016.

Howard Mandelbaum (born 1950) is noted for a different type of library, one specializing in the licensing of still photographs. New York-based Photofest, cofounded by Mandelbaum and Carlos Clarens (1930–1987), is a familiar name to anyone purchasing a film book, for which it has provided so many illustrations for editorial use. Its owner is an addictive collector, but also an organized one, and he uses the licensing of his photographs to raise money to purchase more. He recalls,

Marvin Paige with Anna Lee.

> My friends were influenced by Andrew Sarris and *Movie* magazine from London. We carried a paperback edition of *The American Cinema* [by Sarris] and checked off movies after seeing them. When I helped run film societies, it was satisfying to show movies without reputations. We didn't limit ourselves to lauded directors, showing pictures made by Don Weis, Richard Quine, Phil Karlson, lots of action specialists. That was the golden age of 16mm and a tremendous number of films were being offered by companies like Films Inc. and Universal 16. I worked at the latter in 1971 and recall when *Touch of Evil* went from the budget category, renting for $15 to International Film Classic at $75.[8]

Howard Mandelbaum and his partner, Roger McNiven, would host film screenings at their apartment, and later McNiven opened a commercial theatre, the Thousand Eyes at 425 West Forty-Third Street, between Ninth and

Tenth Avenues, which demonstrated a penchant for the films of Anthony Mann and Nicholas Ray, and survived for a brief six months. As fans of Andrew Sarris, both Mandelbaum and McNiven appreciated the auteurists.

The *Star Wars* franchise has attracted all manner of followers, fans, buffs, and collectors. Described as "without doubt the most successful and renowned *Star Wars* fan collector"[9] is Stephen J. Sansweet, who as of 2009 owned 55,352 items relating to the *Star Wars* series. For fifteen years, until his retirement in 2011, Sansweet served as Director of Content Management and Head of Fan Relations at Lucasfilm. He also created the Rancho Obi-Wan, from a former chicken farm in Sonoma County, California, at which to display his collection. As Lincoln Geraghty rather delightfully describes him, Sansweet has risen from "poacher to gamekeeper, moving from collector to curator."[10]

Similarly, the horror genre attracts its own peculiar breed of film buffs, and their high priest was, and remains, Forrest J [James] Ackerman (1916–2008; he never used a period after the "J" in his name), who had been a literary agent (representing Ray Bradbury among others), editor and publisher of *Famous Monsters of Filmland* (1958–1983), and a major collector of horror and science fiction memorabilia. The latter was housed in the Ackermansion, the Son of Ackermansion, and the Acker-mini-mansion (as he called his various Los Angeles homes). He remains a subject of adulation to many, although I must confess that I found him rather boring, but then I am obsessed neither with horror or science fiction films. Certainly, he knew how to generate an income from his hobby. "I remember going over to the Ackermansion," recalls Rudy Behlmer. "I got a couple of pictures from him, and he said that was $250 a still—just to copy. I thought this guy has to be out of his mind. I think eventually he said, 'You can have that one for $120.' I just thought, this guy is weird."[11]

Any film buff or film enthusiast growing up in the 1950s, 1960s, or 1970s owned copies of Daniel Blum's *A Pictorial History of the Silent Screen* (Grosset & Dunlap, 1953) and *A Pictorial History of the Talkies* (1958). There may have been earlier, similar volumes, such as Deems Taylor's *A Pictorial History of the Movies* (1943), but there was nothing quite like these two coffee-table books by Daniel Blum. They were at once fun to browse and sources of reference, and little wonder that they were reprinted many times by other publishers. And, as I grew more interested in theatre, I discovered that this extraordinary man, Daniel Blum, had also compiled *A Pictorial History of the American Theatre, 1900–1951* (Greenberg, 1951), which was also revised and reprinted through the years.

Forrest J Ackerman.

Just who was this ultimate of ultimate film buffs, who apparently had turned a hobby into a career? Daniel Blum (1900–1965) had first become fascinated with the theatre at the age of ten, and began compiling scrapbooks on the plays and stars that he saw. He embarked on a career as a theatre producer in 1929, while still collecting and expanding his hobby to include the motion picture. One of his favorite stars was Clara Kimball Young, and he dedicated one volume of his annual *Screen World* to her and dutifully sent her inscribed copies of other editions.[12]

By 1949, Daniel Blum had a full-time staff working with him, producing the annual *Theatre World* from 1944 and *Screen World* from 1949, with a year off in 1950. *Opera World* followed briefly, from 1952 to 1954, as did *A Pictorial History of Television* in 1959. A young actor named John Willis (1916–2010) joined company with Daniel Blum, initially as a typist on *Theatre World* after service in the navy during World War II. He took over Blum's editorship after his death,[13] and also founded *Dance World*, which was published from 1966 to 1979. Like Blum, Willis was gay, and like Blum, Willis was perhaps more of a stage buff than a film buff—but you wouldn't know it from what the two men created on the printed page.

A handsome Richard Lamparski photographed in 1974 with Diana Cary, better known as "Baby Peggy" (courtesy of Richard Lamparski).

Richard Lamparski does not consider himself a film buff, but he is someone who quite definitely understood film buffs and how to market his work as part of their culture. Through his interview shows on radio station WBAI and, most importantly for posterity, through the *Whatever Became Of . . . ?* books, published by Crown in eleven volumes from 1966 through 1989, Lamparski proved himself the "connoisseur of has-beens,"[14] not just those in the film industry but from many other areas of American culture, including music, sports, and theatre. Lamparski's inspiration was the song "The Rochelle Hudson Tango" from *Ben Bagley's Shoestring '57*, sung by Dody Goodman.

Long before publication of his books, Lamparski conducted his first interview in 1959 with actor Richard Cromwell—"a very dull interview," he comments.[15] His last interview never actually took place. It was Thanksgiving 1989, and he was in Paris, scheduled to interview Cecile Aubrey. On the journey to her home, he was on the subway, got confused and canceled. "My career was over, and that was God whispering in my ear."[16]

Because of his good looks, Richard Lamparski discovered that many former stars appreciated being with him. He was "the ultimate leading man who liked being with older women." The first such woman was silent star Aileen Pringle; "she was fifty-eight and I was twenty-two."[17]

In Los Angeles, a telephone caller to his home would be greeted with the message that this was Richard Lamparski speaking, "from the heart of Hollywood, a city that has no heart." Copies of his books would always be inscribed with one simple and meaningful word, "Peace." I recall with pleasure dinners with him, Charles Higham, and Curtis Harrington at Hamburger Hamlet on the Sunset Strip. I still enjoy talking with him by telephone, recognizing that we will never actually meet again. In 1989, Lamparski moved to Santa Barbara, and it led him into a life of solitude. Since 2001, he has not socialized in person, never been to a movie theatre or a restaurant. As he recalls, he was standing in line at the beginning of 2001 at his local stationary store, waiting to purchase the annual "day-at-a-glance" diary. There was a line and it was moving slowly. Suddenly, Richard realized there was no point in waiting in line to acquire a book he did not need. He was not going to socialize again. "I decided I wanted to spend all of my days by myself. . . . A very nice feeling after a life of people."[18] He is "a voyeur, an onlooker"—that is how he looks upon life and as far as he is concerned it has been an interesting one, catering to the film buff fraternity.

Film buffs occupy a wide spectrum of those involved in cinema. A perfect example of this can be found with the 1969 Citadel Press book, *The Films of Errol Flynn*. Here is a book definitely aimed at the film buff market, and its three authors are all professionals in the field, and yet all might be classified as film buffs. Tony Thomas (1928–1997) was a noted Canadian broadcaster, musicologist, and author of some thirty books; Rudy Behlmer (born 1926) is a historian with a background in television direction and advertising production; and Clifford McCarty (1929–2005) was also an authority on film music and the owner of a Los Angeles bookstore, Boulevard Books on Pico Boulevard.[19]

Professionals in the museum field are sometimes buffs. An obvious case might be Henri Langlois of the Cinémathèque Francaise, although whether his administration of that film archive can be considered as professional is in doubt. Bob Epstein, cofounder of the UCLA Film and Television Archive, was quite definitely a film buff, but again he had issues with professionalism. Two gentlemen associated with the Los Angeles County Museum of Natural History were both professionals and film buffs. The first is Earl Theisen, who collected motion picture artifacts for a permanent exhibit at what was then called the Los Angeles County Museum in the 1930s, under the sponsorship of the Society of Motion Picture Engineers. Based on contemporary documentation, Theisen's exhibit was worthy but somewhat boring. Far more entertaining was the Movie Gallery, created by John Dewar, after the Los Angeles County Museum had been split into two, with the Los Angeles County Museum of Art moving elsewhere in the city, and the Los Angeles County Museum of Natural History, with all its movie artifacts, remaining in Exposition Park.

John Dewar (1912–2004), who was also responsible for the creation of the William S. Hart Museum at the cowboy star's home in Newhall, California, had been a curator in the museum's History Department and set up a Movie Gallery in the late 1960s, featuring some of the incredible artifacts that had survived at the museum, including Lon Chaney's makeup kit, Mary Pickford's curl, Harold Lloyd's glasses, Buster Keaton's porkpie hat, Chaplin's costume from *Modern Times*, and much more. Amazingly, from today's perspective, John had been forced to hide much of this memorabilia around the museum to avoid its being discovered and discarded by an uncaring museum bureaucracy.

At this point, it might be appropriate to discuss film buffs who became academics. It might be appropriate, but also something of a pointless exercise as most film academics lack the essential emotion necessary to be a film buff. Through the years, I have met a few that have some of the traits identified with film buffs, most notably John Belton, whose film collecting instincts make him quite definitely a film buff, and Richard Koszarski. One academic who is proud to be considered also a buff is Gary Rhodes, whose books cover a variety of subjects and some of which are very much film buff-oriented.[20] As he sees it, he would hope to be considered a film buff first, a film historian second, and a filmmaker third. He writes,

> I grew up in what was basically the last generation of little kids who just had the three networks and PBS, just before VHS hit. Most everyone got home video around 1984 or 1985, when I was 12–13 years old. Before that, if you wanted to see anything, you watched those networks and caught old movies/B&W films all the time. It was amazing. I think home video, the cable TV explosion, etc. meant that everyone just a little younger than me experienced very different viewing in their formative years. And for me, it was a family experience . . . my mother loved Universal horror films during the original Shock Theatre days, and they gripped me as a youngster.

Academic film buff Gary Rhodes with Carla Laemmle (courtesy of Gary Rhodes).

I do know a small number of film buffs in the world of academia. . . . I'd include William K. Everson, of course, and looking to the distant past of folks I didn't know, I'd say Merritt Crawford . . . reading his papers [at the Museum of Modern Art] leads me to think that. These are folks who, like me, seem to glow when talking about movies they love. They have passion and like me, find that passion leading them to research, as well as collecting things like movie posters.

Most academics seem not to be all that interested in cinema, many having outward disdain for film history, others using it for career aims. Quite a few are interested in theory only, and have seen very little of the cinema.

This is certainly my view. I love films and knew as a kid (age 12) reading your work, [Kevin] Brownlow's work, and Everson's that I wanted to be a film historian . . . to devote my career to it. Academia for me has only been a way of making that happen.

In terms of academia, I really don't understand it. Were most academics always devoid of passion for the cinema, even though they went into Film Studies as a career? Or did academia drain them of their passions? In some cases, I'd tend to think the former, as I meet very young academics who seem to have no interest in film at all.[21]

Gary Rhodes is actually repeating something written by legendary critic Pauline Kael: "I underestimated the ability of academics to squeeze the life out of a subject."[22] Kael would probably insist that fans cannot be scholars and vice versa, and yet Rhodes is proof that they can.[23]

Another academic-cum-film buff, with similar interests to those of Gary Rhodes, is Arthur Lennig (born 1933), the author of *The Immortal Count: The Life and Films of Bela Lugosi*, first published in 1974. Arthur was truly eccentric and most dedicated to cinema.[24] Long retired, he was for many years one of the most popular professors at the State University of New York at Albany, in large part perhaps because he never acknowledged the existence of political correctness. He could be found at William K. Everson's Saturday night screenings, usually making very pointed and non-complimentary comments on the other guests, their dress, hygiene, and lack of social graces. Good taste prevents my writing too much about Arthur, but I would note that my most persistent image is of him striding down the street, a cigar in his hand, discoursing on an esoteric aspect of film history, with a female student (with whom he would be in a relationship) trying to keep pace a few yards behind, struggling with two heavy pieces of luggage. Every so often, Arthur would stop, turn around, and demand that the acolyte please keep up.

There is one other very pointed image, and that is Arthur's accompanying Richard Koszarski to the film study department at the Museum of Modern Art, where the latter had an appointment. As Arthur was seen approaching, the head of the department slammed the door in his face and bolted it. I know of no one else ever being physically prevented from entering a film institution, but then Arthur and the Museum of Modern Art never really got along. He was too much of his own man to become part of a clique.[25]

To paraphrase William K. Everson, paraphrasing D. W. Griffith, "Truly Arthur Lennig's life ran in a quaintly way."[26]

Chapter Eleven

# JOE FRANKLIN

ACCORDING TO RICHARD LAMPARSKI, JOE FRANKLIN ALWAYS SAID THAT he would retire after interviewing Garbo. Well, Franklin did eventually semi-retire in August 1993, after 21,425 broadcasts over WWOR-TV (formerly WOR-TV), despite never quite accomplishing his goal, with perhaps the biggest star that he ever interviewed being Barbra Streisand, who appeared on WOR-TV with him on February 14, 1963, along with Rudy Vallee and Jack LaLanne. If anything, it was a typical Franklin mix of guests, and what may be considered a typical assortment of advertisers, Chase & Sanborn Coffee, Fleischmann's Margarine, and Royal Gelatin, all of which were promoted with typical Joe Franklin aplomb. There is something very surreal at looking at photographs from old Joe Franklin shows, with Ethel Waters, Leopold Stokowski,[1] and Salvador Dali, seated behind a display of Nabisco Shredded Wheat.

The last group may be considered some of the greatest celebrities one could entice to appear on a talk show, but as Franklin's son, Brad, explained,

> People always commented that Joe Franklin was the only truly accessible celebrity. Anyone could (and everyone did) walk off the street right into his office and hang out with him. His two telephones rang continuously and he loved answering them. Sometimes it was his childhood pal Tony Curtis, or John Lennon, or a wannabe producer trying to raise money for a movie, or a lonely 93-year-old fan in a nursing home, or a lounge singer from New Jersey trying to get on TV. Dad gave them all equal time. And if the lounge singer was persistent and kept calling, he did get to appear on real television![2]

Just as this examination of the film buff begins to a large extent with Chaw Mank, so it seems somewhat appropriate to end it with Joe Franklin. The two men had little in common and yet both were films buffs who turned a hobby, a love of entertainment, into a highly personalized business proposition. Both, in very different ways, catered to other film buffs, understanding a market and an opportunity. In fact, Joe Franklin would boast, with some conviction, that he was in large part responsible for the nostalgia craze. Popular culture perhaps began with him.

Just as Chaw Mank reveled in his running of so many fan clubs, so did Joe Franklin enjoy being Joe Franklin. His son, Brad, recalls, "You hear of celebrities avoiding paparazzi and the public. Not my Dad! He would stop anytime, anywhere for a photo or for one of his fans. In the middle of dinner he would eagerly push away his lamb chops and sign autographs, tell them jokes, make them happy."[3]

The man who, in the words of the *New York Times*, "became a New York institution by presiding over one of the most compellingly low-rent television programs in history,"[4] was born Joseph Fortgang in the Bronx on March 9, 1926. He had a passion for all aspects of entertainment, and, as a child, would spend most days at a movie theatre in company with his friend, Bernard Schwartz, who later changed his name to Tony Curtis. At the age of nineteen, in 1945, Franklin was hired as a writer and "technical advisor" for Kate Smith's radio show; at WNEW-AM he selected records for *Make-Believe Ballroom* with disc jockey Martin Block,[5] and soon had his own program, *Vaudeville Isn't Dead*. He was also the host of *Main Street Memories* and *Antique Record Shop* on WMCA. He was now Joe Franklin, a name he adopted at the age of twenty-one.

Franklin made his television debut in January 1951 with a daytime show, *Joe Franklin—Disc Jockey*, on WJZ-TV, and the following year, also on WJZ-TV, he began presenting a program of film clips on Sunday evenings titled *Joe Franklin's Memory Lane*. He continued on WJZ-TV when, in 1953, it changed its call letters to WABC-TV. The show was now a daytime program.

*Joe Franklin's Memory Lane* began airing on WOR-TV in 1962, changing its name in 1967 to the *Joe Franklin Show*, and continuing for three decades, moving with the station from New York to Secaucus, New Jersey, where it changed its name to WWOR-TV.[6] The show was available to 2,537 cable stations, with 12 million viewers in all fifty states, Guam, and Puerto Rico, so it could not in any way be identified as simply a New York phenomenon or a program peculiar to that city. In New York initially, the show was recorded in a small studio on West Sixty-Seventh Street, "twice the size of a cab," as Franklin described it, with guests including such illustrious names as John F. Kennedy, Woody Allen, Elvis Presley, Bing Crosby, Dustin Hoffman, Bill Cosby, Paul Newman, Lisa Minnelli, Robert Redford, and Michael Jackson,

Joe Franklin.

as well as newcomers such as Bette Midler and Barry Manilow. Franklin would proudly proclaim that "I never rehearsed my show, never read the authors' books, just glanced at their jackets. I guess I was the only talk show on the air that was not rehearsed."[7]

Joe Franklin's show was aired at various times of the day and night, depending almost upon the whim of the station management. As Franklin once commented, "You needed a compass to find me."[8]

The record for appearances with Joe Franklin belongs to a busy but largely forgotten painter named Morris Katz, who was a prolific guest, having

Joe Franklin with guest Debbie Reynolds.

been on the show some 800 times. Second in terms of appearances is Otto Preminger with 155, followed by George Jessel, with 125, and Rudy Vallee, with eighty-five.

On November 5, 1985, to celebrate his fortieth anniversary in broadcasting, Franklin taped an interview with himself, using a split screen. "This is the first time I've interviewed myself in all those years," he told the *New York Times* (November 5, 1988).

> I got a few questions I'm planning to surprise myself with. I tell you, I'm gonna be incisive, penetrating. I'm gonna hit myself with a couple of heavy ones.
>
> I wanted to get Greta Garbo, Sinatra or maybe Springsteen to conduct it. They weren't available. So I'll have to do the split screener with myself.

Whether the show aired live or was later taped in New York or Secaucus, New Jersey, Joe Franklin maintained his office in Manhattan. The first space

Franklin rented was in the basement of the Hotel Wentworth on West Forty-Seventh Street. From the Wentworth, Franklin moved to 152 West Forty-Second Street, then to a fourth floor space at 147 West Forty-Second Street, and finally to Eighth Avenue and Forty-Third Street (first in a five-room suite and then, after downsizing in 2000, to Room 305).

The Joe Franklin offices were legendary for the amount of unsorted, uncatalogued memorabilia that they contained, much of it gifts from the thousands who had appeared on his show. Among the artifacts were photographs, recordings, films, posters, and all manner of paper memorabilia. The *New York Times* (November 5, 1988) reported, "The room is so jammed with memorabilia that Mr. Franklin can conduct interviews only by opening his office door and seating the interviewer partly in the hall under a sign that says 'Memory Lane.'"

Joe Franklin was a prolific author of titles intended primarily for the film buff market. Aside from a couple of autobiographical volumes, *A Gift for People* (Lippincott, 1978) and *Up Late with Joe Franklin* (Scribner, 1995), and *Joe Franklin's Encyclopedia of Comedians* (Lyle Stuart, 1979), the majority of the books are minor works[9]—with two exceptions. Franklin's first book, coauthored with Laurie Palmer, in 1953, containing a mere sixty-three pages and retailing for $1 in paperback and $2 in hardcover, is *The Marilyn Monroe Story: The Intimate Inside Story of Hollywood's Hottest Glamor Girl*, the first book-length study of the actress.

> It was the first book I had ever written and I was excited that it was coming out.
>
> Well the day it was schedule to be published, Rudolph Field, the publisher died! The book had a much more limited printing and distribution because of Field's untimely death.[10]

In his autobiography, *Up Late with Joe Franklin*, the author maintains that the book was initially co-written with Monroe, but when she had to leave New York for California, the interview sessions with her obviously ceased, and the volume was published as little more than a collection of press releases, blurbs, and publicity stories, with Laurie Palmer the primary author, even if not so recognized on the title page.[11]

As far as most film buffs are concerned, Joe Franklin has his name on only one major volume, and that is *Classics of the Silent Screen*, first published by Citadel Press in 1959. Film buffs would always insist that the book was actually written by William K. Everson, who certainly was responsible for the research, and who is acknowledged at the start of the volume. The true authorship cannot be confirmed, but Franklin's son, Brad, notes,

> Dad did tell me that *Valley of the Dolls* was not written by Jacqueline Susann, but that attributing it to her was a brilliant marketing move. He also had a Yogi Berra-esque saying: "Most bestselling books weren't written by the author who wrote them."
>
> Many years ago Dad came back from a trip to Hollywood, where he had visited a bookstore, possibly a movie or show business bookstore. The owner greeted Dad personally and showed him the sales sheet for *Classics of the Silent Screen*. Dad was amazed, because the sales from that single store in Hollywood exceeded the total global sales reported on his royalty statement![12]

William K. Everson's daughter, Bambi, comments, "I know he ghostwrote the book but it is a 'secret' even when I met Joe Franklin a few years ago and he was introducing me to other people, he was [saying] that my dad helped him write the book."[13]

Just as Bambi Everson has fond memories of growing up with a film buff father, so does Joe Franklin's son, Brad:

> My Dad wasn't perfect, he was nuanced like all of us. But my childhood memories are of a wonderful father and endless fun. He often spent all day with me, just being a dad.
>
> On Sundays he would drop everything and take me to 96th Street and Broadway to let me spend an hour buying a huge stack of comic books.
>
> He would then take me to Playland and for hours give me dimes for the Skee-Ball and pinball machines. . . .
>
> My dad often took me to Coney Island, went on all the rides with me, and we played all the games, especially throwing darts at balloons and winning prizes. We always stayed at the boardwalk all day and rode the subway home together, happy and loaded down with our loot—kewpie dolls, live goldfish and Turkish Taffy.
>
> Best of all were the many days spent in his legendary show-biz office. I was befriended by a utopian collection of characters . . . There was Joe Green and his amazing dog Bee Bee (who could spell and perform mathematical calculations better than most humans) . . . Jack Walsh, the World's Strongest Man, who let trucks run over his chest, lifted motorcycles with one finger, and bent coins with his teeth . . . not to mention baseball players,

belly dancers, magicians, ventriloquists, a man who hypnotized live rabbits, and a dentist who whistled through his nose!"[14]

The demise of Joe Franklin's television show did not mean the end of his career as a broadcaster; he returned to radio, continuing on air almost until his death. In November 1987, Joe Franklin Productions became a publicly held company, marketing everything from sweatshirts to cheesecake, and in 2000, he loaned his name to a restaurant at Eighth Avenue and Forty-Fifth Street, which later housed Joe Franklin's Comedy Club.

In April 2016, an anonymous collector who had acquired various pieces of memorabilia put some of them up for sale at Saco River Auctions, a relatively small company located in Biddeford, Maine. A baseball glove belonging to Babe Ruth sold for $118,000, while a homburg-style hat and harmonica belonging to Janis Joplin sold for $33,000, and Jimi Hendrix's cowboy hat sold for $22,000. In total, the auction generated half-a-million dollars.

When he became a publicly owned company, most of the expensive memorabilia that Joe Franklin had collected passed out of his hands, and it is that which generally appears for sale at auction. Indeed, one has the strong feeling that the overcrowded office which Joe Franklin inhabited contained little of any major financial, or for that matter archival, worth.

A close friend, Cliff Adam, recalls that the memorabilia was considered an asset of the new company and moved by president Gary Paperman to a Pennsylvania storage unit.[15] Son Brad tells that his father had a barn or storage building in Florida, in which was a large collection of 78 rpm recordings and bound volumes of magazines.[16] There was also memorabilia at Franklin's Thirtieth Street apartment.

It was Cliff Adam who helped "revive" Franklin's career after the demise of his television show. He persuaded Columbia Records to release a four CD set, *The Joe Franklin Nostalgia Collection*, on the Legacy label. Franklin appeared on the CVC network and sold some 10,000 copies. Adam also put together Joe Franklin Memory Lane Orchestra, fronted by the broadcaster, who would make a speech and tell a few jokes, while appearing at dinner-dance locations on the East Coast. Also contributing to the evening's entertainment was Misha Dabich, perhaps best remembered for the fifty-one years he was the boyfriend of millionairess Lillian Booth.

If anyone should doubt that Joe Franklin should be acknowledged as a film buff, his autobiography confirms the description, with his comment, "Memorabilia is my number one love."[17] Here he writes of purchasing 16mm film prints from long-forgotten but film buff-memorialized New

York outlets, such as Peerless and Mogul. He acknowledges as one of his best friends, Mark Ricci, owner of the Memory Shop, adding a comment of which any true film buff would approve: "I'd take memorabilia over a love affair. You can always find romance, but you're not always able to purchase the exact memorabilia you're seeking."[18]

Chapter Twelve

# STALKERS

ORIT KAMIR HAS PERCEPTIVELY POINTED OUT THAT FILM ALLOWS ONE TO stalk a film actor or actress without being exposed to their gaze. He continued,

> Film viewers, therefore, practice stalking when they assume their targets' inherent consent. And as the cinematic object is usually a woman, movies train their viewers to pursue women, assuming their implicit consent. Every on-screen woman is always available to the viewer. If the viewer needs reassurance, movies make sure to have their women viewed and stalked on screen by male characters.[1]

The only issue facing the viewer/stalker, and it is really an insurmountable one, is that there is a fixed barrier between the viewer and the object of his/her desire. They are on screen, and you are in the audience, one of an anonymous many. "A permanent distance between viewer and object is inherent to the cinematic experience."[2]

In a sense, all film buffs and film fans are stalkers, but, happily for the objects of their desire, they seldom put their instincts into practice. However, it is a new era for film buffs and stalkers thanks to social media. Technology has made it easier to be a celebrity, no talent required, but, equally, it has made it more difficult for leading members of the film industry to hold onto their privacy. "Stars can attract millions of 'followers' and 'friends' with social media accounts,"[3] but there are consequences. The film buff lurks in a hotel lobby, the doorway of a nightclub or restaurant, by the side of a red carpet at a movie premiere with but one thought in his head: the possibility of a brief moment with *his* star, captured on a "selfie" or through a signature on a photograph or in an autograph book. It is all relatively harmless—part of what being a star requires or, for that matter, what is required of a film buff—but there is always the danger that lurking can so easily turn into stalking. And then what?

One male film buff was fixated with Judy Garland—and not alone in his attachment—but slowly his obsession turned to abnormality. He could not sleep with the "star" as she was no longer around, but he determined on the next best solution to his problem. He would sleep with one of her leading men. Quickly, he began stalking an elderly gentleman who had once been Garland's love interest in one of her 1940s movies. The former star in question was not averse to young male companionship, and the fan achieved his dream. Stalking? Yes. But no harm done in that the elderly gentleman received the best blow job he had had in years, and the star had a close encounter with genitalia that had supposedly once been in contact with Judy Garland.[4]

There are obviously many recorded, and unrecorded, instances of stalking in the film industry dating back to the early twentieth century. In 1936, the *Washington Post* reported on "movie crazy kids" making their way to Hollywood to meet their favorite stars. The Travelers' Aid Society came to the help of many stranded in Los Angeles. When one John Boles fan said that she would not return to her hometown until she had met her idol, the society telephoned the actor, he said to send her over to the studio, gave her an autographed photograph, and she willingly went back to where she belonged. One nineteen-year-old from New Jersey was desperate to meet Errol Flynn. When he read the Flynn played tennis at a specific club, the teenager purchased a racket and hired the court next to the one on which the star was playing. "He met Flynn and told him his story. That was all there was to it; he went back to New Jersey."[5]

Teenagers would arrive at the gates of the studios, desperate to come face-to-face with their favorite stars. One young lady from Oregon insisted that if she met George Raft she would marry him, but he was out of town. Another schoolgirl went to M-G-M, claiming she knew Jean Harlow and William Powell. Alas, the acquaintance was only via the screen, and she was refused admission. One well-dressed young man telephoned M-G-M on some twenty-five separate occasions seeking a meeting with Greta Garbo. Subsequently, he visited the studio every day for six weeks, bringing an expensive bouquet of flowers for the star. "But she never saw him."[6]

One highly persistent early stalker was Albert F. Holland, and his target was Bebe Daniels, a delightful star of both silent and sound films. Holland believed that he and Daniels had known each other as children and that they had married in 1925. In 1931, he entered her hotel room in San Francisco, was arrested, and sentenced to be committed to the Arizona State Asylum. He escaped from there in August 1932, and began to send the

Bebe Daniels shakes hands with Superior Court Judge J. J. Van Nostrand at a November 1931 San Francisco court appearance. Looking on are her attorney E. E. Morris, husband Ben Lyon, and Mrs. Lionel Barrymore.

actress threatening letters. He was again arrested, tried, committed, and then released. After a third confrontation between Holland and Daniels in 1934, the former was permanently committed to a mental institution.

The one positive outcome from Holland's stalking of Bebe Daniels was that she decided to leave Hollywood, and go with her baby daughter, Barbara, to England, where she would star on screen in British films. Eventually, she, Barbara, and husband Ben Lyon decided to stay in England, and became, along with adopted son, Richard, a prominent part of British life, thanks to their wartime activities and the radio series *Life with the Lyons*. The Lyons were always held in fond and high regard.

Two notorious attacks by stalkers involved actresses of far lesser fame than Garbo or Jean Harlow. Rebecca Schaeffer (1967–1989) was a young actress with a handful of television credits and only a couple of screen appearances, including a part cut from Woody Allen's *Radio Days* (1987). She came to fame thanks to her role as the sister of Pam Dawber's character in the sitcom *My Sister Sam*, of which more than forty episodes were aired between 1986 and 1988. Since the start of the series, she had been stalked by a

Publicity shot for *My Sister Sam*, with Rebecca Schaeffer (left) and Pam Dawber.

fan named Robert John Bardo. He wrote her many letters, one of which was apparently answered by a service used by the actress to handle her fan mail. In 1987, Bardo on two occasions attempted to visit the actress at Warner Bros., where she was taping *My Sister Sam*, but he was turned away by security guards.

For a while, Bardo lost interest in Schaeffer but when he saw her in a scene in bed with another actor in *Scenes from the Class Struggle in Beverly Hills* (1989), he determined to punish her for being "another Hollywood whore."[7] He hired a private detective in Tucson, where he was living, to find Schaeffer's home address. After being first turned away by the actress, Bardo

Theresa Saldana.

returned to her Los Angeles apartment, took out a gun and shot her; she was dead within thirty minutes. He was sentenced to life imprisonment.

An earlier stalker named Arthur Richard Jackson had used a similar method to locate the actress with whom he was obsessed, Theresa Saldana (1954–2016). A better-known actress than Rebecca Schaeffer, Saldana had costarred in the television series *The Commish* from 1991 to 1996 and had appeared in a number of prominent films, including *I Wanna Hold Your Hand* (1978) and *Raging Bull* (1980). Scottish-born Jackson had a private detective find the unlisted telephone number of Saldana's mother. He called, claiming to be an assistant to Martin Scorsese, and was given the actress's home address in West Hollywood. Here, he stabbed Saldana ten times and might well have killed her had he not been interrupted by a neighbor. Theresa Saldana's recovery took more than four months, and she replayed the incident on camera for the 1984 NBC made-for-television movie,

*Victims for Victims: The Theresa Saldana Story*. After fourteen years in prison, Arthur Richard Jackson was extradited to the United Kingdom, where he was tried for an earlier crime and committed to a psychiatric hospital, where he died in 2004. That same year, Saldana stopped acting; she died twelve years later of complications from pneumonia.

The most famous of stalked stars and the most famous of stalkers are, respectively, Jodie Foster and John Hinckley Jr. Despite her sterling work as both an actress and a director (perhaps to a lesser extent), Foster's place in history will always be as the woman whose stalker shot the president of the United States. It all started with the 1976 feature film, *Taxi Driver*, in which she plays a child prostitute. Hinckley became obsessed with the actress—in true film buff fashion—and even moved to New Haven, Connecticut, when she entered Yale University, stalking her on campus and placing notes and poems under the door of her room.

His obsession unrecognized by the actress he worshipped, Hinckley determined to do something that would gain her attention, and perhaps influenced by *Taxi Driver*, in which the leading character, played by Robert De Niro, plots to assassinate a presidential candidate, he determined to kill an American president; initially it was to be Jimmy Carter, but when that became less of a possibility, he took the obvious next step and targeted the man who succeeded Carter, Ronald Reagan.

He wrote,

> At one time Miss Foster was a star and I was the insignificant fan. Now everything is changed. I am Napoleon and she is Josephine. I am Romeo and she is Juliet. I am John Hinckley, Jr. and she is Jodie Foster. The world can't touch us. Society can't bring us down. Jodie can't ignore history.
>
> She will never escape me. I may be in prison and she may be making a movie in Paris or Hollywood but Jodie and I will always be together, in life and in death.[8]

On March 30, 1981, John W. Hinckley Jr. fired six shots at President Reagan as he left the Hilton Hotel in Washington, DC. In addition to Reagan, three others were injured, including press secretary James Brady. Hinckley was tried and found not guilty by reason of insanity. Am I callous, insensitive, and unfeeling in my belief that a similar verdict might be rendered against many of today's pseudo-anonymous film buffs who overpopulate Internet blog sites?

Jodie Foster.

Jodie Foster has an unfortunate penchant for attracting stalkers. John W. Hinckley Jr. was the first, but he was closely followed by Edward Richardson, who also stalked her while she was a student at Yale. His intention was perhaps more severe as regards the actress' well-being, but in time he decided that, after Hinckley, she was "too beautiful to kill."

A third stalker was Michael Smegal, who first became attracted to Foster in 2004, and continued his stalking for four years. It began with his mailing a prepaid cellphone to the actress, demanding that she call a specific number. Smegal's behavior was somewhat similar to that of Hinckley in that he was determined to prove his adoration for Jodie Foster by hurting others—this time with a bomb attack, foiled, on Van Nuys Airport in Los Angeles. As with Hinckley, a court determined that Smegal was mentally ill.

Apparently, Jodie Foster was not the only celebrity for whom overenthusiastic fans had an infatuation, and certainly there are other actors and actresses who have had to deal with stalkers. In April 1997, aging actor Richard Crenna was forced to take out a restraining order against a fan from the Czech Republic, named Veronika Kuncova, who claimed to be Veronika Crenna and live at the actor's home. Interestingly, it was suggested in court that she was a danger to Richard Crenna in that police had found on her person a listing of every film appearance the actor had made. If this is the only evidence that is needed to obtain a restraining order, a good many film buffs had best be careful of what lists they carry around with them.

Obsessed fan and shipping clerk Tina Marie Ledbetter of Camarillo, California, was found guilty in December 1989 of mailing a reported 6,000 threatening letters to Michael J. Fox. Apparently, Ledbetter hated Fox's wife, Tracy Pollan, and was furious when he married her. There can be bilateral damage, as John Hinckley Jr.'s killing spree proves, and as does the December 1987 killing of two security guards at the main gate of Universal Studios, when a former mental patient, Nathan Nicholas Trupp, attempted to get to Michael Landon. The latter's son was also the subject of stalking—by Christopher James Taylor—in 1991.

In 2000, Dante Michael Soiu was convicted of stalking Gwyneth Paltrow. In 2008, Jack Jordan was convicted of stalking Uma Thurman. On June 8, 2014, a thirty-nine-year-old named Joshua Corbett managed to climb the fence surrounding the home of Sandra Bullock and confront the actress. He was carrying several photographs of Bullock, along with a number of handwritten love letters, including one that read, "I will forever be thinking of you and [Bullock's son] Louie, my son, as you are my wife by law, the law of God and you belong to me and me to you." Dawnette Knight, who claimed to have been in a relationship with Michael Douglas, wrote some nineteen letters in 2004 to the actor's wife, Catherine Zeta-Jones, threatening to chop her into pieces. Michael Douglas should have learned from *Fatal Attraction* just how difficult it is to take "no" for an answer. In 2013 and 2014, Alec Baldwin was stalked by a forty-one-year-old Canadian actress named Genevieve Sabourin, who sent him voice mails and emails. It was a German stalker, Ursula Reichert-Habbishaw, who sent Richard Gere more than 1,000 faxes, not only declaring her devotion for him but also warning that she had a gun with which she would kill herself. At her 2002 trial in New York, she voluntarily agreed to return to Germany. When Edward Van Tassel tried repeatedly to deliver a letter to Tom Cruise, asking for help for veterans of the Iraq War, he was served in 2008 with a restraining order. Van Tassel's lawyer actually made it clear that his client was not "some sort of star-obsessed fan," but rather "seeking remedies for soldiers of the Iraq war."

In 2001, Nicole Kidman took out a restraining order against Matthew Hooker, who claimed to be in a "flirty" relationship with her. In 2004, Halle Berry obtained a restraining order against a Louisiana native named Greg Broussard, who believed himself to be her fiancé and had even sent her an engagement ring. Broussard was not the first male against whom the actress had obtained a restraining order; similar action was taken against her first husband, baseball player David Justice, claiming harassment. In the summer of 2012, Ellen Page was subjected to stalking via Twitter, with threats to take her life if she did not stop dating Alexander Skarsgaard.

Nineteen-year-old Athena Marie Rolando broke into Brad Pitt's Hollywood home in 1999, carrying what she claimed to be a doll as a gift for him, and as the actor was not in residence, she decided to try on his clothes. She stayed a full ten hours in the house. Pitt obtained a temporary restraining order against the would-be actress, pointing out she had been making "bizarre, disturbing, ominous and threatening statements" to him since 1996. Mel Gibson took out a restraining order in 2004 against Zach Sinclair, who would show up at the actor's Malibu home, asking that they pray together. In that Gibson had just produced and directed *The Passion of the Christ*, Sinclair's interest is not entirely inexplicable. In 2014, Ryan Gosling took out a restraining order to prevent stalker Gracie Marie Del Villar from getting too close to him; she claimed to be his "twin soul."

In 1983, Jerry Lewis was seen on screen as Jerry Langford, the central character in Martin Scorsese's *The King of Comedy*.[9] He is kidnapped by a mentally deranged stand-up comic and autograph collector named Rupert Pupkin, played by Robert De Niro. It is one of Lewis's best films, described by the British weekly *Time Out* as the "creepiest movie of the year in every sense and one of the best." Equally creepy is that from 1989 to 1994, Lewis was stalked and harassed by a diagnosed chronic schizophrenic Gary Benson, of whom the comedian claimed to live in fear. Benson served six years in prison, but eight months after his release in 2000, he sent Lewis a letter, reading simply, "Dear Jerry. Your [*sic*] Dead. Your Friend, Gary Benson." Re-arrested and awaiting trial, Benson was found dead in his cell in August 2001.

If nothing else, the long-term stalking of Jerry Lewis is proof that one does not need to be a young and female celebrity to face such harassment. But it does help.

There are celebrity stalkers who do not limit their activities to just one celebrity. A case in point is that of Diana Louisa Napolis, who used the online pseudonym of "Karen Curlo Jones." In 2001, director Steven Spielberg took out a restraining order against her after she had made threatening telephone calls accusing him and his wife of being part of a satanic cult. A year later, Napolis approached Jennifer Love Hewitt at the Grammy Awards, beginning a series of confrontations with the actress. Again, Napolis was obsessed with the notion that Jennifer Love Hewitt was a member of a satanic cult. This time around, she was arrested.

Steven Spielberg had a more serious encounter with a stalker in June and July 1997, when Jonathan Norman tried to break into his Pacific Palisades, Los Angeles, home, with the intention to rape him. The director was working on *Saving Private Ryan* in Ireland at the time. Norman, a bodybuilder, was apparently sexually obsessed with Spielberg, and in June 1998, he was sentenced to a twenty-five-year jail term. Spielberg told the court, "Had I not been out of town on the first of July, I genuinely, in my heart of hearts, believe I would have been raped or maimed or killed, and the same would have happened to my wife and kids."

In an example of life imitating life in the film world, actor James Farentino (1938–2012) was charged with stalking his ex-girlfriend, Tina Sinatra (the youngest daughter of the legendary singer), in the summer of 1993. Apparently, he sent her sixteen faxes and made thirty telephone calls, threatening her life. The actor's life had started unraveling two years earlier when he was arrested for cocaine possession in Canada.

If it is any consolation to members of the motion picture fraternity and sorority, in recent years they have evoked lesser interest from stalkers than have their colleagues, including Justin Bieber, Madonna, and Selena, in the music field. Indeed, it was perhaps always so if one sadly recalls the 1980 murder of John Lennon by Mark David Chapman.

The threat of celebrity stalkers in Los Angeles has become such a major issue that the Los Angeles Police Department established a Threats Management Unit, and the Los Angeles District Attorney's Office created a Stalking and Threat Assessment Team. A third group, unrelated directly to the police and law officials, is the Association of Threat Assessment Professionals (ATAP). As a result of the Rebecca Schaeffer murder, in 1990

California became the first state to pass an anti-stalking law (Penal Code 646.9), which defines stalking and sets harsh penalties.

As an aid to stalkers in general, as well as film buffs and film fans, the Stalkers Homepage was created in the mid-1990s. The basic concept was to bring together a variety of Internet sources, and thus make it easier to locate addresses, telephone numbers, Social Security information, and the like. Put simply, Facebook is good for two things: staying in touch with others, and stalking them.[10]

## Chapter Thirteen

# THE FILM BUFF, THE INTERNET, AND THE NEW AGE

A CHAPTER ON THE FILM BUFF AT PRESENT MUST, OF NECESSITY, BE SOMEwhat short—not because there is little to write on the subject, but rather because much of what could and should be discussed is possibly libelous. While film buffs do not care that what they write or say about others—individuals often with a professional standing—might be libelous or scandalous, there is no doubt that if the tables are turned they will not be happy at the result.

There is one fundamental difference between film buffs of the past and those who are identified as such today. Unquestionably, film buffs from the 1980s and earlier were often older gentleman, and all with a kindly disposition and an enthusiasm to share their hobby with others. There was no spite or animosity visible in their demeanor. They did not spew hatred or venom, as do their younger counterparts in the twenty-first century. And, of course, they did not have blog sites to help in their campaign against all who did not agree with them.

The film buffs of the past relied on published books, newspapers, and periodicals for their information, as well as the films themselves. They would happily spend hours in libraries, researching the arcane and irrelevant. Today's film buffs have the Internet, and they also have the Internet Movie Database (IMDb) as a primary source of information. It is the one Internet site used by just about everybody as a quick, usually (but not always) accurate source of information. As of 2016, it is reported there were 3.6 million titles and seven million individuals to be found there.

And, of course, the IMDb exists thanks to a self-confessed "film geek" named Col Needham (born 1967), a Hitchcock-obsessed film buff (favorite film: *Vertigo*) who, like many of his kind, kept a record of all the films he had seen. Needham recounts his company's history on its own website, in a posting celebrating IMDb's twentieth birthday, dated October 17, 2010:

> You might wonder how it is possible for IMDb to be 20 since the first web browser wasn't really available until 1991. Well, on October 17th in 1990 I published a series of scripts which allowed you to search a list of credits collected by a wonderful USENET group called "rec.arts.movies." Though the naming was still four years off IMDb was, in essence, born.

The company, operating out of Needham's Bristol home, was incorporated in the United Kingdom in 1996 as Internet Movie Database, Ltd., and became a subsidiary of Amazon.com in 1998. It must be exciting for all those anonymous film buffs out there on blog sites to know that IMDb operates much like a secret society, with no information as to the individuals who compile its data and their sources (although quite obviously one for older films is the *American Film Institute Catalog*).[1] "It's as if everybody behind IMDb is in the FBI's Witness Protection Program," commented one journalist.[2]

The IMDb's uses are varied. As the *Guardian* (November 5, 2004) noted, a somewhat original one is in the form of a dating tool, providing clarification as to whether a prospective date did actually appear in a certain film or whether he or she is about to appear in a well-known director's latest work.

For the film buffs, who are probably not known for their dating skills, it is one source of credit information, but often not the definitive one, and it provides many of them with the opportunity to post reviews of films, which they have not always seen—obviously so when the film no longer survives. The IMDb is the only film buff-founded entity that survives, prospers, and at times infuriates:

> It settles screaming matches, decides friendly bets, and solves nagging questions. It's a globally recognized authority, yet it had humble beginnings. It's rarely wrong, always up to date and sometimes even ahead of the curve. In fact, it's not too much of an exaggeration to say it functions in its field like a god (God, with a capital G, even had his own credits page, albeit briefly), deciding when life is created or mutated or ended—which is why we bow and scrape to its all-knowing supremacy and celebrate its uniqueness. We need it, we love it and we applaud it. Heck, if it were a drug, we'd be hopelessly addicted to it.[3]

In much the same way that the IMDb has changed research habits, so has eBay changed how one buys and sells all manner of goods and services. Founded in 1995 by Pierre Omidyar and Jeff Skoll, and initially operating out of the living room of the former's San Jose home, the major expansion of the company took place in 1998, when Harvard Business School graduate Meg Whitman came on board. Thanks to eBay's outreach, it is the primary source for all types of low-priced movie memorabilia and its success has led to the demise of virtually all storefront establishments in the field. Catering as much to investors as to film buffs and film fans are auction houses, such as Los Angeles-based Profiles in History (founded in 1985), Dallas-based Heritage Auctions (established in 1976), and Bruce Hershenson's eMoviePoster.com (established in 1999), and just as eBay has swamped walk-in businesses, so have these auction houses forced the better-known auction houses of Christie's and Sotheby's to pull back on their entertainment-related sales.

On one issue film buffs are united in disunity. They have their favorite stars or directors, and acclaim for such individuals can never be met with indifference or, worse, criticism. Film buffs will never accept the reality of gossip columnist Liz Smith assessment that "celebrity evaluation is a case of 'to each his own.' Or one man's star is another man's yawn."[4] Film buffs have been barred from contributing to the various blogs catering to them thanks to negative opinions they have expressed in regard to one celebrity or another. And the lesser the star name, the more vehement the perceived insult. In 2012, for example, controversy erupted on the film buff website, silentcomedymafia.com, as to whether John Wayne might have appeared in *Careful Please*, a 1926 film, starring a silent comedian named Lloyd Hamilton whom nobody except film buffs remembers—and with good reason.

Today's film buffs are perhaps comparable to the Senior League, a group founded in San Francisco by some 750 fans in 1946, with the sole intention "to denounce the bobbysoxers and rescue film fandom as a respectable pursuit."[5] Or, perhaps not, in that under the control of modern film buffs, film fandom can hardly be so described.

There is little doubt that thanks to the Internet, and the various outlets thereon, film buffs have found a new lease on life. They can gossip, offend, ridicule, insult, and generally cause havoc, to their hearts' content. The only limitation is, of course, that they can only communicate with each other. The frenzied obsessive fans who rioted at a movie premiere in Nathaniel West's *The Day of the Locust* have now become the obsessive film buffs, quietly, or at least soundlessly, fulminating on the Internet.

These Internet-savvy film buffs represent, in the words of playwright Alan Bennett, "millions of opinionated and empty-headed people," who regale the world "with their fatuities."[6]

It is more than evident that the film buffs of today are not the sweet, gentle, and kind film buffs of the past. The likes of Thomas Fulbright or DeWitt Bodeen were sincere, friendly individuals, anxious to share their enthusiasm with others—although—truth be told—perhaps because of their homosexuality, more willing to share their interests with young, good-looking men. There is little if any comparison between them and the majority of today's film buffs, who are ignorant of scholarship and serious research, living in a world inhabited by their own kind, and willing always to be negative and cruel towards those who do not share their interests. Generally, they are bitter men, undeserving of encouragement.

A comparison might be made between today's motion picture history-related blogsites and some of the fan-oriented clubs of the past, such as the Scroll Motion Picture Correspondence Club, based in St. Louis, Missouri, and active in the 1920s. It had occasional problems with abusive members, such as Mrs. Minnie Leiby of Los Angeles, who took it upon herself to write offensive letters to fellow and sister Scrollers, and whose $1 membership fee was refunded. She was told, in a lesson that today's bloggers might take to heart,

> It is a task indeed to acquire real friends. It requires, among other things, that first we be a friend to ourselves, and treat ourselves real nice. Then it requires sacrifice; even sometimes being pleasant to those we don't especially regard very tenderly! "To have a friend, we must be a friend."[7]

There is no accurate record of the number of film buff-oriented blog sites to be found on the Internet. There are, however, two groups, the Classic Movie Blog Association, with seventy-one member blogs as of 2016, and the Vintage Association of Motion Picture Blogs, with a reported thirty-six member blogs. Obviously, visitors to many of the blogs are little more than casual observers, with just a slight interest in a specific topic, too grounded in reality to be identified and dismissed as hardened film buffs.

Film buffs are not well read. The vast numbers of academic texts on film history are unknown to them. Indeed, they might be quite shocked to discover much of the revisionist documentation to be found there. The only books they read are those glorifying one of their favorite stars, written by fellow fans and produced by small publishing houses, such as BearManor Media, in equally small numbers. A star biography by a major critic or author, published by a major outlet, such as Knopf or Simon and Schuster, will generally be shunned because it will provide too close and too unacceptable a study of a life for which they have already determined a false reality.

Nothing upsets a film buff more than evidence of a gay sexual identity for a star that they worship as heterosexual. One female writer managed to produce an entire book on actor Raymond Burr, with no hint as to the actor's homosexuality or his long-term domestic partner. When such a relationship was revealed by another author, the lady of the first part denounced such writing as unsubstantiated and nothing more than an effort to destroy a reputation. Not once did the writer consider that one's sexual orientation did not make an individual in any way inferior or a lesser person (or star). I, myself, have been denounced at length because I wrote of actor Ralph Graves's having "enjoyed" gay sex on quite a few occasions, including a two-year relationship with producer Mack Sennett. Despite Graves himself having told me of this, I have read that such information is unsubstantiated, unproven, or perhaps worse, because we were both drinking gins and tonic at the time. That Ralph Graves was actually drinking vodka, and I was not drinking anything, is an irrelevancy.

One critic, Richard Schickel, has generally escaped the negative attention of the modern film buff, and yet he is exemplary of everything they hate.[8] Had the film buffs read the opening comment to one of his book reviews in the *New York Times* (December 3, 2006), there would have been a mass uprising, similar to the torch-bearing procession of villagers in the 1931 film version of *Frankenstein*:

> A surprising number of essentially affectless people—George Raft, Richard Dix, Nelson Eddy, to name but a few old-timers—have been movie stars. Or at any rate, so proclaimed by Hollywood, at least for a moment. These are triumphs of good looks over good sense, for generally speaking, handsome blankness leads, sooner rather than later, to B pictures, television guest shots and an inevitable drift out of all but the most cultish of consciousness.

Schickel's comments on film buffs and the like are untempered and unqualified in their opinion, matched only by those of the film buffs themselves: "What I see of Internet reviewing is people of just surpassing ignorance about the medium expressing themselves on the medium."[9] He continued, writing in the *Los Angeles Times*,

> Let me put this bluntly, in language even a busy blogger can understand: Criticism—and its humble cousin reviewing—is not a democratic activity. It is, or should be, an elite enterprise, ideally undertaken by individuals

> who bring something to the party beyond their hasty, instinctive opinions of a book (or any other cultural object). It is a work that requires disciplined taste, historical and theoretical knowledge and a fairly deep sense of the author's (or filmmaker's or painter's) entire body of work, among other qualities.[10]

While film buffs might well agree with Schickel in regard to undemocratic activity, they would not agree with his requirement as to an intellectual and disciplined approach. Indeed, in support of the film buffs, it could be argued that the motion picture is perhaps the only democratic art form, and, therefore, writing on it should be open to all—not just the educated critics. "The movies are always there when you want them," as one sociologist commented.[11]

Certainly it must be accepted that those film buffs who contribute unsolicited "reviews" to Amazon.com often seem of limited intelligence, assigning two stars to a book for such extraordinary reasons as it was a used copy and not in good condition, the type was too small, and, my favorite, the "reviewer" had yet to finish the volume and, therefore, could only give it two stars.

We are living, or perhaps at most existing, in a world of mediocrity, terror, and tragedy, to which film buffs contribute little that can help relieve the often sad reality of life. Two topics that film buffs not only avoid but also become embarrassed at when they are brought into a conversation are religion and politics. As Richard Lamparski points out, such topics might go towards a notion to be shunned of humanizing an individual.[12] There are no world events affecting the lives or thoughts of film buffs. They do not mourn on 9/11. Rather, the dates they celebrate are film-related. October 21, 2015, was recognized by film buffs as the day on which the world would be full of flying cars and "hovering hoverboards," at least according to *Back to the Future*. On March 6, it is time to celebrate the Day of the Dude, recalling the original release date of *The Big Lebowski*. On January 12, one honors the day back in 1992 on which the computer Hal from *2001: A Space Odyssey* was supposedly invented. There are even those who recognize *Star Wars* on May 4, for the sole reason that "May the Fourth" sounds like "may the force."

One may understand a yearning for past films, as identified back in 1974 by Richard Galligan:

> Those aging flicks you saw anywhere from 5 to 20 years ago. Those old "B" American movies that we sometimes run across on the late-late show, or

> at "Nostalgia Night" at college film societies. Those sentimental or western shoot-outs or World War II mini-epics that have fallen out with prevailing tastes, but stand like benchmarks in your own life, reminding you of the good times when you first saw them. (Your first kiss in the Bijou? Your last night in Poughkeepsie?)[13]

All that is well and good—all clean and healthy. A nostalgia for moments in one's past life that will not come again but will remain strong in the memory. But what does one make of the "tastes" of some film buffs, such as John Holmstrom, from North Wales, who "assembled with love" a major collection of photographs of little boys on screen from the 1910s onwards, and whose archive was published after his death as *The Moving Picture Boy Gallery*.[14] Am I the only individual who felt unclean looking through the volume at the library? At least one film bookseller told me that he could not in all decency stock it.

Perhaps the one hopeful sign is that the influence and obsession of the film buff is steadily being eroded thanks to a new generation of fans, for whom the film buffs must have little affection. For example, there has always been a strong showing from football (in the non-American sense) fans, and in the second decade of the new century, catering to such individuals has become a major industry. The popular German club F. C. Bayern Munchen publishes a 340-page catalog of souvenirs, including clothes, school supplies, backpacks, coffee mugs, jewelry, golfing accessories, and children's attire. Would be that fans of Richard Dix or J. Warren Kerrigan might have such a choice. And F. C. Bayern Munchen does not even need to hire or borrow a handsome Dix or Kerrigan to show off its clothing line; its players are far more handsome than many a male model. F. C. Bayern Munchen and its film star-like players cannot interest a film buff, who answers more to the sobriquet of "couch potato" than "goal-scorer."

Interest today has moved away from the movie sphere to the sports and music arenas. The new brand of stars communicate with the fans on social media, which, as a psychology professor quoted in the *New York Times* (March 4, 2014) noted, "allows celebrities to give their fans 'access' or, at the very least, the illusion of success." The blogs of film buffs have followers in the hundreds, while Beyoncé has more than thirteen million Twitter followers known as the "Bey Hive"; the "Britney Army," as they call themselves, is more than thirty-six million strong for Britney Spears; Lady Gaga's "Little Monsters" numbers more than forty-one million; Katy Perry's "KatyCats" number in excess of fifty-one million; and then there are the fifty million or so "Beliebers" following Justin Bieber.

The followers of almost all major music stars have a name: the "Swifties" (Taylor Swift), the "Directioners" (One Direction), the "Simpsonizers" (Cody Simpson), the "Selenators" (Selena Gomez), the "Animals" (Kesha), "Team Breezy" (Chris Brown), the "Smilers" (Miley Cyrus), and the "Barbz" (Nicki Minaj). One is reminded of the early books by James Robert Parish, who probably does not qualify as a full-blown film buff, despite such titles as *The Fox Girls* and *The RKO Girls*, not to mention *The Funsters* and *Jason Biggs: Hollywood's Newest Cutie-Pie!* At least, Parish did not give us *The Republic Rascals* or *The Columbia Cuties*.

Recognition should also be made of the San Diego-based Comic-Con, which, since 1970 has brought together fans not only of comic books but also of relevant movies and science fiction fare. It has certainly generated more press and achieved more fame than any film buff can have imagined in his Vera Hruba Ralston-ridden dreams or, as *New York Times* critic Bosley Crowther described them, "self-identifying dreams."[15]

Film buffs—their sites, their publications, their conventions—cater only to a limited few—numbering in the hundreds rather than the thousands. Comic-Con and music star celebrants inhabit a far different world, with far different goals and ambitions. Films buffs will never completely vanish, and it seems remarkable that their number does not diminish with old age and death, but, rather, that they seem to replenish themselves. The "synthetic flesh" of *The Mystery of the Wax Museum* (1933) is apparently always available to replicate their number. Only in the field of the "B" Western does the film buff genuinely seem to be bound by age; it you did not see Gene Autry or Roy Rogers on screen when they were in their prime, you cannot be, or more accurately do not want to be, a Western buff.

In the June 3, 1991, issue of the *New Yorker*, Mark Singer wrote a brilliant study of the National Tom Mix Festival held at the Imperial Palace Hotel, Las Vegas, and hosted by Dr. Richard Sieverling. The writer summed it up so perfectly with the simple comment: "Crowd control was not an issue." Even a die-hard fan such as Bud Norris had to admit, "His fans are rapidly dying out, literally, and new generations have never heard of him."[16]

There is a 1971 *Peanuts* cartoon by Charles Schulz in which Snoopy and Lucy are seen watching television. In the last frame of the cartoon, after Snoopy has suddenly kissed Lucy, he is shown thinking, "Old movies sort of affect me that way." Old movies on Turner Classic Movies certainly do affect many of us that way. Sadly, today's film buffs are immune to that sort of love of film and all it represents (be it the storyline, the technique, the acting, the stars, the character players, and, yes, even those who write authoritatively and intelligently about the motion picture).

The film buff has matured, increased in number, decreased in intelligence, and generally moved far, far away from the original concept of the film buff as expressed more than a century ago in the pages of *Motion Picture Story Magazine*, which seems almost prescient in its reference to the Turner Classic Movies phenomenon of nightly movies if somewhat generous in its belief in a film buff's discernment and critical appreciation: "To us in the audience, the day of being merely entertained has passed . . . as the photoplay becomes a nightly habit, familiar faces on the screen must breed either respect, toleration or contempt . . . we have become an audience, accustomed, discerning, critical and appreciative."[17]

# NOTES

## INTRODUCTION

1. Tom Stempel, *American Audiences on Movies and Moviegoing*, p. xi.

2. Robert Osborne died on March 6, 2017, at the age of eighty-four.

3. "George Canham," p. 5. George Canham, who died in April 1964, at the age of sixty-one, is a forgotten film buff who was obviously held in high regard. A published tribute to him contains comments not only by Everson, but also Gerald D. McDonald, Kirk Bond, and Charles Shibuk. The tribute contains a delightful story about a screening of Mrs. Wallace Reid's *The Red Kimono*. At its conclusion, Mrs. Reid appears on screen and a title reads, "And so, in the immortal words of the Carpenter of Nazareth," which was followed not by an inspirational comment but a jump cut, and immediately afterwards, "The End." George Canham's favorite film was *The Birth of a Nation*, and it was the last film he saw at a theatre—the New Yorker—in the winter of 1963.

4. Video interview provided to me by Richard Lamparski.

5. Matt Hills, *Fan Culture*, p. xi.

6. Ibid., p. xii.

7. Burt Prelutsky, "Queen of the Movie Fans," *Hollywood Studio Magazine*, August 1978, p. 16.

8. Ibid.

9. As reported in *Hollywood Studio Magazine*, October 1990, p. 28.

10. "Meet No. 1 All Time Movie Fan," p. 11.

11. "The Brothers Who Befriended Hollywood," www.express.co.uk/.

12. Published by Antique Collectors Club.

13. When the good brother wants to marry Marian Marsh, he is killed by the bad brother who adopts his identity, including the paralyzed arm.

14. Mike Hawks, interview with Anthony Slide, August 1, 2016.

15. John Cocchi authored two books, *The Western: A Picture Quiz Book* (Dover, 1976) and *Second Feature: The Best of the B's* (Citadel Press, 1991), and is also credited as a coauthor on a number of titles, primarily written by James Robert Parish.

16. Corey Kilgannon, "Froggy's Last Story."

17. Barry Brown contributed a number of articles to *Films in Review* and other publications. His brother, James Brown, wrote a novel, *Final Performance* (William Morrow, 1988),

and *The Los Angeles Diaries* (HarperCollins, 2003), based on his family and discussing also the 1997 suicide of his sister, Marilyn.

18. I should also perhaps mention Kirk Hammett, lead guitarist and songwriter with the heavy metal group Metallica. He has had a lifelong interest in horror and monster movies, and in 2012, he shared his substantial collection in *Too Much Horror Business*, coauthored with Stefan Chirazi (New York: Harry N. Abrams).

19. Jaq Greenspan, *Careers for Film Buffs*, VGM Career Horizons, 1994 (reprinted as *Careers for Film Buffs and Other Hollywood Types*, McGraw Hill, 2003) and Katie Haegle, *Cool Careers without College for Film and Television Buffs* (Rosen Publishing Group, 2002).

20. Quoted in Samantha Barbas, *Movie Crazy: Fans, Stars, and the Cult of Celebrity*, p. 166.

21. Ibid., p. 168.

22. Louis E. Bisch, "Are We Morons?" p. 50.

23. Ibid., p. 90.

24. This story was told to me by the RKO executive, Vernon Harbin, who was the last in such a position at RKO.

25. Former actor Tom Tryon based his novella, *Fedora*, part of the trilogy, *Crowned Heads* (Knopf, 1976), on Corinne Griffith; it was filmed by Billy Wilder in 1978.

26. The 1984 film *Garbo Talks*, directed by Sidney Lumet and with Betty Comden uncredited as the title character, is set in the present and concerns the efforts of a dutiful son to fulfill his dying mother's last wish that she meet Garbo. There were insufficient film buffs to help make the film a success.

27. Leonard Maltin, interview with Anthony Slide, July 1, 2016.

28. Reported in *Hollywood Reporter*, "Rambling Reporter" column, October 14, 1935, p. 2.

## CHAPTER 1: ENTER THE FILM BUFF

1. "Boys" suggests a gay connotation, which is of interest in that so many film buffs are gay.

2. Mark Duffet, *Understanding Fandom: An Introduction to the Study of Media Fan Culture*, p. 5.

3. Gladwin Hill, "Silent-Film Buff Shows His Wares," p. 33.

4. *New York Times*, December 1, 1968, p. D1.

5. Charles Champlin, "Random List of Gift Books for Film Buffs," December 23, 1969, p. E1.

6. "The Random Shots of a Picture Fan," p. 198.

7. *Moving Picture World*, December 2, 1911, p. 738.

8. "Letters and Answers," *New York Dramatic Mirror*, July 5, 1911, p. 19. The column continues on page 22.

9. Ibid.

10. "Musings of the Photoplay Philosopher," p. 137.

11. Richard Koszarski, "Richard Hoffman: A Collector's Archive," p. 520.

12. Ibid., p. 500.

13. I have no evidence of this, but it is claimed that one of Hoffman's three children was Secretary of the Army Martin R. Hoffman (1932–2014).

14. Hugo Munsterberg, *The Photoplay: A Psychological Study*, p. 97.

15. Anna Steese Richardson, "Filmitis: The Modern Malady," p. 12.

16. Samantha Barbas, *Movie Crazy: Fans, Stars and the Cult of Celebrity*, p. 2.

17. George Walsh to Dorothea Savithes, letter dated September 25, 1917, original in the Anthony Slide Collection.

18. Bessie Love at the Fine Arts Film Co. to Ceceila [*sic*] Wry, Des Moines, Iowa, letter dated October 17, 1916, copy in the Anthony Slide Collection.

19. Lee Graham, "Man About Town," *Hollywood Studio Magazine*, October 1970, p. 4.

20. Letter to "Mr. Schuessler," undated, original in the Anthony Slide Collection.

21. "Right Idea," *Exhibitors Trade Review*, March 25, 1922, p. 1189.

22. Letter to Vivian A. Nordeen, sold by RR Auctions (Boston), July 2013. Because the typed letter appears actually to have been signed by the star, it sold for $1,118.40.

23. Mark Larkin, "What Happens to Fan Mail?" p. 130.

24. Ibid., p. 130.

25. Frances Clark, "Their Funniest Fan Letters," p. 63.

26. According to the website www.garboforever.com.

27. The history of Ross Verlag can be found at the site cinemaplayerspostalantiquities .com.

28. Quoted in John Hegenberger, *Collector's Guide to Treasures from the Silver Screen*, p. viii.

29. Margaret Farrand Thorp, *America at the Movies*, p. 136.

30. The George Eastman House stills collection began with a core collection of 120,000 items from Huff, James Card, and a motion picture poster artist named Ray Rueby.

31. "The Still and Its Mission," p. 240.

32. Ralph Rugoff, "Fantasia," p. 37.

33. Richard Lamparski, telephone conversation with Anthony Slide, March 28, 2016.

34. Dallas Bower, *Plan for Cinema*, p. 34.

35. "Hays Office Probes Bootleg of Studio Publicity Stills," p. 6.

36. Quoted in John Hegenberger, *Collector's Guide to Treasures from the Silver Screen*, p. xii.

37. Mike Hawks, interview with Anthony Slide, August 1, 2016; later quotes from same source.

38. Director Quentin Tarantino thanks Eddie Brandt in the credits of his 2004 film, *Kill Bill: Vol. 2*.

39. Ricci is coauthor, with Mark Conway, of *The Films of Marilyn Monroe* (Secaucus, NJ: Citadel Press, 1964), with Boris Zmijewsky and Steve Zmijewsky, of *The Films of John Wayne* (Secaucus, NJ: Citadel Press, 1970), and, with Jerry Vermilye, of *The Films of Elizabeth Taylor* (Secaucus, NJ: Citadel Press, 1976).

40. Leonard Maltin, interview with Anthony Slide, July 1, 2016.

41. "Leonard for a Day," www.austinchronicle.com/.

42. Patricia Ward Biederman, "Years Later, He's Still a Poster Boy for Films," articles. latimes.com/.

43. Mark Jacobson, "In Praise of Film Freaks," p. 82.

44. Jerry Vermilye to Anthony Slide, letter dated May 22, 2016.

45. A new edition of the recordings can be downloaded at dionmcgregor.bandcamp .com.

46. Joe Franklin, *Up Late with Joe Franklin*, p. 241.

47. Jeremiah Moss, "The Last Picture Shop," www.newyorker.com/.

48. According to the *Las Vegas World News* (July 31, 2012), there is some mystery as to the company's true identity. It was perhaps actually named Desert Collectibles Corporation, owned by Stuart Scheinman. The newspaper noted, "it is unclear if Scheinman purchased the collection outright or not. Maybe it is some type of commission deal or even a distress sale since the New York owner said the upkeep was very expensive."

## CHAPTER 2: FAN CLUBS AND FAN MAIL

1. Morton M. Hunt, "Our Drooling Movie Fans," p. 79.

2. Samantha Barbas, *Movie Crazy: Fans, Stars, and the Cult of Celebrity*, pp. 183, 184.

3. Alberta Vaughn (1904–1992) and Adamae Vaughn (1905–1943).

4. Undated letter from Adamae Vaughn, Anthony Slide Collection, written after she had completed the 1925 film *The Last Edition*, in which she played a stenographer.

5. Mark Larkin, "What Happens to Fan Mail?" *Photoplay*, August 1928, pp. 38–40, 130–34.

6. An anecdote found in Denis Norden's *Clips from Life* (London: Fourth Estate, 2008).

7. Membership was $1 a year, with a life membership available at $10.

8. Margaret Farrand Thorp, *America at the Movies*, p. 67.

9. Jimmie Fiddler to Chaw Mank, letter dated January 31, 1933, in the Anthony Slide Collection.

10. A film buff with similar, undivided devotion for one star is Lou Valentino, with a reported 20,000 photographs of Lana Turner. He authored *The Films of Lana Turner* (Citadel Press, 1976) and was even featured on the television series, *To Tell the Truth*, in 1970 as Lana Turner's No. 1 Fan.

11. Bob Thomas, "When Covering Hollywood Was More Personal," penultimate paragraph.

12. Reported in the *New York Times*, August 28, 1926, p. 6.

13. I was invited to present the keynote address at the Eighty-Fourth Rudolph Valentino Memorial on August 23, 2011.

14. For those seeking more information on Leslie Flint, I would recommend his autobiography, *Voices in the Dark: My Life as a Medium* (London: Macmillan, 1971). For information on the Leslie Flint Educational Trust, readers should check out www.leslieflint.com/, which also reproduces an excellent obituary on Leslie, written by film critic Alexander Walker, and published originally in the *Independent*.

15. http://www.basingstoke-canal.org.uk/archive/booklets/bkltarc9-9.htm.

16. Philip Jenkinson (1935–2012) was a British film buff and film collector who regularly appeared on television, and is outrageously parodied by the Monty Python troupe, although American viewers will not understand what it is all about. American film buffs will find far greater amusement in Jenkinson's interview with John Ford, in which the director savages him. Jenkinson was quite homophobic; in one wonderful, undated letter to film collector David Bradley, he writes of a group of ten or twelve "limp-wristed . . . Judy Garland crazed bum boys," film buffs who hang around London's National Film Theatre.

17. Philip Castanza, *The Complete Films of Jeanette MacDonald and Nelson Eddy*, p. 48.

18. Mackenzie Carpenter, "Fan Clubs Keep the Flame Alive for Stars Fading from Memory," www.post-gazette.com/.

19. Irene Lacher, "MacDonald-Eddy: Stoking the Passions of New Fans," articles.latimes .com/.

20. The Appreciating Jeanette MacDonald Club publishes a quarterly magazine, has regular membership meetings, and sponsors the Jeanette MacDonald Operetta Scholarship and Performance Fund at the USC Thornton School of Music.

21. "Deanna Durbin Lovers in Conflict with Devoters," www.thecrimson.com/.

22. Randy Henderson, "Wayne Martin—Judy's Number One Fan," p. 11.

23. Ibid., p. 9.

24. Richard Schickel, *Intimate Strangers: The Culture of Celebrity*, p. 85.

25. Lora Kelly, "How One Girl Built up a Fan Club," p. 72.

26. Ibid., p. 73.

27. Mike Hawks, interview with Anthony Slide, August 1, 2016. The only film that comes to mind in which a lighthouse is prominently featured is *Portrait of Jennie* (1948).

28. Margaret Farrand Thorp, *America at the Movies*, p. 61.

## CHAPTER 3: CHAW MANK

1. Like so many statements that Chaw Mank made in interviews given in old age, it is impossible to confirm the details.

2. Brad Steiger and Chaw Mank, *Valentino*, p. 7.

3. Karen R. Marshall, "Chaw Mank: The Ultimate Fan," p. 5.

4. New York: Popular Library, 1970, with Jeanyne Bezoier, and under the editorship of Brad Steiger.

5. H. Crump, secretary, to Chaw Mank, letter dated July 8, 1926, in the Anthony Slide Collection.

6. Virginia Kellogg, secretary, to Chaw Mank, letter dated August 21, 1926, in the Anthony Slide Collection.

7. Jimmie Fiddler noted that both he and Mank "have a common yen for the red-headed gal, Peggy Shannon," Jimmie Fiddler to Chaw Mank, undated letter, in the Anthony Slide Collection.

8. Application form dated November 13, in the Anthony Slide Collection.

9. I am currently the proud owner of the tie, which I am more than happy to relinquish to a Minna Gombell fan with cash in hand.

10. Virginia R. Lewis, secretary, to Chaw Mank, letter dated February 9, 1939, in the Anthony Slide Collection. Rosalind Russell had her own fan club, with which Chaw Mank does not appear to have been involved, and which was located in Buffalo, New York, the hometown of its president, Lucille Robbins. I have Chaw Mank's membership cards to two other fan clubs, for Nina Foch (1949) and Marie Windsor (1951); Mank's involvement in them is not clear.

11. Letter to Chaw Mank, dated May 24, 1940, in the Anthony Slide Collection.

12. Letter to Chaw Mank, dated July 11, 1940, in the Anthony Slide Collection.

13. Mina Borg to Chaw Mank, letter dated July 30, 1941. Mrs. Borg complains that Chaw Mank's typewriter needs a new ribbon, and apologizes for having to handwrite a letter to him, but "my neighbor has my typewriter & I hate to bother her this a.m. since she's busy."

14. Albert Conti to Chaw Mank, letter dated November 8, 1932, in the Anthony Slide Collection.

15. Bodil Rosing to Chaw Mank, letter dated September 3, 1933, copy in the Anthony Slide Collection.

16. Harmony Haynes to Chaw Mank, undated letter, in the Anthony Slide Collection.

17. Monroe M. Goldstein, secretary, to Chaw Mank, letter dated February 9, 1936, in the Anthony Slide Collection.

18. Monroe M. Goldstein, secretary, to Chaw Mank, letter dated October 15, 1937, in the Anthony Slide Collection.

19. Karen K. Marshall, "Chaw Mank: The Ultimate Fan," p. 5.

20. It was claimed in *Hollywood Studio Magazine*, September 1980, that Mank was sending out 25,000 letters a year.

21. Ibid., p. 11.

22. Brad Steiger, email to Anthony Slide, March 1, 2016.

23. Brad Steiger and Chaw Mank, *Valentino*, p. 80.

24. Brad Steiger, email to Anthony Slide, March 1, 2016.

25. *Classic Film Collector*, April 1982, p. 17.

## CHAPTER 4: FILM BUFF SCREENINGS

1. Haidee Wasson, *Museum Movies: The Museum of Modern Art and the Birth of Art Cinema*, p. 2.

2. Huff's attitude towards communism is not based on any ideological disagreement, but rather because the Soviets would emphasize the work of Russian directors, such as Eisenstein, over that of D. W. Griffith.

3. Letter from Theodore Huff to D. W. Griffith, August 1, 1940, copy in the Anthony Slide Collection.

4. Charles Shibuk to Anthony Slide, letter dated March 7, 2016.

5. Charles Shibuk to Anthony Slide, letter dated March 31, 2016.

6. The other featured film buffs in the documentary are Eric Chadbourne, Bill Heidbreder, and Harvey Schwartz.

7. Seymour Stern to David Bradley, letter in the Anthony Slide Collection.

8. "Theodore Huff In Memoriam," p. 212.

9. Ibid., p. 214.

10. Mark Jacobson, "In Praise of Film Freaks," p. 82.

11. Ed Maguire to Anthony Slide, March 23, 2016.

12. Louis Black, "Leonard for a Day," www.austinchronicle.com/.

13. Leonard Maltin, interview with Anthony Slide, July 1, 2016.

14. Charles L. Turner (1915–1999) was primarily an industrial filmmaker, but he could also operate a 35mm projector, which came in handy.

15. William Simpson Kenly III retired as a publicist with New York's Paramount office after more than forty years with the company. He was one of the most helpful individuals with the company. He had earlier managed New York's Fifth Avenue Cinema, and had a major film collection, from which he selected titles for private screening at the West Village apartment that he shared with his companion of thirty-three years, Richard Buban.

16. Ronald S. Magliozzi, "Witnessing the Development of Independent Film Culture in New York: An Interview with Charles L. Turner," p. 86.

17. George J. Mitchell, interview with Anthony Slide, May 31, 1990.

18. William K. Everson, "The Theodore Huff Memorial Film Society: A Brief History," p. 2.

19. Ibid., p. 1.

20. Mark Jacobson, "In Praise of Film Freaks," p. 82.

21. Charles Shibuk to Anthony Slide, letter dated March 9, 2016. Shibuk is best known for his work in the field of mystery novels and stories, and is coauthor of *Detectionary* (Woodstock, NY: Overlook Press, 1977).

22. Charles Shibuk to Anthony Slide, letter dated March 31, 2016.

23. Charles Shibuk attended William K. Everson's screenings from 1956 through the 1980s, and he has provided me with the following record of attendees, decade by decade. 1950s: Gerald D. McDonald (1905–1970), chief of special collections at the New York Public Library; Edward Connor; illustrator and artist Edward Gorey (1925–2000); and Richard Kraft. 1960s: Jack Wolcott; Dorothy Lovell; George Canham, a typesetter with the *New York Daily News*, who was obsessed with *The Birth of a Nation* and *Intolerance* and would never miss a screening; Fran Morris, who served as Everson's secretary; and Alan Barbour. 1970s and later: Gary Collins, a student who supervised Everson's screenings at the New School; Romano Tozzi; sound editor Ed and his wife Peta Smith; and Chester Wiskowski, a film collector whose collection was divided at his death between New York University and the Luxembourg Cinémathèque.

24. *A Tribute to William K. Everson by a Few of His Friends*, p. 22. Arthur does not mention that each time George O'Brien took off his shirt, he would also quite visibly hold in his stomach in an effort to contain oncoming flab.

25. Leonard Maltin, interview with Anthony Slide, July 1, 2016.

26. Everson's papers were donated by his widow to the university, which has made his program notes available online.

27. In all probability, Everson had borrowed the print from a collector/dealer named William Donnachie located in Philadelphia. Donnachie was an interesting character, a Scotsman who had served with the Argyle and Sutherland Highlanders during World War I. He owned prints of a number of M-G-M films, including *The Kiss*, *The Scarlet Letter*, and *White Shadows in the South Seas*.

28. George J. Mitchell, interview with Anthony Slide, May 11, 1990.

29. The story is retold by Eugene Stavis in "In Memoriam: William K. Everson," p. 124.

30. *A Tribute to William K. Everson by a Few of His Friends*, p. 21.

31. *The Biscuit Eater* is a 1940 sentimental Paramount film concerning two small boys and their dog.

32. Bambi Everson, email to Anthony Slide, dated April 19, 2016.

33. *A Tribute to William K. Everson by a Few of His Friends*, p. 29.

34. John Griggs should not be confused with another New Yorker Named John Griggs (1941–1981), who had been a research assistant to critic Judith Crist, and wrote *The Films of Gregory Peck* (1984) and coauthored *The Films of World War Two* (1973).

35. She is referring to 16mm footage shot between 1931 and 1973 by Ray Knight of Jacksonville, Florida, who would sneak his camera into New York theatres.

36. Eleanor Knowles Dugan, email to Anthony Slide, dated April 8, 2016.

37. Richard Lamparski to Anthony Slide, telephone conversation, June 19, 2016.

38. Jim Cronin, "Revived Celluloid in NYC," p. 15.

39. David E. James and Adam Hyman, eds., *Experimental Projections: Experimental Films in Los Angeles, 1945–1980*, p. 184.

40. Richard Lamparski, *Hollywood Diary*, p. 148.

41. Tim Lanza, "Raymond Rohauer and the Society of Cinema Arts (1948–1962): Giving the Devil His Due," p. 131.

42. In 2006, the Vagabond again became a legitimate theatre, the Hayworth.

43. Charles Champlin, "An Appreciation: The Two Garys—Zealots with a Passion for Film," articles.laltimes.com/.

44. Joan Cohen, email to Anthony Slide, dated April 21, 2016.

45. Todd McCarthy, *Howard Hawks: The Grey Fox of Hollywood*, New York: Grove Press, 1997.

46. Joseph McBride, *Hawks on Hawks* (Berkeley, CA: University of California Press, 1982) and *Frank Capra: The Catastrophe of Success* (New York: Simon and Schuster, 1992). McBride was also a film critic with *Daily Variety*, and has authored books on John Ford, Kirk Douglas, and Orson Welles.

47. 1991.

48. Joan Cohen, email to Anthony Slide, dated April 21, 2016.

## CHAPTER 5: DAVID BRADLEY AND HERB GRAFF AND THE FILM COLLECTOR AS FILM BUFF

1. Advertisement in *The Film Spectator*, July 9, 1927, p. 4.

2. Marie Seton, "Ancient Rome in Gangster Town," p. 172.

3. Credit for the costumes goes to Bradley's mother, Katharine.

4. In the early 1950s, Bradley had also formed a company, Oceanic Productions, Inc., which was to film Paul Gaugin's Tahitian journal, *Noa Noa*, with James Agee writing the script. The latter does survive, but the project failed to materialize.

5. Copy in the Anthony Slide Collection.

6. Ibid.

7. Letter dated May 3, 1989, copy in the Anthony Slide Collection.

8. The first time I attended was January 1, 1976, when guests included Madge Bellamy, Fritz Feld, and Tay Garnett.

9. *The Silent Clowns* (New York: Alfred A. Knopf, 1975).

10. Herb Graff's friendship with Adolph Green is interesting in that in 1938 Judy Holliday began her career as part of a nightclub act which included Green, in 1956, she starred in *Bells Are Ringing*, co-written by Green and Betty Comden, and at some point in the 1940s, she and Herb Graff apparently had a relationship.

11. Being a New Yorker, Herb could never understand why the deli, when confronted with a party of five or six, would have one wait until two tables could be put together. As he explained, in New York, the deli would simply add two more seats to a table for four.

12. Leonard Maltin, interview with Anthony Slide, July 1, 2016.

13. Ibid.

14. Ibid.

15. Douglas Watt, "Profiles: Film Resource," p. 59.

16. Leonard Maltin points out in an interview, July 1, 2016, that wife Anita was "long suffering. It was kind of sad because they actually loved each other when they got married. Had three children. But when he got really hooked on movies and found you could collect them and show them, they grew more and more apart. She liked movies but not in the same way as Herb. She was also a very feisty woman, a sharp tongue. I liked her, and I think she liked me. She came to a sad end. She dropped dead on the street and her body went unclaimed for several days."

17. Leonard Maltin, interview with Anthony Slide, July 1, 2016.

18. Douglas Watt, "Profiles: Film Resource," p. 62.

19. Leonard Maltin, interview with Anthony Slide, July 1, 2016.

20. Douglas Watts, "Profiles: Film Resource," p. 59.

21. Founded in 1978 by Julian Schlossberg, Castle Hill closed down in 2009, and its assets were acquired by Westchester Films, also owned by Schlossberg.

22. Douglas Watt. "Profiles: Film Resource," p. 65.

23. Leonard Maltin, interview with Anthony Slide, July 1, 2016.

24. Douglas Watts, "Profiles: Film Resource," p. 61.

## CHAPTER 6: FILM BUFF MEETS FILM SCHOLAR

1. Little is known about Turner, except that, according to his obituary in the *New York Times*, he was an art patron and advisor to various British and American publishers. Presumably, his position as editor of *Films in Review* was a non-paying one.

2. He also authored *Dr. Barnes of Merion: An Appreciation* (New York: Farrar, Straus, 1963), a tribute to the Philadelphia art collector.

3. Jerry Vermilye to Anthony Slide, letter dated May 22, 2016.

4. Henry Hart to Dudley Nichols, July 1, 1958, original letter in the Anthony Slide Collection.

5. Ronald S. Magliozzi, "Witnessing the Development of Independent Film Culture in New York: An Interview with Charles L. Turner," p. 91.

6. Rudy Behlmer, interview with Anthony Slide, April 20, 2016.

7. Ibid.

8. The *Films in Review* essays were collected in two volumes: *From Hollywood: The Careers of 15 Great American Stars* (South Brunswick, NJ: A. S. Barnes, 1976) and *More from Hollywood: The Careers of 15 Great American Stars* (South Brunswick, NJ: A. S. Barnes, 1977). DeWitt Bodeen also authored a highly entertaining novel based on the William Desmond Taylor murder mystery, *13 Castle Walk* (New York: Pyramid Books, 1975), as well as *Ladies of the* Footlight (Pasadena: Logan, 1937), *The Films of Cecil B. DeMille*, with Gene Ringgold (Secaucus, NJ: Citadel Press, 1969), *Chevalier: The Films and Career of Maurice Chevalier*, with Gene Ringgold (Secaucus, NJ: Citadel Press, 1973),

9. George Geltzer's papers are at the Library of Congress. He was a strange character, extremely knowledgeable about silent films, but with a paranoia and an obsession with imagined slights, perhaps influenced by his being a deaf mute.

10. Romano Tozzi to Anthony Slide, letter dated March 25, 2016.

11. Kenneth G. Laurence wrote on "The Academy Retrospective" in the January 1970 issue.

12. Herbert G. Luft's papers are at the American Heritage Center of the University of Wyoming.

13. Originally published by Popular Library, the book was later considerably expanded as *Don Miller's Hollywood Corral: A Comprehensive B-Western Roundup*, and published in 1993 by Riverwood Press, with additional commentary by others and a foreword by Gene Autry.

14. Romano Tozzi to Anthony Slide, letter dated March 25, 2016.

15. The blogger is actually actor/singer/composer Bruce Kimmel hiding behind the pseudonym of Guy Haines. This and other quotes on Page Cook are taken from the Film Score blog site, http://www.filmscoremonthly.com/boards.posts/cfm?threadID=47637 (accessed March 2016).

16. Rudy Behlmer, conversation with Anthony Slide, March 26, 2016, after a chance meeting in the Studio City branch of Gelson's Supermarket. Film buffs will be delighted to know that this same store was the supermarket of choice of Nancy Davis Reagan, who once declared it the one thing she missed most in Los Angeles while residing at the White House.

17. In the September–October 1992 issue, Page Cook wrote a glowing review of Ken Darby's quite wonderful memoir, *Hollywood Holyland: The Filming and Scoring of The Greatest Story Ever Told* (Scarecrow Press, 1992), which I had the good fortune to edit.

18. An anthology of Page Cook's writing is long overdue. His papers are at Brigham Young University.

19. There are 119 boxes of Roi Uselton's papers at Emory University.

20. Roi Uselton, "Cooperative Scholarship," *Films in Review*, January 1972, pp. 23–27.

21. Jerry Vermilye to Anthony Slide, letter dated April 10, 2016. He is the author of many books, including four published by Pyramid, *Bette Davis* (1973), *Cary Grant*, with Ted Sennett (1975), *Barbara Stanwyck* (1976), and *Ida Lupino* (1977), and a number of Citadel Press titles, *The Films of Charles Bronson* (1981), *Films of the Thirties* (1982), *More Films of the Thirties* (1989), *The Films of Elizabeth Taylor*, with Marc Ricci (1989), *Films of the Twenties* (1990), *Great Italian Films* (1994), *The Complete Films of Audrey Hepburn* (2000). He is also the author of *Ingmar Bergman: His Life and Films* (McFarland, 2007), which stemmed from a *Films in Review* article, "An Index to the Films of Ingmar Bergman," and editor of *The 500 Best British and Foreign Films to Buy, Rent, or Videotape: Selected by the National Board of Review of Motion Pictures and the Editors of Films in Review* (William Morrow, 1988). He was one of the first people I came across who had been a member of the National Board of Review.

22. Jerry Vermilye to Anthony Slide, letter dated July 19, 2016.

23. *Films in Review*, August–September 1962, p. 430.

24. Ibid., January 1963, p. 43.

25. Ibid., April 1963, p. 243.

26. Ibid., August–September 1970, p. 442.

27. Ibid., June–July 1965, p. 382.

28. Ibid., June–July 1969, p. 375.

29. Ibid., August–September 1971, p. 441.

30. Ibid., March 1964, p. 176.

31. Andrew Sarris, "The Farthest-Out Movie Goers," p. 14–15.

32. *Films in Review*, May 1958, p. 244.

33. Ibid., May 1961, p. 261.

34. Ibid., May 1962, p. 263.

35. Ibid., May 1963, p. 277 and p. 279.

36. Ibid., May 1964, p. 281.

37. Ibid., May 1965, p. 267.

38. Ibid., May 1966, p. 270.

39. Ibid., May 1967, p. 262.

40. Ibid., May 1968, p. 261.

41. Ibid., May 1969, p. 266.

42. Ibid., May 1972, p. 260.

43. Ibid., May 1970, p. 262.

44. "Astaire on Chambers," p. 445.

45. Charles Higham, *In and Out of Hollywood: A Biographer's Memoir*, p. 128.

46. Many years after his retirement, Henry Hart learned that I was involved with Martin Sopocy in raising the funds to have a lilac named in honor of Blanche Sweet. Henry shipped all the spare copies of *Films in Review* that he still had in his possession and asked me to sell them to raise whatever we could. It was the sort of gesture, not only on Henry's part but also on my own, that no self-absorbed, rude, and arrogant film buff today would understand.

47. Ronald Bowers, email to Anthony Slide, dated March 31, 2016.

48. Ronald Bowers, email to Anthony Slide, dated April 1, 2016.

49. Harry Pearson Jr., self-described as "a queer boy from the South," published *The Perfect Vision* and *The Absolute Sound.*

50. Lewis Frumkes (born 1939), educator, humorist, and writer.

51. Marsha McCreadie, email to Anthony Slide, dated April 24, 2016.

52. A discussion of the current status of the National Board of Review is outside the scope of this book. Hopefully, one day there will be a major exposé of the present-day National Board of Review, the makeup of its membership, and why anyone in the Hollywood community should care about its awards and its opinions.

53. An article by Louise Tanner in February 1994 provides a short history of *Films in Review*, which is quite incredible for its lack of knowledge of the publication or even of when it began. At one point, she writes of its reviewing *City Lights* in 1931, and that Robert Giroux began as a "junior" critic for the magazine in 1928. She credits the National Board of Review as responsible for removing "offensive racist scenes" from *The Birth of a Nation*, and then writes glowingly of the board's annual D. W. Griffith Life Achievement Award, first presented in 1979 to Myrna Loy. I wonder if Tanner was alive in 1999, when the Directors Guild of America removed Griffith's name from its life achievement award, and the National Board of Review, quietly and shamefully, followed suit.

54. Named for the 1933 Laurel and Hardy feature film, the Sons of the Desert was founded in 1965 by the couple's biographer, John McCabe, a truly honorable and decent man.

55. Al Kilgore (1927–1983) worked on the "Bullwinkle" and "Hoppity Hooper" comic scripts. He certainly qualifies as a film buff, thanks to his appearance in *Captain Celluloid vs. the Film Pirates* and his involvement in the founding of the Laurel and Hardy organization, the Sons of the Desert.

56. Catherine Barbour, email to Anthony Slide, dated April 9, 2016.

57. He wrote a massive, 568-page volume based on his memories, *Saturday Afternoon at the Movies*, published in 1987 by Random House.

58. The Alan G. Barbour Screen Facts and Screen Nostalgia Illustrated Collection is available on microfiche from ProQuest.

59. March 28, 2003, http://groups.google.com/forum/#!topic/alt.movies.silent/QghOzqMFwUs (accessed March 2016).

## CHAPTER 7: PUBLISHING, PUBLICATIONS, AND BOOKSTORES FOR THE FILM BUFF

1. Lyle Stuart's papers are at Columbia University.

2. Barricade Books, press release, dated January 27, 2011.

3. Linda Carlson, "Today's Self-Publishing Pathways," July 2014.

4. Ben Ohmart, email to Anthony Slide, dated March 7, 2016.

5. All of Lee's books are published by A. S. Barnes out of South Brunswick, New York.

6. Texas-born Lee Graham gave new meaning to the word "smarm," and always had a penchant for being photographed, with a sickly smile on his face, beside one aging actress or another. He had at one time been an actor and married to a dancer named Evelyn Fahrney; his obituaries reported the sad but expected news that there were "no survivors."

7. Tom Scalzo, "Wallace Reid," February 1988, p. 7.

8. Robert Rosterman, "Looking Back: at Lon McCallister," November 1989.

9. Currently, the Margaret Herrick Library of the Academy of Motion Picture Arts and Sciences has only one issue, September 1973, and that is the only copy that I have seen.

10. Toronto is also home to the Toronto Film Society, founded in 1948 and the oldest in Canada. Obviously, it is a venue for film buffs. For example, in 1978, it celebrated Deanna Durbin's birthday with a screening of *100 Men and a Girl*. The star herself contacted the society, commenting, "when I think of all you film buffs looking at me as I was in 1937, I consider that this is the nicest way to stay young . . . no make up, no hairdo, just roll the projector and there I am."

11. Stephen Rebello, "State of Siege," p. 43.

12. Published in 1964 by the University of Oklahoma Press. Lahue's other film-related volumes are: *World of Laughter: The Motion Picture Comedy Short, 1910–1930* (Norman, OK: University of Oklahoma Press, 1966); *Kops and Custards: Legend of Keystone Films*, with Terry Brewer (Norman, OK: University of Oklahoma Press, 1968); *Clown Princes and Court Jesters*, with Sam Gill (South Brunswick, NJ: A. S. Barnes, 1970); *Bound and Gagged*; *Collecting Classic Films* (New York: Hastings House, 1970); *Winners of the West: Sagebrush Heroes of the Silent Screen* (South Brunswick, NJ: A. S. Barnes, 1971); *Ladies in Distress* (South Brunswick, NJ: A. S. Barnes, 1971); *Dreams for Sale: Rise and Fall of the Triangle Corporation* (South Brunswick, NJ: A. S. Barnes, 1971); *Gentlemen to the Rescue: The Heroes of the Silent Screen* (South Brunswick, NJ: A. S. Barnes, 1972); *Riders of the Range: The Sagebrush Heroes of the Sound Screen* (South Brunswick, NJ: A. S. Barnes, 1973); and *Motion Picture Pioneer: Story of the Selig Polyscope Company* (South Brunswick, NJ: A. S. Barnes, 1973).

13. Not to be confused with CineCon, the annual convention of the National Association of Theatre Owners.

14. Anonymous, email to Anthony Slide, dated September 18, 2016.

15. "Interview with Former AMC TV Host Bob Dorian," gofatherhood.com (accessed March 2016).

16. The book was eventually published by Grove Press in 1983. Luboviski and the Miller estate shared the royalties.

17. Edwin McDowell, "1942 Miller Worth Being Published," *New York Times*, June 7, 1983, www.nytimes.com/.

18. Kenneth Turan, "Filmland's Book World," *Arizona Republic*, February 26, 1978, p. N5.

19. Mike Hawks, interview with Anthony Slide, August 1, 2016.

20. Ibid.

21. Hollywood Book and Poster was founded by Eric Caidin (1952–2015), who cofounded the Grindhouse Film Festival, which operated at various locations until 2002, when it became permanently established at the New Beverly Cinema, now owned by film director-film buff Quentin Tarantino. Caidin's father was Beverly Hills entertainment lawyer Stan Caidin, who had a magnificent collection of vintage film posters, and can definitely be classified as a film buff.

22. Owner Edward Gilbert, then seventy, sold the business in 1984, fed up with the tawdry clientele in and around his store. He told the *Spokesman-Review* (Spokane, Washington), January 16, 1984, "I delivered books to Ronald Colman, Bette Davis, Joan Crawford, Greta Garbo and Bing Crosby. Ginger Rogers and Lew Ayres used to smooch in the corner."

23. Sol Chaneles, *Collecting Movie Memorabilia*, pp. 162–63.

24. "Cinemabilia," p. 47.

25. Matt Harvey, "The East Village Isn't What It Used to Be. And It Never was," *Strausmedia*.

## CHAPTER 8: THE SILENT MOVIE THEATRE

1. Rip Rense, "Serial Box," *Los Angeles Herald-Examiner*.

2. Dale D. Drum, "Silent Movies in Los Angeles," p. 453.

3. Ron Russell and Victor Mejía, "The Last Picture Show," p. 10.

4. "Silents Glorified at Old-Time Theater," Part III, p. 10.

5. Philip K. Scheuer, "Unique Theater Shows Only Silent Pictures," p. C3.

6. Anonymous source.

7. *John Hampton and Dorothy Hampton, Appellants, v. Paramount Pictures Corporation and Eastman Kodak Company, Appellees*, 279 F.2d 100 (9th Circ. 1960).

8. It has been pointed out to me just how amazing it is that A. C. Lyles could survive at Paramount from 1937 until his death, through one regime change after another. He must truly has known how to toady to the right executives.

9. Hampton always claimed that it was these chemicals that caused the cancer that was to kill him, but there is no proof of this.

10. Hampton's brother Gilbert and his son Lenn tried to carry out John Hampton's wishes, with Lenn's spending some time disposing of an undetermined number of films, posters, lobby cards, and still photographs in an effort to make the theatre and living accommodation a little less cluttered.

11. Ron Russell and Victor Mejía, "The Last Picture Show," p. 8.

12. Ibid., p. 7.

13. Anonymous source.

14. Valerie Yaros, "My Experience at the Silent Movie Theatre on Friday, January 17, 1997."

15. Hillel Aron, "Harry Major Took in Ex-Cons for Sex and Friendship. Then He Turned Up Dead."

16. Andy Klein, "The Silent Remains Silent," p. 32.

17. Scott Timberg, "Reviled Revivalist," p. 13.

18. Robin Rauzi, "Silent Calling," p. 12.

## CHAPTER 9: SEX AND THE FILM BUFF

1. Mike Hawks, interview with Anthony Slide, August 1, 2016.

2. Louis Black, "Leonard for a Day," www.austinchronicle.com/.

3. Gloria G. Brame and William D. Brame, "Leather Hall of Fame," leatherhalloffame .com/.

4. Ibid.

5. Josh Becker, *Rushes*, p. 40.

6. Christopher Isherwood and Don Bachardy, *October*, p. 32.

7. Sam Frank, *Ronald Colman: A Bio-Bibliography*, p. i.

8. Rudy Behlmer, interview with Anthony Slide, April 20, 2016.

9. Joan Cohen, email to Anthony Slide, dated April 21, 2016.

10. Leonard Maltin, interview with Anthony Slide, July 1, 2016.

11. Robert Gitt, conversation with Anthony Slide, April 20, 2016.

12. Leonard Maltin, interview with Anthony Slide, July 1, 2016.

13. Sam Frank authored one other book, *Buyer's Guide to Fifty Years of TV on Video* (New York: Prometheus Books, 1999).

14. p. 23.

15. "thirteenbyseven," July 9, 2004, http://www.lpsg.com/threads/the-hung-jury-and-the -infamous-sam-frank.16759/ (accessed January 2016). A posting by this member (no pun intended) on the same date provides a fascinating account of his meeting with an affluent couple from Nevada, his lack of social skills in a restaurant, and his efforts to obtain an appropriate-size erection.

16. Christine Carlisle to Jonathan Ross, *Americana* television program, 1992.

17. Ibid., Jonathan Ross narration.

18. Leonard Maltin, interview with Anthony Slide, July 1, 2016.

## CHAPTER 10: ORGANIZED FILM BUFFS

1. Kreuger is the author of *Showboat: The Story of a Classic American Musical* (New York: Oxford University Press, 1978).

2. I wrote of John LeBold and his museum in the British annual, *Film Review*, and among the other costumes I identified as being there are those worn by Chaplin in *The Great Dictator*, Valentino in *Blood and Sand*, Betty Grable in *Coney Island*, Claudette Colbert in *Cleopatra*, Julie Andrews in *The Sound of Music*, Judy Garland in *The Wizard of Oz*, Alice Faye in *Hello, Frisco, Hello*, Hedy Lamarr in *Samson and Delilah*, Bette Davis in *The Private Life of Elizabeth and Essex*, as well as the shorts worn by Sylvester Stallone in *Rocky*.

3. Robert M. Gettemy, "Hobbyist Projects Secret into Open," p. E6.

4. The hotel was named after Beverly Garland (1926–2008), who was usually to be found playing leads in low-budget films. It was developed in 1971 by Garland and her husband, Fillmore Crank. When he died, she took over the operation of the hotel.

5. Chris Epting, p. 14.

6. Sam Sherman was a close friend of Joe Franklin, sharing a mutual interest not only in old films but also old 78 rpm recordings.

7. Richard Lamparski to Anthony Slide, telephone conversation, May 5, 2016.

8. Howard Mandelbaum, email to Anthony Slide, dated March 28, 2016.

9. Lincoln Geraghty, *Cult Collectors: Nostalgia, Fandom and Collecting Popular Culture*, p. 134.

10. Ibid., p. 136.

11. Rudy Behlmer, interview with Anthony Slide, April 20, 2016.

12. As I write this in the summer of 2016, those Clara Kimball Young-owned volumes of *Screen World* are being offered for sale on eBay.

13. Daniel Blum's collection of 440 scrapbooks was purchased by the Wisconsin Historical Society after his death, and is available in its entirety on microfilm.

14. "Whatever Became of . . . Richard Lamparski?: Exclusive Interview with Mr. Yesterday," *Boy Culture*, http://www.boyculture.com/boy_culture/2010/10/richard-lamparski-whatever-became-of-gossip-gay-rumors-books.html/.

15. Video interview provided to me by Richard Lamparski.

16. Ibid.

17. Ibid.

18. Ibid.

19. Rudy Behlmer authored a piece, "Collaboration May Be the Answer," in *Films in Review* (March 1970), on how three authors could work together in the writing of a single book.

20. I am thinking of titles such as *Lugosi* (1997), *Horror at the Drive-In* (2001), and *White Zombie: Anatomy of a Horror Film* (2002), all published by McFarland, and *Tod Browning's Dracula* (Tomahawk Press, 2015).

21. Gary Rhodes, emails to Anthony Slide, dated March 26 and March 30, 2016.

22. Quoted in Tom Stempel, *American Audiences on Movies and Moviegoing*, p. 140.

23. A discussion of this issue can be found in Mat Hills's book *Fan Culture*.

24. His papers are at Brigham Young University.

25. Long before the Museum of Modern Art put together its "restoration" of D. W. Griffith's *Intolerance*, Arthur Lennig scrupulously restored the film in 16mm, using contemporary documentation and all surviving film elements. It was a somewhat variant restoration to that attempted by the museum but infinitely more satisfying from an aesthetic and audience viewpoint.

26. *A Tribute to William K. Everson and a Few of His Friends*, p. 23.

## CHAPTER 11: JOE FRANKLIN

1. I love the notion of Leopold Stokowski explaining to Franklin, "I am not a cow. It is Sto-koff-ski but Sto-cow-ski!"

2. Brad Franklin, email to Anthony Slide, dated May 6, 2016.

3. Ibid.

4. James Barron, "Joe Franklin, Local Talk Show Pioneer, Dies at 88," p. 19.

5. Martin Block (1903–1967) would play records as if he was broadcasting from a ballroom on *Make-Believe Ballroom*, which was first heard on WNEW-New York on February 3, 1935, and which was based on a similar West Coast program hosted by Al Jarvis. Legend has it that columnist Walter Winchell coined the title "disc jockey" to describe Block's work.

6. The name change occurred after the station was purchased from RKO General, Inc., by MCA, Inc., in 1987.

7. Joe Franklin, *Up Late with Joe Franklin*, p. 96.

8. Ibid., p. 161.

9. *Joe Franklin's Memory Lane Cookbook* (Lion Books, 1974), *Joe Franklin's Awfully Corny Joke Book* (Chelsea House, 1980), *Joe Franklin's Movie Trivia* (Hastings House, 1992), and *Joe Franklin's Great Entertainment Trivia* (Square One, 2002). There was also *Joe Franklin's Nostalgia Magazine*, first published March 1990, with Lucille Ball on the cover.

10. "50 Years After Marilyn Monroe's Death—Examining the Books That Were Written about Her While She Was Living." Published by New York-based Rudolph Field, the book was distributed by Greenberg.

11. Joe Franklin, *Up Late with Joe Franklin*, pp. 118–20.

12. Brad Franklin, email to Anthony Slide, dated May 7, 2016.

13. Bambi Everson, email to Anthony Slide, dated May 4, 2016.

14. Brad Franklin, email to Anthony Slide, dated May 6, 2016.

15. Cliff Adam, interview with Anthony Slide, November 29, 2016.

16. Brad Franklin, email to Anthony Slide, dated September 29, 2016.

17. Joe Franklin, *Up Late with Joe Franklin*, p. 239.

18. Ibid., p. 241.

## CHAPTER 12: STALKERS

1. Orit Kamir, *Every Breath You Take: Stalking Narratives and the Law*, p. 114

2. Ibid. The author is quoting Christian Metz.

3. Heather Hunter, "A New Era for Celebrity Stalkers," www.lifezette.com/popsette/a-new-era-for-stalkers/.

4. For obvious reasons, I am not identifying the film buff, who died in 2016, and the leading man, who died some years ago.

5. "One Out of 12 Crashes Barriers Set up Around the movie Stars."

6. Ibid.

7. Robert L. Snow, *Stopping a Stalker: A Cop's Guide to Making the System Work for You*, p. 73.

8. Quoted in Stuart Taylor Jr., "Hinckley Hails 'Historical' Shooting to Win Love," *New York Times*, July 9, 1982, www.nytimes.com/.

9. Aside from *The King of Comedy*, the best-known film concerning a deranged fan is *The Fan* (1981), starring Lauren Bacall as a famous actress stalked by one of her fans, played by Michael Biehn. Ironically, the film was released shortly after the killing of John Lennon, who, like Lauren Bacall, lived at the Dakota Apartments in New York. A later film titled *The*

*Fan*, from 1996, is concerned with an obsessive baseball fan, played by Robert De Niro, who of course played Travis Bickle in *Taxi Driver*, which so influenced John Hinckley Jr.

10. Check out "I'm Not a Stalker, It was on My Homepage" at www.facebook.com/.

## CHAPTER 13: THE FILM BUFF, THE INTERNET, AND THE NEW AGE

1. As obviously the IMDb is aware, one cannot copyright credit information.
2. Nikki Finke, "Do You IMDB?" www.laweekly.com/.
3. Ibid.
4. Liz Smith, "The Celebrity and the Fan—What Price Glory?" p. F11.
5. Mark Duffet, *Understanding Fandom: An Introduction to the Study of Media Fan Culture*, p. 9.
6. Quoted in *The Week*, November 5, 2016, p. 5.
7. *The Scrollogram*, April 10, 1924, p. 6.
8. One blogger who did respond in general to Schickel is a retired college professor living in Florida who does not reveal her name but who hosts the roberttayloractor site. She describes Schickel as "a member of the self-appointed left-wing elite who like to tell the rest of us what to do and what to think." I rather like this lady as she continues, "Schickel is of medium height, fat and sports a bad comb over. These physical attributes might partially explain his extraordinary rancor against Taylor. The opportunity for a homely person to attack one who defined tall, dark and handsome might have been irresistible."
9. Paul Brunick, "Online Film Criticism Part One: The Living and the Dead," p. 37.
10. Richard Schickel, "Not Everybody's a Critic," p. M4.
11. Margaret Farrand Thorp, *America at the Movies*, p. 158.
12. Richard Lamparski to Anthony Slide, telephone conversation, August 2, 2016.
13. Richard Galligan, "Irish Like Their Flicks Clean, Simple—and Old," p. 11.
14. Paul Sutton, *The Moving Picture Boy Gallery* (Cambridge, UK: Buffalo Books, 2014).
15. Bosley Crowther, "Those Amazing Movie Fans," p. 15.
16. Quoted in Samuel K. Rubin, *Moving Pictures and Classic Images: Memories of Forty Years in the Vintage Film Hobby*, p. 106.
17. "Favorite Plays and Players," p. 131.

# BIBLIOGRAPHY


"Actress of Silent Era Paints Great Comics." *Valley News*, February 21, 1974, p. 105.

Almereyda, Michael. "William K. Everson, 1929–1996." In *Projections 7*, eds. John Boorman and Walter Donahue. London: Faber & Faber, 1997.

Amorosi, A. D. "The Party at McFly's—That Must be Some Sort of Victory, Celebrating the Kid from Lancaster?" *Philadelphia City Newspaper*, February 24, 2000, www.citypaper.net/.

Aron, Hillel. "Harry Major Took in Ex-Cons for Sex and Friendship. Then He Turned Up Dead." *LA Weekly*, October 21, 2015, www.laweekly.com/.

Astaire, Fred. "Astaire on Chambers." *Films in Review*, August–September 1970, p. 445.

Austin, Joe, and Michael Nevin Willard, eds. *Generations of Youth*. New York: New York University Press, 1998.

Barbas, Samantha. *Movie Crazy: Fans, Stars, and the Cult of Celebrity*. New York: Palgrave, 2001.

Barron, James. "Joe Franklin, Local Talk Show Pioneer, Dies at 88." *New York Times*, January 25, 2015, p. 19.

Becker, Josh. *Rushes*. New York: PointBlank, 2008.

Biederman, Patricia Ward. "Years Later, He's Still a Poster Boy for Films," December 26, 2003, articles.latimes.com/.

Bisch, Louis E. "Are We Morons?" *Photoplay*, March 1928, pp. 50–51, 90.

Black, Louis. "Leonard for a Day." *Austin Chronicle*, May 24, 2013, www.austinchronicle.com/.

Bower, Dallas. *Plan for Cinema*. London: J. M. Dent, 1936.

Brame, Gloria G., and William D. Brame. "2012 Leather Hall of Fame Inductee Irving Klaw," http://leatherhalloffame.com/index.php/inductees-list/15-irving-klaw (accessed January 2016).

Braun, Jonathan. "Joe Franklin Talk Show King." *Andy Warhol's Interview*, February 1974, pp. 8–9.

Brody, Richard. "Talking with Truffaut." *New Yorker*, August 15, 2010, www.newyorker.com/.

"The Brothers Who Befriended Hollywood," http://express.co.uk/life-style/life/461180 (accessed July 2014).

Brunick, Paul. "The Living and the Dead, Online Versus Old School: Time to Debunk the Myth." *Film Comment*, July–August 2010, pp. 36–39.

Callahan, Dan. "Gene Stavis: Curating and Stargazing," http://chiseler.org/post/48360066860/gene-stavis-curating-and-stargazing (accessed March 2016).

Carlson, Linda. "Today's Self-Publishing Pathways," July 2014, http://www.obpa-online.org/article/todays-self-publishing—pathways/ (accessed April 2016).

Carpenter, Mackenzie. "Fan Clubs Keep the Flame Alive for Stars Fading from Memory." *Pittsburgh Post-Gazette*, May 19, 2013, www.post-gazette.com/.

Castanza, Philip. *The Complete Films of Jeanette MacDonald and Nelson Eddy*. New York: Citadel Press/Carol Publishing, 1990.

Champlin, Charles. "An Appeciation: The Two Garys—Zealots with a Passion for Film." *Los Angeles Times*, December 18, 1992, articles.latimes.com/.

Chaneles, Sol. *Collecting Movie Memorabilia*. New York: Arco, 1977.

"Cinemabilia." *New York*, September 13, 1982, p. 47.

Citron, Alan. "Theater Owner Still Hopes Silents Are Golden." *Los Angeles Times*, June 5, 1988, Part II, p. 16.

Clark, Frances. "Their Funniest Fan Letters." *Photoplay*, April 1929, pp. 63, 138–41.

Cosgrove, Bryony. "The Stuff of Silent Legend." *Sydney Morning Herald*, March 3, 2012, www.smh.com.au/.

Cronin, Jim. "Revived Celluloid in NYC." *Columbia Daily Spectator*, April 6, 1978, p. 15.

Crowther, Bosley. "Those Amazing Movie Fans." *New York Times*, April 24, 1942, p. 15.

"Deanna Durbin Lovers in Conflict with Devoters." *Harvard Crimson*, May 24, 1938, www.thecrimson.com/.

"Deanna Fans Have a 'Devotee' Club." *Life*, October 3, 1938, pp. 33–34.

Deneroff, Harvey. "Bill Everson: Terminal Film Buff," March 22, 2008, http://deneroff.com/blog/2008/03/22/bill-everson-terminal-film-buff/ (accessed March 2016).

Drum, Dale D. "Silent Movies in Los Angeles." *Films in Review*, November 1952, pp. 450–54.

Duffett, Mark. *Understanding Fandom: An Introduction to the Study of Media Fan Culture*. New York: Bloomsbury, 2013.

Epting, Chris. "A Weekend on Planet B: Snapshots from the Far Side of Hollywood Stardom." *Los Angeles Times, West Magazine*, May 6, 2007, pp. 13–15.

Everson, William K. "The Theodore Huff Memorial Film Society," 2-page mimeographed essay, undated.

"Favorite Plays and Players." *Motion Picture Story Magazine*, October 1912, pp. 131–36.

Felchner, William J. "Chaw Mank and the World of Entertainment." *Illinois Magazine*, January–February 1990, pp. 14–17.

"50 Years after Marilyn Monroe's Death—Examining the Books That Were Written about Her While She Was Living," http://Stuffnobodycaresabout.com/2012/08/04/50-years-after-marilyn-monroes-death-examining-the-books/ (accessed May 2016).

Frank, Sam. *Ronald Colman: A Bio-Bibliography*. Westport, CT: Greenwood Press, 1997.

———. *Sex in the Cinema*. Secaucus, NJ: Citadel Press, 1986.

Franklin, Joe, and R. J. Marx. *Up Late with Joe Franklin*. New York: Scribner, 1995.

Finke, Nikki. "Do You IMDB?" *LA Weekly*, August 5, 2004, www.laweekly.com/.

Galligan, Richard. "Irish Like Their Flicks Clean, Simple—and Old." *Los Angeles Times*, September 22, 1974, p. 11.

Gardner, Joel. *Louis Epstein Oral History*. Los Angeles: UCLA Oral History Program, 1977.

"George Canham." Theodore Huff Memorial Film Society, mimeographed tribute, May 15, 1964.

Gettemy, Robert M. "Hobbyist Projects Secret into Open." *Los Angeles Times*, February 23, 1972, p. E6.

Graham, John Ringo. "Mark Ricci the Film Buff's Friend." *Hollywood Studio Magazine*, December 1972, p. 5.

Gussow, Mel. "Herb Graff, 74, Film Devotee and Preservationist, Is Dead." *New York Times*, January 15, 2000, www.nytimes.com/.

Harris, Scott. "Customer Mad as Hell, Ready to Go Postal." *Los Angeles Times*, April 4, 1996, pp. B1, B6.

Hartford, Adelaide. "Gladys Corbin." *Film Fan Monthly*, April 1969, pp. 21–23.

Harvey, Matt. "The East Village Isn't What It Used to Be. And It Never Was." *Strausmedia*, December 10, 2008, www.nypress.com/.

Hayes, Scott. "Star Struck." *Orange County Magazine*, March 1991, pp. 114–20.

"Hays Office Probes Bootleg of Studio Publicity Stills." *Hollywood Reporter*, August 22, 1939, p. 6.

Hegenberger, John. *Collector's Guide to Treasures from the Silver Screen*. Radnor, PA: Wallace Homestead, 1991.

Henderson, Randy. "Wayne Martin—Judy's Number One Fan." *Garlands for Judy*, December 2013, pp. 7–11.

Heritage, Stuart. "Does Every Film Really Need Its Own Fan Day?" *Guardian*, October 21, 2015, p. 2.

Higham, Charles. *In and Out of Hollywood: A Biographer's Memoir*. Madison, WI: Terrace Books, 2009.

Hill, Gladwin. "Silent-Film Buff Shows His Wares." *New York Times*, November 21, 1960, p. 33.

Hillinger, Charles. "Jeanette MacDonald Spirit Lives On." *Los Angeles Times*, November 9, 1980, p. 6.

Hoberman, James. "The Movie Freak's Guide to Film in New York." *New York Magazine*, December 29, 1975, pp. 72–77.

Holbrook, Earl. "Silent Haven." *Daily Variety*, October 29, 1968, pp. 87–88.

"The Hung Jury and the Infamous Sam Frank," http://www.lpsg.com/threads'the-hung-jury-and-the-infamous-sam-frank (accessed January 2016).

Hunt, Morton M. "Our Drooling Movie Fans." *The Woman*, September 1950, pp. 76–79, 118–20.

Hunter, Heather. "A New Era for Celebrity Stalkers." *Popzette*, February 22, 2016, www.lifezette.com/popzette/a-new-era-for-celebrity-stalkers (accessed March 2016).

"'I'll Be Watching You': Celebrities and Their Stalkers," July 17, 2014, www.biography.com/new/famous-celebrity-stalkers (accessed March 2016).

"In Memoriam: William K. Everson." *Films in Review*, July–August 1996, pp. 122–24.

Isherwood, Christopher, and Don Bachardy. *October*. Los Angeles: Twelvetrees Press, 1981.

Jacobson, Mark. "In Praise of Film Freaks." *Village Voice*, June 16, 1975, back page, pp. 81, 82.

Kamir, Orit. *Every Breath You Take: Stalking Narratives and the Law*. Ann Arbor, MI: University of Michigan Press, 2001.

Kasindorf, Jeanie. "Preview Henry." *Andy Warhol's Interview*, October 1973, p. 19.

Kehr, Dave. "A Lavish Busby Berkeley Musical (Is There Any Other Kind?) Displays Its Delicious Colors." *New York Times*, August 12, 2005, www.nytimes.com/.

Kelly, Lora. "How One Girl Built Up a Fan Club." *Picture Play*, December 1925, pp. 72–74.

Kendall, Robert. "Collector Chaw Mank Has a Million Stories to Tell." *Hollywood Studio Magazine*, September 1980, p. 32.

———. "De-Witt [*sic*] Bodeen." *Hollywood Studio Magazine*, September 1980, pp. 14–16.

Kijner, Nadine. "Old Time Movies." *Detour*, September 1999, pp. 100–105.

Kilgannon, Corey. "Froggy's Last Story." *New York Times*, September 10, 2010, www.nytimes.com/.

———. "An Overflow of Memories from a Storied Career." *New York Times*, January 28, 2015, p. A16.

Klein, Andy. "The Silent Remains Silent." *New Times*, January 30, 1997, p. 32.

Koszarski, Richard. "Richard Hoffman: A Collector's Archive." In *A Companion to Early Cinema*, eds. André Gaudreault, Nicolas Dulac, and Santiago Hidalgo. Hoboken, NJ: John Wiley and Sons, 2012, pp. 498–523.

Lacher, Irene. "MacDonald-Eddy: Stoking the Passions of New Fans." *Los Angeles Times*, March 1, 1995, articles.latimes.com/.

Lahue, Kalton C. *Collecting Classic Films*. New York: Hastings House, 1970.

Lamont, Tom. "How Did Two Brothers from Surrey Become Confidantes to the Stars?" *Esquire*, February 14, 2014, www.esquire.co.uk/.

Lamparski, Richard. *Hollywood Diary*. Boalsburg, PA: BearManor Media, 2006.

Lanza, Tim. "Raymond Rohauer and the Society of Cinema Arts (1948–1962): Giving the Devil His Due." In *Alternative Projections: Experimental Film in Los Angeles, 1945–1980*, eds. David E. James and Adam Hyman. New Barnet, UK: John Libbey, 2015, pp. 129–40.

Larkin, Mark. "What Happens to Fan Mail." *Photoplay*, August 1928, pp. 38–40, 130–34.

Lewis, Lisa, ed. *The Adoring Audience: Fan Culture and Popular Medium*. New York: Routledge, 1993.

Lonergan, Elizabeth. "Those Autograph Fiends." *The Picturegoer Summer Annual*, 1934, p. 64.

Magliozzi, Ronald S. "Witnessing the Development of Independent Film Culture in New York: An Interview with Charles L. Turner." *Film History*, vol. 12, no. 1, 2000, pp. 72–96.

Maltin, Leonard. "From a Brooklyn Basement to Yale University." *Indiewire*, June 2, 2015, www.indiewire.com/.

Marshall, Karen K. "Chaw Mank: The Ultimate Fan." *St. Louis Globe-Democrat Magazine*, September 11–12, 1982, pp. 4–5, 11.

McElwee, John. "National Screen Service and Collecting Days Gone By," greenbriarpictureshows.blogspot.com/.

McGahan, Michelle. "The Definitive Guide to Fan Base Nicknames: Beliebers, Directioners, Swifties + More," http:/popcrush.com/fan-nicknames-beliebers-dictioners-swifties-list/ (accessed February 2015).

McGrath, Bonnie. "Lottie Da," January 24, 1991, www.chicagoreader.com/.

McKee, Gerald. *Film Collecting*. South Brunswick, NJ: A. S. Barnes, 1978.

"Meet No. 1 All Time Movie Fan." *Hollywood Studio Magazine*, September 1974, p. 11.

Morley, Hugh R. "Rutherford Couple Face Suit over Millions of Pieces of Hollywood Memorabilia." *North Jersey Record*, November 5, 2014, www.northjersey.com/.

Moss, Jeremiah. "The Last Picture Shop." *New Yorker*, October 24, 2013, www.newyorker.com/.

Munsterberg, Hugo. *The Photoplay: A Psychological Study*. New York: D. Appleton, 1916 (reprinted in 1970 by Dover Publications as *The Film: A Psychological Study*).

"Musings of the Photoplay Philosopher." *Motion Picture Story Magazine*, July 1912, pp. 137–44.

O'Donnell, Michelle. "Man Charged with Raping 5-Year-Old Daughter." *New York Times*, July 29, 2005, www.nytimes.com/.

"One Out of 12 Crashes Barriers Set Up around Movie Stars." Newspaper clipping dated September 6, 1936, source unknown.

Pierce, Ron. "Motion Picture Hall of Fame," http://cinematreasures.org/theaters/40076 (accessed February 2015).

Poffenberger, A. T. "Motion Pictures and Crime." *Scientific Monthly*, April 1921, pp. 336–39.
Posner, Phil. "Kier's—a Reminiscence," www.philposner.com/kiers.htm (accessed July 2016).
Prelutzky, Burt. "Queen of the Movie Fans." *Hollywood Studio Magazine*, August 1978, p. 16.
Raborn, George. *How Hollywood Rates*. Los Altos, CA: Bert Nelson, 1955.
"The Random Shots of a Picture Fan." *Moving Picture World*, October 21, 1911, p. 198.
Ranalli, Ralph. "Film-Flam?" *Boston Globe*, April 26, 2000, pp. B1, B5.
Rauzi, Robin. "Not Just the Silent Treatment on Fairfax." *Los Angeles Times*, June 13, 2006, pp. E1, E5.
———. "Silent Calling." *Los Angeles Times* Calendar, November 4, 1999, pp. 6–10, 12–13.
"Revealed: How the World's Biggest Movie Database Is Run by a 'Self-Confessed Geek' from a House in Bristol." *Daily Mail*, December 31, 2010, www.dailymail.co.uk/.
Reavill, Gil. *Aftermath, Inc.: Cleaning Up after CSI Goes Home*. New York: Gotham Books, 2007.
Rebello, Stephen. "State of Siege." *American Film*, May 1984, pp. 41–45.
Rense, Rip. "Serial Box." *Los Angeles Herald-Examiner*, February 19, 1981.
———. "Sound of Silents Lives On." *Los Angeles Times*, July 5, 1993, pp. F1, F8–F9.
Rich, Sharon. *Sweethearts*. New York: Bell Harbour Press, 2001 (first published 1994).
Rohter, Larry. "Dear Donna: A Pinup So Swell She Kept G.I. Mail." *New York Times*, May 25, 2009, pp. A1, A11.
"Roll the Cameras: Hollywood Coming Here?" *Argus-Press (Michigan)*, July 7, 1993, p. 2.
Ross, Barbara. "Sicko Gets 5 Yrs. In Molest." *New York Daily News*, September 29, 2006, www.newyorkdailynews.com/.
Rubin, Samuel K. *Moving Pictures and Classic Images: Memories of Forty Years in the Vintage Film Hobby*. Jefferson, NC: McFarland, 2004.
Rugoff, Ralph. "Fantasia." *LA Weekly*, February 4, 2000, pp. 36–37.
Russell, Michelle. "Looking for Judy." *Garlands for Judy*, June 2012, pp. 16–18.
Russell, Ron. "Silent Movie Murder, Act 2." *New Times*, April 23, 1998, p. 10.
Russell, Ron, and Víctor S. Mejía. "The Last Picture Show." *New Times*, May 8, 1997, pp. 6–12.
Sarris, Andrew. "The Farthest-Out Movie Goers." *Saturday Review*, December 26, 1964, pp. 14–15.
Saunders, Rhonda B., and Stephen G. Michaud. *Whisper of Fear: The True Story of the Prosecutor Who Stalks the Stalkers*. New York: Berkley True Crime, 2009.
Schelly, Bill. *Founders of Comic Fandom: Profiles of 90 Publishers, Dealers, Collectors, Writers, Artists and Other Luminaries of the 1950s and 1960s*. Jefferson, NC: McFarland, 2010.
Schickel, Richard. *Intimate Strangers: The Culture of Celebrity*. New York: Doubleday, 1985.
——— "Not Everybody's a Critic." *Los Angeles Times*, May 20, 2007, p. M4.
Seton, Marie. "Ancient Rome in Gangster Town." *Sight and Sound*, June 1950, pp. 176–77.
Silberg, Jon. "Silence Is Golden." *Boxoffice*, November 1994, pp. 52–53.
"Silent Movie Theatre." Dead History Project, http://deadhistoryproject.com/other-projects/silent-movie-theater/ (accessed February 2015).
"Silents Glorified at Old-Time Studio." *Los Angeles Times*, November 28, 1960, Part III, pp. 1, 10.
Singer, Mark. "Our Far-Flung Correspondents." *New Yorker*, June 3, 1991, pp. 89–103.
Slide, Anthony, ed. *International Film, Radio, and Television Journals*. Westport, CT: Greenwood Press, 1985.
———. "Letter from Hollywood." In *Film Review 1985–6*, ed. F. Maurice Speed. London: Columbus Books, 1985, pp. 133–38.

Smith, Liz. "The Celebrity and the Fan—What Price Glory?" *Los Angeles Times*, September 2, 1991, p. F11.

Smith, Rick. "Hickory Police Officer Gathers the Stars." *Hickory Daily Record*, date unknown.

Snow, Robert L. *Stopping a Stalker: A Cop's Guide to Making the System Work for You.* Cambridge, MA: Perseus, 1998.

Stahl, Jerry. "Obsession!" *Los Angeles*, October 1982, pp. 162–71, 261–65.

Stanhope, Mercia. "A Valentino Memorial Guild." *Picture Play*, May 1927, pp. 8, 10.

Steiger, Brad, and Chaw Mank. *Valentino*. New York: MacFadden-Bartel, 1966.

Stein, Elliott. "New York 1970: The Year of the Foof." *Sight and Sound*, Autumn 1970, pp. 204–207.

Stempel, Tom. *American Audiences on Movies and Moviegoing*. Lexington, KY: University Press of Kentucky, 2001.

"The Still and Its Mission." *Motion Picture News*, December 27, 1919, p. 240.

Stokes, Melvyn, and Richard Maltby, eds. *American Movie Audiences: From the Turn of the Century to the Early Sound Era*. London: BFI Publishing, 1999.

"Stuff Nobody Cares About," http://stuffnobodycaresabout.com/2012/08/04/50-years-after-marilyn-monroes-death-examining-the-books/ (accessed May 2016).

Tanner, Louise. "A Short History of *Films in Review*." *Films in Review*, January–February 1994, pp. 2–5.

Theisen, E. "The Historical Motion Picture Exhibit at the Los Angeles Museum." *Journal of the Society of Motion Picture Engineers*, March 1936, pp. 259–69.

"This Man Has Seen 5,592 Movies." *Look*, August 9, 1955, pp. 96–98, 101–102.

Thomas, Bob. "Stars and Letter Writers." Associated Press syndicated column, November 14, 2010.

Thorp, Margaret Farrand. *America at the Movies*. London: Faber and Faber, 1946.

Thorpe, Vanessa. "Now No Longer Silent as a Lamb." *Guardian*, December 15, 2007, www.theguardian.com/.

Timberg, Scott. "Reviled Revivalist." *New Times*, January 4, 2001, pp. 13–19.

*A Tribute to William K. Everson by a Few of His Friends*. Vestal, NY: Syracuse Cinephile Society/Vestal Press, 1997.

Turan, Kenneth. "Film Land's Book World." *Arizona Republic*, February 26, 1978, p. N5. Syndicated from the *Washington Post*.

Tuttle, Mike. "Jodie Foster Stalker Walks the Streets Tailed by Secret Service." April 19, 2015, www.webpronews.com/.

Viuker, Steven J. "Television's Master of Memory Lane Goes Public." *New York Times*, November 22, 1987, p. F7.

Wasson, Haidee. *Museum Movies: The Museum of Modern Art and the Birth of Art Cinema*. Berkeley, CA: University of California Press, 2005.

Watt, Douglas. "Profiles: Film Resource." *New Yorker*, November 20, 1989, pp. 59–69.

Weaver, John D. "The Movies Are Silent Again—At Last in One Los Angeles Theater." *Coast*, September 1976, p. W16b.

Weaver, Tom. "Norman, Is That You?" *The Astounding B Monster Archive*, http://www.bmonster.com/horror29.html (accessed February 2016).

Weber, John. "An Outline of Syracuse Cinephile History," March 2015, syracusecinephile.com/history/our-story/ (accessed May 2016).

"Whatever Became of . . . Richard Lamparski?: Exclusive Interview with Mr. Yesterday." October 23, 2012, http://www.boyculture.com/boy_culture/2012/10/richard lamparski-whatever-became-of-gossip-gay-rumors-books.html.

Wilinsky, Barbara. *Sure Seaters: The Emergence of Art House Cinema*. Minneapolis: University of Minnesota Press, 2001.

Wilkins, Barbara. "Jeanette MacDonald Fan Club Lives on after Death of Star," *Toledo Blade*, October 8, 1967, p. 2.

Yaros, Valerie. "My Experience at the Silent Movie Theatre on Friday January 17, 1997," email account.

Wilson, Eric G. "The Most Dangerous Hobby in the World: Film Collecting in the Digital Age." *Virginia Quarterly Review*, Spring 2009, vqronline.

# INDEX


A. J. Caley & Sons, 34
Abrahams, Gary, 91
Abrams, J. J., 144
Academy Awards, 4, 122–23
Academy of Motion Picture Arts and Sciences, 36, 116
Academy of Science Fiction, Fantasy and Horror Films, 58
Ackerman, Forest J, 180
Adam, Cliff, 193
Adler, Renata, 22
American Cinematheque, 90
American Film Institute, 39
*American Film Institute Catalog*, 5, 169, 205
American Movie Classics, 137–39
Ames, Aydelott, 115
Anderson, Pat, 127
Anger, Kenneth, 88
Angstreich, Jack, 75
Appreciating Jeanette MacDonald Club, 56
Arcadia Press, 131
Arkush, Alan, 93
Arnold, Alan, 52
Ashford, Prudence, 121
Asimov, Isaac, 105, 107
Association of Threat Assessment Professionals, 204
Astaire, Fred, 123
auction houses, 208
Austin, Laurence "Larry," 154–58
autograph collectors, 8, 9, 20, 21, 27–29
Ava Gardner Museum, 58
Bachardy, Don, 165
Backlot Books, 40
Baggot, King, 150
Ball, Lucille, 58
Ballard, Paul, 35, 89
Banky, Vilma, 18–19
Barbour, Alan G., 85–86, 128
Bardo, John, 198–99
Barker, Betty, 51
Barricade Books, 131
Barry, Iris, 73, 74
Bateman, Pete, 141
BearManor Media, 131, 209
Beaver, Jim, 129
Beck, Calvin, 76–77
Becker, Adolphe, 48
Beeler, William C., Jr., 136
Behlmer, Rudy, 17, 114–15, 118, 169, 180, 183
Belaney, Ida, 75
Belton, John, 184
*Ben-Hur*, 82
Bennett, Alan, 208
Benson, Gary, 203
Beranger, George "Andre," 95–96
Berlin, Ariel, 163
Berry, Halle, 203
Beverly Garland Howard Johnson Hotel, 176
Beyoncé, 212
Bieber, Justin, 212
*Big Lebowski, The*, 211
*Big Reel*, 134, 177

Birchard, Bob, 136
*Birth of a Nation, The*, 150–51
Bisch, Louis E., 16
*Black Room, The*, 9–10
Blackhawk Films, 137
Bleeker Street Theatre, 87
Blockwell, Mary, 56
Blum, Daniel, 180–81
Boas, Gary, 35–36
Bodeen, DeWitt, 115–17, 127, 128, 165, 209
*Bodil and Her Friends*, 67
Boles, John, 64, 196
Bone, Henry, 6–7
Bonner, Marjorie, 102
Bonner, Priscilla, 102
Book City, 142, 144
books for film buffs, 130–31
Borg, Veda Ann, 66
Bow, Clara, 31, 47, 48, 152
Bowers, Ronald L., 115, 125–26
Boyd, Jim. *See* Frank, Sam
Bradley, David, 75, 77, 97–104
Brandt, Eddie, 38–40
Braverman, Barnett G., 73
Bret, David, 88
Brian, Mary, 31
Britt, Gwenneth, 121
Brock, Patrick, 132
Bronson, Charles, 13
Brooks, Louise, 29, 47, 48
Broussard, Greg, 203
Brown, Barry, 10–11, 125
Brown, Chris, 213
Brown, Leonard, 143
Brownlow, Kevin, 82, 101, 136, 185
Buckley, Michael, 127
Bullock, Sandra, 202
Burns, Ernest D., 144–45
Burr, Raymond, 210

Caidin, Eric, 144
*Captain Celluloid vs. the Film Pirates*, 128
Carlisle, Christine, 172
Carlisle, Kitty, 177
Carnegie Hall Cinema, 87–88
Carol Publishing, 130
Carpenter, Carleton, 43
Casselton, Harold "Rusty," 103
Castanza, Philip, 55
Castle Hill Productions, 110
*Castle of Frankenstein*, 76
*Cesar Romero News*, 63
Chambers, N. C., 122–23
*Chandu on the Magic Isle*, 81
Chaney, Lon, 47, 48, 114, 184
Chapin, Elspeth Burke, 112
Chapin, Harry, 112, 126
Chapin, John, 124
Chaplin, Charlie, 76, 107, 130, 184
Chapman, Mark David, 204
Charles Greenberg & Sons, 108
Chatterton, Robert Wade "Bob," 88–89
Cherokee Bookstore, 144
cigarette cards, 34–35
Cinecon, 109, 110, 135–36
Cinefamily, 161
Cinefest, 136–37
Cinemabilia, 144–46
*Cinemania*, 75
Citadel Press, 41–42, 130–31, 191
Clarens, Carlos, 178
Clarke, Mae, 18
*Classic Film Collector*, 72
*Classic Images*, 134–35
Classic Movie Blog Association, 209
*Classics of the Silent Screen*, 191–92
Clooney, Nick, 138
Cocchi, John, 10, 107, 110
Cohen, Joan, 92, 93, 169
*Coincidence*, 13, 14
Collectors Bookstore, 143–44
Colman, Ronald, 169
Comerford, Adelaide, 121
Comic-Con, 213
Condon, Jack, 40
Connor, Ed, 81, 115, 128
Conti, Albert, 66
Cook, Page, 118–19, 127
Cooper, Gary, 13, 47
Cooper, Merian C., 175

Cooper, Tommy, 90
Corbett, Joshua, 202
Coronet Theatre, 89–90, 101
Count Dracula Society, 57–58
Courts, Ray, 176
Courts, Sharon, 176
*Covered Wagon, The*, 152–53
Crawford, Cis, 52
Crawford, Dale, 119
Crawford, Joan, 7, 48–51, 64, 87, 123, 130
Crawford, Merritt, 185
Crawford, Roz, 52
Crenna, Richard, 202
Criterion, 137
Crivello, Kirk, 132
Cromwell, Richard, 106, 183
Cruise, Tom, 203
Cummins, Samuel, 78
Cushman, Robert, 60
Cyrus, Miley, 213

Da, Lottie, 106
Dabich, Misha, 193
Daniels, Bebe, 196–97
"Dani's Doughnuts," 135
Dante, Joe, 15, 93
Davy, Darryl A., 128
"Day of the Dude," 211
Deanna Durbin Devotees, 56–57
*Deanna's Diary*, 56
Del Villar, Gracie Marie, 203
Delgado, Marcel, 175
Denny, Dorothy H., 132
Detlaff, Alois "Al," 11–12
Dewar, John, 184
Dickens, Homer, 115
Dietrich, Marlene, 9
Dix, Richard, 63, 210, 212
Dommer, Marion, 48
Donaldson, Ted, 144, 145
Donnachie, William, 135
Dorian, Bob, 138–39
Douglas, Michael, 202
Doyle, Bill H., 119
*Dream World of Dion McGregor, The*, 43
Drowne, Tatiana Balkoff, 121, 123
Du Main, Ken, 103
Durbin, Deanna, 56–57, 177
Durfee, Minta, 18, 152

Eastin, Kent D., 137
eBay, 207–8
*Ecstasy*, 78
Eddie Brandt's Saturday Matinee, 38–40
Eddy, Nelson, 55, 210
Edmund, Lawrence O'Connell "Larry," 139–40
Edwards, Christopher, 12–13
Edwards, Susan, 12–13
*8mm Collector*, 134–35
Eighth Street Theatre, 87
Electric Theatre Movie Museum, Inc., 174
Em Gee Film Library, 137
EMO Movie Club, 48
eMoviePoster.com, 208
Entertainment Collectibles, 44
Epstein, Bob, 90, 183
Epstein, Louis, 144
Essert, Gary, 91–92
Essex Film Club, 84
Evans, Robert A., 119
Everson, Bambi, 82–83, 192
Everson, William K., 4, 34, 37, 42, 77, 78–83, 97, 101, 104, 115, 125, 127, 128, 163, 177, 185, 191–92

F. C. Bayern Muchen, 212
Fairbanks, Douglas, 46, 47
*Famous Monsters of Filmland*, 180
Fan Club Guild, 65
fan clubs, 45–60, 61–72
fan mail, 45–60
Farentino, James, 204
Fayette, Madeleine, 7, 8
Feldman, Gwen, 141
Fiddler, Jimmie, 49
*Film Buff*, 134
film buff, origin of term, 21–22
film collectors, 15, 95–110
*Film Fan Monthly*, 128–29

Film Guild Cinema, 87
Film Security Office, 94, 134
Filmavens, 109
Filmex, 91
*Films in Review*, 111–29, 165, 166, 177
*Films of Errol Flynn, The*, 183
Fiorentino, Nick, 137
Flame, Ditra, 53
Flicker Alley, 137
Flint, Leslie, 51–52, 54
Flynn, Errol, 196
FOOFS, 88
Foster, Jodie, 200–202
Fox, Michael J., 202
Francis, Kay, 162
Frank, Sam, 168–72
Franklin, Joe, 43, 132, 187–94
Freeman, Isidore "Dore," 50
Frumkes, Roy, 126, 127
Fulbright, Tom, 173, 209

Gable, Clark, 28
Gallagher, John, 127
*Gang's All Here, The*, 177
Garbo, Greta, 19, 32, 33, 38, 196, 197
Gardner, Ava, 58
Garland, Judy, 57, 60, 93, 196
Garland, Sue, 56
Geffen, Sid, 87
Geltzer, George, 77, 115, 117
Gent family, 8
Gere, Richard, 202
Gibson, Mel, 203
Gilbert's Books, 144
Giles, Mary, 156, 157
Giroux, Robert, 123–24, 125
Gish, Lillian, 9, 29, 82, 112
Gitt, Robert, 100, 101, 106
Glass, Murray, 137
Glenn Photo, 137
*Golden Comet, The*, 55
Gombel, Minna, 65, 69
Gomez, Selena, 213
Gordon, Alex, 177
Gordon, Richard, 177
Gorey, Edward, 42, 79
Gosling, Ryan, 203
Goudal, Jetta, 152, 173
Graff, Herb, 82, 104–10, 162
Graham, Lee, 28, 132
Grapevine Video, 137
Graves, Ralph, 210
Gray, Bert, 76
Gray, Sabin, 40
Greenhill, Mary, 54
Griffith, Corinne, 19
Griffith, D. W., 73, 89, 95, 112, 142, 185
Griggs, John, 84, 85, 96

Haines, Chauncey, 100
Hall, Michael, 52
Hamilton, Lloyd, 208
Hampton, Dorothy, 147–55, 158, 160
Hampton, Gilbert, 147, 158, 159
Hampton, John, 22, 147–54, 158, 159
Hanson, Patricia King, 169
Harding, Ann, 29
Hardy, Jack, 137
Harkman, Dan, 161
Harkman, Sammy, 161
Harlow, Jean, 67–68, 133, 195, 197
Harrington, Curtis, 166, 183
Harron, Robert, 13, 14
Hart, Doug, 40
Hart, Henry, 112–14, 117, 118, 119–20, 121–24, 125, 129
Harvard University, 56
Hathcock, Luther, 8–9
Haver, Ron, 92–94, 137, 170
Hawks, Mike, 9–10, 38–39, 141–42, 144, 162–63
Hayworth, Rita, 90
*Heaven's Gate*, 7
Heckman, Samuel, 15
Hell, Richard, 145
Herbert, Hugh, 28
Heritage Auctions, 208
Herman, Pee-wee (Paul Reubens), 176
Heston, Charlton, 77, 97, 98
Hewitt, Jennifer Love, 204

Higham, Charles, 100, 123, 183
Hill, Roberta, 75
Hinckley, John W., Jr., 200–201
Hoaglin, Jess L., 132
Hoffman, Richard, 25–26
Holland, Albert F., 196–97
Holland, Larry Lee, 116, 127, 165–66, 167
Hollywood, Ken, 38
Hollywood Book and Poster, 144
"Hollywood Legends Collection," 173–74
Hollywood Museum, 173
*Hollywood Studio Magazine*, 132–34
Holmstrom, Jack, 212
Homan, Audrey, 52–54
*Home Maker, The*, 150
homosexuality, 55, 95, 103, 121, 132, 155, 162, 166–68, 210
Hooker, Matthew, 203
Hope, Lee, 100
*How Hollywood Rates*, 6
Howe, Quincy, 123
Hudson, Rochelle, 67
Hudson, Rock, 96
Huff, Theodore, 35, 74, 75–76, 113
Hung Jury, 171–72

Impact Promotion and Publishing, 134
Ince, Thomas H., 150
Inman, Mary, 56
International Wizard of Oz Club, 57–58
Internet, 206–14
Internet Movie Database, 206–7
Isherwood, Christopher, 165

Jackson, Arthur Richard, 199–200
Jacobs, Jack, 115
Jacobsen Publishing Co., Inc., 31
James, Ronnie, 177
Jeanette MacDonald Fan Club, 55–56
JEFF Films, 137
Jenkinson, Philip, 54
Jentz, Marian, 56
Jerry's Deli, 106
Jessel, George, 190
*Joe Franklin Show*, 188–91
*Joe Franklin's Memory Lane*, 188–91
Joe's Place, 87
John Boles Golden Voice Club, 63
John Player & Sons, 34
Joseph, Jeff, 177
Judice, Joe, 87
*Julius Caesar*, 77, 97, 98
Justice, David, 203

Kael, Pauline, 185
Kalish, Bob, 75
Kaplan, Mike, 41, 145
Karnbad, Roger, 36
Katz, Morris, 189
Kearns, Marty, 135
Kenly, Bill, 77
Kerr, Walter, 105
Kerrigan, J. Warren, 212
Kidman, Nicole, 203
Kier, Henry, 40
Killiam, Paul, 81
*King Kong*, 37, 137, 175
*King of Kings*, 148
Klaw, Irving, 43–44, 163–65
Klaw, Paula, 43–44, 163
Knauer, Audrey Jean, 13
Knight, Dawnette, 202
Knight, Ray, 173
Knowles, Eleanor, 84–85
Kodascope Library, 152
Koll, Don, 84–85, 117
Koszarski, Richard, 25, 184, 185
Kralian, Scott, 158
Kramborg, Arlene, 121
Kreuger, Miles, 84, 173
Kuncova, Veronika, 202

Lady Gaga, 212
Laemmle, Carl, 22–24
Lahue, Kalton C., 135
Lake, Alice, 28
Lake, Arthur, 28
Lamparski, Richard, 5, 36, 88, 178, 182–83, 211
Lanchbery, John, 53

Landis, John, 15, 144
Landon, Michael, 202
Langlois, Henri, 183
Lanza, Mario, 58
Larry Edmunds Bookstore, 9, 39, 128, 139–43
Larson, Milt, 89
Larson, Ted, 103
Laserdisc, 137
Laurence, Kenneth G., 117
Lawrence, Florence, 22–24
Ledbetter, Tina Marie, 202
LeBold, John, 173–74
Lee, Anna, 178, 179
Lee, Raymond, 133
Lee, Robert E., 84
Leiby, Minnie, 209
Lennig, Arthur, 80–81, 185
Lennon, John, 204
"Lest We Forget" clubs, 63, 64
Lewis, Jerry, 203–4
Lewis, Spike, 158
Lewton, Val, 115
Liberace, 28, 69
list keeping, 5, 25
Little, Robin, 126, 127
Lloyd, Norman, 100
Lloyd, Peggy, 100
Lloyd, Richard, 145
Los Angeles County Museum of Art, 92–93
Los Angeles County Museum of Natural History, 183–84
Los Angeles Film Exposition, 91
Los Angeles Police Department, 204
Love, Bessie, 28
Lovell, Dorothy, 79
Loy, Myrna, 109, 125
Luboviski, Din, 141–42
Luboviski, Git, 140, 141
Luboviski, Milt, 140, 141
Luboviski, Phil, 141–42
Lucky Girl and Boy shirts, 108
Luft, Herbert G., 117, 127
Lustman, Charles, 159–61
Lyles, A. C., 153
MacDonald, Jeanette, 55–56
Mac/Eddy Club, 55
MacIntyre, Diane, 158
MacIntyre, F. "Froggy" Gwynplaine, 10
Madison, Guy, 27
Magill, Marcia, 127
Maguire, Edward, 74, 75
Maguire, Mary, 74, 75
Major, Harry, 158
Maltin, Alice, 107, 170
Maltin, Leonard, 19, 21, 41, 77, 80, 104, 106–7, 108, 109, 110, 128–29, 135, 163, 170–71
Mancini, Henry, 118
Mandelbaum, Howard, 178–80
Mank, Chaw, 61–72, 187, 188
Mantor, Jeffrey, 142
*Marilyn Monroe Story: The Intimate Inside Story of Hollywood's Hottest Glamor Girl, The*, 191
Mario Lanza Institute, 58
Marrill, Alvin H., 115, 117, 127, 128
Martin, Dean, 58
Martin, Wayne, 57
Marx, Groucho, 169
Masino, Jeffery, 137
McBride, Joseph, 93
McCarthy, Todd, 93, 103
McCarty, Clifford, 183
McClelland, Doug, 132
McCormick, Constance, 7–8
McDowall, Roddy, 96
McGregory, Dion, 42
McMahon, Louis, 97, 128
McNiven, Roger, 179–80
McPhail, Addie, 18
Meginnis, I. K., 136, 137
Meisel, Myron, 93
*Merton of the Movies*, 26
Miller, Henry, 140
Miller, Mary, 55
Miller, Norman, 117
Miller, Roger, 128
Minaj, Nicki, 213
Minot Films, 137
Minter, Mary Miles, 115

Mitchell, Bob, 154
Mitchell, George J., 78, 82
Mitchell, Rick, 177
Mix, Tom, 213
Monroe, Marilyn, 191
Mora, Dean, 156, 157
Morgan, Paul, 8
Motion Picture & Television Research Archive, 178
Motion Picture Country House, 9, 18
Motion Picture Hall of Fame, 174–76
*Motion Picture Story Magazine*, 25
Movie Club Guild, 48
*Movie Collector's World*, 134
*Movie Crazy*, 26
Movie Fans Friendship Club, 61, 64, 67
*Movie Fans' News*, 63
Movie Photo Co., 30
Movie Star News, 38, 42, 43–44, 163–65
*Moving Picture Boy Gallery, The*, 212
Moving Picture Club of America, Inc., 48
*Moving Picture World*, 24
Mullins, "Moon," 37
Munsterberg, Hugo, 26
Museum of Modern Art, 73–75, 101, 107, 117, 148–49, 184
Mutti-Mewse, Austin, 9
Mutti-Mewse, Howard, 9
Myers, Carmel, 63

Nangle, John, 127
Napolis, Diana Louisa, 204
National Board of Review of Motion Pictures, Inc., 111, 123, 124, 126, 127, 129
National Screen Service, 37
National Tom Mix Festival, 213
Neagle, Anna, 66
Needham, Col, 206
Neville, Margaret, 54
"New Star Shines in Heaven, A," 67–68
*New York Dramatic Mirror*, 24
New Yorker Theatre, 87
Nichols, Dudley, 113
Niles Films, 137
Nolan, Doris, 65
Nolan, Jack Edmund, 115
Norma Talmadge Club, 60
Norman, Jonathan, 204
Norris, Bud 213
Novarro, Ramon, 52–55

Oberon, Merle, 52
O'Brien, George, 81
O'Dell, Paul, 52
Ohlinger, Jerry, 43
Ohmart, Ben, 131
Omidyar, Pierre, 207
Ork, Terry, 145
Orowitz, E. M., 48
Osborne, Robert, 3, 138
otaku, 22
Otway, Howard, 87
"Our Gang," 47, 157

Packard, David W., 159
Page, Bettie, 164–65
Page, Ellen, 203
Paige, Marvin, 178, 179
Palmer, Laurie, 191
"paper" shows, 176
Paperman, Gary, 193
Paramount Pictures, 152
Parish, James Robert, 117, 213
Parlour Cinema, 88
*Peanuts* cartoon, 213
Pearson, Alice Canby, 121
Pearson, Harry, Jr., 126
Peeples, Samuel A., 124
Penner, Joe, 67
Perry, Katy, 212
*Phantom of the Opera, The*, 150
Philbin, Mary, 102, 142
photographs, 36–37
*Photoplay*, 16, 29
*Photoplay: A Psychological Study, The*, 26
Pickford, Mary, 46, 60, 61, 184
Pickwick Books, 144
Pierson, Harry, 35
Pitt, Brad, 203
Poffenberger, A. T., 16

Porter, Darwin, 88
postcards, 32–34
posters, 37
Power, Tyrone, 60
Preminger, Otto, 190
"Preview Henry." *See* Bone, Henry
Price, Vincent, 171
Pringle, Aileen, 183
Profiles in History, 208

Quine, Robert, 145
Quirk, James R., 16

Raborn, George, 6
Raft, George, 48, 196, 210
Ramon Novarro Fan Club, 52–55
Raymond, Gene, 55
Reagan, Ronald, 200
Reed, Donald A., 58
Reichert-Habbishaw, Ursula, 202
Reilly, Charles Phillips, 124–25, 126
Resnick, Ira M., 145
Reynolds, Debbie, 60, 174
Rhodes, Clara, 55, 56
Rhodes, Gary, 184–85
Ricci, Mark, 40–43, 194
Rich, Sharon, 55
Richardson, Anna Steese, 26–27
Richardson, Edward, 201
Ringgold, Gene, 115, 117, 128
Riquier, Constance, 59
*Rise and Fall of Free Speech in America, The*, 143
*River, The*, 177
Riviera Capri Theatre, 89
Robert Taylor Friendship Club, 64
Robert Wade Chatterton's Memorable Film Society, 89
*Rocky Horror Picture Show, The*, 90
Rodrigues, Christian, 156, 157–58
Rogers, Ginger, 9, 28
Rohauer, Raymond, 89, 101
Roland, Athena Marie, 203
Roman, Robert L., 115
Romero, Cesar, 63
Rosemary Award Association, 173
Rosing, Bodil, 67
Ross, Heinrich, 32
Ross Verlag, 32–34
Rothschild, Elaine, 121
Rubin, Samuel K., 134–36
running times, 5, 117
Russell, Lynn, 52

Saldana, Theresa, 199–200
Salinger, J. D., 96–97
Sandford, Rick, 165–69
Sansweet, Stephen J., 180
Saunders, Mary Jane, 59
Scaramazza, Paul, 145
Schaeffer, Rebecca, 197–99
Schickel, Richard, 59, 60, 210–11
Schneider, Don, 174
Schrader, Paul, 142, 143
Scorsese, Martin, 15, 199
Scott, Peggy, 51
scrapbooks, 7–8
Screen Art Studios, 32
*Screen Facts*, 128, 142
Scroll Motion Picture Correspondence Club, 209
Seller, Tom, 135
Selznick, David O., 114–15
Semon, Larry, 156,
Senior League, 208
Serling, Phil, 137
*Sex in the Cinema*, 171
Sherman, Eric, 19
Sherman, Sam, 176
Shibuk, Charles, 75, 79
Sidney, Sylvia, 19, 132
Sieverling, Richard, 213
Silent Movie Theatre, 22, 147–61
"Silents Majority, The," 158
Simpson, Cody, 213
Sinatra, Frank, 9
Sinatra, Tina, 204
Sinclair, Zach, 203
Singer, Mark, 213
Sinkler, Eunice, 121

Skarsgaard, Alexander, 203
Skoll, Jeff, 207
Slancy, Marguerite, 56
Smegal, Michael, 201–2
Smith, Albert E., 28
Smith, Liz, 208
Smith, Packy, 176
Society for Cinephiles, Ltd., 109, 135–36
Sofu, Dante Michael, 202
Sons of the Desert, 128
Sorkin, Miles, 130
Spears, Britney, 212
Spears, Jack, 117
Spielberg, Steven, 304
Spilker, Eric, 177
stalkers, 195–205
Stanhope, Marcia, 51
*Star Dust Magazine*, 48
*Star Is Born, A*, 93
*Star Wars*, 180, 211
Stavis, Gene, 109
Steiger, Brad, 69–70
Stein, Elliott, 88
Stein, Jeanne, 120–21
Stern, Seymour, 75, 77, 112
still photographs. *See* photographs
Struthers, Sally, 176
Stuart, Lyle, 130–31
Suber, Howard, 98, 100
suicides of film buffs, 10–11
*Sunrise*, 156
Sutcliffe, Molly, 54
Sutton Cinema Society, 84
Swanson, Gloria, 109, 125
Sweet, Blanche, 125, 129
Swift, Taylor, 213

Talbot, Dan, 87
*Talk about a Stranger*, 97
Talmadge, Norma, 20, 59–60
Tarantino, Quentin, 15, 144
Tatum, Channing, 28
*Taxi Driver*, 200
Taylor, Christopher James, 202
Taylor, Robert, 64
Taylor, Ted, 140
Thalia Theatre, 87
Theatre 80 St. Marks 80, 87
Theisen, Earl, 183–84
Then and There Media, 126
Theodore Huff Memorial Film Society, 4, 19, 77–80, 107–8, 163
"There's a New Star in Heaven Tonight," 13
*They Saved Hitler's Brain*, 98
Thomas, Bob, 50
Thomas, Tony, 183
Thorp, Margaret Farrand, 35
*Thousand Eyes Cinema Guide, The*, 87–88
Three Stooges, 48
Thunderbird Films, 137
Thurman, Uma, 202
Tiffany Theatre, 90
Tozzi, Romano, 115, 118
Tracy, Spencer, 66
Truffaut, François, 142, 143, 145, 175
Trupp, Nathan Nicholas, 202
Turner, Charles L., 77, 114
Turner, John B., 112
Turner Classic Movies, 3, 84, 137–39, 213, 214
Twelvetrees, Helen, 109
Twitter, 212–13
*2001: A Space Odyssey*, 211

UCLA Film and Television Archive, 90, 91, 100, 183
Universal Studios Tour, 24
Uselton, Roi, 115, 119

Vagabond Theatre, 90
*Valentino*, 69–71
Valentino, Lou, 132
Valentino, Rudolph, 13–14, 26, 30–31, 51–52, 53, 61, 66, 69–70
Valentino Memorial Guild, 51–52, 54
Vallee, Rudy, 190
Van Ness, Mary Lou, 59
Van Sickle, James, 155–58
Van Tassel, Edward, 203
Vaughn, Adamae, 45–46

Vaughn, Alberta, 45–46
Vermilye, Jerry, 41, 119–20, 129
*Victims for Victims: The Theresa Saldana Story*, 200
Vintage Association of Motion Picture Blogs, 209
Virzi, Jon, 36
*Voice, The*, 69

W. D. and H. O. Wills, 34
Wagenknecht, Edward, 125
Walsh, George, 28
Ward, Brendan, 126
Webster, Tom, 100
Weinberg, Herman G., 77, 84, 115
We-Love-Deanna-Durbin Club, 56–57
West, Adam, 176
West, Mae, 152
Wharton, Flavia, 121
*Whatever Became Of . . .?* books, 5, 36, 182–83
"Whispering Suzy," 36
Whitney, Doug, 43
Williams, Tessa, 55
Willis, John, 181
Willits, Malcolm, 143–44
Willoughby, Mark, 143, 144
Wilson, Allan J., 130–31
Wise, Robert, 11
Withers, Jane, 60
Wong, Anna May, 28
Woods, Frank, 24–25
Wright, Doug, 174–76
*Wrong Road, The*, 106
Wyanoak Publishing Co., 30

Yaros, Valerie, 156–57
Youngson, Robert, 77

Zeta-Jones, Catherine, 202

# CON PRECISIÓN

# CON PRECISIÓN

## *El listón de la hermenéutica bíblica*

JAIME FASOLD

Tyndale House Publishers, Inc.
Carol Stream, Illinois, EE. UU.

Visite Tyndale en Internet: www.tyndaleespanol.com y www.BibliaNTV.com.

*TYNDALE* y el logotipo de la pluma son marcas registradas de Tyndale House Publishers, Inc.

*Con precisión: El listón de la hermenéutica bíblica*



Para información acerca de descuentos especiales para compras al por mayor, por favor contacte a Tyndale House Publishers a través de espanol@tyndale.com.

ISBN 978-1-4964-2738-0

Impreso en Estados Unidos de América
Printed in the United States of America

25 24 23 22 21 20
9 8 7 6 5 4

A Carolina,
mi maravillosa esposa
por 51 años

# Recomendación

de Samuel Pérez Millos

La hermenéutica, como ciencia y arte de la interpretación bíblica, es determinante para el correcto conocimiento de las Escrituras, y resulta en una definición precisa de la fe. Esta interpretación ha de hacerse de un modo preciso si queremos que tanto el fundamento como la práctica de la vida cristiana sean consecuentes con la verdad revelada por Dios a través del trabajo de hombres seleccionados por él a lo largo del tiempo. Una imperfecta aplicación de los principios de la hermenéutica bíblica trae como consecuencia una fe sin fundamento y una vida sin orientación. De ahí la necesidad de un enfoque que sea correcto.

Sin duda uno de los problemas actuales tiene que ver con los métodos de interpretación incorrectos que alteran el sentido de pasajes de las Escrituras. Por esta razón, tanto el alegorismo como el literalismo, unidos a la dependencia del dogmatismo teológico, han producido una teología humanista, en el amplio sentido de la palabra. A esto se une también la llamada interpretación espiritualista, basada en sentimientos personales a los que se da carácter hermenéutico. La alta crítica aporta otro elemento distorsionante al negar autoría, inspiración e inerrancia, cuestionando la autoridad suprema de la Palabra. Todo esto hace necesario y urgente el retorno a la hermenéutica basada en una interpretación detallada y pormenorizada del texto bíblico, coordinada y en armonía con la totalidad de las Escrituras que, teniendo en cuenta las figuras del lenguaje, los tipos y símbolos, enseña que la Biblia tiene una sola interpretación, sin olvidar las muchas aplicaciones que pueden obtenerse del análisis de su texto.

Esto hace que el libro del profesor y amigo Jaime Fasold sea de suma importancia. Redactado en forma ordenada, lleva al lector a entender con toda claridad la ciencia hermenéutica, guiándolo como sabe hacerlo quien ha dedicado su vida a la formación de centenares de creyentes, hombres y mujeres, que están ejerciendo importantes funciones en el campo pastoral o educativo en iglesias y entidades académicas. Este espíritu de maestro se aprecia ya desde el primer momento con las recomendaciones para un mejor aprovechamiento del estudio del libro. Sigue luego un desarrollo progresivo con una síntesis histórica de la hermenéutica, estudiando asuntos capitales como revelación, inspiración e inerrancia. Aborda también asuntos de la crítica textual, considerando aspectos del texto griego y hebreo, de los manuscritos, variantes textuales, etcétera, que permiten establecer una correcta elección de las alternativas de lectura. No deja de abordar otros asuntos como el lenguaje figurado y la tipología en sus múltiples formas. Finalmente es de destacar la precisión sobre el método hermenéutico gramático-histórico-cultural, que permite una correcta interpretación. Estos y otros muchos aspectos hacen de este libro un tratado de estudio de gran importancia y de elevado contenido bíblico-científico para una correcta interpretación de las Escrituras.

He tenido el privilegio de colaborar con Jaime Fasold durante años en el Instituto Bíblico y Seminario Teológico de España, tanto en el aula como en la Junta Rectora. Estas tareas me han permitido conocer al maestro, pero sobre todo al amigo. De ahí que recomendar su libro sea un honor, aunque una obra como esta no necesita de mi recomendación, ya que por sí misma es suficiente para tal menester. Estoy seguro del éxito editorial, pero mucho más de la bendición que supondrá para todo estudioso de la Biblia. Es un libro que no debe faltar en la biblioteca de pastores, maestros, predicadores y, en general, de creyentes que desean conocer con mayor profundidad la

Palabra para vivir conforme a su enseñanza. Tan solo me resta pedir que el Señor use este tratado de hermenéutica como instrumento bajo el poder de su Espíritu para la mejor formación de creyentes que sean «idóneos para enseñar también a otros» (2 Ti. 2:2, LBLA). Todo para la gloria de Dios.

Samuel Pérez Millos
*Vigo, España*

# Índice

INTRODUCCIÓN

Prólogo .......... 19
Conceptos clave .......... 23

## Sección I
## LA BIBLIA: LIBRO DIVINO

1. Revelación .......... 39
2. Inspiración .......... 49
3. Inerrancia (I) .......... 71
4. Inerrancia (II) .......... 87
5. Iluminación .......... 103

## Sección II
## HERMENÉUTICA GENERAL

6. El método histórico-gramático-cultural .......... 117
7. Géneros literarios .......... 127
8. Trasfondo histórico y cultural .......... 135
9. Tema del libro .......... 147
10. La organización del libro .......... 153
11. Contexto .......... 161
12. Palabras .......... 169
13. Gramática .......... 183
14. El propósito y plan divino .......... 191

# Sección III
# HERMENÉUTICA ESPECIAL


15. Modismos hebreos .......................... 207
16. Lenguaje figurado .......................... 213
17. Poesía hebrea .......................... 225
18. Parábolas (I) .......................... 235
19. Parábolas (II) .......................... 249
20. Símbolos .......................... 263
21. Tipos .......................... 277
22. Profecía (I) .......................... 291
23. Profecía (II) .......................... 303


# Sección IV
# LA APLICACIÓN DE LAS ESCRITURAS


24. Textos que contienen expresiones culturales ...... 331
25. La aplicación personal .......................... 349


# Sección V
# APÉNDICES


A. La ley de la probabilidad .......................... 361
B. El papel de la fe y el intelecto .......................... 365
C. Crítica textual del A.T. .......................... 371
D. Crítica textual del N.T. .......................... 391
E. La historia de la crítica textual del N.T. ............ 405
F. La relación entre una parábola y una alegoría ...... 423
G. La cuestión del *sensus plenior* .......................... 437
H. La contextualización y la homosexualidad ........ 441

Guía de estudio .......................... 445
Índice de textos bíblicos .......................... 469
Índice temático .......................... 483
Bibliografía .......................... 491

# Agradecimientos

Aunque solamente figura un nombre en la portada de este libro, *Con precisión* es el producto de la valiosa aportación de muchas personas. Por ejemplo, familiares, amigos e iglesias de España, Irlanda, México, Puerto Rico y EE. UU. que me apoyaron con sus oraciones, palabras de ánimo y, en muchos casos, con un rincón en sus casas para que pudiera escribir este libro mientras mi esposa y un servidor dábamos conferencias en sus iglesias.

También quiero expresar mi gratitud a unos hermanos muy entrañables que han trabajado conmigo de una forma muy personal y práctica. A Pedro González y a mi yerno Jonatán Schuster por ayudarme a encontrar buena parte de los libros que figuran en la bibliografía de *Con precisión.* A Carlos Piedad, Debbie Vila, Juan Triviño y su esposa Febe por su ayuda técnica para la publicación de este libro. A Amparo Guillem, Laura Pérez y Antonia Vera por su revisión del texto y las sugerencias tan valiosas que hicieron. Y a Samuel Pérez Millos, un «compañero de batallas» desde hace muchos años, cuyo ánimo y consejos me han servido de mucho.

Pero más que a nadie, estoy agradecido a mi esposa Carolina. Es una mujer francamente excepcional, como confirmarán todos los que la conocen. Siempre se ha caracterizado por un compromiso incondicional con el reino de Dios por encima de sus propios deseos. Siempre me ha animado durante los nueve años que me ha costado escribir *Con precisión* en los huecos que tenía entre los diferentes ministerios que llevamos. Además, ha leído los múltiples borradores de cada capítulo, corrigiendo los errores gramaticales y asegurándose de que un servidor había explicado lo más claramente posible los conceptos que surgen en el terreno de la hermenéutica bíblica. Le agradezco muchísimo su ayuda.

Mi deseo es que todos estos amigos míos tengan la oportunidad de ver con sus propios ojos cómo su trabajo ayuda a muchos hermanos nuestros a entender mejor la Palabra de Dios, con el resultado de que estos últimos tengan una vida y un ministerio más grato y útil al Señor.

Jaime Fasold

# Introducción

## Prólogo
## Conceptos clave

# Prólogo

El estudio de las Escrituras es imprescindible porque ellas nos hacen sabios para la salvación y para una vida agradable a Dios (2 Ti. 3:15). Pero para que ese propósito divino se logre, es importante que interpretemos la Palabra de Dios «con precisión» (2 Ti. 2:15, LBLA), porque hay una forma correcta de interpretar la Biblia y otra incorrecta. Y es precisamente aquí donde la hermenéutica juega un papel tan importante.

Tanto los seminaristas como los creyentes que desean ampliar su entendimiento de cómo estudiar la Biblia pueden sacar provecho de este libro. Solo depende de cuánto deseen profundizar en el tema.

***El texto principal*** explica lo básico de cada tema. El principiante en el tema de la hermenéutica puede limitarse a leer el texto principal de cada capítulo. Seguramente habrá uno o dos capítulos cuyos temas le resultarán más interesantes que otros. Pero puesto que el contenido nuevo de cada capítulo descansa sobre el entendimiento que el lector ha adquirido en los capítulos anteriores, sugiero que lea los capítulos en orden sin saltarse ninguno. Este principio será especialmente importante con el capítulo «Conceptos clave».

***Los trabajos de repaso.*** Al final de cada capítulo hay una sección titulada «Trabajo para realizar». El primer trabajo siempre consiste en unas preguntas sobre los puntos principales de dicho capítulo. Recomiendo que cada lector se tome el tiempo necesario para contestar estas preguntas de repaso. Si desea profundizar más, puede contestar todas las preguntas y hacer los trabajos prácticos indicados.

***Las notas a pie de página.*** Aparte de los datos bibliográficos, las notas a pie de página contienen aclaraciones, anécdotas interesantes, sugerencias de libros excelentes para indagar en ciertos temas e información más amplia y técnica.

***Apéndices.*** En algunos capítulos uno de los trabajos a realizar consiste en leer alguno de los apéndices, donde hay información adicional y más técnica para quienes deseen profundizar más sobre algún tema o pregunta que surge en dichos capítulos. Por ejemplo, en el capítulo sobre la inspiración de las Escrituras, afirmamos que solamente los manuscritos originales de los libros bíblicos son inspirados. Pero si no tenemos ni siquiera un fragmento de ninguno de los 66 libros, ¿de qué sirve la Biblia que tenemos en nuestras manos? El lector encontrará la respuesta en los apéndices indicados.

***La bibliografía.*** Los libros y artículos que he leído en la preparación para escribir *Con precisión* se encuentran en la bibliografía. He colocado los libros en categorías para facilitar la búsqueda de aquellos que tratan un tema de especial interés para el lector.

Aparte de las típicas abreviaturas de los dos Testamentos y los libros bíblicos, el autor se ha limitado a cinco abreviaturas. La Septuaginta (LXX) es la traducción del A.T. al griego realizada c. 250 a. C. por unos setenta eruditos judíos. La LXX representa una fuente importante en la tarea de identificar el texto original del A.T.

Las cuatro versiones de la Biblia citadas representan dos clases de traducciones. Para traducir un texto original de la Biblia, el traductor necesariamente ha de interpretar lo que el autor quería decir con sus palabras que empleó. Sin embargo, la Biblia de las Américas (LBLA) y la Reina Valera Revisada de 1960 (RVR60) tienden a limitarse a lo que el autor dice, traduciendo el texto bíblico palabra por palabra. De ahí que se llaman traducciones literales. Por otro lado, los traductores de la Nueva Traducción Viviente (NTV) y la Nueva Versión Internacional (NVI) emplean el método de la equivalencia dinámica, traduciendo palabras bíblicas difíciles de entender por el lector moderno con palabras que sean fácilmente entendidas, las cuales en la opinión del traductor corresponden a lo que el autor bíblico quería decir.

Cada clase de traducción tiene sus ventajas y desventajas. El lector haría bien en adquirir una copia de la RVR60, LBLA[1], NTV y NVI. En caso de no ser posible, el lector puede consultar el texto de estas y muchas otras versiones de la Biblia en español en Internet (biblegateway.com).

La primera vez que aparece en cada capítulo el nombre de un personaje importante de la historia se incluye su fecha biográfica para que el lector pueda situarlo en la época histórica a la cual pertenece.

Finalmente, cuando ha sido necesario citar una palabra griega he sustituido sus letras por las correspondientes letras españolas según el cuadro que figura a continuación. Quienes han tenido la posibilidad de cursar al menos una asignatura de griego sabrán reconvertir esas letras españolas para localizar dicha palabra en un léxico griego.

| | | | | | |
|---|---|---|---|---|---|
| Α | α | a | Ν | ν | n |
| Β | β | b | Ξ | ξ | x |
| Γ | γ | g | Ο | ο | o |
| Δ | δ | d | Π | π | p |
| Ε | ε | e | Ρ | ρ | r |
| Ζ | ζ | ds | Σ | ς/σ | s |
| Η | η | e | Τ | τ | t |
| Θ | θ | z | Υ | υ | u |
| Ι | ι | i | Φ | φ | f |
| Κ | κ | k/c | Χ | χ | k/ch |
| Λ | λ | l | Ψ | ψ | ps |
| Μ | μ | m | Ω | ω | o |

1. Es importante que el lector adquiera la versión que contiene referencias de texto y aclaraciones sobre el texto hebreo y griego en el margen, no una versión que se limita a presentar el texto.

# Conceptos clave

Hay varios términos y conceptos que se repetirán frecuentemente a lo largo de este libro. Para que el lector entienda y aproveche al máximo el contenido de cada capítulo es imprescindible que conozca estos términos y conceptos.

## A. HERMENÉUTICA

En la mitología griega, Hermes era el dios de la ciencia, oratoria, elocuencia, escritura y lectura. Como tal, servía como el mensajero de los dioses a los hombres, transmitiendo e interpretando para ellos los misterios de los dioses. De ahí que los verbos usados en el N.T. como *ermeneuo*, *diermeneuo* y *mezermeneuo* signifiquen *interpretar*, *explicar* o *traducir* según el texto en que se emplean. Cuando Pablo sanó en Listra a un hombre cojo de nacimiento, los habitantes de la ciudad creyeron que los dioses los habían visitado. Como Hermes era el mensajero de los dioses, «Decidieron que Bernabé era el dios griego Zeus y que Pablo era Hermes por ser el orador principal» (Hch. 14:12, NTV).

La hermenéutica se ha definido como la interpretación de cualquier literatura, antigua o moderna, religiosa o secular. No es el coto privado de la interpretación de la Biblia. Sin embargo, puesto que las normas, reglas, métodos y principios de la hermenéutica han sido debatidos y desarrollados mayormente en el campo de la interpretación bíblica, ha llegado a definirse como la ciencia objetiva de las leyes, normas y principios de la interpretación que hacen posible descubrir el significado de un texto bíblico. Es una ciencia porque provee una clasificación lógica y ordenada de sus leyes, reglas y principios. Es objetiva e imparcial porque excluye cualquier originalidad o creatividad por parte del intérprete. De la misma forma en que no existe la química protestante o católica, un uso correcto de la hermenéutica no admite las opiniones del intérprete. Su tarea es la de descubrir lo que el texto significa en lugar de imponer sobre ello sus preferencias y lo que quiere que diga.

Tradicionalmente, la hermenéutica se ha dividido en dos categorías[2]. La hermenéutica general trata los principios y las leyes para interpretar toda la Biblia en general. Puesto que la mente humana y las características básicas de cada idioma funcionan de la misma manera, hay ciertas leyes que son comunes para la interpretación de cualquier clase de literatura, no importa el siglo, cultura o idioma en que ha sido escrita. La hermenéutica especial trata las reglas y normas requeridas para interpretar las formas de la comunicación que no son literales (lenguaje figurativo, poesía, modismos, etcétera).

## B. SIGNIFICADO

Toda comunicación cuenta con tres elementos: el autor de dicha comunicación, las palabras que emplea y el lector u oyente que interpreta esas palabras. Esta sección trata dos preguntas cuyas respuestas jugarán un papel crítico en la interpretación que el lector haga de las Escrituras. (1) ¿Quién determina lo que significa una comunicación? ¿El autor, sus palabras o el lector? (2) ¿Puede un pasaje bíblico o cualquier otra comunicación tener más de un significado?[3] La ciencia de la comunicación, igual que cualquier otra ciencia, descansa sobre axiomas, verdades que no necesitan defenderse por ser evidentes y obvias. A medida que el lector avance a través de los capítulos de este libro, será más consciente de la gran importancia que tienen

2. Ver un excelente resumen del uso del término «hermenéutica» a lo largo de la historia en el libro de Richard N. Soulen, *Handbook of Biblical Criticism* (Atlanta: John Knox Press, 1981), pp. 82–86.

3. Para una definición filosófica de «significado» ver el libro de Norman L. Geisler y William C. Roach, *Defending Inerrancy* (Grand Rapids: Baker, 2011), pp. 265–270.

los axiomas citados a continuación para interpretar «con precisión» (2 Ti. 2:15, LBLA) la Palabra de Dios.

## El propósito del lenguaje es el de impartir una idea

Cuando una persona pronuncia unas palabras lo hace con el propósito de comunicar una idea. Puede que ese pensamiento sea significativo o carezca de importancia, que sea verídico o falso, que pretenda insultar o agradar a la persona a quien va dirigido. Pero lo claro es que la persona que habla quiere comunicar una idea o pensamiento a otra persona. Las tres personas de la Trinidad se comunican entre sí. No es extraño, entonces, que cuando Dios creó al ser humano a su imagen, lo hizo con la capacidad de pensar, tener ideas y comunicar esas ideas a otras personas. El deseo y la habilidad de comunicarse con otras personas es una de las características más innatas y comunes al ser humano.

## Toda comunicación está sujeta a las leyes del lenguaje

Si el autor de unas palabras quiere que sus oyentes o lectores entiendan lo que quiere comunicarles, tiene que someterse a las leyes del lenguaje establecidas por la sociedad en que ellos viven. Un vistazo a un diccionario demostrará que muchas palabras tienen más de un significado. La palabra «carrera» es un ejemplo. Al decir o escribir algo, el autor tiene que limitarse a los significados que la palabra «carrera» tiene en ese momento histórico de su cultura, porque las palabras van adquiriendo nuevos significados con el tiempo. No puede inventar un nuevo significado a no ser que avise a sus oyentes o lectores lo que hace. Además, tiene que seguir las leyes de la gramática, las cuales le indicarán en qué parte de la frase puede colocar la palabra «carrera» para que tenga sentido. No puede introducirla donde más le plazca. De igual modo, el intérprete no puede elegir el significado de «carrera» que más le guste, sino que tiene que entender esa palabra a la luz del contexto en que aparece. Si el autor está hablando de deportes, «carrera» significará una cosa. Pero si está hablando de su hijo que acaba de comenzar sus estudios universitarios, significará algo totalmente distinto. El hecho de que cada comunicación está sujeta a las leyes del lenguaje hace posible saber lo que el autor quiere decir.

## El lenguaje es eficaz como medio de comunicación

Aunque toda comunicación cuenta con tres elementos (el autor, sus palabras, el intérprete), el hecho es que los autores bíblicos ya no están entre nosotros. Siendo este el caso, hay quienes afirman que no podemos saber con precisión lo que un autor bíblico quiso decir y que, por tanto, el lector tiene que determinar lo que el texto significa. Evidentemente, el lector tiene que interpretar el texto bíblico. Pero si se convierte en el propietario de ese texto como si fuera el autor del mismo, dándole el significado que cree más conveniente, entonces no podemos estar seguros de nada y nos hundimos en la pura relatividad, porque la verdad cambiará según la opinión de cada intérprete.

Uno de los axiomas de la comunicación es que se puede saber lo que piensa una persona al estudiar las palabras que emplea. El hecho de que dos personas puedan entenderse mediante una conversación o cartas es una prueba de que el lenguaje es un medio eficaz de comunicación. Si no fuera así, no podríamos fiarnos de ningún documento legal que pretenda recoger con absoluta precisión lo que dos personas han acordado. Evidentemente, a diferencia de un documento legal que no admite opiniones, los periódicos y las noticias de la radio, televisión e Internet representan, en primera instancia, la opinión de los periodistas y locutores sobre los sucesos políticos, sociales, deportivos, religiosos, etcétera. Sus opiniones pueden corresponder o no a la verdad. Pero la veracidad de sus declaraciones no es la cuestión, sino el hecho de que podemos saber con precisión cuál es su opinión. Negar el axioma de que el lenguaje es un medio eficaz de comunicación nos obligaría a tirar por tierra cada ley que se haya establecido, cada dato que figure en los libros de historia, cada carta o comunicación electrónica que hayamos recibido y cada conversación que hayamos tenido durante nuestra vida. No se podría estar seguro de nada. Pero la realidad es que el lenguaje es un medio eficaz de comunicación. Y, puesto que Dios quería que el ser humano entendiera su revelación, le habló en su propio idioma en lugar de en un idioma celestial. Por tanto, Dios se sometió a las leyes gramaticales del hebreo, arameo y griego koiné.

## El significado de una comunicación se encuentra en la mente del autor

Un padre dice a su hijo: «No quiero que juegues fútbol en la calle». Su hijo le responde: «¿Por qué no quieres que coma chocolatinas?». Y su padre, con una frustración incontenible, le pregunta: «¿No has entendido lo que te he dicho?». ¿Quién determina lo que el padre quería decir? ¿El padre o el hijo? Si el significado de las palabras de ese padre es determinado por su hijo, acabamos de crear un caos y una anarquía impresionante en esa familia porque ese padre y su hijo acaban de perder la posibilidad de comunicarse el uno con el otro. Las reglas del lenguaje y el sentido común exigen que sea el padre el que determine el significado de sus palabras, que lo que él quería decir sea la única interpretación válida y correcta.

Una vez dichas las palabras «No quiero que juegues fútbol en la calle», el significado de las mismas queda fijado; no se puede cambiar. Es lo que el padre quiso decir cuando pronunció esas palabras. Más tarde tendrá el derecho a reconocer que ha sido demasiado duro con su hijo y permitirle jugar fútbol en la calle durante las horas de menos tráfico. Pero sus primeras palabras siempre significarán lo que quiso decir en el momento en que las pronunció. La misma dinámica debe aplicarse a un autor bíblico por cuanto sus palabras están ancladas en la historia. El significado de lo que dijo en un momento determinado de la historia no puede cambiarse. El significado de esas palabras siempre se encuentra en la mente del autor porque él es su propietario. El intérprete nunca puede determinar el significado de un texto bíblico, sino solamente interpretar lo que el autor ha dicho. El autor es el que comunica y el intérprete el que interpreta.

El sentido común exige que aceptemos las palabras de otra persona por lo que son, aunque el intérprete no sea capaz de introducirse en la mente o el estado anímico del autor. Este cuarto axioma afirma que las palabras son un reflejo fidedigno de lo que su autor quiso decir. Por tanto, es improcedente, si no imposible, divorciar sus palabras de lo que quiso decir. Para descubrir lo que un autor bíblico quiso decir, el intérprete puede fiarse de las palabras que el autor empleó porque las escogió con cuidado para que expresaran las ideas que quería comunicar.

## Cada comunicación tiene solamente un significado

Durante un período de la historia de la iglesia muchos creyentes sinceros interpretaron las Escrituras de forma alegórica, viendo supuestas enseñanzas espirituales detrás del texto que no eran evidentes a primera vista para los indoctos o menos espirituales. Esa forma de interpretar las Escrituras permitía al intérprete ver más de un significado en un texto. La Reforma del siglo XVI desenmascaró los grandes errores de ese sistema de interpretación.

Hay dos argumentos que sirven como base del axioma de que cada comunicación solo puede tener un significado. (1) Si una comunicación puede tener más de un significado, destruimos la posibilidad de comunicarnos con otras personas porque no queda ningún mecanismo para entendernos. (2) Es psicológicamente imposible para el ser humano decir una palabra o frase y querer decir dos cosas diferentes a la vez. Aun en el caso de emplear una palabra que tiene más de un significado, el ser humano puede mantener en su mente solamente uno de esos dos significados a la vez[4]. Hay quienes argumentan que Dios es capaz de decir algo y tener en su mente dos significados. Hay dos argumentos que desacreditan esa teoría. Primero, si Dios hubiera elegido comunicarse con nosotros de esa forma, entonces estaríamos totalmente perdidos porque nuestra mente es incapaz de funcionar de esa forma. Segundo, no encontramos ningún texto bíblico que demuestre que Dios haya dicho una cosa pero que quería comunicarnos dos ideas totalmente diferentes[5].

---

4. Una palabra puede tener más de un significado según el contexto en que se emplea. El humor de cada país es distinto. En España muchos chistes se basan sobre un juego de palabras en el cual alguien emplea una palabra o frase fuera de su contexto habitual, lo cual hace que sea graciosa y hasta escandalosa. En eso consiste el chiste. El que cuenta el chiste tiene en mente un significado, pero el contexto en que emplea el término anima a los oyentes a pensar en otro significado que esa palabra tiene en otro contexto, aunque entienden perfectamente bien cuál es el significado que el autor del chiste tiene en mente. En ese sentido no existe el «doble sentido», sino un solo significado; a saber, lo que hay en la mente del autor del chiste.

5. El tipo es el fenómeno de la profecía bíblica que más se parece a la teoría de que un texto puede tener más de un significado. En el capítulo 21 el autor insistirá en que hay una diferencia entre un *significado* múltiple y un *cumplimiento* múltiple.

| Axiomas del lenguaje |
|---|
| 1. El propósito del lenguaje es el de impartir una idea. |
| 2. Toda comunicación está sujeta a las leyes del lenguaje. |
| 3. El lenguaje es eficaz como medio de comunicación. |
| 4. El significado de una comunicación se encuentra en la mente del autor. |
| 5. Cada comunicación tiene solamente un significado. |

Si un texto bíblico puede tener más de un significado, entonces abrimos la puerta a que el intérprete encuentre en las Escrituras lo que él quiere en lugar de lo que Dios quiere comunicarle. Por eso dijo John Owen (1616–1683), un puritano, teólogo, pastor y rector de la Universidad de Oxford: «Si las Escrituras tienen más de un significado, no tienen ningún significado en absoluto»[6]. Terry (1840–1914) afirmó lo mismo en su obra clásica de la hermenéutica: «Un principio fundamental de la exposición gramático-histórica es que las palabras y frases pueden tener tan solo un significado en un determinado texto. En el momento que abandonamos este principio, nuestro barco es llevado por cualquier viento sobre un mar de incertidumbre y conjetura»[7].

E. D. Hirsch es uno de los eruditos más conocidos en los círculos seculares de la teoría literaria actual. Aunque sus posiciones no son aceptadas por todos sus colegas, sus teorías han sido recibidas con mucho interés por los evangélicos. Hirsch mantiene que: (1) el significado de un texto se encuentra en la mente del autor y lo que pretendía comunicar de forma consciente cuando escribía dicho texto; (2) cada comunicación tiene tan solo un significado; y (3) la interpretación literal de cualquier texto es la más correcta a no ser que el texto indique lo contrario, como en el caso del lenguaje figurado[8].

---

6. Muchos autores citan esta frase de Owen, pero ninguno dice dónde se encuentra en los muchos escritos de Owen.

7. Milton S. Terry, *Biblical Hermeneutics* (Grand Rapids: Zondervan, 1969), p. 205.

8. Ver E. D. Hirsch, *Validity in Interpretation* (New Haven: Yale University Press, 1967).

## C. EXÉGESIS

Las palabras «exégesis» e «interpretación» son a todos los efectos sinónimas. Por ese motivo se emplearán en ese sentido a lo largo de este libro.

*1. La meta de la exégesis.* Una exégesis honesta y correcta de un texto bíblico busca lo que el autor pretendía comunicar a sus primeros lectores. Aceptar o rechazar como verídico o falso lo que dice es un paso posterior. Como dijo el gran reformador Juan Calvino (1509–1564): «La primera tarea del intérprete es permitir al autor que diga lo que quiere decir en lugar de atribuirle lo que piensa que debería decir»[9].

*2. El papel y los desafíos de los presupuestos.* Cuando una persona interpreta la Biblia, está influida por los presupuestos o presuposiciones (valores, prejuicios, creencias, etcétera) que han sido forjados a lo largo de su vida por la enseñanza y opiniones de sus padres, profesores, amigos, la sociedad en que vive, su propia experiencia, etcétera[10]. No importa si sus presuposiciones se corresponden con la verdad o no; van a afectar a cómo interpreta la Biblia y a lo que está dispuesto a creer. Si uno lleva gafas de color rojo, todo lo que ve le parecerá de color rojo. Sin embargo, la exégesis legítima de las Escrituras busca de forma consciente lo que había en la mente del autor y lo que pretendía comunicar a los lectores originales en lugar de imponer sus presuposiciones sobre el texto.

Para evitar la posibilidad de que el intérprete imponga sus presupuestos sobre el texto, hay quienes sugieren que debe acercarse al texto bíblico con una mente en blanco. Sin embargo, el ser humano es incapaz de desprenderse de sus presupuestos. Además, muchos eruditos insisten en que esas presuposiciones son necesarias para que el intérprete tenga un marco que le oriente[11]. Entonces, ¿qué puede

---

9. Muchos libros sobre la hermenéutica citan esta frase de Calvino, pero ninguno identifica su fuente bibliográfica.

10. Algunos eruditos llaman a esos presupuestos el «entendimiento previo» o el «horizonte» del intérprete.

11. Ver Anthony C. Thiselton, un filósofo evangélico que ha hecho una gran aportación a este tema con sus libros *The Two Horizons: New Testament Description with Special Reference to Heidegger, Bultmann, Gadamar, and Wittgenstein* (Exeter: Paternoster Press, 1980) y *New Horizons in Hermeneutics* (Grand Rapids: Zondervan, 1992).

y debe hacer el intérprete para evitar el error de imponer sus propios presupuestos sobre el texto bíblico? La respuesta a esa pregunta se encuentra en una dinámica que se llama «el círculo» o «la espiral» de la hermenéutica[12].

Todos aceptan el axioma de la comunicación de que no se puede entender una palabra sin tener en cuenta la frase en la cual se emplea. Pero tampoco se puede entender una frase al margen del párrafo en el cual aparece, ni entender un párrafo sin tener en cuenta el mensaje principal del libro del cual forma parte. También es verdad lo inverso: a saber, que no se puede entender el mensaje principal de un libro sin entender los párrafos del mismo, ni un párrafo sin tener en cuenta las frases que componen ese párrafo, ni ninguna frase sin sus palabras. Así se crea un círculo en el cual una parte de las Escrituras (palabras, párrafos, libros) nos ayuda a entender el mensaje global de las Escrituras y viceversa.

El intérprete honesto permitirá que el texto bíblico cambie sus presuposiciones. Si realmente quiere conocer la verdad, cada vez que lea e interprete las Escrituras dejará que estas confirmen, desafíen, corrijan y amplíen sus presuposiciones. Entonces, cuando vuelva a interpretar las Escrituras, lo hará con unas presuposiciones más correctas. De nuevo, la verdad de la Palabra confirmará, desafiará, corregirá o ampliará otras presuposiciones suyas. Así se creará una dinámica en la cual el intérprete va descubriendo progresivamente la verdad. El intérprete honrado siempre estará dispuesto a abandonar una interpretación suya cuando

12. El filólogo alemán Friedrich Ast (1778–1841) empleó por primera vez la frase «el círculo de la hermenéutica» para describir este proceso. Con el tiempo los eruditos prefirieron emplear el término «espiral» por considerar que «círculo» conllevaba la idea de algo cerrado o vicioso, como el hámster que corre todo el día sobre una rueda en su jaula pero que nunca llega a ninguna parte. La palabra «espiral» conlleva la idea de progreso hacia arriba, de un movimiento hacia algo mejor. De ahí el título del libro de Grant R. Osborne, *The Hermeneutical Spiral* (Downers Grove: InterVarsity Press, 1991). El teólogo y filósofo alemán Friedrich Schleiermacher (1768–1834), llamado por muchos el padre de la hermenéutica moderna, dijo que la única forma de adquirir un entendimiento de un texto en toda su plenitud es prestar la máxima atención a los detalles de dicho texto. Pero para apreciar debidamente el significado de todos esos detalles se ha de tener un conocimiento básico del documento en su totalidad.

se le muestra que descansa sobre un presupuesto erróneo. La meta de la exégesis es entender lo que el autor nos quiso comunicar.

## D. APLICACIÓN

Mientras que la exégesis o interpretación procura descubrir el significado de un texto para los lectores originales, la aplicación pretende contestar la pregunta: ¿qué tiene que ver el significado de este texto con mi vida hoy? El orden siempre debe ser primero la exégesis y después la aplicación. Si el intérprete determina primero lo que el texto significaba para los lectores originales, su aplicación tendrá más probabilidades de ser correcta. Cada creyente se encuentra en algún momento asediado por problemas, necesidades y decisiones importantes. La Biblia tiene mucho que decirle. Pero es importante que entienda primero lo que el texto significaba para los lectores originales antes de aplicarlo a su situación. De ese modo su aplicación será correcta. De lo contrario, su aplicación correrá el riesgo de ser incorrecta y podría tomar una decisión equivocada.

Aunque existe solo un significado para cualquier texto bíblico, puede haber muchas aplicaciones del mismo. Jesús nos mandó: «ámense unos a otros. Tal como yo los he amado, ustedes deben amarse unos a otros.» (Jn. 13:34). Este mandamiento tiene solamente un significado; a saber, los creyentes deben amarse mutuamente. No hay otro significado. Sin embargo, este mandamiento tiene muchas aplicaciones. Por ejemplo, los hermanos deben saludarse de forma sincera y cariñosa (Ro. 16:16), soportarse mutuamente con paciencia (Ef. 4:2), ayudar al necesitado (Ef. 4:28), orar el uno por el otro (Ef. 6:18-19), etcétera.

## E. PADRES DE LA IGLESIA

Tras el fallecimiento de los autores del N.T., los creyentes que tenían el don de enseñanza adquirieron una importancia considerable. Y como era de esperar, aquellos que destacaban por su ministerio docente en la iglesia local se convirtieron con el tiempo en maestros y líderes a nivel regional. Los historiadores han dado el título de «padres de la iglesia» a unos setenta teólogos, obispos y autores de los primeros cinco siglos de la historia de la iglesia cuyos pensamientos y escritos tuvieron una influencia marcada sobre la iglesia durante los primeros siglos. Estos hombres no siempre acertaban en su interpretación de las doctrinas del N.T. porque eran nuevas para ellos y no contaban con el gran caudal de comentarios bíblicos que tenemos a nuestra disposición en el siglo XXI. No obstante, no debemos menospreciarlos. Entre ellos había hombres formidables y brillantes con un compromiso y testimonio incuestionables. Además, muchas de sus interpretaciones eran acertadas.

## F. EVANGÉLICO

Muchas palabras adquieren significados adicionales con el tiempo. Originalmente, la palabra «evangélico» se refería a quienes creían en la inspiración plenaria y verbal de las Escrituras. Sin embargo, con el tiempo ha habido quienes se llamaban a sí mismos evangélicos pero que se distanciaban de esa posición original sobre las Escrituras. A lo largo de este libro, el autor empleará la palabra «evangélico» para referirse a quienes creen en las doctrinas fundamentales de la fe cristiana y, muy en particular, en la inspiración plenaria y verbal de las Escrituras. El autor cree que toda la Biblia es inspirada por Dios, palabra por palabra en los manuscritos originales, y, por tanto, es inerrante; o sea, sin error.

## G. BAJA Y ALTA CRÍTICA

Cuando los teólogos debaten un aspecto complejo o polémico de una doctrina suelen elegir una o dos palabras que recogen la esencia de ese aspecto doctrinal. Por ejemplo: depravación total, gracia eficaz, dones carismáticos, etcétera. De esa forma, no tienen que emplear muchas palabras para informar a sus lectores u oyentes sobre lo que están hablando. Es una práctica completamente legítima y necesaria. Pero a veces las palabras elegidas crean más confusión que claridad. Este es el caso con «baja crítica» y «alta crítica». Para muchos principiantes, la palabra «crítica» conlleva una idea negativa. Además, las palabras «baja» y «alta» hacen pensar que hay una clase de crítica que es superior a la otra.

En el ámbito de las disciplinas bíblicas, la palabra «crítica» se refiere a una reflexión y estudio serio en dos disciplinas concretas. La «baja crítica», llamada también «crítica textual» (el término que se empleará a partir de este capítulo), es la ciencia que procura identificar el texto original de una obra antigua de la cual no tenemos el manuscrito original, como es el caso de la Biblia. Puesto que la tarea del crítico textual no es la de determinar la veracidad del texto bíblico sino solo lo que dice el texto original, su trabajo suele ser muy objetivo. Tiene poca posibilidad de imponer sus preferencias teológicas sobre el texto porque un verbo es un verbo; no hay posibilidad de convertirlo en un sustantivo.

La «alta crítica» tiene como meta identificar al autor de un libro, la fecha y lugar en que lo escribió, la ocasión que lo motivó a escribirlo, los receptores originales, los datos históricos y culturales citados en el texto, etcétera[13]. Muchos altos críticos han rechazado las contundentes e irrefutables declaraciones de las Escrituras en cuanto a su origen y naturaleza divina. Sin embargo, cuando se emplea de forma correcta, la alta crítica representa una de las mejores apologías o defensas que el evangélico tiene a su alcance[14].

Aunque las palabras «alta» y «baja» dan la impresión de que la labor del crítico textual (baja crítica) es inferior o más sencilla y fácil que la labor del alto crítico, la realidad es que la baja crítica requiere una capacidad lingüística y técnica que supera con creces los requisitos de un alto crítico. El crítico textual tiene que dominar el hebreo, arameo y griego koiné. La crítica textual es «baja» solamente en el sentido de que sirve como el fundamento del trabajo del alto crítico.

---

13. Originalmente, los eruditos bíblicos se dedicaban a la baja crítica (crítica textual) y la alta crítica a la vez, llamando a la baja crítica simplemente «crítica» y a la alta crítica «hermenéutica». Pero con el tiempo adoptaron los términos «baja» y «alta» para distinguir las dos disciplinas.

14. El libro de George E. Ladd, *Crítica del Nuevo Testamento* (El Paso: Editorial Mundo Hispano, 1990), demuestra la validez y necesidad de estudio crítico de las Escrituras.

## *Trabajo para realizar*

En la sección «Significado», dijimos que la ciencia de la comunicación se basa en varios axiomas. Citamos cinco de ellos que tienen una relevancia especial para la interpretación bíblica. Cite al menos tres de ellos y explíquelos en sus propias palabras. ¿Cuál es la meta primordial de la exégesis bíblica? ¿Quiénes son los padres de la iglesia y qué papel jugaban? ¿A qué labor se dedica la baja crítica? ¿A qué labor se dedica la alta crítica?

## Sección I

# La Biblia: libro divino

Es imprescindible que el intérprete de la Biblia sepa que el libro que tiene en sus manos es de origen y naturaleza divinos. Por tanto, necesita leyes y normas divinas para interpretarla correctamente.

1. Revelación
2. Inspiración
3. Inerrancia (I)
4. Inerrancia (II)
5. Iluminación

# 1 Revelación

El método que se emplea para interpretar cualquier literatura siempre tiene que depender de la naturaleza de la misma. Por ejemplo, nadie interpreta un cómic de forma literal porque entiende que es pura ficción que pretende entretener al lector. En cambio, un libro de fórmulas químicas tiene que interpretarse con una precisión absoluta porque su naturaleza es científica. Las doctrinas bíblicas de la revelación, inspiración e inerrancia demuestran que la Biblia es de origen divino. Por tanto, hacen falta unas normas divinas o espirituales para interpretarla correctamente. La doctrina de la iluminación identifica esas normas para que el intérprete «entienda» las Escrituras de tal forma que se produzca vida espiritual en él.

Para entender el origen divino de las Escrituras es necesario entender la doctrina de la revelación divina al ser humano. Dios ha empleado varios métodos para darse a conocer al ser humano, los cuales los teólogos los han colocado en dos categorías: la revelación general y la revelación especial.

## A. REVELACIÓN GENERAL

La revelación general tiene que ver con las verdades generales que Dios ha dado a conocer a toda persona en cada siglo y cultura mediante tres fuentes de información.

## La naturaleza del ser humano

Dios ha creado al ser humano a su imagen. Ha escrito su ley sobre su corazón y le ha dado una conciencia para saber la diferencia entre lo bueno y lo malo (Ro. 2:12-16). Le ha dado un intelecto para razonar, una voluntad para tomar decisiones y unas emociones para que pueda sentir alegría y gozo, además de tristeza. El ser humano solo tiene que mirarse a sí mismo para saber algo de cómo es Dios. Aunque esa imagen fue terriblemente manchada y distorsionada por el pecado, no fue destruida del todo. Por eso, Moisés afirmó de nuevo en Génesis 9:6 que el ser humano fue creado a la imagen de Dios, aunque la caída de Adán y Eva había ocurrido muchos años antes. Cuando una persona se convierte a Cristo, Dios restaura progresivamente su imagen en él. Por ejemplo, el Espíritu Santo renueva la mente del creyente (Ro. 12:2; Ef. 4:23) con el fin de que la emplee como Dios pretendía que lo hiciera cuando lo creó. Dios ha dado al ser humano un intelecto con el propósito de que lo use. Por tanto, es esencial que el ser humano haga uso de su capacidad intelectual cuando interpreta las Escrituras.

## La creación

El universo y la naturaleza que rodea al ser humano le revelan otras verdades acerca de Dios. Salmo 19:1-6, texto clásico del A.T., dice que los cielos revelan la gloria de Dios. En el N.T., Hch. 14:15-17; 17:22-29 y Ro. 1:18-21 identifican cinco verdades que la creación revela al ser humano. Primera, Dios existe y ha creado todo lo que se ve (Hch. 17:23-24; Ro. 1:20). Al observar la creación, la lógica exige que el ser humano concluya que existe un creador. Su experiencia le ha enseñado que no hay nada que llegue a existir por sí solo, sino que cada objeto tiene un creador. Segunda, Dios gobierna y sustenta todas las cosas (Hch. 14:17; 17:25-26, 28). Tercera, Dios es santo y por tanto exige que el ser humano sea santo. «Por medio de todo lo que Dios hizo, ellos pueden ver a simple vista las cualidades invisibles de Dios: su poder eterno y su naturaleza divina.» (Ro. 1:20, NTV). Por eso, las tribus en las junglas más remotas del mundo ofrecen sacrificios en un intento de apaciguar la ira de Dios contra su pecado. Cuarta, Dios debe ser alabado de una forma digna (Hch. 17:24-25). Quinta, puesto que el ser humano ha creado imágenes de hombres, aves, cuadrúpedos y reptiles, y les ha dado culto (Ro. 1:21, 23; Is. 40:18-26), sabe que está sin excusa y que será juzgado por su pecado (Ro. 1:20, 32; 2:1).

> «Por medio de todo lo que Dios hizo, ellos pueden ver a simple vista las cualidades invisibles de Dios: su poder eterno y su naturaleza divina. Así que no tienen ninguna excusa para no conocer a Dios. Es cierto, ellos conocieron a Dios pero no quisieron adorarlo como Dios ni darle gracias. En cambio, comenzaron a inventar ideas necias sobre Dios. Como resultado, la mente les quedó en oscuridad y confusión».
>
> **(Ro. 1:20-21, NTV)**

## La historia

Daniel observó que Dios «quita reyes, y pone reyes» (Dn. 2:19-21), la misma observación que hizo Isaías (10:13). Hay cosas que ocurren en la historia que no pueden atribuirse a la mera coincidencia. Por ejemplo, el hecho de que el pueblo judío haya sobrevivido y mantenido su identidad a pesar de ser perseguido a lo largo de los siglos es una de las muchas indicaciones de que Dios existe y vela por su pueblo elegido. Lamentablemente, los estragos que el pecado ha causado en el ser humano hacen difícil, si no imposible, que interprete correctamente lo que observa en la creación, la ley que Dios ha escrito en su corazón y los actos de Dios en la historia.

A pesar de lo mucho que la naturaleza del hombre, la creación y la historia revelan al ser humano, la revelación general tiene dos limitaciones considerables. Primera, no se ha comunicado con palabras. Como resultado, hay un alto grado de probabilidad de que el ser humano se equivoque en su interpretación de lo que observa de Dios en sí mismo, la creación y los eventos históricos. Segunda, la revelación general comunica al ser humano que es un pecador, pero no le provee ninguna salida, ningún plan para salvarse. De ahí que haga falta una revelación especial.

## B. REVELACIÓN ESPECIAL

En contraste con la revelación general, la cual siempre ha estado presente y al alcance de todo ser humano en cada siglo y cultura, la revelación especial fue dada solamente a Israel en el A.T. y a la Iglesia en el N.T. Esta revelación cuenta con tres características significativas.

### La revelación especial se dio en tres etapas

*1. El Antiguo Testamento.* En el N.T. la palabra *apokalupto* (traducida como «revelar», «manifestar», etcétera) tiene varios significados según el contexto en que se emplea. Dos de ellos tienen que ver con la formulación de las Escrituras[1]. El primero tiene que ver con el acto divino de revelar el momento en que un evento futuro ocurrirá (Ro. 2:5; 8:18; 1 P. 4:13; 5:1). El segundo se trata del acto divino de revelar verdades espirituales y eventos futuros que no se conocían anteriormente y que no se podían conocer sin una revelación especial. Por ejemplo, en el A.T. Dios reveló a los profetas información sobre el Mesías venidero (1 P. 1:12).

*2. La encarnación de Jesucristo.* Aunque Dios empleó varios métodos en la revelación general y especial para darse a conocer al ser humano, el método supremo fue la encarnación de Cristo, la segunda persona de la Trinidad, el Verbo que «fue hecho carne, y habitó entre nosotros» (Jn. 1:14), y que declaró que «el que me ha visto a mí, ha visto al Padre» (Jn. 14:9). Pero, lejos de ser simplemente el método superior, Cristo es el centro, el eje alrededor del cual gira todo lo que Dios ha comunicado al ser humano «para que en todo tenga la preeminencia» (Col. 1:18).

*3. El Nuevo Testamento.* Mientras que la encarnación de Cristo es la corona suprema de toda la revelación de Dios, el N.T. es la culminación de ella. Puesto que Jesús ya no está entre nosotros, los autores

---

1. La palabra *apokalupto* tiene otros tres significados. Primero, el acto divino de dar entendimiento (iluminar) a un creyente sobre una verdad espiritual ya revelada (Mt. 16:17; Ef. 1:17-19; Flp. 3:15; 1 Co. 2:9-10). Segundo, el acto divino de dar entendimiento (iluminar) a un no creyente sobre verdades relacionadas con la salvación (Lc. 10:22; Jn. 12:37-40; Gá. 1:15-16). Tercero, en Gálatas 2:1-2, parece que Pablo emplea *apokalupto* como una referencia a la guía de Dios en su vida.

| Revelación | |
|---|---|
| General | • La naturaleza del ser humano<br>• La creación<br>• La historia |
| Especial | • El A.T.<br>• La encarnación de Jesucristo<br>• El N.T. |

bíblicos subrayan la importancia de las Escrituras. Los reformadores del siglo XVI insistieron en el principio de *Sola Scriptura,* no porque rechazaban la revelación general ni la importancia de la encarnación de Cristo, sino en protesta por la posición de la Iglesia Católica Romana que afirmaba que la autoridad final en la Iglesia residía en las Escrituras *y la tradición.* «Lutero no menospreció la autoridad eclesiástica ni repudió los concilios como si no tuvieran ningún valor. Lutero y los reformadores no quisieron decir por *Sola Scriptura* que la Biblia es la única autoridad en la Iglesia, sino que es la única autoridad *infalible* en ella»[2].

En el N.T. Dios reveló verdades espirituales e información sobre eventos futuros al apóstol Pablo (Ro. 16:25; 2 Co. 12:1, 7; Gá. 1:11-12; Ef. 3:3, 5), al apóstol Juan (Ap. 1:1), a otros apóstoles y personas íntimamente asociadas con ellos y a creyentes con el don de profecía (Ef. 3:5)[3].

## La revelación especial se dio de forma progresiva

«Revelación progresiva»[4] es un término creado por los teólogos para expresar el concepto de que Dios ha revelado los detalles de ciertas verdades y doctrinas poco a poco a lo largo de la historia. El hecho de que el N.T. es la culminación de esa revelación especial no quiere decir

---

2. R. C. Sproul, «Sola Scriptura: Crucial to Evangelicalism» en *The Foundation of Biblical Authority* (Grand Rapids: Zondervan, 1978), pp. 104, 107.

3. Existen al menos seis definiciones en cuanto a la naturaleza del don de profecía. El autor cree que consistía en el acto de Dios de revelar a ciertos miembros de las iglesias unas verdades que no se podían saber de otro modo, con el fin de dar el contenido de esa revelación especial a las iglesias mientras se escribía el N.T. Para más información, ver el libro de Jaime Fasold, *Dones espirituales* (Grand Rapids: Portavoz, 2000), pp. 147–151.

4. En su libro *Cómo interpretar las Escrituras* (San Luis: Editorial Concordia, 2007), p. 42, Herbert Mayer emplea la palabra «acumulativa», quizás un término más preciso.

que el A.T. sea impreciso o esté equivocado, sino que Dios simplemente fue revelando información adicional sobre ciertas verdades y doctrinas de forma paulatina. Aunque la revelación que los judíos habían recibido en el A.T. era parcial e incompleta, la revelación completa del N.T. no contradice ni corrige la revelación que Dios dio en tiempos del A.T.

Por ejemplo, los eruditos bíblicos creen que el libro de Job fue escrito antes que el Pentateuco, convirtiéndolo en el libro más antiguo del A.T. En 19:25-26 Job afirma que hay vida después de la muerte («Pero en cuanto a mí, sé que mi Redentor vive, y un día por fin estará sobre la tierra. Y después que mi cuerpo se haya descompuesto, ¡todavía en mi cuerpo veré a Dios!», NTV). Si nuestro entendimiento de la doctrina de la resurrección se limitara a este texto, podríamos concluir que solo los creyentes resucitarán. Pero siglos más tarde Daniel habló de una resurrección que tendrá lugar después de un tiempo de tribulación que padecerá el pueblo de Dios (12:1-2). Algunos serán resucitados «para vida eterna y otros para vergüenza y deshonra eterna» (NTV). Por tanto, los no creyentes resucitarán también. Toda la información que Dios nos ha dado sobre una doctrina en particular no se encuentra en un solo capítulo, sino en varios pasajes. No obstante, suele haber un capítulo o pasaje que nos provee de más información que cualquier otro, y a esto lo llamamos la «mención plena» de esa doctrina. Por ejemplo, 1 Corintios 15 es la mención plena de la doctrina de la resurrección, Filipenses 2 la de la encarnación de Cristo, etcétera.

## La revelación especial se dio de forma verbal

Con la revelación general, Dios hizo al hombre a su imagen y escribió su ley sobre su corazón. Sin embargo, con la entrada del pecado en el mundo, muchos rechazan repetidamente esa ley, lo cual hace que el ser humano sea incapaz de discernir entre el bien y el mal (1 Ti. 4:2). Al observar lo que nos rodea en la Tierra y las estrellas en los cielos, lo lógico es llegar a la conclusión de que hay un creador y que él es santo (Ro. 1:20). Sin embargo, algunos rechazan a sabiendas a ese creador, mientras que otros simplemente no le «ven» mediante la creación. Finalmente, Dios controla la historia, quitando y poniendo a los reyes de las naciones según su voluntad (Is. 10:13; Dn. 2:19-21).

Pero ¿cómo podemos discernir entre un evento producido por la intervención de Dios y los muchos sucesos de la vida que son una mera coincidencia?

Es precisamente aquí donde entra en escena la revelación especial. Mediante las Escrituras, Dios comunica con palabras (de forma verbal) quién es él, el estado espiritual del ser humano y cuál es su plan para redimirle. También comunica de forma verbal qué clase de vida exige del ser humano y cuál es el significado de los eventos históricos en los cuales él ha intervenido[5].

Sin embargo, a principios del siglo XX teólogos como Karl Barth (1886–1968), Paul Tillich (1886–1965), C. H. Dodd (1884–1973), Emil Brunner (1889–1966) y John Baillie (1886–1960) propusieron que cuando Dios se reveló al ser humano se limitó a actuar de forma poderosa en la historia, el alma humana, la naturaleza y, sobre todo, en Jesucristo, pero nunca con ideas, conceptos, verdades, doctrinas e instrucciones en forma de palabras[6]. Por tanto, la Biblia no es un libro divino con autoridad absoluta en cuanto a la verdad, sino simplemente un relato de las experiencias religiosas que ciertas personas tuvieron en los siglos pasados. Quienes abrazan esta posición acusan a los evangélicos de convertir la Biblia en un «papa de papel» por su posición sobre la inspiración de las Escrituras. Esta teoría sobre la revelación de Dios al ser humano es rechazada por el evangélico por varios motivos.

Primero, un acto histórico no es capaz de comunicar significado por sí solo; requiere que la persona que produjo dicho acto explique lo que pretendía comunicarnos con ello. Si Dios ha realizado actos poderosos, entonces Dios tiene que decirnos lo que quiso comunicarnos a través de ellos. Si no dice nada, el ser humano no puede

---

5. Los teólogos evangélicos de habla inglesa llaman a este aspecto de la revelación especial *propositional truth* (verdad proposicional).

6. Por ejemplo, en las palabras de John Baillie en su libro *The Idea of Revelation in Recent Thought* (Nueva York: Columbia University Press, 1956), p. 62, «Toda revelación es dada, no en la forma de conocimiento que se comunica directamente, sino a través de eventos que ocurren en la experiencia histórica de la humanidad, eventos que son percibidos por fe como los "actos poderosos" de Dios, los cuales entonces engendran en la mente del hombre un conocimiento de Dios que se le ha permitido poseer». En este libro Baillie, un teólogo escocés, documenta la historia de esta posición.

saber cuáles son los eventos históricos en los cuales Dios ha intervenido y cuáles son una mera coincidencia. Los egipcios y romanos no tenían una copia de las Escrituras. Por eso, Henry hace la observación de que los «analistas egipcios ignoraron el éxodo de los judíos y los historiadores romanos prácticamente ignoraron a Jesucristo. Lo que la historiografía secular no puede hacer, las Escrituras inspiradas sí pueden y de hecho lo hacen: declaran la dirección y la meta de la historia e identifican los eventos importantes y su significado para la redención del ser humano»[7]. Si Dios no nos explica qué ha hecho y por qué razón lo ha hecho, nos quedamos sin saber qué quería decir y sin saber qué creer. «La revelación de los actos poderosos de Dios sin una revelación del significado de esos actos es como un programa de televisión que carece de sonido; deja al ser humano desamparado ante sus adivinanzas humanas en cuanto al significado de lo que Dios está haciendo»[8]. Segundo, la opinión de Barth, Tillick y otros que afirman que Dios nunca se reveló de forma verbal al hombre sustituye la revelación especial de Dios por la revelación general, y choca frontalmente con lo que dicen las Escrituras. En palabras de Henry:

> Decir que la revelación divina no se da en la forma de palabra-revelación contradice de forma tan descarada el testimonio bíblico que roza en lo increíble. Los profetas del A.T. afirman «así dice Jehová» unas 1200 veces no solo para acreditar la fuente de su enseñanza, sino también y con frecuencia para contradecir las ideas paganas de dioses paganos. Hay algo peculiar en una investigación histórica de la Biblia que puede ignorar tan fácilmente las afirmaciones insistentes de las Escrituras de que dentro de los actos de Dios está incluida la revelación de su Palabra a través de portavoces elegidos por Dios[9].

---

7. Carl F. H. Henry, *God, Revelation and Authority: God Who Speaks and Shows,* tomo II (Waco: Word Books, 1976), p. 320.

8. Kenneth S. Kantzer, «The Christ-Revelation as Act and Interpretation» en *Jesus of Nazareth: Savior and Lord* (Londres: Tyndale Press, 1966), p. 252.

9. Henry, ob. cit., pp. 304–305.

## *Trabajo para realizar*

1. ¿Cuáles son las tres formas en que Dios se ha revelado al ser humano de una forma general y cuáles son las tres formas en que se ha revelado de forma especial?
2. Los autores bíblicos afirman que Dios intervino en la historia para darse a conocer al ser humano y que entre los diferentes métodos que empleó figuran los 66 libros que ellos escribieron bajo la inspiración del Espíritu Santo y cuyas palabras representan las mismas palabras de Dios. Pero ¿cómo podemos saber si esos autores decían la verdad? ¿Hemos de aceptar lo que dicen simplemente porque ellos lo dicen? ¿Qué mecanismos podemos emplear para asegurarnos de que decían la verdad? ¿Existe una base sólida sobre la cual podemos fundamentar nuestras creencias con respecto a las verdades espirituales? Lea el Apéndice A sobre «La ley de la probabilidad».
3. Sin embargo, después de emplear la ley de la probabilidad, muchas personas aún se quedan con dudas. Entonces, ¿debemos abandonar el uso de nuestro intelecto y fiarnos solamente de nuestra fe para determinar qué declaraciones son verídicas? O ¿acaso es una cuestión de emplear tanto el intelecto como la fe? Para ver cómo grandes hombres de Dios han luchado con esta cuestión y las conclusiones a las cuales han llegado, lea «El papel de la fe y el intelecto» en el Apéndice B.

# 2

# Inspiración

La palabra «inspiración» tiene diferentes significados según el contexto en que se emplea. Los autores de novelas y compositores de música hablan de momentos en que se sienten inspirados. En esos instantes su creatividad fluye libremente. Otros se sienten inspirados y conmovidos al escuchar a un gran orador. Pero cuando el apóstol Pablo dice que «toda la Escritura es inspirada por Dios» (2 Ti. 3:16), quiere decir algo completamente diferente. La doctrina bíblica de la inspiración cuenta con cuatro elementos principales: (1) las Escrituras son de origen divino; (2) toda Escritura es inspirada; (3) cada palabra en los manuscritos originales es inspirada; y (4) no hay omisiones.

## A. LAS ESCRITURAS SON DE ORIGEN DIVINO

Hay dos preguntas que el intérprete debe hacerse con respecto al origen de la Biblia. Primera, ¿qué dice la Biblia al respecto? Porque si la Biblia no reclama ser de origen divino, con toda probabilidad no lo es. Pero si por el contrario dice que Dios es su autor, el intérprete debería saber qué argumentos emplea para apoyar esa declaración. Segunda, ¿quién es Jesús? Porque si Jesús es Dios, entonces su posición sobre las Escrituras debe ser aceptada como decisiva y autoritativa.

## El Antiguo Testamento

Cuando Jesús y los autores del N.T. afirmaban que las Escrituras son de origen divino, con toda probabilidad se referían al A.T., porque algunos de los autores del N.T. ni siquiera habían empezado a escribir sus respectivos libros.

*La posición de Jesús.* Jesús creía que el A.T. es de origen divino al reconocer en varias ocasiones que las palabras pronunciadas por los autores del A.T. eran las palabras de Dios. Por ejemplo, atribuyó las palabras «Honra a tu padre y a tu madre» a Moisés en Marcos 7:10, pero en Mateo 15:4 dijo que procedían de Dios, hasta tal punto que Éxodo 32:16 parece indicar que Dios mismo escribió las palabras de los Diez Mandamientos sobre las tablas de piedra. También atribuyó a Dios (Mt. 19:4-5) unas palabras que fueron dichas por Moisés (Gn. 2:24). Puesto que Dios eligió a algunos hombres para poner por escrito lo que les había revelado, es imposible divorciar las palabras de los autores humanos de las palabras de Dios. Hasta los teólogos que rechazan la inspiración y origen divinos de las Escrituras admiten que Jesús creía en ellos, aunque creen que se equivocaba.

*La posición de los autores del A.T.* Pache afirma que en 3808 ocasiones los autores del A.T. declaran que están transmitiendo las mismas palabras de Dios[1]. «El SEÑOR le dio este mensaje» es la frase que se encuentra frecuentemente en los primeros versículos de varios libros proféticos del A.T. Al observar las primeras palabras de los autores de los libros proféticos del A.T. (ver la NTV), es más que evidente que eran conscientes de que hablaban y escribían las palabras de Dios.

*La posición de los autores del N.T.* Por su claridad, 2 Timoteo 3:16 y 2 Pedro 1:20-21 son los textos más importantes sobre el origen divino del A.T. Pablo afirma que «toda la Escritura es inspirada *por Dios*» (2 Ti. 3:16, énfasis añadido). Y Pedro declara: «Entendiendo primero esto, que ninguna profecía de la Escritura es de interpretación privada, porque nunca la profecía fue traída por voluntad

---

1. Ver René Pache, *The Inspiration and Authority of Scripture* (Chicago: Moody Press, 1978), p. 21. Otros sugieren la cifra de más de dos mil veces. En cualquier caso, la cifra es impresionante y abrumadora.

| Afirmaciones de autores del A.T. | |
|---|---|
| **Isaías** | «Esto dice el SEÑOR:...» (66:1) |
| **Jeremías** | «El SEÑOR le dio mensajes a...» (1:2) |
| **Ezequiel** | «Se abrieron los cielos y tuve visiones de Dios» (1:1) |
| **Oseas** | «El SEÑOR le dio este mensaje a Oseas...» (1:1) |
| **Joel** | «El SEÑOR le dio el siguiente mensaje a Joel...» (1:1) |
| **Amós** | «Esto es lo que dice el SEÑOR...» (1:3) |
| **Abdías** | «Hemos oído un mensaje del SEÑOR...» (1:1) |
| **Jonás** | «El SEÑOR le dio el siguiente mensaje a Jonás...» (1:1) |
| **Miqueas** | «El SEÑOR le dio el siguiente mensaje a Miqueas...» (1:1) |
| **Sofonías** | «El SEÑOR le dio este mensaje a Sofonías...» (1:1) |
| **Hageo** | «El SEÑOR dio un mensaje por medio del profeta Hageo...» (1:1) |
| **Zacarías** | «El SEÑOR le dio este mensaje al profeta Zacarías...» (1:1) |
| **Malaquías** | «Este es el mensaje que el SEÑOR dio... por medio del profeta Malaquías» (1:1) |

humana, sino que santos hombres de Dios hablaron siendo inspirados *por el Espíritu Santo*» (2 P. 1:20-21, énfasis añadido). El v. 21 declara claramente que Dios es el autor del A.T. Pero, ¿qué quiere decir cuando afirma que «ninguna profecía de la Escritura es de interpretación "privada" (RVR60), "particular" (NVI), "personal" (LBLA) o de "comprensión personal"» (NTV)? Evidentemente, cada creyente tiene que interpretar las Escrituras y llegar a una conclusión en cuanto a lo que enseñan porque es el primer responsable de lo que cree. Y es evidente que algunos creyentes entienden más que otros sobre lo que enseñan las Escrituras porque han invertido más tiempo en estudiarlas. Pero nadie tiene el derecho de presumir de tener el monopolio sobre la verdad, de pensar que sus interpretaciones son las correctas, por la sencilla razón de que las Escrituras proceden de Dios, no del ser humano. El creyente ha de interpretar las Escrituras, pero el significado del texto bíblico se encuentra en la mente de Dios, el autor de las Escrituras, no en la mente del intérprete.

## El Nuevo Testamento

Los 27 libros del N.T. son tan inspirados como los 39 del A.T. Esta conclusión se basa en la autoridad que Cristo dio a sus discípulos, los cuales se convertirían en los apóstoles después de su resurrección y ascensión al cielo.

*1. Jesús profetizó que sus discípulos recibirían un ministerio especial del Espíritu Santo.* En preparación para el día en que tendrían que defenderse ante tribunales hostiles, Jesús prometió que el Espíritu Santo les daría las palabras que necesitaran para defenderse (Mt. 10:19-20; Mc. 13:11). Aunque esta promesa no hace ninguna referencia a los libros del N.T. que algunos de ellos escribirían en el futuro, representa un primer ladrillo en el fundamento del hecho de que estos hombres tendrían un ministerio muy especial en el futuro.

*2. Jesús los comisionó para propagar la nueva fe cristiana.* En Mateo 28:19-20 Jesús comisionó a sus discípulos para evangelizar y discipular a todas las naciones. Ya les había hablado en Juan 15:16 del fruto que tendrían en sus respectivos ministerios futuros. Para llevar a cabo estas tareas, les prometió que su ministerio sería confirmado por señales (Mc. 16:16-20), una promesa que fue cumplida a lo largo del libro de Hechos (Heb. 2:3-4). Aunque solemos aplicar Juan 15:16 y Mateo 28:19-20 a todos los creyentes, su primera aplicación tiene que ver con los discípulos.

*3. Jesús prometió que guiaría a sus discípulos «a toda la verdad» (Jn. 16:13).* Es importante entender el papel que juega el artículo definido griego (el, la) en lo que Jesús está diciendo en este texto. El artículo definido existía en el griego koiné, pero no se empleaba con mucha frecuencia, por lo que cuando se hacía servía para señalar o llamar la atención sobre algo o alguien. Por ejemplo, en los Evangelios el nombre «Cristo» sin artículo se refiere a Jesús como hombre; pero cuando aparece con el artículo («*el* Cristo») lo señala como el Mesías. Así que cuando Jesús prometió a sus discípulos que el Espíritu Santo los guiaría a «toda *la* verdad», no hablaba de verdades en general, sino de una verdad muy concreta; a saber, una verdad espiritual no conocida anteriormente y la labor que algunos de ellos tendrían de poner por escrito esa verdad. De ahí que Juan 16:13 acabe con las palabras: «Os hará saber las cosas que habrán de venir». Esta promesa coincide con la promesa de Juan 14:26 de que el Espíritu Santo «os enseñará todas las cosas», una clara referencia a la revelación especial. También les promete en

14:26 que el Espíritu Santo «os recordará todo lo que yo os he dicho». Así que, para escribir los libros del N.T., los discípulos iban a necesitar no solamente una revelación especial de Dios, sino también una buena memoria de las obras y enseñanzas de Jesús que habían visto y oído por haber acompañado a Jesús durante tres años.

> «Cuando venga el Espíritu de verdad, él los guiará a toda la verdad. Él no hablará por su propia cuenta, sino que les dirá lo que ha oído y les contará lo que sucederá en el futuro».
>
> **(Jn. 16:13, NTV)**

*4. Los discípulos entendieron Juan 16:13 como una referencia a su labor de escribir el N.T.* En comparación con la gran cantidad de textos en los dos Testamentos que hablan sobre el origen divino del A.T., los autores de las Epístolas dicen muy poco sobre sí mismos, los libros que están escribiendo y los demás autores del N.T. En la opinión de Broomall, no es un hecho extraño. «Puesto que todos los apóstoles recibieron su autoridad del Señor resucitado, no les hacía falta confirmar esa autoridad mediante el testimonio de otro apóstol»[2]. No obstante, igual que tantos autores del A.T., los autores del N.T. afirman que sus escritos son las palabras de Dios.

Pablo declara que recibió revelación especial de Dios (1 Co. 14:37; Gá. 1:1, 12). Luego, da gracias a Dios porque los tesalonicenses recibieron sus palabras «no como palabra de hombres, sino según es en verdad, la palabra de Dios» (1 Ts. 2:13). Asegura a los corintios que «habla Cristo en mí» (2 Co. 13:3) y que su autoridad se basa en la labor del Espíritu Santo (1 Co. 2.13). Juan explica cómo Dios le dio instrucciones para escribir el libro de Apocalipsis (1:1-2, 11, 19; 22:18-19). En cuanto a las Epístolas de Pablo, Pedro dice que hay

2. Wick Broomall, *Biblical Criticism* (Grand Rapids: Zondervan, 1957), pp. 47–48. Broomall hace una excelente exposición de este tema en las pp. 42–53 de su libro.

algunas cosas en ellas que son «difíciles de entender, las cuales los indoctos e inconstantes tuercen, como también *las otras Escrituras*» (2 P. 3:16, énfasis añadido), incluyendo así sus Epístolas en ese conjunto de libros llamados «Escrituras». Cabe la posibilidad de que se refiriera también a libros de otros autores del N.T. que habían sido escritos y que circulaban entre las iglesias.

Efesios 2:20 dice que la Iglesia se funda sobre «los apóstoles y profetas», sin lugar a dudas una referencia a la enseñanza de los apóstoles y a los libros que escribían. Al citar a los profetas después de los apóstoles, Pablo da a entender que no se refiere a los profetas del A.T., sino a los que tienen el don de profecía en el N.T., y que estos no llegan al mismo nivel de importancia que los apóstoles. A la vez, al citarlos *conjuntamente* con los apóstoles, es evidente que tienen algo en común con ellos. El autor cree que el don de profecía en el N.T. consistía en la responsabilidad que el Espíritu Santo dio a ciertos miembros de las iglesias de recibir revelación directa de Dios y compartirla con sus respectivas iglesias mientras los apóstoles escribían el N.T.[3]

| El N.T. es inspirado por Dios |
|---|
| 1. Jesús profetizó que sus discípulos recibirían un ministerio especial del E. S.<br>2. Jesús les comisionó para propagar la nueva fe cristiana.<br>3. Jesús prometió que guiaría a sus discípulos «a toda la verdad» (Juan 16:13).<br>4. Los discípulos entendieron Juan 16:13 como una referencia a su labor de escribir el N.T. |

Los apóstoles escribieron con autoridad porque creían que hablaban de parte de Dios. Por eso Pablo insistió en que sus Epístolas fueran leídas no solamente en las iglesias a las cuales fueron dirigidas, sino también en las demás iglesias (1 Co. 14:37; Col. 4:16; 1 Ts. 5:27). Hasta mandó que sus cartas a individuos fueran leídas por otras personas y en las iglesias (notar la palabra «vosotros» en 2 Timoteo 4:22).

## B. TODA ESCRITURA ES INSPIRADA

Los teólogos evangélicos emplean el término «inspiración plenaria» para expresar el concepto de que todas las Escrituras son inspiradas. En Mateo 23:30-31 Jesús condena a los escribas y fariseos por afirmar que

3. Para más información sobre el don de profecía, ver el libro de Jaime Fasold, *Dones espirituales* (Grand Rapids: Portavoz, 2000), pp. 147–151.

ellos no habrían sido cómplices de aquellos que mataron a los profetas en el A.T. si hubiesen vivido en esos tiempos. En el v. 35 les dice que son iguales que esos asesinos. Por tanto, toda la ira de Dios caerá también sobre ellos por toda la «sangre justa que se ha derramado sobre la tierra, desde la sangre de Abel el justo hasta la sangre de Zacarías hijo de Berequías, a quien matasteis entre el templo y el altar». Para apreciar lo que Jesús está diciendo con respecto a la inspiración plenaria de las Escrituras, conviene saber que el orden en que los judíos colocaron los libros del A.T. era diferente al nuestro. Génesis era el primer libro y 2 Crónicas el último. Al reconocer la historicidad de los asesinatos de Abel en Génesis 4:8 y Zacarías en 2 Crónicas 24:21, Jesús reconocía en efecto que todo el A.T. es inspirado, «de tapa a tapa», de principio a fin. En el camino a Emaús Jesús riñe a los dos discípulos por no «creer *todo* lo que los profetas han dicho» (Lc. 24:25, énfasis añadido). Luego, Pablo declara que «*Toda* la Escritura es inspirada por Dios» (2 Ti. 3:16, énfasis añadido). Y cuando se defiende ante Félix, afirma que cree «*todas las cosas* que en la ley y en los profetas están escritas» (Hch. 24:14, énfasis añadido).

Hay quienes proponen que son inspirados solamente aquellos pasajes que tratan sobre doctrina y cuestiones éticas, y que no lo son los pasajes históricos, referencias científicas, fechas, números, cronologías, etcétera. Pero Jesús no limitó la inspiración solamente a los pasajes doctrinales y morales. En sus muchas referencias al A.T., incluyó incluso aquellos eventos cuya historicidad ha sido más cuestionada por los teólogos liberales. Por ejemplo: el diluvio en tiempos de Noé (Mt. 24:37-39; Lc. 17:26-27); Jonás, el gran pez y el arrepentimiento de Nínive (Mt. 12:39-41; Lc. 11:29-32); Sodoma y Gomorra (Mt. 10:15; 11:23-24); etcétera. Jesús citó una y otra vez textos del A.T. sin ninguna insinuación de que algunos eran inspirados y otros no. Otra muestra de su confianza en la inspiración de todo el A.T. fue el hecho de que citó textos de 31 de los 39 libros del A.T. para apoyar su enseñanza. Las Escrituras no eran una cosa secundaria en su vida y ministerio, sino una parte fundamental. Las empleó como la autoridad definitiva en sus discusiones con las personas que rechazaban su enseñanza. Además de las declaraciones de Jesús, textos como 2 Timoteo 3:16 y 2 Pedro 1:20-21 demuestran que Pablo y los demás apóstoles creían en la inspiración plenaria de las Escrituras. Ninguno de ellos declara ni insinúa que solamente son inspiradas algunas partes de ellas.

No obstante, aunque cada parte de la Biblia es igualmente inspirada, todos los textos no son igualmente útiles. Aunque la descripción del reinado de Ezequías en 2 Reyes 18:1–10:21 es tan inspirada como la descripción de la justificación por la fe en Romanos 4–5, la utilidad de Romanos para el creyente y la Iglesia es muy superior a la de 2 Reyes. No es que Romanos goce de una inspiración diferente o superior, sino que «las diferentes partes del canon deben considerarse como los instrumentos musicales de una orquestra sinfónica. Algunos pueden ser más prominentes que otros, pero cada uno es esencial e imprescindible para la armonía de la totalidad»[4]. Hay quienes consideran la petición de Pablo a Timoteo de que le traiga su capote, libros y pergaminos (2 Ti. 4:13) como detalles demasiado triviales para ser inspirados. Pero Harris cree que olvidan…

> …que el Dios que cuida de los gorriones se preocupa mucho más de que su apóstol ya avanzado en edad tenga ropa caliente y un lugar para ubicarse. Si Dios pudo controlar una flecha disparada «a la ventura», la cual hirió al rey Acab «entre las junturas y el coselete» para que se cumpliera la profecía de Miqueas (2 Cr. 18:33), sin lugar a dudas tiene interés también en nuestros pequeños problemas[5].

En algunas ocasiones los autores del N.T. citan las ideas de filósofos conocidas en aquellos tiempos. No es que avalasen dichas ideas, sino que consideraron útil citarlas como una ilustración o elemento esencial de algún argumento teológico.

## El texto es inspirado, no los autores

Cuando un erudito traduce la Biblia, procura elegir la palabra en su idioma materno que mejor representa el significado de cada palabra

4. James Emery White, «Inspiration and Authority of Scripture» en *Foundations for Biblical Interpretation* (Nashville: Broadman & Holman Publishers, 1994), p. 23.

5. R. Laird Harris, *Inspiration and Canonicity of the Bible* (Grand Rapids: Zondervan, 1977), p. 83.

en el texto original. No es una tarea fácil. A veces no existe una palabra exacta en su idioma materno, y tampoco tiene la opción de emplear tres o cuatro palabras en su traducción para que el significado de la palabra original quede claro. Este es el caso de *zeopneustos* en 2 Timoteo 3:16, el único sitio donde esa palabra aparece en todo el N.T. La RVR60, LBLA, NVI y NTV la traducen como «inspirada», con toda probabilidad la mejor palabra disponible en español. Sin embargo, el significado literal de *zeopneustos* es «espirada». De la misma forma en que el ser humano respira y espira, Dios espiró el texto bíblico. De ahí que la LBLA indique en el margen que *zeopneustos* significa literalmente «dada por el aliento de Dios». La NVI coincide, diciendo en el margen que significa «espirada, "soplada" por Dios».

> «Ni por iniciativa humana. Al contrario, fue el Espíritu Santo quien impulsó a los profetas y ellos hablaron de parte de Dios».
>
> **(2 P. 1:21, NTV)**

Segunda de Pedro 1:21 dice que los autores humanos de la Biblia fueron «inspirados por el Espíritu Santo» (RVR60, LBLA), dando a entender que no solo el texto bíblico sino también los autores fueron inspirados. Una vez más nos encontramos ante un problema de traducción. La palabra empleada en 2 Pedro 1:21 no es *zeopneustos* (como en 2 Timoteo 3:16), sino *feromenoi*, la cual significa «llevar, mover o impulsar a algo o a alguien». De ahí que la LBLA indique que *feromenoi* significa «literalmente *llevados* o movidos» (énfasis añadido), mientras que la NVI incluye en el mismo texto del v. 21 las palabras «los profetas hablaron de parte de Dios *impulsados por* el Espíritu Santo», y la NTV las palabras «fue el Espíritu Santo *quien impulsó a los profetas*» (énfasis añadido). El verbo *feromenoi* se usaba en aquella época para describir el impulso que el viento da a un barco de vela. Mientras que 2 Timoteo 3:16 declara que las Escrituras son el producto del aliento o espiración de Dios, 2 Pedro 1:21 subraya el papel del Espíritu Santo de impulsar o llevar, como si fuera en brazos, a los autores humanos mientras escribían las Escrituras. A la luz de estas observaciones es evidente que la inspiración se refiere al texto bíblico, no a los hombres elegidos por Dios para escribirlo[6].

La Biblia subraya el *hecho* de la inspiración, no el *método* que Dios empleó. No nos explica cómo Dios espiró el texto bíblico sin anular la personalidad, vocabulario y estilo literario de los autores bíblicos. La única pista que tenemos es 2 Pedro 1:21, que simplemente dice que el Espíritu Santo impulsó o llevó a los autores. Lo que da a las Escrituras su increíble unidad —a pesar de contar con más de treinta autores que vivieron en diferentes culturas a lo largo de aproximadamente mil quinientos años— es el hecho de que hay un solo autor principal, Dios mismo.

En algunos casos hubo *inspiración sin revelación*. Moisés no necesitaba una revelación especial de Dios para describir la salida de los judíos de Egipto y su viaje por el desierto por cuanto participó en esos eventos. Los autores de los libros históricos hicieron uso de documentos oficiales del gobierno para escribir una gran porción de sus libros. Josué 10:13 y 2 Samuel 1:1-18 citan el libro de Jaser. Primera de Reyes 11:41 indica que alguna de su información proviene del libro de los hechos de Salomón. El autor o autores citan al menos nueve fuentes extrabíblicas que emplearon para relatar la información que aparece en 1 y 2 Crónicas[7]. La información que aparece en Esdras 7:11-26 fue

6. En su libro *Protestant Biblical Interpretation* (Grand Rapids: Baker, 1978), p. 129, Bernard Ramm dice: «Una de las palabras más polémicas del N.T. es "inspirada" (*zeopneustos*). Cuando se añade *-tos* a una palabra griega, ¿qué es lo que pretende indicar? Los eruditos alemanes han puesto el énfasis sobre el estado interno del profeta: es un hombre inspirado. Después de una investigación exhaustiva sobre palabras que terminan con *-tos,* Warfield llegó a la conclusión de que hacía énfasis sobre un producto inspirado, las Sagradas Escrituras. Por tanto, *zeopneustos* no se trata del hombre siendo inspirado por Dios (aunque no está excluido este concepto), sino de un libro que Dios produce».

7. Las nueve fuentes seculares citadas por el autor o autores de 1 y 2 Crónicas son: (1) El libro de los reyes de Judá y de Israel: 2 Crónicas 20:34; 24:27; 25:26; 28:26. No puede referirse a los libros canónicos de 1 Reyes y 2 Reyes ya que algunos eventos citados en 2 Crónicas 25 y 28 no se encuentran en esos libros. (2) El libro de las crónicas de Samuel vidente: 1 Crónicas 29:29. (3) Las crónicas del profeta Natán: 1 Crónicas 29:29; 2 Crónicas 9:29. (4) Las crónicas de Gad vidente: 1 Crónicas 29:29. (5) La profecía de Ahías silonita: 2 Crónicas 9:29. (6) La profecía del vidente Iddo: 2 Crónicas 9:29; 12:15. (7) Los libros del profeta Semaías: 2 Crónicas 12:15. (8) Las palabras de Jehú hijo de Hanani: 2 Crónicas 20:34. (9) Los escritos del profeta Isaías sobre el rey

sacada de los archivos de los persas. Dios no tuvo que conceder a Mateo una revelación especial para que escribiera la genealogía de Jesús (1:1-16), la cual era de conocimiento público. Para escribir una parte de su Evangelio, era suficiente que Lucas realizara una investigación de los documentos que ya existían y una entrevista con las personas que habían presenciado la vida y ministerio de Jesús (Lc. 1:1-3). Lo que Dios sí hizo fue guiar y supervisar a los autores bíblicos de tal manera que incluyeran en el texto bíblico la información que Dios quería que figurara, y que dicha información fuera fidedigna y sin error.

En otros casos hubo *inspiración con revelación*. Cabe dentro de esta categoría toda la información que los profetas del A.T. y los apóstoles del N.T. recibieron por revelación directa sobre verdades espirituales y eventos futuros que no se podían conocer de otro modo. Juan escribió el libro de Apocalipsis exclusivamente con base en la inspiración con revelación.

## C. CADA PALABRA EN LOS MANUSCRITOS ORIGINALES ES INSPIRADA

Los teólogos evangélicos emplean el término «inspiración verbal» para expresar el concepto de que cada una de las palabras que aparecen en los manuscritos originales es inspirada, no solamente la idea expresada por dicha palabra. Hay quienes afirman que los conceptos bíblicos son inspirados, pero no las palabras. Pero por lógica, la inspiración plenaria se extiende hasta las palabras, porque las ideas son explicadas con palabras. Si las palabras no son precisas y correctas, tampoco son precisos y correctos los conceptos que pretenden comunicar. En palabras de Pache:

> El sentido de la revelación divina está inextricablemente vinculado al lenguaje de las Escrituras; su contenido no puede expresarse aparte de palabras. Así que, si no podemos afirmar que las palabras de las Escrituras son dadas por Dios, tampoco podemos afirmar

---

Uzías: 2 Crónicas 26:22. Las pocas referencias a Uzías y la escasa información que se da de él en el libro canónico de Isaías (1:1; 6:1; 7:1) nos empujan a creer que 2 Crónicas 26:22 se refiere a un libro no canónico. La referencia a Isaías en 2 Crónicas 32:32 como el autor de la historia del rey Ezequías fácilmente podría referirse a su libro canónico.

> que las Escrituras lo son, porque consisten de palabras. Nunca podremos estar seguros de lo que el Espíritu de Dios quiere decir en las Escrituras hasta que podamos estar seguros de que las palabras del texto fueron dadas expresamente por él. Lutero tenía mucha razón al decir: «Cristo no dijo que sus pensamientos, sino que sus palabras son espíritu y vida» (Jn. 6:63)[8].

Además, hay demasiados textos bíblicos que apoyan de forma clara la inspiración de las palabras. Vemos algunos ejemplos.

## La posición de Jesús

En varias ocasiones Jesús cita una sola palabra de un texto del A.T. para apoyar una enseñanza suya. En Mateo 22:23-32 los saduceos discuten con Jesús el tema de la resurrección, una doctrina que ellos rechazaban. Como prueba de la veracidad de esa doctrina, Jesús cita en el v. 32 las palabras de Dios a Moisés «Yo *soy* el Dios de Abraham» (Éx. 3:6, énfasis añadido) en lugar de «Yo *era...*» para indicar que Abraham, Isaac y Jacob vivían en aquel momento, aunque habían muerto siglos antes. O sea, hay vida después de la muerte.

> «No malinterpreten la razón por la cual he venido. No vine para abolir la ley de Moisés o los escritos de los profetas. Al contrario, vine para cumplir sus propósitos. Les digo la verdad, hasta que desaparezcan el cielo y la tierra, no desaparecerá ni el más mínimo detalle de la ley de Dios hasta que su propósito se cumpla.».
>
> **(Mt. 5:17-18, NTV)**

En Mateo 5:17-18 Jesús afirma que no ha venido para anular la Ley, sino para cumplirla, y que antes de desaparecer el cielo y la tierra, se cumplirá todo lo que Dios ha dicho en la ley y en los libros proféticos, hasta lo que se encuentra en cada jota y tilde (Lc. 16:17). La jota es

8. René Pache, *The Inspiration and Authority of Scripture* (Chicago: Moody Press, 1978), pp. 73–74, 75.

la letra hebrea *yod,* la más pequeña del alfabeto hebreo. Aunque no es tan clara la identidad de la tilde, muchos eruditos piensan que se refiere a la raya que se parece a un acento y que es prácticamente imperceptible. Se empleaba para distinguir ciertas letras hebreas de otras. Es evidente que en Mateo 5:18 Jesús hace uso de una hipérbole, porque no existen profecías en las jotas y tildes. Igual que una palabra no tiene sentido si no forma parte de una frase, una letra no tiene significado aparte de una palabra. Lo que Jesús quiere decir es que todas las Escrituras son inspiradas por Dios, hasta en los detalles más insignificantes. Por eso, Jesús declaró que «la Escritura no puede ser quebrantada» (Jn. 10:35). No se podrá probar falsa ni quedará corta en ninguna cosa que las Escrituras afirmen y profeticen. Cada profecía se cumplirá.

## La posición de Pablo

Pablo también creía en la inspiración verbal de las Escrituras. En Gálatas 3:16 fundamenta su argumento sobre el hecho de que la palabra «simiente» aparece en singular, no en plural («Ahora bien, a Abraham fueron hechas las promesas, y a su simiente. No dice: Y a las simientes, como si hablase de muchos, sino como de uno: Y a tu simiente, la cual es Cristo»). Para basar su argumento sobre el hecho de que una palabra aparece en singular en lugar de plural, tenía que creer en la inspiración verbal de las Escrituras[9]. En 1 Corintios 2:13 afirma que la eficacia de sus palabras no se debe a la sabiduría humana, sino a «las (palabras) que enseña el Espíritu». Algunos teólogos evangélicos creen que 1 Corintios 2:13 es el texto más claro del N.T. en cuanto a la inspiración verbal de las Escrituras.

---

9. En Romanos 15:8-12 Pablo hace descansar su argumento teológico sobre una sola palabra. En este pasaje enseña que los gentiles también tienen entrada en el reino de Dios, haciendo hincapié en una sola palabra —*gentil*— que aparece en varios textos del A.T. En el v. 9 cita a 2 Samuel 22:50 y Salmo 18:49. En el v. 10 llama la atención a Deuteronomio 32:43. Hace lo mismo en el v. 11 (Sal. 117:1) y el v. 12 (Is. 11:10). En ninguno de los textos del A.T. citados por Pablo aparece la palabra «gentiles» en la RVR60, sino «naciones» o «pueblos». Al citar estos textos Pablo emplea la palabra «gentiles» porque todas las naciones y pueblos aparte de la nación de Israel se componían de gentiles. Por tanto, se tomó la libertad de emplear la palabra «gentiles».

La inspiración se extiende solamente a los manuscritos originales, no a las copias y traducciones a otros idiomas que se han hecho a lo largo de los siglos. Es precisamente aquí donde se plantea una pregunta muy legítima. Si no tenemos ni siquiera un trocito del manuscrito original de ninguno de los 66 libros bíblicos, ¿de qué sirve la doctrina de la inspiración verbal? La respuesta a esa pregunta se dará en los Apéndices C, D y E, los cuales forman parte del «Trabajo para realizar» en este capítulo y en los dos próximos. De momento, es suficiente decir que, debido a la existencia de tantos manuscritos y a la labor tan precisa y completa de los críticos textuales, estamos *absolutamente seguros,* en un 99 por ciento, de lo que dice el texto original. En cuanto al restante 1 por ciento, cada año se va reduciendo. Además, sabemos dónde se encuentra exactamente y cuáles son las dos o tres opciones que hay en cuanto a lo que dice el texto original, que en la mayoría de los casos tienen que ver con cuestiones gramaticales insignificantes. Señalar, finalmente, que no hay ninguna doctrina en juego en ese 1 por ciento.

*La inspiración verbal de las Escrituras es una conclusión lógica, necesaria y a todos los efectos obligatoria.* Si las Escrituras son de origen divino por haber sido «espiradas» por Dios (2 Ti. 3:16), si Jesús y los autores bíblicos reconocieron que todas las Escrituras y cada palabra fueron inspiradas por Dios, y si Dios es verdad y no puede mentir (Nm. 23:19; 1 Ts. 1:9; Tito 1:2; Heb. 6:18; 1 Jn. 5:20), entonces la inspiración verbal de las Escrituras en los manuscritos originales es la única conclusión lógica a la que podemos llegar. Esta conclusión cae por su propio peso; la lógica es prácticamente hermética. Además, no hay ningún texto bíblico que declare que algún texto contenga un error. Y este silencio total de las Escrituras en cuanto a supuestos errores por parte de sus autores conlleva un peso considerable. Por eso, es lógico que todas las ramas del cristianismo aceptaran la inspiración e infalibilidad de las Escrituras desde los tiempos apostólicos hasta finales del siglo XVIII, cuando algunos filósofos seculares y teólogos comenzaron a cuestionar y rechazar la inspiración verbal de las Escrituras además de otras doctrinas fundamentales de la fe cristiana.

Aunque no es la percepción que existe ni la impresión que se da en ciertos círculos teológicos, «no hay otra doctrina, con la excepción de las doctrinas de la Trinidad y la deidad de Cristo, que se ha mantenido de forma tan extendida a lo largo de la historia de la Iglesia como la inspiración verbal»[10] de las Escrituras. La percepción de que esta doctrina es una novedad que ha surgido en tiempos modernos se debe en parte a que los *ataques* contra esa doctrina son modernos, aunque es más que evidente que Jesús y los apóstoles creían en ella. La inspiración verbal no recibió mucha atención durante la era medieval (siglos V–XV). Aunque la Iglesia mantenía esa doctrina, la alegorización como método de interpretación bíblica permitía al intérprete sacar del texto lo que quisiera. Pero la doctrina de la inspiración verbal recibió de nuevo su debido énfasis y atención durante la Reforma (siglo XVI).

## El texto no fue dictado

El hecho de que se puede notar el vocabulario propio y el estilo literario de los autores bíblicos demuestra que Dios no dictó el texto bíblico. Ladd dice que «la mayor parte del Nuevo Testamento está escrito en un griego relativamente suave, pero algunos libros, tales como Marcos y 2 Pedro, son ásperos y pesados. El libro de Apocalipsis está repleto de construcciones sintácticas intolerables en griego»[11]. Es de esperar que Pedro empleara un griego basto y rudimentario, ya que era un pescador sin estudios formales. En la opinión de muchos eruditos, Lucas, Santiago y el autor de Hebreos emplean el mejor griego. Hay ocasiones en que el griego de Pablo se acerca a la elegancia por cuanto estudió bajo Gamaliel, un erudito eminente de la Ley (Hch. 22:3). No obstante, uno de los argumentos que lo elimina como candidato a ser el autor de Hebreos es que su griego no llega a la altura del griego tan fino y exquisito de esa Epístola. ¿Es posible que Apolos, «un orador elocuente» (Hch. 18:24, NTV), fuera el autor? Al hablar de la diferencia en vocabulario que existe entre los autores del A.T., Kaiser dice que el traductor desgastará «un léxico buscando nuevas palabras hebreas en Job y Oseas, pero leerá Génesis y Hageo con una facilidad y velocidad deliciosa»[12]. Todas estas observaciones

---

10. Harris, ob. cit., (1977), p. 72.

11. George Eldon Ladd, *Crítica del Nuevo Testamento* (El Paso: Editorial Mundo Hispano, 1990), p. 19.

12. Walter C. Kaiser, «Legitimate Hermeneutics» en *Inerrancy* (Grand Rapids: Zondervan, 1980), p. 122.

nos obligan a concluir que Dios no dictó las palabras que figuran en los manuscritos originales, aunque las «espiró».

Los padres de la iglesia mantenían que las Escrituras eran verbalmente inspiradas. Solamente un par de teólogos llevaron esa doctrina al extremo de creer que Dios había dictado el texto. Quizás los más destacados fueron Filón de Alejandría (20 a. C.–50 d. C.) y Tertuliano (c. 160–c. 220). Esta teoría brotó de nuevo en el siglo XVI. Desde entonces muchos teólogos liberales han acusado a los evangélicos de creer que el texto fue dictado, argumentando que la inspiración verbal sería posible solo en el caso de que Dios llevara un control férreo sobre los autores, en efecto dictando el texto[13]. Pero el hecho de que se puede observar el vocabulario y estilo literario tan diferente de cada autor contradice esa teoría.

Evidentemente, hay un par de textos como los Diez Mandamientos que fueron dictados por Dios. Pero no representan un argumento suficiente para sugerir que *todas* las Escrituras fueron dictadas. Las Escrituras subrayan el *hecho* de la inspiración verbal, no el *método* que Dios empleó. Por tanto, no sabemos cómo Dios inspiró el texto sin convertir a los autores en unos simples escribas que tomaban dictado. No obstante, es más que evidente que Jesús y el apóstol Pablo creían en la inspiración verbal de las Escrituras.

## A veces los autores emplearon escribas

El hecho de que las Escrituras son inspiradas por Dios no implica que los autores tenían que escribir el texto con su propio puño y letra. Tenían la libertad de dictar el texto a un escriba (amanuense). Parece que Silvano sirvió como amanuense de Pedro (1 P. 5:12) y que Tercio hizo lo mismo para Pablo cuando escribió Romanos (Ro. 16:22). El hecho de decir a varias iglesias que les ha escrito con su propia mano (1 Co. 16:21; Col. 4:18; 2 Ts. 3:17) indica que usaba un amanuense en otras ocasiones[14]. En Gálatas 6:11 Pablo dice: «Mirad con cuán

13. Los teólogos liberales llaman a esta supuesta posición «inspiración mecánica» o «la teoría del dictado».

14. Mientras que el concepto de que algunos autores bíblicos emplearon un amanuense es aceptado por todos, hay mucho debate en cuanto a si el amanuense hizo más que tomar dictado. La evidente diferencia entre el estilo y vocabulario

grandes letras os escribo de mi propia mano». Las letras grandes son características de niños que están aprendiendo a escribir y de ancianos cuya vista falla. Algunos sugieren que el «aguijón» (2 Co. 12:7) que Pablo sufría en su carne consistía en un problema de la vista. Es posible que Pablo necesitara un amanuense porque estaba encadenado a un guardia pretoriano (2 Ti. 1:16)[15] o debido a una salud precaria, frágil, deteriorada y gastada por los rigores de sus prisiones. En cualquiera de estos posibles casos, un amanuense sería una necesidad práctica.

## D. NO HAY OMISIONES

| La inspiración de las escrituras |
|---|
| 1. Las escrituras son de origen divino.<br>2. Toda escritura es inspirada.<br>3. Cada palabra en los manuscritos originales es inspirada.<br>4. No hay omisiones. |

La Biblia protestante cuenta con 66 libros, mientras que la Biblia católica-romana incluye siete libros adicionales llamados apócrifos[16]. Aunque los evangélicos no los consideran canónicos, estos libros nos proveen de una información valiosa sobre la historia y las creencias de los judíos durante los llamados «400 años de silencio» entre los dos Testamentos. Nos permiten saber quiénes son y cómo surgieron los diferentes grupos religiosos y movimientos políticos que aparecen en los Evangelios. Los libros de 1 y 2 Macabeos son nuestra principal fuente histórica de esa época.

Los libros apócrifos no eran los únicos escritos que circulaban durante el primer siglo. En 1945 los arqueólogos descubrieron en la

---

de 1 y 2 Pedro podría explicarse si Pedro permitió a Silvano escribir el texto, el cual después Pedro aprobaría. Es precisamente en este punto donde el debate comienza. Para la opinión de un evangélico muy reconocido sobre esta cuestión, ver el libro de Grant Osborne, *The Hermeneutical Spiral* (Downers Grove: InterVarsity Press, 1991), pp. 256–257.

15. La NVI y la NTV sugieren esta posibilidad.

16. Llamados los libros deuterocanónicos por la Iglesia Católica Romana. Incluyen los libros de Tobit, Judit, 1 y 2 Macabeos, Sabiduría de Salomón, Eclesiastés (o Sirac) y Baruc. Para una lista más extensa ver el libro de Köstenberger y Patterson, *Invitation to Biblical Interpretation* (Grand Rapids: Kregel, 2001), p. 121.

ciudad de Nag Hammadi (Egipto) una colección de 57 escritos «cristianos»[17]. Entre ellos se encuentran títulos como *La exégesis del alma*, *El Apocalipsis de Adán*, *Los Hechos de Pedro* y *El Evangelio de Tomás*, libro que contiene 114 dichos de Jesús sin ningún contexto ni narración y cuya mitad, aproximadamente, refleja el texto bíblico, mientras que la otra mitad roza en la fantasía. Los primeros cristianos estaban informados de la existencia de esta literatura, mucha de la cual contradice la enseñanza de Jesús y la información histórica de los cuatro Evangelios. No obstante, esta literatura plantea dos preguntas legítimas. ¿Es posible que haya un libro inspirado por Dios y que deba figurar en nuestra Biblia que se haya perdido? Y, ¿quién decidió qué libros debían formar parte de la Biblia que tenemos? Hay dos áreas de estudio que contestan estas preguntas y nos llevan a la conclusión de que no falta ningún libro en nuestra Biblia.

## El canon

Uno de los significados de la palabra griega *kanon* es el de «caña o trozo recto de madera que se emplea para medir». De ahí que la palabra «canon» llegara a referirse a los criterios que se emplearon para identificar los libros inspirados por Dios y posteriormente a los 66 libros que cumplían dichos criterios.

*El canon del* A.T. Los 39 libros del A.T. fueron definidos como canónicos antes del primer siglo[18]. Cuando Pablo hace referencia al conocimiento que Timoteo tenía de las Sagradas Escrituras desde su niñez (2 Ti. 3:15), ya hacía más de 200 años que todo el A.T. existía y circulaba entre las comunidades judías. Los muchos textos en el N.T. que hacen referencia a «las Escrituras» (Jn. 5:39), la «palabra de Dios» (Ro. 3:2, RVR60) y otras frases parecidas demuestran que había un cuerpo definido de libros que era reconocido por los judíos y los primeros

17. Estos 57 escritos son antiguos. Aunque algunos de ellos afirman haber sido escritos al final del primer siglo, los eruditos afirman que es muy difícil determinar la fecha de su composición.

18. En el Apéndice I de su libro *Hermenéutica: Entendiendo la Palabra de Dios* (Viladecavalls: CLIE, 2008), J. Scott Duvall y J. Daniel Hays hacen un excelente repaso de la doctrina de la inspiración, el canon y los libros apócrifos. Este libro combina muy bien lo erudito con lo práctico.

cristianos como canónicos. Aunque Jesús no tenía la obligación de citar textos de los 39 libros del A.T. para que creyéramos en la inspiración de los mismos, citó al menos 31 de ellos. Los autores del N.T. citan 300 textos del A.T. Hay solamente ocho libros que Jesús y los autores del N.T. no citan. El historiador judío Josefo (c. 37–100 d. C.) fue el primero en hacer una distinción entre los libros canónicos del A.T. y otros libros religiosos que existían en el primer siglo. Su lista es significativa porque era fariseo y, como tal, representaba la corriente principal de los judíos en cuanto al A.T. Aunque no había un acuerdo en cuanto al orden en que debían colocarse los 39 libros, su lista coincide con las listas de Melitón, obispo de Sardes (siglo II), y Orígenes (siglo III).

*El canon del N.T.* Hubo varios factores que empujaron a los primeros creyentes a identificar los libros que deberían formar parte del N.T. Al principio querían identificar los libros que representaban la nueva revelación que Dios había dado a la Iglesia. Luego, hacía falta un criterio para distinguir entre los libros que eran la Palabra de Dios y los escritos «cristianos», algunos de los cuales promulgaban herejías. Por último, puesto que sufrían tanta persecución, en algunos casos hasta la muerte, querían asegurarse de que sus creencias se fundamentaban en los libros dados por Dios.

Hacia finales del siglo IV todas las iglesias habían recibido una copia de los 27 libros del N.T. y habían llegado a la convicción unánime de que eran canónicos. Cuando hablamos del canon solemos pensar en los concilios de los siglos II y IV en los que participaron líderes como Ireneo (c. 130–c. 202) y Atanasio (293–373), los cuales tomaron decisiones en nombre de todos los creyentes con respecto al canon. Y, aunque es cierto que los concilios sirvieron para aclarar ciertas doctrinas, en el caso del canon simplemente confirmaron y formalizaron lo que ya había sido decidido por los miembros de las iglesias. Nos puede parecer que 300 años es un tiempo excesivamente largo para identificar qué libros son canónicos, pero la gran mayoría de los 27 libros ya fueron aceptados como tales antes del final del siglo II. La iglesia simplemente necesitaba unos años más para llegar a una posición unánime al respecto, ya que no contaba con la tecnología del siglo XXI que hace posible la comunicación instantánea.

Para ser canónico un libro tenía que cumplir ciertos requisitos. (1) Ser escrito por un apóstol o alguien avalado o íntimamente relacionado con un apóstol. Eusebio (280–340), obispo de Cesarea, era un hombre con un afán por las listas; le encantaba hacer listas. En uno de sus escritos c. 325 dice que los miembros de las iglesias, sin la necesidad de recurrir a mucha discusión, reconocieron como canónicos los cuatro Evangelios, Hechos, las Epístolas de Pablo y las Epístolas de 1 Pedro y 1 Juan. Aunque muchas iglesias aceptaron como libros canónicos 2 Pedro, 2 y 3 Juan y Judas, otras no se quedaron convencidas y disputaban su lugar en el canon, aunque luego los aceptaron[19]. (2) Ser escrito con autoridad. Lo que más convenció a los primeros creyentes de que los 27 libros del N.T. eran canónicos era la autoridad con la cual hablaban de Jesús y las doctrinas cristianas. (3) Coincidir con la enseñanza de Jesús, los apóstoles y el A.T. Los primeros creyentes dieron por sentado que Pablo no podía contradecirse a sí mismo ni contradecir lo que Pedro había escrito. Tenía que haber una unidad y acuerdo entre todos los libros canónicos del N.T. (4) Contar con cierta antigüedad. Evidentemente, la mejor prueba de que un evento histórico ha ocurrido es el testimonio de personas que han presenciado dicho evento. Muchos de los autores del N.T. conocían a Jesús personalmente, habían escuchado sus enseñanzas en persona y lo habían visto después de su resurrección. (5) Haber sido usado y aceptado por los miembros de las iglesias.

## La lógica

En 1 Corintios 5:9 Pablo hace mención de una carta —que no tenemos— que envió a la iglesia en Corinto antes de su Primera Epístola. Segunda de Corintios 7:8 indica que les envió otra carta que tampoco tenemos. ¿No deberíamos concluir que estas dos cartas representan un ejemplo de Epístolas inspiradas por Dios que se han perdido y, por tanto, debieran formar parte de nuestra Biblia? No hay ninguna duda de que Pablo escribió esas cartas con toda su autoridad apostólica. A la vez es razonable pensar que los libros y Epístolas que figuran en el N.T. no son los únicos libros que escribieron Pablo y los demás autores. Cabe la posibilidad de que el contenido de las cartas a los

19. Ver Richard B. Gaffin Jr., «The New Testament: How Do We Know For Sure?» en *Christianity Today* (5 febrero 1988), p. 31.

corintios que no tenemos tratara un problema tan local de los lectores originales que no tendría una aplicación suficientemente amplia para ser útil para la iglesia a lo largo de los siglos. A la vez debemos dar por sentado que, si Dios ha sido capaz de crear la Tierra y el universo, es capaz de asegurar que ninguna revelación suya se pierda.

## *Trabajo para realizar*

1. Puesto que la doctrina de la inspiración es la base de todo estudio bíblico, repase los cuatro elementos de esta doctrina citados en este capítulo hasta memorizarlos.
2. La inspiración se extiende solamente a los manuscritos originales, no a las copias y traducciones a otros idiomas que se han hecho a lo largo de los siglos. Pero si no tenemos ni siquiera un trocito del manuscrito original de ninguno de los 66 libros bíblicos, ¿de qué sirve la doctrina de la inspiración verbal? Lea el Apéndice C («Crítica textual del A.T.»), el primero de los tres apéndices que contestan esta pregunta tan importante.

# 3

# Inerrancia (I)

La doctrina de la inerrancia afirma que cada palabra en los manuscritos originales de las Escrituras está exenta de error de la clase que sea. Esta doctrina es la conclusión lógica de los primeros tres pilares de la doctrina de la inspiración; a saber, que las Escrituras son de origen divino, que toda Escritura es inspirada y que cada palabra es inspirada. Aunque algunos detractores han sugerido que la doctrina de la inerrancia nació después de la Reforma del siglo XVI, varios historiadores han demostrado que ya era aceptada por las iglesias y los teólogos destacados de todas las ramas del cristianismo durante los primeros dieciocho siglos de la era cristiana[1]. Es verdad que los credos más antiguos no emplearon las palabras «inspiración» e «inerrancia». Sin embargo, estas doctrinas estaban claramente presentes en los mismos.

Los padres de la iglesia «eran conscientes de las aparentes discrepancias y dificultades encontradas en ciertos textos. Sin embargo, siguieron convencidos —como dijo Agustín— de que la verdad está presente en las Escrituras de forma "absoluta". Las Escrituras no

1. La Iglesia Católica mantuvo la posición de inerrancia hasta el Segundo Concilio Vaticano (1962–1965), cuando eligió considerar como inerrantes solamente aquellos pasajes pertinentes a la salvación. Para más información ver John H. Gerstner, «The Church's Doctrine of Biblical Inspiration» en *The Foundation of Biblical Authority* (Grand Rapids: Zondervan, 1978), p. 50.

pueden mentir. Por eso pueden describirse como "sagradas, infalibles y absolutamente fiables"»[2]. Es más, los padres creían tanto en la inspiración verbal e inerrancia de las Escrituras que algunos de ellos estaban convencidos de que Dios había dictado el texto[3].

## A. EL TRASFONDO HISTÓRICO DEL RECHAZO DE LA INERRANCIA

El rechazo de la inerrancia de las Escrituras no comenzó como un desafío frontal, sino como el resultado de unas reformas que se produjeron en la sociedad europea. Al final del siglo XVII y principio del XVIII, intelectuales como el físico Isaac Newton (1643–1727) y filósofos como Baruch Spinoza (1632–1677), John Locke (1632–1704) y Voltaire (1694–1778) se opusieron a la superstición, intolerancia y abusos cometidos por la Iglesia y el Estado. De este movimiento cultural, llamado el Siglo de la Razón[4], nacieron unos valores como el aprecio del intelecto humano, la ciencia del conocimiento (epistemología), la separación de la Iglesia y el Estado, las libertades civiles, la libertad religiosa y el derecho a la libre expresión. Todos estos cambios eran necesarios y positivos. Sin embargo, a finales del siglo XVIII algunos filósofos, motivados y apoyados por el nuevo aprecio de la capacidad del intelecto humano, empezaron a rechazar abiertamente el origen divino e inspiración de las Escrituras, argumentando que no era intelectualmente razonable creer en los milagros, la profecía, la resurrección, los demonios, etcétera.

Este desafío coincidió con el nacimiento formal de la ciencia de la alta crítica a finales del siglo XVIII. Aunque su cometido es el de identificar la autoría de un libro bíblico, la fecha en que fue escrito, su contexto histórico y trasfondo cultural, etcétera, desde su

---

2. Geoffrey W. Bromiley, «The Church Fathers and the Holy Scripture» en *Scripture and Truth* (Grand Rapids: Baker, 1992), p. 206. En su libro *The Battle for the Bible* (Grand Rapids: Zondervan, 1976), pp. 46–59, Harold Lindsell presenta una lista de personas —desde el historiador judío Josefo (primer siglo) hasta Juan Calvino (1509–1564)— que creían en la inerrancia de las Escrituras.

3. Quizás los más destacados fueran Filón de Alejandría (20 a. C.–50 d. C.) y Tertuliano (c. 160–c. 220).

4. Llamado también el Siglo de las Luces y el Siglo de la Ilustración.

nacimiento y durante muchas décadas después, tanto la alta crítica como la crítica textual fueron realizadas por teólogos liberales, los cuales rechazaban la inerrancia de las Escrituras igual que otras doctrinas fundamentales de la fe cristiana como la deidad y resurrección de Cristo, etcétera. Mientras que los críticos textuales tenían poca oportunidad de promover sus posiciones teológicas, los altos críticos tenían una puerta abierta para manipular la información que los arqueólogos descubrían, proponiendo teorías e interpretaciones —a veces de forma deshonesta y caprichosa— que echaban por tierra las declaraciones bíblicas sobre datos históricos, costumbres del tiempo, la autoría de libros bíblicos, etcétera.

Por ejemplo, Benjamín Jowett (1817–1893) creía que la Biblia es un libro humano como cualquier otro. Y aunque hay que estudiarla en sus idiomas originales, no es un libro sobrenatural. Ferdinand C. Baur (1792–1860), el padre de la «Escuela de Tubinga», creía que el cristianismo no era el resultado de una intervención divina, sino del desarrollo progresivo del judaísmo. David F. Strauss (1808–1874) interpretaba la Biblia con el método mitológico, lo cual lo llevó a rechazar una interpretación gramático-histórico-cultural de las Escrituras. También rechazaba los milagros. Julius Wellhausen (1844–1918) no creía que el Pentateuco haya sido escrito por Moisés, sino por cuatro autores diferentes. También creía que el judaísmo evolucionó desde el politeísmo al animismo, y luego desde el animismo al monoteísmo. En tiempos más recientes los altos críticos que abrazan una teología liberal han rechazado la autoría paulina de las Epístolas Pastorales (1 y 2 Timoteo, Tito) y han considerado la enseñanza paulina sobre la sumisión de la esposa a su marido en Efesios 5:22-24, 33; Colosenses 3:18; Tito 2:4-5; y 1 Pedro 3:1-2 un reflejo de una posición machista, anticuada y retrógrada de la cultura judía del primer siglo.

Frente al gran número de eruditos que rechazaban tantas doctrinas que la iglesia había abrazado a lo largo de los siglos, muchos evangélicos rechazaron la ciencia de la alta crítica, colgándole la etiqueta de «alta crítica destructiva». Pero en el proceso muchos de ellos adoptaron un antiintelectualismo, negándose a reconocer ciertos problemas en la Biblia que merecían y tenían una explicación o solución. A la vez, dejaron que su afán por defender la inspiración de las Escrituras los cegara en cuanto a su naturaleza humana y la validez de la crítica textual. Afortunadamente, durante las últimas décadas la mayoría de los evangélicos se han dado cuenta de que no hay nada que temer de la alta crítica ni de la crítica textual. Para entender las Escrituras es absolutamente necesario saber quién es el autor de un libro, cuál era la situación que le motivó a escribir su libro, quiénes eran los primeros lectores, cómo era la geografía y cultura dentro de la cual escribió su libro, etcétera. Muchos han descubierto también que, cuando la alta crítica es empleada de forma correcta, representa una de las mejores herramientas apologéticas que el evangélico tiene a su alcance[5]. Como resultado, los evangélicos han producido unas obras formidables en el área de la alta crítica que han desbancado sistemática y progresivamente las teorías erróneas de la alta crítica destructiva.

## B. EL DEBATE SOBRE LA INERRANCIA

El debate sobre la inerrancia ha sido muy intenso porque lo que está en juego es la autoridad de las Escrituras. Si la Biblia contiene errores reales, entonces tiene poca, por no decir ninguna, autoridad sobre lo que creemos y cómo vivimos. Pero si es de origen divino, todo cambia radicalmente. El debate sobre la inerrancia ha pasado por cinco etapas.

### Primera etapa (1880–1890)

Los primeros debates sobre la inerrancia tuvieron lugar durante las décadas de los 80 y 90 del siglo XIX entre Benjamin B. Warfield (1851–1921) y Charles A. Briggs (1841–1913). Warfield era rector y profesor del Princeton Theological Seminary (PTS) y defendía la inerrancia de las Escrituras[6]. Le acompañó en su posición A. A. Hodge (1823–1886), teólogo, rector del PTS durante un tiempo e hijo del teólogo reformado Charles Hodge (1797–1878)[7]. Briggs era un erudito del A.T. y profesor del Union Theological Seminary (UTS). Creía que la alta crítica

5. El libro de George E. Ladd, *Crítica del Nuevo Testamento* (El Paso: Editorial Mundo Hispano, 1990) demuestra la validez y necesidad del estudio crítico de las Escrituras.

6. Su libro *The Inspiration and Authority of the Bible* (Filadelfia: Presbyterian and Reformed Publishing Co., 1964) es una obra clásica sobre el tema.

7. Charles Hodge había servido también como rector del PTS (1851–1878).

había demostrado que la Biblia contiene errores. Unos años antes había comenzado a abandonar sus posiciones ortodoxas después de realizar estudios teológicos en Alemania. Phillip Schaff, profesor de Historia de la iglesia en el UTS y autor de varios libros sobre ese tema, era amigo íntimo de Briggs y compartía su posición teológica.

## Segunda etapa (1910–1930)

A principios del siglo XX la teología modernista (llamada más tarde «teología liberal») era la teología dominante en Europa y EE. UU. Los modernistas creían que la Biblia contenía errores en cuestiones de ciencia, números, cronologías, datos históricos, etcétera, pero que era infalible en cuestiones de doctrina y ética. Con el tiempo, algunos modernistas rechazaron doctrinas tan fundamentales de la fe cristiana como la concepción virginal y la resurrección de Cristo.

Para contrarrestar la teología modernista varios autores evangélicos publicaron entre 1910 y 1912 doce volúmenes titulados *The Fundamentals: A Testimony to the Truth* [Los fundamentos: Un testimonio de la verdad], los cuales dieron el nombre al movimiento fundamentalista. El debate se intensificó en las décadas de los años 20 y 30, llegando a conocerse como la controversia fundamentalista-modernista. La mayor parte del debate se centraba en la inerrancia de las Escrituras. El erudito que lideraba la defensa de la inerrancia de las Escrituras fue J. Gresham Machen (1881–1937), profesor en el PTS[8]. Pero en 1929 la Presbyterian Church USA, la denominación que auspiciaba el PTS, tomó la decisión de aceptar la posición modernista. A partir de ese momento contrató solamente a profesores que mantenían esa posición. En protesta, Machen se marchó del PTS, acompañado por algunos profesores y estudiantes, y fundó ese mismo año el Westminster Theological Seminary. Aunque los fundamentalistas contaban con hombres brillantes como Warfield y Machen, lamentablemente adoptaron un antiintelectualismo en cuanto a la interpretación bíblica. Además, se separaron no solamente de las personas que mantenían una teología modernista, sino también de aquellos evangélicos que no se separaban de los teólogos modernistas.

8. Su libro *The Virgin Birth of Christ* sigue siendo la obra clásica sobre ese tema.

## Tercera etapa (1940–1960)

Durante estas décadas muchos seminarios estadounidenses recomendaron a sus graduados que continuaran sus estudios en universidades europeas, donde fueron influenciados por la neoortodoxia del teólogo suizo Karl Barth (1886–1968). Barth creía que la Biblia no es *en sí* la Palabra de Dios, sino el testimonio falible de la experiencia espiritual que los personajes bíblicos tuvieron con Dios. No obstante, aunque la Biblia contiene errores, puede llegar a ser la Palabra de Dios si le habla a una persona y produce en ella una experiencia existencial con Dios. Bajo esa posición, cualquier libro podría llegar a ser la Palabra de Dios para una persona si Dios le hablara a través de dicho libro. La mayoría de los teólogos neoortodoxos creían que Dios quiere hablarle al ser humano. En ese sentido no pretendían atacar la Biblia. Sin embargo, puesto que la mayoría de ellos creían que el lenguaje humano es incapaz de comunicar verdad absoluta, inmutable e inerrante, consideraban la Biblia un mero libro humano.

En 1947 Harold Ockenga (1905–1985) y otros evangélicos fundaron el Fuller Theological Seminary (FTS), empujados por el gran número de seminarios que habían abrazado una teología liberal. Un año después Ockenga predicó un sermón que muchos consideran el nacimiento del movimiento neoevangélico. En él animó a los evangélicos a involucrarse en la obra social en lugar de abdicar ese ministerio a las iglesias y pastores modernistas, pero sin abandonar ninguna doctrina fundamental de las Escrituras. Este sermón coincidió con un momento en que muchos evangélicos se encontraban incómodos con el énfasis antiintelectual y separatista de los llamados «fundamentalistas». Creían que la fe cristiana es razonable y lógica y, por lo tanto, querían entrar en diálogo con los teólogos modernistas. Creían que era posible convencerlos de que la teología evangélica era más coherente y bíblica. Eruditos de renombre como Edward Carnell (1919–1967), Harold Lindsell (1913–1998), Carl F. H. Henry (1913–2003), Gleason Archer (1916–2004) y Kenneth Kantzer (1917–2002) secundaron la propuesta de Ockenga. De acuerdo con esta filosofía, el evangelista Billy Graham fundó en 1956 la revista *Christianity Today* con el propósito de contrarrestar la influencia de *The Christian Century*, la revista de los teólogos liberales. Con el tiempo los eruditos evangélicos se ganaron el respeto de los eruditos de otras tendencias teológicas, hasta el punto de que sus comentarios bíblicos y sus obras de referencia teológica, filosófica y lingüística ocupan un espacio significativo en la biblioteca de muchos seminarios no evangélicos.

## Cuarta etapa (década de 1970)

La década de los 70 fue un tiempo muy movido. La neoortodoxia se había convertido en la posición de los pastores e iglesias de las denominaciones protestantes tradicionales en EE. UU., las cuales habían abandonado la doctrina de la inspiración e inerrancia de las Escrituras. Al mismo tiempo, durante esta década los teólogos y profesores de seminarios evangélicos comenzaron a denunciar el abandono de esa doctrina. Lo que más los movilizó fue la decisión del FTS de eliminar de su Declaración de Fe en 1970 las palabras que afirmaban que la Biblia estaba «libre de error en todo o en parte». Esa decisión provocó el éxodo de muchos de sus profesores más destacados.

En 1976 Harold Lindsell, editor de *Christianity Today* y uno de los profesores que se habían marchado del FTS, escribió el libro *The Battle for the Bible* [La batalla por la Biblia]. En él identificó por nombre a los teólogos, profesores, seminarios y denominaciones que habían abandonado la doctrina de la inerrancia. También mostró las consecuencias negativas de esa decisión en esos seminarios y denominaciones. Lógicamente, ese libro produjo una fuerte reacción. Sin embargo, «ninguna de las acusaciones de Lindsell fue refutada de forma sustantiva»[9]. A la vez, *The Battle for the Bible* animó a muchos pastores y teólogos que creían en la inerrancia de las Escrituras pero que se habían callado, intimidados por la burla y crítica de los liberales. En 1977 unos cincuenta teólogos y líderes evangélicos crearon el International Council on Biblical Inerrancy (ICBI, Consejo Internacional sobre la Inerrancia Bíblica) y redactaron un borrador sobre esa doctrina. Al año siguiente el ICBI convocó en Chicago una conferencia a la cual asistieron unos trescientos teólogos, líderes y pastores evangélicos de renombre para evaluar y revisar ese borrador. El documento que

---

9. Jay Grimstead, «How the International Council on Biblical Inerrancy Began». Este artículo se encuentra en Internet.

aprobaron («The Chicago Statement on Biblical Inerrancy») es considerado la definición más clara y completa hasta el momento de la doctrina de la inerrancia[10].

## Quinta etapa (desde 1980)

En la opinión de Geisler y Roach, los evangélicos que recibieron a partir de la década de los 80 su educación teológica en seminarios que promovían las interpretaciones de la alta crítica destructiva y filosofías modernas y postmodernas protagonizan la quinta etapa del debate sobre la inerrancia desde una perspectiva filosófica[11].

> El verdadero problema con los desvíos contemporáneos en cuanto a la inerrancia no se trata de hechos probados sino de filosofía. No es que se han encontrado nuevos datos o evidencias que hacen increíble el punto de vista histórico de la inerrancia de toda la Biblia, sino que la nueva generación de eruditos ha sido impregnada —algunos de forma inocente, otros no tanto— de nuevas filosofías que son incompatibles con la posición tradicional de la inerrancia. Algunas de esas nuevas ideas proceden de la filosofía del significado o sentido, algunas de la filosofía del lenguaje y algunas de la filosofía de la hermenéutica. Pero en el fondo todas son problemas filosóficos[12].

---

10. Se puede encontrar este y otros documentos pertinentes en Internet. Este documento produjo al menos tres resultados. (1) Se convirtió en la posición de la gran mayoría de los evangélicos en Estados Unidos. (2) Jugó un papel significativo en la decisión de la Southern Baptist Convention (SBC) de adoptar la inerrancia de las Escrituras, una posición que había abandonado. La SBC es la denominación bautista más grande del mundo. En 2010 contaba en EE. UU. con más de dieciséis millones de miembros. (3) Hizo que la membresía de la Evangelical Theological Society —la agrupación de eruditos evangélicos de mayor número, influencia y prestigio en EE. UU.— creciera de mil a cuatro mil miembros.

11. Para una evaluación de la posición de teólogos actuales (Peter Enns, Kenton Sparks, Kevin Vanhoozer, Andrew McGowan, Stanley Grenz y Brian McLaren) que han recogido el testigo de Clark Pinnock, ver los capítulos dedicados a cada uno de ellos en el libro de Norman L. Geisler y William C. Roach, *Defending Inerrancy* (Grand Rapids: Baker, 2011).

12. Norman L. Geisler y William C. Roach, *Defending Inerrancy* (Grand Rapids: Baker, 2011), pp. 343–344.

De ahí la necesidad de que el lector tenga una comprensión clara de los axiomas de la comunicación y el lenguaje, del papel de las presuposiciones en la interpretación bíblica y del proceso de llegar a conocer las verdades espirituales.

## C. TRES POSICIONES SOBRE LA INERRANCIA

Cuando surge la necesidad de definir más detalladamente una doctrina, los teólogos buscan una palabra que, en su opinión, capte mejor la esencia de la nueva clarificación para no tener que usar muchas palabras. No obstante, la selección de una palabra que sea adecuada y clara no es fácil. En el debate sobre la inerrancia los eruditos han usado palabras como *inerrante, infalible, fiable, incapaz de engañar, veraz, autoritativa, suficiente, verídica.* Una de las dificultades en este debate es entender los matices que los teólogos afirman que estas palabras conllevan. A veces rizan el rizo de tal forma que dejan confundidos y perplejos no solamente a los principiantes, sino también a quienes tienen una buena preparación teológica y muchos años de experiencia en el ministerio[13]. Al final, los eruditos se han quedado con las palabras *infalible* e *inerrante.* Hay tres posiciones en cuanto a la inerrancia de las Escrituras.

### Inerrancia total

Esta posición del «Chicago Statement on Biblical Inerrancy» afirma que no existen errores reales en los manuscritos originales. Si las Escrituras son de origen divino, habiendo sido inspiradas («espiradas») por Dios (2 Ti. 3:16), y si Jesús y los autores bíblicos creían en la inspiración plenaria y verbal de las Escrituras, entonces no puede haber errores reales. De hecho, muchos de los supuestos problemas han

---

13. Por ejemplo, en su libro *Evangelicals at an Impasse* (Atlanta: John Knox Press, 1984), p. 36, Johnston dice que «"inerrante" implica que el texto teológico bajo consideración no tiene ningún error en todo lo que afirma. "Infalible" sugiere que el texto es incapaz de enseñar engaño o falsedades. La primera subraya el concepto de precisión; la segunda, la fiabilidad. La primera hace énfasis en estar libre de error; la segunda, en la autoridad indefectible. La primera insiste en la pureza original del texto; la otra, en su poder continuo de dar vida».

sido resueltos, y la mayoría de los que quedan tienen una explicación razonable. En cuanto a los poquísimos «errores» que quedan, los partidarios de la inerrancia total creen que existe la posibilidad de que se resuelvan cuando se descubra información que no tenemos en este momento. Igualmente, puede que nunca se descubra el trasfondo histórico y cultural que resolvería dichos «errores». En cualquier caso, adoptan como punto de partida la posición de que la Biblia es inerrante y luego procuran resolver los problemas en lugar de comenzar con la premisa de que la Biblia es falible.

## Infalibilidad parcial

Esta posición se encuentra en el polo opuesto de la inerrancia total, afirmando que existen errores reales en la Biblia. La inspiración se extiende solamente a los textos que tratan la fe y doctrina cristiana, no a los datos históricos, cronológicos, científicos, etcétera. El testimonio de los autores bíblicos en cuanto al evangelio es fiable y autoritativo porque dichos errores no afectan los elementos esenciales del mismo. De ahí que los partidarios de la infalibilidad parcial se consideran libres de rechazar como no históricos eventos sobrenaturales como la concepción virginal de Cristo, su resurrección, etcétera, y a la vez aceptar el mensaje de la salvación como verídico. Además, no creen que el lenguaje humano sea capaz de expresar ideas con una precisión adecuada o total. Por eso, acusan a quienes abrazan la inerrancia total de ser ingenuos por fijarse tanto en los manuscritos originales.

Esta posición cuenta con cuatro problemas evidentes. Primero, decir que las Escrituras son infalibles solo en parte contradice la enseñanza de Cristo y del apóstol Pablo sobre la inspiración plenaria de las Escrituras. Segundo, ¿quién decide lo que es falible e infalible, y qué criterio emplea para tomar esa decisión? Puesto que los partidarios de esta posición no ofrecen una respuesta a estas preguntas, el intérprete suele tomar esa decisión con base en su propia experiencia subjetiva, a lo que la sociedad contemporánea considera razonable, a la posición de su denominación o a una combinación de estos y otros criterios externos a las Escrituras. Tercero, reconocer como infalibles los pasajes que tratan la doctrina, pero no los que describen eventos históricos, mina las doctrinas bíblicas porque están íntimamente ligados a la historia. Si el relato bíblico de eventos históricos como la encarnación y resurrección de Cristo es erróneo, ¿qué garantía tenemos de que la explicación del significado de esos eventos no sea errónea también? Los eventos citados en la profecía de Jonás son de los más discutidos por los teólogos liberales en cuanto a su historicidad se refiere. No obstante, Cristo empleó precisamente la estancia de Jonás en el vientre del gran pez durante tres días y tres noches como un tipo de su muerte y resurrección (Mt. 12:40). Si esa experiencia de Jonás nunca ocurrió históricamente por ser un mito, ¿qué garantía tenemos de que la resurrección de Cristo es un hecho histórico? Cuarto, insistimos en que el lenguaje es capaz de comunicar ideas con precisión. De lo contrario ninguna comunicación sería posible.

## Infalibilidad total

Daniel P. Fuller (1925– )[14], David A. Hubbard (1927–1996)[15] y Clark Pinnock (1937–2010)[16] son los teólogos más representativos de esta posición que pretende ser más flexible y menos polémica. Por eso Johnston la llama «inerrancia irénica»[17]. Esta posición afirma que la Biblia es inerrante, pero que tiene errores. De entrada, la terminología es confusa. ¿Cómo puede ser inerrante un documento y a la vez tener errores? De ahí que algunos llaman a esta posición «inerrancia limitada». Pero, puesto que Fuller, Hubbard y Pinnock quieren evitar la palabra «inerrante», emplean la palabra «infalible».

*1. La posición de Pinnock.* Pinnock era por naturaleza un hombre pacífico que quería promover la paz entre los evangélicos. Por tanto,

---

14. Daniel Fuller es el hijo de Charles Fuller, cofundador del FTS con Harold Ockenga (1905–1985). Sirvió como decano de la facultad y profesor del Fuller Theological Seminary (1953–1993).

15. Como presidente del FTS en 1970, Hubbard presidió el cambio de la Declaración de Fe del FTS en la cual se eliminaron las palabras «libre de error en todo o en parte» en referencia a las Escrituras. Los datos disponibles no clarifican si nació en 1927 o 1928.

16. Pinnock fue profesor de Teología de varios seminarios en EE. UU. y Canadá.

17. O sea, «pacífica». Ver Robert K. Johnston, *Evangelicals at an Impasse* (Atlanta: John Knox Press, 1984), p. 23.

rechazó el uso de la palabra «inerrante» por considerarla provocativa y de poca ayuda en el debate sobre la inerrancia. No obstante, creía que la doctrina de la inspiración de las Escrituras es una garantía de su infalibilidad (es incapaz de engañar) e inerrancia (sin error en todo lo que afirma). Así pues, parece que sustituye la palabra «inerrancia» por «infalibilidad» por razones pragmáticas en lugar de teológicas, aunque su uso de la palabra «inerrancia» nos deja perplejos[18]. Los que abrazan esta posición dicen que debemos dejar que las normas de la comunicación que existían en tiempos bíblicos determinen nuestro entendimiento de la doctrina de la inspiración. Dentro de ese marco, Pinnock sugiere que debemos tomar en cuenta la intención del autor humano y lo que pretendía decirnos, no los errores que cometió al escribir ciertos textos. Bajo este enfoque Pinnock cree que la Biblia «contiene errores, pero no enseña ninguno».

Hay varios problemas con la posición de Pinnock. Primero, ¿cómo se puede creer en la inspiración plenaria y verbal de las Escrituras y a la vez admitir que contiene errores? Segundo, en efecto, Pinnock dice que la intención del autor es lo que cuenta, no las palabras que emplea. Sin embargo, la única forma de entender la intención de un autor y lo que hay en su mente es a través de las palabras que emplea. No se pueden separar las intenciones de un autor de sus palabras. Tercero, aunque Pinnock no hace de forma explícita una distinción entre pasajes inspirados y no inspirados como los partidarios de la infalibilidad parcial, sí la hace de hecho cuando dice que la Biblia «contiene errores, pero no enseña ninguno». Si un autor cometía un error cuando escribía sobre la historia, la ciencia, etcétera, ¿qué garantía tenemos de que no cometía otro error cuando escribía sobre un tema doctrinal? En este aspecto la posición de Pinnock se parece mucho a la de la infalibilidad parcial. Cuarto, Pinnock siembra confusión y roza la deshonestidad al decir que la Biblia «contiene errores, pero no enseña

---

18. Aparte de la obra clásica de B. B. Warfield (*The Inspiration and Authority of the Bible*), el autor considera el libro de Pinnock (*Biblical Revelation*) el mejor libro en tiempos modernos sobre la inspiración e inerrancia de las Escrituras. Pinnock presenta algunos de los argumentos más completos y contundentes contra la posición de la infalibilidad total. Sin embargo, unos años más tarde abrazó precisamente esa posición.

ninguno». En efecto, otorga un significado a la palabra «inerrancia» que difiere de la definición que tiene y que todos entienden. Si quería emplear la palabra «inerrancia», habría sido más honesto llamar a su posición «inerrancia redefinida». Su deseo de promover la unidad entre los evangélicos es noble, pero en los debates sobre un tema tan importante como la inerrancia de las Escrituras la claridad vale más que el acuerdo.

*2. La posición de Fuller.* Mientras que Pinnock se centra en las intenciones del autor, Fuller hace énfasis en las intenciones de Dios. «A través de las Escrituras Dios pretendía dar al ser humano "la sabiduría para recibir la salvación"» (2 Ti. 3:15, NTV), el versículo que introduce el texto clásico sobre la inspiración de las Escrituras (v. 16). Fuller cree que toda la Biblia representa la revelación de Dios y es inerrante en cuanto a lograr la meta de proveer salvación al ser humano. Sin embargo, aquellos textos que no tratan específicamente la salvación no deben considerarse como «revelación». Por tanto, la inerrancia no trata de la veracidad de los datos históricos, científicos, cronológicos, etcétera citados en la Biblia, sino del propósito divino de redimir al ser humano. Cuando Dios guiaba a los autores bíblicos a escribir la Biblia, les permitía emplear información equivocada que existía en su día para hacer más comprensibles las verdades espirituales que habían recibido por revelación especial.

Muchos de los problemas de la posición de Fuller son los mismos que tiene la de Pinnock, por cuanto sus explicaciones son dos caras de una misma moneda. Pero la posición de Fuller tiene tres problemas adicionales. Primero, al afirmar que 2 Timoteo 3:15-16 enseña que el propósito de la Biblia es el de hacer al ser humano sabio para la salvación y que, por tanto, solamente aquellos pasajes que tratan de la salvación son inspirados y libres de error, contradice la enseñanza de que «*toda* la Escritura es inspirada por Dios». Segundo, confunde el propósito *principal* de la Biblia («hacer sabio para la salvación») con su propósito *total*. La epístola que Pablo escribió a Filemón trata la cuestión de qué hacer con un esclavo prófugo que se había convertido. ¿Acaso es menos inspirada esa epístola por no tratar directamente el tema de la salvación? Tercero, permite a Jesús y a los autores del N.T. acomodarse a los errores del primer siglo con la excusa de no distraer a sus oyentes del mensaje que les predicaba. O sea, evitaron el uso de vocabulario científico preciso porque los lectores originales no lo habrían entendido. Evidentemente, los autores bíblicos se acomodaron a los tiempos en que vivían al hablar el idioma que todos entendían, emplear ilustraciones cuyos detalles eran conocidos y entendidos por todos, redondear datos numéricos de acuerdo con la práctica de su época, etcétera. Pero la clase de acomodación que propone Fuller permite a Jesús y a los autores del N.T. acomodarse a los errores de su día para lograr un bien mayor. Este entendimiento de la acomodación tiene tres problemas. (1) Jesús no era un conformista. Por esto rechazó rotundamente las opiniones equivocadas del público general y de las tradiciones e interpretaciones equivocadas de los líderes religiosos[19]. (2) Si Jesús se equivocó o si comunicó falsedades a sabiendas con respecto a datos botánicos, históricos, etcétera, ¿qué garantía tenemos de que no se acomodó a los errores sobre conceptos espirituales que existían en su día? (3) En efecto, la posición de Fuller se conforma a la idea errónea de que el fin justifica los medios.

Tradicionalmente, la palabra «acomodar» se usaba para expresar la idea de que Dios se sometió a las reglas de la comunicación y del lenguaje humano cuando se reveló a través de las Escrituras. El cambio de significado que Fuller y otros han impuesto a esta palabra en años recientes nos obliga a emplear la palabra «adaptar». Dios se adaptó a la forma humana de comunicarse, pero nunca dejó que los autores bíblicos se acomodaran consciente o inconscientemente a los errores que sus contemporáneos mantenían con respecto a cualquier tema.

*3. La posición de Hubbard.* Hubbard afirma que cree en la inspiración y autoridad de las Escrituras, pero que prefiere emplear la palabra «infalibilidad» porque «inerrancia» tiene varios problemas. Primero, conlleva un concepto de la precisión que es ajeno a la mente de los autores bíblicos y su uso de las Escrituras. Segundo, anima a una investigación superficial de la Biblia que ignora problemas reales que

19. En su Sermón del monte en Mateo, dijo en seis ocasiones: «Han oído [...], pero yo digo» (Mt. 5:21-22, 27-28, 31-32, 33-34, 38-39, 43-44, NTV). Acto seguido corrigió las interpretaciones equivocadas de los rabinos que le habían precedido. Y aunque en muchos otros versículos de ese sermón no empleó la frase «Han oído que fue dicho», es evidente que corregía las interpretaciones equivocadas que el pueblo había oído.

existen. Tercero, provoca un debate que desvía a la iglesia del mensaje salvífico de la Biblia para ir tras cuestiones secundarias. Hubbard cree que la infalibilidad de las Escrituras se acepta por fe, es confirmada por el Espíritu Santo y recibe el testimonio de la investigación seria y erudita de las mismas. Pero igual que Pinnock y Fuller, Hubbard se queda corto al insistir en que la Biblia es infalible en cuanto a su intención, pero no en cuanto a la inspiración del texto en sí.

Quienes creen en la infalibilidad parcial afirman que existen errores *reales* en los manuscritos originales. Los que creen en la infalibilidad total toman la posición de que la Biblia es inerrante, pero que tiene errores. El autor de *Con precisión* cree que no existen errores *reales* en los manuscritos originales y que, por tanto, cada creyente puede tener absoluta confianza en lo que Dios dice en su Palabra.

## *Trabajo para realizar*

1. Describa la diferencia que existe entre las tres posiciones de la inerrancia total, la infalibilidad parcial y la infalibilidad total.
2. La inspiración se extiende solamente a los manuscritos originales, no a las copias y traducciones a otros idiomas que se han hecho a lo largo de los siglos. Pero si no tenemos ni siquiera un trocito del manuscrito original de ninguno de los 66 libros bíblicos, ¿de qué sirve la doctrina de la inspiración verbal? Lea el Apéndice D («Crítica textual del N.T.»), el segundo de los tres apéndices que contestan esta pregunta tan importante.

# 4

# Inerrancia (II)

¿Cuáles son los supuestos errores que han puesto en tela de juicio la inerrancia de las Escrituras? Antes de examinar algunos ejemplos, conviene hacer dos observaciones. Primera, estos supuestos errores no representan un problema nuevo. Desde los primeros siglos de la era cristiana, teólogos de la talla de Jerónimo (c. 340–420) y Agustín (354–430) eran conscientes de estos problemas e intentaron resolverlos. Segunda, es fácil decir que existen errores, pero es difícil probarlo. Tanto es así que alguien ha sugerido que un comité de eruditos que representara diferentes tendencias teológicas sería incapaz de redactar una lista de los errores que existen en la Biblia porque sus definiciones de lo que constituye un error serían diferentes. De tal manera que, mientras que el teólogo liberal afirmaría que un texto bíblico contiene un error sin remedio, el evangélico ofrecería una explicación razonable para dicho «error». Así que lo que sería una solución y explicación razonable para un teólogo, no lo sería para otro.

## A. ¿ERRORES SUPUESTOS O REALES?

El espacio disponible nos permite dar solamente un par de ejemplos de supuestos errores en cada una de las cuatro categorías a continuación. Más ejemplos, y cómo los eruditos evangélicos los han resuelto, pueden encontrarse en libros dedicados exclusivamente a este tema, libros de «introducción»[1] y los comentarios críticos[2] más recientes, puesto que los arqueólogos siguen descubriendo nueva información que nos permite resolver esos «errores».

## Pueblos y costumbres antiguos

Antes de que la arqueología bíblica se estableciera como una ciencia a principios del siglo XIX, había quienes rechazaban la inspiración e inerrancia de las Escrituras porque muchos de sus datos históricos no podían confirmarse por medio de fuentes extrabíblicas. Por ejemplo, a principios del siglo XIX no se sabía nada de los hititas excepto por los trece libros del A.T. que hacen referencia a ellos. Por tanto, había quienes dudaban de su existencia y de la fiabilidad de las Escrituras. Teólogos y eruditos de otras disciplinas sugirieron que, si los hititas existieron, tenían que haber sido un pueblo más pequeño que Judá. Pero en la segunda mitad del siglo XIX los arqueólogos comenzaron a descubrir enseres y documentos antiguos que hablaban de los hititas. Desde entonces se ha comprobado que el Imperio hitita, que ocupaba una gran parte de lo que hoy es Turquía, era igual de grande en poder político, geográfico y militar que el reino dividido de Egipto. Por tanto, es muy precario el argumento de que un dato bíblico no es verídico hasta que es confirmado por una fuente extrabíblica, pues existe el riesgo constante de que sea desacreditado por cada nuevo descubrimiento arqueológico. Por eso, hace muchos años que se ha dejado de emplear esta clase de argumento.

Hubo un tiempo en que se cuestionaba la veracidad del entorno histórico y cultural de los patriarcas tal y como Moisés lo describe en Génesis. Pero los descubrimientos arqueológicos en Ugarit (1928) y Mari (1993) demostraron que la vida y costumbres de aquella época de la historia coinciden con la descripción bíblica. Igualmente, los

---

1. En el ámbito teológico la palabra «introducción» se refiere a cuestiones de la alta crítica (autor, receptores, fecha en que fue escrito un libro bíblico, etcétera). Por tanto, cualquier libro cuyo título contiene la palabra «introducción» suele tratar problemas de la alta crítica a no ser que el autor pretenda dar un resumen del contenido de grandes secciones de la Biblia.

2. O sea, comentarios que tratan cuestiones técnicas como el texto original, problemas teológicos, etcétera en contraste con comentarios devocionales.

arqueólogos han confirmado los eventos históricos, lugares geográficos, nombres de reyes e imperios y costumbres de los tiempos bíblicos más antiguos. Este material puede encontrarse en los excelentes libros de Archer[3], Kaiser[4], Kitchen[5] y otros. La evidencia es tan convincente y contundente que los eruditos de todas las tendencias teológicas no han tenido más alternativa que admitir que la Biblia es una fuente fiable. Y lo es hasta tal punto que Broomall afirma:

> A la luz del aumento rápido de nuestro conocimiento en cuanto a los tiempos antiguos gracias a las excavaciones y descubrimientos modernos, sería un acto temerario afirmar que existen errores históricos en la Biblia que no tengan solución. Y, mientras que los supuestos errores históricos en la Biblia se acercan a cero en número, lo mismo puede decirse con respecto a otros errores que algunos dicen haber encontrado en las porciones didácticas y proféticas de las Escrituras[6].

## Cronologías y datos biográficos

Las cronologías de la Biblia, en particular las del A.T., presentan problemas difíciles de resolver. Algunos tienen una explicación razonable, pero otros resisten cualquier solución. Por ejemplo, 2 Reyes 24:8 dice que Joaquín tenía dieciocho años de edad cuando ascendió al trono y que reinó solo tres meses cuando fue tomado cautivo. Pero 2 Crónicas 36:9 dice que tenía ocho años cuando comenzó a reinar y que reinó tres meses y diez días antes de ser llevado cautivo a Babilonia por Nabucodonosor. Harris admite que:

> Sin lugar a dudas existe una clara contradicción, pero es evidente que se trata de un problema de un error de copia. El número diez

3. Gleason L. Archer, *Encyclopedia of Bible Difficulties* (Grand Rapids: Zondervan, 1982).
4. Walter C. Kaiser, Jr., *The Old Testament Documents; Are They Reliable and Relevant?* (Downers Grove: InterVarsity Press, 2001).
5. K. A. Kitchen, *On the Reliability of the Old Testament* (Grand Rapids: Eerdmans, 2003).
6. Wick Broomall, *Biblical Criticism* (Grand Rapids: Zondervan, 1957), p. 46.

de la expresión «dieciocho años» en Reyes fue omitido o perdido en Crónicas y reaparece en la mención de los diez días. En hebreo «dieciocho» se escribe como «ocho y diez». La palabra «diez» probablemente se perdió. Algunos manuscritos de la LXX y la traducción siriaca de Crónicas dicen que Joaquín tenía dieciocho años, tal y como el manuscrito original seguramente dijo. Hasta 2 Reyes 24:15 dice que las esposas de Joaquín fueron llevadas cautivas con él[7].

Pero no todos los problemas encontrados en las cronologías y los datos biográficos se deben a errores de transmisión de los manuscritos originales. Daniel 1:1 dice que Nabucodonosor sitió la ciudad de Jerusalén en el tercer año del reinado de Joacim mientras que Jeremías 25:1 dice que ocurrió en el cuarto año. Hasta un erudito evangélico del A.T. tan eminente como Edward J. Young (1907–1968) tuvo que confesar que «parece casi imposible encontrar una solución satisfactoria para algunos problemas planteados por las cronologías del A.T.»[8]. En algunos casos el supuesto error se debe a que todavía existe mucho desconocimiento sobre la forma en que los hebreos calculaban y contaban el número de años en que sus reyes gobernaban. No contaban con un calendario fijo ni universal. Por tanto, cabe la posibilidad de que los judíos y los babilonios emplearan dos sistemas diferentes.

## Ciencia natural

Quizás los errores relacionados con la ciencia natural (astronomía, biología, física, etcétera) sean los más mencionados por quienes rechazan la inerrancia de las Escrituras. Desde el siglo XIX la ciencia se ha erigido en la mente de muchas personas como el árbitro final de lo que es verdad y de lo que es falso, incluso en el terreno de la religión.

*1. Salmo 19:4, 6; Eclesiastés 1:5.* Hay quienes citan estos textos como ejemplo de un error científico por cuanto David y Salomón dicen que el Sol gira alrededor de la Tierra cuando la verdad es justo lo contrario. Pero ¿representan estos textos una afirmación científica?

---

7. R. Laird Harris, *Inspiration and Canonicity of the Bible* (Grand Rapids: Zondervan, 1977), p. 105.

8. Edward J. Young, «Are the Scriptures Inerrant?» en *The Bible: The Living Word of Revelation* (Grand Rapids: Zondervan, 1977), p. 110.

¿No es razonable entender que David y Salomón están hablando desde la perspectiva de cómo el ser humano percibe el movimiento del Sol en lugar de hacer una declaración técnica y científica? El autor lee cada día *El Periódico de Catalunya* en el cual se encuentra una página dedicada al tiempo que incluye una sección titulada «Salida y puesta del Sol y la Luna», una frase que da a entender que el sol y la luna giran alrededor de la Tierra. Sin embargo, nadie acusa al editor de esa página de mentir, de propagar falsedades o de estar en un error científico. Todos entendemos que dicha frase refleja la impresión que el ser humano tiene al observar el movimiento de esos astros. Los teólogos se refieren a esta clase de «error» como lenguaje fenomenológico. Una cosa es cómo los astros *son percibidos* por el ojo humano sin ninguna clase de ayuda; otra cosa es cómo *son realmente* para el científico que está mirando a través de un telescopio.

Los autores bíblicos hablan como portavoces de Dios en todo lo que dicen, especialmente cuando tratan cuestiones morales y doctrinales. Sin embargo, a veces en sus pasajes narrativos describen lo que observan desde una perspectiva humana sin que esos pasajes sean menos inspirados. Es imprescindible que el intérprete sepa distinguir entre estas dos formas de hablar. El teólogo Kenneth Kantzer (1917–2002), que fue un pilar del movimiento neoevangélico en EE. UU., además de un pensador agudo que tenía la habilidad de explicar conceptos polémicos con ilustraciones sencillas que todos podían entender, hablando del lenguaje fenomenológico dijo:

> Un hombre que se pone entre dos vías del tren podría afirmar que se juntan. Esta declaración sería verdad desde su punto de vista; las dos vías parecen converger en la distancia. El piloto de un avión podría declarar que las vías del tren son paralelas de forma exacta y él también tendría razón. Pero un científico podría medir con un micrómetro la distancia entre las vías y declarar que no tienen curvas, no se juntan, ni son exactamente paralelas, sino que son serradas y desiguales. Y ese científico también tendría razón. La pregunta en este caso es la misma que hemos de hacernos en todos los demás casos: ¿a qué clase de precisión se compromete la Biblia?[9]

9. Kenneth Kantzer, notas de clase de la asignatura Revelación e Inspiración en la Trinity Evangelical Divinity School (1964–1965), p. 133.

Los autores bíblicos hablan frecuentemente del corazón, las entrañas y hasta los huesos como el centro de las emociones humanas. Aunque los científicos descartan esta clase de expresiones como científicamente erróneas, tampoco son capaces de identificar el lugar donde residen las emociones humanas. Lo que hemos de entender es que los autores bíblicos simplemente hacían uso de las expresiones propias de su época en lugar de comunicarnos un dato con un lenguaje que fuera científicamente preciso.

*2. El grano de mostaza (Mt. 13:32).* Hay quienes encuentran un error en las palabras de Jesús cuando dice que el grano de mostaza «es la más pequeña de todas las semillas», puesto que la más pequeña es la semilla de una especie de orquídea que crece en las selvas tropicales. Pero ¿no es razonable entender que Jesús está comparando el grano de la semilla de mostaza que existía en Palestina con las demás semillas de ese país en lugar de con las semillas de otras partes del mundo? De hecho, la semilla de mostaza es la semilla más pequeña de Palestina.

*3. Creación vs. evolución.* El debate entre el creacionismo y la teoría de la evolución comenzó a principios del siglo XX. Muchos de los problemas que rodearon los inicios de este debate se debieron a errores cometidos por los proponentes de las dos posiciones. En su afán de probar que la Biblia tiene razón, algunos creyentes impusieron interpretaciones científicas sobre ciertos textos bíblicos que una exégesis correcta de los mismos no admitía. La Biblia no es ni pretende ser un libro de texto científico. Y cuando dice algo de índole científico, tampoco provee muchos detalles porque su interés es otro. No obstante, Génesis 1–2 nos dice de forma muy clara que Dios es el creador, nos cuenta el orden en que creó todo lo que existe y nos ofrece algunos detalles más. Pero nada más. El consejo de Ramm es muy sabio y acertado cuando dice:

> Génesis 1 existe en forma de bosquejo. Obras contemporáneas que procuran dibujar los datos más importantes del universo llegan hasta 500 páginas. Génesis da un resumen de la creación en 34 versículos (1:1–2:3). La brevedad extrema del relato debe suavizar nuestra exégesis de ello. Intentar encontrar demasiados detalles específicos en este dibujo puede causar un conflicto innecesario con la ciencia. Siempre es problemático pasar de los «haya» de Génesis

> al *modus operandi.* Pertenece a la ciencia el papel de proveer los detalles para el bosquejo bíblico. La ciencia no debería apropiarse o usurpar *los primeros principios* del relato bíblico, pero tampoco deben los teólogos intentar dictar a los científicos los detalles empíricos sobre los cuales la Biblia se queda en silencio[10].

Tampoco quedan libres de censura los científicos que promueven la teoría de la evolución. Cada científico tiene derecho a proponer la teoría que quiera. Pero sabe que no tiene derecho a presentar y propagar una teoría como si fuera un hecho probado hasta que haya datos irrefutables de que dicha teoría se corresponde con la realidad. La teoría de la evolución no ha sido probada. Además, existen muchos datos en su contra. Sin embargo, muchos científicos la presentan como si fuera un hecho probado, lo cual es una clara transgresión de su propia ética científica. Lamentablemente, una persona corriente, al ver que la teoría de la evolución es presentada continuamente en las aulas académicas y en los medios de comunicación como si fuera un hecho probado, la acepta como tal.

> «Porque, por medio de él, Dios creó todo lo que existe en los lugares celestiales y en la tierra. Hizo las cosas que podemos ver y las que no podemos ver, tales como tronos, reinos, gobernantes y autoridades del mundo invisible. Todo fue creado por medio de él y para él.».
>
> **(Col. 1:16, NTV)**

El creacionista no puede probar que Dios creó el mundo porque nadie estuvo presente cuando lo hizo. Por eso el autor de Hebreos dice que «por la fe entendemos haber sido constituido el universo por la palabra de Dios» (11:3). Pero al observar todos los obstáculos y problemas que la teoría de la evolución tiene que superar para demostrar que es un hecho probado, uno se da cuenta de que requiere más fe creer

10. Bernard Ramm, *Protestant Biblical Interpretation* (Grand Rapids: Baker, 1978), p. 212.

en la teoría de la evolución que en la creación. No cabe duda de que ha habido una «microevolución» o desarrollo natural dentro de cada especie que ha producido diferentes clases de perros, gatos, caballos, peces, aves, etcétera. Pero la idea de que el ser humano haya salido de otra especie —o sea, una macroevolución— sigue siendo una teoría y contradice el claro énfasis de Génesis 1 en la RVR60 de que la hierba, los árboles, los grandes monstruos marinos, las aves, las serpientes y los animales fueron creados por Dios «según su género» (vv. 11, 12, 21, 24, 25), «según su naturaleza» (v. 12), «según su especie» (vv. 21, 24, 25). Pero Dios creó al ser humano «*a su imagen, a imagen de* Dios» (v. 27, énfasis añdido). Si ha habido una macroevolución entre las especies, ¿dónde están los eslabones para demostrarlo? No se han encontrado a pesar de que se han hallado millones de esqueletos y fósiles de peces, aves, otros animales y de seres humanos. De ahí que muchos científicos no creyentes rechacen la teoría de la evolución, aunque la promuevan como si fuera un hecho probado. En algunos casos lo hacen porque la universidad donde enseñan así lo exige y defender el creacionismo les supondría la pérdida del empleo; en otros casos, porque no encuentran otra teoría alternativa aparte del creacionismo, y esta les exige un compromiso espiritual que no están dispuestos a tomar.

En un intento de compaginar la ciencia y la enseñanza bíblica, hay quienes sugieren que Génesis 1 es un pasaje poético y, por tanto, no debe interpretarse de forma literal. El mayor problema de esta interpretación es que ese capítulo no reúne las características de la poesía[11]. Otros han adoptado la posición de la evolución teísta, la cual afirma que Dios empleó el proceso de la evolución para crear al ser humano. Pero a la luz de los problemas mencionados arriba, vemos que unen su teoría a una falsedad porque la evolución sigue siendo una teoría; no ha sido probada. Además, adquieren unos problemas teológicos muy serios. La Biblia afirma que el ser humano fue creado a la imagen de Dios. Si el ser humano evolucionó a lo largo de millones de años desde una especie inferior, ¿en qué momento recibió esa imagen? ¿En qué momento pasó de ser una criatura de una especie inferior a ser un ser

---

11. Ver Young, ob. cit., p. 105, y el capítulo 4 del libro de Walter C. Kaiser, Jr., *The Old Testament Documents; Are They Reliable and Relevant?* (Downers Grove: InterVarsity Press, 2001).

humano con la capacidad de tener una relación con Dios? ¿Y en qué momento rompió esa relación mediante su caída en el pecado? Estas no son preguntas frívolas, sino absolutamente básicas y fundamentales en cuanto a la naturaleza del ser humano, su origen, las consecuencias del pecado y la salvación del ser humano.

El creyente no tiene nada que temer de la ciencia porque es imposible que haya una contradicción entre la forma en que Dios creó el universo y las leyes naturales que hizo para controlarlo por un lado, y lo que la ciencia puede descubrir y probar por otro.

> No existe ningún conflicto entre las declaraciones de la Biblia y los descubrimientos de los científicos. No quiere decir que no existan problemas ni que la solución para cada dificultad sea aparente de forma inmediata. Lo que sí quiere decir es que no existen contradicciones reales. Es obligatorio que quienes afirman que hay errores reales en las Escrituras lo demuestren con pruebas. El simple hecho de llamar la atención sobre las dificultades no bastará[12].

Científicos evangélicos han escrito un buen número de libros y artículos sobre el creacionismo y la teoría de la evolución de un nivel académico y científicamente alto[13]. Puesto que este tema involucra a prácticamente todas las ciencias naturales, es lógico que muchos lectores tengan que hacer un esfuerzo mental para entenderlos, aunque hayan cursado una carrera universitaria en alguna rama de las ciencias naturales. Pero vale la pena que el lector haga un esfuerzo para ampliar su conocimiento en este tema.

## Pasajes paralelos

En la sección anterior titulada «Cronologías y datos biográficos» hemos visto unos ejemplos de textos paralelos en 1–2 Reyes y 1–2 Crónicas que presentan un problema. Sin embargo, cuando hablamos

12. Ibid., Young, p. 109.

13. Por ejemplo, CLIE publicó entre 1973 y 1981 una serie de libritos bajo el título *Creación y ciencia*, escritos por científicos evangélicos, que demuestran que la rama de la ciencia en la cual ellos son especialistas apoya el creacionismo. Se pueden encontrar artículos más recientes en la página web www.creacionismo.net.

de «pasajes paralelos», el debate se centra más bien en los Evangelios sinópticos (Mateo, Marcos, Lucas). Por ejemplo: el orden en que ocurrieron las tres tentaciones de Jesús en Mateo 4:1-11 difiere del orden en que aparecen en Lucas 4:1-13; los cuatro evangelistas citan un texto diferente del letrero que fue colgado en la cruz de Cristo (Mt. 27:37; Mc. 15:26; Lc. 23:38; Jn.19:19); etcétera.

Todos los eruditos bíblicos están de acuerdo en que Mateo, Marcos y Lucas escribieron sus Evangelios para un grupo de personas en concreto. Este hecho hizo que cada evangelista seleccionara de la extensa información que tenía a su disposición la que mejor apoyaba el mensaje que quería comunicar a ese grupo (Jn. 21:25). Por ejemplo, es evidente que Mateo dirigió su Evangelio a los judíos, ya que da por sentado que el lector entiende las costumbres, geografía, fiestas, etcétera de los judíos; se preocupa más que cualquier otro evangelista por demostrar que Cristo es el cumplimiento de las profecías mesiánicas del A.T.; e incluye en su Evangelio la genealogía de Jesús, cosa muy aburrida para otros grupos étnicos, pero de suma importancia para los judíos. Es evidente, también, que los tres evangelistas no colocaron los eventos de la vida de Jesús en un orden estrictamente cronológico, sino de acuerdo con el énfasis o tema que querían comunicar a sus respectivos lectores. Mateo es el menos cronológico de los Evangelios sinópticos, mientras que Juan es el evangelista que más atención presta al orden en que los eventos ocurrieron.

Lo que tenemos en los Evangelios, entonces, son descripciones de los mismos eventos desde perspectivas diferentes. Este hecho tiene dos ventajas. Primera, si tres testigos en un juicio contaran la misma historia palabra por palabra, se les acusaría de confabulación y su testimonio sería desestimado. Lo mismo puede decirse de los evangelistas. Aunque escribieron bajo la supervisión del Espíritu Santo, ese hecho no los convirtió en loros o magnetófonos. Segunda, varios testigos de un mismo evento suelen señalar diferentes detalles del mismo. Este hecho no quiere decir que mientan o que se equivoquen, sino que su personalidad e intereses los hacen apreciar ciertos elementos de ese evento que otros testigos no aprecian tanto. Por ejemplo, cuando Jesús y los discípulos llegaron a la tierra de los gadarenos, Mateo 8:28 dice que dos endemoniados vinieron a su encuentro, pero Marcos 5:2 y Lucas 8:27 dicen que había solo uno. Concluir que existe un error en

Mateo es precipitarse. Muchos eruditos sugieren que había dos endemoniados como dice Mateo, pero que Marcos y Lucas se centran en solo uno de ellos, quizás por ser el más violento o por ser la persona que habló con Jesús. Es una explicación razonable que elimina la necesidad de concluir que Mateo se equivocó[14].

Hay textos paralelos donde los evangelistas recogen las palabras que Jesús pronunció en el mismo contexto, pero cuyas palabras no coinciden. Hay varios factores que explican estas diferencias. Primero, Jesús hablaba en arameo. Sin embargo, el N.T. fue escrito en griego koiné. Quienes dominan dos o más idiomas saben que no se puede traducir palabra por palabra una frase de un idioma a otro. La traducción sería torpe o podría carecer de sentido. De ahí que dos evangelistas que traducen las palabras de Jesús del arameo al griego puedan producir dos textos ligeramente diferentes, pero que correspondan de forma fidedigna a lo que Jesús dijo.

Segundo, es muy probable que Jesús repitiera la misma enseñanza en más de una ocasión. En ese caso las palabras, el orden en que aparecen las ideas y las aplicaciones de las mismas podrían variar. Por ejemplo, aunque muchos no clasificarían el texto de Mateo 7:7-11 como una parábola, estos versículos contienen la misma aplicación que Jesús hace de la parábola del amigo que pide pan a su vecino (Lc. 11:5-13). Pero en Mateo 7:11 Jesús dice que Dios dará «buenas cosas» a quienes se lo pidan, mientras que en Lucas 11:13 dice que Dios dará «el Espíritu Santo». Si estos dos textos describen lo que Jesús dijo en una sola ocasión, entonces los detalles se complementan y el lector tiene un relato más completo de lo que Jesús dijo. Pero si los dos representan ocasiones diferentes en las que Jesús dio la misma enseñanza, es probable que la diferencia se deba a que hizo una aplicación diferente según las necesidades diferentes que percibía en sus oyentes. Un grupo necesitaba «buenas cosas» mientras que el otro precisaba un toque especial del Espíritu Santo en sus vidas.

Tercero, aunque el sistema pedagógico de los rabinos exigía que sus oyentes memorizaran lo que decían, los evangelistas no pudieron memorizar todo lo que Jesús dijo. Cuarto, en el primer siglo no se empleaban comillas para indicar que un autor citaba palabra por palabra

14. Harris, ob. cit., p. 106.

lo que otra persona había dicho. Por tanto, no hemos de suponer que los evangelistas citasen literalmente lo que Jesús dijo. Quinto, si la enseñanza de Cristo era extensa, el evangelista podría hacer un resumen de la misma. Además, podría elegir de toda esa enseñanza lo que más le interesara subrayar para sus lectores, mientras que otro evangelista haría lo mismo señalando un énfasis diferente.

> Un extracto o resumen no es necesariamente incorrecto. Un extracto fidedigno de un discurso largo es preferible a un par de citas exactas de las palabras pronunciadas que no dan en el blanco de la enseñanza principal. «Jesús dijo» no siempre tiene que significar «Jesús dijo estas palabras», sino que el relato a continuación es un reportaje fidedigno de todo el discurso que Jesús pronunció[15].

## En resumen

Los eruditos evangélicos afirman que la gran mayoría de los supuestos errores en la Biblia ya han sido resueltos, muchos de ellos por los descubrimientos arqueológicos que han rellenado las grietas en nuestra comprensión de la historia y el trasfondo cultural de los tiempos bíblicos. Puede resultar una sorpresa para el lector saber que la lista de errores que no han sido resueltos de forma satisfactoria es tan pequeña que Ramm dijo en 1953, hace más de medio siglo:

> A pesar de la mucha atención que han recibido las supuestas contradicciones en las Escrituras, es sorprendente el número tan pequeño de ejemplos que existen que tienen algún mérito y cuán difícil es montar un argumento serio con base en dichos ejemplos. Para ser más específico, Dods[16] cita seis contradicciones en los Evangelios como base para rechazar su inerrancia, y Kenyon[17] nos provee otra

15. Ibid., p. 107.
16. Marcus Dods (1834–1909) era un pastor y erudito bíblico escocés.
17. Frederic George Kenyon (1863–1952) era un erudito de mucho renombre de los idiomas antiguos y de la crítica textual del N.T. Aunque no aceptó la inerrancia de las Escrituras, estaba convencido de la realidad histórica de los Evangelios y afirmó que cualquier duda en cuanto al texto original del N.T. había sido resuelta por la crítica textual.

> lista de contradicciones que según él demuestran que las Escrituras son errantes. En ambos casos se descubrirá que existen explicaciones razonables y convincentes en comentarios conservadores para cada una de estas supuestas contradicciones[18].

Más tarde, en 1977 Harris afirmó que, después de todos los estudios exhaustivos que muchos eruditos han realizado, «la mayoría de las "contradicciones" y "errores" se han reducido a unos meros "problemas". No queda nada que un hombre de fe y sabiduría no podría aceptar»[19]. En 2009 Grudem dijo que «hay muchos eruditos bíblicos evangélicos hoy que dicen que en el presente no tienen conocimiento de ningún texto problemático para el cual no exista una solución satisfactoria»[20].

## B. ¿QUÉ HAY EN JUEGO?

¿Es la inerrancia una doctrina fundamental o secundaria? El autor insiste en que es absolutamente fundamental porque es lo que Jesús y los apóstoles creían y enseñaban. Al abandonar esa posición, se ponen en marcha al menos dos consecuencias muy serias. Primera, se elimina el concepto de autoridad divina. Una vez abandonada la inerrancia de todas las Escrituras, el creyente se ve obligado a buscar otro fundamento sobre el cual basar sus creencias y comportamiento. No tardará mucho en convertir su propia opinión y lo que la sociedad esté dispuesta a aceptar como la última autoridad de su fe y práctica. Parece que vivimos en una época de la historia humana en la cual «las personas no quieren ser atadas por un versículo bíblico, una colección de doctrinas bíblicas o una religión paternalista y autoritativa. Una Biblia sin error apretaría su mente de tal forma que las obligaría a vivir con una camisa de fuerza insoportable. La experiencia muestra que la conciencia y la razón no quieren capitular ante ninguna autoridad»[21].

18. Bernard Ramm, ob. cit., p. 205.

19. R. Laird Harris, «The Problem of Communication» en *The Bible: The Living Word of Revelation* (Grand Rapids: Zondervan, 1977), p. 100.

20. Wayne Grudem, *Teología sistemática* (Miami, Vida: 2009), p. 102.

21. René Pache, *The Inspiration and Authority of Scripture* (Chicago: Moody Press, 1978), p. 131.

Segunda, se corre el riesgo de abandonar otras doctrinas fundamentales. En su libro *The Battle for the Bible*, Lindsell describe cómo en tiempos modernos algunos de los teólogos, seminarios y denominaciones que abandonaron la doctrina de la inerrancia, con el tiempo abandonaron también otras doctrinas fundamentales de la fe cristiana. Aunque hay quienes rechazan la «teoría del dominó», la cual afirma que el derrumbamiento de una cosa resultará inevitablemente en el derrumbamiento de otras cosas, es difícil negar la historia. Si una persona cuestiona la inerrancia de un texto, no tardará mucho tiempo en cuestionar la inerrancia de otros textos y las doctrinas encontradas en dichos textos. El debate sobre la inerrancia ha sido tan intenso porque hay mucho en juego.

La iglesia ha mantenido durante muchos siglos, y como una doctrina fundamental de la fe cristiana, que las Escrituras son inerrantes en sus manuscritos originales. Sin una Biblia inerrante, el creyente carece de una autoridad divina y absoluta en su vida y se expone a los caprichos y exigencias de su propia naturaleza pecaminosa y de la sociedad en la cual vive.

## *Trabajo para realizar*

1. Se dieron cinco factores que podrían explicar por qué los evangelistas no siempre coinciden en sus relatos sobre lo que Jesús hizo y dijo. Cite al menos tres de esos factores.
2. Una persona puede entender la Biblia porque está escrita en un idioma que entiende. Sin embargo, dicho entendimiento no producirá vida espiritual en ella por sí solo. Hace falta la iluminación del Espíritu Santo. Antes de tratar esa doctrina en el próximo capítulo, lea los tres pasajes mencionados a continuación en la RVR60 y, con la ayuda de las preguntas, identifique las tres leyes espirituales o requisitos (uno en cada pasaje) que una persona tiene que cumplir para que la iluminación se efectúe en su vida. Todas las preguntas a continuación se refieren al texto de la RVR60.

*Mateo 13:10-17.* ¿Ha observado que este pasaje trata el tema de la interpretación de las palabras de Cristo (v. 10)? ¿Por qué algunos entendieron sus palabras y otros no (vv. 11, 13-15)? El v. 12 es difícil de entender a primera vista. ¿Qué es lo que se tiene o no se tiene? Si tiene la posibilidad de hacerlo, consulte dos o tres comentarios para contestar esta pregunta. Después, identifique la ley espiritual que el intérprete ha de emplear para que Dios le conceda la posibilidad de «saber los misterios del reino de los cielos» (v. 11).

*Mateo 11:25-30.* «Estas cosas» se refieren a las enseñanzas y milagros que Jesús realizó en las ciudades mencionadas en los vv. 20-24. ¿Por qué no produjeron los resultados deseados? ¿Quiénes son los dos grupos citados en el v. 25? ¿Debemos entender de forma literal los nombres que Jesús emplea para ellos? Fijándose en el nombre que Cristo emplea para describir a esas personas, ¿cuáles son las características principales de ellas a la hora de interpretar las palabras de Cristo? Después, identifique la actitud o predisposición que el intérprete ha de tener o la ley espiritual que ha de emplear para que el Padre le revele «estas cosas».

*1 Corintios 2:6-16.* Este pasaje es la mención plena del tema de la iluminación del Espíritu Santo, el pasaje que más información nos da sobre la interpretación bíblica. Primero, note que las palabras y frases que Mateo emplea en 13:10-17 y 11:25-30 son las mismas que emplea Pablo en este pasaje. Luego, diga cuál es la actitud o predisposición que el intérprete ha de tener o la ley espiritual que ha de emplear para que pueda percibir «las cosas que son del Espíritu de Dios» (v. 14). ¿Ha notado las diferentes frases que Pablo emplea para esa ley o requisito en los vv. 6-16?

**3.** La inspiración se extiende solamente a los manuscritos originales, no a las copias y traducciones a otros idiomas que se han hecho a lo largo de los siglos. Pero si no tenemos ni siquiera un trocito del manuscrito original de ninguno de los 66 libros bíblicos, ¿de qué sirve la doctrina de la inspiración verbal? Lea el Apéndice E («La historia de la crítica textual del N.T.»), el último apéndice de los tres que contestan esta pregunta tan importante.

# 5

# Iluminación

Se puede probar que Cristo murió y resucitó porque son eventos históricos que pueden ser comprobados. Lo que no se puede probar es el significado de esos eventos; a saber, que Cristo murió *por nuestros pecados* y que resucitó *para justificarnos.* Para que un no creyente se quede convencido de que esas declaraciones bíblicas son verídicas, necesita que Dios lo ilumine[1]. Después de su conversión a Cristo, seguirá necesitando la iluminación del Espíritu para entender otras verdades bíblicas. Por eso, Pablo ora que Dios alumbre los ojos de los efesios para que se den cuenta de todo lo que tienen en Cristo (Ef. 1:18).

## A. EN EL NO CREYENTE

En el tercer año de su ministerio Jesús preguntó a sus discípulos: «¿Quién dicen los hombres que es el Hijo del Hombre?» (Mt. 16:13). Le contestaron que muchos lo consideraban un profeta como Elías, Jeremías o Juan el Bautista; o sea, un mero hombre, aunque su categoría de profeta lo colocaba por encima de los demás. Cuando Jesús les preguntó qué opinión tenían ellos, Pedro respondió: «Tú eres el Cristo, el Hijo del Dios viviente» (v. 16). Su uso del artículo definido («*el* Cristo») indica que creía que Jesús era el Mesías; o sea, Dios

1. La palabra «iluminación» no se encuentra en la Biblia, sino que es, en opinión de los teólogos, la palabra que mejor conlleva la idea bíblica de esa obra divina.

mismo. Entonces, Jesús le dijo: «Bienaventurado eres, Simón, hijo de Jonás, porque no te lo reveló carne ni sangre, sino mi Padre que está en los cielos» (v. 17). Pedro no llegó a la convicción de que Jesús era el Mesías por su inteligencia («carne ni sangre»), sino porque el Padre se lo «reveló». Puesto que Cristo ya se había identificado como el Mesías en presencia de Pedro y los demás discípulos en al menos cuatro ocasiones[2], la revelación que recibió no se trataba de una revelación especial de una verdad desconocida anteriormente, sino de la iluminación sobre algo que Cristo ya le había dicho. En algún momento de su relación con Cristo, el Padre le dio la convicción de que Cristo realmente era el Mesías.

## Requisitos de la iluminación (Mt. 11:25-30)

¿Por qué el Padre iluminó a Pedro en lugar de a alguna de esas personas que consideraban a Jesús como un mero hombre? ¿Qué es lo que el Padre vio en Pedro que no estaba presente en esas personas? ¿Cuáles son los requisitos que el no creyente tiene que cumplir para que Dios le ilumine y se convierta a Cristo?

*1. Humildad (Mt. 11:20-26).* En Mateo 11:20-24, Jesús recrimina a los habitantes de Corazín y Capernaúm que, a pesar de la cantidad de milagros que había realizado en sus ciudades, no se habían arrepentido.

En su oración al Padre, Jesús le da las gracias por haber escondido «estas cosas de los sabios y de los entendidos» (vv. 25-26). A primera vista parece que Jesús menosprecia el papel de la inteligencia humana

---

2. Según los libros (llamados «armonías») que colocan en orden cronológico la vida y enseñanza de Cristo. Primero, después de que la mujer samaritana se quedó convencida de que Jesús era el Mesías, ella invitó a todos los habitantes de su pueblo a conocerle personalmente y comprobar por sí mismos que Jesús era el Mesías (Jn. 4:25-30, 39-42). Segundo, en el primer siglo los judíos creían que el Mesías venidero proveería pan para su pueblo elegido, igual que Dios lo hizo cuando los judíos atravesaban el desierto hacia Canaán. En Juan 6:30-42 Jesús se identifica como el verdadero pan enviado por el Padre desde el cielo. Tercero, cuando Juan el Bautista se encontraba en la cárcel y a punto de ser ejecutado, envió a unos discípulos suyos para preguntar a Jesús: «¿Eres tú aquel que había de venir, o esperaremos a otro?» (Mt. 11:3). La respuesta de Jesús, afirmando que Él era el Mesías tan esperado, fue oída por Pedro. Cuarto, en Lucas 5:20 Jesús dice al paralítico: «Hombre, tus pecados te son perdonados». Cuando los escribas y fariseos protestan que solo Dios puede perdonar pecados, Jesús defiende lo que ha dicho, afirmando así su deidad.

para entender y aceptar las verdades espirituales. Pero cuando Jesús compara a los sabios y entendidos con los niños, es evidente que no está hablando en términos literales de personas de poca edad, sino de personas que adoptan la actitud propia de un niño. Los niños suelen ser humildes y creer lo que un adulto les dice. Las enseñanzas de Cristo son reveladas a aquellas personas que son humildes, que se dan cuenta de que necesitan la ayuda de Dios para entenderlas. Por tanto, el problema de los sabios y entendidos no era su capacidad intelectual en sí, sino la autosuficiencia que esa capacidad provocaba en ellos[3].

La inteligencia es un maravilloso don de Dios, pero no es suficiente para convencer a una persona de que Cristo murió por sus pecados. Por eso hay eruditos no creyentes que pueden elaborar un bosquejo inmejorable de Romanos. Entienden los argumentos teológicos de Pablo, pero al no cumplir los requisitos para que la iluminación tome lugar en sus vidas nunca entenderán las verdades bíblicas de tal manera que las acepten como verídicas, se arrepientan y reciban vida eterna. Les falta la humildad para recibir la iluminación de Dios. Hubo ocasiones en que los fariseos entendieron enseguida lo que Cristo decía, mientras que sus propios discípulos seguían sin entender sus palabras. Pero el entendimiento que tenían los fariseos nunca pudo concederles vida eterna. Les faltaba la humildad para entender las palabras de Cristo y convertirse a él. Mientras que el mundo considera la humildad un defecto o debilidad, Dios la considera una virtud y un requisito para que la iluminación divina pueda efectuarse en la vida del no creyente.

*2. Un deseo de conocer la verdad y obedecerla (Mt. 13:10-17; Jn. 7:17).* Si un hombre investigara todas las religiones y sectas que existen en el mundo, ¿qué probabilidades habría de que identificara la única religión verdadera? ¿Qué criterio tendría que emplear para reconocerla?

Durante la fiesta de los tabernáculos los hermanos de Jesús lo animan a subir a Jerusalén. La ciudad iba a rebosar de multitudes de muchas partes del mundo mediterráneo, y Jesús tendría la oportunidad de dirigirse a un público más amplio (Jn. 7:3). Pero Jesús toma la decisión de esperar. Mientras tanto, los líderes religiosos lo buscan con el propósito de enfrentarse con él. El pueblo se ha polarizado en dos opiniones

---

3. Este es el sentido del v. 25 en la NTV, la cual representa una traducción que emplea la equivalencia dinámica.

muy opuestas. Algunos creen que Jesús es un hombre bueno, pero otros siguen la opinión de los líderes religiosos de que engaña al pueblo (v. 12). A mitad de la fiesta Jesús sube a Jerusalén y se dirige al templo para enseñar. Es precisamente en este momento cuando Jesús trata la cuestión de cómo saber si sus enseñanzas son verdaderas o falsas. Jesús identifica el segundo requisito que permite a un no creyente reconocer la verdad. «Todo el que quiera hacer la voluntad de Dios sabrá si lo que enseño proviene de Dios o solo hablo por mi propia cuenta» (v. 17, NTV). Sus palabras contienen dos caras de una misma moneda. Por un lado, identifica de forma muy clara el requisito de desear *hacer* la voluntad de Dios. Y, por otro lado, hay un elemento más que Jesús da por sentado: el deseo de *conocer* la verdad y la voluntad de Dios. Nadie querrá cumplir con la voluntad de Dios si primero no ha tenido un deseo de saber en qué consiste. Los dos requisitos van de la mano. El deseo de obedecer la luz recibida presupone que la persona primero ha querido conocerla. Para entender las Escrituras el no creyente tiene que desear conocer la verdad y obedecerla.

> «Todo el que quiera hacer la voluntad de Dios sabrá si lo que enseño proviene de Dios o solo hablo por mi propia cuenta». **(Jn. 7:17, NTV)**

Mientras que Juan 7:17 subraya el requisito de desear conocer la verdad y obedecerla, Mateo 13:10-17 se centra en las consecuencias de no obedecer la luz recibida. Jesús se encuentra a la orilla del mar con una multitud de personas que se han congregado para escuchar su enseñanza (vv. 1-2). Jesús emplea tantas parábolas en su enseñanza que la curiosidad de los discípulos los empuja a preguntarle: «¿Por qué les hablas por parábolas?» (vv. 3, 10). Jesús responde que los misterios del reino no han sido dados a la multitud, sino a ellos (v. 11). ¿Por qué? ¿Qué es lo que los discípulos habían hecho o lo que las personas de esa multitud no habían hecho para que se les descalifique para entender los misterios del reino?

A primera vista parece que faltara una palabra o dos al final de la frase: «Porque a cualquiera que tiene» (v. 12). ¿Qué es lo que tenían los discípulos que no poseían algunas personas de esa multitud? Para entender el v. 12, conviene mirar primero los vv. 13-15. En respuesta a la pregunta de los discípulos, Jesús les explica que emplea parábolas porque algunas personas ven, pero no «ven»; oyen, pero no «oyen» ni «entienden» (v. 13). Entonces, Jesús cita Isaías 6:9-10 porque, al igual que Jesús, ese profeta tenía el mismo problema con las personas a las cuales predicaba. Entendían sus palabras, pero no las «entendían» porque su corazón «se ha engrosado, y con los oídos oyen pesadamente, y han cerrado sus ojos» (Mt. 13:15). Puesto que consideraban pesados los mandamientos de Dios, tomaron conscientemente la decisión de tapar sus ojos para no verlos. Esta decisión puso en marcha un proceso que Jesús explica en el v. 12. La persona que hace uso de la luz que ya ha recibido recibirá más luz («a cualquiera que [aún] tiene [luz], se le dará [luz], y tendrá más [luz]»). Pero la persona que rechaza la luz que ha recibido, la perderá progresivamente («pero al que no tiene, aun lo que tiene le será quitado»). Por ese motivo sus corazones se habían vuelto insensibles[4]. Parece que Jesús tenía en mente a esa clase de personas cuando contó la parábola del rico y Lázaro a los fariseos y líderes religiosos, personas que habían rechazado una y otra vez sus enseñanzas y declaraciones (Lc. 16:19-31)[5]. En su aplicación de la parábola, Jesús dice que hay personas que no aceptarían la verdad aunque alguien resucitara de la muerte para comunicarles las consecuencias que les esperan si no se arrepienten (vv. 30-31). «No se requiere fe para oír el mensaje bíblico, pero una resistencia consciente y a propósito, y un rechazo de ese mensaje, obstaculizará el entendimiento del mismo»[6].

## Dos clases de no creyentes

Hay dos clases de no creyentes. Por un lado, hay quienes rechazan de forma consciente y constante la ley que Dios ha escrito en su corazón (Ro. 2:14-16), las Escrituras y el testimonio de los creyentes. Aunque

---

4. La NTV, una traducción que emplea la equivalencia dinámica, capta el sentido del v. 12 al traducirlo con la palabra «escuchan» en el sentido de escuchar y obedecer («A los que escuchan mis enseñanzas se les dará más comprensión, y tendrán conocimiento en abundancia, pero a los que no escuchan se les quitará aun lo poco que entiendan»).

5. Las parábolas nunca citan a sus protagonistas por nombre. Sin embargo, Lucas 16:20 identifica al mendigo como Lázaro. Por eso, muchos comentaristas consideran Lucas 16:19-31 una historia real en lugar de una parábola.

6. Elliott E. Johnson, *Expository Homiletics: An Introduction* (Grand Rapids: Zondervan, 1990), p. 53.

hay grados de rebeldía entre esta clase de no creyentes, todos carecen de un deseo de buscar y conocer a Dios. No es que no entiendan la enseñanza bíblica, sino que no quieren doblar la rodilla ante Dios y aceptar la verdad con todas sus implicaciones. Por eso consideran las enseñanzas bíblicas una «ridiculez» (1 Co. 1:18; 2:14, NTV), «puras tonterías» (1:23, NTV). El hecho de considerar el evangelio una «ridiculez» implica haberlo entendido. En las palabras tan gráficas de Clark: «Cuando Adán cayó, la raza humana no se hizo *estúpida*, haciendo así que la verdad fuera difícil de entender, sino *hostil* a la aceptación de la verdad»[7]. Entonces, su rechazo pone en marcha ese proceso de perder progresivamente el entendimiento del evangelio que habían adquirido hasta el momento (Mt. 13:12), invitando así al «dios de este siglo» a cegar aún más su entendimiento (2 Co. 4:3-4). Por tanto, cuando Pablo dice que el hombre natural no «sabe» (1 Co. 2:12), no «percibe», no «entiende» ni «discierne» las cosas de Dios (v. 14), es evidente que no se refiere a que no entiende intelectualmente las cosas de Dios.

Por otro lado, hay no creyentes que tienen un deseo sincero de conocer la verdad y agradar a Dios, pero se enfrentan con el problema de no tener una base suficiente para «probar» que Jesús *murió por sus pecados*. Es precisamente en esta situación que la iluminación de Dios juega un papel tan importante. Este es el énfasis que Pablo hace con respecto a la conversión de los tesalonicenses. «Pues, cuando les llevamos la Buena Noticia, no fue solo con palabras sino también con poder, porque el Espíritu Santo les dio plena certeza de que lo que decíamos era verdad» (1 Ts. 1:5, NTV). La iluminación le permite al no creyente «ver el reino de Dios» (Jn. 3:3). Todos hemos observado a un no creyente que, aunque ha recibido una explicación del evangelio en tantas ocasiones que puede repetirla palabra por palabra, no se convierte hasta que un día declara con un entusiasmo incontenible: «¡Ahora *lo veo*!». ¿Qué ha ocurrido? En un momento que solo Dios sabe, esa persona ha abrazado la luz que ha recibido mediante la obra divina de la iluminación. Entendía a nivel intelectual el mensaje del evangelio, pero no lo había «visto» con los ojos de su alma.

7. Gordon H. Clark, «How May I Know the Bible is Inspired?» en *Can I Trust the Bible?* (Chicago: Moody Press, 1968), p. 28.

## B. EN EL CREYENTE

La iglesia en Corinto era la más problemática de todas las congregaciones del N.T. Entre sus muchos pecados se encontraba el de cuestionar y rechazar el apostolado de Pablo, obligándolo a dedicar una buena parte de 2 Corintios a defender su nombramiento divino. Antes de escribir 2 Corintios, algunos corintios decían que era poco atractivo y que empleaba una forma «menospreciable» y «tosca» de predicar y enseñar (2 Co. 10:10; 11:6). Querían que fuera guapo, que tuviera una personalidad carismática y que predicara con una oratoria atractiva y persuasiva que dejara boquiabiertos a todos sus oyentes. Antes de predicarles el evangelio por primera vez, parece que Pablo era consciente de ese defecto en el carácter de los corintios, ya que en 1 Corintios 2:3 habla de la debilidad y temor que sintió cuando les predicó el evangelio por primera vez. Por eso les dice en los vv. 4-5 que cuando les comunicó el evangelio, «mi mensaje y mi predicación fueron muy sencillos... para que ustedes no confiaran en la sabiduría humana sino en el poder de Dios» (1 Co. 2:4-5, NTV).

### 1 Corintios 2:6-16

Con esta situación como trasfondo, Pablo escribe 1 Co. 2:6-16 diciendo que hay misterios y verdades espirituales que solamente el creyente puede entender. Dios en su misericordia ilumina al no creyente con respecto a las verdades que tienen que ver con la salvación. Pero una vez que se convierte, el Espíritu lo ilumina en cuanto a otras verdades espirituales. En este pasaje, que representa la mención plena de la iluminación del Espíritu Santo, Pablo subraya dos verdades.

> «...alumbrando los ojos de vuestro entendimiento, para que sepáis cuál es la esperanza a que él os ha llamado, y cuáles las riquezas de la gloria de su herencia en los santos...».
>
> **(Ef. 1:18)**

*1. Hace falta la iluminación del Espíritu Santo para entender las Escrituras.* Por eso, Pablo ora que Dios alumbre los ojos de los efesios para que se den cuenta de todo lo que tienen en Cristo (Ef. 1:18). Por eso, David pidió a Dios: «Abre mis ojos, para que vea las maravillas de tu ley». (Sal. 119:18, LBLA).

Mateo 11:25 y 16:17 indican que el Espíritu ilumina, mientras que Mateo 11:27 indica que el Hijo lleva a cabo esa labor. Sin embargo, 1 Corintios 2:6-16 identifica esa obra divina con el Espíritu Santo, hasta tal punto que su nombre aparece en cada versículo desde el v. 10 hasta el v. 14 inclusive. Entonces, ¿cuál de las tres personas de la Trinidad se encarga de la iluminación? Es probable que estemos ante una de esas lagunas que existen en las Escrituras con respecto a la doctrina de la Trinidad. La Biblia enseña de forma clara que hay un solo Dios y que existe en tres personas. Aunque esa matemática no cuadra, el creyente acepta esa enseñanza como verídica. La Biblia indica también que cada persona de la Trinidad tiene unas responsabilidades particulares. Por ejemplo, es el Hijo quien muere en una cruz, no el Padre. Sin embargo, como las tres personas son uno, en un sentido lo que decimos de una de ellas es aplicable también a las otras dos. Por tanto, cabe la posibilidad de que la labor de iluminar sea compartida por las tres personas. También cabe la posibilidad de que el Padre y el Hijo iluminaran a los intérpretes de las Escrituras en tiempos del antiguo pacto (dispensación de la Ley), pero que esa labor fuera delegada al Espíritu Santo en el nuevo pacto (dispensación de la Gracia).

*2. Solamente el creyente puede «entender» las Escrituras.* Este es el gran énfasis de este pasaje. Evidentemente, Pablo no se refiere a las verdades que el no creyente tiene que entender para convertirse a Cristo, sino a todas las demás verdades de las Escrituras. Esas verdades son entendidas solamente por los creyentes, «los que le aman» (v. 9), «nosotros» (v. 10), los que han recibido «el Espíritu que proviene de Dios» (vv. 11-12) y «el (hombre) espiritual» (vv. 14-15). El significado de cualquier comunicación se encuentra en la mente («espíritu») del autor de dicha comunicación (v. 11). Puesto que el creyente tiene acceso a la «mente de Cristo» en la persona del Espíritu Santo que mora en él, puede entender la Palabra de Dios (v. 16). Aunque el no creyente puede entender las Escrituras, nunca podrá «entenderlas» por sí solo. En el v. 9 Pablo emplea el mismo juego de palabras que Isaías y Jesús usaron en Isaías 6:9 y Mateo 13:14. El no creyente puede ver y oír las Escrituras, pero nunca podrá «ver», «oír» o «entender» las Escrituras por sí solo porque la inteligencia y «la sabiduría de los hombres» (vv. 5-6, 13) son incapaces de «ver» y «oír» las «cosas [...] que Dios ha preparado para los que le aman» (v. 9). El «hombre natural no percibe las cosas que son del Espíritu de Dios, porque para él son locura, y no las puede entender, porque se han de discernir espiritualmente» (v. 14).

## Características de la iluminación en el creyente

Hay muchos textos y enseñanzas que el nuevo creyente no entenderá. Por eso, el Espíritu Santo comenzará a iluminarle en cuanto a las enseñanzas y doctrinas más básicas de la vida cristiana. Con el tiempo le ayudará a masticar comida más sólida. Dios pretende iluminarle a lo largo de su vida para que su entendimiento de las Escrituras vaya en aumento (2 Ti. 2:7). Lógicamente, el creyente tiene que seguir cumpliendo con los requisitos de la humildad y tener un deseo de conocer la verdad y obedecerla. La iluminación del Espíritu en el creyente cuenta con siete características que definen qué es y qué no es la iluminación.

*1. Siempre está ligada a las Escrituras.* La iluminación no produce «iluminados» que reciben una revelación especial de Dios cuyo contenido no se encuentra en ninguna parte de las Escrituras. Eso representaría una revelación nueva, cosa que no es posible porque el canon está cerrado. Tampoco llevará al creyente a entender como verdad una idea que es contraria a la Palabra de Dios. La iluminación ayuda al creyente a entender el significado de la revelación que ya se ha dado en las Escrituras.

*2. Nunca es sustituta de una hermenéutica correcta.* El creyente ha de aprender a interpretar «con precisión» la Palabra de Dios (2 Ti. 2:15, LBLA) usando las herramientas que se encuentran en el presente libro y en otros que acepten la inspiración plenaria y verbal de las Escrituras, y que promuevan el método histórico-gramático-cultural de la interpretación bíblica.

*3. Su meta es la de proveer una relación más íntima con Dios y una vida más santa.* Si el creyente estudia las Escrituras simplemente para adquirir un conocimiento más amplio de las mismas, ese conocimiento lo envanecerá (1 Co. 8:1). La meta divina es que estudie las

Escrituras y sea iluminado por el Espíritu con el propósito de cambiar sus actitudes y comportamiento, conformándose así progresivamente a «la medida de la estatura de la plenitud de Cristo» (Ef. 4:13; ver también Flp. 3:15; Col. 1:9-10).

*4. No es sustituta del sudor intelectual.* La naturaleza divina de las Escrituras requiere que el intérprete sea creyente, que sea humilde y que tenga un deseo de conocer la verdad y obedecerla para que el Espíritu Santo pueda iluminarlo. A la vez, su naturaleza humana le requiere que haga un esfuerzo intelectual, que use la inteligencia que Dios le ha dado. La interpretación correcta de un texto bíblico no vendrá por visiones en la noche, sino por el esfuerzo intelectual acompañado por la iluminación del Espíritu Santo. El Espíritu no dará al intérprete el trasfondo cultural e histórico de un texto, el significado de una palabra griega, ni otros datos que se encuentran en léxicos, diccionarios y comentarios bíblicos. El intérprete tendrá que buscar esa información por su propia cuenta.

Aunque la iluminación no le otorgará al creyente un coeficiente intelectual superior al que tenía antes de convertirse, este tiene que utilizar su inteligencia para que el Espíritu realice su labor de iluminación al máximo nivel. Siempre y cuando el creyente use su inteligencia, la iluminación lo ayudará a usarla de una forma más correcta y a juzgar mejor los méritos y fallos de los argumentos de otros a favor de una determinada interpretación. «Mientras que el no creyente es guiado por una razón sin fe, el creyente debe ser guiado por una fe que razona»[8]. Por regla general, el creyente no recibirá ráfagas de luz en cuanto al significado de las Escrituras, sino un entendimiento progresivo, especialmente en los textos y doctrinas más difíciles de entender.

> La historia de la Iglesia y la experiencia diaria atestiguan que una pretendida dependencia del Espíritu divorciada del estudio serio y diligente en la interpretación de la Escritura es frecuentemente causa de extravagancias religiosas o de herejías. La obra del Espíritu Santo es indispensable para la comprensión de la Palabra de Dios; pero no es, por lo general, una obra que nos ahorre la saludable

8. J. I. Packer, *«Fundamentalism» and the Word of God* (Grand Rapids: Eerdmans, 1977), p. 128.

tarea de la hermenéutica. Es guía, no atajo, para llevarnos al conocimiento de la verdad de Dios[9].

*5. El creyente ha de aceptar lo que entiende por la iluminación. Si lo rechaza corre el riesgo de perder la luz que ya tiene.* Cuando el creyente no obedece lo que ha entendido en las Escrituras, pone en marcha la dinámica de Mateo 13:12 («A los que escuchan mis enseñanzas se les dará más comprensión, y tendrán conocimiento en abundancia; pero a los que no escuchan se les quitará aun lo poco que entiendan», NTV). La vida cristiana es como subir una montaña en un automóvil sin frenos. En el momento en que deja de avanzar hacia el pico de esa montaña, vuelve hacia atrás. Cuando el creyente no obedece lo que aprende de la Palabra de Dios, retrocede hacia ese estado espiritual en el cual la única alimentación que es capaz de digerir es la leche de la Palabra de Dios, esas enseñanzas más básicas y fáciles de entender. «Es por eso —lamenta Pache— que nuestras iglesias frecuentemente son guarderías para infantes espirituales en lugar de campos de entrenamiento para hombres maduros, para maestros y para soldados de Jesucristo (Heb. 5:11-14)»[10].

| La iluminación en el creyente |
|---|
| 1. Siempre está ligada a las Escrituras. |
| 2. Nunca es sustituta de una hermenéutica correcta. |
| 3. Su meta es la de proveer una relación más íntima con Dios y una vida más santa. |
| 4. No es sustituta del sudor intelectual. |
| 5. Si lo rechaza, corre el riesgo de perder la luz que ya tiene. |
| 6. No garantiza una interpretación correcta de las Escrituras. |
| 7. No produce un conocimiento completo de las Escrituras. |

*6. No garantiza una interpretación correcta de las Escrituras.* Puede resultar una sorpresa para el principiante descubrir que grandes hombres de Dios difieren en cuanto a su interpretación de ciertos textos. Puede que todos acierten en un elemento de la enseñanza de un texto, pero que se equivoquen en otros. Nadie tiene la posibilidad de acertar

9. José María Martínez, *Hermenéutica bíblica* (Tarrasa: CLIE, 1984), p. 21.

10. René Pache, *The Inspiration and Authority of Scripture* (Chicago: Moody Press, 1978), p. 208. Su capítulo sobre la iluminación y el capítulo que Stein incluye en su libro *A Basic Guide to Interpreting the Bible* (Grand Rapids: Baker, 1994) sobre esa doctrina son dos de las mejores presentaciones que existen sobre la iluminación.

siempre en todas sus interpretaciones por inteligente y piadoso que sea. Nadie tiene el monopolio sobre la verdad. Por tanto, el intérprete haría bien en mantener un alto nivel de humildad y evitar el dogmatismo en aquellos temas bíblicos que sean secundarios o en los cuales la iglesia no ha llegado a un acuerdo.

*7. No produce un conocimiento completo de las Escrituras.* El nivel de entendimiento que la iluminación producirá en el creyente estará condicionado por tres factores. Primero, el nivel de madurez que haya alcanzado hasta el momento. Este factor determinará cuánta información nueva podrá entender y asimilar. Segundo, su nivel intelectual y el esfuerzo que haga en su estudio de las Escrituras. Tercero, el año o siglo en que viva. Grandes estudiosos de la Palabra de Dios tomaron posiciones en su día que hoy día son consideradas erróneas simplemente porque no tenían a su disposición la cantidad de información que tenemos hoy en los léxicos, teologías sistemáticas, diccionarios, los comentarios bíblicos y los nuevos descubrimientos arqueológicos.

La Biblia es de origen y naturaleza divina. Por tanto, hacen falta normas divinas para interpretarla correctamente. Tanto el creyente como el no creyente tienen que ser humildes y tener el deseo de conocer la verdad y obedecerla para recibir la iluminación del Espíritu Santo. La iluminación en el no creyente tendrá que ver con aquellos temas relacionados con su salvación y conversión a Cristo. Pero para el creyente, la iluminación incluirá todos los demás misterios del reino de Dios que se encuentran en las Escrituras.

## *Trabajo para realizar*

¿Cuáles son los dos requisitos espirituales que el no creyente ha de cumplir para que «vea» y «entienda» lo que Dios ha dicho en su Palabra para que la iluminación pueda tomar lugar? Explique de forma breve las siete características de la iluminación en el creyente.

Sección II

# Hermenéutica general

Dios dio una revelación especial a unos hombres escogidos por él con el propósito de que la pusieran por escrito. Las normas para interpretar cualquier literatura de índole literal forman parte de lo que tradicionalmente se llama hermenéutica general.


6. El método histórico-gramático-cultural
7. Géneros literarios
8. Trasfondo histórico y cultural
9. Tema del libro
10. La organización del libro
11. Contexto
12. Palabras
13. Gramática
14. El propósito y plan divino

# 6

# El método gramático-histórico-cultural

La Biblia tiene dos naturalezas. Es un libro divino; por tanto, requiere que el intérprete emplee leyes espirituales para entenderlo. Pero también es un libro humano. Por mucho que los autores bíblicos fueran guiados por el Espíritu Santo, sus libros no dejan de ser humanos en el sentido de que fueron escritos con palabras humanas de idiomas que esos autores hablaban. Por tanto, es necesario emplear un método de interpretación que tenga en cuenta todos los elementos de la comunicación humana que los autores emplearon cuando escribieron sus respectivos libros. El método histórico-gramático-cultural cumple con ese requisito al reconocer que la Biblia está anclada en la historia, al hacer énfasis en la gramática de los idiomas originales empleados por sus autores y al tener en cuenta el trasfondo cultural del texto[1].

*1. La historia.* La Biblia cita en sus páginas a más personas, eventos y lugares históricos que cualquier otra literatura religiosa antigua. Sus autores hacen referencia a eventos históricos que ocurrieron a lo largo de unos 1500 años. Isaías comienza su profecía diciendo que

1. Aunque I. Howard Marshall llama al término «histórico-gramático-cultural» un «trabalenguas» en su libro *Biblical Inspiration* (Vancouver: Regent College Publishing, 2004), p. 86, es el término que todos los evangélicos han adoptado.

la escribió «en días de Uzías, Jotam, Acaz y Ezequías, reyes de Judá» (1:1), dando así un marco histórico dentro del cual quiere que sus lectores interpreten su profecía. Por tanto, para entender el libro de Isaías el intérprete debe empaparse de la historia de esos reyes que se encuentra en 1–2 Reyes y 1–2 Crónicas y de cualquier dato que pueda encontrar en fuentes extrabíblicas.

El cristianismo está anclado en la historia. Además de ser verídicos los datos históricos que cita, ciertos eventos históricos como la crucifixión y resurrección de Cristo forman una parte indispensable y fundamental de la revelación divina. El cristianismo no es una religión histórica solamente por tener su comienzo en un momento determinado de la historia humana, sino también en el sentido de que el Dios del universo intervino en la historia humana, se reveló al hombre en medio de esa historia, fundamentó su obra redentora sobre eventos históricos, controla la historia (Dn. 2:21; Hch. 17:26), la emplea para llevar a cabo sus propósitos (Gn. 50:20; Éx. 12:36: Is. 10:5-6) y la llevará a su culminación con la segunda venida de Cristo (2 Ts. 1:6-8). Es prácticamente imposible no notar el gran énfasis que los autores bíblicos hacen sobre los eventos históricos. No se puede investigar la veracidad de los mitos y fábulas porque no se basan ni ocurrieron dentro de la historia humana. Carecen de credenciales históricas. Por el contrario, el cristianismo está basado en eventos históricos.

*2. La gramática.* El método histórico-gramático-cultural descansa sobre el axioma de la comunicación humana que afirma que cada persona que quiere comunicar una idea tiene que sujetarse a las leyes del lenguaje. Para que sus lectores los entendieran, los autores bíblicos tuvieron que someterse a las leyes generales del lenguaje —las cuales son aplicables a todos los idiomas— y a las leyes particulares de la gramática del idioma que emplearon.

El estudio de la gramática obliga al intérprete a centrarse en lo que el autor dice en lugar de en lo que él quiere que diga. Algunos opinan que hay que hacer una distinción entre lo que el autor dijo (el significado del texto) y lo que pretendía decir. Pero no hay forma de saber lo que hay en la mente de un autor si prescindimos de las palabras que ha escrito, porque no existe la posibilidad de introducirse dentro de su mente para descubrir lo que pretendía comunicar a sus primeros lectores. Sería un ejercicio de pura especulación psicológica.

El método histórico-gramático-cultural se centra en las palabras del autor con base en el axioma del lenguaje humano de que el autor es capaz de comunicar a sus lectores lo que hay en su mente. Tanto énfasis sobre la gramática no quiere decir que el texto sea más importante que el autor o que el texto cobre una vida propia al margen de lo que el autor pretendía decir, como algunos eruditos modernos de la nueva hermenéutica quieren hacernos creer, sino que el lenguaje es un medio eficaz de comunicación. Nos puede indicar de forma fidedigna lo que el autor quería y pretendía decirnos.

*3. La cultura.* La cultura tiene que ver con muchos aspectos de la vida cotidiana de un pueblo: su forma de pensar, los artefactos que produce y emplea, la geografía, las cronologías, las prácticas de los comerciantes, las estructuras militares y los métodos de guerra, las estructuras políticas, los sistemas monetarios, los sistemas legales, el trato de los esclavos y prisioneros, la arquitectura, las prácticas agrícolas, los medios de transporte, los grupos religiosos y sus respectivas prácticas, las bodas, los entierros, las características de las ciudades donde hubo una iglesia que recibió una epístola, etcétera.

El método histórico-gramático-cultural de la interpretación bíblica cuenta con tres características básicas.

## A. UNA INTERPRETACIÓN LITERAL

Quizás la característica que mejor describe el método histórico-gramático-cultural sea su interpretación literal de las Escrituras excepto cuando el texto indica que el autor bíblico está empleando una forma no literal de comunicación. Esta característica se basa en los axiomas del lenguaje que vimos en el apartado titulado «Conceptos clave» y en el consenso de los eruditos de la teoría literaria que afirman que la interpretación literal de cualquier texto, sea de la Biblia o de cualquier otro libro, es la más correcta.

La palabra «literal» ha sido atacada por quienes no aceptan el origen divino e inspiración de la Biblia. Acusan a los evangélicos de hacer un dios de la interpretación literal a expensas de las diferentes formas no literales de escritura empleadas por los autores bíblicos. El problema no es que los evangélicos sean «literalistas», sino que sus detractores no quieren aceptar la enseñanza bíblica con todas sus implicaciones y, para esquivarlas, interpretan algunos pasajes bíblicos como si fueran mitos, leyendas o símbolos de experiencias espirituales en lugar de eventos y personas históricas. Por ejemplo, dicen que la caída de Adán y Eva descrita en Génesis no es un evento histórico, sino un reflejo del estado pecaminoso del ser humano. Esta forma de interpretar las Escrituras les permite imponer sobre el texto bíblico el significado que ellos quieren.

Los evangélicos siguen firmes en su decisión de emplear la palabra «literal» porque, después de considerar todas las alternativas, sigue siendo la mejor palabra para definir la *primera* manera en que el intérprete debe acercarse al texto bíblico. Es la forma más obvia, sencilla, directa, normal y natural[2]. Las razones son más que convincentes. En primer lugar, el lenguaje literal es la forma habitual que los seres humanos emplean para comunicarse entre sí. En segundo lugar, una comunicación no literal se fundamenta y descansa sobre un entendimiento literal de las palabras que emplea. «El significado no literal es siempre un significado secundario que toma por sentado un entendimiento literal que ya existe de la literatura. Este nivel del lenguaje es el punto de partida *necesario* para la interpretación de toda literatura»[3]. Por ejemplo, si el autor de *Con precisión* dijera «Mi automóvil es una lata», el lector no sabría lo que quiere decir si no entiende el significado literal de las palabras «automóvil» y «lata». ¿Qué es una lata y cuál es su conexión con el automóvil en cuestión? Las latas que se encuentran

---

2. En su libro *Toward an Exegetical Theology*, ob. cit., pp. 87–88, Kaiser dice que «desde el tratado en latín de Karl A. G. Keil (1788) y su libro de texto en alemán sobre la hermenéutica del N.T. (1810), los exégetas en general han adoptado su término, "el método gramático-histórico" de interpretación, como descriptivo de su propio acercamiento a la tarea exegética. La meta del método gramático-histórico es la de determinar el significado requerido por las leyes de la gramática y los hechos de la historia. Sin embargo, el término "gramático" es algo desorientador puesto que solemos usar la palabra "gramática" para referirnos al orden en que colocamos las palabras y la construcción de frases. Pero Keil tenía en mente la palabra griega *gramma*, y su uso del término *gramático* se aproxima a lo que nosotros entendemos por el término *literal* (para emplear un término derivado del latín). Así que el sentido gramático, en el entendimiento de Keil, es el sentido simple, directo, ordinario, llano y literal de las frases».

3. Bernard Ramm, *Protestant Biblical Interpretation* (Grand Rapids: Baker, 1978), p. 123.

en las estanterías de las tiendas de comestibles se hacen de estaño, un metal que resiste la oxidación. Por tanto, es ideal para la conservación de vegetales, frutas, etcétera durante mucho tiempo. Además, por ser un metal tan abundante, no es caro. Sabiendo esto, decir que «Mi automóvil es una lata» es una forma no literal de decir literalmente que el automóvil del autor no vale mucho. En tercer lugar, cuando un autor emplea una forma de comunicación no literal, lo que dice no es literal, pero *lo que quiere decir sí.*

El método literal de interpretación no excluye ni ignora las formas no literales de la comunicación, sino simplemente reconoce que el método literal es aceptado universalmente como el punto de partida de la interpretación de cualquier literatura. El intérprete sabe que tiene delante un texto figurativo en lugar de literal cuando el texto: (1) Emplea una clase de lenguaje figurado. Veremos las diferentes clases de lenguaje figurado en el capítulo 16. (2) Expresa una idea disparatada. Por ejemplo: «A menos que coman la carne del Hijo del Hombre y beban su sangre, no podrán tener vida eterna en ustedes» (Jn. 6:53, NTV). (3) Contradice la clara enseñanza de otros textos bíblicos.

La comunicación literal es la forma más lógica y apropiada que Dios podría haber empleado para revelarnos la verdad espiritual. No hay ambigüedad. Además, la interpretación literal es el único control que existe contra las interpretaciones y aplicaciones alegóricas y fantasiosas, una práctica muy común durante la Edad Media (siglos V–XV) y por parte de las sectas hoy. Los reformadores del siglo XVI rechazaron de forma tajante la interpretación alegórica de las Escrituras e insistieron en una interpretación literal de las mismas.

## B. UN MÉTODO INDUCTIVO

Con el método *deductivo* el intérprete acepta como verdad lo que un mentor espiritual, comentario bíblico, etcétera dice en cuanto a lo que la Biblia enseña sobre un tema, y luego busca textos que apoyen dicha enseñanza. Es un método legítimo cuando se trata de enseñar verdades bíblicas a niños o a nuevos creyentes que no están en posición de realizar un estudio inductivo completo de las Escrituras por su propia cuenta. Con el método *inductivo*, el intérprete estudia primero un texto o tema bíblico y luego consulta lo que otros opinan sobre dicho texto o tema. Mientras que cada creyente debe consultar las opiniones de personas que tienen un conocimiento bíblico más amplio que él, cada creyente es el primer responsable de lo que cree. El método inductivo presta atención a tres tareas.

Primera, observar. ¿Qué dice el texto? ¿Quiénes son las personas, cuáles los lugares geográficos, el trasfondo histórico, los detalles culturales, los problemas, las bendiciones, los avisos, etcétera que surgen del texto? Si el intérprete está estudiando los milagros de Jesús le convendría preguntar: ¿en qué consistió el milagro y cuál era su naturaleza? ¿En qué ocasión se realizó? ¿Quiénes eran las personas que se beneficiaron de él? ¿Cómo realizó Jesús el milagro y cómo reaccionaron aquellos que lo observaron? En este primer paso el intérprete simplemente hace preguntas y recoge información. Las respuestas a sus preguntas le proveerán la materia prima que necesita para hacer una interpretación correcta del pasaje en cuestión.

Segunda, interpretar. En este paso el intérprete procura contestar la pregunta: ¿qué es lo que el autor quiso comunicar a sus primeros lectores? La tarea del intérprete se parece mucho al trabajo de un detective: tiene que recoger las huellas y demás evidencias forenses del escenario de un crimen, distinguir entre aquellos detalles que constituyen una evidencia y prueba indiscutible y los que son meramente circunstanciales, interpretar correctamente el valor de dicha evidencia, sistematizarla y llegar a unas conclusiones válidas. No debe precipitarse ni proceder de forma errática, sino con mucho cuidado para no perjudicar los resultados de su trabajo. De la misma manera el intérprete ha de emplear un procedimiento que le permita trabajar con seriedad y orden. Ha de saber analizar la enseñanza de un texto sin entrar en conflicto con la clara enseñanza de otros textos. Una vez que haya realizado su propio estudio del texto —y solo entonces— deberá consultar varios comentarios bíblicos, porque ningún comentarista es infalible ni experto en todos los pasajes. Estos comentarios desafiarán ciertas conclusiones del intérprete y le darán un entendimiento más amplio del texto.

Tercera, aplicar. La aplicación es la meta de todo estudio bíblico. Un conocimiento más amplio de la Biblia no es un fin en sí mismo, sino el vehículo cuya misión es la de llevar al intérprete a una vida más santa. Recordemos que uno de los requisitos para una mayor comprensión de las Escrituras (iluminación) es la disposición a obedecerlas (Mt. 13:10-17; Jn. 7:17). En este paso el intérprete procura contestar la pregunta: ¿qué aplicación tiene este texto a mi propia vida? A la vez que los tres pasos de observar, interpretar y aplicar están estrechamente relacionados y a veces se solapan, representan el orden lógico y correcto en que el intérprete debería proceder. Antes de hacer una aplicación de un texto, el intérprete debe identificar el significado de dicho texto.

## C. PREMISAS BASADAS EN EL SENTIDO COMÚN

El método histórico-gramático-cultural se basa sobre varias premisas que son de sentido común. Prueba de la validez de estas premisas es el hecho de que son empleadas por las personas de cualquier cultura, lugar y siglo sin importar la clase de literatura que interpreten.

1. *El autor no se contradice a sí mismo.* Cuando los lectores de cualquier libro encuentran una aparente contradicción, suelen dar al autor el beneficio de la duda y buscar una explicación razonable, a no ser que haya un claro consenso por parte de muchos de que el autor es un mentiroso empedernido o de que sufrió un serio lapsus mental cuando escribió dicho libro. Desafortunadamente, algunos intérpretes que no aceptan el origen e inspiración divina de las Escrituras se niegan a dar a los autores bíblicos el mismo beneficio de la duda que dan sin reservas a otros autores. El sentido común nos lleva a creer que un autor no se contradice a sí mismo.

*2. El contexto es de suma importancia.* Puesto que ciertas palabras adquieren significados adicionales a lo largo de su historia, y puesto que el contexto es lo que identifica el significado que el autor tenía en mente cuando empleaba una palabra que tenía varios significados, es menester que el intérprete preste mucha atención al contexto.

*3. Lo difícil debe interpretarse a la luz de lo evidente.* Es de sentido común comenzar con los textos claros y luego procurar entender los textos más difíciles. A veces, la dificultad de entender un texto se debe a que el creyente es nuevo en la fe y no está preparado para digerir otra cosa que la leche de la Palabra de Dios (1 Co. 3:1-2; 1 P. 2:2). En otras ocasiones se debe a que el intérprete desconoce el trasfondo histórico y cultural, o porque el texto es simplemente difícil.

*4. Las partes deben interpretarse a la luz de la totalidad.* No es lícito obligar a una frase o texto a significar algo que la totalidad de la enseñanza bíblica niega. Por ejemplo, el hecho de que Dios amó de tal manera al mundo que dio a su Hijo unigénito para morir en una cruz por nuestros pecados, no nos permite creer que el infierno no existe o que Dios concederá a los no creyentes una segunda oportunidad de convertirse a Cristo después de su muerte.

*5. La interpretación de los lectores originales es con toda probabilidad la más correcta.* Cuando un autor bíblico escribió a una iglesia o persona, pretendía atender una necesidad o situación que había surgido, resolver un problema, corregir un error, contestar una pregunta, etcétera. Por lógica, los lectores originales sabían a qué se refería el autor. Por tanto, es de sentido común dar por sentado que en la gran mayoría de los casos los lectores originales entendieron lo que el autor quiso comunicarles. De lo contrario, el autor habría hecho un esfuerzo para aclarar cualquier concepto difícil de entender. Siendo este el caso, cualquier interpretación que los lectores originales nunca podrían haber entendido es con toda probabilidad una interpretación errónea. De ahí que la explicación más sencilla de un texto suela ser la correcta. Las interpretaciones excesivamente creativas y fantasiosas raras veces reflejan lo que el autor pretendía comunicar y, por tanto, deben considerarse sospechosas.

| **El método histórico-gramático-cultural** | |
|---|---|
| Una interpretación literal | Se interpreta cada pasaje de forma literal a no ser que el autor bíblico esté empleando una forma no literal de comunicación. |
| Un método inductivo | 1. Observar. ¿Qué dice el texto?<br>2. Interpretar. ¿Qué es lo que el autor quiso comunicar a sus primeros lectores?<br>3. Aplicar. ¿Qué aplicación tiene este texto a mi propia vida? |
| Premisas basadas en el sentido común | 1. El autor no se contradice a sí mismo.<br>2. El contexto es de suma importancia.<br>3. Lo difícil debe interpretarse a la luz de lo claro.<br>4. Las partes deben interpretarse a la luz de la totalidad.<br>5. La interpretación de los lectores originales es con toda probabilidad la más correcta. |

Esto no quiere decir que los primeros lectores siempre entendieron lo que oían o leían. Adán y Eva no pudieron haber entendido todo el alcance de la profecía de que la descendencia de Eva heriría mortalmente a la descendencia de la serpiente (Gn. 3:15, NTV). Algunos profetas no entendieron ciertos aspectos de las profecías que ellos mismos pusieron por escrito (1 P. 1:10-12). Cuando Jesús dijo a sus discípulos, «Guardaos de la levadura de los fariseos y de los saduceos», ellos pensaban que se refería a que no habían traído pan (Mt. 16:6-7). Y cuando Jesús respondió a una pregunta de Pedro sobre la vida futura de Juan en Juan 21:22-23 («Si quiero que él siga vivo hasta que yo regrese, ¿qué tiene que ver contigo?», NTV), algunos discípulos creyeron que Jesús decía que el apóstol Juan nunca moriría. No obstante, estos casos son la excepción. Si un texto es ambiguo, la interpretación preferida será la que habría tenido más sentido para los lectores originales.

## *Trabajo para realizar*

Una interpretación literal de cualquier libro es la más lógica y correcta por tres razones. Explique dos de esos argumentos. No obstante, existen formas no literales de escritura que la Biblia emplea, igual que muchos otros libros. Hay al menos tres maneras de saber cuándo un texto bíblico emplea una de esas formas no literales. Explique dos de ellas. ¿Cuál es la diferencia entre un estudio inductivo y un estudio deductivo de las Escrituras?

# 7

# Géneros literarios

Después de identificar el método histórico-gramático-cultural como el sistema de interpretación que mejor abarca y toma en cuenta todos los diferentes elementos de la comunicación empleados en las Escrituras, nos dedicamos en primer lugar a aquellas formas del lenguaje que son generales. Más tarde, veremos las formas especiales y no literales (la poesía, los símbolos, etcétera) o las que únicamente aparecen en las Escrituras (profecía, tipos). Este capítulo enfocará la interpretación bíblica desde la óptica más amplia posible de los géneros o clases literarias que los autores bíblicos emplearon[1]. Después, los seis capítulos siguientes llevarán al lector de forma progresiva hacia los aspectos más detallados de la interpretación gramático-histórico-cultural de un texto bíblico. Finalmente, el último capítulo de esta sección invitará al lector a dar un paso hacia atrás para ver el cuadro completo de la Biblia e identificar la forma en que Dios llevó a cabo su plan para la salvación del hombre.

Los autores bíblicos emplearon varios géneros literarios para comunicar su mensaje a sus lectores. Antes de interpretar cualquier texto bíblico, el intérprete debe identificar a qué clase de literatura pertenece, porque cada género tiene distintas características y limitaciones, además de reglas propias para su interpretación.

---

1. Muchos libros y artículos emplean el término *genre*, una palabra francesa que significa «clase de».

## A. LOS GÉNEROS LITERARIOS EMPLEADOS EN LA BIBLIA

Aunque varios eruditos bíblicos en los siglos pasados investigaron y estudiaron el tema de los géneros literarios, fueron voces muy aisladas[2]. Sin embargo, en la década de los 70 del siglo pasado este tema empezó a recibir su merecida atención, y en la de los 90 se convirtió en uno de los temas que más atención recibía.

¿Cuántos géneros literarios hay? Todos reconocen la diferencia entre los géneros de epístola, poesía y parábola, por nombrar algunos. Sin embargo, no existe un consenso entre los eruditos sobre la identificación de los diferentes géneros, el número de los que se utilizan en las Escrituras, ni cuáles son géneros principales y cuáles subgéneros de estos. Esta situación se debe en parte a que varios géneros se solapan, compartiendo algunas de sus características[3]. Además, cada erudito coloca en categorías los géneros que ha identificado con el propósito de ordenar más fácilmente la gran cantidad de material que existe en las Escrituras[4]. Lógicamente, si los eruditos no han podido llegar a un

---

2. Por ejemplo, Robert Lowth (1710–1787), obispo de la Iglesia de Inglaterra y profesor de Poesía de la Universidad de Oxford, fue el primero en emplear el término «paralelismo» para describir la característica fundamental de la poesía hebrea. Años después, Charles A. Briggs (1841–1913), erudito del A.T. y profesor del Union Theological Seminary, se quejó en su libro *General Introduction to the Study of the Holy Scripture* (Grand Rapids: Baker, 1970), p. 328, de que «ha habido una gran negligencia en cuanto al estudio de las Sagradas Escrituras como literatura en la sinagoga y en la iglesia. Pocos eruditos han prestado su atención a este tema».

3. Por ejemplo, aunque la profecía y el apocalíptico tienen mucho en común, son diferentes. De ahí que algunos los consideren dos géneros diferentes, siendo el apocalíptico una subcategoría de la profecía, mientras que otros creen que representan dos aspectos del mismo género (profético-apocalíptico).

4. Por ejemplo, en su libro *Hermenéutica: Entendiendo la Palabra de Dios* (Viladecavalls: CLIE, 2008), Duvall y Hays sugieren que el N.T. contiene cuatro géneros básicos: cartas (Epístolas), Evangelios, Hechos y Apocalipsis (pp. 309–421). En cuanto al A.T. Giese sugiere en su capítulo titulado «Literary Forms of the Old Testament» en *Cracking Old Testament Codes,* editado por Brent Sandy y Ronald Giese (Nashville: Broadman & Holman, 1995), que «la prosa es mejor vista como tres diferentes géneros: narración, historia y ley. La profecía, que típicamente es una combinación de prosa y poesía, es mejor vista como tres diferentes géneros: oráculos de salvación, declaraciones de juicio y apocalíptico. La poesía es mejor dividida en salmos de lamento y salmos de alabanza. Y la sabiduría es dividida en proverbial y sabiduría no proverbial» (p. 19).

consenso en cuanto a la identificación y número de géneros que existen en las Escrituras, aún menos consenso existe sobre su definición y número de categorías. No obstante, lo importante es que el intérprete sepa distinguir entre un género y otro, que sepa cuáles son las limitaciones y aportaciones de cada uno y cuáles son las reglas que debe emplear para interpretar correctamente cada uno de ellos. Un autor bíblico puede emplear varios géneros distintos en el mismo libro.

| **Algunos géneros en el libro de Isaías (NTV)** | |
|---|---|
| Historia | «Estas son las visiones que tuvo Isaías, hijo de Amoz, acerca de Judá y Jerusalén durante los años en que Uzías, Jotam, Acaz y Ezequías eran reyes de Judá.». (1:1) |
| Poesía | «¡Santo, santo, santo es el SEÑOR de los Ejércitos Celestiales! ¡Toda la tierra está llena de su gloria!». (6:3) |
| Profecía | «Fue oprimido y tratado con crueldad, sin embargo, no dijo ni una sola palabra. Como cordero fue llevado al matadero. Y como oveja en silencio ante sus trasquiladores, no abrió su boca.». (53:7 y Mt. 27:12; Lc. 23:9) |
| Parábola | «Ahora cantaré para aquel a quien amo un canto acerca de su viña. Mi amado tenía una viña en una colina rica y fértil...». (5:1-7) |
| Lenguaje figurado | «Vengan ahora. Vamos a resolver este asunto –dice el SEÑOR–. Aunque sus pecados sean como la escarlata, yo los haré tan blancos como la nieve. Aunque sean rojos como el carmesí, yo los haré tan blancos como la lana». (1:18) |
| Proverbio | «Pero los generosos proponen hacer lo que es generoso y se mantienen firmes en su generosidad». (32:8) |

Los dos géneros literarios más comunes en las Escrituras y más fácilmente reconocidos en cualquier literatura son la prosa y la poesía. Cuando un autor quiere comunicar un concepto con base en sus emociones, emplea la poesía, haciendo mucho uso del lenguaje figurado. Pero cuando quiere comunicar una idea con base en su intelecto, emplea la prosa, diciendo con un lenguaje literal lo que quiere decir. En la Biblia la prosa es empleada en géneros como la genealogía, epístola, ley, narración, etcétera, los cuales sirven como subgéneros de la prosa. De todos los subgéneros de la prosa, la narración predomina, ocupando más del 40 por ciento del A.T. y el 65 por ciento del N.T. Dado el amplio espacio que ocupa la narración, es menester que el intérprete sepa cómo funciona, qué es lo que puede aportar y cómo debe interpretarla. Trataremos otros géneros en próximos capítulos.

## B. LA NARRACIÓN

Los pasajes narrativos que describen eventos históricos ilustran varios conceptos teológicos. Por ejemplo: Dios ha intervenido repetidas veces en la historia humana; Dios ama a su pueblo y siempre busca lo mejor para él; aunque Dios odia el pecado, es pronto para perdonar los pecados de su pueblo cuando se arrepiente; y Dios está al control de la historia humana[5]. En cuanto a los pasajes narrativos que describen los actos y experiencias de los personajes bíblicos, Pablo afirma que fueron incluidos en las Escrituras «para nuestra enseñanza» (Ro. 15:4) y «para amonestarnos a nosotros» (1 Co. 10:11; ver también vv. 6-10). De ahí que los pasajes narrativos hayan servido como guía, consuelo, ánimo y corrección para el creyente.

Los autores de pasajes narrativos tratan los actos de estas personas de tres formas. Los autores de Reyes y Crónicas aportan un juicio *explícito* sobre los actos de los reyes de Israel y Judá, además de describir las consecuencias o bendiciones de esos actos para el pueblo de Dios. Pero en prácticamente todos los demás pasajes narrativos del A.T. el autor no dice nada explícito. A veces su juicio es más bien *implícito*. Por ejemplo, en Génesis 19:4-8 Moisés describe las pretensiones homosexuales de los varones de Sodoma con los dos ángeles que visitaban a Lot, y la decisión de Lot de ofrecerles sus dos hijas vírgenes para satisfacer sus apetitos sexuales. Aunque Moisés no condena explícitamente las pretensiones de estos hombres ni la sugerencia de Lot, es imposible leer este pasaje sin quedarse con la clara impresión de que

---

5. Doriani hace un énfasis sobre el elemento teológico de la narración en las pp. 87–89 de su libro *Putting the Truth to Work: The Theory and Practice of Biblical Application* (Phillipsburg: R. & R. Publishing, 2001). Pero en las pp. 193–194 lleva ese énfasis al extremo de rechazar la premisa de que los pasajes didácticos tienen preferencia sobre la narración a la hora de interpretar las Escrituras. No obstante, su libro tiene mucho que ofrecer. Para un repaso del movimiento de «la teología de la narración», lo cual encaja con el énfasis de Doriani, ver el artículo de Leslie Leland Fields, «Gospel is More Than Story» en *Christianity Today* (julio-agosto 2012), pp. 39–43.

las condena de forma implícita. La ceguera con la cual los ángeles afligieron a los hombres de Sodoma sería un detalle que apoya esa impresión. Pero frecuentemente los autores no indican de forma explícita ni implícita si los protagonistas actuaron correctamente o no. En ese caso el intérprete debe contar con la enseñanza clara de los textos didácticos de las Escrituras para evaluar los actos de dichas personas, porque el género epistolar pretende *explicar* conceptos éticos y teológicos con una precisión absoluta, mientras que en muchos casos la narración simplemente *describe* sus actos. El intérprete no debe concluir que el silencio del autor representa una aprobación de dichos actos.

## ¿Cuánto es normativo en Hechos?

Los pasajes narrativos del A.T. son tan inspirados por Dios como los del N.T. Sin embargo, todos suelen considerar los pasajes narrativos del N.T., y muy en particular los del libro de Hechos, como más válidos y aplicables a la iglesia y a su vida personal. Eso sucede probablemente porque el N.T. es la revelación final de Dios y, por tanto, la más completa, y porque trata el tema de la iglesia en lugar de Israel. El mayor reto de los pasajes narrativos de Hechos es el de determinar si lo que observamos es normativo para todas las iglesias y creyentes en cualquier siglo y cultura. Al tomar esa decisión, el intérprete tendrá que recordar que los primeros creyentes pasaban por un período de transición entre el antiguo y el nuevo pacto, lo cual provocó circunstancias y situaciones que difícilmente podrían repetirse en otros siglos y culturas.

Hay tres criterios que permiten al intérprete identificar lo que es normativo. Primero, si un acto fue provocado por una circunstancia puntual es muy probable que no sea normativo. Por ejemplo, unos días después del nacimiento de la iglesia en Hechos 2, los creyentes en Jerusalén decidieron tener todas sus pertenencias en común (Hch. 2:44-45). ¿A qué se debió esta decisión? Una de las posibles explicaciones de esa decisión es que muchos judíos de otros países habían llegado a Jerusalén para la fiesta de la Pascua. Durante su estancia allí presenciaron la crucifixión de Cristo, las señales que acompañaron ese evento, el milagro de las lenguas en el día de Pentecostés y la predicación de Pedro. Cuando muchos de ellos se convirtieron a Cristo, era lógico que muchos de ellos quisieran quedarse para ver lo que iba a ocurrir a continuación. Pero llegó el momento en que se agotaron sus recursos porque su plan original contemplaba un viaje de poca duración. ¿Qué iban a hacer los habitantes de Jerusalén con estos centenares de nuevos creyentes que no tenían qué comer? Cabe la posibilidad de que decidieran tener todas sus posesiones en común para suplir sus necesidades. Independientemente de cuál fuera la explicación correcta de su decisión, el hecho es que las iglesias en otros lugares no la consideraron normativa. Efesios 4:28 dice que el creyente debe trabajar no solamente para poner pan en su propia mesa, sino también para tener algo que compartir con quienes tengan necesidad, lo cual indica que los creyentes en Éfeso no consideraban como normativa la decisión de sus hermanos en Jerusalén. No obstante, este texto indica que el principio que motivó esa decisión seguía vigente; a saber, que todo creyente en cualquier siglo y cultura tiene la responsabilidad de suplir las necesidades de sus hermanos.

Segundo, si un acto es repetido a lo largo de varios años, ese hecho indicaría que se trata de una norma. Por ejemplo, aunque no existe ningún mandamiento explícito en Hechos o en las Epístolas de que los creyentes debían celebrar sus cultos el domingo, varios textos indican que es lo que hacían los apóstoles y las iglesias (Hch. 20:7). Luego, el mandamiento de Pablo unos años más tarde de que los corintios debían traer a la iglesia sus ofrendas el primer día de la semana indica que las iglesias seguían reuniéndose los domingos (1 Co. 16:1-2).

Tercero, el principio detrás de un acto podrá ser normativo para todo creyente en cualquier siglo y cultura, pero la expresión cultural de ese acto podrá ser diferente según cada cultura. Este criterio será tratado más ampliamente en el capítulo 24.

## La aplicación personal

¿Hasta qué punto es legítimo hacer una aplicación personal de la experiencia de un personaje bíblico cuando no se trata de una cuestión moral o teológica? Por ejemplo, Hechos 18:1-6 describe cómo Pablo evangelizaba en la ciudad de Corinto. Pero, al ver tanta oposición y tan pocos resultados, tomó la decisión de marcharse a otra ciudad al día siguiente. Sin embargo, esa noche el Señor le dijo en una visión:

«¡No tengas miedo! ¡Habla con libertad! ¡No te quedes callado! Pues yo estoy contigo, y nadie te atacará ni te hará daño, porque mucha gente de esta ciudad me pertenece» (Hch. 18:9-10, NTV). Antes de hacer una aplicación personal de esta clase de narración, el intérprete debe tener en cuenta dos principios. Primero, las experiencias muy personales de los personajes bíblicos en las cuales no está en juego ninguna cuestión moral ni teológica son precisamente eso; a saber, muy personales. Hacer una aplicación *directa* de un texto bíblico de esta naturaleza es muy cuestionable y arriesgado. Segundo, los pasajes didácticos deben interpretar los pasajes narrativos y tener preferencia sobre ellos porque su cometido principal es el de *enseñar* la verdad de Dios con toda claridad, mientras que los pasajes narrativos se limitan a *describir* las experiencias de los personajes bíblicos. Cualquier aplicación que se hace de una narración debe ser secundada por la enseñanza de un pasaje didáctico para evitar la pura subjetividad.

Por ejemplo, supongamos que un siervo de Dios que evangeliza en una ciudad se encuentra con las mismas circunstancias con las cuales se enfrentó el apóstol Pablo. Un día en su tiempo devocional le toca leer Hechos 18:9-10. ¿Debe entender que Dios lo está guiando a quedarse en esa ciudad? Decir que «sí» porque ha leído ese texto precisamente en ese momento es una respuesta muy inadecuada por dos motivos. (1) No existe ningún elemento moral ni teológico en la experiencia de Pablo en Corinto. Por tanto, no puede tener una aplicación para todos los siervos de Dios que pasan por la misma experiencia como si fuera un modelo a seguir. El mensaje que Pablo recibió en esa visión representaba la guía de Dios para él, no para cada siervo de Dios que leyera ese texto mientras se encontraba en circunstancias parecidas. (2) Si damos por sentado que este texto puede aplicarse a cualquier siervo de Dios, no existe ningún criterio objetivo para determinar si su lectura de este texto precisamente en ese momento representa la verdadera guía de Dios o una mera coincidencia. Como consecuencia, el intérprete corre el peligro de caer en la pura subjetividad, aplicando las palabras de cualquier texto sin tener en cuenta la intención del autor bíblico.

Es legítimo que un siervo de Dios abandone un ministerio en un lugar concreto si cree que ha hecho todo lo que está en su mano hacer, y que más vale ofrecer dicho ministerio a otras personas que posiblemente estén abiertas a recibirlo. Pero no con base en Hechos 18:9-10. No obstante, estos textos tienen una aplicación general. Por ejemplo, la experiencia de Pablo ilustra el hecho de que es posible equivocarse al abandonar precipitadamente un ministerio porque a veces Dios está realizando una obra que el siervo de Dios no puede ver en ese momento. A veces las apariencias engañan.

Puesto que los autores de los pasajes narrativos no siempre evaluaron explícitamente los actos y experiencias de los personajes, el intérprete debe apoyar su interpretación de esos actos y experiencias en los pasajes didácticos de las Escrituras. Aunque el género de epístola ocupa mucho menos espacio en la Biblia, su propósito es el de explicar de forma clara y explícita el comportamiento que Dios espera de sus hijos. Aunque ninguno de los capítulos encontrados en esta sección de la hermenéutica general lleva el título de «Epístola», en ellos se tratan los principios requeridos para interpretar correctamente ese género.

En este capítulo hemos visto las características, aportaciones y limitaciones del género de la narración. En los capítulos siguientes consideraremos otros géneros.

## *Trabajo para realizar*

¿Cuáles son las tres formas en que los autores bíblicos tratan los actos y experiencias de los personajes bíblicos? ¿Cuáles son los tres criterios que permiten al intérprete identificar lo que es normativo para la iglesia y para su vida personal en un pasaje narrativo?

# 8

# Trasfondo histórico y cultural

El 30 de septiembre de 1993 apareció en *El Periódico de Catalunya*[1] una viñeta humorística en la cual un hombre decía: «Después de los JJ. OO., resulta que soy de BCN y vivo en la V.O. Además, tengo un VW, mis discos son CD, el video VHS y veo las TN en la TV. Un hijo estudia EGB, el otro BUP y el tercero COU. Mi mujer trabaja en la IBM, yo soy ATS, pero ahora cobro del INEM. Fumo L&M y bebo J&B. Admiro a los EE. UU. Confío en la CE, pero no apoyo a la OTAN, aunque me cae bien la ONU. Voto PSC, soy de CC. OO. y odio al PP».

¿Cuántas de estas abreviaturas podría identificar *hoy un catalán*? ¿Cuántas un *español* que vive en otra región de España *dentro de un año*? Y, ¿cuántas un *japonés* que reside en su país y no conoce el español *dentro de 2000 a 3400 años?*[2] ¡Esta es precisamente la situación en

---

1. Un diario que se vende en las cuatro provincias catalanas de España.

2. JJ. OO. (Juegos Olímpicos, los cuales se celebraron en Barcelona en 1992); BCN (Barcelona); V.O. (Villa Olímpica donde se hospedaron los atletas); VW (Volkswagen); CD (Compact disc); VHS (Videocassette Home System, un sistema de video que ya ha quedado obsoleto); TN (*Telenoticias*, un programa de noticias de la televisión española); TV (televisión); EGB (Educación General Básica); BUP (Bachillerato Unificado Polivalente); COU (Curso de Orientación Universitaria); IBM

la cual el intérprete de la Biblia se encuentra hoy! Puesto que Moisés escribió el Pentateuco c. 1400 a. C. y Juan el libro de Apocalipsis c. 90–95 d. C., existe una distancia histórica y cultural de unos veinte a treinta y cinco siglos entre el intérprete del siglo XXI y los autores bíblicos. Frente a ese desafío, hay quienes creen que es imposible entender la Biblia. Sin embargo, esa opinión es derrumbada por dos hechos.

Primero, mucho de nuestro conocimiento del trasfondo histórico y cultural de los tiempos bíblicos se encuentra en la propia Biblia. Hay un consenso entre los eruditos bíblicos de que Marcos dirigió su Evangelio a los romanos. Por eso, explica ciertas costumbres de los judíos que un romano típico no entendería (7:2-4; 14:12; 15:42), traduce palabras arameas (5:41; 7:11, 34; 12:42; 15:22, 34), dice que el Jordán es un río (1:5) e indica que el monte de los Olivos está delante del templo (13:3). Y cuando los fariseos y escribas preguntan por qué Jesús y sus discípulos no lavan sus manos antes de comer, Marcos explica que no se trata de una cuestión de higiene, sino de una ceremonia religiosa establecida por los fariseos (7:1-5).

Segundo, la Biblia no es la historia de todo lo que ha pasado, sino la historia de la redención del ser humano. Por tanto, no explica el trasfondo histórico y cultural de cada pasaje. No obstante, desde el nacimiento de la ciencia de la arqueología a comienzos del siglo XIX, los arqueólogos han hecho tantos descubrimientos que ha sido posible identificar el trasfondo histórico y cultural de la gran mayoría de los textos bíblicos. Y, en los pocos pasajes donde queda alguna incógnita, no hay en juego ninguna doctrina ni enseñanza esencial de la Biblia.

## A. EL IMPORTANTE PAPEL DE LA ARQUEOLOGÍA

Cuando la ciencia de la arqueología comenzaba a establecerse a principios del siglo XIX, los eruditos bíblicos evangélicos estaban divididos

---

(International Business Machines); ATS (Ayudante Técnico Sanitario); INEM (Instituto Nacional de Empleo); L&M (la marca de tabaco Liggett & Myers); J&B (la marca de whisky escocés Justerini & Brooks, Ltd.); EE. UU. (Estados Unidos); CE (Comunidad Europea); OTAN (Organización del Tratado del Atlántico del Norte); ONU (Organización de las Naciones Unidas); PSC (el partido político Partido Socialista de Cataluña); CC. OO. (el sindicado laboral Comisiones Obreras); PP (el partido político Partido Popular).

en cuanto a su utilidad para la interpretación de la Biblia. Algunos la rechazaron porque tenían un aprecio tan alto por el estudio literario y lingüístico de las Escrituras que eran incapaces de ver la gran aportación que podía hacer a su entendimiento de los idiomas bíblicos y del trasfondo histórico y cultural de la Biblia. Pero otros la abrazaron con entusiasmo como un medio para demostrar con pruebas tangibles que la Biblia tenía razón.

Al principio del siglo XX los arqueólogos evangélicos habían llegado a creer que los descubrimientos arqueológicos apoyarían los datos bíblicos y nunca los contradecirían, una posición que todos los evangélicos mantienen hoy. Pero igual que los altos críticos manipulaban los descubrimientos arqueológicos para rechazar las afirmaciones bíblicas, algunos evangélicos llegaron al otro extremo de reclamar pruebas de la veracidad de la Biblia donde no existían. Por ejemplo, en la década de los 30 el arqueólogo John Garstang afirmó que había encontrado los muros de Jericó que cayeron cuando los judíos conquistaron Canaán (Jos. 6). Los evangélicos estaban eufóricos, hasta que otro arqueólogo demostró en la década de los 50 que dichas ruinas pertenecían a ¡un milenio después de los tiempos de Josué!

Era un error fácil de cometer puesto que las normas y técnicas de la ciencia de la arqueología aún eran rudimentarias. Pero este ejemplo y otros similares plantean una pregunta muy importante: ¿cuál es la aportación principal que la arqueología puede hacer a la interpretación bíblica y cuáles son sus limitaciones? Su mayor aportación es la de proveer una información general sobre el trasfondo histórico y cultural de los tiempos bíblicos. Sin esa información muchos pasajes serían difíciles de entender. Además, es capaz de confirmar los datos bíblicos. Por ejemplo, en 1854 comenzaron las excavaciones de la ciudad antigua de Ur de los caldeos en el sur de Mesopotamia (hoy Iraq), donde vivía Abraham antes de marcharse a Canaán. Los arqueólogos demostraron que la ciudad contaba con una sociedad muy desarrollada. En 1928 fue descubierta la ciudad fenicia portuaria de Ugarit en la costa este del Mediterráneo, además de Mari, una ciudad encontrada a la orilla del río Éufrates en Siria. Algunos altos críticos habían afirmado que la descripción del entorno social y económico de Abraham en Génesis no era histórica, sino una leyenda folklórica. Sin embargo, las excavaciones en Ugarit y Mari demostraron que dicha descripción coincidía con las costumbres del tiempo. En 1896 los arqueólogos encontraron unas tablas en Nuzi, una ciudad antigua de Mesopotamia que fue fundada a finales del siglo XXIII a. C. Las excavaciones comenzaron en serio en 1925. Desde entonces se han encontrado unas cinco mil tablas, la mayoría de ellas del siglo XXII a. C., la época en que Abraham vivía.

> La búsqueda por parte de Sara de un heredero mediante su sierva egipcia Agar, su acto legal de echar a Agar de la casa cuando nació Isaac, el acto de Abraham de adoptar a Eliezer como su heredero, la venta despreciativa de Esaú de su primogenitura, los acuerdos que hicieron Labán y Jacob, el intento por parte de Raquel de confirmar la sucesión al robar el terafín[3] y el otorgamiento irrevocable de la bendición de Isaac, todos estos datos encuentran un paralelo detallado en las tablas de Nuzi. Las historias de los patriarcas son evidentemente historias auténticas que necesitan interpretarse como tal. El relato de Génesis es vindicado como un relato fiable[4].

Lo que la arqueología no puede hacer es probar que Abraham vivía en Ur ni que los patriarcas realmente existieron. Como dice Hoerth: «En el caso de que se pudiera probar que los autores bíblicos fueran historiadores infalibles, este hecho aumentaría la *probabilidad* de que su mensaje teológico fuera verdad, pero nada más»[5]. La arqueología puede descubrir ciudades escondidas bajo el desierto durante siglos enteros y confirmar que los datos bíblicos sobre esas ciudades son verídicos. Pero «una evidencia material es raras veces capaz siquiera de confirmar que un evento específico ocurrió y aún menos proveernos de guía en cuanto al significado o una interpretación de ese evento»[6].

---

3. Esta palabra es traducida como «dioses» en la RVR60 y LBLA.
4. E. M. Blaiklock, «The Use of Archaeology in Interpretation» en *Hermeneutics* (Grand Rapids: Baker, 1972), p. 57.
5. Alfred J. Hoerth, «Archaeology and the Christian Mind» en *Interpreting the Word of God* (Chicago: Moody Press, 1970), p. 35.
6. V. Phillips Long, «History and Hermeneutics: How Then Should We Read the Bible "Historically"?» en *Foundations of Contemporary Interpretation*, ed. Moisés Silva (Grand Rapids: Zondervan, 1996), p. 401.

La arqueología no es en sí una herramienta apologética de nuestra fe, sino una fuente de información que puede confirmar ciertos datos históricos e informarnos sobre detalles culturales. No obstante, no deja de tener un gran valor apologético cuando confirma lo que dijo la Biblia hace muchos siglos. Por ejemplo, W. M. Ramsay (1851–1939), que era un gran historiador británico, por ser agnóstico se dedicó a demostrar que la Biblia estaba equivocada. Pero al descubrir que toda la evidencia arqueológica confirmaba los datos históricos y culturales citados en Lucas y Hechos, se convirtió a Cristo y llegó a ser un eminente erudito del N.T.[7]

## B. NORMAS PARA EL USO CORRECTO DEL TRASFONDO HISTÓRICO Y CULTURAL

No todos los textos bíblicos requieren que el intérprete sepa algo de su trasfondo histórico o cultural para entenderlos, porque en muchos casos la cultura del intérprete y la de los tiempos bíblicos tienen mucho en común. Las necesidades del hombre son iguales en todos los siglos y culturas. No obstante, ese trasfondo actúa como un muro de contención contra la tendencia del ser humano de imponer sobre el texto su propia cultura. Al recoger y emplear material sobre el trasfondo de un texto bíblico, hay varios principios que el intérprete debe respetar.

*1. Asegurar que el material sea aplicable al texto que está interpretando.* Fee dice que esta norma «es con creces el paso más crucial de la exégesis, pero a la vez el más difícil de "enseñar" y sobre el que hacer reglas»[8]. Por ejemplo, el contexto de los Evangelios y Hechos 1–12 es netamente judío, mientras que las Epístolas y Apocalipsis se sitúan en un mundo greco-romano. Aunque estos dos mundos se solapan a

7. De los muchos libros que Ramsey escribió, tres de los más apreciados son *St. Paul the Traveler and Roman Citizen* (1895), *The Cities of Paul* (1907) y *Letters to the Seven Churches of Asia* (1904). Todos son una mina de información sobre el trasfondo histórico y cultural del primer siglo. Desafortunadamente, estos libros no han sido traducidos al español.

8. Gordon D. Fee, *New Testament Exegesis* (Louisville: Westminster/John Knox Press, 1993), p. 121.

veces, representan dos contextos culturales diferentes. Por tanto, no se debe aplicar un detalle de un contexto judío en Palestina a una congregación de gentiles ubicada en una ciudad romana.

También hay textos que tienen una aplicación local, pero no universal. Algunos eruditos bíblicos creen que el trasfondo cultural detrás de la exhortación de Pablo de que las mujeres que profetizan en el culto deben cubrir su cabeza (1 Co. 11:26) es el gran número de prostitutas que servían como sacerdotisas en el templo de la diosa griega Afrodita en Corinto. Esas sacerdotisas llevaban el pelo suelto. Pablo no quería que un no creyente entrara en la iglesia y pensara que las mujeres cristianas eran iguales que las de la secta de la diosa Afrodita. Pablo no quería que las mujeres creyentes se pareciesen a las prostitutas. Si este es el caso, la exhortación de Pablo no tendría una aplicación universal, sino solamente local.

*2. Dejar que el texto tenga preferencia sobre el trasfondo histórico y cultural.* El texto es lo importante, no el trasfondo, por necesario, interesante y espectacular que este sea. El trasfondo puede iluminar un texto, pero nunca debe colocarse en un lugar de preeminencia. El trasfondo es el siervo del texto, no al revés.

*3. Resistir la tentación de precipitarse en el uso de un nuevo descubrimiento arqueológico como prueba de una afirmación bíblica.* En demasiadas ocasiones ha aparecido más tarde una información más completa que ha desacreditado la supuesta prueba. Cuando esto ocurre, las demás interpretaciones de la persona en cuestión son colocadas en tela de juicio. El consejo de Fee al respecto es muy sabio:

> Debería notarse como medida de precaución que mucha de la literatura sobre el trasfondo bíblico nos ha llegado por circunstancias fortuitas y que mucha de la información a nuestra disposición ha sido recogida y organizada con base en una variedad de fuentes que reflejan solamente un porcentaje pequeño de todo lo que fue escrito en la antigüedad. Mientras que es legítimo sacar conclusiones de la información que tenemos, en muchas ocasiones esas conclusiones deberían presentarse con menos dogmatismo de lo que los eruditos del N.T. están propensos a hacer[9].

9. Ibid., p. 123.

| **Normas para el uso del trasfondo histórico y cultural** |
|---|
| 1. Asegurar que el material sea aplicable al texto que está interpretando.<br>2. Dejar que el texto tenga preferencia sobre el trasfondo histórico y cultural.<br>3. Resistir la tentación de precipitarse en el uso de un nuevo descubrimiento arqueológico como prueba de una afirmación bíblica.<br>4. Emplear con precisión y honestidad la información sobre el trasfondo. |

*4. Emplear con precisión y honestidad la información sobre el trasfondo.* Hay quienes han defendido la homosexualidad argumentando que Pablo la condenó porque en el primer siglo la homosexualidad se practicaba en el contexto de la idolatría. Y, puesto que los homosexuales que afirman ser creyentes no practican la homosexualidad dentro de ese entorno, concluyen que la homosexualidad es legítima. Es verdad que la prostitución masculina se practicaba en ciertas sectas paganas del primer siglo. Sin embargo, también es verdad que la homosexualidad estaba muy extendida en la sociedad griega y en ciertos sectores de la sociedad romana donde no se asociaba de ninguna forma con ritos idólatras. Y, puesto que Pablo no distingue entre la homosexualidad que se practica en un contexto religioso y los actos homosexuales cometidos en un entorno privado, la condenación del apóstol es aplicable a los dos contextos.

## C. TRES LLAVES QUE ABREN LA PUERTA DEL TRASFONDO

Si un texto bíblico tiene un trasfondo histórico o cultural que el intérprete necesita conocer para interpretarlo correctamente, este tiene a su disposición tres llaves para abrir la puerta de ese trasfondo. En algunos textos necesitará solamente una de estas llaves, mientras que en otros textos puede que necesite más de una.

### La ocasión

¿Cuál era el problema que motivó al autor bíblico a escribir su libro? ¿Cuál era la pregunta que los primeros lectores habían pedido que contestara o la dificultad o situación en la cual se encontraban? Esta llave es especialmente útil para abrir la puerta del fondo histórico y cultural de los libros proféticos del A.T. y las Epístolas del N.T. por ser muy ocasionales. Por ejemplo, Pablo consuela a los efesios con respecto a su encarcelamiento ¡en tres ocasiones! (Ef. 3:1, 13; 4:1), con toda probabilidad porque uno de los miembros de esa congregación tuvo algo que ver con sus prisiones (Hch. 21:27-29). ¿Cómo se sentiría usted si el predicador o evangelista más reconocido de su país estuviera en la cárcel por algo que había hecho uno de los miembros de su congregación? Esta es precisamente la situación de la iglesia en Éfeso.

Muchos profetas identifican en los primeros versículos de sus libros a los reyes que gobernaban cuando ellos escribieron su profecía. En efecto, estos profetas ruegan al intérprete que consulte 1–2 Reyes, 1–2 Crónicas y cualquier fuente extrabíblica disponible para informarse de la situación espiritual y política de esos reyes. Isaías dice que profetizó durante los reinados de Uzías, Jotam, Acaz y Ezequías, reyes de Judá (1:1). Limitándonos al rey Uzías (Azarías), observamos:

| **Uzías/Azarías** | |
|---|---|
| *Situación espiritual* | *Situación política* |
| 1. «Hizo lo que era agradable» (2 R. 15:3, NTV)<br>• «Mientras el rey buscó la dirección del SEÑOR, Dios le dio éxito» (2 Cr. 26:5, NTV).<br>• Bendecido hasta que se hizo poderoso (2 Cr. 26:15-16).<br>2. Sus pecados<br>• Dejó los lugares altos (2 R. 15:4).<br>• Entró en el templo para ofrecer incienso sobre el altar de incienso (2 Cr. 26:16-18).<br>3. Los profetas<br>• Isaías (2 Cr. 26:22) y Zacarías (no del libro canónico), «quien le enseñó a temer a Dios» (2 Cr. 26:5, NTV). Era un profeta «entendido en visiones de Dios» (RVR60).<br>• Is. 1:1; Os. 1:1; Am. 1:1. | 1. Hijo de Amasías. Reinó 52 años (2 R. 15:1-2).<br>2. Recupera Elat para Judá (2 R. 14:22; 2 Cr. 26:2).<br>3. Derrota a los filisteos y árabes (2 Cr. 26:7).<br>4. Los amonitas le daban «presentes»; (2 Cr. 26:8, RVR-60); o sea, «le pagaban un tributo anual» (NTV).<br>5. Se hizo muy poderoso (2 Cr. 26:8).<br>6. Hizo muchas obras públicas (2 Cr. 26:10). |

Toda esta información provee una base para entender el libro de Isaías. Lamentablemente, hay quienes no quieren realizar todo este trabajo y se lanzan a interpretar el texto. Pero, por desconocer el trasfondo histórico de este libro, no entienden a qué se refiere el profeta. Como resultado, caen fácilmente en la tentación de espiritualizar o alegorizar dichos textos. Todo este proceso ilustra el hecho de que no hay atajos en el verdadero estudio de las Escrituras.

## La situación o estado inmediato del autor

¿Dónde se encuentra el autor? ¿Qué hace? ¿Cuál es su estado anímico? Esta llave es especialmente útil para abrir la puerta del fondo histórico y cultural de los libros poéticos (en particular Job y Salmos), puesto que destacan la vida, experiencia y sentimientos del autor.

Sin entender la situación inmediata del autor, las palabras del Salmo 3:5 tienen poco sentido («Yo me acosté y dormí, y desperté, porque Jehová me sustentaba»), puesto que hay millones de personas que se acuestan cada noche y se despiertan la mañana siguiente sin contar con la ayuda de Dios. La tradición hebrea que encabeza este salmo sugiere que se trata de aquel momento cuando Absalón perseguía a David para matarlo (2 S. 15:7-17). Al acostarse cada noche, David se preguntaba si viviría para ver el amanecer del día siguiente. ¿Cuántas personas no pueden dormir debido a los problemas que tienen? Pablo tuvo ese problema. Su preocupación por las iglesias le quitó mucho sueño (2 Co. 11:27-28). La experiencia de perder el sueño es justificada en algunas situaciones. No obstante, la otra cara de esa moneda es que David dormía muy bien porque confiaba en Dios.

Sabiendo que la Epístola a los Filipenses fue escrita por Pablo desde la cárcel, sus exhortaciones a ser gozoso son muy significativas. Si esas exhortaciones hubiesen sido escritas por un creyente que vivía en un palacio, no tendrían el mismo impacto. Pero ¿cómo se puede tener gozo cuando uno se encuentra en la cárcel? La felicidad y el gozo no son sinónimos. La felicidad se produce cuando todo va bien. Depende de las circunstancias, las cuales no podemos controlar del todo. Por el contrario, el gozo consiste en una tranquilidad y contentamiento que proviene de Dios a pesar de las circunstancias. «Grande es tu fidelidad» es el himno favorito de muchos creyentes en todo el mundo.

Cuando cantamos las palabras «Oh, Dios eterno, tu misericordia ni una sombra de duda tendrá. Tu compasión y bondad nunca fallan y por los siglos el mismo serás», solemos pensar en aquellos momentos de necesidad cuando Dios intervino y nos dio lo que hacía falta. Pero al notar que las palabras de este himno se basan en Lamentaciones 3:22-23, donde Jeremías describe cómo Dios destruye la ciudad de Jerusalén a manos de los babilonios, estas palabras cobran más significado. Dios sigue fiel aun cuando las circunstancias de nuestra vida vayan de mal en peor.

## La cultura

Es imprescindible que el intérprete entienda tanto como pueda de la historia y cultura que hay detrás del texto porque toda la Biblia fue escrita dentro de un contexto histórico y cultural. No hay otro libro religioso que cuente con tanto texto histórico como la Biblia. «La "interpretación literal" cojea sin la ayuda de los estudios sobre la cultura. Igual que la historia bíblica, las cuestiones culturales no son pequeños detalles que podemos buscar si tenemos el tiempo o ignorar bajo la presión del tiempo y las circunstancias. Las cuestiones culturales son indispensables para un entendimiento preciso de las Sagradas Escrituras».

Por ejemplo, en 1 Samuel 12:17 Samuel pide que Dios envíe truenos y lluvias durante el tiempo de la cosecha (desde mediados de abril hasta mediados de mayo). En principio parece ser una petición como cualquier otra, hasta que uno se da cuenta de que nunca llovía entre los meses de abril y octubre. Sabiendo eso, uno concluye que Samuel pedía un verdadero milagro. En Apocalipsis 3:17-18 Jesús critica a los habitantes de Laodicea por su autosuficiencia y arrogancia. Al saber que esa ciudad era famosa por su riqueza, textiles finos y pomadas medicinales, entendemos por qué Jesús los condena precisamente por esos dos pecados; a saber, la autosuficiencia y arrogancia son dos de las mayores tentaciones de los ricos. Los pobres luchan con otras tentaciones propias de su estado económico.

## En resumen

La tarea de recoger información sobre el trasfondo histórico y cultural de los tiempos bíblicos nunca acaba, porque los arqueólogos siguen descubriendo nueva información. Por eso es importante que el intérprete consulte los libros más recientes y mejor documentados. No obstante, a veces una obra publicada hace unos años tendrá una información valiosa que las nuevas publicaciones no incluyen entre sus páginas. Las fuentes que más información aportarán al intérprete, en orden de importancia, son los libros sobre costumbres bíblicas, revistas sobre los descubrimientos arqueológicos, diccionarios y enciclopedias bíblicas y comentarios bíblicos de índole general y técnico.

La aportación que la arqueología ha hecho a nuestro entendimiento de las Escrituras ha sido excepcional. No obstante, no es razonable esperar que los arqueólogos encuentren un número suficiente de enseres, inscripciones y obras literarias con 2000 a 3400 años de antigüedad para resolver todas las incógnitas que existen en la Biblia. Yamauchi, un reconocido arqueólogo evangélico, opina que «no sería una exageración decir que lo que hemos podido encontrar representa una fracción de una fracción de toda la posible evidencia». Solamente un pequeño porcentaje de los objetos que existían en tiempos bíblicos ha sobrevivido. De los que aún existen, solamente un pequeño porcentaje de ellos ha sido localizado. De los que han sido localizados, solamente un pequeño porcentaje ha sido excavado. Y de ese porcentaje tan pequeño que ha sido excavado, solamente un pequeño porcentaje ha sido examinado. Por tanto, Yamauchi calcula que tenemos acceso a solamente un 0,006 por ciento «de toda la posible evidencia». No obstante, conviene recordar que el mensaje principal de la Biblia queda más que claro y que la cantidad de objetos e inscripciones que han sido descubiertos hasta el momento nos han permitido entender una gran parte de los textos que requieren una información que las Escrituras no aportan.

## *Trabajo para realizar*

1. A pesar de la gran aportación que la arqueología hace a nuestro entendimiento de la Biblia, tiene sus limitaciones. Cite algunas de esas limitaciones. Hay tres llaves que el intérprete tiene a su disposición para abrir la puerta del trasfondo histórico y cultural de un texto. ¿Cuáles son?
2. Para que se familiarice con las fuentes que proveen información sobre las costumbres y cultura de los tiempos bíblicos, visite un seminario o librería evangélica y consulte al menos un libro de cada una de estas fuentes sobre la forma en que los judíos celebraban sus bodas. Antes de consultar estas fuentes, el lector debe consultar una concordancia completa para encontrar los textos donde aparecen palabras como *boda, matrimonio, desposar*, etcétera, las cuales aparecen en textos como Mateo 22:1-14; 25:1-13; Lucas 12:35-40; Juan 2:1-12; etcétera.
   - Libros sobre costumbres.
   - Diccionarios bíblicos. Buscar palabras como *boda, matrimonio, desposar*, etcétera.
   - Comentarios bíblicos que sean generales o técnicos, dirigiéndose a los textos donde aparecen palabras como *boda, matrimonio, desposar*, etcétera.

# 9

# Tema del libro

La mayoría de los libros bíblicos tienen un «hilo», un tema principal que une sus párrafos en una composición unida y coherente. Al identificar el tema de un libro, el intérprete verá más claramente la relación que existe entre los párrafos, y las frases y palabras de cada párrafo tendrán más sentido. Juan y Lucas identifican de forma clara cuál es el tema de sus libros (Lc. 1:1-4; Jn. 20:31; Hch. 1:1; 1 Jn. 1:4; 2:1; 5:13). Sin embargo, el intérprete tendrá que excavar como un arqueólogo para descubrir el tema de los demás libros, porque ese tesoro no se encuentra en la superficie. Para descubrir el tema de un libro, el intérprete debe seguir dos pasos, los cuales representan dos caras de una misma moneda y que se realizan simultáneamente.

## A. LEER EL LIBRO REPETIDAS VECES

Una anécdota personal del autor de *Con precisión* ilustra la gran importancia de este paso. En un momento determinado de mi ministerio docente me tocó impartir una asignatura sobre los profetas menores. Después de leer el texto de cada profeta, identificar el tema principal y hacer un bosquejo que reflejaba el tema de cada profeta, consulté los comentarios que tenía en mi biblioteca personal. Tenía dos o tres libros de G. Campbell Morgan (1863–1945), un reconocido pastor y expositor de la Biblia. Uno de ellos era *The Minor Prophets* [Los profetas menores]. Sus páginas son pequeñas, el libro cuenta con solamente

157 páginas, y además reproduce el texto de cada profeta menor. Por tanto, no esperaba encontrar gran cosa. Pero nada más repasar sus bosquejos de cada profeta, me quedé atónito porque Morgan captaba con una precisión impresionante el tema principal de cada libro y la manera en que cada párrafo encajaba dentro de ese tema. No pude hacer otra cosa que decir: «Tiene toda la razón; su bosquejo refleja lo que dice el texto. Es tan obvio. ¿Cómo es que no lo vi yo?». Entonces, recordé que Morgan tenía la costumbre de leer un libro bíblico ¡cincuenta veces! antes de predicar una serie de sermones o enseñar unas clases sobre ello. La respuesta a mi pregunta era obvia: no había leído el texto tantas veces como Morgan.

No existen atajos en el estudio serio de la Biblia. El primer paso que el intérprete tiene que dar para descubrir el tema de un libro *no es* el de consultar unos comentarios bíblicos, sino el de leer una y otra vez el libro hasta dar con dicho tema. Si le cuesta diez lecturas del libro encontrarlo, que sean diez las veces que lo lee. Si quince, pues quince. El sudor intelectual es imprescindible.

## B. FIJARSE EN LAS INDICACIONES DEL AUTOR

Durante su lectura de un libro, hay cuatro preguntas que ayudarán al intérprete a identificar el tema. Primera, ¿indica el autor cuál es el tema de su libro como el apóstol Juan suele hacer? Segunda, ¿cuáles son las palabras, frases y conceptos que se repiten una y otra vez? Es de suponer que una palabra que aparece frecuentemente tendrá algo que ver con el tema principal. Se requerirá una atención más intensa para identificar los conceptos que se repiten, porque cada frase empleará palabras diferentes. Tercera, ¿cuál es el tema que ocupa el mayor número de versículos? Cuarta, ¿cuál era la necesidad que tenían los lectores originales, la pregunta que hicieron al autor, la doctrina que no entendían, etcétera? Veamos cómo emplear este paso en los casos de Filipenses y 1 Juan.

> «Pero estas se escribieron para que ustedes continúen creyendo que Jesús es el Mesías, el Hijo de Dios, y para que, al creer en él, tengan vida por el poder de su nombre».
>
> **(Jn. 20:31, NTV)**

## Filipenses

Pablo escribió esta Epístola para dar las gracias a los filipenses por su donativo (1:4-5; 4:10-19). Sin embargo, dedica la mayor parte del texto a otro tema. Algunos sugieren que el tema principal es «el gozo», por cuanto esa palabra se repite muchas veces (1:4, 18, 25; 2:2, 17-18, 28-29; 4:1, 4, 10). De todas las Epístolas de Pablo, es la que más énfasis hace sobre el gozo. Sin embargo, el autor de *Con precisión* sugiere que el tema es «la unidad» con base en las siguientes consideraciones.

En primer lugar, las exhortaciones a tener «un mismo sentir» (1:27; 2:2; 3:15-16; 4:2). La LBLA traduce estos versículos con las frases *un mismo espíritu, un mismo propósito, una misma actitud, una misma norma, vivan en armonía*, ilustrando el hecho de que a veces el tema de un libro se descubre mediante unas frases que comunican el mismo concepto. En segundo lugar, Pablo saluda a «*todos* los santos» (1:1, énfasis añadido), la única vez que emplea la palabra «todos» en los saludos de sus Epístolas. Al dirigirse a *todos* los miembros de la iglesia en Filipo, promueve la unidad entre los miembros de esa congregación. La idea de «todos» se repite en 1:4, 7-8, 25; 2:17, 26. En tercer lugar, la exhortación de Pablo a Evodia y Síntique a dejar de pelearse (4:2). En cuarto lugar, Pablo incluyó en esta epístola la mención plena de la encarnación de Cristo (2:1-11) no porque existiera un error doctrinal en la iglesia con respeto a esta doctrina, sino porque había algo en la encarnación de Cristo que Pablo quería que los filipenses imitaran: a saber, que Cristo no se quedó en el cielo, velando por sus propios intereses, sino que los dejó a un lado para dedicarse a nuestra necesidad de salvación. «Haya, pues, en vosotros este sentir que hubo también en Cristo Jesús» (2:5), porque una de las cosas que destruye la unidad de una iglesia es la práctica de algunos miembros de velar solamente por sus propios intereses.

## 1 Juan

Algunos sugieren que el tema principal de 1 Juan es «el amor» porque Juan habla repetidamente de ello (2:5, 10, 15; 3:1, 10, 11, 14-18, 23; 4:7-12, 16-21; 5:1-3). Pero si el tema de un libro se determina por la palabra que se repite más, tendría que tener algo que ver con los conceptos tan íntimamente relacionados de «saber, conocer, confianza, asegurar».

- saber: 2:3, 5, 11, 29; 3:2, 5, 14, 15, 20, 24; 5:13, 15, 18, 19, 20
- conocer: 2:3, 4, 3-14, 18, 20, 21; 3:6, 16, 19; 4:2, 6, 7, 8, 13, 16; 5:2, 20
- confianza: 3:21; 4:17; 5:14
- asegurar: 3:19

Mirando el texto más de cerca, notamos que Juan identifica tres temas diferentes: «para que vuestro gozo sea cumplido» (1:4); «para que no pequéis» (2:1); y «para que sepáis que tenéis vida eterna» (5:13). ¿Cómo puede haber más de un tema principal, especialmente en una epístola de solo cinco capítulos?

Hay consenso entre los eruditos bíblicos de que el gnosticismo representa el trasfondo de esta epístola puesto que las doctrinas que Juan subraya contrarrestan las doctrinas de esa secta pagana. Aparentemente, el gnosticismo había hecho tanta mella en los creyentes a quienes Juan escribe que tenían dudas en cuanto a su salvación. Por eso, Juan dice que les escribe «para que sepáis que tenéis vida eterna» (5:13). Es evidente que son creyentes porque se dirige a ellos con las palabras: «vosotros que creéis en el nombre del Hijo de Dios». Pero no estaban seguros de que poseían la salvación. Por eso hace tanto énfasis sobre *conocer, saber, confianza, asegurar.* Tener dudas sobre su salvación roba al creyente su gozo. De ahí que Juan diga que les escribe «para que vuestro gozo sea cumplido» (1:4). Además, los creyentes que dudan de su salvación suelen caer en la trampa de creer que su salvación depende de ellos. Por consiguiente, procuran alcanzar una vida más santa por sus propios esfuerzos. Pero, puesto que la vida cristiana se vive con base en la fe, no en los propios esfuerzos (Col. 2:6), caen una y otra vez en el pecado. De ahí que Juan diga que les escribe «para que no pequéis» (2:1).

Por todos estos motivos el autor cree que el tema principal de 1 Juan es «la certeza de la salvación». Para ayudar a estos creyentes, Juan les da una serie de pruebas objetivas que indican quiénes son de Cristo. (1) El creyente guarda los mandamientos de Dios (2:3-5). No practica el pecado, sino la justicia (3:8-10). Aunque el creyente sigue pecando debido a la naturaleza pecaminosa que todavía tiene, el rumbo de su vida es marcadamente distinto al que tenía cuando no conocía a Cristo como su Salvador. (2) El creyente se congrega con los hermanos (2:18-19). Aquel que dice ser creyente pero nunca se congrega con otros creyentes levanta sospechas legítimas. No obstante, es Dios quien sabe a ciencia cierta quiénes son hijos suyos. (3) El creyente cree que Jesús es el Hijo de Dios, una doctrina que los gnósticos rechazaban (5:4-5). (4) El creyente ama a los hermanos (3:13-14).

Si la certeza de la salvación es el tema de 1 Juan, ¿por qué hace tanto énfasis sobre el amor? Porque de todas las pruebas objetivas que Juan podría haber citado para identificar a quiénes son creyentes, el amor es la prueba suprema. Por algo Juan es el único evangelista que cita las palabras de Jesús: «El amor que tengan unos por otros será la prueba ante el mundo de que son mis discípulos» (Jn. 13:35, NTV).

## *Trabajo para realizar*

1. La tarea de descubrir el tema de un libro bíblico cuenta con dos pasos que en efecto representan dos caras de una misma moneda y que se realizan simultáneamente. ¿Cuáles son esos dos pasos? ¿Por qué es tan importante que el intérprete evite la tentación de saltar directamente a los comentarios bíblicos y ahorrarse mucho tiempo?

2. De todos los trabajos que el autor recomienda que el lector haga en este libro, este y el del capítulo siguiente son, en su opinión, los más importantes. Tienen como propósito introducir al lector en los pasos que ha de seguir para encontrar el tema principal de un libro y la forma en que el autor bíblico desarrolla ese tema (bosquejo). En ningún momento debe el lector consultar libros de bosquejos, comentarios bíblicos o la «Guía de estudio» para realizar este trabajo.

Lea Efesios 1–3 *tres* veces en la RVR60, procurando leer con atención y discernimiento. Esta lectura debe realizarse de una vez. Si tiene la posibilidad de fotocopiar Efesios 1–3 en la RVR60, LBLA y NTV, el autor le recomienda que subraye las palabras, frases y conceptos que se repiten una y otra vez.

Lea Efesios 1–3 *tres* veces en la NTV. Esta lectura debe realizarse de un tirón. Con esta lectura el lector debe comenzar a reconocer palabras o una combinación de dos o tres palabras que se refieren al mismo tema.

Lea Efesios 1–3 *tres* veces en la LBLA. Esta lectura debe realizarse de un tirón. Si el lector no tiene acceso a una copia de la LBLA, puede encontrarla en Internet (www.BibleGateway.com).

Habiendo llegado a este punto, el lector debe tomar una decisión en cuanto a lo que considera el tema principal de Efesios. Si conoce a otra persona que ha hecho este trabajo, sería útil intercambiar impresiones sobre el tema de esta Epístola. Si quiere, el lector puede cambiar o retocar su conclusión.

Ahora, el lector debe consultar la «Guía de estudio» al final de este libro para ver cómo el autor ha llevado a cabo este trabajo en base al texto de la RVR60.

10

# La organización del libro

Para identificar la forma en que un autor bíblico desarrolla el tema principal de su libro el intérprete tiene que empaparse primero del texto. Entonces, y solo entonces, estará en posición de entender cómo el tema de cada párrafo desarrolla el tema principal del libro. Un bosquejo bien hecho es una de las herramientas más importantes que el intérprete puede emplear en su entendimiento de cada versículo. Para encontrar el bosquejo de un libro el intérprete necesita seguir los pasos que se detallarán a continuación.

## A. IDENTIFICAR LOS PÁRRAFOS

Un párrafo es un bloque de versículos en el cual el autor desarrolla un pensamiento. Por eso el párrafo es la unidad ideal para realizar un estudio sobre cualquier tema bíblico. Al determinar dónde comienza y dónde termina cada párrafo, el intérprete debe recordar que no existían capítulos ni versículos en los manuscritos originales. La división del A.T. en versículos se atribuye a la familia masoreta de ben Asher c. 900 d. C.[1] Dos siglos más tarde, Stephen Langton (1150–1228),

1. Ver Robert L. Plummer, *Preguntas y respuestas sobre cómo interpretar la Biblia* (Grand Rapids: Portavoz, 2013), p. 26.

arzobispo de Canterbury de la Iglesia de Inglaterra, dividió toda la Biblia en capítulos en su edición de la Vulgata Latina de 1228. Aunque la gran mayoría de las divisiones de los capítulos son correctas, muchos eruditos bíblicos coinciden en que hay pasajes dondeLangton introdujo una división entre un capítulo y otro que no es natural, cortando en seco el tema que el autor desarrollaba. A estas alturas sería imposible cambiar esas divisiones. Por tanto, el intérprete tendrá que discernir dónde empieza y termina cada párrafo. La división del N.T. en versículos[2] se produjo en el año 1550 cuando Robertus Stephanus (1503–1559) publicó su tercera edición del N.T. griego[3].

| **Palabras de transición** | |
|---|---|
| Por esta causa | Ef. 3:1 |
| Por lo cual | 1 Ts. 2:13; 3:1; Flm. 8; 2 P. 3:14 |
| Por tanto | Flp. 2:1, 12; He. 12:1; 1 P. 1:13 |
| Por esto | 2 P. 1:12 |
| Tú, pues | 2 Ti. 2:1 |
| Puesto que | 1 P. 4:1 |
| Así que | 2 Co. 7:1 |
| Pero | 1 Co. 15:12; Gá. 4:1 |

Los autores bíblicos proveen dos pistas para identificar los párrafos de sus libros. Primero, palabras de transición (pero, por tanto, pues, etcétera) que actúan como los pasillos de una casa que llevan al ocupante de una habitación a otra. Segundo, a veces el autor identifica el tema en el primer versículo del párrafo. Una vez que el intérprete haya seguido estas pistas, el autor sugiere que consulte una versión completa de la LBLA: o sea, una versión que tiene en el margen los textos de referencia y los comentarios de los editores sobre palabras hebreas y griegas. Casi todas las versiones de la Biblia introducen títulos en ciertos puntos del texto. Pero a veces hay más de un

2. Robert L. Plummer, *Forty Questions About Interpreting the Bible* (Grand Rapids: Kregel, 2010), p. 28.

3. Este hecho ha dado pie a la leyenda de que Stephanus realizó su trabajo mientras cabalgaba entre París y Lyon. Un tropiezo o movimiento brusco del caballo resultaba en la creación de ciertas divisiones. En su libro *Forty Questions About Interpreting the Bible* (Grand Rapids: Kregel, 2010), p. 28, Plummer sugiere que esta tradición se basa en un comentario no muy claro del hijo de Stephanus que, con toda probabilidad, quería decir que su padre estableció la división de los capítulos del N.T. mientras pernoctaba en diferentes posadas a lo largo de su viaje.

párrafo entre un título y otro. La ventaja de la LBLA es que coloca en negrita el número del primer versículo de cada párrafo[4].

## B. DAR UN TÍTULO A CADA PÁRRAFO

Para identificar dónde comienza y termina cada párrafo, el intérprete debe identificar los bloques de texto que tratan un tema en particular. Por eso, este segundo paso y el paso anterior se solapan en muchos sentidos. Es de esperar que este segundo paso sea el más fácil de los dos. Sin embargo, Osborne opina justo lo contrario. Después de observar a muchos seminaristas en sus clases de hermenéutica, dice que «la cosa más difícil de aprender por parte del principiante es a dar un vistazo general a cada párrafo para hacer un resumen de su punto central. Las personas se atascan y se enredan con los detalles de tal manera que parece que nunca suben a la superficie para tomar aire»[5]. El intérprete debe recordar que tiene que contestar solamente una pregunta: ¿cuál es el tema que predomina en este párrafo? Tener que dar un título a cada párrafo lo obligará a identificar lo más importante del párrafo.

## C. REDACTAR UN BOSQUEJO DEL LIBRO

Este tercer paso obliga al intérprete a observar detenidamente lo que el autor dice. Un buen bosquejo no consiste en una lista de párrafos con sus respectivos títulos, sino en una presentación organizada que sea coherente y clara, y que demuestre de forma visual cómo cada párrafo encaja con los demás. Para lograr esta meta, el intérprete ha de identificar los puntos principales que definen, apoyan o explican el tema principal del libro. Suponiendo que el tema principal es «Comida», un buen bosquejo tendrá la forma expuesta a continuación. Los puntos principales son los números 1–5, los cuales cuentan con

---

4. A veces un nuevo párrafo se encuentra en medio de una larga sección de texto. Este es el caso de Efesios 4:25, el cual se encuentra en una sección que comienza en el 4:17 y termina en el 4:32. Los editores opinan que este bloque de texto contiene dos párrafos (4:17-24 y 4:25-32).

5. Grant R. Osborne, *The Hermeneutical Spiral* (Downers Grove: InterVarsity Press, 1991), p. 23.

subpuntos (a–b) que definen más detalladamente en qué consisten los números 3 y 5.

COMIDA (1:3-14)
1. Frutas (vv. 3-4)
2. Vegetales (vv. 5-8)
3. Mariscos (vv. 9-11)
   a. Calamares (v. 9)
   b. Gambas (v. 10)
4. Carnes (v. 12)
5. Helados (vv. 13-14)
   a. Chocolate (v. 13)
   b. Vainilla (v. 14)

Un bosquejo debe ser breve, pero lo suficientemente claro para que cualquier persona pueda entender a primera vista cuál es el tema del libro y cómo se desarrolla. Un buen bosquejo no repite todo el texto bíblico, sino que lo resume en pocas palabras. La creatividad del intérprete no juega ningún papel en la tarea de redactar un bosquejo. Su único interés es entrar en la mente del autor.

Hay quienes enfocan sus bosquejos desde la perspectiva histórica, doctrinal, devocional, etcétera de un libro para facilitar su enseñanza o predicación sobre un tema en concreto. Por ejemplo, un bosquejo que refleja lo que Santiago dice sobre «la oración». Pero el mejor bosquejo es el que se ciñe al texto: o sea, un bosquejo exegético, porque para captar los matices y énfasis que Santiago hace con respecto a «la oración» en los versículos pertinentes, el intérprete tiene que haber entendido primero cómo esos versículos encajan en el desarrollo del tema principal de Santiago.

## D. CONSULTAR VARIOS COMENTARIOS BÍBLICOS

Después de haber hecho su propio estudio inductivo del texto, el intérprete debe consultar lo que el Espíritu Santo ha enseñado a otros creyentes, muchos de los cuales han destacado por su entendimiento de las Escrituras. Un buen comentario bíblico proveerá información a la cual el intérprete no tiene acceso, hará preguntas que a él no se le ha ocurrido plantear y propondrá interpretaciones que reten las suyas.

Si los comentarios bíblicos discrepan entre sí sobre el tema de un libro, discreparán aún más en su bosquejo de ese libro. Mientras que el intérprete nunca debe aceptar el bosquejo completo de nadie, con la excepción de aquellos párrafos en los cuales todos coinciden con el mismo bosquejo, es apropiado que adopte ciertas ideas que considere mejores que las suyas y que haga los cambios pertinentes en su propio bosquejo. Para eso ha consultado los comentarios. Lo importante es que haya hecho primero su propio trabajo de identificar el tema y bosquejo de un libro, porque entonces, y solo entonces, estará en posición de evaluar las opiniones de los demás.

**Pasos para redactar un bosquejo**

1. Identificar los párrafos.
2. Dar un título a cada párrafo.
3. Redactar un bosquejo del libro.
4. Consultar varios comentarios bíblicos.

No hay atajos en el verdadero estudio bíblico, especialmente cuando se trata de buscar el tema principal de un libro y la forma en que el autor desarrolla ese tema. No obstante, es uno de los trabajos más útiles y fructíferos que el intérprete puede realizar.

## *Trabajo para realizar*

1. ¿Cuáles son los cuatro pasos que el intérprete debe seguir para redactar un buen bosquejo? ¿Por qué es tan importante redactar un bosquejo exegético antes que un bosquejo que subraye un tema encontrado en un libro?
2. Este trabajo será el más largo y arduo de todos los trabajos de este libro. No obstante, si el lector logra dominar los pasos necesarios para encontrar el bosquejo de un libro, habrá hecho un paso significativo en su capacidad de interpretar «con precisión la palabra de verdad» (2 Ti. 2:15, LBLA). El lector no debe consultar libros de bosquejos, comentarios bíblicos o la «Guía de estudio» antes de que el autor lo indique. Puesto que este trabajo será una experiencia nueva para muchos lectores, el autor seguirá los párrafos sugeridos por la LBLA[6].

Trabajando exclusivamente con una copia de la RVR60, dé un título a los siguientes párrafos: Efesios 1:3-14; 1:15-23; 2:1-10; 2:11-22; 3:1-13; y 3:14-21. Recuerde que el título debe abarcar todo el contenido de cada párrafo. Después, redacte un bosquejo, incluyendo los subpuntos de los puntos principales. Para ayudar al lector en esta tarea, el autor plantea varias preguntas con base en el texto de la RVR60.

- **1:3-14:** ¿A quién se refieren las frases «en él» (vv. 4, 11, 13) y «en el Amado» (v. 6)? ¿Ha detectado la presencia de las tres personas de la Trinidad en este párrafo, las distintas obras que cada uno realiza y el propósito con el cual cada uno lleva a cabo sus respectivas obras?
- **1:15-23:** ¿Cuál es el tema principal de esta oración? ¿Puede identificar las cosas que Pablo pide que Dios conceda a los efesios?

6. La única excepción es que el autor de *Con precisión* incluye la doxología de 3:20-21 en la oración de 3:14-19.

- **2:1-10:** ¿Ha observado la diferencia de énfasis que Pablo hace entre los vv. 1-3, 4-6 y los vv. 7-10? ¿Ha notado el tiempo de los verbos en los vv. 1-3? El v. 4 comienza con «pero», indicando que Pablo va a hacer un cambio en su explicación del tema principal de este párrafo. ¿Ve la diferencia en el tiempo verbal de los vv. 4-6 con respecto a la idea que se expone en el v. 7? El v. 7 también plantea el tema de la gracia de Dios, el cual se desarrolla en los vv. 8-10.

- **2:11-22:** En este párrafo vemos algo similar al párrafo anterior. ¿A qué tiempo se refieren los vv. 11-12 y qué puede decir en cuanto a ello? El v. 13 comienza con «pero», indicando que habrá un contraste o cambio de dirección. ¿Cuál es el tema de los vv. 13-22?

- **3:1-13:** El autor sugiere que este párrafo está íntimamente ligado con 2:11-22. Si 2:11-12, 13-22 y 3:1-13 son tres aspectos de un mismo tema, ¿cuál es el tema de 3:1-13 y qué relación guarda con 2:11-12 y los vv. 13-22?

- **3:14-21:** Este párrafo representa la segunda oración de Pablo en los primeros tres capítulos de Efesios. ¿Puede identificar las tres peticiones concretas del apóstol?

Ahora, consulte los bosquejos encontrados en la «Guía de estudio» («Capítulo 10: La organización del libro [I]»). Aunque fueron escritos por autores de una generación anterior, servirán para ilustrar varios elementos positivos y negativos de un bosquejo. Antes de realizar cualquier cambio que crea conveniente en su propio bosquejo, lea la «Nota del autor» al final de los bosquejos.

Finalmente, lea la «Guía de estudio» («Capítulo 10: La organización del libro [II]») donde el autor explica cómo ha llegado a formular su bosquejo de Efesios 1–3.

# 11

# Contexto

Alguien ha dicho que «un texto sin contexto es un pretexto», una frase que expresa de forma escueta y fácil de recordar lo que ocurre cuando alguien ignora el contexto del versículo o pasaje que interpreta; a saber, en lugar de identificar lo que el autor pretendía comunicar a los lectores originales, impone sobre el texto su propia opinión. La Biblia puede probar cualquier idea, siempre que el intérprete no tenga en cuenta el contexto. Cuando esto ocurre, la Palabra de Dios se convierte en una fuente de confusión y caos en lugar de una lámpara a los pies (Sal. 119:105). Para descubrir lo que un autor quiere decir es imprescindible que el intérprete tenga en cuenta el contexto de un pasaje.

¿Qué es el «contexto»? Esta palabra proviene de las dos palabras latinas *con* (prefijo que señala convergencia, unión) y *textus* (tejer, enlazar). De ahí que se refiera a lo que precede y sigue a un texto, y lo que está directamente relacionado con ello. Sin embargo, hay porciones de las Escrituras que no encajan con esta definición. Por ejemplo, los primeros diez capítulos de Proverbios cuentan con secciones dedicadas a la sabiduría, las virtudes del hombre justo en contraste con el impío y unas advertencias contra el adulterio y las rameras. Pero los demás capítulos son un popurrí de versículos que no guardan ninguna relación entre sí, salvo un par de agrupaciones de dos o tres versículos que tratan el mismo tema. Lo mismo ocurre en pasajes como Romanos 12:9-21, donde se encuentra una lista de exhortaciones. No obstante, la gran mayoría de los textos bíblicos encajan con esta definición de «contexto». Procediendo desde el contexto más amplio hasta el más detallado, hay siete clases de contextos en las Escrituras.

## Toda la Biblia

Toda la Biblia representa un contexto porque todos sus pasajes forman un conjunto de lo que Dios quería comunicar al ser humano. Por ese motivo el intérprete tiene que asegurarse de que la enseñanza o doctrina que cree observar en un texto esté de acuerdo con lo que dicen los demás textos bíblicos sobre el tema en cuestión. Por ejemplo, los textos que parecen indicar que Dios quiere que seamos ricos y prósperos deben equilibrarse con los textos que afirman que el aprender a contentarse con poco es una virtud (Flp. 4:12-13), que Dios usa también a los pobres para su gloria (Hch. 3:1-6), etcétera. La Biblia *entera* es el árbitro final de la veracidad o falsedad de una idea, enseñanza o doctrina. Dios no va a decir algo en un texto y contradecirse en otro. Quienes mantienen una posición equivocada sobre una doctrina suelen cometer el error de no tener en cuenta *todo* lo que dice la Biblia sobre dicha doctrina.

## El Testamento

El Testamento en el que se encuentra un texto determinará en muchos casos si tiene o no una aplicación para el creyente hoy. Después de pecar con Betsabé, David oró: «No me eches de delante de ti, y no quites de mí tu santo Espíritu» (Sal. 51:11). En el A.T. el Espíritu Santo venía sobre ciertas personas según el ministerio que Dios les había asignado. Pero el Espíritu solo moraba en la persona hasta que la misión había sido cumplida. A partir de Hechos 2 el Espíritu Santo mora de forma permanente en cada creyente. Cuando el creyente peca, el Espíritu Santo es entristecido (Ef. 4:30), pero no se retira de él. Por tanto, en lugar de pedir que Dios no le quite el Espíritu Santo, el creyente de hoy debe pedir perdón cuando peca[1].

---

1. Para una explicación de las diferencias que existen entre la obra del Espíritu Santo en el A.T. y el N.T. ver el libro de Jaime Fasold, *Dones espirituales* (Grand Rapids: Portavoz, 2000), pp. 77–87.

## El libro

En su Epístola a los Romanos, Pablo subraya el hecho de que la salvación no se consigue por obras, sino por fe (Ro. 4:5). Sin embargo, Santiago dice que «La fe por sí sola no es suficiente. A menos que produzca buenas acciones» y que «se nos declara justos a los ojos de Dios por lo que hacemos y no solo por la fe» (Stg. 2:17, 24, NTV). A primera vista parece que Santiago contradice a Pablo. Sin embargo, si nos quedamos con el énfasis que Santiago quiere hacer en su Epístola, nos damos cuenta de que está exhortando a los creyentes a ser consecuentes, a que su vida se corresponda con lo que creen. Aunque las obras nunca pueden producir ni mantener la salvación, la salvación siempre produce obras buenas en el creyente[2]. Ningún texto se encuentra solo, sino que forma parte del libro en el cual se encuentra. Por tanto, la enseñanza de cualquier versículo o pasaje ha de entenderse a la luz de la enseñanza de todo el libro en el cual se encuentra.

## El contexto inmediato

El contexto inmediato se refiere al párrafo que precede y al que sigue a un párrafo o versículo. Cada párrafo y los versículos que contiene guardan una relación con los párrafos que los rodean. Uno de los grandes valores de hacer un bosquejo de un libro —y en particular de una epístola— es que obliga al intérprete a identificar el desarrollo del pensamiento del autor al pasar de un párrafo a otro. Por ejemplo, Efesios 1:3-14 trata tres de las diversas obras que las tres personas de la Trinidad realizan en la vida de una persona cuando se convierte a Cristo. En el párrafo siguiente (1:15-23), Pablo dice que cuando ora por los efesios pide que Dios alumbre los ojos de su entendimiento (v. 18). ¿Por qué? Para que se den cuenta de todo lo que tienen en Cristo Jesús. ¿De qué sirve a un creyente todo lo que tiene en Cristo (vv. 3-14) si no sabe que lo tiene ni lo aprovecha? La

---

2. Martín Lutero se convirtió al estudiar la Epístola a los Romanos. Su gran aprecio por el énfasis de Romanos sobre «la salvación por fe sin obras» lo empujó a rechazar la epístola de Santiago como canónica. Aparentemente, no pudo distinguir entre los matices que Pablo y Santiago hacían en sus respectivas epístolas.

conexión entre 1:15-23 con el párrafo anterior (1:3-14) es más que evidente[3].

## El mismo párrafo

El estudio del mismo párrafo es especialmente útil en las Epístolas. Por ejemplo, la promesa de Filipenses 4:19 («Mi Dios, pues, suplirá todo lo que os falta conforme a sus riquezas en gloria en Cristo Jesús») ha sido memorizada y reclamada en algún momento por cada creyente. Sin embargo, muchos ignoran que esta promesa contiene una condición que ha de cumplirse. En el mismo párrafo (vv. 10-18) Pablo agradece a los filipenses su donativo. Entonces, cuando comienza el v. 19 con la palabra «pues», en efecto les está diciendo: «Puesto que vosotros habéis suplido mi necesidad, Dios suplirá vuestras necesidades». Por tanto, Filipenses 4:19 no es una promesa gratuita. Solo la pueden reclamar quienes cumplen con su responsabilidad de sostener a los obreros y la obra de Dios. Si suplen las necesidades de la obra de Dios, él promete suplir las suyas. Es la misma enseñanza que encontramos en Isaías 58:10-11. Si el creyente cumple la condición (en cursiva), Dios cumplirá con su promesa[4].

> *Alimenten a los hambrientos y ayuden a los que están en apuros.* Entonces su luz resplandecerá desde la oscuridad, y la oscuridad que los rodea será tan radiante como el mediodía. El SEÑOR los guiará continuamente, les dará agua cuando tengan sed y restaurará sus fuerzas. Serán como un huerto bien regado, como un manantial que nunca se seca. NTV

---

3. Aunque la relación entre la oración de Pablo en Efesios 1:15-23 con el párrafo anterior (vv. 3-14) parece clara, no es tan clara la relación entre su segunda oración en 3:14-21 con el párrafo anterior (2:11–3:13), el cual trata la obra de Dios de acercar a los gentiles al reino de Dios y el ministerio especial que Dios encomendó a Pablo de proclamar ese misterio. En su libro *The Hermeneutical Spiral* (Downers Grove: InterVarsity Press, 1991), p. 345, Osborne sugiere que «la situación que hay detrás de la oración de 3:16-19 es la falta de unidad entre las facciones judías y gentiles en la iglesia de Éfeso (ver 2:11-12)». Es una interpretación que merece ser considerada.

4. Ver también Proverbios 3:9-10; 11:24-25; Malaquías 3:10; 2 Corintios 9:6 como ejemplos de textos que conllevan una condición o requisito en cuanto a la bendición de Dios sobre las finanzas de sus hijos.

Filipenses 4:13 («Pues todo lo puedo hacer por medio de Cristo», NTV) es una promesa que muchos creyentes han aplicado a muchas circunstancias de su vida. Pero lo que muchos ignoran es que su *primera* aplicación es a una situación que padecía Pablo. En su caso, Dios lo había fortalecido de tal manera que había aprendido a contentarse, fuera cual fuera su situación económica: «He aprendido a estar contento con lo que tengo. Sé vivir con casi nada o con todo lo necesario. He aprendido el secreto de vivir en cualquier situación, sea con el estómago lleno o vacío, con mucho o con poco» (vv. 11-12). Evidentemente, este texto puede aplicarse a muchas situaciones de la vida. Pero al ignorar el contexto de este versículo, muchos lo aplican a cualquier cosa menos a la pobreza o la riqueza.

Cuando una persona habla de «contexto», normalmente se refiere inconscientemente al contexto inmediato (el párrafo que precede y el que sigue) o al mismo párrafo. Los dos son muy importantes. Cuando un intérprete se fija en el contexto de un pasaje, notará cómo Dios crea en él un aprecio mayor por la autoridad de las Escrituras.

## Pasajes paralelos

Un pasaje paralelo es una serie de versículos o un párrafo en otro libro o epístola que aporta la misma enseñanza, especialmente cuando los dos son escritos por el mismo autor. Por ejemplo, aunque 1–2 Reyes

| Contexto | |
|---|---|
| Toda la Biblia | ¿Coincide mi interpretación con la enseñanza de toda la Biblia? |
| El Testamento | ¿Coincide mi interpretación con lo que la revelación progresiva ha desvelado hasta el momento del texto que interpreto? |
| El libro | ¿Cómo encaja la enseñanza de este pasaje con el tema principal del libro? |
| El contexto inmediato | ¿Cómo encaja mi interpretación de este pasaje con lo que dicen el párrafo anterior y el que sigue? |
| El mismo párrafo | ¿Cómo encaja mi interpretación de este texto con el fluir del pensamiento del autor en este párrafo? |
| Pasajes paralelos | ¿Qué información adicional pueden aportar los pasajes en otros lugares que tratan el mismo tema con más de un versículo? |
| Citas de referencia | ¿Qué información adicional pueden aportar versículos sueltos de otros pasajes que tratan este mismo tema? |

y 1–2 Crónicas hacen diferentes énfasis en cuanto a la vida espiritual del pueblo de Dios, los dos juegos de libros describen a los mismos reyes de Israel y Judá. Los cuatro Evangelios, y en particular los Evangelios sinópticos (Mateo, Marcos, Lucas), proveen pasajes paralelos sobre la enseñanza y los eventos en la vida de Jesús. Colosenses 3:18–4:1 y Efesios 5:21-6:9 son pasajes paralelos porque tratan las responsabilidades que tienen los dos cónyuges el uno con el otro, las responsabilidades de los hijos hacia sus padres y las responsabilidades de los siervos hacia sus amos.

## Citas de referencia

Una cita de referencia es un versículo —en contraste con los pasajes paralelos que cuentan con varios versículos— que se encuentra en otro pasaje y que trata el mismo tema. Una cita de referencia puede aclarar un texto oscuro. Pero quizás el mayor valor de las citas de referencia sea que permiten al intérprete saber lo que toda la Biblia enseña sobre cierto tema. Se pueden encontrar citas de referencia en el margen de muchas versiones de la Biblia, diccionarios temáticos de la Biblia y comentarios bíblicos. Una vez reunidos todos los textos que tratan el mismo tema, el intérprete debe estudiar cada uno en su propio contexto, llegar a una conclusión en cuanto a lo que cada texto enseña y finalmente compaginar la enseñanza de todos[5].

De todos los temas tratados en esta Sección II sobre la hermenéutica general, la cuestión de tomar en cuenta el contexto al interpretar un pasaje bíblico es quizás la más importante, porque permite al intérprete ver el «hilo» del mensaje que el autor quería comunicar a los lectores originales.

5. *The Treasury of Scripture Knowledge* (Westwood, Nueva Jersey: Fleming H. Revell Company) fue publicado c. 1830. Es un libro de referencia muy útil por contar con unas 500.000 citas de referencia. Identifica las palabras importantes de cada versículo y luego indica dónde se encuentran textos sobre el mismo tema. Aunque este libro no ha sido traducido al español, cualquier lector podrá adivinar qué palabra es señalada como importante y reconocer los nombres de los libros bíblicos donde se encuentran las citas de referencia.

## *Trabajo para realizar*

Cite las siete clases de contexto que existen en la Biblia. Luego, escoja cuatro de esos contextos y dé un ejemplo de cómo el contexto en cuestión ayuda al intérprete a entender «con precisión» un texto bíblico.

# 12

# Palabras

La Biblia es inspirada por Dios de forma verbal en los manuscritos originales. Aunque el Espíritu Santo no dictó a los autores bíblicos las palabras que emplearon, los supervisó en las palabras que seleccionaron de su propio vocabulario para que estas expresaran con precisión las verdades que Dios les había revelado. De ahí que el estudio de las palabras empleadas en la Biblia cobre tanta importancia.

## A. CARACTERÍSTICAS DE LAS PALABRAS

Las palabras empleadas en la Biblia tienen las mismas características y funcionan bajo las mismas leyes que las palabras encontradas en cualquier literatura secular, porque todos los idiomas funcionan de acuerdo con las mismas leyes del lenguaje. Un conocimiento de cuatro características en particular ayudará al intérprete a interpretar con precisión las palabras bíblicas.

*1. Solas y aisladas las palabras no tienen un significado claro.* Entendemos lo que significa «¡Corre!». Pero tal y como aparece esa palabra, carece de sentido porque le falta un contexto. No sabemos si ha sido pronunciada por un entrenador que anima a un atleta a correr más de prisa o por una madre que empuja a su hijo a darse prisa para que no llegue tarde al colegio. Solas y aisladas las palabras son incapaces de comunicar un significado claro.

*2. Con el tiempo las palabras adquieren significados adicionales.* Una ojeada a cualquier diccionario demostrará que muchas palabras tienen más de un significado. Por ejemplo, la palabra «llevar» tiene ¡diecinueve significados diferentes! A veces el N.T. añade un significado adicional o más amplio a una palabra que el A.T. emplea. Por ejemplo, la palabra «justicia» en Salmo 18:20 se refiere al carácter moral de David[1], mientras que esa misma palabra en Romanos 5:17 tiene que ver con la justicia de Cristo, la cual es imputada al creyente.

*3. Aunque dos palabras pueden ser muy similares, tienen matices distintos.* Los filólogos afirman que no hay dos palabras que sean cien por cien sinónimas. Aunque las dos tengan un significado muy similar, cada una tiene un matiz que la hace diferente a la otra. Por ejemplo, ¿cuál es la diferencia entre las palabras *redargüir, reprender* y *exhortar* en 2 Timoteo 4:2? Al identificar esos matices, el intérprete entenderá con más precisión cuál era el ministerio que Pablo le encomendaba a Timoteo.

*4. Los autores del N.T. dieron a ciertas palabras un significado teológico.* En el primer siglo la palabra «redimir» se refería al acto de comprar un esclavo con el propósito de liberarlo. Los autores del N.T. creían que esa palabra describía con mucha precisión lo que ocurre cuando una persona confía en Cristo como su Salvador. Antes era esclava del pecado y estaba expuesta a la condenación eterna, pero al depositar su confianza en Cristo, es redimida por el precio que Cristo pagó en la cruz y librada de la condenación eterna por su pecado.

## B. ¿DÓNDE SE ENCUENTRA EL SIGNIFICADO DE UNA PALABRA?

El primer paso que el intérprete ha de dar para descubrir el significado de una palabra es el de identificar las palabras que merecen una investigación seria. Puede identificar esas palabras al contestar cuatro preguntas. Primera, ¿cuáles son las palabras de este párrafo que tienen una importancia teológica? En Efesios 1:3-14 las palabras *escogió, predestinado, adoptados, redención, gracia* y *sellados* encajarían en ese perfil. Segunda, ¿cuál es la palabra que juega un papel significativo en el

1. Por eso, la NTV traduce este texto como «El Señor me recompensó por hacer lo correcto».

énfasis de este párrafo? Tercera, ¿hay una palabra ambigua o difícil de entender? Cuarta, ¿hay una palabra que las diferentes versiones de la Biblia traduzcan de forma diferente? Una vez identificada una palabra importante, el intérprete debe dirigirse a las siguientes fuentes de investigación, las cuales aparecen en orden de importancia y prioridad.

## El contexto inmediato

Los libros de hermenéutica suelen emplear el término *usus loquendi* para referirse al uso o significado que una palabra tiene en el pasaje o párrafo donde es empleada. Ese significado coincidirá con el uso que hacían de esa palabra los primeros lectores y la sociedad en que vivían en ese momento, puesto que ningún autor dejaría de lado el entendimiento que su sociedad tiene de una palabra sin dar una explicación del nuevo significado que él ha dado a dicha palabra. El párrafo (contexto inmediato) determina el significado de una palabra y sirve como árbitro de cómo el intérprete debe entenderla. Por eso, el estudio del párrafo tiene prioridad sobre todas las demás fuentes citadas a continuación.

Por regla general, una palabra que se encuentra más de una vez en el mismo párrafo tendrá el mismo significado a no ser que el autor indique de alguna forma que la está empleando en dos sentidos diferentes. Por ejemplo, es obvio que Ezequiel emplea la palabra «casa» para referirse al templo (44:5) y a la nación de Israel (44:6), aunque emplee esa palabra en dos sentidos diferentes en el espacio de tan solo dos versículos. En 1 Corintios 2:14-15 Pablo emplea la palabra «espiritual» para describir al creyente en contraste con el no creyente, pero dos versículos después la usa para describir al creyente maduro en contraste con el creyente inmaduro (3:1). Aunque no es frecuente que un autor bíblico emplee una palabra en dos sentidos diferentes en el mismo párrafo, el intérprete debe ser consciente de ello y estar atento a esa posibilidad.

En alguna ocasión el autor dará una definición de alguna palabra que emplee. Por ejemplo, Pablo dice que las Escrituras son útiles para hacer que «el hombre de Dios sea perfecto» (2 Ti. 3:17). ¿Acaso está diciendo que se puede alcanzar la perfección en este lado de la eternidad? Pero en la frase siguiente («enteramente preparado para toda buena obra») Pablo indica que está hablando de la madurez espiritual, no de una supuesta perfección absoluta.

Para investigar el significado de una palabra en un párrafo concreto, el intérprete tiene a su disposición dos, posiblemente tres, clases de libros.

*1. Un diccionario secular.* Para descubrir el significado de una palabra como «sellados» (Ef. 1:13), muchos se dirigen sin más a un diccionario secular. Es un paso lógico porque los traductores de las diferentes versiones de la Biblia tuvieron que elegir la palabra española que mejor expresara el significado de *esfragiszete,* la palabra griega que aparece en Efesios 1:13. Sin embargo, aunque un diccionario secular puede orientar al intérprete sobre los diferentes significados que adquirió la palabra española («sellados») a lo largo de su historia, no le dará los significados que *esfragiszete* acumuló con el tiempo, ni mucho menos su significado teológico. Lo que más importancia tiene es el significado de *esfragiszete,* no el significado de «sellado». Pero ¿qué puede hacer una persona que no ha tenido la posibilidad de estudiar griego?[2] Es precisamente aquí donde dicha persona debe hacer uso de la siguiente clase de libro.

*2. Concordancia exhaustiva de la Biblia* (CEB). Si el intérprete no tiene un conocimiento suficiente del griego para dirigirse directamente a un N.T. griego para descubrir cuál es la palabra griega que es traducida como «sellado» en Efesios 1:13, puede conseguir esa misma información en la CEB de James Strong. Allí encontrará una lista de todas las veces que «sellar» o «sellado» aparece en la RVR60. En los textos del N.T. donde figuran esas palabras, encontrará uno de estos tres números (2696, 4972, 4973) al final de cada versículo, porque los traductores de la RVR60 emplearon la palabra «sellar» para traducir tres palabras griegas diferentes. De las tres, 4972 es el que se emplea en Efesios 1:13. Al buscar ese número en el *Diccionario de las palabras griegas* al final de la CEB, encontrará la palabra *esfragiszete*[3].

2. Puesto que existe un consenso entre los entendidos de que un conocimiento básico del hebreo es mucho más difícil de conseguir que un conocimiento básico del griego, el autor citará los pasos requeridos para descubrir el significado de una palabra griega.

3. Otra posible concordancia sería la de Pedro Ortiz, *Concordancia manual y diccionario griego-español del Nuevo Testamento* (Madrid: Sociedad Bíblica, 2006), la cual sigue el mismo sistema para localizar una palabra.

Quienes han estudiado griego tendrán la posibilidad de consultar un léxico griego, donde encontrarán registrados los diferentes significados que una palabra ha tenido a lo largo de su historia y los textos bíblicos donde, en opinión de los editores, se utiliza un significado concreto. Algunos léxicos más completos incluirán los textos de fuentes extrabíblicas[4].

Los editores y autores de los léxicos son unos verdaderos eruditos lingüísticos. En principio, el intérprete puede fiarse de las opiniones de los léxicos en cuanto a los diversos significados que una palabra ha adquirido a lo largo de su historia. Pero en el momento en que identifican los textos donde esos significados son empleados, se convierten en comentaristas bíblicos y sus propios prejuicios y presuposiciones o presupuestos entran en juego. Por eso, el intérprete haría bien en recordar que los léxicos no son infalibles, sino simplemente comentarios bíblicos muy técnicos. Hablando del *Theological Dictionary of the New Testament*[5], el cual es considerado por los eruditos de todas las posiciones teológicas como el léxico de referencia que supera con creces todos los demás, Virkler nos advierte que «la posición teológica de sus autores varía considerablemente, y la influencia de presuposiciones liberales en algunos de los artículos es significativa»[6]. Berkhof (1873–1957) decía lo mismo unos cuantos años antes con respecto a los léxicos en general.

---

4. El intérprete ha de tener en cuenta que los léxicos registran las palabras de forma genérica, no con las desinencias que la palabra presenta dentro de un versículo. Por ejemplo, si queremos saber el significado de «fuisteis sellados» no buscaremos estas palabras en el diccionario español así, sino que buscaremos la forma «sellar» (el verbo, sin desinencias). Lo mismo ocurre en griego.

5. El *Theological Dictionary of the New Testament* (Grand Rapids: Eerdmans, 1964) de Gerhard Kittel y Gerhard Friedrich es una obra monumental que cuenta con diez tomos grandes. Esta obra fue editada por Geoffrey W. Bromiley. Fue escrita originalmente en alemán y luego traducida al inglés. Muchos de sus artículos sobre palabras importantes cuentan con quince páginas o más. Puesto que el precio del TDNT supera los recursos de muchos pastores y estudiantes, se publicó una versión de un solo tomo en inglés, la cual fue traducida al español con el título *Diccionario teológico del Nuevo Testamento* (Grand Rapids: Libros Desafío, 2002).

6. Henry A. Virkler, *Hermeneutics: Principles and Processes of Biblical Interpretation* (Grand Rapids: Baker, 1988), p. 104. La sección titulada «Theological Wordbooks» donde aparecen estas palabras de Virkler no ha sido incluida en la traducción de este libro al español.

> Es necesario tener presente que los léxicos o diccionarios no son dignos de confianza de un modo absoluto, por lo menos cuando descienden a detalles particulares. Generalmente estos libros contienen los resultados de labores exegéticas de varios intérpretes, y a menudo revelan opiniones diferentes. Es posible, y en algunos casos perfectamente evidente, que la elección de significado (de una palabra) fue determinada por prejuicios dogmáticos del autor[7].

Una vez que el intérprete sepa cuáles son los significados de «sellado», estará en posición de determinar cuál de ellos es el que tenía en mente el autor cuando empleó el término en Efesios 1:13. En principio, el significado elegido debe ser apoyado por algún detalle del contexto inmediato. Cuando dicho apoyo no exista o no quede claro, el intérprete debe dirigirse a la siguiente fuente.

## Otros textos del mismo libro

La palabra «sellados» figura no solamente en Efesios 1:13, sino también en 4:30. Estas son las únicas ocasiones en que Pablo emplea una forma de *sfragdso* en Efesios. Para saber lo que «sellado» significa en 4:30, el intérprete tiene que estudiar el contexto inmediato (párrafo) de 4:17-32.

## Otros libros escritos por el mismo autor

El lector notará en la *Concordancia* de Strong que hay unos 34 versículos además de Efesios donde se emplea alguna forma de *sfragdso*. Sin embargo, una lectura rápida de esos textos demostrará que no tienen un sentido teológico como es el caso en Efesios 1:13 y 4:30, con la excepción de 2 Corintios 1:22. Una vez más, el intérprete estudiará el uso de esa palabra en su contexto inmediato para descubrir su significado.

## Libros escritos por otros autores bíblicos

El significado de palabras teológicas como «justificación», «santificación», etcétera conlleva varios matices. Por eso, un autor podría subrayar

---

7. Louis Berkhof, *Principios de interpretación bíblica* (Tarrasa: CLIE, 1973), p. 81.

un aspecto o matiz de una doctrina mientras que otro autor haría énfasis en otro elemento de esa palabra. En este caso la enseñanza de los dos autores se complementará. Pero hay otros casos donde dos autores emplean diferentes significados de una misma palabra. Por ejemplo, cuando Pablo habla de «obras», casi siempre se refiere a las buenas obras que muchos no creyentes creen necesarias para conseguir la salvación. Pero cuando Santiago emplea esa palabra, se refiere a los actos éticos que son normales y automáticos en la persona que se ha convertido a Cristo. Esas obras no consiguen ni guardan su salvación, sino que se hacen manifiestas en las vidas de quienes son hijos de Dios.

## Paralelismo hebreo

El paralelismo hebreo es una herramienta muy útil en la interpretación de las palabras que figuran en el género literario de la poesía, especialmente en el A.T., donde encontramos muchos pasajes poéticos. El paralelismo se tratará en el capítulo 17.

## Libros de sinónimos

Los lingüistas afirman que no hay dos palabras que sean sinónimas de forma absoluta, sino que cada una conlleva un matiz que la hace distinta. Con el tiempo los lingüistas y eruditos bíblicos han logrado identificar esos matices sin perder de vista las similitudes que dos palabras «sinónimas» puedan compartir. Para evitar la tentación de ver distinciones, matices y énfasis donde no existen[8], el consejo de Mickelsen es muy sabio. «Cuando aparecen sinónimos en el texto bíblico, el intérprete debe fijarse en cómo añaden fuerza a la idea que es comunicada en dicho pasaje. Si el contexto apoya ese matiz, entonces se aumenta la luz sobre la idea comunicada. Pero en la práctica muchos "descubrimientos ingeniosos" carecen de fundamento textual»[9]. Las dos obras más conocidas y apreciadas sobre los sinónimos bíblicos son

---

8. En las generaciones anteriores hubo un entusiasmo desenfrenado por el estudio de los sinónimos, lo cual llevó a algunos a ver diferencias y significados muy marcados entre una palabra y otra.

9. A. Berkeley Mickelsen, *Interpreting the Bible* (Grand Rapids: Eerdmans, 1963), p. 129.

*Sinónimos del Antiguo Testamento* de R. B. Girdlestone (1836–1923) y *Synonyms of the New Testament* [Sinónimos del Nuevo Testamento] de R. C. Trench (1807–1886). Aunque fueron publicadas hace muchos años y no incluyen la información más reciente que nos han proporcionado los descubrimientos arqueológicos, su aportación sigue siendo muy apreciada.

## Fuentes extrabíblicas

El contexto inmediato (el mismo párrafo) es la fuente más importante a la hora de determinar el significado de una palabra. Pero cuando una palabra bíblica aparece solamente una o dos veces en las Escrituras, el intérprete solo cuenta con uno o dos contextos sobre los cuales basar sus conclusiones en cuanto a su significado. Si ese significado no queda claro, la única fuente que le queda son las fuentes extrabíblicas, las cuales son válidas por cuanto los autores bíblicos usaban las mismas palabras que se hablaban en los países donde vivían.

Para encontrar el significado de una palabra hebrea en fuentes extrabíblicas, los lexicógrafos estudian varias clases de literatura antigua hebrea. Pero la fuente más apreciada es la LXX, la traducción del A.T. al griego c. 250 a. C., seguida en importancia por la Vulgata Latina, la traducción de la Biblia al latín de Jerónimo (c. 340–420) en 405. Puesto que los traductores de estas dos obras estaban altamente comprometidos con la inspiración de las Escrituras, podemos dar por sentado que hicieran el mayor esfuerzo posible para encontrar la palabra griega o latina que mejor representaba el significado de cada palabra hebrea.

En cuanto a las fuentes extrabíblicas para palabras griegas, el intérprete encontrará información en varias fuentes. La «otra literatura cristiana temprana» a la cual se refiere el título del léxico de Walter Bauer (*A Greek-English Lexicon of the New Testament and Other Early Christian Literature*) [Léxico griego-español del Nuevo Testamento y otra literatura cristiana temprana] incluye varias fuentes. Entre ellas se encuentra toda la literatura cristiana de los primeros siglos, la cual incluye las obras de los padres apostólicos y los escritos de algunos autores heréticos. El título «padre apostólico» nació en el siglo XVII, y se refiere a aquellos hombres que vivieron en la segunda mitad del primer siglo y la primera mitad del siglo II que tuvieron —a ciencia cierta o en toda probabilidad— contacto con al menos uno de los doce apóstoles, o que fueron tan influenciados por uno de ellos que sus escritos son considerados un reflejo de la enseñanza apostólica. Los padres apostólicos fueron los primeros padres de la Iglesia[10].

Igual que con los léxicos bíblicos, el intérprete que investiga las fuentes extrabíblicas para descubrir el significado de una palabra haría bien en seguir el sabio consejo de Osborne y Woodward de «estudiar los artículos con mucho cuidado y negarse a dar por sentado la veracidad de los datos. Como cualquier otro ser humano, los eruditos caen presos de sus prejuicios y frecuentemente prestan poca atención a la evidencia contraria a sus conclusiones. Es sabio comparar varias opiniones, evaluar la discusión, tomar nota de los pasajes que cada erudito emplea para apoyar sus conclusiones y averiguar con mucho cuidado si los datos lo llevan o no a sus conclusiones»[11].

## La etimología de la palabra

La etimología es el estudio del origen de una palabra y cómo adquirió significados adicionales con el tiempo. Suele ser fascinante. No obstante, aunque hay quienes se dirigen primero a la etimología de una palabra para determinar su significado, la colocamos a la cola de las diferentes fuentes de investigación porque cuenta con más dificultades y peligros que beneficios.

El origen de algunas palabras es totalmente desconocido, como es el caso de *diakonos,* la palabra griega para «diácono» (1 Ti. 3:8). En un intento de definir el trabajo de los diáconos, muchos los asocian con los siete hombres en Hechos 6 que repartieron la comida a las viudas griegas porque *diakonos* es de la misma raíz que la palabra *diakonein,* traducida como «servir» en Hechos 6:2. De ahí que muchos

10. Aunque no hay un consenso en cuanto al número de personas que conformaban el grupo de los padres apostólicos, hay cinco nombres que aparecen en casi cada lista: Clemente de Roma (murió c. 97); Ignacio de Antioquía (nació entre el 25 y 28, y murió entre el 98 y 110); Policarpo de Esmirna (c. 69–c. 155); y los autores desconocidos de la *Didaché* y el *Pastor de Hermas.*

11. Grant R. Osborne y Stephen B. Woodward, *Handbook for Bible Study* (Grand Rapids: Baker, 1983), p. 147.

consideren el servicio en cuestiones cotidianas como la labor a la que se dedicaban los diáconos en las iglesias del primer siglo. Sin embargo, esta es una base muy pobre. Como dice Silva, «[...] en cualquier caso, la especificación del significado de una palabra basándonos únicamente en la etimología nunca puede ser más que una conjetura fundamentada»[12]. No obstante, hasta Silva reconoce que a veces no le queda otra opción al intérprete.

En otros casos la historia de una palabra es tan complicada que no hay manera de sacar una conclusión clara en cuanto a su significado. Y cuando dicha historia queda clara, descubrimos que la etimología raras veces refleja el significado de dicha palabra hoy día debido a que las palabras adquieren significados adicionales con el paso del tiempo. Es verdad que en algunos casos la etimología de una palabra se parece a su significado actual. Pero si el intérprete insiste en cada detalle de la misma, puede llegar a ideas erróneas. La etimología de la palabra griega en Hebreos 13:7, 17, 24, la cual es traducida como *pastores* (RVR60, LBLA) *dirigentes* (NVI), *guías* (LBLA) y *líderes* (NTV), hace referencia a un jefe militar. En este caso vemos fácilmente la conexión entre la autoridad de un jefe militar y la de un líder de la iglesia. Los pastores y líderes de una congregación deben gobernar con la autoridad que Dios les ha dado (1 Ti. 5:17). No obstante, sería inapropiado llevar esa analogía más lejos, porque ningún pastor tiene derecho a gritar órdenes como un jefe militar ni a esperar que los miembros de su iglesia le obedezcan cada vez que expresa su opinión.

En respuesta a estos problemas, Stein opina que la etimología es útil en solamente dos casos. Primero, cuando una palabra aparece solamente una o dos veces en la Biblia. Segundo, cuando los personajes bíblicos dieron nombres a ciertas personas en momentos importantes o críticos[13]. Por ejemplo, Dios mandó al profeta Oseas que nombrara a su hijo Jezreel, «porque de aquí a poco yo castigaré a la casa de Jehú por causa de la sangre de Jezreel» (1:4). José nombró a su hijo «Jesús» (*Yehoshua* en hebreo) porque salvaría (*Yasha*) a su

12. Estas palabras de Silva, que aparecen en su libro *Biblical Words and Their Meanings* (Grand Rapids: Zondervan, 1983), p. 42 son citadas por Donald A. Carson en *Falacias exegéticas* (Viladecavalls: CLIE, 1996), p. 39.

13. Robert H. Stein, *A Basic Guide to Interpreting the Bible* (Grand Rapids: Baker, 1994), p. 173.

pueblo de sus pecados (Mt. 1:21). El nombre «Jesús» es el equivalente griego del nombre hebreo «Josué», cuya etimología significa «Yahveh es salvación». Dos versículos más adelante Jesús es llamado «Emanuel», cuya etimología significa «Dios con nosotros». Sin embargo, si las mismas Escrituras no indican que un personaje recibió su nombre en un momento importante de su vida o de la del pueblo de Dios, es dudoso que Dios quiera subrayar alguna verdad.

En algunos casos la etimología puede proveer al predicador una buena ilustración. Por ejemplo, la etimología de la palabra «sincera» sale de las carpinterías y talleres de cerámica. Al fabricar un mueble o vasija, podía haber un desperfecto que se cubría con cera. Pero si ningún mueble o vasija sufría un percance, el carpintero o artesano sellaba su producto con las palabras «sin cera». De ahí que una persona sincera sea alguien transparente, sin engaño, auténtica, genuina, «sin cera». La etimología de la palabra «irritarse» nació en las granjas. Las personas que cuidaban las vacas afilaban un palo y con él las guiaban en la dirección que querían. En 1 Corintios 13:5, la frase «el amor [...] no se irrita», no se deja provocar por el mal que otra persona le puede hacer, hace referencia a esa imagen. A pesar de lo interesantes y legítimas que sean estas ilustraciones en particular, el predicador tiene que recordar que el contexto inmediato (párrafo) determina el significado de una palabra, no una ilustración que encaja muy bien en un sermón. ¡El *usus loquendi* es siempre mucho más importante que la etimología!

| **Pasos para encontrar el significado de una palabra** |
|---|
| 1. El contexto inmediato |
| 2. Otros textos del mismo libro |
| 3. Otros libros escritos por el mismo autor |
| 4. Libros escritos por otros autores bíblicos |
| 5. Paralelismo hebreo |
| 6. Libros de sinónimos |
| 7. Fuentes extrabíblicas |
| 8. La etimología de la palabra |

Al finalizar este capítulo, debe ser evidente para el lector que un conocimiento básico de griego representa una gran ventaja al investigar el significado de una palabra. Cuanto más conocimiento del griego tiene el intérprete, más posibilidades tendrá de profundizar en el estudio de las palabras bíblicas. No obstante, el 95 por ciento de la enseñanza bíblica y el significado esencial de cualquier pasaje pueden conseguirse mediante dos o tres buenas versiones de la Biblia, una concordancia completa, un léxico y unos comentarios que expliquen los matices de ciertas palabras hebreas y griegas.

## *Trabajo para realizar*

1. Cite al menos seis de las ocho fuentes que el intérprete puede emplear para descubrir el significado de una palabra. ¿Cuáles son las dos fuentes más importantes y fiables para lograr esa meta?

2. La palabra «sellar» formaba parte del vocabulario del primer siglo. Contaba con cuatro usos. (1) La señal de una transacción terminada, igual que el recibo que se da a un comprador cuando paga el precio de un producto. (2) Una señal de posesión, como la «M» que aparece en unas vacas para indicar que pertenecen a Francisco Martínez. (3) Una garantía de que lo que se entrega *ahora* está completo. Es como el camión lleno de género que viaja desde un gran almacén hasta un centro comercial. Si el precinto en sus puertas traseras está intacto, es una garantía de que todo el género ha llegado sano y salvo. (4) Un pago y señal, que sirve como garantía de que lo que queda por pagar se entregará *en el futuro.*

   Pablo pidió prestado *uno* de esos significados y lo cargó con un concepto teológico. La pregunta es: ¿cuál de los cuatro significados tenía «sellar»? Pablo emplea esa palabra solamente tres veces en sus Epístolas (2 Co. 1:22; Ef. 1:13-14; 4:30). En teoría, cada texto podría emplear un significado diferente. Pero puesto que los tres textos tratan la misma doctrina y han sido escritos por el mismo autor, es lógico suponer que tengan el mismo significado a no ser que el contexto inmediato indique lo contrario.

   Trabajando exclusivamente con una copia de la RVR60, estudie los tres textos en el orden en que aparecen a continuación e identifique el significado que Pablo tenía en mente en cada texto. Las preguntas lo ayudarán en esa tarea.

**2 Corintios 1:22**

El v. 22 forma parte de una frase que comienza en el v. 21. ¿Quién es la persona de la Trinidad que realiza la obra citada en el v. 21? ¿Es la misma persona que «nos ha sellado» en el v. 22? ¿Qué quiere decir la palabra «arras» (v. 22)? El lector haría bien en buscar esa palabra en un diccionario secular. La LBLA traduce la palabra griega para «arras» como «garantía», aunque en el margen dice «O, arras». De los tres textos, 2 Corintios 1:22 es el menos claro. Sin embargo, si el lector tuviera que determinar el significado de «sellar» con base en este texto, ¿cuáles de los cuatro significados citados arriba serían los mejores candidatos?

**Efesios 4:30**

Este versículo no pretende tratar la doctrina de «sellar», sino exhortar al creyente a no contristar al Espíritu Santo. No obstante, la siguiente frase («*con* el cual fuisteis sellados», énfasis añadido) aporta algo a nuestro entendimiento de esa doctrina. ¿Qué diferencia habría si el texto bíblico dijera que el creyente ha sido sellado «*por*» el Espíritu Santo? Este versículo indica también que el Padre ha sellado al creyente con el Espíritu «para el día de la redención». ¿A qué día se refiere y qué tiene que ver el acto de sellar al creyente para ese día?

**Efesios 1:13-14**

De los tres textos, este es el más claro debido a la mayor cantidad de información que nos da. Según el v. 13, ¿en qué momento se efectúa la obra de sellar al creyente? Igual que Efesios 4:30, el v. 13 dice que el creyente ha sido sellado «*con* el Espíritu Santo», no «*por* el Espíritu Santo». Entonces, ¿quién sella y en qué consiste ese sello? ¿A qué o a quién se refiere la palabra «arras»? Sea cual sea la respuesta correcta a esa pregunta, esas «arras» sirven al creyente en algo «hasta la redención de la posesión adquirida», lo cual tiene algo que ver con la herencia que espera al creyente.

Ahora, tome una posición en cuanto a la definición de la doctrina de «sellar». Luego, consulte la «Guía de estudio».

# 13

# Gramática

Pocas personas se entusiasman con la gramática. Sin embargo, este capítulo, conjuntamente con los pasos explicados en los seis capítulos anteriores, han ido preparando al lector para contestar con la máxima precisión posible la pregunta: ¿qué es lo que el autor quiso decir en este texto? No fijarse en la gramática de un pasaje sería parecido a correr un maratón de 42 km y a solo 10 metros de la meta ¡tirar la toalla! Por eso el gran reformador alemán Philipp Melanchthon (1497–1560), colaborador de Martín Lutero y el primer teólogo sistemático de la Reforma, dijo: «No se pueden entender las Escrituras de forma teológica hasta que hayan sido entendidas de forma gramatical»[1].

## A. CUATRO FACETAS DE LA GRAMÁTICA

El estudio gramatical de un texto bíblico incluye cuatro áreas de investigación:

*1. La lexicografía* identifica el significado de una palabra. Como vimos en el capítulo anterior, un léxico completo registrará los diferentes significados que una palabra ha adquirido con el tiempo y dónde, en la opinión de los editores, esos significados aparecen en las Escrituras.

1. Walter C. Kaiser, *Toward an Exegetical Theology* (Grand Rapids: Baker, 1981), pp. 26–27.

*2. La sintaxis* trata la relación que existe entre las palabras, proveyendo un uso consistente entre ellas para que un autor pueda decir algo que tenga sentido[2]. Las palabras nunca se encuentran solas, sino siempre en relación con otras palabras. Por ejemplo, si mezclásemos las palabras de Juan 3:16 ignorando la sintaxis, aparecería como «él mundo aquel manera mas Hijo para vida amó de tenga dado al porque Dios que su a todo unigénito pierda se no eterna que todo en he tal». Evidentemente, no entenderíamos nada porque no habríamos respetado la sintaxis, la cual establece una relación correcta entre las palabras.

*3. La gramática* presta atención al grupo al cual una palabra pertenece y a cómo funcionan las palabras en cada grupo. Un sustantivo designa personas, lugares y cosas. Un verbo indica acción o estado. Un pronombre (yo, tú, aquellos, etcétera) sustituye a un sustantivo. Un adjetivo modifica o describe un sustantivo. Un adverbio califica, limita o describe verbos, preposiciones y otros adverbios. Una preposición muestra la relación de un sustantivo con otra palabra con palabras como «encima de, dentro de, por, de, sobre», etcétera. Y una conjunción une palabras o frases.

*4. La morfología* presta atención a la forma de las palabras. Al estudiar un segundo idioma, no se tarda mucho en descubrir que las normas gramaticales de ese idioma son diferentes a las de la lengua materna. Una de las diferencias más importantes de la gramática del griego koiné son sus verbos. Mientras que los verbos en el español expresan tiempo (ayer *estudiaba*, hoy *estudio*, mañana *estudiaré*), en el griego los verbos subrayan el estado de una acción[3]. Por ejemplo, un verbo en:

---

2. En su libro *The Hermeneutical Spiral* (Downers Grove: InterVarsity Press, 1991), p. 93, Osborne dice que «en su sentido más restringido, la sintaxis se refiere a la relación entre las palabras de una frase u oración y es a todos los efectos sinónimo de la gramática. En su sentido más amplio, la sintaxis se refiere a las relaciones entre todas las palabras dentro de una frase u oración como un método de determinar el significado de una unidad total».

3. Algunos eruditos prefieren usar la palabra «aspecto» en lugar de «tiempo», puesto que los verbos griegos funcionan en base al estado de la acción que toma lugar, no el tiempo. Sin embargo, debido a que la palabra «tiempo» ha sido empleada durante tantos años, muchos eruditos prefieren usarla en lugar de intentar cambiar esa tradición tan arraigada.

a. *Presente* indica acción continua. La palabra *plero* en Efesios 5:18 está en el tiempo presente de imperativo, indicando acción continua. Por tanto, técnicamente debería ser traducida como «seguid siendo llenados». Pero puesto que los traductores no pueden permitirse el lujo de emplear tantas palabras para traducir una sola, la han traducido como «sed llenos». Este detalle hace una gran aportación a nuestra comprensión de la doctrina de la plenitud del Espíritu Santo; a saber, que el creyente puede y debe ser llenado continuamente del Espíritu Santo.
b. *Imperfecto* normalmente indica acción continua en el pasado.
c. *Perfecto* denota una acción que ocurrió en un momento puntual en el pasado, pero cuyos resultados, beneficios o consecuencias continúan en el presente.
d. *Pluscuamperfecto* indica una acción puntual en el pasado cuyos resultados tuvieron lugar solamente en el pasado.
e. *Futuro* es una acción indefinida por cuanto puede indicar una acción puntual o continua que ocurrirá en el futuro.
f. *Aoristo* denota una acción puntual. Aunque hay quienes cometen el error de limitar el estado del aoristo a una acción puntual en el pasado, el hecho es que el aoristo no define claramente cuál es la duración de dicha acción[4]. «El tiempo aoristo es como una fotografía instantánea que muestra (expresa) que una acción ocurre, mientras que la acción del tiempo presente es como una película que continúa»[5]. Esto no elimina la posibilidad de que, según el contexto inmediato, se refiera a una acción que ha ocurrido una vez y para siempre. Pero esta interpretación no puede sostenerse automáticamente en cada contexto.

---

4. Para una explicación excelente sobre la falacia de que el aoristo siempre indica que una acción haya sido realizada «una vez y para siempre», ver el libro de Donald A. Carson, *Falacias exegéticas* (Viladecavalls: CLIE, 1996), pp. 74–79.

5. Kay Arthur, *Cómo estudiar tu Biblia* (Chattanooga: Ministerios Precepto Internacional, 2002), p. 165.

Por ejemplo, hay una gran diferencia entre decir que «ninguna condenación *hay* para los que están en Cristo Jesús» (Ro. 8:1, énfasis añadido) y «ninguna condenación *habrá*...». La primera frase significa que el creyente ya está libre de toda condenación eterna, mientras que la segunda dice que será libre en un futuro. Si la segunda frase fuera la que apareciera en los manuscritos originales de Romanos, el creyente se quedaría con muchas dudas en cuanto a su estado eterno.

En la edición del N.T. de 1973 de la LBLA, Efesios 5:21 fue traducido como «*Someteos* unos a otros en el temor de Cristo» (énfasis añadido). «Someteos» es un imperativo, un mandamiento. No obstante, una nota en el margen indicaba que esa palabra significa literalmente «sometiéndoos». O sea, en español un gerundio que sirve para describir al verbo principal[6]. El verbo principal es «sed llenos» (v. 18). Entonces, Pablo emplea cuatro gerundios para describir cómo actúa el creyente que está lleno o controlado por el Espíritu Santo:

- «*hablando* entre vosotros con salmos, himnos y cantos espirituales» (v. 19);
- «*cantando y alabando* con vuestro corazón al Señor» (v. 19);
- «*dando* siempre gracias por todo» (v. 20); y
- «*sometiéndoos* unos a otros en el temor de Cristo» (v. 21, énfasis añadido)[7].

Para realizar un estudio gramatical de las Escrituras, el intérprete tiene que dominar no solamente estas diferencias en los verbos griegos, sino también los demás elementos de la gramática griega y hebrea. Este conocimiento le permitirá identificar el desarrollo del pensamiento del autor y así hacer una interpretación más precisa del pasaje. Sin embargo, este requisito no es una opción realista para la gran mayoría de los lectores. No obstante, hay al menos tres cosas que puede y, por tanto, debe hacer.

Primera, debe adoptar la costumbre de esquematizar el párrafo que estudia si se encuentra en una epístola. (El autor sugerirá a continuación un método para realizar esta tarea). Segunda, debe consultar al menos

---

6. En griego este gerundio corresponde a un participio con valor adverbial.

7. Con la publicación de la versión que incluía el A.T. el texto fue cambiado a «sometiéndoos».

dos versiones que pretenden recoger las palabras literales de los manuscritos originales (por ejemplo, la RVR60 y LBLA) y dos que procuran encontrar una equivalencia dinámica de esas palabras (por ejemplo, la NVI y NTV). Si en una o dos de esas versiones hay una palabra o frase que es marcadamente diferente a otras versiones, el lector puede estar seguro de que los eruditos bíblicos han debatido el tema de qué palabra o frase figuraba en el manuscrito original. Tercera, el lector debe consultar comentarios bíblicos técnicos, los cuales han sido escritos por eruditos que han pasado la mayor parte de sus vidas estudiando el griego y el hebreo.

| **Cuatro facetas de la gramática** | |
|---|---|
| Lexicografía | ¿Cuál es el significado de una palabra en su contexto inmediato? |
| Sintaxis | ¿Cuál es la relación que existe entre las diversas palabras de un párrafo? ¿Y entre las palabras de este párrafo y el siguiente? |
| Gramática | ¿A qué categoría gramatical pertenece una palabra? ¿Es un sustantivo, verbo, pronombre, adjetivo, adverbio, preposición, conjunción, etc.? |
| Morfología | ¿Cuál es la forma de una palabra? ¿El Padre nos bendijo, nos bendice o nos bendecirá con toda bendición espiritual en Cristo (Ef. 1:3)? |

## B. CÓMO ESQUEMATIZAR UN PÁRRAFO

Al esquematizar un párrafo, el intérprete tiene más posibilidades de identificar el desarrollo del pensamiento del autor. Hacer el esquema de un párrafo se limita casi exclusivamente a las Epístolas del N.T. puesto que son textos didácticos y pretenden comunicar ideas de forma lógica, en contraste con un pasaje histórico, poético o narrativo. Pero las Epístolas de Pablo pueden resultar difíciles de esquematizar porque el apóstol tiene la tendencia de escribir oraciones muy largas y desviarse frecuentemente por sendas que parecen no tener nada que ver con el desarrollo de su pensamiento principal. Por ejemplo, Colosenses 1:9-20 es una sola frase en el texto original. Y, aunque las diferentes versiones del N.T. introducen comas y puntos finales, a veces es difícil seguir el desarrollo de su pensamiento[8].

8. La RVR60 introduce cuatro puntos finales, la LBLA siete, la NVI diez y la NTV diecisiete en su traducción de este pasaje.

Una forma sencilla y muy eficaz de esquematizar un párrafo, ilustrado a continuación con Romanos 1:1-7, consiste en escribir de nuevo el texto, separando las oraciones independientes de las frases dependientes. Hay cinco normas que el intérprete debe seguir. Primera, el párrafo es la unidad de pensamiento que se debe esquematizar, no un par de versículos ni capítulos enteros. Segunda, las declaraciones u oraciones principales se colocan al extremo izquierdo. Tercera, cuando existe solamente una oración subordinada, debe colocarse en la misma línea que la frase independiente. Cuarta, cuando existen dos o más frases subordinadas, estas son colocadas debajo de la oración principal y sangradas. Quinta, normalmente las conjunciones *y*, *pero*, *ni tampoco*, *por eso*, etcétera introducen una frase que debe ser tratada como una entidad entera y colocada debajo de la línea principal que la precede.

**I. PABLO**

- A. siervo de Jesucristo
- B. llamado a ser apóstol
- C. apartado para el evangelio de Dios
    - 1. que él ya había prometido
        - a. por medio de sus profetas
        - b. en las santas Escrituras
    - 2. acerca de su Hijo
        - a. nuestro Señor Jesucristo
        - b. que nació de la descendencia de David según la carne
        - c. y que fue declarado Hijo de Dios
            - con poder
            - conforme al Espíritu de santidad
            - por la resurrección de entre los muertos
        - d. por medio de quien hemos recibido la gracia y el apostolado
            - para promover la obediencia a la fe entre los gentiles por amor a su nombre
            - entre los cuales estáis también vosotros, llamados de Jesucristo

**II. A TODOS LOS AMADOS DE DIOS**

- A. que están en Roma
- B. llamados a ser santos

**III. GRACIA A VOSOTROS Y PAZ**

- A. de parte de Dios nuestro Padre
- B. y del Señor Jesucristo

Según este esquema, el pensamiento principal de Romanos 1:1-7 es: «Pablo, a todos los amados de Dios, gracia a vosotros y paz». Al notar las frases que modifican estos tres conceptos principales, vemos que Pablo es identificado de tres maneras, los creyentes en Roma son identificados de dos maneras, y la gracia y paz cuentan con dos orígenes o fuentes. El siguiente nivel de frases sangradas muestra que el evangelio trata de lo que Dios «ya había prometido», «acerca de su Hijo», que es el cumplimiento de la promesa que Dios dio «por medio de sus profetas», la cual se encuentra «en las santas Escrituras». Además, su Hijo es identificado de cuatro maneras. La relación de las frases modificadoras más allá de este nivel normalmente está abierta a discusión y diferencias de opinión.

El estudio de la gramática es un trabajo laborioso. Pero el esfuerzo valdrá la pena porque abrirá los ojos del intérprete al significado del texto como ningún otro ejercicio puede hacerlo.

## *Trabajo para realizar*

La gramática cuenta con cuatro aspectos o áreas de investigación. Explique cuáles son y la tarea a la que se dedica cada uno. Puesto que el lector verá con cierta frecuencia estas cuatro palabras cuando consulte los comentarios bíblicos, es importante que domine el significado de cada una.

14

# El propósito y plan divino

La Biblia no es la historia de todo lo que ha ocurrido, sino de todo lo que es pertinente para el *propósito* de Dios de que «todos los hombres sean salvos y vengan al pleno conocimiento de la verdad» (1 Ti. 2:4, LBLA). Al llegar a este último capítulo de esta sección sobre la hermenéutica general, es el momento ideal para echar la vista atrás, contemplar el cuadro global de las Escrituras y contestar una pregunta muy importante: ¿cuál era el *plan* que Dios empleó para llevar a cabo ese propósito?

> «Oh SEÑOR, honraré y alabaré tu nombre, porque tú eres mi Dios. ¡Tú haces cosas maravillosas! Las planeaste hace mucho tiempo, y ahora las has realizado».
>
> **(Is. 25:1, NTV)**

¿Por qué es tan importante que el intérprete sepa en qué consistía ese plan? El mayor beneficio es que le proveerá un organigrama, un sistema, una estructura dentro de la cual podrá colocar la gran cantidad de eventos históricos, información y enseñanza que encuentra en las

Escrituras. Sin entender ese plan, muchos textos bíblicos le quedarán con incógnitas. Cuando pensamos en el plan de Dios para salvar al ser humano, solemos pensar en la muerte y resurrección de Cristo y en su segunda venida. Sin embargo, el plan de Dios contaba con muchos otros elementos, como la elección de los judíos como pueblo suyo, el Estado de Israel, la sustitución de Israel por la iglesia como el canal de la redención, etcétera.

## A. LOS TRES PLANES PRINCIPALES

Los evangélicos están de acuerdo en su convicción de que el propósito de Dios siempre ha sido la redención del ser humano. Sin embargo, discrepan sobre el plan que empleó para llevar a cabo ese propósito. El debate gira alrededor de unas preguntas muy relacionadas entre sí; a saber, ¿cuál es la relación entre la iglesia e Israel? ¿Son organismos diferentes o forman parte de una misma entidad? Aunque algunos creerán que estas preguntas son de poco valor práctico, la verdad es todo lo contrario. La respuesta que se dé a estas preguntas afectará dos doctrinas en particular.

1. *Soteriología.* En el A.T., cada hijo que nacía de padres judíos era incluido automáticamente en los pactos que Dios había hecho con todo el pueblo judío. ¿Es igual para los hijos de los creyentes hoy? O sea, ¿es creyente un bebé por ser hijo de padres creyentes? ¿Se debe evangelizar a los niños? ¿Es el bautismo de un bebé un sustituto o una extensión de la circuncisión que se practicaba en el A.T.? ¿Debemos bautizar a los bebés? Si bautizamos a los bebés, ¿qué es lo que representa dicho acto y qué es lo que logra?

2. *Escatología.* ¿Figura el pueblo judío en los planes futuros de Dios? ¿Son literales o espirituales las promesas que Dios les hizo sobre su vuelta futura a la Tierra Prometida? ¿Reinará Cristo durante mil años de forma literal en la tierra, o es su reino en esencia espiritual? ¿Habrá una Gran Tribulación literal? ¿Pasará la iglesia por ella? ¿Se cumplen en la iglesia las promesas que Dios hizo a Israel en el N.T.?

Entre los evangélicos existen tres ideas diferentes en cuanto al plan que Dios empleó para llevar a cabo su propósito de salvar al ser humano. Y más concretamente, sobre la relación que existe entre Israel y la iglesia, los dos medios que Dios ha empleado como canales de la redención. Esos tres planes se llaman la teología del pacto, el dispensacionalismo y el eclecticismo. Aunque la teología del pacto ha existido desde los primeros siglos de la iglesia, no fue sistematizada hasta la Reforma del siglo XVII por los teólogos holandeses Herman Witsius (1636–1708) y Johannes Cocceius (1603–1669). El dispensacionalismo nació a mitad del siglo XIX, tomando posición en el polo opuesto a la teología del pacto. El eclecticismo ha existido desde los primeros siglos de la iglesia; sin embargo, no jugó un papel significativo en el debate sobre el plan de Dios hasta mediados del siglo XX.

## Teología del pacto

La teología del pacto toma su nombre del pacto que Dios hizo con Adán antes de la Caída en Génesis 3 y de su pacto de gracia con el hombre después de ella. Afirma que Dios tiene una sola operación desde el principio hasta el final de la historia humana, ilustrada por las dos líneas que van en aumento en el dibujo de abajo. No existen diferencias en esta operación. La gracia de Dios es la misma en todas las edades, y la fe es el único requisito para salvarse, tanto en el A.T. como en el N.T. Abraham se salvó por la fe igual que cualquier creyente del siglo XXI. Por tanto, el pueblo de Dios en el A.T. es el mismo pueblo que encontramos en el N.T. No hay ninguna diferencia entre los ciudadanos de Israel que eran creyentes y los miembros de la iglesia. Israel es como la semilla de una planta que va creciendo y que vemos completamente desarrollada en el N.T. De ahí que los teólogos del pacto hablen de «la iglesia en el A.T.». Además, afirman que las promesas que Dios dio a Israel son aplicables a la iglesia.

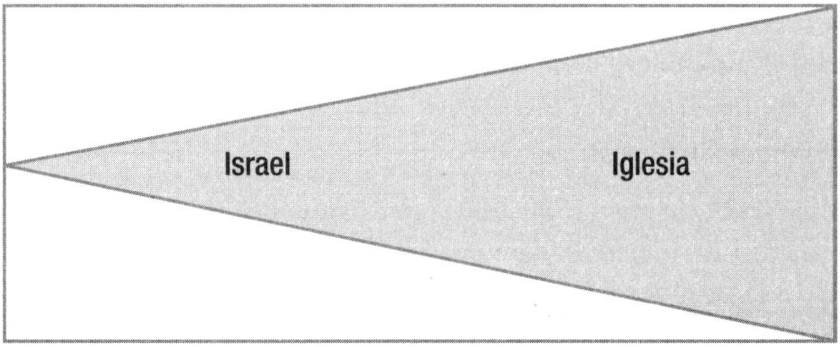

Los dispensacionalistas y eclécticos llaman la atención sobre varios problemas de este planteamiento, entre los cuales destacan dos. Primero, todos los evangélicos creen que es legítimo aplicar a la iglesia los textos del A.T. que hablan del amor y perdón de Dios. Puesto que Dios no cambia en cuanto a su carácter se refiere, los miembros de la iglesia pueden contar con ese mismo amor y perdón. Pero ¿cómo se pueden aplicar a la iglesia las promesas sobre la vuelta futura de los judíos a Palestina y su restauración como nación? Puesto que estas promesas fueron dadas en el contexto histórico de la destrucción de Israel y Judá como naciones, una interpretación literal es la única forma en que los judíos de aquel entonces las habrían entendido. Los teólogos del pacto son unos defensores ardientes de la interpretación literal de las Escrituras, excepto en estos temas escatológicos. Para aplicarlos a la iglesia, tienen que alegorizar o espiritualizar esos textos.

Segundo, su práctica de bautizar a los bebés delata una incoherencia en su definición del bautismo. Decir que el bautismo *salva* al infante contradice la fe que ejerció Abraham, haciendo uso de su inteligencia y voluntad de creer lo que Dios le había dicho. Un bebé no tiene uso de razón. Decir que es un *símbolo* de la salvación por cuanto el bebé ya forma parte del pueblo de Dios los obliga a explicar cómo llegó a ser creyente. ¿Simplemente por ser hijo de creyentes de la misma forma en que un niño judío en el A.T. formaba parte del pueblo de Dios por nacer de padres judíos? Decir que es un *acto de dedicación* en el cual los padres piden que Dios proteja a su hijo hasta que llegue a la edad en que pueda tomar su propia decisión en cuanto a Cristo contradice lo que dicen los textos didácticos del N.T. en cuanto a la naturaleza y propósito del bautismo. La definición que una iglesia y sus miembros hagan en cuanto al bautismo afectará su ministerio entre los niños. ¿Están perdidos? ¿Deben ser evangelizados? ¿Deben bautizarse de nuevo como mayores si se convierten?

## Dispensacionalismo

John Nelson Darby (1800–1882) es el padre del dispensacionalismo. Comenzó su ministerio como pastor anglicano en Irlanda del Norte. En 1845 abandonó la Iglesia de Inglaterra, convencido de que esta había abandonado el mensaje de la gracia y salvación en Cristo Jesús, que no tenía un concepto bíblico de la iglesia local y que había caído en la apostasía. A raíz de esa convicción, Darby y otros salieron de la Iglesia de Inglaterra y fundaron los Hermanos en Plymouth[1].

Darby no inventó la palabra «dispensación», sino que era la palabra que Tertuliano (c. 160-c. 220) empleaba para traducir la palabra *oikonomia* de 1 Corintios 9:17; Efesios 1:10; 3:2, 9; Colosenses 1:25[2]. En la cultura griega del primer siglo un *oikonomos* era un siervo que administraba las actividades de una casa. La palabra *oikonomia* se refería a su oficio o a la actividad que desempeñaba[3]. Con el tiempo *oikonomos* y *oikonomia* llegaron a referirse a cualquier clase de administración o administrador[4]. El dispensacionalismo define la dispensación como un período de la historia humana en el cual Dios administra o gobierna el mundo de una forma diferente a como lo hace en los tiempos anteriores y posteriores. Aunque Efesios 1:10 («...de reunir todas las cosas en Cristo, en la dispensación del cumplimiento de los tiempos...») es el

---

1. Las iglesias de este grupo son llamadas Asambleas de Hermanos en muchos países. En las pp. 13–14 de su libro *Understanding Dispensationalists* (Phillipsburg: R & R Publishing, 1994), Vern S. Poythress sugiere que había un factor adicional que animó a Darby y otros a marcharse de la Iglesia de Inglaterra (anglicana). «Los distintivos del dispensacionalismo surgieron por primera vez en el siglo XIX en un momento cuando buena parte de la teología ortodoxa, y en particular la teología sistemática, no hacía un énfasis suficiente en el carácter histórico y progresivo de la revelación bíblica. Al preocuparse tanto por lo que dice la Biblia sobre un tema en particular, la teología sistemática puede ignorar la diversidad y carácter dinámico con los que la Palabra de Dios ha llegado al hombre en las diferentes épocas de la historia. El dispensacionalismo surgió en parte como un intento de reconocer esas diferencias y diversidades. Procuró colocar en un sistema que fuera coherente e inteligible dichas diferencias que, de otro modo, podrían entenderse como tensiones y hasta contradicciones dentro de la misma Palabra de Dios».

2. Tertuliano estableció mucho del vocabulario teológico que la iglesia latina empleó durante los siglos siguientes.

3. De ahí que *oikonomia* se traduzca en la RVR60 como «comisión» (1 Co. 9:17), «dispensación» (Ef. 1:10; 3:9) y «administración» (Ef. 3:2; Col. 1:25).

4. En la p. 107 de su libro *Progressive Dispensationalism* (Grand Rapids: Baker, 1993), Craig A. Blaising y Darrell L. Bock dicen que «no solamente el administrador de una finca, sino también un cocinero podría ser designado como un *oikonomos*. Este título fue empleado para oficiales públicos y políticos desde los procuradores romanos hasta los tesoreros de las ciudades, y hasta los administradores de los baños públicos».

único texto donde *oikonomia* parece tener ese significado teológico, el hecho es que este texto existe y ha de tomarse en cuenta. La mayoría de los dispensacionalistas creen que hay siete dispensaciones[5].

Hay cuatro distintivos que caracterizan el dispensacionalismo. Primero, su interpretación literal de las Escrituras, especialmente aquellos pasajes que tratan el futuro escatológico de Israel. A partir de Agustín (354–430) predominó la idea de que las profecías sobre la restauración futura de Israel tenían que ver con el alcance del evangelio durante el tiempo actual de la iglesia. Para llegar a esa interpretación, el intérprete tenía que espiritualizar los textos pertinentes. El dispensacionalismo insiste en que esos textos han de interpretarse de forma literal.

Segundo, su interés por la profecía. En los siglos anteriores a Darby la iglesia creía en la segunda venida de Cristo, la condenación eterna de los perdidos y el futuro glorioso de los creyentes. Pero poco más. No indagaba más en la escatología por considerar los textos proféticos demasiado difíciles de entender. Además, estaban ocupados con otras doctrinas. La interpretación literal de los textos proféticos por Darby demostró que se podían entender, lo cual a su vez promovió un interés por los temas proféticos entre los dispensacionalistas. Como consecuencia, la gran mayoría de los libros escritos sobre temas proféticos durante muchas décadas han procedido de autores dispensacionalistas. Los gráficos que han creado para mostrar la cronología de los eventos futuros han sido muy apreciados por muchos creyentes

5. En su *Systematic Theology* (Grand Rapids: Eerdmans, 1997), tomo II, pp. 373–377, Charles Hodge (1797–1878) reconoció cuatro dispensaciones: de Adán hasta Abraham; de Abraham hasta Moisés; de Moisés hasta Cristo; y la dispensación del evangelio. No obstante, el típico dispensacionalista reconoce entre siete y nueve dispensaciones: (1) Inocencia o libertad: desde la creación hasta la Caída; (2) Conciencia: desde la Caída hasta el Diluvio; (3) Gobierno humano: desde el Diluvio hasta la torre de Babel; (4) Promesa: desde la promesa hecha a Abraham hasta el Éxodo; (5) Ley: desde el monte Sinaí hasta el Calvario; (6) Gracia. Todos los dispensacionalistas creen que esta dispensación comenzó el día de Pentecostés en Hechos 2. Algunos creen que la dispensación actual terminará con el arrebatamiento de la iglesia antes de la Gran Tribulación, y añaden una séptima dispensación de Juicio, la cual comenzará con el arrebatamiento y se extenderá hasta la segunda venida de Cristo al final de la Gran Tribulación. (7) Reino: desde el milenio hasta el gran trono blanco. Normalmente, la eternidad futura no es considerada una dispensación.

porque les han permitido colocar todas las piezas de su conocimiento profético dentro de un sistema.

Tercero, su énfasis sobre la revelación progresiva. Este principio obliga al intérprete a tomar en cuenta el momento histórico en que cada revelación fue dada. Por ejemplo, la forma tan diferente en que el Espíritu Santo se relacionaba con los creyentes en las dispensaciones de la Ley y la Gracia. Antes de Hechos 2, el Espíritu Santo venía solamente sobre aquellas personas que Dios había elegido para llevar a cabo una misión. Una vez cumplida esa misión, se retiraba. Pero en la dispensación de la Gracia, el Espíritu Santo mora en cada creyente de forma permanente[6]. Un texto encontrado en la dispensación de la Ley no debe aplicarse a la iglesia que se encuentra en la dispensación de la Gracia, ni viceversa.

Cuarto, su distinción muy marcada entre Israel y la iglesia. Con base en el tercer énfasis del párrafo anterior, los dispensacionalistas hacen una distinción muy clara entre el plan que Dios tiene para Israel y su plan para la iglesia. Aunque los autores dispensacionalistas reconocen las similitudes que existen entre el pueblo de Dios en el A.T. y los miembros de la iglesia en el N.T., a la hora de escribir artículos y libros sobre temas proféticos dejan de mencionar dichas similitudes.

A la luz de estos distintivos, el dispensacionalismo cree que el plan original de Dios para la redención del ser humano contaba con la colaboración de los judíos, su pueblo elegido. Pero puesto que insistieron en desobedecerlo, Dios levantó a la iglesia como su nuevo colaborador, abandonando así de momento a Israel. La iglesia representa un segundo plan, un paréntesis entre la primera y la segunda parte de su plan original. Por tanto, el plan de Dios cuenta con dos operaciones. El dispensacionalismo cree que la iglesia comenzó en Hechos 2 y culminará cuando sea arrebatada justo antes de la Gran Tribulación, tiempo durante el cual los judíos serán perseguidos a escala mundial y se convertirán en masa a Cristo, su Mesías. La iglesia no pasará por la Gran Tribulación puesto que es un tiempo de aflicción para «Jacob»; o sea, Israel (Jer. 30:7). Al final de la Gran Tribulación, Cristo volverá

---

6. Para más información sobre la obra distinta del Espíritu Santo en el A.T. y N.T., ver el libro de Jaime Fasold, *Dones espirituales* (Grand Rapids: Portavoz, 2000), pp. 77–87.

a la tierra con la iglesia y reinará sobre todas las naciones desde Jerusalén durante mil años. Al final de ese reino ocurrirán ciertos eventos y después todos pasarán a la eternidad. En todo este planteamiento el dispensacionalismo hace una distinción muy marcada entre Israel y la iglesia como entidades diferentes, aunque tienen ciertas similitudes.

Este dibujo del dispensacionalismo y el del eclecticismo más adelante reflejan el orden cronológico en que ocurrirán los eventos citados, no el tiempo que durará cada uno de ellos. Por ejemplo, el tiempo que han durado Israel y la Iglesia ha sido de muchos siglos, mientras que el cuadro de «Israel restaurado» ocurrirá a lo largo de los siete años de la Gran Tribulación (G.T.).

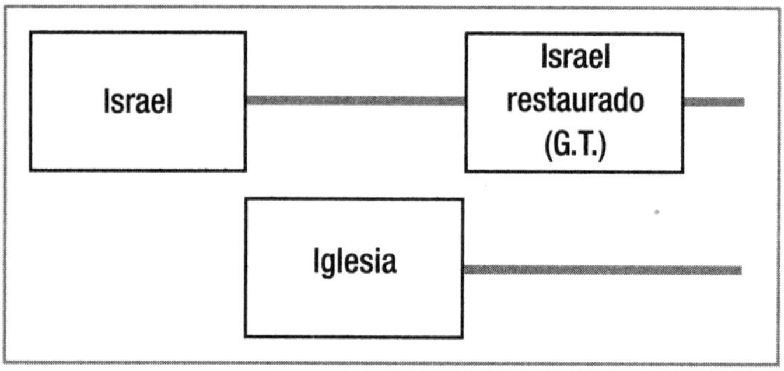


En cualquier debate el mayor peso para demostrar que alguien tiene razón recae sobre la persona cuya interpretación es más detallada. Puesto que el dispensacionalismo es la más detallada de las tres posiciones, ha sido también la más escudriñada y criticada. Por ejemplo, en referencia a su posición de que la iglesia será arrebatada antes de comenzar la Gran Tribulación, Gundry dice que «la novedad de una posición escatológica requiere que la evidencia presentada a su favor tenga más peso de lo normal puesto que es dudoso que eruditos santos y muy formados, o la gran masa de los creyentes piadosos, hayan malinterpretado la enseñanza de las Escrituras en un área tan importante como la esperanza gloriosa y que lo hayan hecho durante siglos enteros»[7].

7. Robert H. Gundry, *The Church and the Tribulation* (Grand Rapids: Zondervan, 1973), p. 172.

## Eclecticismo

El eclecticismo aprecia y acepta ciertos elementos de la teología del pacto y del dispensacionalismo[8], pero no acepta la totalidad de ninguno de los dos. Para el eclecticismo, Dios tiene un solo programa. Igual que el dispensacionalismo, cree que Israel y la iglesia son dos entidades distintas. Por eso, no se refiere a Israel como «la iglesia en el A.T.». No obstante, mientras que no llega tan lejos como la teología del pacto, cree que existe una relación íntima entre Israel y la iglesia. Igual que el dispensacionalismo, el eclecticismo cree que la iglesia comenzó en Hechos 2. Pero al contrario que los dispensacionalistas, los eclécticos creen que la Iglesia pasará por la Gran Tribulación. Durante la Gran Tribulación los judíos reconocerán a Cristo como el Mesías. En su segunda venida al final de la Gran Tribulación, Cristo arrebatará a su iglesia para encontrarse con ella en el aire. Entonces, en lugar de ser llevada al cielo, la iglesia acompañará a Cristo hasta la tierra, donde él reinará durante mil años desde Jerusalén con la iglesia e Israel presentes[9].

| Israel | / / / / / | Iglesia | / / / / / | Iglesia e Israel |
|---|---|---|---|---|

Hay varios pasajes que apoyan el concepto de que existe una relación íntima entre Israel y la iglesia, aunque son entidades distintas. En Romanos 11:16-24 los gentiles que se convierten a Cristo son descritos como injertos silvestres en el mismo árbol que representa a Israel. Como hay un solo árbol, este texto deja la clara impresión de que hay un solo programa en el plan de Dios para redimir al ser humano. Sin

8. En el capítulo 5 de su libro *Hermenéutica: principios y procedimientos de interpretación bíblica* (Miami: Editorial Vida, 1994), Henry A. Virkler describe lo que creen la teología del pacto, el dispensacionalismo, el eclecticismo (lo cual llama «el modelo epigenético») y el modelo luterano.

9. O sea, el arrebatamiento de la iglesia y la segunda venida de Cristo ocurren simultáneamente.

embargo, los vv. 1 y 13 hablan de los israelitas y los gentiles de la iglesia en Roma como dos pueblos diferentes en el contexto de ese único programa (especialmente en los vv. 17, 19, 23-24).

Las palabras de Jeremías 31:31-34 sobre el nuevo pacto que Dios establecerá en el futuro con su pueblo elegido están dirigidas a Israel (v. 1). Sin embargo, Jesús declaró que la copa es «el nuevo pacto en mi sangre» (1 Co. 11:25). Pero esta copa forma parte de la celebración de la Santa Cena, una ordenanza de la iglesia.

Joel profetizó que en el futuro Dios derramaría su Espíritu sobre su pueblo de Israel, y tanto jóvenes como ancianos profetizarían y recibirían sueños y visiones (2:28-32). Esta promesa fue dada a Israel. Sin embargo, Pedro declara en el día de Pentecostés que esa profecía se cumplió en aquel momento, justamente el día en que los dispensacionalistas y eclécticos creen que la iglesia nació (Hch. 2:16-21). Si la promesa fue dada a Israel, ¿cómo es que se cumplió en la iglesia, a no ser que los dos estén íntimamente relacionados?

Romanos 9 y Gálatas 3 dan la clara impresión de que los gentiles que se han convertido a Cristo en la dispensación de la Gracia, el tiempo de la iglesia, son herederos de las promesas que Dios dio originalmente a Israel. A la luz de estos dos capítulos y los textos citados anteriormente, nos enfrentamos con dos opciones. O tenemos que ignorar o minimizar los pasajes del N.T. que declaran que ciertas profecías dirigidas a Israel fueron cumplidas en la iglesia, o tenemos que reconocer que Israel y la iglesia están íntimamente relacionadas, aunque sean entidades diferentes.

## B. LA CUESTIÓN FUNDAMENTAL

¿Cuántos programas tiene Dios? El autor de *Con precisión* cree que Dios tiene solamente un programa o plan para redimir al ser humano. Tanto los creyentes del A.T. como los del N.T. se salvaron por la fe, no por obras. Sin embargo, existe una diferencia entre Israel y la iglesia. Son dos entidades distintas. Entonces, ¿cuál es la relación entre Israel y la iglesia? ¡Esa es la cuestión fundamental! En cualquier consideración del plan que Dios empleó para redimir al ser humano, conviene mantener en mente tres observaciones importantes.

*1. Los tres sistemas no afectan ni tratan de doctrinas fundamentales.* Mientras que el *propósito* de Dios es que «todos los hombres sean salvos y vengan al pleno conocimiento de la verdad» (1 Ti. 2:4, LBLA), lo cual es una doctrina fundamental, su *plan* para llevar a cabo ese propósito no es una cuestión fundamental. Por tanto, ninguno de los tres sistemas representa una desviación doctrinal. Los tres representan interpretaciones evangélicas. Luego, la posición que otro hermano en Cristo mantiene sobre el plan de Dios no debería ser un criterio para tener comunión o no con él.

*2. Durante las últimas décadas la teología del pacto y el dispensacionalismo se han acercado en sus posiciones.* Desde que Witsius y Cocceius sistematizaron la teología del pacto en el siglo XVII, y desde que Darby introdujo el dispensacionalismo en la última mitad del siglo XIX, los teólogos del pacto[10] y los dispensacionalistas[11] han

---

10. Los teólogos actuales del pacto creen que el milenio ocurre ahora en el cielo o en el corazón del creyente. Por tanto, es espiritual en esencia. Sin embargo, al hacer más énfasis en la promesa bíblica de un cielo y una *tierra* nueva (Ap. 21:1), algunos de ellos se han acercado a la posición dispensacionalista de que Cristo establecerá un reino en la tierra a partir de su segunda venida. Para más información al respecto, ver el libro de Anthony A. Hoekema, *The Bible and the Future* (Grand Rapids: Eerdmans, 1979).

11. Ha habido tres etapas en el desarrollo del dispensacionalismo. La primera, llamada el dispensacionalismo clásico o tradicional, fue fundada por John Nelson Darby y secundada por C. I. Scofield (1843–1921), un reconocido erudito bíblico estadounidense cuyo apoyo dio ímpetu al dispensacionalismo. Durante esta etapa se hizo énfasis en las distintas dispensaciones. La segunda etapa comenzó en la década de los 60, en gran parte gracias al trabajo de Charles C. Ryrie, autor de *Dispensacionalismo hoy* (Barcelona: Portavoz Evangélico, 1974). [En su libro *Four Views on the Book of Revelation* (Grand Rapids: Zondervan, 1998), p. 30, C. Marvin Pate (ed.) dice que esta segunda etapa es llamada a veces la etapa clásica o tradicional.] Ryrie y otros clarificaron que los hombres de todas las edades son salvados por la fe, no por obras. También hicieron énfasis en el método literal de interpretación como la hermenéutica del dispensacionalismo. Durante la década de los 80 surgió la tercera etapa, llamada el dispensacionalismo progresivo o modificado, una posición explicada por Craig A. Blaising y Darrell L. Bock en su libro *Progressive Dispensationalism* (Grand Rapids: Baker, 1993). Mientras que los dispensacionalistas se reparten entre las posiciones mantenidas durante las tres etapas de su historia, muchos en la actualidad no hacen una distinción tan marcada entre Israel y la iglesia como en tiempos pasados. A la vez creen que la iglesia participa en las promesas hechas a Abraham

continuado investigando los textos pertinentes para entender mejor el plan de Dios para redimir al ser humano. Como resultado los dos sistemas se han acercado en ciertos temas.

*3. La exégesis es más importante que el sistema que produce.* Cada sistema es el producto de la exégesis de los textos pertinentes. Con base en su exégesis de estos textos, el intérprete formula un sistema que, en su opinión, explica mejor el plan que Dios empleó para llevar a cabo su propósito de redimir al ser humano. Entre esos textos habrá unos que le parezcan claros y otros más difíciles de entender. El sistema que adopte el intérprete lo ayudará a entender mejor aquellos textos difíciles. Hasta este punto el procedimiento que ha seguido el intérprete es correcto y legítimo. Sin embargo, ¿qué debe hacer cuando un texto contradiga las conclusiones de su sistema? ¿A qué se deberá esta contradicción? Es probable que el intérprete haya cometido uno de los siguientes tres errores.

Primero, que se haya equivocado en su exégesis de los textos pertinentes; entonces, los problemas planteados por un texto lo obligarán a retocar su sistema.

> La posición protestante histórica es que la teología debe fundarse sobre la exégesis bíblica. Un sistema teológico debe ser construido por la exégesis ladrillo a ladrillo. De ahí que la teología no sea mejor que la exégesis sobre la cual descansa. La tarea del teólogo sistemático es la de comenzar con estos ladrillos identificados mediante la exégesis y construir el templo de su sistema teológico. Sin embargo, solo después de estar seguro de cada ladrillo puede el intérprete hacer las generalizaciones necesarias y llevar a cabo la actividad creativa que es necesaria para la construcción de un sistema teológico[12].

---

debido a su unión con Cristo, quien es el cumplimiento de esas promesas. No obstante, creen que el cumplimiento completo y literal de esas promesas ocurrirá en el futuro. Contrario al dispensacionalismo clásico o tradicional, el dispensacionalismo progresivo no considera como tan importante el momento en que ocurrirá el arrebatamiento de la iglesia.

12. Bernard Ramm, *Protestant Biblical Interpretation* (Grand Rapids: Baker, 1978), p. 169.

Segundo, que haya impuesto sobre algunos textos la interpretación que otros le han enseñado, la cual no puede ser sostenida por dichos textos. Es lógico y comprensible que el intérprete adopte el sistema que otros le han enseñado. Pero es imposible que las tres posiciones sean correctas. Si el intérprete va a reconocer las Escrituras como la última autoridad en todo lo que cree, tendrá que dar prioridad a la exégesis y reconocer al sistema como siervo de ella.

> Los sistemas no son intrínsecamente malos. Funcionan para hacer que la interpretación sea un poco más fácil y un poco más realista; significa que no hay que volver a las bases en cada punto. Si la tradición es, en líneas generales, ortodoxa, el sistema ayuda a alejarse de interpretaciones heterodoxas. Pero un sistema puede ser tan estrechamente controlado que no permite, en sí mismo, ser corregido por las Escrituras, modificado por las Escrituras o incluso rechazado por las Escrituras[13].

Tercero, que haya estudiado ciertos textos pertinentes dejando otros en el tintero. La solución de este problema es evidente: tiene que estudiar todos los pasajes pertinentes de un tema antes de tomar una posición.

Es legítimo, importante y hasta necesario que el intérprete emplee un sistema para interpretar las Escrituras. Pero ha de recordar también que el sistema que abraza es de fabricación humana y que prima la exégesis de los textos pertinentes. Dios tiene un plan para salvar al ser humano y lo está llevando a cabo en este momento. En esto todos los evangélicos están de acuerdo.

---

13. Donald A. Carson, «¿Debo aprender a interpretar la Biblia?» en *Idea*, revista de la Alianza Evangélica Española (septiembre–diciembre 2008), p. 15.

## *Trabajo para realizar*

1. Describa las creencias básicas de los tres sistemas que los teólogos han propuesto para explicar el plan que Dios está empleando para llevar a cabo su propósito de salvar al ser humano de su pecado. ¿Cuáles son las creencias principales de cada uno? ¿Cuáles son las dos doctrinas más afectadas por el plan que el intérprete adopta?

2. Para comparar los distintivos del dispensacionalismo y de la teología del pacto, lea las páginas indicadas de los libros de Ryrie y Berkhof.

   - Charles C. Ryrie, *Dispensacionalismo hoy* (Barcelona: Portavoz Evangélico, 1974). Lea los capítulos titulados «La Iglesia en el dispensacionalismo» y «La teología del pacto». Ryrie es dispensacionalista.

   - Louis Berkhof, *Teología sistemática* (Grand Rapids: Tell, 1976). Lea las páginas 345–357, 661–683 y 754–768, prestando atención especial a las pp. 680–683 y 754–768. Berkhof es un teólogo del pacto.

## Sección III

# Hermenéutica especial

Los géneros literarios tratados en la tradicionalmente llamada hermenéutica especial son aquellos que no admiten una interpretación literal, la forma habitual de interpretar cualquier comunicación humana. Y dos de ellos —la profecía y los tipos— se encuentran solamente en las Escrituras.


15. Modismos hebreos
16. Lenguaje figurado
17. Poesía hebrea
18. Parábolas (I)
19. Parábolas (II)
20. Símbolos
21. Tipos
22. Profecía (I)
23. Profecía (II)

# 15

# Modismos hebreos

En esta sección trataremos algunos de los géneros literarios que tradicionalmente han formado parte de la hermenéutica especial. Todos estos géneros son especiales por dos motivos. Primero, porque no emplean una forma literal de comunicación. Por tanto, se requieren normas especiales para interpretarlos. Segundo, porque algunos de ellos, como la profecía y los tipos, se encuentran solamente en las Escrituras. Ningún libro secular emplea el género de tipos, y solamente las Escrituras incluyen la verdadera profecía. Este primer capítulo tratará los modismos hebreos más comunes por ser los más fáciles de entender. Los capítulos siguientes procederán paso a paso hasta los géneros más difíciles empleados por los autores bíblicos.

Un modismo es una frase o expresión que es peculiar del idioma de un pueblo en un lugar geográfico específico, porque funciona de forma contraria a las normas de dicho idioma. El significado del modismo no se encuentra en sus palabras, sino en el uso de una frase que ese pueblo entiende, que supone un significado especial. Los modismos abundan en cada idioma. Cuatro de los modismos hebreos más comunes son los siguientes.

## A. «PARA SIEMPRE»

Por regla general, en las Escrituras «para siempre» significa «para la eternidad». Por ejemplo, Pablo dice: «Luego, junto con ellos, nosotros, los que aún sigamos vivos sobre la tierra, seremos arrebatados en las nubes para encontrarnos con el Señor en el aire. Entonces estaremos con el Señor para siempre» (1 Ts. 4:17, NTV; ver también 2 Co. 9:9 y 1 P. 1:25). Pero cuando «para siempre» es empleado como modismo, significa «el resto de la vida terrenal» de una persona. En Deuteronomio 15:12-18 la Ley dicta cómo un amo debe tratar a un judío que se ha vendido a sí mismo como esclavo porque no puede pagar sus deudas. Cuando el esclavo ha cumplido seis años de trabajo, el amo tiene que liberarlo. Pero si el esclavo quiere quedarse como tal, Dios dice al amo: «Entonces tomarás una lesna, y horadarás su oreja contra la puerta, y será tu siervo *para siempre*; así también harás a tu criada» (v. 17, énfasis añadido). Evidentemente, «para siempre» no significa por toda la eternidad, sino hasta que muera el esclavo. Con este texto como trasfondo, Jesús emplea este modismo al decir que «el esclavo no queda en la casa para siempre; el hijo sí queda para siempre» (Jn. 8:35).

## B. «HIJO DE» O SU EQUIVALENTE

Este modismo tiene cuatro expresiones. Primero, se emplea para describir a una persona que posee la característica de alguien o algo. En Efesios 5:8 Pablo exhorta a los efesios a vivir como «hijos de luz», obedeciendo la luz que se encuentra en las Escrituras. En Lucas 7:35 Jesús afirma que la sabiduría es «justificada por todos sus hijos». Antes de enviar a los setenta evangelistas a predicar en las ciudades donde pensaba hacer una visita, Jesús les habló de los «hijos de paz», personas pacíficas (o posiblemente creyentes) que encontrarían por el camino (Lc. 10:6). Otros ejemplos incluyen:

| | |
|---|---|
| «Hijos del Trueno» (Mc. 3:17) | Los hermanos Jacobo y Juan eran hombres violentos y vengativos. |
| «Hijo de consolación» (Hch. 4:36) | Bernabé era un hombre con un ministerio especial de consolación. |
| «hijos de desobediencia» (Ef. 2:2) | Antes de convertirse, los efesios desobedecían las leyes de Dios. |
| «hijos de ira» (Ef. 2.3) | Antes de convertirse, los efesios eran caracterizados por la ira. |

| | |
|---|---|
| «hijo de perdición» (Jn. 17:12) | Cristo guardó a todos sus discípulos con la excepción de Judas porque este estaba condenado a perderse. |
| «hijos de luz e hijos del día» (1 Ts. 5:5) | Los tesalonicenses andaban en la luz, obedeciendo al Padre celestial. |
| «para que seáis hijos de vuestro Padre» (Mt. 5:45) | El que ama y ora por sus enemigos es un hijo de Dios, quien hace que el sol se levante y la lluvia caiga también sobre los injustos igual que sobre los justos. |

Segundo, «hijo de» se refiere a «alguien que pertenece a la familia espiritual de...». En Gálatas 3:7 Pablo dice que todas las personas que creen en Cristo son «hijos de Abraham». Abraham se destaca como un hombre de fe. Creyó la promesa que Dios le hizo en cuanto al nacimiento de su primer hijo Isaac «y el SEÑOR lo consideró justo» (Gn. 15:6, NTV). Por tanto, es un hijo de Abraham todo aquel que cree lo que Dios dice en cuanto a su Hijo Jesucristo y aprovecha la salvación que le ofrece.

Tercero, se emplea para los seguidores o discípulos de una persona. En Mateo 12:22-32 los fariseos acusan a Jesús de echar un demonio por el poder de Satanás. Jesús les responde con una pregunta: «Si yo echo fuera los demonios por Beelzebú, ¿por quién los echan vuestros hijos?» (v. 27). Evidentemente, Jesús se refiere a los discípulos de los fariseos, no a los hijos que han tenido con sus respectivas esposas.

Pero es el cuarto uso de «hijo de» el que suele crear la mayor confusión. En este caso las palabras «hijo de», o palabras como «engendrar», «padre de», etcétera, pueden referirse a descendientes lejanos, no solamente a hijos inmediatos. El autor de 2 Reyes 9:20 habla de Jehú como el hijo de Nimsi cuando en realidad es su *nieto* (v. 2). En Génesis 30:11, 13 y 46:16-18 Gad y Aser son identificados como los *hijos* de Zilpa, cuando en realidad son sus *nietos*. Heber y Malquiel son identificados como los hijos de Bería (un hijo de Aser), aunque eran *bisnietos* suyos. Es posible que los setenta hijos e hijas que Jacob engendró incluyeran *bisnietos* (Éx. 1:5). En 2 Reyes 8:26 Atalía es llamada la hija de Omri, mientras que el v. 18 la identifica como la hija de Acab. En este caso Atalía era la hija de Acab y la *nieta* de Omri.

## C. LO ABSOLUTO POR LO RELATIVO

Una declaración absoluta emplea palabras como «todos, nadie, siempre, nunca, no, ninguno», las cuales no admiten ninguna excepción. Una declaración relativa emplea palabras como *más que, más de, mucho, poco, prefiere*, las cuales admiten otras posibilidades, comparaciones, grados y niveles. Una declaración relativa solo tiene sentido cuando se hace una comparación con otra cosa.

Cuando los autores bíblicos emplean el modismo de lo absoluto por lo relativo, dicen algo de forma absoluta, algo que no admite ninguna excepción, pero quieren que sus lectores entiendan sus palabras de forma relativa. Su propósito es llevarlos de una posición extrema y equivocada en la cual han caído a una posición equilibrada y bíblica. Para lograr esa meta el autor les manda realizar un acto que se encuentra en el polo opuesto, lo cual es igualmente erróneo. Entender este modismo de forma literal llevaría al intérprete a caer en una interpretación absurda que a la vez contradeciría la enseñanza de otros textos bíblicos.

Por ejemplo, en Lucas 14:12-13 Jesús dice al hombre que le ha invitado a comer en su casa: «Cuando ofrezcas un almuerzo o des un banquete, no invites a tus amigos, hermanos, parientes y vecinos ricos. Pues ellos también te invitarán a ti, y esa será tu única recompensa. Al contrario, invita al pobre, al lisiado, al cojo y al ciego» (NTV). A primera vista, parece que Jesús le prohíbe invitar a sus amigos y familiares a casa para cenar. Pero lo que quiere decir a ese anfitrión es que no debería invitar solamente a aquellas personas que le podrán devolver el favor, sino también a los pobres que realmente necesitan la comida que pone en su mesa.

Otro ejemplo se encuentra en Proverbios 8:10 donde Salomón dice a su hijo (y otros): «Elijan mi instrucción en lugar de la plata y el conocimiento antes que el oro puro» (NTV). No está diciendo que su hijo deba menospreciar o rechazar el valor del dinero o un empleo, sino que sus consejos y el conocimiento (ciencia) son más importantes que el dinero.

En Jeremías 7:2 Dios manda a Jeremías a ponerse a la entrada del templo y decir a los habitantes de Jerusalén: «No hablé yo con vuestros padres, ni nada les mandé acerca de holocaustos y de víctimas el día que los saqué de la tierra de Egipto. Mas esto les mandé, diciendo: Escuchad mi voz, y seré a vosotros por Dios, y vosotros me seréis por pueblo; y andad en todo camino que os mande, para que os vaya bien» (vv. 22-23). Si interpretáramos este texto de forma literal, tendríamos que eliminar una gran parte del Pentateuco. Lo que Dios quiere decir es que todos los holocaustos, sacrificios, etcétera no sirven de nada si su pueblo no lo obedece, si su corazón está lejos de él. Ser un verdadero adorador de Jehová implica una vida consecuente de obediencia. No se trata simplemente de cumplir con las formas externas de lo que significa ser creyente.

En 1 Pedro 3:3-4 el apóstol dice a las mujeres: «Vuestro atavío *no* sea el externo de peinados ostentosos, de adornos de oro o de vestidos lujosos, sino el interno, el del corazón, en el incorruptible ornato de un espíritu afable y apacible, que es de grande estima delante de Dios» (énfasis añadido). En este texto Pedro se dirige a aquellas mujeres cuyo interés y afán principal es embellecer su aspecto exterior sin prestar ninguna atención al estado de su alma. Para llevarlas a una posición equilibrada, Pedro se va al otro extremo. Sin embargo, no está diciendo que estas mujeres deberían descuidar su aspecto exterior, no usar maquillaje, no vestirse de ropa atractiva ni llevar joyas de la clase que sea (incluyendo anillos de boda), sino que presten atención a su belleza interior, que es mucho más valiosa que la belleza exterior.

Cuando un autor bíblico emplea este modismo, está haciendo un énfasis exagerado sobre una actividad, pensamiento o actitud con el fin de recuperar un valor que se ha perdido por el camino. Cuando la interpretación literal de un texto resulta absurda, es muy posible que se trate de este modismo de lo absoluto por lo relativo o de una clase de lenguaje figurado. No obstante, el intérprete no debe abusar de este principio, eliminando la fuerza y enseñanza de pasajes literales al considerarlos un ejemplo de este modismo.

## D. MODISMO DEL TIEMPO

Uno de los textos que ha dejado perplejo a más de un creyente es Mateo 12:40 donde Jesús dijo que estaría «en el corazón de la tierra tres días y tres noches». A primera vista parece que este texto es un error porque Jesús pasó solamente la noche del viernes, todo el sábado y parte de la mañana del domingo en la tumba. Pero este texto y otros parecidos contienen un modismo hebreo. Para los occidentales, un día consiste en un período de veinticuatro horas. Pero para los judíos la parte de un día o noche se contaba como si fuera un día completo. Por tanto, una parte del viernes, todo el sábado y una parte del domingo equivalían a tres días.

Reconocer la existencia de estos y otros modismos hebreos en las Escrituras no representa un rechazo del principio de la interpretación literal de un texto, sino la comprensión de que cada idioma tiene sus frases y expresiones que a primera vista no tienen ningún sentido, pero que sí tienen mucho sentido para el pueblo de un lugar geográfico específico.

## *Trabajo para realizar*

De los cuatro modismos citados arriba, el que más aplicación tendrá para la vida diaria del creyente es el del absoluto por el relativo. Explique qué es lo que el autor bíblico pretende lograr con este modismo y cite algunos ejemplos bíblicos donde es utilizado.

# 16

# Lenguaje figurado

El lenguaje figurado es un género literario común a todos los idiomas. Sin embargo, juega un papel muy significativo en los idiomas de Medio Oriente y en los países del Mediterráneo. De ahí que se encuentren muchas figuras del lenguaje en la Biblia, especialmente en los libros poéticos y proféticos del A.T.[1] El lenguaje figurado es fascinante porque es como un rompecabezas que desafía al intérprete a resolver la incógnita de lo que el autor pretendía comunicar.

## A. INTRODUCCIÓN

Antes de ver las formas del lenguaje figurado más comunes en las Escrituras, hay tres preguntas que merecen una respuesta.

*1. ¿Por qué existe el lenguaje figurado?* Algunos lingüistas sugieren que el lenguaje figurado nació durante las primeras épocas del desarrollo de cada idioma debido a la falta de palabras para expresar ciertas ideas. Con el tiempo otros factores motivaron su uso. Por ejemplo, el deseo natural del ser humano de hacer comparaciones. Además, el lenguaje figurado añade color a cualquier mensaje, haciendo que sea más ameno, atractivo e impactante que un mensaje literal, llamando así la atención y despertando el interés del lector u oyente. También,

1. En su libro *Interpreting the Bible* (Grand Rapids: Eerdmans, 1963), A. Berkeley Mickelsen dedica dos páginas enteras (pp. 180–181) a las ocasiones en que Jesús empleó el lenguaje figurado.

a veces, el lenguaje figurado es más capaz de comunicar una idea abstracta y difícil de entender que una comunicación literal.

*2. ¿Cuántas figuras del lenguaje hay?* La respuesta a esta pregunta variará según el idioma, la clase de literatura y la definición que se da al término «lenguaje figurado». En principio el lenguaje figurado es simplemente el uso de una palabra fuera de su sentido normal o literal. Cabe en esa definición un gran número de formas del lenguaje figurado. Por eso, se identifican más de cincuenta formas en la literatura secular y hasta la mitad de ese número en la Biblia.

*3. ¿Cómo debe interpretarse el lenguaje figurado?* Aunque algunas formas del lenguaje figurado mencionadas a continuación requieren unas normas especiales para ser interpretadas correctamente, hay al menos tres normas generales que el intérprete debe respetar.

En primer lugar, debe estar atento a su posible uso en cualquier texto. Muchas de las personas que escuchaban las palabras y enseñanzas de Jesús las interpretaban de forma literal cuando en realidad estaba empleando una figura del lenguaje figurado. Por ejemplo, cuando Jesús dijo a la mujer samaritana que «el que bebiere del agua que yo le daré, no tendrá sed jamás» (Jn. 4:14), ella creía que Jesús poseía un agua que eliminaría su trabajo de sacar agua del pozo comunitario del pueblo. Y cuando Jesús dijo que «el que come mi carne y bebe mi sangre, tiene vida eterna; y yo le resucitaré en el día postrero» (Jn. 6:54), muchos dejaron de seguirle por creer que lo decía de forma literal. O cuando dijo a sus propios discípulos que debían guardarse «de la levadura de los fariseos» (Mt. 16:6), ellos pensaron que los criticaba por haberse olvidado de comprar pan para el camino. Como observa Berkhof:

> Hay ciertos escritos en los cuales el uso del lenguaje figurado es imposible *a priori*. Entre tales escritos están las leyes y toda clase de instrumentos legales, escritos históricos, obras estrictamente filosóficas y científicas y confesiones de fe. Tales escritos tienen como propósito primario la mayor precisión y claridad, y en ellos la belleza de lenguaje es una consideración secundaria. Sin embargo, es necesario tener presente que la prosa de los orientales es mucho más figurativa que la de los pueblos occidentales[2].

2. Louis Berkhof, *Principios de interpretación bíblica* (Tarrasa: CLIE, 1973), pp. 101–102.

En segundo lugar, el intérprete debe entender un texto de forma literal a no ser que: (1) carezca de sentido o sea absurdo; (2) contradiga la clara enseñanza de otros textos bíblicos; (3) promueva un acto inmoral; o (4) sea interpretado como lenguaje figurado por el mismo autor u otro autor bíblico. No obstante, la gran mayoría de la literatura bíblica y secular es literal. Lo único que hace el lenguaje figurado es adornar una idea literal. Por tanto, en lugar de interpretar literalmente el adorno, el intérprete tiene que mirar más allá de él para captar el significado literal del autor.

En tercer lugar, el intérprete debe recordar que el significado de una palabra que se emplea en una frase del lenguaje figurado puede cambiar de pasaje en pasaje. En Isaías 53:6 la palabra «oveja» se refiere a la ignorancia y tendencia del ser humano a apartarse de Dios, pero en el versículo siguiente alude a la sumisión de Cristo cuando fue llevado a la cruz. La Biblia describe tanto a Israel como a la iglesia como «esposa». A primera vista parece que este hecho favorece la posición de la teología del pacto, que entiende que las dos entidades son iguales. Pero los dispensacionalistas y los eclécticos, que creen que Israel y la iglesia son entidades diferentes, apoyan su posición en el hecho de que el significado de una palabra en un texto no necesariamente significa lo mismo en otro.

## B. FIGURAS DEL LENGUAJE

Se encuentran aproximadamente unas veinte figuras del lenguaje en la Biblia. Para los eruditos bíblicos un símil es fácil de definir; pero con otras figuras del lenguaje no han podido llegar a un acuerdo en cuanto a su definición. Por ejemplo, mientras que algunos consideran el antropomorfismo como un modismo hebreo, otros creen que tiene su propia identidad. Lo importante no es tanto la etiqueta que se pone a cada clase de figura del lenguaje, sino saber reconocerla por lo que es y saber interpretarla correctamente. Hay bastante acuerdo entre los eruditos en cuanto a la definición de las figuras mencionadas a continuación, que también son las más utilizadas en las Escrituras.

## Símil

Un símil es una comparación entre dos cosas totalmente diferentes. Usa palabras como *así, como, semejante a, parecido a*. Es típico de los autores hebreos emplear más de un símil en un solo texto. Por ejemplo, Isaías 1:18 cuenta con cuatro: «Vengan ahora. Vamos a resolver este asunto —dice el SEÑOR—. Aunque sus pecados sean como la escarlata, yo los haré tan blancos como la nieve. Aunque sean rojos como el carmesí, yo los haré tan blancos como la lana» (NTV). Un símil no suele ser demasiado difícil de interpretar. Los autores de cualquier literatura hacen mucho uso del símil porque saben que sus lectores reconocen las similitudes entre las dos cosas comparadas.

## Metáfora

Una metáfora funciona igual que un símil con la única excepción de que emplea solamente el verbo «ser». A veces el verbo «ser» es insinuado. Por ejemplo, en Jeremías 2:13 Dios se compara con una fuente: «Pues mi pueblo ha cometido dos maldades: me ha abandonado a mí —la fuente de agua viva— y ha cavado para sí cisternas rotas ¡que jamás pueden retener el agua!» (NTV).

Mientras que el símil hace una comparación de forma clara (A es *como* B), la metáfora insinúa dicha comparación (A *es* B). Cuando un autor emplea una metáfora, parece que está diciendo que una cosa es igual a la otra. A veces, esta característica de la metáfora deja al intérprete con la duda de si debe interpretar un texto de forma literal o como una metáfora. En algunos textos la insinuación es clara. Cuando Jesús dice «Yo soy la puerta» (Jn. 10:9), todos entienden que no es una tabla de madera, sino la entrada al reino de Dios. Pero cuando Jesús dijo a sus discípulos «Tomad, comed; esto es mi cuerpo» (Mt. 26:26), ¿qué quería decir? La interpretación de este texto ha provocado mucho debate a lo largo de la historia del cristianismo. Por un lado, la iglesia católica entiende estas palabras de forma literal, mientras que los evangélicos insisten en que son una metáfora. En todos los idiomas, la metáfora es empleada más frecuentemente que el símil[3].

---

3. Ver Milton S. Terry, *Biblical Hermeneutics* (Grand Rapids: Zondervan, 1969), p. 258.

Puesto que el símil y la metáfora funcionan de la misma forma, los principios para su interpretación son los mismos. Después de identificar las cosas que se comparan y las diferentes maneras en que se parecen, el intérprete debe elegir la similitud que cree que el autor bíblico tenía en mente cuando escribió el símil o la metáfora. Hay textos donde el autor emplea dos metáforas o símiles. Puede que los dos se refieran a la misma similitud o cada uno a una similitud diferente. El Salmo 133:1-3 (énfasis añadido) nos servirá para ilustrar estos pasos.

> ¡Mirad cuán bueno y cuán delicioso es habitar los hermanos juntos en armonía! *Es como el buen óleo* sobre la cabeza, el cual desciende sobre la barba, la barba de Aarón, y baja hasta el borde de sus vestiduras. *Como el rocío de Hermón*, que desciende sobre los montes de Sion; porque allí envía Jehová bendición, y vida eterna.

En este Salmo David emplea dos metáforas, comparando la armonía entre hermanos con el óleo que descendió sobre la barba de Aarón y el rocío que desciende de Hermón. Pero ¿quién era Aarón? ¿Para qué se empleaba el óleo en tiempos bíblicos? ¿Qué es Hermón, y qué importancia tenía el rocío que bajaba del Hermón sobre los montes de Sion?

Al indagar en los usos que se hacían del óleo en los tiempos bíblicos, descubrimos que servía en las lámparas para alumbrar y que también se usaba para guisar y como medicina[4]. Un cuarto uso era como hidratante y perfume. Puesto que Palestina es una tierra muy cálida con temperaturas muy elevadas, sus habitantes calzaban sandalias. Por tanto, el judío que quería visitar a un amigo que vivía a cierta distancia solía llegar a su casa sudado y con los pies llenos de polvo y barro porque los caminos no estaban pavimentados. También es muy probable que desprendiera un olor desagradable. Para remediar hasta cierto punto esta situación, en la cultura judía cada visitante era recibido con tres cortesías. Su anfitrión le daba un beso de bienvenida. Entonces, un siervo o esclavo le lavaba los pies. En Juan 13:1-17 Jesús realizó esta labor para enseñar a sus discípulos que debían servir a sus hermanos hasta en las tareas más desagradables. Finalmente, se le daba

4. Ver este uso del óleo en la parábola del buen samaritano (Lc. 10:34).

un poco de óleo para refrescar su piel, lo cual servía también como perfume o desodorante. En quinto lugar, el óleo se empleaba para ungir a un nuevo sumo sacerdote.

¿Quién era Aarón? Aarón era el hermano de Moisés (Éx. 7:1). Cuando los judíos salieron de Egipto, Dios lo nombró como el portavoz y asistente de Moisés (Éx. 4:10-16). En el monte Sinaí Dios mandó a Moisés que nombrara a Aarón sumo sacerdote y a sus cuatro hijos sacerdotes (Éx. 28:1-4). En la ceremonia de su investidura fue ungido con óleo «para santificarlo» (Lv. 8:12). David habla del óleo que descendía de la cabeza de Aarón hasta su barba, y luego hasta el borde de sus vestiduras. Por tanto, es muy probable que el v. 2 se refiera a esa ceremonia. En este caso el óleo representaba de forma simbólica el derramamiento de la bendición divina sobre Aarón como sumo sacerdote. De la misma forma, cuando unos hermanos viven en armonía, «allí envía Jehová bendición, y vida eterna» (v. 3). Parece que esta es la similitud que David tenía en mente.

En la segunda metáfora que David emplea en este Salmo, dice que la armonía entre hermanos es «*como el rocío de Hermón*, que desciende sobre los montes de Sion[5]; porque allí envía Jehová bendición, y vida eterna». Hermón es la montaña más alta de Israel, con una altura de 2814 metros por encima del mar. De ahí que esté cubierta de nieve durante el invierno[6] (énfasis añadido). Y durante los meses tan cálidos de julio y agosto, goza de una temperatura tan fresca que los israelitas y turistas que quieren subir a su cima han de abrigarse. El rocío que baja del monte Hermón refresca la tierra árida en los alrededores. Parece evidente que el rocío que desciende del monte Hermón y que refrigera y alivia las tierras de alrededor del calor tan sofocante de Palestina es una ilustración muy acertada de lo que siente una persona que pertenece a una familia en la cual reina la armonía.

---

5. Sion se refiere a Jerusalén. Era el nombre de la fortaleza de los jebuseos que David conquistó en 2 Samuel 5:7. A partir de ese momento se llamó la Ciudad de David (1 R. 8:1). Más tarde, el nombre de la ciudad fue cambiado a Jerusalén.

6. Hermón forma parte de una cordillera que pasa también por el Líbano y Siria, y está situado justamente donde las fronteras de Israel y esos dos países se juntan.

En este Salmo David emplea dos metáforas como ilustraciones de dos verdades distintas, aunque evidentemente muy relacionadas. Lo que no sería legítimo sería imponer *dos o más* significados sobre un solo símil o metáfora. ¿Por qué solamente uno? Porque cuando las Escrituras interpretan los símiles y metáforas que aparecen en sus páginas, siempre se centran en una sola similitud. También porque es psicológicamente imposible para el ser humano tener en su mente más de un significado a la vez. Finalmente, porque uno de los axiomas del lenguaje es que un mensaje tiene solamente un significado. Los símiles y las metáforas añaden una riqueza especial a nuestro entendimiento cuando seguimos este principio.

## Metonimia

Una metonimia es el uso de una palabra que sugiere una idea debido a la relación lógica, relación íntima o asociación natural que esa palabra tiene con esa idea. Hay diferentes clases de metonimia:

*1. La señal por lo señalado.* En Levítico 19:32 Moisés manda a los judíos: «Delante de las canas te levantarás, y honrarás el rostro del anciano». Si tuviéramos solamente la primera frase, la cual es una metonimia, podríamos concluir que Moisés manda que mostremos respeto a las personas ancianas, puesto que «canas» nos hace pensar en una persona de edad avanzada. Pero al añadir la frase «y honrarás el rostro del anciano», Moisés deja aún más claro que se refiere a una persona de edad avanzada[7]. En Mateo 16:19 Jesús dice a Pedro: «A ti te daré las llaves del reino de los cielos; y todo lo que atares en la tierra será atado en los cielos; y todo lo que desatares en la tierra será desatado en los cielos». Una llave se emplea para abrir y cerrar puertas. Es muy probable que esta metonimia se refiera al hecho de que Pedro fue la primera persona en predicar el evangelio a los judíos (Hch. 2) y a los gentiles (Hch. 10), abriendo así las puertas del cielo a estos dos grupos étnicos.

*2. El recipiente por lo que contiene.* Al entrar en una tienda y pedir «una lata de Coca-Cola», el cliente tiene interés en adquirir ese refresco, no en el recipiente en el cual se vende al público. En Oseas 1:2

7. Esta segunda frase es una sinécdoque en la cual una parte de una persona u objeto sirve para la totalidad del mismo.

Dios dice al profeta: «Ve, tómate una mujer fornicaria, e hijos de fornicación; porque la tierra fornica apartándose de Jehová». Evidentemente, la «tierra» no fornica, sino el pueblo que vive en ella.

*3. El autor por su libro.* En la parábola del rico y Lázaro, el rico pide a Abraham que envíe a Lázaro para advertir a sus cinco hermanos de lo que les espera si no se arrepienten. Abraham niega su petición porque «a Moisés y a los profetas tienen; óiganlos» (Lc. 16:29). O sea, tienen los libros escritos por Moisés y los profetas.

## Sinécdoque

Con una sinécdoque el autor habla de una parte de algo, pero quiere que el lector entienda que está hablando de su totalidad[8]. Cuando Pedro dice a Safira que «los pies» de los que ya han enterrado a su marido van a enterrarla a ella (Hch. 5:9), evidentemente se refiere al cuerpo entero de esos hombres. Habla de sus pies porque oye el sonido de sus pasos que vienen por Safira. Cuando Lucas dice que los primeros creyentes partían «el pan» (Hch. 2:42; 20:7) en su celebración de la Cena del Señor, tiene también en mente el vino.

Los libros proféticos hablan frecuentemente de Efraín, una de las diez tribus del reino del norte (Israel). En un alto porcentaje de las veces que Efraín es mencionado, el profeta tiene en mente las diez tribus de Israel (Jer. 31:18, 20; etcétera). Cuando el Mesías reine sobre toda la tierra, las naciones «martillarán sus espadas para azadones, y sus lanzas para hoces; no alzará espada nación contra nación, ni se ensayarán más para la guerra» (Mi. 4:3). Seguramente las naciones en tiempos del profeta Miqueas contaban con otras armas bélicas aparte de las espadas y lanzas. Pero basta que hable de espadas y lanzas para que el lector entienda que está hablando de todas sus armas bélicas.

La metonimia y la sinécdoque son dos figuras del lenguaje que funcionan con base en la asociación. Con la metonimia la asociación viene a través de una relación sugerida. Con la sinécdoque la asociación es literal.

---

8. Una sinécdoque puede hablar de la totalidad de algo pero referirse solamente a una parte de ello. Sin embargo, no hay muchos ejemplos de este uso de la sinécdoque.

## Hipérbole

El significado literal de la palabra «hipérbole» es el de tirar más allá del blanco. Una hipérbole es una exageración de tal magnitud que no hay ninguna duda en cuanto a lo que el autor quiere decir. La hipérbole se emplea para aumentar un objeto o idea más allá de la realidad con el fin de hacer énfasis en algún aspecto de ese objeto o idea. Con una hipérbole el autor puede comunicar no solamente datos objetivos, sino también emociones, haciendo un impacto que no es posible con una comunicación literal. Una hipérbole no es una mentira, puesto que todos reconocen que el autor está exagerando; todos intuyen cuándo está exagerando y cuándo no. Por el contrario, una mentira engaña al oyente porque eso es precisamente lo que el mentiroso pretende lograr.

La hipérbole es particularmente común en los libros poéticos y proféticos. Hay diferentes grados de dificultad en detectar si un texto debe interpretarse literalmente o como una hipérbole. Es más que evidente que las palabras de Dios a Faraón son una hipérbole: «Pondré tus carnes sobre los montes, y llenaré los valles de tus cadáveres» (Ez. 32:5). Menos claras son las palabras de Jesús: «Si quieres ser mi discípulo, debes aborrecer a los demás —a tu padre y madre, esposa e hijos, hermanos y hermanas— sí, hasta tu propia vida. De lo contrario, no puedes ser mi discípulo» (Lc. 14:26, NTV). Por sentido común entendemos que los discípulos de Cristo no deben odiar a sus padres. Pero cuando hay un conflicto entre los deseos de su Padre celestial y los de sus padres terrenales, los de su Padre celestial siempre tienen preferencia. Con otros textos el intérprete puede quedarse con la duda de si tiene entre manos un texto literal o una hipérbole. No obstante, el intérprete puede correr el peligro inverso de interpretar pasajes literales como si fueran una hipérbole. «Hace falta tener cuidado al identificar una hipérbole para no suavizar las demandas radicales ni las promesas de la Biblia. A veces la Biblia puede dar la impresión de que está empleando una hipérbole cuando en realidad es simplemente radical en lo que dice. Cuando Jesús dice que nuestra justicia tiene que ser mayor que la de los fariseos, no es una hipérbole»[9].

---

9. Dan McCartney y Charles Clayton, *Let the Reader Understand* (Wheaton: Victor Books, 1994), p. 121.

## Ironía y sarcasmo

La ironía consiste en decir justamente lo contrario de lo que se quiere decir con el propósito de subrayar lo absurdo de algo. La ironía contiene cierto elemento de burla, una forma sutil de poner en ridículo a una persona o idea. El sarcasmo hace más impacto porque suele ser más severo en el tono y normalmente se emplea para herir. En ese sentido, la ironía y el sarcasmo son diferentes. Algunos sugieren que la ironía y el sarcasmo representan el lenguaje de la frustración, el dolor o la pena cuando un oyente o lector no ve lo obvio o cuando no responde adecuadamente a una situación que no admite otra explicación.

Los ejemplos más claros de ironía o sarcasmo provienen de Elías y Pablo. Primera de Reyes 18:27 dice: «Cerca del mediodía, Elías comenzó a burlarse de ellos. "Tendrán que gritar más fuerte —se mofaba—, ¡sin duda que es un dios! ¡Tal vez esté soñando despierto o quizá esté haciendo sus necesidades! ¡Seguramente salió de viaje o se quedó dormido y necesita que alguien lo despierte!"» (NTV). En 1 Corintios 4:8 Pablo dice a los corintios: «Ya estáis saciados, ya estáis ricos, sin nosotros reináis. ¡Y ojalá reinaseis, para que nosotros reinásemos también juntamente con vosotros!». Los corintios se creían tan sabios y ricos en conocimiento espiritual que se atrevían a juzgar al apóstol Pablo.

La hipérbole y la ironía son dos figuras del lenguaje que funcionan con base en la exageración. Mientras que la hipérbole exagera hasta un punto *extremo* para hacer énfasis, la ironía exagera hasta el punto totalmente *opuesto* para poner en ridículo una idea, actitud o acción.

## Personificación

La personificación proyecta sobre objetos inanimados (montañas, ideas, etcétera) acciones y características de los seres humanos[10]. Por ejemplo, en el libro de Proverbios la «sabiduría» se describe como un heraldo (1:20-21; 8:1-2) y un anfitrión (9:1-2). La Biblia está llena de otros ejemplos que el intérprete identificará con facilidad.

---

10. Algunos eruditos bíblicos aceptan la posibilidad de que la personificación se emplee con animales.

## Antropomorfismo

La palabra «antropomorfismo» quiere decir «forma de hombre». Mientras que la personificación proyecta sobre objetos inanimados acciones y características del ser humano, el antropomorfismo hace lo mismo con Dios. El Salmo 34:15 habla de «los ojos de Jehová». Aunque Dios no tiene ojos por ser espíritu, lo que el salmista quiere comunicarnos es que a Dios no se le escapa nada; sabe todo lo que hacemos, hasta las motivaciones que hay detrás de cada acto nuestro. En Juan 10:29 Jesús habla de «la mano» del Padre, haciendo referencia al poder del Padre para proteger a sus hijos. Por regla general, es fácil reconocer e interpretar correctamente los pasajes donde se emplean la personificación o el antropomorfismo[11].

## Eufemismo

Un eufemismo es una palabra o frase que se usa para referirse de forma suave, vaga e indirecta a un hecho, idea o situación que si se dijera claramente podría resultar vulgar, ofensiva o inapropiada para la cultura o el contexto. En el A.T. los autores suelen emplear la palabra «conocer» para referirse al acto sexual. En Levítico 18:6 Dios manda a su pueblo: «Ningún varón se llegue a parienta próxima alguna, para descubrir su desnudez». En este texto las palabras «llegue» y «descubrir su desnudez» (LBLA, RVR60) también se refieren al acto sexual. Las palabras «parienta próxima», que no son un eufemismo sino palabras literales, se refieren a familiares de primer o segundo grado[12]. De ahí que la NTV y la NVI traduzcan esa frase como «tener relaciones sexuales». En 1 Samuel 24:3 la RVR60 dice que Saúl entró en una cueva para «cubrir sus pies». Pero la LBLA, NVI y la NTV dicen que entró en esa cueva «para hacer sus necesidades». En 1 Tesalonicenses 4:13 Pablo habla de los creyentes que «duermen», un término más suave que Jesús también empleó (Jn. 11:11), en lugar de decir que están muertos[13].

---

11. Uno de los errores que las sectas cometen es que interpretan de forma literal textos bíblicos que contienen una personificación o un antropomorfismo, o viceversa. Por ejemplo, los mormones creen que Dios tiene un cuerpo físico porque hay muchos textos que hablan de sus brazos, ojos, etcétera.

12. Los vv. 7-16 citan al padre, madre, hermana, hermano, nieta, tía, tío, nuera y cuñada.

13. Mateo 9:24 y Marcos 5:39 son más discutibles en cuanto a si la persona en cuestión había fallecido o no.

## *Trabajo para realizar*

1. ¿Cuál es la diferencia entre un símil y una metáfora? ¿Qué es una metonimia? ¿Cuáles son las tres formas en que la Biblia emplea una metonimia? ¿Cuál es la diferencia entre una hipérbole y la mentira? ¿Cuál es la diferencia entre la hipérbole y la ironía?

2. Trabajando exclusivamente con la RVR60, identifique la clase de lenguaje figurado que se emplea en los textos de abajo. Los textos que llevan un (+) emplean dos clases diferentes de lenguaje figurado en el mismo versículo. Primera de Corintios 10:21 lleva un (*) porque es un texto difícil. Por tanto, el lector haría bien en consultar Marcos 10:38 y el contexto inmediato de 1 Corintios 10:21 antes de llegar a una conclusión en cuanto a la clase de lenguaje figurado que se emplea. Al terminar este trabajo, consulte la «Guía de estudio» para ver la opinión del autor sobre la forma de lenguaje figurado que se emplea en cada texto.

Gn. 49:17
Nm. 16:32
1 S. 17:7
1 R. 18:27
Job 12:2+
Sal. 18:1
Sal. 23:4+
Sal. 84:11
Sal. 90:1
Sal. 114:3
Sal. 119:105+
Pr. 25:25
Cnt. 2:2
Cnt. 2:9
Is. 1:8+
Os. 7:8+
Os. 13:3
Os. 13:7
Os. 14:5+
Am. 2:13
Am. 4:4
Hab. 3:10
Hab. 3:19+
Mt. 7:15+
Lc. 13:32
Jn. 6:48
Jn. 10:7
Jn. 14:6
Jn. 15:1
Jn. 21:25
1 Co. 4:8
1 Co. 10:21*
1 Co. 13:1
2 Co. 12:13
Gá. 2:9

17

# Poesía hebrea

La poesía ocupa un espacio significativo en las Escrituras. El N.T. contiene una selección limitada de pasajes poéticos. Por ejemplo, Lucas incluye en su Evangelio las poesías de María (1:46-55), Zacarías (1:68-79) y Simeón (2:29-32). Pablo cita la letra de un credo (1 Ti. 3:16) y un himno que las iglesias cantaban en sus cultos (Ef. 5:14). Y Juan incluye una cantidad considerable de pasajes poéticos en el Apocalipsis (4:8, 11; 5:9-10, 12-13; etcétera). Pero es en el A.T. donde encontramos la mayoría de los pasajes poéticos. Tanto es así que una tercera parte del A.T. es poesía[1]. Aunque el Pentateuco y los libros históricos están escritos en prosa, encontramos porciones significativas de poesía entre sus páginas. De los cinco libros poéticos, Salmos, Proverbios y Cantares están escritos por completo en poesía. De los 42 capítulos de Job, todos ellos están escritos en poesía con la excepción de 48 versículos (1:1-20; 2:1-13; 32:1-5; 42:7-16). El 55 por ciento de Eclesiastés es poesía. Pero lo que sorprende a muchos es que la poesía ocupa el 45 por ciento de los libros proféticos[2].

---

1. En su libro *Reading Biblical Poetry: An Introductory Guide* (Louisville: Westminster John Knox Press, 2000), p. 1, Jan P. Fokkelman sugiere la cifra más específica del 37 por ciento. Mientras que otros sugieren la cifra del 50 por ciento, prácticamente todos se limitan a decir aproximadamente una tercera parte.

2. De los 5259 versículos encontrados en los libros proféticos, 2370 son de poesía. Aunque no hay ni un solo versículo de poesía entre los 38 versículos de

# A. EL PARALELISMO

Es fácil reconocer la poesía en cualquier idioma, pero difícil definirla. No obstante, siempre hay ciertas características que la señalan. Mucha de la poesía occidental se caracteriza por el ritmo y la rima. Note, por ejemplo, el ritmo en esta sección del *Romancero gitano* de Federico García Lorca titulada «Muerto de amor».

> ¿Qué es aquello que reluce
> por los altos corredores?
> Cierra la puerta, hijo mío,
> acaban de dar las once.

La característica que más destaca en la poesía hebrea es el paralelismo[3]. Hay muchas clases de paralelismo, algunas de ellas muy complejas[4]. No obstante, las tres formas más comunes de paralelismo nos permiten captar la esencia de la poesía hebrea[5].

## Paralelismo sinónimo

En el paralelismo sinónimo el autor repite con otras palabras en la segunda frase de un versículo lo que acaba de decir en la primera. Si

---

Hageo, y aunque hay solamente dos de los 55 versículos de Malaquías (4%) y 16 de los 248 de Daniel (7%) que son poesía, el porcentaje de textos poéticos encontrado en los demás profetas es considerable: Abdías (100%); Nahúm (100%); Habacuc (100%); Sofonías (100%); Lamentaciones (100%); Miqueas (99%); Joel (92%); Oseas (91%); Amós (87%); Isaías (85%); Jeremías (46%); Zacarías (17%); Jonás (14%) y Ezequiel (10%).

3. La poesía hebrea tiene ritmo, pero no rima. El término «paralelismo» fue empleado por primera vez en 1753 por Robert Lowth (1710–1787), obispo de la Iglesia de Inglaterra y profesor de Poesía en la Universidad de Oxford.

4. Por ejemplo, el quiasmo es una estructura en la cual la primera línea presenta dos ideas (A y B) y la segunda presenta esas mismas ideas en orden inverso (B y A). O sea, es un paralelismo del revés. Según Robert H. Stein en su libro *A Basic Guide to Interpreting the Bible* (Grand Rapids: Baker, 1994), p. 113, se encuentran posibles ejemplos de quiasmo en Mateo 6:24; 23:12; Marcos 8:35.

5. Algunos eruditos han debatido la validez de estos términos. Sin embargo, han sido tan aceptados que la gran mayoría de sus opositores no creen que merezca la pena intentar introducir otras designaciones.

la primera frase queda oscura, la segunda la clarificará al decir lo mismo con otras palabras. En algunos casos la segunda frase aporta una idea que es similar, pero no exactamente igual que la primera[6]. Los textos a continuación son un ejemplo de paralelismo sinónimo.

> Te has enlazado con las palabras de tu boca,
> y has quedado preso en los dichos de tus labios. (Pr. 6:2)
>
> Y dijo Lamec a sus mujeres: Ada y Zila, oíd mi voz;
> mujeres de Lamec, escuchad mi dicho:
> que un varón mataré por mi herida,
> y un joven por mi golpe. (Gn. 4:23)
>
> ¿Cómo podré abandonarte, oh Efraín?
> ¿Te entregaré yo, Israel? (Os. 11:8)
>
> El Espíritu de Jehová ha hablado por mí,
> y su palabra ha estado en mi lengua.
> El Dios de Israel ha dicho,
> me habló la Roca de Israel. (2 S. 23:2-3)

Hay textos poéticos como Proverbios 6:2 y Génesis 4:23 (citados arriba) que no tratan ningún tema teológico. Pero hay ocasiones en las cuales el paralelismo sinónimo representa una herramienta importante de la interpretación bíblica. Por ejemplo, el A.T. hace un énfasis sobre el papel del Padre sin hacer ninguna distinción entre las tres personas de la Trinidad. Israel estaba rodeado de naciones idólatras. Si el A.T. hubiese hecho dicha distinción, esas naciones habrían acusado a los judíos de practicar la idolatría por tener tres dioses. No obstante, el paralelismo sinónimo de 2 Samuel 23:2-3 dice claramente que el «Espíritu de Jehová» es Dios, «el Dios de Israel».

---

6. En su libro *The Hermeneutical Spiral* (Downers Grove: InterVarsity Press, 1991), p. 178, Grant R. Osborne dice que sus estudios de la poesía hebrea le han llevado a la conclusión de que el paralelismo sinónimo muestra también ciertos matices del paralelismo sintético.

## Paralelismo antitético

En el paralelismo antitético la segunda frase de un versículo dice lo contrario de lo que afirma la primera. Si hay alguna duda en cuanto al significado de la primera, el intérprete simplemente tiene que identificar lo que dice la segunda frase y luego buscar el concepto opuesto, lo cual representará el significado de la primera frase. Normalmente la segunda frase comienza con las palabras «mas» o «pero». Stein hace la observación de que el paralelismo antitético «es la forma más común de paralelismo en la Biblia. Limitándonos solamente a las enseñanzas de Jesús tenemos más de 130 ejemplos de ello. En el libro de Proverbios hay capítulos enteros dedicados a esta forma literaria»[7]. Los textos de Proverbios citados a continuación son un ejemplo de paralelismo antitético donde la segunda frase contrasta con la primera.

> La blanda respuesta quita la ira;
> mas la palabra áspera hace subir el furor.
> La lengua de los sabios adornará la sabiduría,
> mas la boca de los necios hablará sandeces. (15:1-2)

> Las riquezas de los sabios son su corona;
> pero la insensatez de los necios es infatuación. (14:24)

> La justicia engrandece a la nación;
> mas el pecado es afrenta de las naciones. (14:34)

## Paralelismo sintético

En el paralelismo sintético el pensamiento de la primera frase es desarrollado o ampliado en las frases sucesivas, las cuales incluyen información adicional. Lógicamente, el paralelismo sintético requiere que haya al menos tres frases. El ejemplo clásico es el Salmo 1:1. El v. 2 emplea el paralelismo sinónimo, puesto que la segunda frase repite el concepto de la primera con otras palabras.

---

7. Robert H. Stein, *A Basic Guide to Interpreting the Bible* (Grand Rapids: Baker, 1994), p. 111.

Bienaventurado el varón que no anduvo en consejo de malos,
ni estuvo en camino de pecadores,
ni en silla de escarnecedores se ha sentado; (v. 1)

sino que en la ley de Jehová está su delicia,
y en su ley medita de día y de noche. (v. 2)

La poesía hebrea aporta dos grandes ventajas. Primera, facilita la labor de su traducción a otros idiomas. El traductor no tiene que alterar el contenido del texto con tal de que su traducción rime o tenga cierto ritmo. Si tuviera que hacerlo, dicha traducción no sería un reflejo fidedigno de lo que dice el manuscrito original. Pero al no tener que preocuparse por el ritmo y la rima tan característicos de la poesía occidental, no se pierde nada de lo que Dios dice en el texto. Segunda, la poesía hebrea se presta a clarificar el significado del texto para que haya mayor entendimiento.

| Tres clases de paralelismo hebreo | |
|---|---|
| Sinónimo | La idea de la segunda frase es igual a la de la primera frase. |
| Antitético | La idea de la segunda frase contrasta con la de la primera frase. |
| Sintético | La segunda y otras frases sucesivas amplían la idea de la primera frase. |

## B. CÓMO INTERPRETAR LA POESÍA HEBREA

Hay tres normas que han de emplearse en la interpretación de la poesía hebrea, no importa en qué parte de las Escrituras se encuentre. Primera, el intérprete tiene que darse cuenta de su existencia. Será más fácil identificar la poesía si utiliza una versión de la Biblia que coloque los pasajes poéticos en un formato que la distinga de la prosa. Segunda, el intérprete debe tener en cuenta que la identificación del tipo de paralelismo que un autor emplea es una de las herramientas más útiles para entender el significado de un texto poético, y que el paralelismo sinónimo es el que más ayuda le aportará. Después de identificar la clase de paralelismo empleado por el autor bíblico, debe interpretar el texto de acuerdo con esa clase de paralelismo. Tercera, el intérprete debe ser sensible al espíritu y la emoción de las palabras porque la poesía es emotiva.

## Salmos

Hasta donde sea posible, el intérprete debe identificar el trasfondo histórico del Salmo que interpreta. De vez en cuando el contenido de un Salmo proveerá ese fondo histórico. En otras ocasiones los títulos que llevan ciertos Salmos lo indicarán. Estos títulos no figuraban en el manuscrito original de los Salmos, sino que fueron añadidos más tarde. Aunque no son inspirados, la tradición judía es bastante fiable. Puesto que algunos cuestionan hasta qué punto uno puede fiarse de esos títulos, Mickelsen ofrece el siguiente consejo al respecto.

> Estos títulos no deben ignorarse como si fueran la obra de unos fanáticos o incondicionales del autor que querían aumentar su fama. El contenido de un Salmo y su título frecuentemente pueden proveer luz en cuanto a la situación histórica del autor original, y a veces dicha luz hace que algunas partes del Salmo sean más significativas. Pero es mejor admitir nuestra ignorancia en cuanto al contexto de un Salmo en lugar de asignarlo arbitrariamente a una ocasión histórica si no existe evidencia suficiente para justificar dicha clasificación[8].

Sin embargo, en la mayoría de los casos, el contenido de un Salmo identificará el tema general del mismo, pero no el trasfondo histórico específico. En muchos Salmos no existe ningún título, o el título que existe se limita a indicar la música o el instrumento musical que debe emplearse al cantarlo.

Una segunda norma que el intérprete debe tomar en cuenta es que los Salmos se dedican a expresar las emociones más íntimas y profundas de los autores, las cuales han sido provocadas tanto por los problemas que padecen como por la alegría y el gozo que sienten. Aunque los Salmos contienen conceptos doctrinales, su propósito no es el de presentar las grandes doctrinas de la fe, sino acercar al lector a Dios mediante las angustias, dolores, frustraciones, penas, gozo, tristeza, alegría y demás emociones de sus autores. Mientras que las Epístolas se acercan a la verdad desde una perspectiva intelectual y lógica, los Salmos lo hacen con base en las emociones humanas. De ahí que no se pueda hacer la misma exégesis de un Salmo que de un pasaje de

---

8. A. Berkeley Mickelsen, *Interpreting the Bible* (Grand Rapids: Eerdmans, 1963), pp. 352–353.

Romanos. Mientras que el cometido de una Epístola es describir y establecer la doctrina de la fe cristiana con un vocabulario que emplea la máxima precisión, la poesía de los Salmos hace un impacto en las emociones de una persona mediante un lenguaje artístico y muy emotivo.

> El uso que se hizo de la poesía en tiempos antiguos, como en nuestro tiempo, indica que el autor está menos preocupado por una descripción exacta o una precisión científica que por evocar emociones y crear ciertas impresiones. Los médicos no emplean poesía para describir los problemas médicos de sus pacientes, pero los enamorados sí la emplean cuando expresan su amor el uno hacia el otro[9].

| Algunas emociones expresadas por los salmistas | |
|---|---|
| **Gozo** | «Me regocijo en tu palabra como el que halla muchos despojos». (119:162) |
| **Dolor y terror** | «Mi corazón está dolorido dentro de mí, y terrores de muerte sobre mí han caído». (55:4) |
| **Traición** | «Porque no me afrentó un enemigo, lo cual habría soportado; ni se alzó contra mí el que me aborrecía, porque me hubiera ocultado de él; sino tú, hombre, al parecer íntimo mío, mi guía, y mi familiar». (55:12-13) |
| **Temor** | «En el día que temo, yo en ti confío (56:3). En Dios he confiado; no temeré; ¿qué puede hacerme el hombre?» (56:11) |
| **Reposo, paz** | «Alma mía, en Dios solamente reposa, porque de él es mi esperanza». (62:5) |
| **Ansiedad** | «No me deseches en el tiempo de la vejez; cuando mi fuerza se acabare, no me desampares». (71:9) |
| **Envidia** | «Porque tuve envidia de los arrogantes, viendo la prosperidad de los impíos». (73:3) |
| **Ira** | «Pon sobre él al impío, y Satanás esté a su diestra. Cuando fuere juzgado, salga culpable, y su oración sea para pecado. Sean sus días pocos; tome otro su oficio. Sean sus hijos huérfanos, y su mujer viuda. Anden sus hijos vagabundos, y mendiguen; y procuren su pan lejos de sus desolados hogares. Que el acreedor se apodere de todo lo que tiene; y extraños saqueen su trabajo». (109:6-11) |
| **Angustia** | «A Jehová clamé estando en angustia, y él me respondió». (120:1) |
| **Confianza** | «Dios mío, en ti confío». (25:2) |

9. Stein, ob. cit., p. 102.

Por último, los llamados Salmos imprecatorios (5, 10, 17, 35, 58-59, 69-70, 79, 83, 109, 129, 137, 140) requieren un trato cauteloso y especial. En ellos los autores reclaman el juicio de Dios contra sus enemigos con un lenguaje que parece muy vengativo, un detalle muy inusual en las Escrituras. Una vez más, Mickelsen provee una observación muy razonable y equilibrada.

> Al tratar los elementos imprecatorios en los Salmos el intérprete debe considerarlos como expresiones poéticas de unas personas que estaban enfurecidas con la tiranía del mal, pero cuya actitud en cuanto a la retribución está tan influenciada por su sentido de ser maltratadas o por la blasfemia que se ha cometido, que hablan con un lenguaje que está muy lejos de la enseñanza de que se debe dejar el juicio a Dios, o de las declaraciones de Jesús en cuanto a cómo tratar a los enemigos (ver Salmo 109:13). Pero ¡ningún poeta del A.T. conocía las enseñanzas de Jesús![10]

## Proverbios

Hay secciones en el libro de Proverbios donde Salomón agrupa varios versículos que tratan un mismo tema, como la sabiduría (1:20-33), el adulterio (cap. 5), etcétera. Cuando este sea el caso, el intérprete debe estudiar los textos conjuntamente. Pero en la mayoría de ocasiones, el tema de un versículo no tiene nada que ver con el tema del versículo anterior o posterior. Por tanto, la mejor manera de estudiar el libro de Proverbios es reunir todos los versículos que tratan el mismo tema y estudiarlos como un conjunto.

Quizás el principio de interpretación más importante para el libro de Proverbios es que el intérprete debe darse cuenta de que sus versículos tratan de principios, no de promesas. Por regla general, la enseñanza de cada versículo promueve un comportamiento que resultará en bendición. Pero hay excepciones. En ese sentido los proverbios de este libro poético no son promesas como Juan 3:16, sino principios. Por ejemplo, Proverbios 3:13, 16 afirma que «largura de días» está en la mano derecha del «hombre que halla la sabiduría». Sin embargo, de vez en cuando nos enteramos de que una persona que ha cometido los

10. Mickelsen, ob. cit., p. 353.

crímenes más monstruosos acaba de cumplir noventa y tantos años de edad, o de que un creyente joven muy comprometido acaba de morir en un accidente de automóvil que él no provocó. Los proverbios son principios, no promesas.

Durante mi investigación para escribir *Con precisión*, leí varios libros que hacían mención de este principio. Y hubo algo que me llamó la atención. Aunque Proverbios cuenta con 925 versículos, todos los autores de esos libros, casi sin excepción, emplearon el mismo texto para ilustrar este principio: «Dirige a tus hijos por el camino correcto, y cuando sean mayores, no lo abandonarán» (22:6, NTV). ¿Por qué, cuando hay otros 924 que podrían haber servido de ejemplo? Muy probablemente porque conocían a unos padres excelentes —padres perfectos no existen— que hicieron todo lo posible para que sus hijos siguieran al Señor, pero alguno de ellos no quiso rendirse a Cristo. Desde entonces esos padres se han culpado a sí mismos, preguntándose continuamente: «¿Qué hemos hecho mal? ¿No promete Proverbios 22:6 que...?». Y ese es precisamente el problema. Muchos no entienden que Proverbios 22:6 enseña que, por regla general, un niño seguirá los pasos que sus padres han trazado para él. Pero siempre habrá alguna excepción, porque cada niño tiene una voluntad propia. Aunque esta verdad no eliminará el dolor que esos padres sienten por su hijo, al menos el dolor que sienten no vendrá de una fuente falsa.

## Libros proféticos

Si un pasaje poético se encuentra en un libro profético, el primer paso que el intérprete debe dar es el de estudiar el trasfondo histórico y cultural de dicho libro. Por ejemplo, para entender el libro de Isaías en general, y en particular sus pasajes poéticos, el intérprete debe informarse de la situación política y espiritual de los reinados de «Uzías, Jotam, Acaz y Ezequías, reyes de Judá» (Is. 1:1). Hemos visto un ejemplo de cómo realizar esta clase de investigación en el capítulo 8. A continuación, debe seguir las normas generales para los pasajes poéticos que se encuentran en cualquier lugar de las Escrituras.

Una gran porción de la Biblia es poesía. No debe sorprendernos, porque Dios tiene emociones. Y puesto que hemos sido creados a la imagen de Dios, cada ser humano cuenta con emociones. Aunque algunos muestran sus emociones más que otros, todos tienen emociones. Una de las cosas que hacen que el tiempo de alabanza en los cultos sea de tanta bendición es que la música en esencia es emotiva. Los Salmos eran el himnario de los judíos. Por eso, algunos de los títulos que encabezan algunos de los Salmos indican la clase de música o el instrumento musical que debía emplearse. Cuando Dios quiere comunicarse a través de nuestro intelecto, emplea las Epístolas. Pero cuando quiere tocar nuestras emociones, emplea la poesía.

## *Trabajo para realizar*

Identifique las tres clases básicas de paralelismo y explique cómo funciona cada una. ¿Qué es lo que pretende lograr un pasaje poético en comparación con el propósito de una epístola? Cite dos principios de interpretación para el libro de Proverbios.

# 18

# Parábolas (I)

Justo antes de llegar a España, el autor de *Con precisión* era el pastor de los jóvenes de una iglesia en Chicago. Durante ese tiempo impartió unos estudios sobre las parábolas. Cuarenta y dos años después, uno de esos jóvenes le escribió diciendo: «Lo que más recuerdo de aquellos años son los estudios que dio sobre las parábolas». Y unos años después ocurrió lo mismo en España. Antes de predicar en una iglesia, el pastor lo presentó a la congregación diciendo: «Jaime y un servidor nos conocemos desde hace más de cuarenta años. Aún guardo los apuntes del estudio sobre las parábolas que dio cuando yo era un joven».

Las parábolas no son fascinantes solamente para los creyentes, por muy jóvenes que sean, sino también para los no creyentes, muchos de los cuales se interesan por ellas y entienden el significado de términos como «buen samaritano» e «hijo pródigo». Desafortunadamente, las parábolas han sido el objeto de mucho abuso interpretativo a lo largo de la historia de la Iglesia, lo cual ha provocado mucho debate entre los eruditos del N.T. Ese debate ha girado alrededor de tres cuestiones, a saber: el propósito que Jesús tenía al emplearlas en su enseñanza, la definición de una parábola y la relación que existe entre una parábola y una alegoría. Ese debate ha sido tan largo e intenso, que un autor ha dicho que «la literatura sobre este tema es tan extensa que puede llevar al intérprete a la desesperación»[1]. No obstante, las repuestas a esas tres preguntas son muy claras.

## A. EL PROPÓSITO DE JESÚS AL EMPLEAR PARÁBOLAS

Jesús es conocido en el mundo entero por dos hechos principales: su crucifixión y su amplio uso de las parábolas, las cuales ocupan un 35 por ciento de su enseñanza en los Evangelios sinópticos (Mateo, Marcos y Lucas). Jesús no fue el primer rabino que empleó parábolas. Pertenecía a una tradición muy larga de rabinos que empleaban parábolas en su enseñanza del A.T. Dos de los más famosos son Hilel (c. 70 a. C.–c. 10 d. C.) y Shamai (50 a. C.–30 d. C.). Sin embargo, Jesús no era como los demás rabinos de su época, quienes enseñaban el Pentateuco y en particular la Ley con base en las interpretaciones de los rabinos que les habían precedido. Además, daban una importancia tan excesiva a los detalles de la Ley que su enseñanza era muy teórica, pedante, pesada y aburrida. En contraste con ellos, Jesús no repetía lo que otros habían dicho, sino que hablaba con autoridad. Dijo varias veces en su Sermón del monte: «Oísteis que fue dicho..., pero *yo os digo...*» (Mt. 5:21-22, 27-28, 31-32, 33-34, 38-39, 43-44, énfasis añadido). Sus parábolas eran interesantes, creativas y fáciles de entender. Pero ¿por qué hizo tanto uso de ellas? La primera razón se basa en la lógica. Los Evangelios sinópticos identifican cuatro razones adicionales.

### Captar y mantener la atención de los oyentes

Como buen maestro que era, Jesús sabía que una presentación sosa y aburrida no despertaría ni mantendría el interés de nadie. Pero Jesús no empleaba las parábolas simplemente para entretener a las multitudes, sino porque representaban una forma muy eficaz de comunicar las actitudes y el comportamiento que se requerían de los ciudadanos del reino de Dios. En ese sentido las parábolas representaban un buen método pedagógico. Había ocasiones en que

---

1. Kenneth E. Bailey, *Las parábolas de Lucas* (Miami: Editorial Vida, 2009), p. 23. De hecho, cuando el autor de *Con precisión* consultó varias bibliotecas en preparación para escribir este libro, encontró más libros sobre las parábolas que sobre cualquier otro tema relacionado con la hermenéutica.

Jesús enseñaba durante horas enteras. El uso de parábolas hacía que ese tiempo fuera más ameno. En otras ocasiones tenía solamente unos minutos para enseñar una verdad. El uso de parábolas hacía que quienes lo escuchaban recordaran mejor lo que había dicho. Por tanto, uno de los motivos para usar parábolas era que despertaban y mantenían el interés de sus oyentes y los ayudaban a recordar lo que había dicho.

## Ilustrar las verdades enseñadas

«Una vez, Jesús estaba orando en cierto lugar. Cuando terminó, uno de sus discípulos se le acercó y le dijo: —Señor, enséñanos a orar, así como Juan les enseñó a sus discípulos» (Lc. 11:1, NTV). Entonces, Jesús les enseñó una oración modélica que se conoce como el Padre Nuestro (vv. 2-4). Acto seguido, les contó la parábola del amigo que llega a medianoche (vv. 5-13) para ilustrar la necesidad de perseverar en la oración. Las parábolas servían como excelentes ilustraciones de sus enseñanzas.

Por regla general, las personas encuentran más fácil entender y aceptar una verdad vestida de una ilustración que un discurso comunicado con lenguaje literal, especialmente si ese discurso representa una reprimenda. El ejemplo clásico es la conversación que el profeta Natán tuvo con David después de su adulterio con Betsabé (2 S. 12:1-13). Natán le contó la parábola de un hombre rico que tenía mucho ganado. Un día llegó a su casa una visita inesperada. Pero en lugar de tomar una de sus muchas reses para darle de comer, confiscó el corderito de una familia pobre y con él preparó una buena comida para su visita. Cuando Natán llegó al final de esta parábola, David estaba tan enfurecido que quería ajusticiar a dicho hombre en el acto. Entonces, Natán le dijo: «Tú eres aquel hombre» (v. 7). David no tenía escapatoria y tardó poco tiempo en confesar: «Pequé contra Jehová» (v. 13). A veces una parábola llega más rápida y eficazmente al alma de una persona que una reprimenda comunicada directamente con un lenguaje literal.

## Revelar la verdad a quienes deseaban conocerla y obedecerla

Al principio de su ministerio Jesús captaba el interés de las multitudes «porque lo hacía con verdadera autoridad, algo completamente diferente de lo que hacían los maestros de la ley religiosa» (Mt. 7:29; Mc. 1:22; Lc. 4:32, 36, NTV). También le seguían porque en algunas ocasiones su enseñanza iba acompañada de milagros. Pero a medida que las multitudes entendían lo que se requería de ellas si querían ser ciudadanos del reino de Dios, y que el concepto que Jesús tenía de ese reino no incluía la expulsión inmediata de los ejércitos romanos de Palestina, lo fueron abandonando muchas personas.

Simultáneamente, crecía la oposición a su persona, en particular por parte de los líderes religiosos. Jesús se opuso a la doctrina de los saduceos sobre la resurrección (Mc. 12:18-27), convirtiéndose así en una amenaza a su autoridad civil y religiosa. En varias ocasiones llamó a los fariseos «hipócritas» (Mt. 23:13-16) y los acusó de sustituir la Palabra de Dios por sus tradiciones (Mc. 7:1-13). Así que los líderes religiosos comenzaron a criticarlo abiertamente en público. Por ejemplo, al sanar a un paralítico en una casa en Capernaúm (Mc. 2:1), Jesús declaró que tenía poder para perdonar pecados. Enseguida los fariseos y escribas, «los cuales habían venido de todas las aldeas de Galilea, y de Judea y Jerusalén» (Lc. 5:17), lo acusaron de blasfemar porque solamente Dios es capaz de perdonar el pecado. Luego, en casa de Leví, los fariseos y escribas le echaron en cara el hecho de que comía con publicanos y pecadores y que sus discípulos no ayunaban como los discípulos suyos y los de Juan el Bautista (Mc. 2:16, 18).

Poco tiempo después, Jesús se sentó en una barca a la orilla del mar para enseñar a la multitud que se había congregado, y «les enseñaba por parábolas muchas cosas» (Mc. 4:1-2). Los Evangelios no siguen de forma estricta la cronología de la vida de Jesús. Los eruditos que han reconstruido esa cronología dicen que este encuentro con la multitud, descrito en Marcos 4:1-20 y sus pasajes paralelos de Mateo 13:1-23 y Lucas 8:4-15, representa el momento en que la hostilidad contra Jesús llegó a su apogeo. Es precisamente en este momento cuando Jesús toma la decisión de enseñar a través de parábolas. Al final de ese capítulo Marcos dice que «con muchas parábolas como estas les hablaba la palabra, conforme a lo que podían oír. Y sin parábolas no les hablaba; aunque a sus discípulos en particular les declaraba todo» (Mc. 4:33-34). La frase «y sin parábolas no les hablaba» es con toda probabilidad una hipérbole por parte de Marcos. No es que Jesús nunca había empleado parábolas antes, sino que a partir de este momento las empleaba como su forma principal de enseñanza.

«Cuando estuvo solo, los que estaban cerca de él con los doce le preguntaron sobre la parábola» (Mc. 4:10). Puesto que los tres Evangelios sinópticos recogen la interpretación de Jesús sobre la parábola del sembrador, es evidente que de todas las parábolas que Jesús contó aquel día, esta fue la que los dejó más intrigados y perplejos. Además de preguntarle acerca del significado de esa parábola, querían saber por qué hablaba a las multitudes con parábolas (Mt. 13:10). Los discípulos lo habían acompañado a todos los sitios hasta este momento y habían notado este cambio en su forma de enseñar. Jesús les respondió: «Porque a vosotros os es dado saber los misterios del reino de los cielos; mas a ellos no les es dado. Porque a cualquiera que tiene, se le dará, y tendrá más; pero al que no tiene, aun lo que tiene le será quitado» (Mt. 13:11-12).

O sea, su uso de las parábolas tenía como propósito otorgarles un entendimiento de los misterios del reino de Dios porque poseían algo que los demás no tenían. Y, por tenerlo, ganarían más entendimiento, mientras que los demás perderían lo que poseían. ¿Qué es lo que tenían los discípulos y seguidores de Jesús que los demás no tenían? Habría ocasiones en el futuro próximo en que los fariseos y líderes religiosos entenderían perfectamente algunas parábolas, mientras que los propios discípulos se quedarían perplejos (Lc. 16:14-15). Pero existía una gran diferencia entre ellos y los líderes religiosos. Los discípulos querían entender y obedecer la enseñanza de Jesús, uno de los requisitos de la iluminación. Aunque algunas parábolas no tendrían mucho sentido de entrada para ellos, con el tiempo las entenderían. Su deseo de entenderlas les empujaría a meditar sobre ellas, y con el tiempo los ojos de su entendimiento se abrirían. Los detractores de Jesús entenderían las parábolas de Jesús en términos generales, pero dicho entendimiento nunca produciría un cambio espiritual en ellos. «Pues ellos miran, pero en realidad no ven. Oyen, pero en realidad no escuchan ni entienden» (Mt. 13:13, NTV). Justo lo contrario de lo que ocurriría con los seguidores de Cristo, aunque les costara entender al principio los misterios del reino de Dios.

## Esconder la verdad a quienes no querían aceptarla

De los cuatro propósitos que Jesús tenía al usar parábolas en su enseñanza, este es el único que ha provocado polémica. El debate gira alrededor de la frase: «Porque a vosotros os es dado saber los misterios del reino de los cielos; *mas a ellos no les es dado*» (Mt. 13:11, énfasis añadido). No obstante, de los cuatro propósitos que Jesús tenía al emplear parábolas en su enseñanza, este cuarto es el que goza de más apoyo bíblico. Mateo 13:11 y sus pasajes paralelos (Mc. 4:11; Lc. 8:10) son muy explícitos. Sin embargo, son a la vez los textos más difíciles de interpretar. ¿Cómo podría el Padre enviar al Hijo a morir sobre una cruz con tal de ofrecer la salvación eterna a todos, pero a la vez no permitir que algunos entiendan esa verdad para que sean salvos? ¿Tenemos un Dios que ciega los ojos de algunos hombres, quitándoles así la posibilidad de entender la verdad y responder positivamente a ella para salvarse? ¿Es posible que Dios condene a algunos mientras que extiende una mano salvífica a otros? Estas preguntas han motivado a algunos evangélicos a rechazar este cuarto propósito[2].

> «Cuando ustedes oigan lo que digo, no entenderán. Cuando vean lo que hago, no comprenderán. Pues el corazón de este pueblo está endurecido, y sus oídos no pueden oír, y han cerrado los ojos».
>
> **(Mt. 13:14-15, NTV)**

Sin embargo, en el fondo este debate representa un problema más teológico que exegético. O sea, el texto es claro, lo difícil es

2. Por ejemplo, en su libro *The Parables of the Kingdom* (Londres: Hodder and Stoughton, 1907), pp. 9–22, G. Campbell Morgan insiste en que Jesús no hablaba en parábolas para esconder la verdad de aquellas personas que habían endurecido sus corazones, sino precisamente para ayudarlos a entenderla, usando uno de los medios más eficaces para comunicar un concepto nuevo o difícil. Así que el cambio pedagógico de dejar un lenguaje literal a favor de las parábolas era una muestra de la gracia y misericordia de Dios, dando a dichas personas una segunda oportunidad para entender y responder positivamente a la verdad. Otros han hecho una exégesis de las palabras clave de Mateo 13:13-15, Marcos 4:12 y Lucas 8:10 con el propósito de mostrar cuán errónea es la interpretación tradicional de que las parábolas servían para cegar los ojos de algunos. Pero a pesar de su trabajo exegético tan completo y respetable, sus argumentos no han convencido a todos.

encontrar cómo encaja la verdad de este texto con las demás verdades bíblicas sobre la salvación. Siempre ha sido difícil encontrar el equilibrio entre ciertos aspectos doctrinales. Por ejemplo, Jesús invita a todos los que quieran ser salvos a venir a él para recibir la salvación que les ofrece. Pero por otro lado declara que nadie puede acercarse a él sin que el Padre lo traiga (Jn. 6:44). Pero ¿por qué traería Dios a algunos y a otros no? En el fondo, la respuesta es que Dios es soberano y hace lo que le place. No obstante, en términos prácticos, en algunos casos se debe a la dureza de corazón que algunos han cultivado de forma consciente, consistente y voluntaria. Hay ejemplos suficientes de esta dinámica en las Escrituras para convencernos de que este cuarto propósito no es una interpretación errónea y que Jesús usaba parábolas precisamente para esconder la verdad a quienes no querían aceptarla[3].

| **Jesus empleó parábolas para...** |
|---|
| 1. Captar y mantener la atención de los oyentes. |
| 2. Ilustrar las verdades enseñadas. |
| 3. Revelar la verdad a quienes deseaban conocerla y obedecerla. |
| 4. Esconder la verdad a quienes no querían aceptarla. |

3. Por ejemplo, la lucha que Dios mantuvo con Faraón para que dejara a los israelitas marcharse de Egipto. Antes de entrar en esa lucha, Dios informó a Moisés de que iba a endurecer el corazón de Faraón (Éx. 4:21; 7:3). Pero no lo hizo desde el principio. En dos ocasiones Faraón endureció su propio corazón (8:15, 32). En tres ocasiones el texto dice que «el corazón de Faraón se endureció» (7:13-14, 22; 8:19). Aunque Moisés no identifica quién lo endureció, es lógico concluir que Faraón fue el primer responsable. En 9:34 Faraón endureció su corazón de nuevo, siendo él con toda probabilidad el culpable del endurecimiento que se cita en los vv. 7 y 35. Pero es ahora en este capítulo, después de que Faraón endureció su propio corazón en tantas ocasiones, que Dios interviene *por primera vez* y endurece su corazón (9:12). Después de tantas oportunidades que Dios le había dado para cambiar de opinión al ver los estragos que las plagas hacían en su país, Faraón siguió negándose a arrodillarse ante el Dios del universo. Así que Dios toma la iniciativa de endurecer el corazón de Faraón aún más (10:1, 20, 27; 11:10; 14:8) y de empujar el proceso que Faraón había puesto en marcha para que llegara cuanto antes a su fin. Cuando los israelitas se encontraban frente al mar Rojo, Dios endureció el corazón de Faraón por última vez (14:8).

Cuando Dios llamó a Isaías para que le sirviera como profeta, le informó de que lo enviaba a predicar a un pueblo que no aceptaría su mensaje (Is. 6:9-13). Mateo 13:14-15 cita una porción de esa conversación de Dios con Isaías (Is. 6:9-10). En Romanos 1:17-32 Pablo describe la depravación total del ser humano. Este, a pesar de todas las pruebas que puede observar de que Dios existe y es santo, insiste en seguir en su pecado. Así que cuando llega el momento en que no hay vuelta atrás, un momento que solamente Dios conoce, Dios entrega a esas personas «a la inmundicia» (v. 24), «a pasiones vergonzosas» (v. 26) y «a una mente reprobada» (v. 28), dándoles rienda suelta para que lleguen cuanto antes a su destino de condenación.

Las parábolas de Jesús llevaban la fe de algunos a una fe más profunda y la incredulidad de otros a una incredulidad mayor. Mientras que Cristo empleaba las parábolas para ilustrar y revelar las verdades a quienes estaban dispuestos a entenderlas y obedecerlas, también las empleaba para esconder la verdad a quienes no querían aceptarla. En efecto, las parábolas ponían a prueba el carácter de una persona y su disposición para aceptar la verdad. El mismo sol que endurece el barro de los caminos hace blando el alquitrán en las grietas de las calles.

Además de esconder la verdad a sus detractores, las parábolas protegían a Jesús de una posible violencia contra su persona antes de su viaje a Jerusalén para morir. Si Jesús hubiera presentado su enseñanza sobre el reino de Dios —y a él mismo como el Rey de ese reino— con un lenguaje literal que no dejara lugar a dudas en cuanto a lo que decía, esto habría sido más que suficiente para convencer a las autoridades romanas de que era culpable de sedición. Pero debido al carácter ambiguo de sus parábolas, sus oponentes encontraban difícil acusarlo con argumentos convincentes. A la vez, sus parábolas eran capaces de mantener el interés de sus detractores hasta que Jesús pudiera poner el dedo en la llaga. Esto es precisamente lo que ocurrió cuando Jesús contó la parábola de los labradores malvados (Mt. 21:33-44). Los principales sacerdotes y los fariseos sabían que Jesús hablaba de ellos y por ello buscaban la forma de arrestarlo (v. 46). Pero por temor a la reacción de la multitud desistieron en su deseo. Terry hace un resumen inmejorable del primer y cuarto propósito que Jesús tenía al usar parábolas.

Muchas lecciones morales, si son predicadas en un estilo completamente literal, se olvidan rápidamente. Pero vestidas de una parábola despiertan el interés y se pegan a la memoria. Muchos reproches y avisos directos pueden vestirse de una parábola y así ofender menos, pero a la vez ser más efectivos que una declaración muy clara que va al grano. Algunas de las parábolas más claras del Señor contra los judíos —parábolas que percibieron como dirigidas contra ellos— conllevaban una reprensión. Sin embargo, debido a su forma y adorno, sirvieron para protegerlo de una violencia en potencia (Mt. 21:45; Mc. 12:12; Lc. 20:19)[4].

## B. DEFINICIÓN DE PARÁBOLA

La palabra *parabole* proviene de las palabras *para* (al lado de) y *balo* (arrojar). De ahí que conlleve la idea de «colocar al lado de» con el propósito de comparar una cosa con otra. En el N.T. *parabole* aparece solamente en los Evangelios sinópticos (47 veces)[5], y siempre es traducida en la RVR60 como «parábolas»[6].

---

4. Milton S. Terry, *Biblical Hermeneutics* (Grand Rapids: Zondervan, 1969), pp. 277–278.

5. Algunos libros dicen que aparece 48 veces. Pero la *Concordancia de las Sagradas Escrituras* de C. P. Denyer (San José: Caribe, 1969) indica que aparece 47 veces, teniendo en cuenta que *parabole* aparece dos veces en Mateo 13:34 y Marcos 4:13. Aunque la *Exhaustive Concordance of the Bible* de James Strong (Gordonsville: Dugan Publisher's Inc., s. f.) es reconocida por todos como una obra excelente, presenta el aparente error de no incluir Mateo 13:31 y Marcos 4:30 en la lista de textos donde se emplea la palabra *parabole*.

6. Juan nunca emplea la palabra *parabole*, sino *paroimia* (10:6; 16:25, 29). Segunda de Pedro 2:22 es el otro versículo donde aparece *paroimia*. Es interesante notar cómo la RVR60, LBLA, NTV y NVI traducen *paroimia*. En 2 Pedro 2:22 todos lo traducen como «proverbio» o «proverbios». En Juan 10:6, la RVR60 y la LBLA lo traducen como «alegoría», pero la NTV y NVI lo hace como «ejemplo». Pero en Juan 16:25 la diversidad entre estas versiones se dispara: RVR60 («alegorías»); NVI («comparaciones»); NTV («lenguaje figurativo»); LBLA («lenguaje figurado» con una nota en el margen que dice «Lit. *en proverbios o figuras del lenguaje*»). Dicha diversidad se ve también en Juan 16:29: RVR60 («alegoría»); LBLA («lenguaje figurado» con una nota en el margen que dice «Lit. *un proverbio*»); NVI («sin vueltas ni rodeos»); NTV («en sentido figurado»). La LXX se refiere a *paroimia* como un proverbio o parábola que se basa en objetos comunes y acciones típicas de la vida cotidiana.

Los eruditos están de acuerdo en que el concepto que tenían Jesús y los evangelistas de una parábola no vino del mundo clásico griego sino del A.T., donde la palabra hebrea *mashal* se empleaba para varias formas figurativas de comunicación. Por ejemplo, proverbios, dichos enigmáticos, adivinanzas, fábulas, símiles, alegorías, parábolas (historias con un argumento), etcétera. Cuando los traductores de la LXX encontraban la palabra *mashal*, siempre la traducían con la palabra griega *parabole*. Puesto que muchos judíos del primer siglo no podían leer el hebreo, la LXX era su versión preferida del A.T. Por tanto, cuando Mateo, Marcos y Lucas escribieron sus Evangelios, emplearon la palabra *parabole* para al menos cinco de esas clases de comunicación figurativa.

*1. Símiles*. Muchos eruditos afirman que cuando un símil es ampliado, extendido o alargado con más detalles, se convierte en una parábola (una historia con un argumento). Este es el caso en las parábolas de la semilla de mostaza (Mt. 13:31-32) y la levadura (13:33). La parábola de la mostaza es un puro símil. Pero la parábola de la levadura añade dos frases más para describir lo que la mujer hizo con la levadura: «El reino del cielo es como la levadura que utilizó una mujer para hacer pan. Aunque puso solo una pequeña porción de levadura en tres medidas de harina, la levadura impregnó toda la masa» (NTV). Pero ¿cuántos detalles hacen falta para convertir un símil en una parábola? ¿Dos, tres, cuatro? Es difícil, si no imposible, dar una respuesta a esa pregunta que sea aceptada por todos. Este es uno de los factores que ha hecho difícil que los eruditos lleguen a un acuerdo sobre la definición de una parábola.

*2. Señales, ilustraciones*. Jesús dijo: «De la higuera aprended la parábola: Cuando ya su rama está tierna, y brotan las hojas, sabéis que el verano está cerca» (Mt. 24:32). O sea, cuando los creyentes vean ciertas señales, sabrán que la segunda venida de Cristo está cerca.

*3. Principios espirituales*. Cuando Jesús dijo en referencia a los fariseos que «toda planta que no plantó mi Padre celestial, será desarraigada» (Mt. 15:13), Pedro le pidió que explicara esta parábola (v. 15)[7]. Evidentemente, se trata de un principio espiritual. En Lucas 14:7-8 Jesús asiste

7. Marcos 7:17 indica que los «discípulos» pidieron una interpretación de la parábola. Una explicación razonable es que todos tenían la misma pregunta, pero que Pedro actuaba como el portavoz de todos.

a un convite. Al observar cómo algunos buscaban los mejores asientos, «refirió a los convidados una parábola, diciéndoles: Cuando fueres convidado por alguno a bodas, no te sientes en el primer lugar».

*4. Proverbios.* O sea, argumentos basados en el sentido común. Por ejemplo: Satanás no lucha contra sí mismo; un reino y una casa divididos contra sí mismos no prevalecerán; el hombre que entra en una casa para robar, primero tiene que atar al propietario (Mc. 3:23-27 a la luz del v. 22); un ciego no puede guiar a otros ciegos (Lc. 6:39); nadie cose un pedazo de un vestido nuevo en un vestido viejo, ni nadie mete vino nuevo en odres viejos (Lc. 5:36-39); etcétera.

*5. Una historia con un argumento.* Este es el uso de *mashal* en que pensamos cuando decimos que una parábola es «una historia terrenal con un significado celestial»[8]. Es una historia ficticia que en verdad podría haber ocurrido, puesto que refleja las costumbres y la vida cotidiana de los palestinos del primer siglo. Para crear y contar una historia se requiere cierta cantidad de detalles, algunos de los cuales no tendrán ningún significado especial[9].

Estos ejemplos demuestran que cuando los judíos del primer siglo empleaban la palabra *parabole* no hacían ninguna distinción entre estas diferentes formas figurativas de la comunicación. Sin embargo, el hecho de que no *hicieran* ninguna distinción no significa que no *exista* una distinción entre ellas. El hecho de que existan palabras distintas para todas estas formas de comunicación figurativa en el español y otros

8. En su libro *The Parables of the Kingdom* (Londres: Hodder and Stoughton, 1907) G. Campbell Morgan dice que oyó esta definición en la escuela dominical cuando era un niño. Escribió este libro en 1907 cuando tenía 44 años (p. 13). Si restamos unos 34 años, Morgan aprendió esta definición c. 1873. Aunque hay quienes quieren descartar esta definición en favor de una más técnica, es por algo que esta definición sencilla ha perdurado tantos años.

9. Aunque las historias del tesoro escondido (Mt. 13:44), la perla de gran precio (Mt. 13:45-46) y la red (Mt. 13:47-48) no son llamadas *parábolas* en el texto bíblico, y pese a que cuentan con un mínimo de detalles, el autor cree que son parábolas en el sentido de que cuentan una historia con un argumento porque forman parte de un capítulo repleto de parábolas de esa clase. No sabemos a qué clase de «parábola» se referían Mateo (v. 3), los discípulos (v. 10) y Jesús (v. 13), puesto que no figuran en el capítulo 13 todas las parábolas que Jesús contó a las multitudes aquel día.

idiomas es una prueba de que no son iguales y de que cada una conlleva un matiz que la distingue de las demás. Por ejemplo, una fábula no es una parábola. Hay solamente dos ejemplos claros de fábulas en la Biblia. En Jueces 9:7-20 Jotam, el hijo menor de los muchos que tenía Gedeón y el único que no fue asesinado por Abimelec, lo denuncia con una fábula. En 2 Reyes 14:9 Joás, rey de Israel, envía una fábula a Amasías, rey de Judá, en un intento de evitar que ataque a Israel. Estas fábulas fueron citadas por los autores de Jueces y 2 Reyes bajo la inspiración del Espíritu Santo. Pero no tienen como propósito comunicar una verdad espiritual que Dios quiere transmitir a su pueblo[10]. Aunque el N.T. no contiene ninguna fábula, condena las «fábulas [...] interminables» (1 Ti. 1:4), las «fábulas profanas» (1 Ti. 4:7), las «fábulas judaicas» (Tit. 1:14) y las «fábulas artificiosas» (2 P. 1:16). Mientras que las fábulas y las parábolas son ficticias en el sentido de que las historias que cuentan nunca ocurrieron, no tienen nada más en común[11].

10. En su libro *Interpreting the Bible* (Grand Rapids: Eerdmans, 1963), p. 204, Mickelsen sugiere que las palabras del profeta Ezequiel en el capítulo 17 son «una alegoría y fábula» o «una fábula parabólica». Si es así, representaría un ejemplo único en el cual Dios emplea una fábula para comunicar algo a su pueblo. No obstante, los casos de Jueces 9:7-20 y 2 Reyes 14:9 son los únicos casos que podrían clasificarse como fábulas en un sentido técnico de esa palabra.

11. En su libro *The Parables of Jesus* (Grand Rapids: Baker, 1979), p. xvi, George A. Buttrick sugiere que Jesús nunca empleó una fábula en su enseñanza porque «una fábula es "fabulosa". Rompe con las fronteras de lo natural, otorga poderes humanos a los árboles y animales y se somete a lo grotesco. La mente de Jesús era demasiado natural y normal desde una perspectiva divina, demasiado sensible al mundo de los goces y lágrimas humanas para estar aficionada a lo fabuloso. La fábula enseña una virtud meramente prudencial. La fábula recomienda la cautela, el uso cuidadoso de nuestro dinero, el estar prevenido, y lo hace desde una perspectiva de las consecuencias humanas si no cumplimos. Se mueve en una línea horizontal; su mérito es de hombre a hombre. Pero la parábola siempre se mueve en una línea vertical; tiene "un significado celestial". Evidentemente, una parábola puede instarnos a amar a nuestro prójimo como a nosotros mismos. Pero esa exhortación siempre depende de otra: "Amarás al Señor tu Dios"».

## *Trabajo para realizar*

1. ¿Cuáles son las cuatro razones que motivaron a Jesús a emplear tantas parábolas en su ministerio docente? Cuando los traductores de la LXX se encontraban con la palabra hebrea *mashal,* la tradujeron con la palabra *parabole.* Sin embargo, *mashal* se empleaba para referirse a varias clases de lenguaje figurado. Los evangelistas emplearon *parabole* para cinco de esas clases. ¿Cuáles son?

2. En las últimas décadas los eruditos del N.T. han debatido tres cuestiones. Han llegado a un acuerdo en cuanto al propósito que tenía Jesús al emplear las parábolas en su enseñanza y la definición de una parábola. Lo que no ha sido tan fácil ha sido ponerse de acuerdo en cuanto a la cuestión de la relación que existe entre una parábola y una alegoría. Todas las formas figuradas de la comunicación tienen cosas en común. Por eso, a veces se solapan y actúan de la misma forma. Pero esta característica es más frecuente y evidente con las parábolas y alegorías. Lea «La relación entre una parábola y una alegoría» en el Apéndice F, el cual describe la interesante historia y debate que hay detrás de los principios que han sido establecidos para la interpretación de las parábolas, los cuales veremos en el capítulo 19.

# 19

# Parábolas (II)

Cuando los setenta eruditos judíos tradujeron el A.T. al griego (LXX) c. 250 a. C. emplearon la palabra *parabole* para traducir la palabra hebrea *mashal*, una palabra que incluía varias formas de comunicación figurativa, incluyendo la parábola. De acuerdo con la definición de que una parábola es una historia con un argumento, se encuentran cuarenta parábolas en los Evangelios sinópticos[1].

| | Mateo | Marcos | Lucas |
|---|---|---|---|
| 1. La oveja perdida | 18:12-14 | | 15:3-7 |
| 2. La moneda perdida | | | 15:8-10 |
| 3. El hijo pródigo | | | 15:11-32 |
| 4. El amigo de medianoche | | | 11:5-13 |
| 5. Los dos hijos y la viña | 21:28-32 | | |
| 6. Los labradores malvados | 21:33-46 | 12:1-12 | 20:9-18 |
| 7. La fiesta de bodas | 22:1-14 (R) | | |
| 8. La viuda y el juez injusto | | | 18:1-8 |

1. Están incluidas en esta lista las parábolas identificadas por Jesús y los evangelistas como una *parabole* además de aquellos pasajes que tienen un mínimo de argumento, aunque la palabra *parabole* no aparezca. Los versículos incluidos en esta lista corresponden a cada parábola en sí y a cualquier interpretación o aplicación que Jesús hace de ella. Puesto que las parábolas nunca dan nombres a sus personajes, el relato del rico y Lázaro (Lc. 16:19-31) no figura en esta lista. Si este texto no es una parábola, entonces describe un evento real.

| | Mateo | Marcos | Lucas |
|---|---|---|---|
| 9. El acreedor y los dos deudores | | | 7:41-43 |
| 10. El candelero | | 4:21-25 | 8:16-18 |
| 11. El sembrador | 13:3-8, 18-23 | 4:3-8, 14-20 | 8:5-8, 11-15 |
| 12. El trigo y la cizaña | 13:24-30, 36-43 (R) | | |
| 13. La semilla de mostaza | 13:31-32 (R) | 4:30-34 (R) | 13:18-19 (R) |
| 14. La levadura | 13:33 (R) | | 13:20-21 (R) |
| 15. El tesoro escondido | 13:44 (R) | | |
| 16. La perla de gran precio | 13:45-46 (R) | | |
| 17. La red | 13:47-50 (R) | | |
| 18. El siervo sin misericordia | 18:23-35 (R) | | |
| 19. Los obreros de la viña | 20:1-16 (R) | | |
| 20. Las diez vírgenes | 25:1-13 (R) | | |
| 21. Los talentos | 25:14-30 (R) | | |
| 22. El crecimiento de la semilla | | 4:26-29 (R) | |
| 23. El buen samaritano | | | 10:30-37 |
| 24. El rico insensato | | | 12:16-21 |
| 25. La higuera estéril | | | 13:6-9 |
| 26. La gran cena | | | 14:16-24 |
| 27. El mayordomo infiel | | | 16:1-13 |
| 28. El deber del siervo | | | 17:7-10 |
| 29. El fariseo y el publicano | | | 18:9-14 |
| 30. Las diez minas | | | 19:11-27 (R) |
| 31. Los vestidos y los odres | 9:16-17 | 2:21-22 | 5:36-39 |
| 32. Los convidados a las bodas | | | 14:7-15 |
| 33. El siervo vigilante | | | 12:35-40 |
| 34. El siervo infiel | | | 12:41-48 |

| | Mateo | Marcos | Lucas |
|---|---|---|---|
| 35. La edificación de una torre | | | 14:28-30 |
| 36. El rey que hace guerra | | | 14:31-32 |
| 37. Los dos cimientos | 7:24-27 | | 6:48-49 |
| 38. Las cosas nuevas y viejas | 13:51-53 (R) | | |
| 39. La puerta estrecha | | | 13:23-40 |
| 40. Las ovejas y los cabritos | 25:31-46 | | |

En sus estudios de las parábolas, Dodd (1884–1973) y Jeremias (1900–1979) llegaron a la conclusión de que su mensaje principal es el reino de Dios, una conclusión compartida por todos los eruditos del N.T. En el cuadro de arriba, las parábolas que Jesús introduce con las palabras «El reino de Dios [o de los cielos] es como...» son identificadas con una (R). Aunque Jesús contó las demás parábolas en respuesta a una petición, pregunta, acusación o crítica contra su persona o sus discípulos, todas ellas tocan algún aspecto del reino de Dios. Hay siete normas que el intérprete debe emplear al interpretar una parábola.

## A. TOMAR EN CUENTA EL CONTEXTO HISTÓRICO

El contexto histórico trata de la situación, petición, pregunta, problema, injusticia, crítica o acusación que motivó a Jesús a contar una parábola. Cerciorarse del contexto histórico es el primer paso que el intérprete debe dar para hacer una interpretación correcta de una parábola. Además, este paso limitará el peligro de que el intérprete imponga sobre una parábola un significado que Jesús nunca pretendió comunicar a los primeros oyentes. Cuando los evangelistas no identifican el contexto histórico, por regla general el tema y el punto principal de la parábola son evidentes.

Normalmente, el contexto histórico se encuentra justo antes de la parábola. Cuando una parábola es precedida por otra parábola, esa parábola representa un contexto, pero no el contexto *histórico*. Por tanto, el intérprete tendrá que volver hacia atrás hasta que lo encuentre. Por ejemplo, la parábola del hijo pródigo (Lc. 15:11-32) es precedida por dos parábolas, la de la moneda perdida (vv. 8-10) y la de la oveja perdida (vv. 3-7). El contexto histórico de las tres se encuentra en los vv. 1-2, donde los fariseos y escribas murmuran porque Jesús «a los pecadores recibe, y con ellos come». Hasta que el intérprete no haya identificado el contexto histórico de una parábola, no estará en posición de interpretarla correctamente.

El autor de *Con precisión* cree que el punto central de la parábola del hijo pródigo es que «Jesús ama a los pecadores». Por eso estaba dispuesto a sentarse con ellos. Pero ¿por qué contó *tres* parábolas para comunicar *una* sola verdad? A veces hay dos o tres parábolas que aparecen juntas en las cuales sus respectivos puntos centrales presentan tres aspectos de un mismo punto central, o tres ideas diferentes pero íntimamente relacionadas. Las tres parábolas de Lucas 15 presentan tres aspectos de una misma verdad. Puesto que la respuesta que Jesús da a la pregunta insinuada de los fariseos y escribas hace énfasis en que «Jesús *ama* a los pecadores»[2], el autor de *Con precisión* opina que las tres parábolas subrayan tres aspectos del amor de Dios. Lo que llama la atención en la parábola de la oveja perdida es que Dios ama a cada pecador en particular, aunque tenga muchas otras ovejas. Si bien Cristo murió por el pecado de todos, salva a cada pecador individualmente. En la parábola de la moneda perdida el énfasis recae sobre el amor que persevera. La mujer buscó esa moneda «con diligencia hasta encontrarla» (v. 8). ¡Menos mal que Cristo perseveró con algunas personas que por fin lo aceptaron como su Salvador después de muchos años de rechazarlo! Lo que destaca en la parábola del hijo pródigo es que

2. Algunos serán tentados a creer que el énfasis recae sobre «*Jesús* ama a los pecadores» y que las tres parábolas representan las tres personas de la Trinidad: Jesús es el buen pastor en la parábola de la oveja perdida, el Padre es el padre en la parábola del hijo pródigo y el Espíritu Santo es la mujer en la parábola de la moneda perdida... ¡porque es la única persona de la Trinidad que queda! Pero es difícil, si no imposible, entender cómo la mujer representa el Espíritu Santo. Tampoco recae el énfasis sobre «Jesús ama a los *pecadores*», representando así tres clases de pecadores: los que pecan por ignorancia (oveja perdida), el pecador rebelde que sabe lo que hace (hijo pródigo) y el pecador que intenta hacer lo correcto pero es incapaz de hacerlo (Ro. 7:18-19), quien es representado por... ¡otra vez la parábola de la moneda perdida porque es la única que queda! No hay manera de entender cómo una moneda que cae, rueda y se esconde fuera de la vista de su propietaria puede representar esa clase de pecador.

nadie se encuentra más allá del alcance del amor de Cristo debido a la cantidad o seriedad de los pecados que haya cometido.

En el caso de la parábola de la oveja perdida, Mateo y Lucas citan dos contextos históricos y dos puntos centrales completamente diferentes. Lucas 15:1-7 indica que esta parábola fue dirigida a los fariseos y escribas, mientras que Mateo 18:1, 12-14 dice que Jesús la contó a sus discípulos. En Lucas el punto central es que Jesús ama a los pecadores. Pero en Mateo, Jesús dice que no quiere que ningún niño se pierda eternamente. Las explicaciones que algunos dan a estas diferencias representan un claro rechazo de las doctrinas de la revelación, inspiración e inerrancia de las Escrituras. Sugieren que Mateo o Lucas —o quizás los dos— fabricaron dichos contextos históricos y atribuyeron a Jesús parábolas que nunca contó, y que lo hicieron con el propósito de apoyar el mensaje que querían comunicar a sus respectivos lectores[3].

Sin embargo, es mucho más razonable pensar que Jesús repitió ciertas parábolas, lo cual explicaría dos contextos históricos diferentes. Además, es más que razonable suponer que Jesús utilizó más de una vez la misma historia, creada por él, para ilustrar verdades diferentes de acuerdo con las necesidades diferentes de las personas que tenía delante. No estaba obligado a hacer que el punto central de una parábola que ya había contado una vez tuviese el mismo punto central cada vez que la contaba a un grupo distinto.

## B. INVESTIGAR EL FONDO HISTÓRICO Y CULTURAL DE LOS DETALLES

Aunque las historias de las parábolas nunca ocurrieron, reflejan las costumbres y la vida cotidiana de los primeros oyentes. Pero no todos

3. En su artículo «Interpretación de parábolas» en el *Diccionario de la teología práctica: hermenéutica* (Grand Rapids: Subcomisión Literatura Cristiana de la Iglesia Cristiana Reformada, 1984), pp. 35–36, Wallace roza esta clase de explicación al decir que las parábolas de la gran cena (Lc. 14:16-24) y la fiesta de bodas (Mt. 22:1-14) eran originalmente una sola parábola, pero que Mateo y Lucas las retocaron para hacer un énfasis que atendiera a una necesidad de los grupos a los cuales escribían. En el caso de Mateo quería atender a la controversia que había entre los judíos y los primeros cristianos, mientras que Lucas quería hacer énfasis sobre el banquete que se celebrará en un futuro escatológico.

los detalles son realistas. De vez en cuando Jesús añadía un detalle que distaba mucho de la realidad con tal de causar un impacto en el punto central de su parábola. Por ejemplo, es muy poco probable que alguien que vivía en Palestina en el primer siglo tuviera una deuda que ascendiera a 10.000 talentos (millones y millones de euros o dólares) como en el caso de la parábola del siervo sin misericordia (Mt. 18:23-35). El intérprete que ignora el fondo histórico y cultural de los detalles de una parábola no se dará cuenta del impacto que dicha parábola causaba en los primeros oyentes.

Un entendimiento de la topografía de Palestina es muy útil para entender una parábola como la del buen samaritano (Lc. 10:30-37). Un hombre descendía de Jerusalén a Jericó, un recorrido de unos 33 km. Era un viaje arduo porque Jericó estaba situada unos 1097 metros más abajo, y el camino pasaba por una zona montañosa. Los ladrones aprovechaban los muchos sectores estrechos de ese camino para robar a los viajeros. En el siglo V Jerónimo (c. 340–420) dijo que ese recorrido se llamaba el Camino Sangriento. Y aún en el siglo XIX los viajeros tenían que pagar una «tasa de seguridad» a los jeques que controlaban la zona. Varias parábolas contienen un elemento de *shock*. Al quedar cautivados con las parábolas de Jesús, los oyentes creían saber cómo acabaría la historia. Y cuando menos lo esperaban, Jesús introducía el punto central, el cual tomaba un rumbo que nadie esperaba y que dejaba a todos atónitos. Para apreciar el elemento de *shock* que esta parábola representaba para los primeros oyentes, el intérprete tiene que conocer los orígenes de los samaritanos[4] y la discriminación que los judíos y los samaritanos practicaban los unos contra los otros. Para estos primeros oyentes suponía un tremendo *shock* que un samaritano fuera el único que se parara a socorrer al viajero herido, que además era judío.

Otras parábolas requieren que el intérprete conozca algo acerca de los escribas, saduceos, fariseos, publicanos, zelotes, herodianos, etcétera[5], grupos que ya existían durante los 400 años que transcurrieron

4. Ver la sección «El Pentateuco samaritano» del Apéndice C para una explicación de los orígenes de los samaritanos.

5. El nombre de los saduceos se toma de Sadoc, el sumo sacerdote durante los días de David y Salomón. Los hijos de Sadoc ocupaban la jerarquía sacerdotal durante la cautividad babilónica (2 Cr. 31:10; Ez. 40:46; 44:15; 48:11). Aunque no

entre los dos Testamentos. Por ejemplo, la parábola del fariseo y el publicano (Lc. 18:9-14) requiere que el intérprete sepa quiénes son estos dos grupos. La secta de los fariseos, cuyo nombre viene del verbo *parash*, que significa «separar», nació durante los días de los Macabeos (c. 167 a. C.) como una reacción contra la cultura griega (helenismo) con sus lujos, comodidades, adoración del cuerpo desnudo, etcétera. Los fariseos eran separatistas y puristas. En tiempos de Jesús eran el grupo que hacía ostentación de más miembros e influencia. Creían en la Ley de Moisés y la interpretaban literalmente. Creían en los ángeles y los espíritus, la inmortalidad del espíritu y la resurrección del cuerpo. Pero creían también en las tradiciones orales, las interpretaciones que los rabinos habían hecho de la Ley a lo largo de los siglos, las cuales consideraban iguales en valor a las Escrituras (Mt. 15:2-6; Mc. 7:1-13).

Además, los fariseos se caracterizaban por el legalismo. Puesto que la Ley no permitía el trabajo en el día de reposo, los fariseos prohibían a sus miembros escupir en el día de reposo por si acaso se movía el polvo de la tierra, lo cual sería igual que ararla. No se les permitía a las mujeres mirarse en el espejo por si acaso veían una cana y la quitaban, trabajando así en el día de reposo. Tampoco permitían comer huevos puestos por las gallinas en el día de reposo, ni llevar ropa en los brazos. Si su casa se incendiaba, tenían que ponerse la ropa que querían salvaguardar para sacarla fuera de la casa. Llevarla en brazos representaría trabajo. No podían viajar más de aproximadamente un kilómetro el día de reposo. Para esquivar esta ley, el día antes algunos miembros de esta secta judía depositaban comida a un kilómetro de

---

tenían tantos miembros como los fariseos, ostentaban el poder político y gobernaban en los asuntos civiles de Palestina bajo los Herodes. Mientras que los fariseos y escribas eran de la clase media, los saduceos representaban la aristocracia y contaban entre sus filas con las familias más ricas y relevantes de la sociedad. Por tanto, tenían mucha influencia. Los saduceos eran oportunistas políticos. Abrazaban el helenismo con sus lujos, placeres y comodidades. La mayoría de los saduceos pertenecían al sacerdocio. Interpretaban las Escrituras de forma literal y creían en la Ley de Moisés. Sin embargo, abrazaban una teología liberal, rechazando todo lo sobrenatural como la resurrección, los espíritus y la inmortalidad. Rechazaban la tradición oral de los fariseos. Eran escépticos y mundanos; mantenían una ética muy fría. Jesús no tenía mucho que ver con ellos.

su casa. Entonces, podían viajar un kilómetro más allá de ese lugar, argumentando que su hogar se encontraba donde ellos se alimentaban.

Al otro extremo se encontraban los publicanos. No eran una secta ni un partido político, sino un grupo de personas marginadas de la sociedad debido a la repulsión que producía su profesión. Eran judíos que trabajaban para el Imperio romano como cobradores de impuestos. Agentes enviados por Roma dividían las provincias (Palestina era una provincia) en distritos y otorgaban el puesto de cobrador de impuestos al que prometía la mayor cantidad de impuestos. Al final del año el publicano tenía que pagar a Roma la cantidad pactada. Lo que quedaba representaba su sueldo para el año. Jesús llamó a los publicanos «gentiles», o sea, paganos (Mt. 18:17). Los mismos romanos decían que «donde están los publicanos no hay respeto por la ley ni por la libertad de los aliados». Había varias clases de impuestos, por ejemplo un impuesto imperial (Mt. 22:15-22). José y María inscribieron sus nombres en la lista de impuestos imperiales de Belén puesto que sus familias procedían de esa ciudad (Lc. 2:1-4). Además, había un impuesto de aduanas, que era aún más detestado por los judíos. Los publicanos montaban unas cabinas en puntos estratégicos de las carreteras principales y allí cobraban a los comerciantes según el género que llevaban. Los publicanos tenían la orden de inspeccionar todos los paquetes y cobrar lo que les parecía justo. Pero siempre cobraban de más. Aunque estaban respaldados por Roma, eran odiados por los judíos.

El creyente del siglo XXI considera hipócrita al fariseo que daba gracias a Dios por no ser como «los otros hombres, ladrones, injustos, adúlteros, ni aun como este publicano» (Lc. 18:11). Pero el judío del primer siglo aplaudía a los fariseos por haber hecho el esfuerzo de ser hombres rectos. Por tanto, cuando Jesús llegó al final de la parábola y dijo que el publicano «descendió a su casa justificado antes que el otro (el fariseo)», ese punto central estalló entre los oyentes como una bomba. Este detalle se le escapa al intérprete que no dedica tiempo a investigar el fondo histórico y cultural de los detalles de una parábola.

## C. IDENTIFICAR LOS PUNTOS DE COMPARACIÓN

A veces hay más personas en una parábola que en su contexto histórico, o viceversa. No obstante, por regla general es fácil identificar quiénes son las personas a las que se refiere la parábola. Por ejemplo, la parábola del hijo pródigo (Lc. 5:11-32) hace mención a seis personas o grupos: el padre, el hijo mayor, el hijo menor, las rameras con las cuales el hijo gastó su herencia (v. 30), el propietario de los cerdos, y los jornaleros (siervos, criados) del padre. Sin embargo, el contexto histórico (vv. 1-2) cuenta con solamente tres: Jesús, los publicanos y pecadores, y los fariseos y escribas. No obstante, es evidente que Jesús es representado por el padre, los publicanos y pecadores por el hijo menor, y los fariseos y escribas por el hijo mayor.

En la mayoría de las parábolas se hace una *comparación* entre las personas del contexto histórico y la parábola, y en un par de parábolas se hace un *contraste*. Por ejemplo, en la parábola del amigo que llega a medianoche (Lc. 11:5-7), el hombre que necesita pan representa a los discípulos. El vecino que tiene pan, pero que se resiste a dárselo, representa a Dios. A primera vista parece que esta parábola sugiere que hemos de perseverar en la oración porque Dios no quiere darnos lo que necesitamos. Pero en la interpretación que Jesús hace de esta parábola, explica que Dios es justo lo contrario a ese vecino. Si Dios nos requiere que perseveremos en oración con ciertas peticiones no es porque no quiera responder a esas oraciones.

## D. RECORDAR QUE HABRÁ DETALLES QUE NO TIENEN NINGÚN SIGNIFICADO

¿Cuántos detalles de una parábola tienen significado? Desde los primeros siglos del cristianismo, la mayoría de los líderes rechazaban una interpretación literal de las Escrituras en favor de la alegorización de las mismas, y muy en particular de las parábolas. Con la alegorización cada detalle tenía un significado, como lo muestra (en la página siguiente) la interpretación que Tertuliano (c. 160–c. 220) hizo de la parábola del hijo pródigo.

Los eruditos están de acuerdo en que la parábola del sembrador (Mt. 13:3-8, 18-23) y la del trigo y la cizaña (Mt. 13:24-30, 36-43) son las primeras que Jesús pronunció. Puesto que él las interpretó, esa interpretación nos es muy instructiva. En la parábola del sembrador identificó la semilla con la Palabra de Dios y las cuatro clases de tierra con los diferentes grados de disposición que caracterizan a las personas que la reciben. No hay cuatro puntos centrales, sino uno; a saber, que el crecimiento de la semilla y el fruto que se produce será diferente en cada caso porque dependerá de la receptividad de cada persona. En la parábola del trigo y la cizaña Jesús indica que el enemigo de nuestra alma siempre está sembrando confusión y error. Como resultado, no todos los que dicen ser creyentes lo son. Pero al final Dios separará el trigo de la cizaña. La iglesia no debería dedicarse a esa labor para no arrancar al trigo por error. En esta parábola Jesús da atención especial al sembrador, al campo, a la buena semilla, al trigo, a la cizaña, al enemigo, a los que cosechaban y al juicio final cuando Dios separará el trigo de la cizaña. Pero deja varios detalles en el tintero: los hombres que durmieron, los siervos del padre de familia, las preguntas que esos siervos hicieron, el crecimiento del trigo y la cizaña y el fruto que produjeron. Estos detalles no tienen ningún significado especial. Haciendo un resumen de cómo Jesús interpretó estas parábolas, Virkler dice:

| **La parábola del hijo pródigo (según Tertuliano)** | |
|---|---|
| **Detalles** | **Interpretación** |
| El hijo menor | El creyente |
| El hijo mayor | El pueblo judío |
| El dueño de los cerdos | Satanás |
| El vestido que recibió el hijo menor | La posición de Adán antes de pecar |
| El anillo | El bautismo |
| El banquete para el hijo menor | La Cena del Señor |
| La Santa Cena | Cristo, quien fue sacrificado por nosotros |

> En el propio análisis de Jesús es posible determinar tanto una idea central o focal, y un énfasis significativo en detalles, *según están relacionados con la idea focal.* El análisis de Jesús de los detalles de la parábola contrasta con la práctica de quienes les dan significado a los detalles de manera tal que los detalles enseñan lecciones adicionales sin relación con el punto central de la parábola. Por tanto, si se pueden sacar algunas inferencias de la interpretación de Cristo de sus propias parábolas, son que (1) hay un punto central o focal de enseñanza en las parábolas de Cristo, y (2) los detalles tienen importancia según estén relacionados con la enseñanza focal. Los

detalles no están para tener significado que sea independiente de la enseñanza principal de una parábola[6].

## E. INTERPRETAR A LA LUZ DE LA INTERPRETACIÓN DE JESÚS

Jesús no siempre interpreta sus parábolas. Pero cuando lo hace el intérprete queda obligado a aceptar esa interpretación como la única correcta. A veces los discípulos le piden que explique una parábola; en otras ocasiones Jesús toma la iniciativa de hacerlo. Cuando el punto central es evidente, a veces Jesús se dirige directamente a una aplicación de esa enseñanza principal. Aunque hay solamente un punto central en cada parábola, puede haber muchas aplicaciones. Para entender aún mejor cualquier interpretación que Jesús hace de una parábola suya, el intérprete debe prestar atención a la reacción de los primeros oyentes, la cual puede indicar lo que Jesús quería decir.

## F. LIMITARSE A UN PUNTO CENTRAL

Ramm dice que «se podría llamar a este principio la ley de oro de la interpretación de una parábola, porque prácticamente todos los escritos sobre el tema hacen mención de ello y con mucho énfasis»[7]. Aunque hay algunos evangélicos que no aceptan esta norma, el debate que ha tenido lugar durante las últimas décadas ha convencido a la gran mayoría de que cada parábola tiene tan solo un punto central, aunque Jesús puede identificar muchas aplicaciones del punto principal de una parábola[8]. A la luz de todos los abusos de interpretación que se han cometido en siglos pasados con la alegorización de las parábolas y la búsqueda de más de un punto

---

6. Henry A. Virkler, *Hermenéutica: principios y procedimientos de interpretación bíblica* (Miami: Editorial Vida, 1994), pp. 145–146.

7. Bernard Ramm, *Protestant Biblical Interpretation* (Grand Rapids: Eerdmans, 1963), p. 283.

8. Por ejemplo, David Wenham, *The Parables of Jesus* (Downers Grove: InterVarsity Press, 1989), p. 17; Grant R. Osborne, *The Hermeneutical Spiral* (Downers Grove: InterVarsity Press, 1991), p. 250; Klyne Snodgrass, *Stories with Intent: A Comprehensive Guide to the Parables of Jesus* (Grand Rapids: Eerdmans, 2008), pp. 28–29.

central, la responsabilidad de demostrar que tienen razón descansa sobre quienes creen que una parábola puede tener más de un punto central.

## G. CONFIRMAR CUALQUIER ENSEÑANZA DOCTRINAL CON PASAJES DIDÁCTICOS

Algunos han sugerido que se debe excluir a las parábolas como una fuente de enseñanza doctrinal porque una parábola simplemente ilustra una verdad. Evidentemente, uno de los mayores problemas de una ilustración es que es capaz de ilustrar solamente un punto central. En el momento en que una persona mira con lupa cada detalle, la ilustración deja de funcionar como tal porque su cometido es el de dejar al intérprete con una primera impresión. Nada más. No obstante, una ilustración es un medio valioso para enseñar una verdad. El intérprete nunca debe hacer que una doctrina *descanse exclusivamente* sobre una parábola. Por eso, cualquier doctrina enseñada por una parábola debe ser confirmada por la enseñanza clara de pasajes didácticos del N.T. Como dice Trench:

> Las parábolas no deben convertirse en fuentes primarias de doctrina. Las doctrinas que han sido fundamentadas por otras fuentes pueden ser ilustradas y confirmadas por ellas, pero la doctrina no debe ser constituida en primera instancia por ellas. Las parábolas pueden servir como el borde ornamental exterior, pero no como la textura principal o como la prueba. Porque de lo literal a lo figurativo, de lo claro a lo más oscuro, es lo que siempre ha sido reconocido como la ley de la interpretación bíblica. Sin embargo, esta regla frecuentemente ha sido olvidada, y los que viven de la controversia, buscando argumentos para sostener una posición personal para la cual no encuentran apoyo en las Escrituras, frecuentemente inventan apoyos para ellas en las parábolas[9].

9. Richard Chenevix Trench, *Notes on the Parables of Our Lord* (Nueva York: D. Appleton & Company, 1850), p. 39.

El estudio de las parábolas resulta muy ameno porque se trata de historias llenas de detalles interesantes y a veces sorprendentes. Sin embargo, es imprescindible que el intérprete respete las normas y principios que se han establecido después de mucho debate para no solamente evitar los abusos que se han cometido con las parábolas en el pasado, sino también para entender las enseñanzas importantes que se encuentran en ellas.

| **Normas para interpretar una parábola** |
|---|
| 1. Tomar en cuenta el contexto histórico. |
| 2. Investigar el fondo histórico y cultural de los detalles. |
| 3. Identificar los puntos de comparación. |
| 4. Recordar que habrá detalles que no tienen ningún significado. |
| 5. Interpretar a la luz de la interpretación de Jesús. |
| 6. Limitarse a un punto central. |
| 7. Confirmar cualquier enseñanza doctrinal con pasajes didácticos. |

## *Trabajo para realizar*

**1.** ¿Por qué es tan importante que el intérprete identifique el contexto histórico de una parábola? ¿Por qué es tan importante que investigue el fondo histórico y cultural de los detalles citados en una parábola? ¿Cuántos puntos centrales puede haber en una parábola? ¿Cuántas aplicaciones pueden haber?

**2.** En Mateo 22:2-14 Jesús cuenta la parábola de la fiesta de unas bodas. El contexto histórico de esta parábola se encuentra en 22:1, lo cual indica que Jesús contó esta parábola en respuesta a una pregunta que alguien le hizo. Pero este texto no identifica esa pregunta. Encuentre el contexto histórico donde se encuentra esa pregunta. Después, consulte el comentario que se encuentra en la «Guía de estudio».

# 20

# Símbolos

Los símbolos forman parte de cada cultura: desde las estatuas que aparecen en las plazas principales de una ciudad hasta los colores y objetos que figuran en las banderas de cada país. Los capítulos anteriores de esta sección sobre la hermenéutica especial han tratado de los modismos hebreos, el lenguaje figurado, la poesía hebrea y las parábolas. Los tres temas que quedan —símbolos, tipos y profecía— son más difíciles de entender. Además, están íntimamente relacionados entre sí. Los símbolos se encuentran casi exclusivamente en los libros proféticos, principalmente en Ezequiel, Daniel, Zacarías y Apocalipsis, y los tipos son una especie de profecía.

## A. CARACTERÍSTICAS DE UN SÍMBOLO

Un símbolo bíblico es un objeto o cualidad de un objeto que es visible y que representa una verdad espiritual dada su asociación íntima con lo que simboliza. El símbolo puede ser algo natural que se ve en la vida diaria o algo visto en una visión o sueño. Puede tratarse de objetos, acciones, ordenanzas, materiales, números, animales, colores, nombres, metales, joyas, etcétera. Quizás el símbolo bíblico más conocido es el pan y el vino que se emplean en la ordenanza de la Cena del Señor, los cuales son símbolos del cuerpo y la sangre de Cristo.

*1. Un símbolo es visible.* Para servir como símbolo, el objeto en cuestión tiene que ser visible. Si no se ve, no es un símbolo. Esta característica es importante porque nos permite distinguir entre un símbolo y el lenguaje figurado. Un símbolo es una figura *vista*, mientras que las diferentes formas del lenguaje figurado son figuras *dichas*. Cuando Dios quiere hablarnos a través de nuestros oídos hace uso del lenguaje figurado. Cuando quiere comunicarnos una verdad a través de nuestros ojos emplea un símbolo. Por ejemplo, cuando Jesús advirtió a sus discípulos de la necesidad de guardarse «de la levadura de los fariseos» (Mt. 16:5-6), ellos pensaron que dicha exhortación se debía a que se habían olvidado de traer pan. En este caso la levadura no es un símbolo sino una metonimia, la más parecida de todas las formas del lenguaje figurado a un símbolo por sugerir una idea. Pero cuando Jesús tomó el pan y dijo a sus discípulos «Tómenlo y cómanlo, porque esto es mi cuerpo» (Mt. 26:26, NTV), se trataba de un símbolo porque ellos veían el pan.

*2. Un símbolo representa una verdad espiritual.* Como veremos en los ejemplos a continuación, los símbolos son empleados para comunicar una verdad espiritual que tiene que ver con Israel o la Iglesia. En muchos casos el símbolo sirve para describir un evento que ocurrirá en el futuro inmediato o lejano.

*3. En un símbolo el punto de comparación es obvio.* Cuando Dios o un autor bíblico explica el significado de un símbolo, el intérprete tendrá pocas dificultades para entender ese significado. Pero cuando falte esa explicación, el intérprete deberá partir de la premisa de que el símbolo guardaba una relación lo suficientemente obvia con la verdad que ilustraba como para que fuera entendida por los primeros lectores. Para que el símbolo comunique una verdad no puede ser arbitrario; tiene que haber una conexión lógica, una comparación obvia entre el símbolo y lo que este simboliza, algo que los primeros lectores entenderían a la luz de su cultura y contexto histórico. Si no existiera dicha relación sería imposible interpretar el símbolo. Las Escrituras emplean el león como símbolo del Imperio babilónico con todo su poderío y violencia, el candelero como símbolo de la iglesia por su responsabilidad de servir como luz (Ap. 1:12) y el pan y el vino como símbolos del cuerpo y la sangre de Cristo (Mt. 26:26-28).

No obstante, la Biblia contiene símbolos oscuros y difíciles de interpretar. Por regla general, esos símbolos tienen que ver con profecías que aún están por cumplirse. Por ejemplo, ¿a qué se refiere el número 666 en Ap. 13:18? Aunque se han sugerido muchas interpretaciones, nadie sabe a ciencia cierta lo que significa. Por lógica, ha de haber una conexión entre ese número y lo que simboliza. En el caso de símbolos oscuros como el 666, hemos de dar por sentado que las personas que estarán presentes cuando se cumplan las profecías relacionadas con esos símbolos serán capaces de reconocer lo que simbolizan.

## B. CLASES DE SÍMBOLOS

En las Escrituras los símbolos se presentan de varias formas y con diferentes características. De ahí que se puedan catalogar de la siguiente forma.

### Símbolos cotidianos

Un símbolo cotidiano trata de objetos reales de la vida cotidiana que el autor bíblico ve en contraste con objetos que se ven en sueños o visiones, muchos de los cuales corresponden a cosas irreales. El profeta Jeremías vio cuatro símbolos cotidianos. El primero fue una vara de almendro que Dios le mostró cuando lo llamó al ministerio profético (Jer. 1:11-12)[1]. Hay un juego de palabras entre las palabras hebreas *shaqued* («almendro») y *shoqued* («apresuro»). El almendro es el primer árbol frutal que produce flores en la primavera. La palabra *shaqued*, traducida por la RVR60 como «almendro»[2], significa literalmente «despierto». Podríamos decir que el almendro es un árbol que se apresura para despertarse después del invierno y dar fruto lo más pronto posible. Este símbolo pretendía asegurarle a Jeremías que Dios se apresuraría para cumplir con el mensaje que él mismo le daría para predicar al pueblo. Dios nunca llega tarde.

### Actos simbólicos

Los actos simbólicos son visibles, pero no en el mismo sentido que la visión que tuvo Daniel de «un varón vestido de lino, y ceñidos sus lomos de oro de Ufaz» (Dn. 10:5). En este caso el lino y el oro

1. Los otros tres símbolos cotidianos son una olla que hierve (1:13-16), el alfarero y el barro (18:1-11) y dos cestas de higos (cap. 24).

2. La LBLA traduce *shoqued* como «velo».

son símbolos. Con los actos simbólicos el profeta ve el símbolo en primera persona como si fuera el actor principal, el protagonista en una obra de teatro.

Jeremías participó en ocho actos simbólicos. Por ejemplo, su encuentro con los recabitas (Jer. 35)[3], los cuales eran un grupo puritano, seguidores de Jonadab, hijo de Recab (2 R. 10:15-16, 23). Vivían en el desierto con el propósito de abstenerse de lo que ellos consideraban actividades corruptas como beber vino o ser propietario de una casa. Los recabitas ayudaron a Jehú a eliminar la religión de Baal de Israel (2 R. 10:1-28). Cuando Nabucodonosor invadió Judá huyeron a Jerusalén para protegerse. En este acto simbólico Dios manda a Jeremías a animarlos a beber vino. Pero se niegan a hacerlo porque su antepasado Jonadab les había prohibido tomar vino (Jer. 35:2-6). Dios no los condena por sus ideas tan extremas. Al contrario, los alaba por su tenacidad y perseverancia en llevar a la práctica sus creencias. El mensaje que Dios quiere comunicar a su pueblo a través de este acto simbólico es que los recabitas obedecen a un mero hombre, pero vosotros no me obedecéis aunque soy Dios y a pesar de que os hablé «desde temprano y sin cesar»[4]. Jeremías promete a los recabitas que siempre habrá alguien de la familia de Jonadab, hijo de Recab, que estará en la presencia de Dios (vv. 18-19).

| Los actos simbólicos de Jeremías | |
|---|---|
| **Acto simbólico** | **Significado** |
| El cinto de lino podrido (13:1-11) | Se pudrirá la soberbia de Judá y Jerusalén (v. 9) |
| La vasija rota (cap. 19) | Dios romperá al pueblo y a la ciudad de Jerusalén (v. 11) |
| Jeremías pone un yugo sobre su cuello (cap. 27) | Dios ha puesto sobre Judá a Nabucodonosor y los judíos le servirán (v. 6 y ss.) |

3. Los recabitas se citan por primera vez en 1 Crónicas 2:55.

4. En los vv. 14-15 Dios emplea la frase «desde temprano y sin cesar», una frase que se repite en 7:13, 25; 26:5; 29:19; 44:4.

| Los actos simbólicos de Jeremías | |
|---|---|
| El profeta Hananías quita el yugo del cuello de Jeremías y lo rompe (28:12-17) | Puesto que la profecía de Hananías era falsa, dando esperanzas falsas a los judíos, Dios le quitará la vida (vv. 15-16) |
| Compra de un campo en Anatot (32:1-15) | En el futuro Israel volverá a la tierra y comprará campos y viñas (v. 15) |
| Los recabitas (cap. 35) | *Ver interpretación más atrás* |
| Esconder piedras grandes en la entrada del palacio de Faraón en Tafnes (43:8-13) | Nabucodonosor reinaría en Egipto (vv. 10-11) |
| Leer el texto de un rollo y después tirarlo al río Éufrates (51:59-64) | Dios hundiría a Babilonia (v. 64) |

## Símbolos irreales

Esta clase de símbolos se ven en visiones y sueños. Aunque contienen elementos realistas, lo que predominan son los elementos irreales y ajenos a la experiencia humana. Por ejemplo, Juan ve un trono rodeado de otros 24 tronos sobre los cuales están sentados 24 ancianos «vestidos de ropas blancas, con coronas de oro en sus cabezas» (Ap. 4:1-4). Aunque sería poco usual ver todos los elementos de esta escena en nuestra vida cotidiana, no es una imposibilidad. Pero en el v. 5 Juan dice que del trono «salían relámpagos y truenos y voces; y delante del trono ardían siete lámparas de fuego». No hay nada extraño en relámpagos, truenos, voces y lámparas de fuego en sí. ¿Pero saliendo de un trono? Eso sí cae fuera de nuestra experiencia humana. Pero *todos* los elementos que Juan describe en el v. 6 son irreales. «Y delante del trono había como un mar de vidrio semejante al cristal; y junto al trono, y alrededor del trono, cuatro seres vivientes llenos de ojos delante y detrás». Los símbolos que se ven en visiones y sueños suelen ser irreales.

## Símbolos de culto

Los símbolos de culto tienen que ver con los actos religiosos que los judíos celebraban en el A.T. y los miembros de las iglesias en el N.T. En el A.T. había varios elementos simbólicos en el tabernáculo y el templo. Por ejemplo, Dios mandó a Moisés fabricar el propiciatorio con dos querubines en los dos extremos y colocarlo encima del arca del testimonio (Éx. 25:17-21). Desde allí Dios hablaba con Moisés y el pueblo (Éx. 25:18-22) puesto que Dios moraba entre los querubines (1 S. 4:4; 2 S. 6:2; 2 R. 19:15; Is. 37:16). Cuando el templo fue construido, el arca fue colocada en el lugar santísimo. Las referencias a la morada de Dios entre los querubines y el hecho de que estaba en el lugar santísimo, un lugar inaccesible para todos excepto el sumo sacerdote, y aun así solamente una vez al año, parece indicar que los querubines tienen mucho que ver con la santidad de Dios. Es probable que haya más símbolos en el tabernáculo y el templo. En el N.T. el pan y vino de la Cena del Señor son símbolos del cuerpo y la sangre de Cristo (Mt. 26:26-28; 1 Co. 11:23-26), y el bautismo por inmersión simboliza el entierro de la antigua vida del nuevo creyente y su resurrección a una nueva vida en Cristo (Ro. 6:1-4).

## Colores, metales, joyas, nombres, animales y números

Con esta categoría de símbolos entramos en un terreno complicado y resbaladizo debido a la tendencia de algunos en el pasado a identificar como simbólicos los detalles más insignificantes de los números, colores, metales y ciertos eventos o instituciones como el tabernáculo y el templo. Por algo, prácticamente todos los autores modernos que escriben sobre el tema advierten a sus lectores del peligro de ver más significados de los que realmente existen en esta clase de símbolos. Por ejemplo, Mickelsen introduce su comentario sobre esta clase de símbolos diciendo que «raras veces podemos estar seguros de que algunos ejemplos concretos de esta categoría conlleven un simbolismo. Sin embargo, hay momentos en que el intérprete se pregunta si es posible que un significado simbólico coexista con su significado literal. En otros pasajes es claramente el caso»[5]. Puesto que muchos eruditos dudan seriamente de que Dios pretendiera comunicarnos algo a través de muchos de estos objetos, es razonable

5. A. Berkeley Mickelsen, *Interpreting the Bible* (Grand Rapids: Eerdmans, 1963), p. 272.

que el intérprete sea cauteloso y simplemente sugiera que un color, número, etcétera. *podría* servir como un símbolo, en lugar de afirmar tajantemente que sirve como tal.

*1. Colores.* El color blanco es quizás el color cuyo simbolismo es más evidente y seguro, representando la pureza y la santidad, porque hay objetos, seres humanos y seres celestiales que están vestidos de blanco o asociados con ese color de alguna forma y que a la vez son caracterizados por esas dos particularidades (Dn. 7:9; Mt. 17:2; 28:3; Hch. 1:10; Ap. 1:14; 4:4; 6:11; 7:9, 13-14; 19:14; 20:11). Dios hace uso del color blanco cuando dice: «Vengan ahora. Vamos a resolver este asunto —dice el SEÑOR—. Aunque sus pecados sean como la escarlata, yo los haré tan blancos como la nieve. Aunque sean rojos como el carmesí, yo los haré tan blancos como la lana» (Is. 1:18, NTV). Pero en este caso se trata de lenguaje figurado (símil), no de un símbolo, ¡porque un símbolo siempre se puede ver!

Si el intérprete identifica equivocadamente Isaías 1:18 con un símbolo, su interpretación —al menos en ese caso— será la misma. El problema viene cuando el intérprete procura ver un significado en un texto que va más allá de su significado literal. Por ejemplo, en Ester 1 el autor describe cómo Asuero, después de ser afirmado como rey, toma 180 días para mostrar las riquezas de su reino al pueblo y a unos dignatarios que había invitado a la capital en Susa. Entre otras descripciones, el autor del libro de Ester dice que el pabellón donde se celebró un banquete era blanco, verde y azul. Aunque este texto es inspirado por Dios, lo único que quiere comunicar el autor con este texto es que la decoración de ese pabellón era blanca, verde y azul. Nada menos, pero tampoco ¡nada más! De ahí que Zuck haga la sugerencia, muy acertada, de que «no debemos sacar significados de otros colores como el azul, rojo, escarlata, negro o amarillo, puesto que las Escrituras no parecen apuntar claramente hacia sus significados por las asociaciones que tienen. Por tanto, los estudiantes de la Biblia no deben encontrar en las Escrituras cosas que no se encuentran allí»[6].

*2. Metales.* No hay un acuerdo entre los eruditos bíblicos en cuanto a lo que los metales podrían simbolizar. No obstante, parece

6. Roy B. Zuck, *Basic Bible Interpretation* (Colorado Springs: Victor, 1991), p. 193.

que algunos simbolizan conceptos muy básicos y evidentes. Daniel 2 describe el sueño que Nabucodonosor tuvo sobre un hombre cuya cabeza era de hierro, su pecho y brazos de plata, su vientre y muslos de bronce, sus piernas de oro y sus pies de una mezcla de hierro y barro. Daniel interpreta este sueño identificando la cabeza de oro como un símbolo del reino poderoso y glorioso de Nabucodonosor, y las demás partes del cuerpo como los reinos e imperios que sucederán al Imperio babilónico con sus respectivas características de fuerza (hierro), debilidad (barro), etcétera.

En tiempos del A.T. la plata era la «moneda» común con la cual se pagaban productos y servicios costosos (2 Cr. 25:6; etcétera.). La plata también se empleaba para redimir a una persona. De ahí que llegara a llamarse «el dinero de la redención». Dado este trasfondo histórico, hay quienes consideran la plata como símbolo de la redención. Pero muchos intérpretes no quedan convencidos. De ahí que sugieran que el único mensaje que un metal puede simbolizar está asociado con su *valor* en el contexto donde se encuentra.

El oro es el metal que la Biblia cita frecuentemente. Por eso, algunos lo consideran como simbólico. De acuerdo con las instrucciones que Moisés recibió de Dios en Éxodo 25, se fabricaron con oro o fueron cubiertos de oro el arca del testimonio (vv. 10-11), el propiciatorio (v. 17) y los dos querubines de los dos extremos del propiciatorio (v. 18), todo lo cual fue colocado encima del arca (v. 21). Luego, la mesa para el pan de la propiciación (vv. 23-24), las varas de madera y los utensilios empleados en la mesa para el pan de la propiciación (vv. 28-29) y el candelero (v. 31). La implicación del uso del oro en un lugar tan preeminente en el tabernáculo podría simbolizar la gloria de Dios o quizás el hecho de que debemos adorar y servir a Dios con lo mejor que tenemos. Terry sugiere que los metales inferiores empleados en otras partes del tabernáculo simbolizaban la inferioridad de esos lugares en comparación con el lugar santísimo. Pero a la vez insiste en que el intérprete no debe buscar un significado específico para cada metal, color o joya, porque con toda probabilidad saldrá con interpretaciones que serán «monstruos de pura fantasía»[7]. Por eso, lo máximo

7. Milton S. Terry, *Biblical Hermeneutics* (Grand Rapids: Zondervan, 1969), p. 395.

que los eruditos bíblicos más reconocidos están dispuestos a hacer es sugerir lo que un par de metales podrían simbolizar.

*3. Joyas.* Las joyas son parecidas a los metales en el sentido de que aparecen frecuentemente en enumeraciones, dejando al intérprete con la incógnita de si debe buscar un significado para cada metal o joya o si la lista como un conjunto representa una sola verdad espiritual. De ahí que los metales y joyas representen la clase de símbolo más difícil de interpretar en el supuesto caso de que sirvan como símbolos. El pectoral del juicio que llevaba el sumo sacerdote tenía doce joyas preciosas que representaban las doce tribus de Israel (Éx. 28:15-21). El muro de la nueva Jerusalén lleva doce puertas y doce cimientos, los cuales representan las doce tribus de Israel y los doce apóstoles respectivamente (Ap. 21:2, 12-14). Una vez más, Terry nos advierte contra cualquier intento de identificar la tribu que simboliza cada puerta o el apóstol que representa cada cimiento porque «llevaría al intérprete a especulaciones no autorizadas, las cuales solo lograrían confundir y desconcertar en lugar de proveer una lección valiosa»[8].

*4. Nombres.* Era una práctica común de los padres judíos poner a sus hijos un nombre que correspondía o reflejaba las circunstancias bajo las cuales había nacido, o una verdad, valor o defecto que creían que sería una característica suya como adulto. En el caso del profeta Isaías, Dios le mandó llamar a su hijo *Maher-salal-hasbaz*, que significa «el despojo se apresura», porque antes de que el niño supiera decir «papá» o «mamá», «será quitada la riqueza de Damasco y los despojos de Samaria delante del rey de Asiria» (Is. 8:1-4). Dios tomó la iniciativa de cambiar el nombre de Abram («padre exaltado») a Abraham («padre de muchas personas», Gn. 17:5). Pero en muchos casos el nombre que los padres dieron a su hijo no tenía ningún significado particular. Por regla general, si un nombre tiene un significado especial, la Biblia lo dirá.

A veces el nombre de un lugar geográfico era cambiado para reflejar algo importante que había ocurrido allí. Cuando el ángel de Jehová apareció a Agar junto a una fuente, le mandó nombrar al hijo que esperaba «Ismael», lo cual significa «Dios oye», porque «Jehová ha oído tu aflicción» (Gn. 16:11). Entonces, Agar nombró el lugar donde se encontraba «Pozo del Viviente-que-me-ve» (v. 14). En otros casos

8. Ibid.

tenemos un claro ejemplo de metonimia. El apóstol Juan emplea los nombres de Sodoma y Egipto para referirse a la ciudad de Jerusalén (Ap. 11:8) porque se caracterizaba por la misma corrupción de esos lugares. Era precisamente en Jerusalén donde Jesús y tantos profetas perdieron sus vidas (11:8). La gran Babilonia (14:8; 16:19; 18:2; etcétera.) es otro nombre simbólico, una metonimia, que todavía carece de una interpretación consensuada por parte de los eruditos.

*5. Animales.* Hay varios animales que sirven como símbolos en las Escrituras, pero nos limitaremos a dos muy conocidos. En Marcos 1:10 la paloma que descendió sobre Jesús en su bautismo es el Espíritu Santo. Cuando Juan el Bautista reconoce a Jesús como el Cordero de Dios (Jn. 1:29), es una metáfora. Pero cuando el apóstol Juan ve un cordero en Apocalipsis 5:6, es un símbolo porque lo vio. Para ser símbolo, un animal u otro objeto tiene que ser visible.

*6. Números.* Hay números que se asocian tan frecuentemente con ciertos conceptos bíblicos que es difícil de ignorar o negar su posible simbolismo. Los números tres, siete, doce y cuarenta son los ejemplos más claros. Muchas veces el *tres* está relacionado con la Trinidad o la unidad y plenitud de Dios (Nm. 6:24-27; Is. 6:3; Mt. 28:19; 2 Co. 13:14; Ap. 4:8). El número *siete* aparece frecuentemente en textos que hacen énfasis en la integridad o la perfección (Gn. 2:2-3; 29:18; 41:2, 18; 50:10; Éx. 12:15; Jos. 6:4; Sal. 119:164; Pr. 24:16; Zac. 4:2; Mt. 12:45; Hch. 6:3; Ap. 1:4, 12; 4:5; 5:1; 8:1; 15:1; 16:1). Con solo decir el número *doce* el creyente piensa en las doce tribus de Israel o los doce apóstoles (Gn. 49:28; Éx. 28:21; Jos. 4:9; Mt 10:1; Ap. 21:12, 14). El número *cuarenta* aparece frecuentemente en el contexto de pruebas o juicio (Gn. 7:4; Éx. 24:18; Nm. 14:34; 32:13; Dt. 8:1-5; Mt. 4:2; Hch. 7:29-30).

Sin embargo, por interesantes que sean estas asociaciones entre ciertos números y conceptos bíblicos, hemos de ser honestos y preguntarnos: ¿las asociaciones que tienen ciertos números realmente nos ayudan a entender mejor las enseñanzas bíblicas que una exégesis sencilla y normal de la Biblia? Hay quienes se lanzan a una búsqueda de otros supuestos números simbólicos que son más bien un reflejo de su imaginación y creatividad[9].

---

9. Por ejemplo, los números 11, 17 y otros en el libro de J. Edwin Hartill, *Manual de interpretación bíblica* (Puebla: Publicaciones Las Américas, 1968), pp. 164–183.

Además, se ha de tener en cuenta que, aunque con algunas interpretaciones simbólicas hay muy poco en juego, por no decir nada, existe otra faceta de la supuesta simbología de los números que conlleva grandes peligros y riesgos. En los siglos anteriores al nacimiento de Cristo los asirios y babilonios habían creado un sistema de numerología llamada *gematría*, que asignaba un valor numérico a cada letra de su alfabeto. Este método fue abrazado por muchos rabinos judíos. Cuando el valor numérico de una palabra equivalía al valor numérico de otra palabra, se establecía una asociación. Por ejemplo, en Lamentaciones 1:16 Jeremías llora la destrucción de Jerusalén, diciendo que «se alejó de mí el consolador». En Zacarías 3:8 el profeta se refiere al Mesías como el «Renuevo» (RVR60, LBLA, NVI) o "Retoño" (NTV). Puesto que el valor numérico de las letras de la palabra «Renuevo» es el mismo que el valor de la palabra «consolador», afirmaban que Jeremías se refería al Mesías en Lamentaciones 1:16, RVR60. Aunque es probable que Jeremías se refiera a Dios, es cuestionable que se refiera explícitamente al Mesías. Pero aun en el caso de que este texto se refiera al Mesías, sería más que cuestionable y peligroso basar nuestra interpretación de las Escrituras sobre la numerología.

Es posible que Pablo se refiriera precisamente a esta clase de manipulación de las Escrituras cuando instruye a Timoteo a advertir a los efesios «que dejen de pelearse por palabras. Esos altercados son inútiles y pueden destruir a los que los oyen» (2 Ti. 2:14, NTV). El autor ha observado que los creyentes que se interesan por esta forma de interpretar la Biblia comienzan creyendo que han descubierto algo nuevo y acaban perdiendo de vista e ignorando las enseñanzas claras de temas mucho más importantes en las Escrituras, y raras veces vuelven a disfrutar de una vida cristiana normal centrada en el amor por el Señor y su Palabra. Aunque hay eruditos bíblicos que creen que puede haber algún simbolismo en los números, a la vez opinan que esta clase de interpretación bíblica tiene un lugar menor en un sistema de hermenéutica que sea sana y coherente.

## C. NORMAS DE INTERPRETACIÓN

Terry comienza su capítulo sobre los símbolos diciendo que «el simbolismo bíblico es, en muchos aspectos, uno de los temas más difíciles de la revelación divina con los cuales el intérprete tiene que tratar»[10]. Son particularmente difíciles de interpretar aquellos símbolos que tienen que ver con las profecías que quedan por cumplirse. Por tanto, es menester que el intérprete emplee con mucha destreza las siguientes normas.

## Estudiar el fondo histórico y la naturaleza del símbolo

El verdadero significado de un símbolo se encuentra en lo que entendían los primeros lectores, no en lo que supone el intérprete moderno. Algunos objetos serán fáciles de entender. Por ejemplo, un león se caracteriza por su agresividad, peligrosidad y dominio sobre la mayoría de los demás animales de su entorno. Desde tiempos antiguos los leones siempre han servido como símbolos de esas características. Pero para apreciar debidamente lo que significaba esa «espada aguda de dos filos» (Ap. 1:16) que salía de la boca del Hijo del Hombre, el intérprete tiene que saber que se trataba de una espada romana de sesenta centímetros de longitud con los dos lados afilados, lo cual hacía que fuera mucho más destructiva que una espada de solo un filo.

## Estudiar el contexto inmediato y el contexto más amplio

Las mejores indicaciones en cuanto al significado de un símbolo siempre se encuentran en el contexto inmediato. En Jeremías 24:1 el profeta se entretiene en definir el contexto histórico en el cual Dios le muestra dos cestas de higos delante del templo. Esa introducción aporta mucho sentido a la explicación que Dios da en los vv. 4-10. Daniel y Apocalipsis, los dos libros proféticos que más símbolos emplean, casi siempre explican sus símbolos en el contexto inmediato. Si el contexto inmediato no aclara el significado de un símbolo, el intérprete debe consultar el uso de ese símbolo en el contexto más amplio de otros textos, en particular pasajes en el A.T. No obstante, el intérprete debe recordar que el significado de un símbolo en un texto no necesariamente será el mismo en otro texto.

---

10. Terry, ob. cit., p. 347.

## Identificar el punto de comparación que tiene significado

Cuando la Biblia interpreta uno de sus símbolos, por regla general encuentra solamente un punto de comparación entre el símbolo y lo que simboliza, aunque pueden existir varias similitudes. Por tanto, el intérprete debe resistir la tentación de identificar como significativo más de un punto de similitud. Para no magnificar detalles pequeños e insignificantes a expensas de la lección principal, el intérprete debe cerciorarse primero de la naturaleza y trasfondo histórico del símbolo, y luego prestar atención a lo que considera la comparación principal. Al igual que las demás formas de la comunicación figurativa, los símbolos tienen como meta dar una impresión, un impacto visual. Por tanto, buscar un significado en cada detalle de un símbolo representa una violación de su naturaleza y propósito. El intérprete debe quedarse con lo más evidente. Como dice Lockhart:

> En el estudio de la visión que tuvo Ezequiel de un valle lleno de huesos secos (37:1-14) observamos una descripción extendida con muchos detalles pequeños; pero la interpretación es breve y sencilla. Al interpretar esta visión sería posible imponer numerosas analogías imaginativas que el autor nunca pretendió y sería fácil encontrar similitudes en muchos de los detalles que tenían como único propósito permitir que la visión fuera más natural y viva. Una interpretación microscópica podría encontrar analogías naturales para cada detalle de la descripción, pero como en el caso de las parábolas, el autor pretendía que solamente los puntos centrales tuviesen significado[11].

## Evitar el dogmatismo, especialmente cuando el símbolo trata de eventos futuros

El intérprete debe evitar el error de ser dogmático cuando las Escrituras no identifican de forma clara un objeto como simbólico, especialmente cuando su significado tiene que ver con eventos futuros. «La Biblia no identifica todos sus símbolos como tales, sino que deja

11. Clinton Lockhart, *Principles of Interpretation* (Fort Worth: S. H. Taylor, 1915), pp. 219–220.

| Normas para interpretar un símbolo |
|---|
| 1. Estudiar el fondo histórico y la naturaleza del símbolo. |
| 2. Estudiar el contexto inmediato y el contexto más amplio. |
| 3. Identificar el punto de comparación que tiene significado. |
| 4. Evitar el dogmatismo, especialmente cuando el símbolo trata de eventos futuros. |

al intérprete identificarlos por sí mismo. Así que tenemos que ser estudiosos, no ignorando los símbolos que sí existen, pero tampoco encontrándolos donde no los hay»[12].

Aunque los pasajes didácticos de las Escrituras son de una importancia incalculable, Dios incluyó también símbolos porque la mente humana suele recordar más fácilmente lo visible que un discurso lógico bien planteado. Por tanto, es importante que estudiemos los símbolos bíblicos empleando los principios y normas de su interpretación expuestos en este capítulo.

## *Trabajo para realizar*

¿Cuáles son las tres características de un símbolo bíblico? Debido a los muchos abusos e interpretaciones fantásticas que se han hecho de los símbolos bíblicos en el pasado, es importante que el lector domine las cuatro normas de su interpretación. Explique en sus propias palabras esas cuatro normas.

12. Bernard Ramm, *Protestant Biblical Interpretation* (Grand Rapids: Eerdmans, 1963), p. 235.

# 21

# Tipos

Cuando Jesús dijo a Nicodemo que de la misma forma en que Moisés levantó una serpiente de bronce sobre un palo en el desierto, «así es necesario que el Hijo del Hombre sea levantado, para que todo aquel que en él cree, no se pierda, mas tenga vida eterna» (Jn. 3:14-15), reconoció ese acto de Moisés como un tipo de su muerte sobre la cruz. ¿Qué es un tipo y cuáles son las normas y principios que han de emplearse para interpretarlo?

> «El sistema antiguo bajo la ley de Moisés era solo una sombra —un tenue anticipo de las cosas buenas por venir— no las cosas buenas en sí mismas. Bajo aquel sistema se repetían los sacrificios una y otra vez, año tras año, pero nunca pudieron limpiar por completo a quienes venían a adorar».
>
> **(Heb. 10:1, NTV)**

## A. DEFINICIÓN

Un tipo es un evento, persona, institución u objeto que existía históricamente en el A.T., que tenía una función en su propio día y que fue planeado por Dios para prefigurar una verdad que se revelaría más tarde en el N.T. La existencia de tipos se debe a que Dios controla la historia y a que la está conduciendo hacia un final que coincide con sus propósitos. Ninguna otra literatura contiene tipos porque solamente Dios controla la historia. Dios, además de haber revelado muchas verdades mediante el lenguaje literal, también ha revelado verdades espirituales mediante formas figurativas del lenguaje, entre ellas el tipo. Pero igual que las parábolas, la tipología ha sufrido mucho abuso a manos de la imaginación y creatividad de algunos intérpretes. De ahí que muchos asocien la tipología con la alegorización e interpretaciones raras y rebuscadas. Por eso, Mickelsen afirma que «no hay otra área de la interpretación bíblica que requiera una definición más precisa que la tipología»[1].

Los autores del N.T. identifican un tipo mediante una de las siguientes cuatro palabras. (1) La palabra «tipo», que proviene de *tupos*. Al igual que muchas palabras en todos los idiomas, *tupos* tiene más de un significado. Por tanto, no siempre se refiere a un tipo[2]. No obstante, hay tres pasajes donde el contexto inmediato demuestra de forma clara que el autor tiene en mente un tipo. En Romanos 5:14 *tupos* es traducido como «figura», en 1 Corintios 10:6, 11 como «ejemplo» y en Hebreos 8:5 como «modelo». (2) La palabra *parabole,* que es traducida en Hebreos 9:9 como «símbolo»[3]. (3) La palabra *skia,* que es traducida como «sombra» en Colosenses 2:17, Hebreos 8:5 y 10:1. (4) Finalmente, *upodeijma,* que es traducido como «figura» en Hebreos 8:5. En este texto el autor emplea tres de estas cuatro palabras.

> Ahora bien, el punto principal de lo que venimos diciendo es que tenemos tal sumo sacerdote, el cual se sentó a la diestra del trono de la Majestad en los cielos, ministro del santuario, y de aquel verdadero

---

1. A. Berkeley Mickelsen, *Interpreting the Bible* (Grand Rapids: Eerdmans, 1963), p. 236.

2. Ver Juan 20:25 y Hechos 7:43 («señal»); Hechos 7:43 («figura»); Filipenses 3:17, 1 Tesalonicenses 1:7, 2 Tesalonicenses 3:9, 1 Timoteo 4:12, Tito 2:7 y 1 Pedro 5:3 («ejemplo»); Romanos 6:17 («forma»); Hechos 7:44 («modelo»); Hechos 23:25 («términos»).

3. El lector debe recordar que en el primer siglo la palabra *parabole* se refería a varias clases de lenguaje figurado. Aunque Hebreos 9:9 emplea la palabra «símbolo», no se trata de un símbolo tal y como se ha definido en el capítulo 20, sino de un tipo.

> tabernáculo que levantó el Señor, y no el hombre. Porque todo sumo sacerdote está constituido para presentar ofrendas y sacrificios; por lo cual es necesario que también este tenga algo que ofrecer. Así que, si estuviese sobre la tierra, ni siquiera sería sacerdote, habiendo aún sacerdotes que presentan las ofrendas según la ley; *los cuales sirven a lo que es figura (upodeijma) y sombra (skia) de las cosas celestiales,* como se le advirtió a Moisés cuando iba a erigir el tabernáculo, diciéndole: Mira, haz todas las cosas conforme *al modelo (tupos)* que se te ha mostrado en el monte (Heb. 8:1-5, énfasis añadido).

Los vv. 1-4 demuestran que el autor tenía en mente un tipo. No obstante, en la mayoría de los casos los autores del N.T. simplemente citan un evento, persona, institución u objeto del A.T. y lo relacionan con una verdad revelada en el N.T., la cual los teólogos llaman «antitipo»[4]. El tipo cuenta con cuatro características principales.

*1. Un tipo es algo que existía o un evento histórico del A.T.* En contraste con el lenguaje figurado, el cual es dicho o hablado, un tipo es algo que existía o un evento que ocurrió en un momento concreto de la historia. Por tanto, el tipo se encuentra en un evento histórico o una cosa que existía (el tabernáculo, etcétera.), no en las palabras de Jesús o un autor del N.T. Un tipo no es una manera de hablar, sino una actividad o un evento. Por ejemplo, el sumo sacerdote entraba una vez al año en el lugar santísimo para ofrecer un sacrificio por los pecados de todo el pueblo. Es un hecho histórico. Por ese motivo, la metodología que se emplea para interpretar un tipo es completamente diferente a la que se usa para una alegoría. La tipología es «la búsqueda de enlaces entre eventos, personas u objetos *dentro del marco histórico de la revelación*, mientras que la alegorización es la búsqueda de significados secundarios y escondidos detrás del significado primario y obvio de una narración»[5]. Mientras que la alegorización menosprecia e ignora la historicidad del texto bíblico, la tipología la reconoce como verídica y de suma importancia.

*2. El tipo tenía una función en su día.* Cada tipo tenía una función contemporánea y servía a un propósito concreto en su día. Por ejemplo, el tabernáculo servía como un lugar de alabanza a Dios. No

4. En Hebreos 9:24 *antitupa* es traducido como «figura», mientras que en 1 Pedro 3:21 es traducido como «corresponde».

5. Mickelsen, ob. cit., p. 238.

obstante, las personas que participaban en el tipo no se daban cuenta de ello, sino que centraban su atención en el propósito que tenía dicha actividad, evento u objeto en su propia época. Al entrar en el lugar santísimo el sumo sacerdote nunca pensaba: «¡Qué tipo más maravilloso!». Tocó a los autores del N.T. identificar ese evento u objeto como tipo (Heb. 9:6-12).

*3. El tipo prefiguraba una verdad importante que se revelaría en el N.T.* La tipología se basa en la premisa de que un evento, persona, institución u objeto encontrará su cumplimiento más pleno en un momento futuro de la historia. En ese sentido estricto de la palabra el tipo es una especie de profecía. Mientras que la profecía de *predecir* comunica con palabras los eventos que ocurrirán en el futuro, el tipo *prefigura*, ilustra o da el perfil de una verdad importante que será revelada en el futuro mediante una similitud significativa que el tipo comparte con el antitipo. Para que un evento, persona, institución u objeto sea considerado un tipo, tiene que conllevar un elemento profético, una mirada hacia el futuro que anticipe algo superior a sí mismo. El antitipo es siempre más importante que el tipo; el Cordero de Dios es mucho más importante que el conjunto de los millones de corderos que fueron sacrificados en tiempos del A.T. «El tipo, dada su naturaleza, tiene que ser inferior al antitipo, porque no podemos esperar que la sombra sea igual a la realidad»[6]. El tipo siempre se centra en la obra de Cristo o en algún aspecto importante de la vida cristiana. Siempre mira desde el A.T. hacia el N.T., nunca desde el A.T. hacia otro pasaje en el A.T., ni desde el N.T. hacia el A.T., tampoco desde el N.T. hacia otro pasaje en el N.T., ni desde el N.T. hacia el futuro.

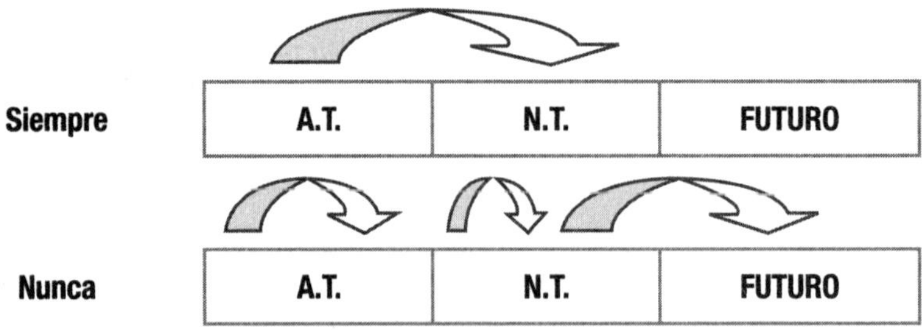


6. Bernard Ramm, *Protestant Biblical Interpretation* (Grand Rapids: Baker, 1978), p. 230.

*4. El tipo es planeado por Dios.* La tipología se basa en la premisa de que Dios está llevando la historia humana hacia el final que él mismo ha determinado según sus planes y propósitos. Por tanto, la historia no es caprichosa o sin propósito, sino algo que Dios tiene bajo su control (Ef. 1:9-10). Lógicamente, los tipos no se encuentran en ninguna literatura fuera de la Biblia. Solamente un autor que recibe una revelación especial de Dios tiene la posibilidad de introducir tipos en sus escritos. Quienes no aceptan las Escrituras como inspiradas por Dios no admiten el concepto ni la existencia de los tipos.

Antes de plantear la pregunta sobre cuántos tipos existen en el A.T., conviene ver dos tipos claramente reconocidos en el N.T. como tal para ver cómo funcionan. En Oseas 11:1 el profeta habla de la salida de los judíos de Egipto cuando «Israel era muchacho», cuando no era más que una multitud desorganizada de personas. Sin embargo, Mateo dice que José, María y Jesús se quedaron en Egipto «hasta la muerte de Herodes; para que se cumpliese lo que dijo el Señor por medio del profeta, cuando dijo: De Egipto llamé a mi Hijo» (2:15). O sea, los judíos salieron de Egipto hacia la tierra prometida (tipo) de la misma forma en que Jesús saldría de Egipto (antitipo) muchos años más tarde[7]. En Jeremías 31:15 el profeta describe el dolor y llanto de las mujeres de Jerusalén cuando sus maridos e hijos fueron muertos por los ejércitos de Nabucodonosor en la destrucción de Jerusalén. Sin embargo, después de la matanza de los infantes en Belén a manos de Herodes, Mateo dice: «Entonces se cumplió lo que fue dicho por el profeta Jeremías, cuando dijo...» (Mt. 2:17). Entonces, cita Jeremías 31:15. De la misma forma en que muchas mujeres de Jerusalén lloraron la muerte de sus hijos (tipo), muchas mujeres de Belén hicieron lo mismo (antitipo).

## B. ¿CUÁNTOS TIPOS HAY?

Los padres de la iglesia (siglos I–V) creían que detrás del texto bíblico se encontraban verdades espirituales profundas que una interpretación literal era incapaz de sacar y que la alegorización era el método de

7. Mientras que algunos eruditos prefieren considerar este texto una ilustración o ejemplo en lugar de un tipo, el lenguaje que Mateo emplea parece indicar que es más que un mero ejemplo o ilustración.

interpretación ideal para lograr esa meta. Puesto que la alegorización se parece mucho a la tipología, era natural que buena parte de la exégesis alegórica en los siglos anteriores fuera dominada por la tipología. La tipología era una herramienta apologética muy útil para demostrar la antigüedad del cristianismo contra quienes lo acusaban de ser una novedad, ya que indicaba que el A.T. apuntaba hacia la persona y obra de Cristo. Desafortunadamente, los padres llevaron la tipología a tal extremo que encontraban tipos por todas partes, incluso donde no existían[8]. No obstante, el excelente resumen de Dana de las circunstancias y desafíos con los cuales estos hombres de Dios tenían que enfrentarse nos lleva a concluir que sería un gran error juzgarlos con demasiada severidad.

> Para el cristianismo del siglo II todas las ideas e instituciones de la religión cristiana encontraban su sombra en el A.T. Era lógico, porque el A.T. era las únicas «Escrituras» que poseían. Además, creía que la totalidad de las verdades religiosas deberían ser enseñadas en las Escrituras. De hecho, algunos elementos del A.T. apuntaban de forma clara y con tipos hacia los grandes hechos y doctrinas de la redención. Por tanto, se daba por sentado que todo el A.T. estaba lleno de tipos, y que toda verdad redentora se enseñaba a través de ellos. Este significado típico es lo que captaba la atención del expositor. Cualquier evento u objeto —aparte de su significado histórico— que sugería cualquier paralelo con algún elemento del pensamiento cristiano era reclamado con afán como un tipo y representaba precisamente la verdad que Dios había propuesto por inspiración divina que se enseñara. Para Clemente de Roma el acto de Rahab de colgar un cordón de grana en su ventana era una sombra de la redención por la sangre de Cristo. En las primeras etapas de este período la tipología no hacía gran daño al desarrollo del pensamiento cristiano porque se empleaba principalmente con fines homiléticos y prácticos. Pero con el tiempo se empleó como prueba de doctrinas y políticas eclesiásticas, llegando así a ser la base de algunas teorías erróneas y dañinas[9].

---

8. Entre otras cosas, Orígenes (185–254) y Jerónimo (c. 340–420) destacaban por sus interpretaciones típicas del A.T.

9. H. E. Dana, *Searching the Scriptures* (Kansas City: Central Seminary Press, 1946), pp. 62–64.

Al otro extremo se encuentran quienes rechazan por completo el concepto de tipos puesto que no creen que la Biblia represente una revelación especial de Dios ni que tenga un autor divino. Tampoco creen en un Dios que interviene en la historia humana. Los evangélicos rechazan como erróneas tanto esta posición como la práctica de encontrar tipos donde no existen. Entonces, ¿cuántos tipos hay? Existen entre los evangélicos dos respuestas a esta pregunta. Algunos creen que los tipos son todos aquellos que son reconocidos de forma explícita e implícita en el N.T., mientras que otros se limitan a solamente aquellos que son reconocidos explícitamente en el N.T.

*1. Todos los tipos reconocidos de forma explícita e implícita en el N.T.* Jesús reconoció de forma explícita y sin lugar a dudas que la serpiente de bronce (Jn. 3:14-15) era un tipo que encontró su cumplimiento en su crucifixión. Pero hay otros textos en los cuales el autor parece indicar que se refiere a un tipo, pero no lo dice explícitamente. Son textos implícitos, no explícitos. Por ejemplo, en la conversación que Cristo tuvo con los dos discípulos en el camino hacia Emaús, los riñó por ser «insensatos, y tardos de corazón para creer todo lo que los profetas han dicho» (Lc. 24:25). Entonces, «comenzando desde Moisés, y siguiendo por todos los profetas, les declaraba en todas las Escrituras lo que de él decían» (v. 27). Este texto nos deja con la clara impresión de que hay tipos que existen en el A.T. que los autores del N.T. no identifican de forma explícita. También tenemos la Epístola a los Hebreos que se dedica casi por completo al tema de los tipos en el A.T. y su antitipo en el N.T. Y finalmente, hay textos como Juan 5:39 y Colosenses 2:16-17 que añaden aún más peso al argumento de que hay más tipos en el A.T. de lo que muchos solemos reconocer. Por ejemplo, dos de los eventos no reconocidos explícitamente como tipos, pero que muchos consideran como tal, son el sacrificio de Isaac (Gn. 22; Heb. 11:17-19) y la experiencia de José de ser rechazado por sus hermanos, humillado y luego exaltado. La experiencia de estas dos personas se parece tanto a la de Jesús que muchos encuentran difícil no reconocerlas como un tipo de Cristo.

Para considerar como tipo a un evento, persona, institución u objeto no reconocido explícitamente como tal por un autor del N.T., la mayoría de los eruditos evangélicos creen que ha de reunir al menos cinco características. (1) Tiene que estar arraigado en la historia igual que el antitipo que pretende prefigurar. (2) Debe tener en común con el antitipo una similitud, correspondencia o paralelismo notable. No puede ser un detalle insignificante. (3) Debe tener una relación real u orgánica[10] con la enseñanza del antitipo que pretende prefigurar. Por ejemplo, existe una función similar, real y orgánica entre los muchos corderos que fueron sacrificados en el A.T. y la obra redentora de Cristo, el Cordero de Dios en el N.T. (4) Tiene que colocar el antitipo en una posición de mayor preeminencia porque el antitipo siempre es más importante que el tipo. (5) La enseñanza que el tipo pretende prefigurar tiene que coincidir con la totalidad de la enseñanza bíblica y la interpretación que las Escrituras hacen de sí mismas. Los teólogos llaman a este concepto «la analogía de las Escrituras» o «la analogía de la fe».

*2. Solamente aquellos tipos reconocidos explícitamente en el N.T.* Aunque muchos evangélicos aceptan en principio la primera opción como legítima, en la práctica abrazan la segunda por no querer abrir de nuevo la puerta a los excesos y abusos que se han cometido en el pasado. Aunque podría parecer fácil identificar los tipos que el N.T. reconoce como tales, la realidad es otra[11]. De ahí que sea difícil encontrar una lista de tipos que todos los evangélicos acepten. No obstante, existe un consenso general de que los siguientes eventos, personas, instituciones y objetos son tipos.

---

10. El término «orgánico» se emplea por los teólogos para referirse a una relación evidente, real y obvia entre el tipo y el antitipo.

11. De ahí que en su libro *Basic Bible Interpretation* (Colorado Springs: Victor, 1991), Zuck no reconozca a Adán, Jonás ni la serpiente de bronce como tipos (ver p. 181), sino como ilustraciones. Aunque una ilustración actúa de la misma forma que un tipo, cuenta con solamente tres de las cinco características de un tipo; a saber, que tiene una similitud, correspondencia o paralelismo notable, que cuenta con una realidad histórica y que es planeado por Dios. Pero una ilustración no prefigura de forma clara el antitipo ni conlleva una expectación que va en aumento y que hace que el antitipo sea más importante que el tipo (ver p. 176).

EVENTOS

1. El Diluvio: el bautismo del creyente (1 P. 3:20-21).
2. El éxodo de Egipto: la salida de Jesús de Egipto (Os. 11:1; Mt. 2:15).
3. El velo de Moisés: la ceguera espiritual de los judíos en tiempos de Jesús y Pablo (2 Co. 3:13-16).
4. La serpiente en el desierto: Cristo levantado sobre una cruz que salva a quienes lo miran con fe (Jn. 3:14; Nm. 21:4-9).
5. El llanto de las mujeres en la destrucción de Jerusalén (586 a. C.): el llanto de las mujeres de Belén en la matanza de los infantes (Jer. 31:15; Mt. 2:17-18).
6. El sumo sacerdote entra una vez al año en el lugar santísimo: a través de Cristo el creyente puede acercarse directamente al Padre (Heb. 10:11-22).

PERSONAS

1. Adán: Cristo es la cabeza de una nueva raza (Ro. 5:12-21; 1 Co. 15:45).
2. Melquisedec: Cristo es un rey y sacerdote eterno (Heb. 7:1-17).
3. Moisés: el ministerio profético de Cristo (Heb. 3:1-6).
4. Aarón: el ministerio sacerdotal de Cristo (Heb. 5:4-5).
5. David y Salomón: Cristo es un rey glorioso (2 S. 7:12-17; Heb. 1:5).
6. David: el sufrimiento de Cristo en la cruz (Sal. 22:1; Mt. 27:46).
7. Elías (Mal. 4:5-6; Mt. 17:10): el ministerio de Juan el Bautista y de Cristo.
8. Jonás: Cristo está tres días en la tumba (Mt. 12:40; Lc. 11:30).

INSTITUCIONES

1. El descanso sabático: el descanso espiritual del creyente (Gn. 2:2-3; Heb. 3:7-11; 4:4-11).
2. El cordero de la Pascua: Cristo es nuestra Pascua, el Cordero de Dios (Éx. 12; Jn. 1:29; 1 Co. 5:7; Heb. 9:1-10:18).
3. El tabernáculo: varias verdades relacionadas con el cielo (Heb. 8:5; 9:24).

OBJETOS

1. El maná: Cristo es el pan de la vida para el creyente (1 Co. 10:3).
2. La roca de la que salió agua en el desierto: Cristo provee refrigerio al creyente (Éx. 17:6; 1 Co. 10:4).

## C. NORMAS DE INTERPRETACIÓN

Los autores del N.T. identifican de forma explícita que algunos eventos, personas, instituciones y cosas del A.T. son tipos de una verdad (antitipo) que el Espíritu Santo les ha revelado a ellos. Todos los evangélicos aceptan la probabilidad de que haya otros tipos, aunque los autores del N.T. no los reconozcan de forma explícita. Sin embargo, antes de lanzarse a un estudio de los textos que contienen un posible tipo, el intérprete debe estudiar aquellos textos donde el tipo es reconocido de forma explícita. Las normas expuestas a continuación servirán tanto para los tipos reconocidos de forma explícita como para los reconocidos de forma implícita.

*1. Identificar el contexto histórico del tipo y la función que tenía en su propia época.* El primer paso que el intérprete debe dar es el de identificar con mucha precisión el contexto en que ocurrió el tipo y la función que tenía en su época, porque tendrá mucho que ver con la verdad enseñada por el antitipo. También debe recordar que los protagonistas no eran conscientes de que tenían un tipo entre manos ni se daban cuenta de la verdad espiritual que prefiguraba. Esta primera norma dará un enfoque más realista al estudio de los tipos.

*2. Identificar los detalles que el tipo y el antitipo no comparten.* Al identificar los detalles que el autor del N.T. no cita, el intérprete evitará más fácilmente la tentación de caer en interpretaciones sensacionalistas, forzadas o ingeniosas identificando como significativos algunos detalles que no tienen ninguna relación con el antitipo. Eso también lo ayudará a discernir cuáles son los pasajes que contienen un tipo y los que no. La Biblia ignora muchos detalles que tendríamos la tendencia a considerar como importantes. Por ejemplo, cuando Jesús hace referencia a la serpiente de bronce (Nm. 21:4-9; Jn. 3:14-15), no hace ninguna mención del pecado que cometieron los israelitas, ni de que Dios mandó serpientes ardientes para matar a muchos de ellos, ni de que el pueblo confesó su pecado, ni de que el bronce sea un símbolo de alguna verdad.

*3. Identificar el punto de comparación que más destaca entre el tipo y el antitipo.* Cuando un autor del N.T. reconoce e interpreta un tipo, en la gran mayoría de los casos señala solamente un punto de comparación entre el tipo y el antitipo, igual que pasaba en las demás formas de la comunicación figurativa. El intérprete debe tener esto en cuenta. El punto de comparación no debe ser una mera coincidencia, sino algo notable que exhibe de forma muy clara el propósito divino tanto en el contexto histórico del tipo como en la enseñanza del antitipo. En un par de casos el autor llamará la atención a dos detalles. Por ejemplo, de la misma forma que la serpiente de bronce fue levantada, Jesús dice que él será levantado (Jn. 3:14), y que todo aquel que cree en el Cristo levantado será salvo (v. 15). Con este segundo detalle Jesús identifica la enseñanza del antitipo; a saber, que todos los que miran por fe a Cristo serán salvados. No obstante, aunque Jesús hace mención de *dos* detalles, los dos están tan relacionados que expresan solamente *una* verdad; a saber, que la salvación se concede a quienes miran con fe al Cristo levantado (crucificado).

En 1 Corintios 5:7 Pablo reconoce al cordero de la fiesta de la Pascua como un tipo de Cristo, «porque nuestra pascua, que es Cristo, ya fue sacrificada por nosotros». Este es el primero de dos detalles que el tipo y el antitipo tienen en común. El segundo detalle que Pablo cita es el pan sin levadura que acompañaba la comida de la Pascua (vv. 6-8). Muchos intérpretes consideran a la levadura como un símbolo del pecado en la mayoría de los textos donde se cita. Una vez más, estos *dos* detalles no suponen dos significados, ideas o verdades completamente distintas, sino solamente *una* verdad; a saber, que el Cristo crucificado demanda una vida santa de sus discípulos. Pablo no hace ninguna mención de que el cordero de la primera Pascua en Egipto tenía que tener un año de edad, tenía que ser seleccionado de entre las ovejas o cabras, tenía que ser sacrificado por la tarde, que su sangre tenía que rociarse por los postes y el dintel de cada casa, que al ver esa sangre Dios no mataría al primogénito de esa familia, que la carne del cordero tenía que ser asada, que los israelitas tenían que comerla apresuradamente con sus lomos ceñidos, sus pies calzados, etcétera, ni que los restos tenían que ser quemados.

Existe solamente un punto central, una enseñanza principal en cada tipo. La persona y obra de Cristo son las verdades que más destacan en los tipos. De ahí que Ramm aconseje que «en la tipología hemos de limitar nuestros esfuerzos a las doctrinas principales, las verdades centrales, las lecciones espirituales clave y los principios morales fundamentales. La tipología que se deja fascinar por detalles pequeños ya está fuera del enfoque de la tipología del N.T.»[12].

*4. Emplear los tipos como ilustraciones, no como textos para apoyar doctrinas.* Un tipo es por naturaleza un simple reflejo de la realidad que se encuentra en el antitipo. Mientras que es legítimo emplear tipos, parábolas y otras formas de la comunicación figurativa como ilustraciones de una doctrina, un tipo nunca debe emplearse como el fundamento ni el texto para probarla. Los autores del N.T. pudieron hacerlo porque escribieron bajo la inspiración del Espíritu Santo. El intérprete no cuenta con esa ventaja.

| **Normas para interpretar un tipo** |
|---|
| 1. Identificar el contexto histórico del tipo y la función que tenía en su propia época. |
| 2. Identificar los detalles que el tipo y el antitipo no comparten. |
| 3. Identificar el punto de comparación que más destaca entre el tipo y el antitipo. |
| 4. Emplear los tipos como ilustraciones, no como textos para apoyar doctrinas. |
| 5. Evitar los peligros propios de un estudio de los tipos. |

*5. Evitar los peligros propios de un estudio de los tipos.* Dados los peligros que conlleva un estudio de los tipos, hay cuatro consejos prácticos que el intérprete haría bien en seguir. Primero, no debe dejarse arrastrar por la tentación de permitir que la tipología se convierta en el tema principal y dominante de su estudio bíblico. «El uso que el N.T. hace de los tipos demuestra que hemos de limitarnos»[13]. Segundo, debe evitar el dogmatismo cuando el N.T. no identifica de forma explícita un evento, persona, institución u objeto como tipo. Tercero, debe evitar la tendencia de ser original. «En el N.T. la tipología era empleada para hacer más prominente el mensaje de la gracia de Dios en

12. Ramm, ob. cit., p. 230.

13. T. Norton Sterret, *How to Understand Your Bible* (Downers Grove, IL: InterVarsity Press, 1975), p. 244.

Cristo, no para exaltar al maestro. Los intérpretes que son fieles al N.T. harán lo mismo»[14]. Cuarto, «los tipos son como las flores silvestres; su belleza se estropea si se cultivan. El intérprete debe evitar la tendencia de inmiscuirse en cada hueco y rincón del tabernáculo o cada faceta de la vida de los patriarcas en una búsqueda de tipos»[15].

## *Trabajo para realizar*

1. ¿Cuáles son los cuatro elementos de la definición de un tipo? De los diecinueve tipos reconocidos explícitamente por un autor del N.T., nombre ocho. ¿Cuáles son las cinco normas que el intérprete debe emplear para interpretar un tipo?
2. Hay quienes han sugerido que el concepto de tipos implica que un texto puede tener dos significados, uno para el autor del A.T. que describe un evento, persona, institución u objeto, y otro para el autor del N.T. que identifica el antitipo de ese evento, persona, institución u objeto. Lea «La cuestión del *sensus plenior*» en el Apéndice G.

14. El autor no ha podido localizar esta declaración de Sidney Soares.
15. Mel Couch, *An Introduction to Classical Evangelical Hermeneutics* (Grand Rapids: Kregel, 2000), pp. 82–83.

# 22

# Profecía (I)

El hecho de que la profecía ocupe una tercera parte de las Escrituras subraya el gran papel que juega en el deseo de Dios de darse a conocer al ser humano. Además, el hecho de que cada una de las profecías bíblicas que tenían que cumplirse hasta el día de hoy se han cumplido al pie de la letra representa uno de los argumentos más contundentes de que la Biblia es de origen y naturaleza divina. Pero es más. Dios no solamente es capaz de ver lo que pasará en el futuro, sino que también controla la historia humana y está llevándola hacia el destino que él mismo ha determinado. Por tanto, mientras que muchas personas consultan horóscopos, brujas y otras formas de profecía falsa con la esperanza de descubrir qué les pasará en el futuro próximo, el creyente puede mirar al futuro con absoluta confianza, sabiendo que su Dios lo controla.

> «Pero ¿acaso no has oído? Yo lo decidí hace mucho tiempo. Hace mucho que lo planifiqué, y ahora lo llevo a cabo».
>
> **(Is. 37:26, NTV)**

Lo que más distinguía al profeta de otros siervos de Dios en el A.T. era que el mensaje que predicaba era recibido por revelación directa de Dios[1]. Al observar el contenido de su mensaje, notamos que en su mayor parte consiste en *predicar* contra el pecado del pueblo de Dios y en promover una vida santa. Este elemento de la profecía bíblica es relativamente fácil de interpretar. En cambio, en ese porcentaje menor que se dedica a *predecir* eventos futuros es donde los intérpretes pueden encontrar más dificultades, porque la profecía que *predice* conlleva por naturaleza cierta ambigüedad puesto que la información que Dios ha elegido darnos es incompleta. En ese sentido la profecía de *predecir* no es la historia escrita de antemano con todo detalle. Con ciertas profecías somos como los judíos que vivían antes del primer siglo. Sabían que el Mesías nacería en Belén (Mi. 5:2), saldría de Egipto (Os. 11:1) y se llamaría nazareno (Mt. 2:23)[2], pero no podían encajar esos tres lugares geográficos tan diferentes en la vida del Mesías.

## A. PRINCIPIOS BÁSICOS DE LA INTERPRETACIÓN PROFÉTICA

Para interpretar con precisión los textos proféticos de las Escrituras, el intérprete necesitará emplear todos los principios y normas de la hermenéutica explicados en los capítulos anteriores. Pero si tuviéramos que hacer un resumen de todos esos principios y normas, nos quedaríamos con tres principios básicos.

*1. Interpretar la profecía de forma literal a no ser que el texto indique lo contrario.* Muchas profecías se han cumplido de forma literal: la concepción virginal de Cristo (Is. 7:14; Mt. 1:22-23); la entrada de Jesús en Jerusalén sobre un asno (Zac. 9:9; Mt. 21:1-5); el nacimiento de Cristo en Belén (Miq. 5:2; Mt. 2:5-12); etcétera. Cuando el profeta emplea lenguaje figurado, poesía, etcétera, el intérprete debe seguir las

1. Para una explicación más amplia de esta definición de un profeta, ver el libro de Jaime Fasold, *Dones Espirituales* (Grand Rapids: Portavoz, 2000), pp. 147–151.

2. Mateo 2:23 dice que los «profetas» (plural) dijeron que el Mesías se llamaría «nazareno». Pero los eruditos no han encontrado ni siquiera *un* texto que haga esa afirmación de forma clara. Aunque algunos citan Isaías 11:1, la verdad es que Mateo 2:23 ha provocado mucha investigación y debate.

normas para la interpretación de esos géneros literarios. De todos los géneros que los profetas emplearon, el apocalíptico es quizás el más difícil de interpretar debido a que los símbolos que emplean y las visiones e imágenes cósmicas que describen son muy extrañas e irreales[3]. Hay libros que dedican capítulos enteros al género apocalíptico, como Isaías 24-27; Daniel 7-12; Ezequiel 38-39; Zacarías 1-6, 9-14; y Apocalipsis 4–22. El hecho de que Ezequiel y Daniel se encontraran en Babilonia, que Zacarías acabara de volver de Babilonia a Jerusalén y que Juan se encontrara en la isla de Patmos donde fue desterrado por Domiciano (51–96)[4], un emperador tiránico que perseguía a los cristianos, explica en parte el gran énfasis que estos tres profetas hacen sobre la lucha que está teniendo lugar entre el reino de Dios y las huestes terrenales y celestiales de Satanás, la realidad de que Dios sigue al control y de que al final de los tiempos Dios mostrará de forma visible la victoria que Jesús consiguió en la cruz sobre Satanás y los suyos.

*2. La exégesis tiene prioridad sobre cualquier sistema de interpretación.* El intérprete necesita emplear un sistema de interpretación (teología del pacto, dispensacionalismo, eclecticismo) para organizar en un conjunto coherente toda la información que la Biblia pone a su disposición. Pero, aunque el sistema que emplee determinará en gran parte su interpretación de los textos proféticos, a veces dos intérpretes que emplean el mismo sistema pueden llegar a interpretaciones distintas. Y esto subraya el hecho de que los tres sistemas, cuyas interpretaciones de los textos escatológicas veremos en el capítulo siguiente, son de fabricación humana. Por tanto, toda interpretación debe basarse principalmente sobre la exégesis del texto bíblico, no sobre un sistema de interpretación por necesario que sea.

*3. La exégesis tiene prioridad sobre argumentos secundarios.* Algunos han defendido sus interpretaciones de ciertos textos proféticos con base en la gran bendición que esas interpretaciones han producido.

3. Hay un consenso entre los eruditos en cuanto a que el género de la profecía cuenta con varios subgéneros, y que el apocalíptico es uno de ellos. Ver el libro de Köstenberger y Patterson, *Invitation to Biblical Interpretation* (Grand Rapids: Kregel, 2011), pp. 321–340, como ejemplo de los subgéneros que algunos autores creen observar bajo el género principal de la profecía.

4. Según los escritos de varios padres de la iglesia.

Pero la historia ha demostrado que es un argumento construido sobre arena. Por ejemplo, el postmilenialismo nació durante los siglos XVII y XVIII. Esta interpretación sobre el reino de Dios afirmaba que el mundo se convertiría progresivamente al cristianismo mediante el poder de la predicación del evangelio, produciendo así un mundo mejor. El postmilenialismo era el motor detrás de unos esfuerzos evangelísticos que lograron un éxito significativo en muchos lugares del mundo. Pero no por eso era correcta esa interpretación sobre la naturaleza del reino de Dios. Las dos guerras mundiales prácticamente enterraron el postmilenialismo al demostrar que el mundo iba de mal en peor[5].

## B. FENÓMENO PROFÉTICO

Hay una larga lista de profecías que se han cumplido de forma literal. Sin embargo, hay otras que desafían una interpretación literal. Aunque no hay muchos ejemplos de estos fenómenos, el intérprete debe ser consciente de su existencia y de cómo los eruditos evangélicos los han interpretado.

### El principio de equivalencia

Cuando los profetas hablaban de cosas y eventos futuros tenían que describirlos en términos comprensibles para ellos y sus lectores. Por ejemplo, al hablar de futuros modos de transporte, no describían aviones, trenes, ni automóviles, sino caballos y camellos, los cuales equivaldrían a esos futuros modos de transporte. Igualmente, no describían carros de combate, ametralladoras y bombas nucleares, sino lanzas, escudos y flechas. Y al describir a los enemigos futuros del pueblo de Dios, hablaban de los filisteos, los moabitas, etcétera, pueblos que desaparecieron hace muchos siglos. En todos estos casos el intérprete debe ser consciente de que el profeta describe algo futuro en términos que equivalen a lo que él y sus lectores pueden entender.

Para muchos eruditos bíblicos la descripción de la restauración espiritual futura de Israel en Ezequiel 40–48 representa un ejemplo

5. No obstante, ha habido un pequeño resurgimiento de personas que abrazan el postmilenialismo.

del principio de equivalencia. Ezequiel se encuentra en la cautividad babilónica. Jerusalén y el templo han sido destruidos hace tiempo y el sistema sacerdotal ya no existe. Al profetizar la futura restauración de Israel, Ezequiel tiene que describirla en términos contemporáneos; o sea, cómo sería si ocurriera en su época. Que los judíos volverán a la tierra prometida (47–48) y que el templo se reedificará (40:1–44:3) no representa en principio ningún problema. Pero la idea de que el sistema sacerdotal se establecerá de nuevo (44:4–45:17) y de que se practicarán de nuevo los ritos levíticos (45:18–46:24) representaría un problema teológico si se cumpliera de forma literal, porque entraría en conflicto con la enseñanza de la Epístola a los Hebreos. Los corderos (tipo) no tienen ningún lugar en el nuevo pacto que Dios ha hecho con su pueblo porque el Cordero de Dios (antitipo) ya se ha presentado. La única solución es entender estos capítulos como un ejemplo del principio de equivalencia.

## Cumplimiento por etapas

Con este fenómeno el profeta cita dos eventos en un mismo versículo o pasaje, dando la impresión de que se cumplirán simultánea o seguidamente. Sin embargo, es evidente que los dos eventos tienen que cumplirse en momentos distintos. «Los profetas comprimieron grandes sucesos en un breve espacio de tiempo. Unieron movimientos trascendentales en un sentido temporal y los presentaron en una sola perspectiva; o sea, bajo una simple mirada. Ellos vieron el futuro como el viajero desde una alta montaña. Todos sabemos que en tales casos el pico de un monte parece estar al lado de otro, cuando en realidad puede haber muchos kilómetros entre uno y otro»[6]. Normalmente, las profecías que se cumplen por etapas tienen que ver con las dos resurrecciones, los dos ministerios de Cristo de morir y reinar, los aspectos actuales y futuros del reino de Dios y las dos venidas de Cristo. Por ejemplo:

*Isaías 9:6-7,* LBLA. Existe un tiempo entre «un niño nos ha nacido» y el momento en que «la soberanía reposará sobre sus hombros» si se toma en cuenta la descripción más detallada de su reino en el v. 7.

6. Louis Berkhof, *Principios de interpretación bíblica* (Tarrasa: CLIE, 1973), p. 181.

Puesto que los dispensacionalistas y eclécticos (términos que se describirán en el capítulo siguiente) creen que Cristo reinará sobre la tierra durante mil años, consideran este texto un ejemplo de una profecía que se cumple por etapas. Los teólogos del pacto rechazan este texto como un ejemplo del cumplimiento por etapas porque creen que el reino de Dios es espiritual por naturaleza y que está teniendo lugar ahora en el cielo o en el corazón del creyente.

*Isaías 61:1-3.* Jesús leyó este texto en una sinagoga en Nazaret para presentarse como el Mesías (Lc. 4:16-21), confirmando que había venido para predicar e inaugurar «el año favorable del SEÑOR» (LBLA). Pero no leyó la siguiente frase («el día de venganza de nuestro Dios») porque ese evento se cumplirá en el futuro.

*Daniel 12:2.* Hablando de la resurrección de cada ser humano, Daniel dice que «muchos de los que duermen en el polvo de la tierra serán despertados, unos para vida eterna, y otros para vergüenza y confusión perpetua», dejando la impresión de que habrá una resurrección general de todos a la vez como creen los teólogos del pacto. Puesto que los dispensacionalistas y eclécticos creen que los creyentes resucitarán al principio del reino terrenal de Cristo y los no creyentes al final del mismo, consideran este texto un ejemplo de una profecía que se cumple por etapas.

## Doble cumplimiento

El fenómeno del doble cumplimiento no significa que un texto tiene dos *significados*, sino dos *cumplimientos*. Hay una gran diferencia entre sentido múltiple y cumplimiento múltiple.

*Jeremías 31:27-40*: El profeta habla del nuevo pacto que Dios hará con «la casa de Israel y la casa de Judá» (v. 27). O sea, los judíos. Sin embargo, Hebreos 8:7-13 y 10:15-17 indican que ese nuevo pacto ya se ha cumplido en la iglesia. Mientras que los dispensacionalistas y eclécticos creen que Dios cumplirá esta promesa en una futura restauración de Israel y el pueblo judío, los teólogos del pacto creen que esta profecía se cumple solamente en la Iglesia. Por tanto, rechazan este texto como un ejemplo de doble cumplimiento.

*Isaías 7:14*: Israel y Siria quieren que Judá se alíe con ellos contra Asiria. Pero cuando Acaz, rey de Judá, rechaza su petición, Israel y

Siria atacan a Judá c. 734 a. C. Isaías aconseja a Acaz que no tema a Rezím, rey de Siria, ni a Peka, rey de Israel, porque los dos son como «dos cabos de tizón que humean» (v. 4). O sea, están por extinguirse. Isaías le promete que Efraín (Israel) dejará de ser pueblo dentro de 65 años (v. 8)[7]. Para que Acaz tenga la confianza de que Israel y Siria no traspasan los muros de Jerusalén, Isaías le manda pedir una señal a Dios. Pero Acaz se niega a hacerlo, no porque no quiera tentar a Jehová, como dice (v. 12; ver Éx. 17:2 y Dt. 6:16), sino porque no quiere depender de él. De hecho, ya había pedido a Asiria que lo ayudara contra Israel y Siria (2 Cr. 28:16-20). Isaías lo riñe y le dice que de todos modos Dios le dará una señal: «He aquí que la virgen concebirá...» (v. 14)[8].

Se han hecho varias sugerencias en cuanto a la identidad de esa virgen. Lo claro es que no puede referirse a María porque el nacimiento virginal de Jesús unos cuantos siglos después no serviría a Acaz como señal. La virgen tenía que ser alguien que él conocía en aquel momento. Algunos argumentan que esta profecía tiene que referirse

7. Acaz reinó en el 735–715 a. C. Isaías dio esta profecía c. 734 a. C. Inscripciones asirias afirman que Asurbanipal conquistó el último remanente de Samaria c. 669–668 a. C., una labor comenzada antes por Salmanasar y Sargón (2 R. 17:6).

8. Algunos eruditos insisten en que *almah* puede referirse a una mujer joven, una doncella, alguien sexualmente maduro o de una edad para casarse. Insisten en que el v. 14 no se refiere a una virgen en el sentido estricto de la palabra. Hasta sugieren que *almah* pueda referirse a una mujer casada. Hay dos palabras hebreas que Isaías podría haber empleado: *almah* y *bethulah*. Algunos sugieren que *bethulah* puede referirse a una mujer casada. Sugieren como ejemplos Deuteronomio 22:24 y Joel 1:8. Pero una lectura de esos textos parece indicar una mujer virgen, no una mujer casada. También insisten en que el autor que emplea *bethulah* en el sentido de virgen debería indicarlo de alguna forma en el contexto. Por ejemplo, Rebeca es llamada *almah* (Gn. 24:43) y *betulah* (Gn. 24:16), y el texto dice que «La joven era muy hermosa, virgen, *ningún hombre la había conocido*» (énfasis añadido). Isaías emplea la palabra *almah* en el v. 14, una palabra mucho más apropiada puesto que se refiere de forma clara a una virgen. La palabra *almah* no requiere frases aclaratorias; se entiende por sí misma. *Almah* encaja en el contexto de textos como Génesis 24:43; Éxodo 2:8; Salmo 68:28; Proverbios 30:19; Cantares 1:3; 6:8. No existe ningún ejemplo en las Escrituras ni en ningún escrito extrabíblico que indique que *almah* pueda referirse a una mujer casada. Cuando *almah* se traduce como «una mujer joven», la implicación es que es soltera y, por tanto, virgen. Los traductores de la LXX así lo entendieron.

exclusivamente a Jesús porque un mero ser humano no podría llamarse «Emanuel», lo cual significa «Dios con nosotros». Sin embargo, el hecho de que ese niño se llamara Emanuel y que naciera de una virgen no significa que fuera Dios, ni que el milagro del nacimiento de Cristo fuera menos milagroso, ni que Cristo fuera menos divino de lo que es, sino que Dios simplemente hizo el mismo milagro dos veces.

*Malaquías 4:5*: Este profeta dijo: «He aquí, yo os envío el profeta Elías, antes que venga el día de Jehová, grande y terrible». En Mateo 11:10-14 Jesús identifica a Juan el Bautista como el cumplimiento de esta profecía. Es evidente que se trata de una metonimia, porque Elías y Juan el Bautista tenían un carácter muy parecido. Esta interpretación coincide con las palabras del ángel a Zacarías de que su hijo (Juan el Bautista) serviría como el heraldo del Mesías e iría «delante de él con el espíritu y el poder de Elías» (Lc. 1:17). Todo esto sucedería «antes que venga el día de Jehová, grande y terrible». Aunque Malaquías no indica cuánto tiempo ha de transcurrir entre la venida de «Elías» y «el día de Jehová», los dispensacionalistas y eclécticos creen que «el día de Jehová» se refiere a la Gran Tribulación.

| **Fenómeno profético** | |
|---|---|
| El principio de equivalencia | La descripción de eventos futuros en términos que los primeros lectores entendían. |
| Cumplimiento por etapas | Los profetas citan en el mismo versículo algunos eventos que se cumplen en dos etapas. |
| Doble cumplimiento | Hay profecías que tienen dos cumplimientos. |

En Mateo 17:1-13 Jesús es transfigurado. Pedro, Jacobo y Juan lo observan hablando con Moisés y Elías. Después, Jesús les manda que no digan nada de lo que han visto hasta que haya resucitado. Entonces le preguntan: «¿Por qué, pues, dicen los escribas que es necesario que Elías venga primero?». Jesús les responde que «Elías ya vino» (v. 12). «Entonces los discípulos comprendieron que les había hablado de Juan el Bautista» (v. 13). Sin embargo, aunque Jesús dijo que Elías «ya vino» (v. 12), también dijo que Elías «restaurará todas las cosas» (v. 11). Aunque el ministerio de Juan el Bautista produjo un avivamiento espiritual, no se podría decir que restauró todas las cosas. Puesto que la profecía dice que Elías vendrá «antes que venga el día de Jehová, grande y terrible», una referencia a los últimos tiempos, y puesto que Dios es el único capaz de restaurar todas las cosas, lo más probable es que se refiera a Cristo y a la obra que realizará en su segunda venida. O sea, la profecía de Malaquías 4:5 se cumple en Juan el Bautista y en Cristo.

## C. EL REINO DE DIOS

El reino de Dios es el tema principal de la profecía bíblica. Por eso Ramm lo llama «el *crux interpretum* de la interpretación profética»[9]. El tema del reino de Dios aparece por primera vez en Génesis 12:1-7 donde Dios promete a Abraham que hará de sus descendientes una gran nación, la cual será una gran bendición para todos los pueblos de la tierra. Luego, Dios lo lleva a Canaán y le dice que esa tierra será el hogar de esa nación futura. Puesto que Génesis 12:1-7 es el primer ladrillo que la revelación progresiva coloca en el edificio del tema del reino de Dios, los datos son escasos y muy básicos.

Muchos años después Dios libra a los judíos de la esclavitud en Egipto. Por el camino hacia Canaán les da la Ley. En esa Ley les da instrucciones sobre la nación que él mismo establecerá. Dios había prometido a Abraham que haría de su descendencia un *pueblo* numeroso y le había indicado la *tierra* que ocuparía. Ahora, Dios añade unas leyes en cuanto a los futuros *reyes* de Israel (Dt. 17:14-20). Este es el elemento que faltaba en Génesis 12:1-7. Si falta uno de estos tres elementos (pueblo, tierra, rey), los dos que quedan no son suficientes para formar un reino. Sin embargo, en la Ley Dios advierte a su pueblo escogido que lo reducirá en número si lo desobedece (Dt. 28:62-63), lo sacará de la tierra que le ha dado y lo esparcirá a los cuatro vientos (Dt. 28:63-68). Evidentemente, los reyes y la soberanía de la nación judía también desaparecerán.

Los judíos conquistan la tierra prometida y pasan por un período de caos político después de la muerte de Josué. El pueblo insiste en tener un rey como las demás naciones. Desafortunadamente, insisten en adelantar el calendario divino y eligen a Saúl como rey. Debido al pecado de Saúl, Dios les quita ese rey y nombra a David como sucesor. Una vez consolidado su reino, David expresa al profeta Natán su deseo

9. Bernard Ramm, *Protestant Biblical Interpretation* (Grand Rapids: Baker, 1978), p. 266.

de construir un templo para Dios. Aunque Dios niega su petición, le dice que establecerá su reino (2 S. 7:11-15), y que «será afirmada tu casa y tu reino para siempre delante de tu rostro, y tu trono será estable eternamente» (v. 16). Si no tuviéramos los demás ladrillos de la revelación progresiva sobre el reino de Dios, podríamos concluir que las palabras «para siempre» y «eternamente» son hipérboles que indican que siempre habrá un rey de la dinastía davídica sobre el trono de Israel. Pero como veremos a continuación, Dios está hablando de un Rey que no es un mero ser humano, sino Dios.

Salomón sucede a David como rey. Pero cuando muere, el reino se divide. Con el tiempo las diez tribus del norte y las dos del sur persisten en su pecado y Dios se ve obligado a destruirlas como naciones. Como resultado, el *pueblo* de los dos reinos es llevado a tierras extranjeras, su *tierra* es ocupada por sus conquistadores y su *gobierno* y soberanía nacional dejan de existir. Sin embargo, en medio de estos eventos históricos, varios profetas dicen que en el futuro los judíos se arrepentirán y volverán a Dios, se convertirán de nuevo en un pueblo numeroso, Dios les traerá de nuevo a la tierra prometida y unirá al reino dividido bajo un solo rey que gobernará a todas las naciones desde Jerusalén (Jer. 23:7-8; 32:36-41; Ez. 28:25-26; 37:15-28; Dn. 2:44; 7:13-14; Os. 1:10-11; Zac. 10:6-10; Ro. 11:25-26). Además, afirman que el Mesías será el Rey de ese reino y que su reino será eterno (Is. 9:6-7; Dn. 2:44; 7:1-14).

En el N.T. Dios coloca unos ladrillos más en el edificio de nuestro entendimiento sobre el reino de Dios. Después del nacimiento de Jesús, un ángel le dice a María que «el Señor Dios le dará el trono de David su padre; y reinará sobre la casa de Jacob para siempre, y su reino no tendrá fin» (Lc. 1:32-33). Más adelante, Jesús habló en muchas ocasiones sobre el reino de Dios, especialmente en sus parábolas. Entre otras cosas, dijo que el reino de Dios se había acercado en el sentido de que el *Rey* de ese reino estaba presente (Mt. 4:17; Mc. 1:15)[10]. En Lucas 17:20-21 dijo que el elemento *pueblo* del reino de

10. En su momento algunos intentaron hacer una distinción entre los términos «reino de Dios» y «reino de los cielos». Pero dicha distinción no se sostenía. Hay un consenso entre los eruditos de que los dos términos son sinónimos. Mateo emplea el término «reino de los cielos» para no ofender a los judíos (a quienes escribió su Evange-

Dios era más importante que el elemento *tierra.* Los fariseos se interesaban solamente por el aspecto *tierra*, queriendo echar a los romanos y recuperar la soberanía nacional de Israel. Aunque Pablo no dedicó un porcentaje tan alto de sus enseñanzas como Jesús al tema del reino de Dios, habló de ello en catorce ocasiones. En la mayoría de esos textos hizo énfasis sobre la ética que deben practicar los miembros (*pueblo*) del reino de Dios.

> «Oh Señor, honraré y alabaré tu nombre, porque tú eres mi Dios. ¡Tú haces cosas maravillosas! Las planeaste hace mucho tiempo, y ahora las has realizado».
>
> **(Is. 25:1, NTV)**

Apocalipsis 11:15 es el penúltimo ladrillo de la revelación progresiva sobre el reino de Dios: «Entonces el séptimo ángel tocó su trompeta, y hubo fuertes voces que gritaban en el cielo: "Ahora el mundo ya es el reino de nuestro Señor y de su Cristo, y él reinará por siempre y para siempre"» (NTV). Este texto declara que los reinos del mundo llegarán a pertenecer a Cristo y que su reino será eterno. Pero ¿reinará Cristo de forma literal sobre todos los reinos del mundo, o es su reino más bien espiritual por naturaleza? Apocalipsis 20:1-6 es el último ladrillo de la revelación progresiva que se coloca en nuestro entendimiento del reino de Dios.

> Luego vi a un ángel que bajaba del cielo con la llave del abismo sin fondo y una pesada cadena en la mano. Sujetó con fuerza al dragón —la serpiente antigua, quien es el diablo, Satanás— y lo encadenó por mil años. El ángel lo lanzó al abismo sin fondo y lo encerró con llave para que Satanás no pudiera engañar más a las naciones hasta

---

lio), quienes tenía la costumbre de no pronunciar el nombre de Dios para no correr el riesgo de tomarlo en vano. Esta conclusión es apoyada por el hecho de que la frase «reino de los cielos» se encuentra 32 veces en Mateo y ni una sola vez en Marcos y Lucas.

> que se cumplieran los mil años. Pasado ese tiempo, debe ser soltado por un poco de tiempo. Después vi tronos, y los que estaban sentados en ellos habían recibido autoridad para juzgar. Vi las almas de aquellos que habían sido decapitados por dar testimonio acerca de Jesús y proclamar la palabra de Dios. Ellos no habían adorado a la bestia ni a su estatua, ni habían aceptado su marca en la frente o en las manos. Volvieron a la vida, y reinaron con Cristo durante mil años. Esta es la primera resurrección. (El resto de los muertos no volvieron a la vida hasta que se cumplieron los mil años). Benditos y santos son aquellos que forman parte de la primera resurrección, porque la segunda muerte no tiene ningún poder sobre ellos, sino que serán sacerdotes de Dios y de Cristo, y reinarán con él durante mil años. (NTV)

Los vv. 4 y 6 declaran que Cristo reinará en la tierra durante mil años. Estos versículos han provocado un debate que ha procurado contestar tres preguntas. ¿Es literal o espiritual ese reino? ¿Dónde tendrá lugar? Y, ¿a partir de qué momento comenzará? Las respuestas a estas preguntas han dado pie a tres posiciones. En el capítulo siguiente veremos cómo interpreta cada posición Apocalipsis 20:1-6.

La profecía bíblica parte de la base de que nuestro Dios no solamente conoce lo que ocurrirá en el futuro, sino que también controla la historia que él ha determinado antes de la fundación del mundo y la está llevando al final. Este hecho no solamente sirve de consuelo y confianza para el creyente, sino que debe servir también como estímulo para estudiar la profecía.

## *Trabajo para realizar*

Describa cómo funciona el principio de equivalencia, las profecías que se cumplen por etapas y el principio del doble cumplimiento.

# 23

# Profecía (II)

Apocalipsis 20:1-6 es un texto clave para nuestra comprensión del reino de Dios. Para facilitar sus referencias a los mil años durante los cuales Cristo reinará, los teólogos emplean el término «milenio». Además, se han creado los términos amilenialismo, postmilenialismo y premilenialismo para referirse a las tres interpretaciones principales sobre ese tiempo. El amilenialismo cree que el milenio es espiritual por naturaleza y que está ocurriendo ahora en el cielo o en el corazón de los creyentes. La segunda venida de Cristo tendrá lugar al final de esta era de la iglesia. El postmilenialismo se parece mucho al amilenialismo. Cree que el milenio es espiritual por naturaleza y que está creciendo ahora mismo en la tierra mediante la conversión de los no creyentes. Llegará una «edad de oro» al final de la cual Cristo volverá. El premilenialismo cree que el milenio cuenta no solamente con aspectos espirituales, sino también literales y terrenales. Cristo volverá por segunda vez al final de la Gran Tribulación para establecer un reino de mil años en la tierra.

## A. EL AMILENIALISMO

Durante los primeros años de la iglesia hubo mucho debate sobre el sistema que debía emplearse para interpretar las Escrituras. Aunque algunos creían que una interpretación literal de las Escrituras era el método correcto, la alegorización y la espiritualización (misticismo) del texto bíblico encontraron una aceptación más amplia. Estos sistemas de interpretación afirmaban que hay unas verdades profundas detrás del texto que una interpretación literal no es capaz de descubrir. Para descubrir esas verdades, la alegorización rechazaba la historicidad del texto bíblico. Aunque la espiritualización aceptaba la historicidad del texto, la ignoraba a la hora de interpretar cualquier texto. Con el tiempo la espiritualización se convirtió en el método preferido de la mayoría[1].

## Historia del amilenialismo

Durante los tres primeros siglos la iglesia creía que el milenio era futuro y que ocurriría en la tierra de forma literal. Uno de los primeros líderes que rechazó esa interpretación fue Ticonio (c. 330–c. 390), un teólogo donatista en el Norte de África[2]. Espiritualizando los textos pertinentes, concluyó que el milenio correspondía al tiempo entre la primera y segunda venida de Cristo. Por tanto, no se trataba de mil años literales en la tierra, sino de un largo período de tiempo. La primera resurrección de Apocalipsis 20:4 correspondería al momento en que una persona se convertía a Cristo, y las referencias al trono que debe ocupar el Mesías corresponderían a la encarnación de Cristo y su reino actual en la iglesia. En base a estas conclusiones, podríamos considerar a Ticonio como el primer amilenialista.

Aunque Ticonio fue el primero en espiritualizar los textos referentes al milenio, Agustín (354–430) fue su promotor más famoso. En lugar de un evento temporal y cronológico, creía que el significado del milenio se encontraba en lo que simbolizaba[3]. Agustín fue el primero en identificar el reino de Dios con la iglesia visible. Hubo tres factores que le llevaron a esa conclusión. Primero, la Iglesia Católica Romana

---

1. Puesto que la alegorización cayó en descrédito hace muchos siglos, hoy día hay pocos eruditos que la utilicen, independientemente de su tendencia teológica. Prácticamente los únicos que alegorizan el texto bíblico son las sectas.

2. Los donatistas se separaban de las demás iglesias por considerarlas apóstatas. Además, creían que el bautismo que practicaban esas iglesias no era válido. Los donatistas se caracterizaban por una disciplina severa y tenían requisitos muy altos para sus pastores. Con el tiempo los donatistas cayeron en varias herejías.

3. Aunque Agustín atacó las doctrinas heréticas de Ticonio y los demás donatistas, adoptó sus ideas básicas en cuanto al milenio.

se consolidaba y experimentaba a diario nuevos logros y éxitos. Segundo, la conversión de Constantino en el año 312 prácticamente convirtió al cristianismo en la religión oficial del Imperio. Tercero, al desintegrarse el Imperio romano, la Iglesia Católica Romana asumió poco a poco prácticamente todas las funciones del Estado. Puesto que Agustín estaba en la vanguardia de muchas áreas de la teología, su influencia sobre los teólogos de los siglos siguientes fue muy grande.

Los reformadores del siglo XVI no prestaron mucha atención a los temas escatológicos puesto que el debate teológico de su día se centraba en otros temas como la justificación por la fe, el sacerdocio de cada creyente o el derecho de cada creyente a interpretar las Escrituras por sí mismo. Creían en la segunda venida de Cristo, el cielo, el infierno, etcétera, pero consideraban los demás temas proféticos demasiado difíciles de interpretar. Por eso, Apocalipsis fue el único libro sobre el cual Juan Calvino (1509–1564) no escribió un comentario. No obstante, creía que el milenio correspondía al estado eterno. Y, puesto que Agustín era un referente muy importante para los reformadores, la gran mayoría de ellos aceptaban sin más su posición amilenialista.

Aunque los amilenialistas modernos reconocen a Agustín como el padre del amilenialismo, creen que hace falta modificar su interpretación y la de Calvino en cuanto al lugar del milenio. Algunos creen que el milenio se encuentra en el corazón de cada creyente que aún vive, mientras que otros creen que se trata del estado de bendición que los creyentes fallecidos disfrutan en el cielo. La mayoría de los amilenialistas modernos abrazan la segunda opción, la cual es considerada una posición más espiritual. En cualquier caso, el amilenialismo cree que el reino de Dios es espiritual por naturaleza y que precede a la segunda venida de Cristo. Después, todos los muertos de todos los siglos resucitarán (R) y pasarán a la eternidad.

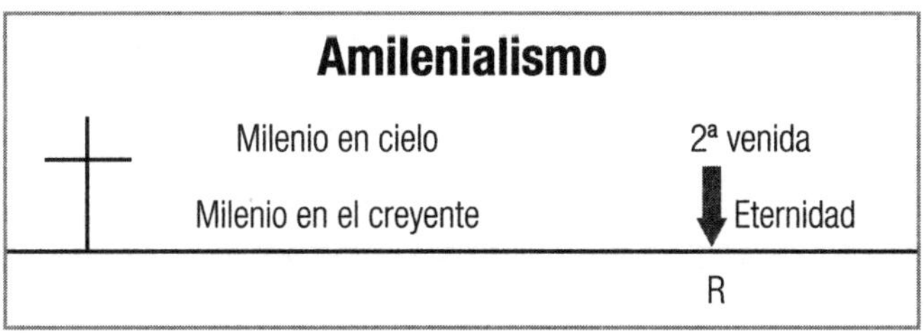

## ¿Cómo interpretan los amilenialistas Apocalipsis 20:1-6?

Muchos amilenialistas emplean la teoría de la recapitulación en su interpretación de Apocalipsis. Según ella, Juan describe en seis ciclos (capítulos 4–7, 8–11, 12–14, 15–16, 17–19 y 20–22) los mismos eventos que ocurren entre la primera y la segunda venida de Cristo. Por tanto, los primeros versículos de cada ciclo describen la primera venida de Cristo, y los últimos versículos de cada ciclo relatan los eventos relacionados con la segunda venida de Cristo. Cada ciclo describe los mismos eventos pero con otros símbolos y figuras. Puesto que Apocalipsis 20 se encuentra al principio del último ciclo, los eventos citados en los vv. 1-10 tienen que ver con la primera venida de Cristo. Por tanto, interpretan la atadura de Satanás y las dos resurrecciones de Apocalipsis 20 de la siguiente forma:

| Teoría de la recapitulación |
|---|
| Caps. 4–7 |
| Caps. 8–11 |
| Caps. 12–14 |
| Caps. 15–16 |
| Caps. 17–19 |
| Caps. 20–22 |

*1. La atadura de Satanás (Ap. 20:1-3).* Agustín creía que era una forma simbólica de decir que Satanás ya no es capaz de seducir ni engañar a los elegidos apoyándose en textos como Mateo 12:25-29; Colosenses 2:15; Apocalipsis 12:7-9; y especialmente Lucas 10:17-20. Pero también creía que existe una lucha entre Dios y Satanás, y que la presencia del pecado y la ineficacia de la Iglesia indica que el tiempo presente no es el cumplimiento de la prometida edad de rectitud y justicia, sino un tiempo de conflicto en el cual parece que Satanás esté ganando la batalla[4]. A pesar de ello, la iglesia triunfará sobre la marcha. Como un reflejo de esa interpretación, Calvino decía que Satanás y los suyos «arrastran sus cadenas por dondequiera que vayan»[5]. Por un lado, Satanás fue atado mediante la obra de Cristo en la cruz. Pero por otro

4. Existe en el amilenialismo una tensión por entender el milenio como algo presente pero a la vez futuro. Por eso, los amilenialistas admiten que el término «milenio» podría considerarse un sinónimo del estado eterno. Calvino era más coherente y consistente por creer que el milenio en todos sus sentidos era sinónimo del estado eterno. No obstante, aunque existe esa tensión entre el milenio como algo presente y a la vez futuro, los amilenialistas tienen una filosofía realista de la historia. Cabe tanto la posibilidad de que las cosas mejoren como que empeoren. No caen en el típico optimismo de los postmilenialistas, pero tampoco en el pesimismo de muchos premilenialistas.

5. Citado por Louis Berkhof, *Teología sistemática* (Grand Rapids: Tell, 1976), p. 176.

lado se le permite cierta actividad. Lutero expresó este concepto con las siguientes palabras de su gran himno *Castillo fuerte es nuestro Dios*.

Y si demonios mil están prontos a devorarnos,
no temeremos, porque Dios sabrá cómo ampararnos.
Que muestre su vigor Satán, y su furor.
Dañarnos no podrá, pues condenado es ya
por la Palabra Santa.

*2. Las dos resurrecciones (Ap. 20:4-6).* La primera resurrección es espiritual y representa uno de los beneficios de la obra de Cristo en la cruz. Algunos amilenialistas creen que se refiere al momento en que una persona se convierte a Cristo, de acuerdo con textos como Ef. 2:1, 5-6 que hablan de la conversión a Cristo como una resurrección espiritual («Que, a pesar de que estábamos muertos por causa de nuestros pecados, nos dio vida... (¡Es solo por la gracia de Dios que ustedes han sido salvados!)», NTV). Pero la mayoría de los amilenialistas creen que se refiere al momento en que el creyente muere y pasa al cielo donde reina con Cristo. Prácticamente todos los amilenialistas creen que la segunda resurrección es física y que ocurrirá simultáneamente con la segunda venida de Cristo o justo después de ella[6].

## Las fuerzas y debilidades del amilenialismo

El amilenialismo cuenta entre sus filas con eruditos y personajes históricos del cristianismo como Juan Calvino (1509–1564), Martín Lutero (1483–1546), Philipp Melanchthon (1497–1560), B. B. Warfield (1851–1921)[7], John Gresham Machen (1881–1937),

6. Para una descripción de un amilenialista que cree que tanto la primera como la segunda resurrección son espirituales, ver la posición de James A. Hughes citado por Millard J. Erikson en su libro *Contemporary Options in Eschatology* (Grand Rapids: Baker, 1977), pp. 79–83, 87–89.

7. En su libro *Contemporary Options in Eschatology* (Grand Rapids: Baker, 1977), p. 61, Erickson dice que Warfield era postmilenialista. Sin embargo, en la p. 69 dice: «Mientras que es algo cuestionable si Warfield fue postmilenialista o amilenialista, su interpretación de los mil años ha sido citada con aprobación por Boettner, un postmilenialista militante». Y en la p. 84 dice que ambos grupos reclaman a Warfield como uno de los suyos.

Louis Berkhof (1873–1957) o Anthony Hoekema (1913–1988). Una de las aportaciones más valiosas que los amilenialistas han hecho al tema del milenio es su énfasis sobre la abundancia de símbolos en la profecía bíblica. Lógicamente, un símbolo no debe ser interpretado literalmente. Sin embargo, el amilenialismo tiene la tendencia a considerar como simbólico lo que en realidad es literal. El hecho de que un pasaje contenga un símbolo no significa que todos los objetos en dicho pasaje sean símbolos. Por eso Zuck pregunta:

> ¿Debemos entender todos los números que (Juan) cita como simbólicos? ¿No tienen significado como números normales y literales? Si los números 7, 42, 1260 no deben entenderse como literales, entonces ¿cómo deberíamos entender la referencia a los dos testigos en 11:3? ¿Con base en qué criterio decimos que 7000 no significa literalmente 7000? Y si mil es un número grande e indefinido, ¿son las referencias a cuatro ángeles (7:1) y siete ángeles (8:6) simplemente números pequeños? Si estos números en el libro de Apocalipsis no tienen un valor normal y numérico, entonces ¿qué hacemos con el principio de una interpretación normal y gramatical? ¿Cómo podemos decir que 144.000 es un número simbólico cuando 7:5-8 se refiere de forma específica a 12.000 personas de las doce tribus de Israel? [8]

Una segunda debilidad de los amilenialistas es su espiritualización de los textos concernientes al milenio y al reino de Dios. Afortunadamente, lo hacen solamente con los textos pertinentes a esos temas. Sin embargo, esa práctica los expone a tres problemas. Primero, se hacen vulnerables a la acusación de ser arbitrarios por espiritualizar solamente aquellos pasajes concernientes al milenio y al reino de Dios. Segundo, la espiritualización deja al intérprete con una libertad total y absoluta; no existen barreras para limitar sus errores de interpretación. No sorprende, entonces, que el amilenialismo haya contado a lo largo de su historia con cuatro diferentes interpretaciones sobre

8. Roy B. Zuck, *Basic Bible Interpretation* (Colorado Springs: Victor, 1991), pp. 244–245.

dónde toma lugar el milenio (la iglesia visible, la eternidad, el cielo, el corazón del creyente), aunque en la actualidad ese número se ha reducido a los dos últimos. Tercero, la espiritualización es un sistema de interpretación que destruiría las doctrinas fundamentales de la fe cristiana si no se limitara al tema del milenio y el reino de Dios. De hecho, algunos amilenialistas han pasado a campos teológicos que no mantienen una teología bíblica sobre algunas doctrinas fundamentales de la fe cristiana.

## B. EL POSTMILENIALISMO

Durante los siglos XVII y XVIII los puritanos que huyeron al nuevo continente para escapar de la persecución religiosa en Europa y los puritanos que se quedaron en Inglaterra creían que era necesario modificar ligeramente el amilenialismo. Las novedades que introdujeron afirmaban que la predicación del evangelio es tan poderosa y eficaz que todo el mundo sería cristianizado antes de la segunda venida de Cristo; que, aunque Cristo reina en el cielo, los textos que hablan del reino de Dios trataban del control y dominio de Cristo en el corazón de los creyentes en la tierra; que cada vez que una persona se convertía a Cristo, allí se establecía el reino de Dios; y que el evangelio es tan poderoso que se producirá una «edad de oro» en el futuro. Esta nueva interpretación del milenio encajaba a la perfección con la ola de libertad intelectual, los logros científicos y el énfasis sobre el progreso del ser humano que caracterizaron al siglo XVIII. Como consecuencia, el postmilenialismo se convirtió en la posición predominante sobre el milenio durante aproximadamente 200 años, cubriendo porciones de los siglos XVIII al XX.

Igual que el amilenialismo, el postmilenialismo cree que las promesas hechas a Israel se cumplen en la iglesia y que, por tanto, Israel no figura en los planes futuros de Dios. También cree que Satanás fue atado en el momento de la crucifixión de Cristo y que la segunda venida de Cristo tendrá lugar después de la «edad de oro» que se producirá como consecuencia de la predicación del evangelio y del gran número de personas que se convertirán a Cristo. Entonces, resucitarán (R) todos los muertos de todos los siglos y pasarán a la eternidad.

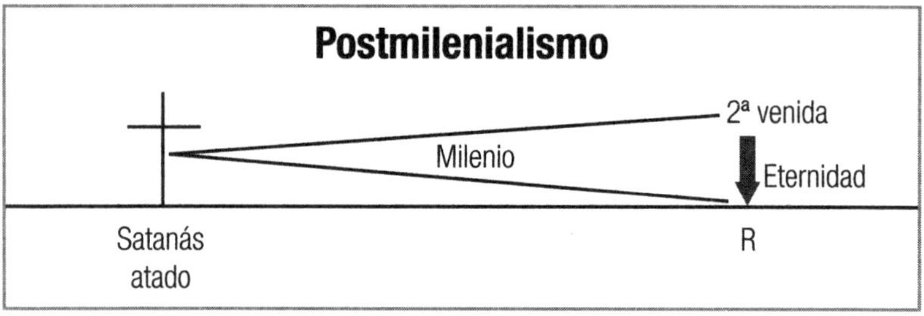


Aunque el reino de Dios tiene lugar en la tierra por encontrarse en el corazón de los creyentes, es invisible y espiritual. No es material o político, no ocupa un área geográfica, no tiene nada que ver con el estado de Israel ni con un trono literal en Jerusalén[9]. La Gran Tribulación no es un período de siete años que tendrá lugar en un futuro, sino que representa la tribulación que sufrieron los judíos entre la crucifixión de Cristo y la destrucción de Jerusalén en el año 70 por haber rechazado a Jesús como el Mesías.

## La base bíblica del postmilenialismo

Para muchos postmilenialistas Mateo 13 describe la transformación que tendrá lugar en la sociedad de todos los países debido a la predicación del evangelio y la conversión de muchos no creyentes. De las siete parábolas de Mateo 13, creen que cuatro de ellas relacionan el reino de Dios con un proceso de crecimiento. La parábola de la levadura (v. 33) enseña que ese crecimiento ocurrirá poco a poco. Por tanto, no vendrá de repente, sino lentamente, casi sin percibirse. Las parábolas del trigo y la cizaña (vv. 24-30) y de la red (vv. 47-50) enseñan que los obstáculos a la predicación del evangelio y al crecimiento del reino no son tan grandes como parecen. En comparación con el trigo, la cizaña es una parte comparativamente pequeña. Además, al final la cizaña se convertirá en trigo. La parábola del grano de mostaza (vv. 31-32) también subraya el concepto de crecimiento.

Charles Hodge (1797–1878), uno de los teólogos evangélicos más destacados del pasado, defendió el postmilenialismo con cinco

9. El postmilenialismo suele relegar a un futuro ambiguo el cumplimiento de los pasajes que hablan del trono de David y de un reino literal en la tierra.

argumentos. Primero, las profecías del A.T. crean esa esperanza. Por ejemplo, aunque Isaías 45:22-25 está dirigido a Israel, habla de una aceptación universal del Mesías. Por tanto, el reino de Dios será universal. Oseas 2:23 parece indicar que muchas personas que vivían en tiempos del profeta recibieron la bendición de Dios aunque no formaban parte del pueblo judío con el cual Dios había hecho un pacto (Jer. 31:27-40). Los Salmos 47, 72 y 110 hablan de un reino universal. Jesús citó Salmo 110:1 como prueba de su deidad (Lc. 20:42-43) y Pedro dijo que esta profecía fue cumplida en Pentecostés (Hch. 2:34-35). Por tanto, el milenio está teniendo lugar durante la edad actual. Segundo, Jesús dijo que el evangelio se predicaría por todo el mundo (Mt. 24:14). ¿No sería extraño que fuese una predicación sin resultados? ¿Qué sentido tendría que esa predicación fracasara? Tercero, la gran comisión tiene este propósito (Mt. 28:18-20). Implícito en la gran comisión está el concepto de que la evangelización producirá resultados abundantes. Cuarto, la gran comisión está investida con la autoridad de Cristo. Por tanto, esa comisión nunca contará con más poder del que tiene en este momento. No tenemos que esperar hasta el futuro para que el reino de Dios se manifieste. Dios es capaz de mostrar su reino ahora. Quinto, la prometida conversión nacional de Israel no ocurrirá «hasta que haya entrado la plenitud de los gentiles» (Ro. 11:25), lo cual indica que tiene que haber una gran cosecha entre los gentiles antes de que se conviertan los judíos.

## Sus fuerzas y debilidades

El postmilenialismo cuenta con unos elementos muy bíblicos, como su énfasis sobre los aspectos actuales y presentes del reino de Dios. Este énfasis promueve un espíritu optimista y un activismo por parte de los creyentes. Prueba de ello es que el postmilenialismo sirvió como el motor del avivamiento evangélico en EE. UU. desde principios del siglo XVIII hasta finales del siglo XIX, y el gran movimiento misionero moderno del siglo XIX. Los creyentes evangelizaban con la confianza de que Dios iba a mostrar su poder de forma visible y abundante. El postmilenialismo también confía en el poder del evangelio para cambiar la sociedad. A medida que los creyentes actúen como sal de la tierra (Mt. 5:13), el mundo irá mejor. Los postmilenlialistas creen que los amilenialistas y los premilenialistas tienen en poco el poder del evangelio.

No obstante, el postmilenialismo cuenta con unas debilidades serias. Primero, aunque cuenta entre sus filas con teólogos de la talla de Charles Hodge, su hermano A. A. Hodge (1823–1886), Loraine Boettner (1901–1990), J. Marcellus Kik (1903–1965) y otros, todos los cuales creían en la inspiración de las Escrituras, el postmilenialismo cuenta también con teólogos liberales. Daniel Whitby (1638–1726), a quien se le atribuye el papel de popularizar el postmilenialismo, no creía en la inspiración de las Escrituras y mantenía posturas heréticas en cuanto a la Trinidad. Por eso, sus libros fueron quemados en público. Además, parece que los postmilenialistas modernos que abrazan una teología liberal son incapaces de distinguir entre lo malo y lo bueno. Creen que el reino de Dios está presente y que obra a través de instituciones seculares y movimientos políticos a pesar de que sean antibíblicos.

Segundo, el postmilenialismo no coincide con lo que observamos en nuestro mundo. Lo que dio un golpe mortal al postmilenialismo fueron las dos guerras mundiales y las muchas guerras regionales que han surgido desde entonces. En la opinión de muchos, estos eventos demostraron que el mundo no mejora, sino que va de mal en peor a pesar de las ráfagas ocasionales de avivamiento espiritual que se producen. Como resultado, en la segunda mitad del siglo XX la mayoría de los postmilenialistas se pasaron al campo amilenialista. Aunque ha habido un pequeño resurgimiento del postmilenialismo desde la última década del siglo XX, las únicas opciones reales que quedan en la actualidad son el amilenialismo y premilenialismo.

Tercero, su exégesis carece de seriedad. Los postmilenialistas ignoran conscientemente aquellos pasajes que contradicen sus conclusiones. Por ejemplo, Mateo 24:9-14 parece indicar que todo irá de mal en peor. Además, en los textos que emplean para apoyar su posición existe una aparente selectividad de detalles. Es verdad que el trigo crece y se hace grande en la parábola del trigo y la cizaña (Mt. 13:24-30), pero lo que ignoran los postmilenialistas es que la cizaña se desarraigará al final, no se convertirá en trigo. Finalmente, su interpretación de Apocalipsis 20 suele ser superficial.

## C. EL PREMILENIALISMO

De las tres posiciones sobre el milenio, el premilenialismo es la que ha desarrollado más sus argumentos. Además, es la posición que el público evangélico conoce mejor debido a que han escrito un mayor número de libros que los defensores de otras posiciones. No obstante, aunque prevalece la impresión de que el premilenialismo es la posición predominante, la realidad es que el amilenialismo sigue siendo la posición de la mayoría a nivel mundial. Como las demás posiciones, el premilenialismo ha pasado por diferentes etapas en su historia.

### Historia del premilenialismo

*El período apostólico.* Hay un consenso entre los historiadores de que el premilenialismo era la posición de la iglesia durante el período apostólico porque los creyentes creían que el fin de la historia humana estaba cerca. Pero cuando los años fueron pasando y Cristo no volvía, cambiaron sus expectativas y aplazaron la segunda venida a un futuro más lejano[10].

*El período postapostólico.* Justino Mártir (c. 100–c. 165) era un apologeta. No obstante, explicó su posición premilenialista solamente en sus escritos teológicos para que las autoridades civiles no le acusaran de provocar una revolución. Mártir creía que quienes no creían en un milenio terrenal estaban muy equivocados. Ireneo (c. 130–c. 202) presentó el premilenialismo de una forma más sistematizada que los demás.

10. Hubo personajes ilustres como Hipólito de Roma (c. 170–c. 236), Lactancio (c. 240–c. 320) y otros que, interpretando simbólicamente los seis días de la creación, creían que la historia de la civilización humana duraría seis mil años y que el milenio comenzaría a partir del séptimo milenio. Bajo este patrón, entendían que la primera venida de Cristo ocurrió durante el sexto milenio y que la segunda venida ocurriría al final del mismo. Así que la segunda venida tenía que ocurrir dentro de mil años como mucho. Muchas fechas fueron sugeridas para el comienzo del milenio, entre ellas: 200, la posición de Lactancio; 204, una fecha basada en la cronología de Daniel; y 500, la posición de Hipólito de Roma que basó sus cálculos en las proporciones del arca. Aunque Agustín era amilenialista, creía que la segunda venida de Cristo podría ocurrir en 650, basando sus cálculos en la cronología de la LXX desde Adán. No obstante, admitió que podría haberse equivocado.

Creía que la victoria de Cristo sobre Satanás en la cruz era incompleta si Cristo no reinaba en la tierra, pues entender que el milenio iba a ocurrir en cualquier otro lugar sería igual que admitir que Cristo no podía con la tierra —donde fue crucificado— y por tanto tuvo que trasladar su reino a otro sitio. Ireneo fue aún más crítico que Mártir con quienes no creían en un milenio terrenal.

No obstante, llegó un momento en que el premilenialismo fue descartado. Algunos teólogos creían que el premilenialismo hacia un énfasis demasiado «judío», mientras que otros como Agustín (354–430) lo rechazaban debido a «las exageraciones locas e ideas extremas encontradas en las descripciones de los milenialistas»[11]. Antes de convertirse, Agustín había llevado una vida disoluta, y por tanto le era prácticamente imposible aceptar un milenio cuya descripción era tan carnal que rozaba el hedonismo. Puesto que Agustín originalmente abrazaba el premilenialismo, era tolerante con aquellos que se excedían en su descripción de los placeres del milenio. Aunque el premilenialismo nunca desapareció del todo, quedó desacreditado como una opción. A partir de Agustín el amilenialismo se estableció como la posición predominante.

*La Edad Media (siglos V–XV).* A veces el premilenialismo era tolerado y a veces condenado como una herejía. Puesto que había sectas que abrazaban el premilenialismo, muchos rechazaron el premilenialismo al emplear la dinámica de la «culpabilidad por asociación».

*El tiempo de la Reforma (siglo XVI).* Los luteranos y reformados siguieron las pautas establecidas por Agustín. Había algunas personas y grupos ilustres de la Reforma, como los anabaptistas, que abrazaban el premilenialismo. Pero, puesto que fueron considerados como radicales, su posición premilenialista también fue rechazada.

*Los siglos XIX–XX.* Durantes estos siglos el premilenialismo experimentó un cambio que dividió esa posición en dos campos: el premilenialismo histórico y el premilenialismo dispensacionalista. El premilenialismo histórico creía que el anticristo se presentaría en algún momento de la historia y provocaría la Gran Tribulación (GT en el cuadro a continuación), la cual consistiría en tres años y medio de paz

11. Carl E. Armerding y W. Ward Gasque (eds.), *Dreams, Visions, and Oracles* (Grand Rapids: Baker, 1977), p. 60.

seguidos por tres años y medio de persecución mundial de los judíos. Al final de la misma, los creyentes fallecidos de todos los tiempos resucitarían (R1) y conjuntamente con los creyentes vivos serían arrebatados para encontrarse con el Señor en el aire y acompañarlo hasta la tierra. Satanás sería atado (SA) para no engañar más a las naciones y Cristo reinaría durante mil años en la tierra[12]. Para el premilenialista histórico el arrebatamiento y la segunda venida de Cristo son dos aspectos de un mismo evento. Al final del milenio Satanás será desatado, reunirá a las naciones en batalla contra Dios y todos serán derrotados. Entonces, los no creyentes de todos los siglos resucitarán (R2), todos serán juzgados[13] y todos los seres humanos pasarán a la eternidad.

Durante los años inmediatamente después de las guerras napoleónicas (1799–1815) coincidieron varios eventos que animaron a muchos creyentes de Inglaterra a abandonar el amilenialismo y el postmilenialismo a favor del premilenialismo histórico. Primero, muchos judíos se convertían al evangelio. Naturalmente, los postmilenialistas interpretaban ese fenómeno con mucho optimismo. Segundo, la labor misionera en muchos países, facilitada por el aparente derrumbamiento de fuerzas opuestas, fomentaba la idea de que el milenio tenía que ser literal. Tercero, se convertían muchos católicos-romanos en

12. Los premilenialistas históricos son llamados premilenialistas-postribulacionistas porque creen que la iglesia pasará por la Gran Tribulación.

13. Es probable que este sea el momento en que son juzgados Satanás, los ángeles caídos (2 P. 2:4; Ap. 20:10) y las naciones (Mt. 25:31-46). La iglesia (2 Co. 5:9-11), Israel (Ez. 20:33-38) y los mártires (Ap. 20:4-6) habrán sido juzgados en algún momento antes.

Irlanda. Cuarto, el Imperio otomano (turco), sede del Islam, daba señales de perder su poder. Si esta impresión era acertada, dejaría abierta la posibilidad de una vuelta de los judíos a Palestina. Por último, existían señales de apostasía en la iglesia. A raíz de esa apostasía, nació un movimiento que promovía una vuelta a los principios del N.T. en cuanto a la naturaleza de la iglesia local, su organización y su función. Como resultado, salieron dos grupos de la iglesia de Inglaterra (anglicana), siendo uno de ellos los Hermanos, que se reunían en Plymouth.

Estos premilenialistas esperaban una obra especial del Espíritu Santo que sería acompañada por una actividad carismática. En 1830 se oyeron noticias de que una joven en Escocia había tenido una experiencia carismática. Este hecho, los eventos citados en el párrafo anterior y la influencia de John Nelson Darby (1800–1882) produjeron un interés casi incontenible por la profecía bíblica. Darby nació en el seno de una familia anglo-irlandesa en Westminster, Inglaterra. Sirvió durante unos años como pastor anglicano en Irlanda. Cuando abandonó la Iglesia de Inglaterra en 1845, fundó las iglesias de los Hermanos de Plymouth en colaboración con hombres destacados como Eduardo Irving y B. W. Newton. En sus estudios de los pasajes proféticos de las Escrituras, Darby interpretó los siete «días» de Daniel como una referencia a los siete años de la Gran Tribulación, adoptó una interpretación futurista del libro de Apocalipsis[14], e hizo una distinción marcada entre Israel y la iglesia. Los premilenialistas históricos

14. En algún momento de su estudio de Apocalipsis, el intérprete tiene que tomar una decisión en cuanto a lo que representan los eventos descritos en ese libro y cuándo tendrán lugar. Tiene cuatro opciones. Una interpretación *futurista* entiende que dichos eventos ocurrirán en los últimos tiempos. Con esta opción, Darby entendió que los capítulos 4–18 describían los siete años de la Gran Tribulación; el capítulo 19 la segunda venida de Cristo; el capítulo 20 el milenio; y los capítulos 21–22 el estado eterno. Una interpretación *preterista* (llamada también «histórico-contemporánea») entiende que los eventos descritos ocurrieron en tiempos del apóstol Juan. Los que adoptan una interpretación *histórica* sugieren que dichos eventos se han ido cumpliendo a lo largo de la historia de la iglesia. Por tanto, algunos ya se han cumplido y otros quedan por cumplir. Una interpretación *idealista-simbólica* quita el sentido histórico de los eventos descritos y los considera símbolos de grandes verdades espirituales. Evidentemente, la opción que el intérprete elija determinará en gran manera su interpretación de Apocalipsis.

aceptaban un cumplimiento literal de las promesas de Dios sobre el futuro de Israel, pero hasta ese momento nadie había hecho una distinción tan marcada entre la Iglesia e Israel.

Debido a su distinción entre Israel y la Iglesia, Darby concluyó que la iglesia no estaría presente durante la Gran Tribulación (GT). Por tanto, tenía que ser arrebatada antes de la misma. Esta posición le llevó a entender que la primera resurrección de Apocalipsis 20:4-6 contaría con dos partes. Según Darby, solamente la iglesia participará en la primera parte de la primera resurrección (R1a) y el arrebatamiento. Los miembros fallecidos y vivos de la iglesia serán arrebatados para encontrar al Señor en el aire y acompañarlo al cielo. Al final de la Gran Tribulación (GT), la iglesia acompañará al Señor en su segunda venida. En ese momento tendrá lugar la segunda parte de la primera resurrección (R1b), la cual incluirá a todos los creyentes del A.T. y los judíos y gentiles que se hayan convertido a Cristo durante la Gran Tribulación. Cristo reinará sobre la tierra durante mil años. Entonces, Satanás será desatado, reunirá a las naciones en batalla contra Dios, serán derrotados, los no creyentes de todos los siglos resucitarán (R2) y serán juzgados, y tanto creyentes como no creyentes pasarán a la eternidad[15].

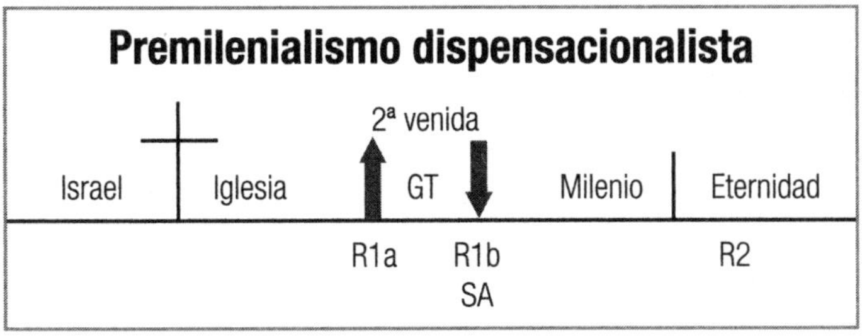


15. Hay quienes creen que el arrebatamiento y la resurrección de la iglesia (R1a) ocurrirá a mitad de la Gran Tribulación puesto que la persecución de los judíos a escala mundial ocurrirá durante los últimos tres años y medio de la misma. Sin embargo, hay muy pocos que abracen esta posición, entre los cuales se encuentra el erudito del A.T. Gleason Archer (1916–2004).

Puesto que el premilenialismo dispensacionalista de Darby fue bastante más allá de lo que el premilenialismo histórico afirmaba, algunos de los líderes que habían acompañado a Darby en la fundación del movimiento de los Hermanos de Plymouth lo abandonaron. Y aunque los premilenialistas históricos no han escrito tantos libros sobre su posición como los premilenialistas dispensacionalistas, cuentan entre sus filas con teólogos destacados como George E. Ladd[16], Wayne Grudem[17] y Robert H. Gundry[18].

En 1862 Darby fue invitado a impartir estudios bíblicos en EE. UU. Su visita coincidió con un tiempo en que muchos líderes evangélicos habían llegado a la convicción de que era necesario establecer unas instituciones teológicas netamente evangélicas, puesto que universidades de renombre como Princeton, las cuales tenían una posición doctrinal evangélica cuando fueron fundadas, habían abandonado sus raíces y abrazado las premisas antibíblicas de la alta crítica. Darby captó la atención y admiración de líderes como Dwight L. Moody (1837–1899), el evangelista que fundó el Instituto Bíblico Moody en 1886, y C. I. Scofield (1843–1921). Era lógico, entonces, que estas instituciones teológicas incluyeran el premilenialismo dispensacionalista en sus declaraciones de fe y que sus graduados promovieran esa posición en sus respectivos ministerios.

## Su hermenéutica

Tanto los premilenialistas históricos como los premilenialistas dispensacionalistas interpretan de forma literal los textos sobre el milenio a no ser que el texto indique lo contrario. Su hermenéutica admite el lenguaje figurado, los símbolos y otras formas de la comunicación figurativa. Lo que no admiten es que se espiritualice el texto bíblico. En contraste con la teoría de la recapitulación de los amilenialistas, creen que Apocalipsis describe los eventos futuros de una forma continuada. Creen que el siguiente bosquejo de los eventos que ocurren entre los capítulos 12 a 20 inclusive apoya esa posición. No hay ninguna

16. Ver *The Blessed Hope* (Grand Rapids: Eerdmans, 1966).
17. Ver *Teología sistemática* (Miami: Vida, 2009), pp. 1194–1198.
18. Ver *The Church and the Tribulation* (Grand Rapids: Zondervan, 1973).

indicación de que 19:21 describa el final de un ciclo ni de que 20:1 describa el comienzo de otro.

| | |
|---|---|
| 12 | Satanás es introducido. |
| 13 | Las bestias son introducidas. |
| 14–16 | El ministerio de los 144.000; la tierra sufre las siete plagas; las siete copas de la ira de Dios. |
| 17 | La ramera es introducida. |
| 18 | La ramera es juzgada. |
| 19 | El Señor desciende del cielo con sus ejércitos (vv. 11, 14).<br>La bestia, los reyes de la tierra y el falso profeta se disponen a luchar (vv. 18-19).<br>La bestia y el falso profeta son echados al lago de fuego (v. 20).<br>Todos son destruidos (v. 21). |
| 20 | Satanás es atado durante mil años (vv. 1-3).<br>Los santos reinan con Cristo mil años (v. 4) después de la primera resurrección (vv. 5-6).<br>Satanás es desatado al final del milenio y engaña a las naciones (vv. 7-8).<br>Satanás reúne a las naciones contra los santos en Jerusalén (v. 9).<br>Satanás y los suyos son derrotados (v. 9).<br>Satanás es echado al lago de fuego donde se encuentran la bestia y el falso profeta (v. 10).<br>El gran trono blanco (v. 11). |

## La atadura de Satanás

Los premilenialistas hacen tres observaciones en cuanto a la atadura de Satanás en Apocalipsis 20:2-3. Primera, es total y a la vez temporal. Satanás es atado por completo al principio del milenio, pero soltado al final del mismo. Al ser atado al principio del milenio, Cristo reinará sin oposición. Después, cuando es soltado, aprovecha su libertad para engañar a las naciones y entrar en batalla contra Dios. Si la atadura de Satanás ocurrió en la cruz, como cree el amilenialismo, en efecto significa que la obra de Cristo en la cruz fue parcial e incompleta porque Satanás sigue vivo y activo. Segunda, esa atadura sucede en el abismo, un lugar geográfico específico. El hecho de que Satanás esté tan activo en el mundo en este momento demuestra que no se encuentra en el abismo. Por muy poderoso que sea Satanás, no goza del atributo de omnipresencia. Tercera, el propósito de su atadura es evitar que engañe a las naciones. En este momento engaña a muchas personas (2 Co. 11:3-4, 13-15; 1 Jn. 2:18, 26), lo cual demuestra que su atadura es aún futura.

## Las dos resurrecciones

El premilenialismo cree que las dos resurrecciones de Apocalipsis 20:4-6 son físicas. Uno de los argumentos más contundentes para apoyar esta interpretación se encuentra en la frase «de los muertos» en Lucas 20:35 (NTV) y 1 Corintios 15:20-26. Aunque estos textos no tratan el tema del milenio, aportan algo importante a nuestra comprensión de las dos resurrecciones de Apocalipsis 20:4-6. Además, el uso de *edsesav*, traducido como «vivieron» en Apocalipsis 20:4 y «volvieron a vivir» en el v. 5, añade aún más peso al argumento de que las dos resurrecciones son físicas.

*Lucas 20:35.* Los saduceos rechazaban la doctrina de la resurrección. En su discusión con Jesús plantean el supuesto caso de un hombre que, en obediencia a la Ley, se casa con la viuda de sus siete hermanos que fallecieron uno tras otro sin tener hijos. Para mostrar lo ridícula que es la doctrina de la resurrección, preguntan: «En la resurrección, pues, ¿de cuál de ellos será mujer, ya que los siete la tuvieron por mujer?» (Lc. 20:33). Jesús responde que «los hijos de este siglo se casan, y se dan en casamiento; mas los que fueren tenidos por dignos de alcanzar aquel siglo y la resurrección de entre los muertos, ni se casan, ni se dan en casamiento» (vv. 34-35). Jesús dice que hay personas que resucitarán «de entre los muertos» por ser dignos de esa resurrección, indicando que habrá otros que se quedarán en el estado de la muerte. ¿Quiénes son? Tienen que ser no creyentes por no ser «dignos de alcanzar aquel siglo y la resurrección de entre los muertos».

Esta interpretación coincide con otros dos textos. Puesto que Daniel 12:1-2 dice que los no creyentes han de resucitar, tiene que haber una segunda resurrección física para aquellos que no fueron tenidos por dignos de alcanzar la primera resurrección. En Lucas 14:14 Jesús hizo referencia a «la resurrección de los justos», dando a entender que tiene que haber otra resurrección de los injustos. Estos dos textos añaden más peso a la interpretación de que tanto la primera como la segunda resurrección de Apocalipsis 20:4-5 son físicas.

*1 Corintios 15:20-26.* La palabra «orden» en este pasaje es un término militar y describe la resurrección como un desfile, cada uno resucitando a su debido tiempo y en su debido orden. Cristo resucitó primero «de entre los muertos» (v. 20, LBLA), «luego los que son de Cristo, en su venida» (v. 23). Aunque este pasaje no habla de los no creyentes, encaja con la posición premilenialista de que tiene que haber una resurrección para los no creyentes en otro momento. O sea, dos resurrecciones físicas.

*El uso de «edsesav» en Apocalipsis 20:4-5.* Cuando una palabra se emplea más de una vez en el mismo versículo o párrafo, por regla general su significado es el mismo a no ser que el autor indique de alguna forma que está empleándola en dos sentidos diferentes. Puesto que *edsesav* se emplea tanto con la primera como con la segunda resurrección en Apocalipsis 20:4-5, sin que el apóstol Juan use un adjetivo o adverbio para indicarnos que está hablando de dos resurrecciones diferentes en naturaleza, cualquier intento de hacer que la primera resurrección sea espiritual y la segunda física es arbitrario. Sería raro que una palabra se entendiera de dos formas completamente distintas en un mismo contexto y mucho menos en dos versículos seguidos. Además, las descripciones de las dos resurrecciones son paralelas, indicando que son físicas.

Es verdad que hay textos donde los conceptos de *vida, muerte, sepultura, resurrección* son empleados en un sentido figurativo (Ro. 6:4; Ef. 2;1, 6; Col. 2:12). Sin embargo, cuando el autor emplea las palabras «vida, muerte, resurrección» en un sentido espiritual, siempre indica en el contexto que ese es el significado que tiene en mente. Puesto que Juan no indica en Apocalipsis 20 que tiene dos clases diferentes de resurrección en mente, lo lógico es concluir que tanto la primera como la segunda resurrección son físicas. Si Apocalipsis 20:5 representa una resurrección física, el v. 4 también tiene que referirse a una resurrección física. De lo contrario, como afirma Ladd, «hemos perdido control de la exégesis». Por ese mismo motivo el erudito hebreo Henry Alford dice:

> Si en un pasaje donde se habla de *dos resurrecciones*, donde ciertas *almas vivieron* solamente al principio y los *demás muertos vivieron* solamente al final de un período específico después de esa primera resurrección —si en dicho pasaje la primera resurrección puede entenderse como un resucitar con Cristo de forma espiritual, mientras que la segunda significa una resurrección literal del sepulcro— entonces hemos llegado al final de todo significado en cuanto al lenguaje y las Escrituras pierden su valor como un testimonio concreto de cualquier cosa[19].

## El futuro de Israel

Los premilenialistas coicinden con los amilenialistas en que las bendiciones que Dios prometió a los judíos en el A.T. se cumplirán solamente en el Israel espiritual (Mt. 3:9; Ro. 2:28-29; 9:6-8) porque nadie recibirá esas bendiciones por el mero hecho de ser judío. Puesto que la Iglesia es identificada como el Israel espiritual (Gá. 3:7; 6:16; Flp. 3:3), las promesas hechas a Israel en el A.T. deben aplicarse a la iglesia. Sin embargo, los premilenialistas también creen que el pacto que Dios hizo con la nación de Israel incluía a todo el pueblo, no solamente a aquellos que eran verdaderos adoradores de Jehová. La promesa de un nuevo pacto (Jer. 31:31-33) incluía a los no creyentes precisamente por ser quienes habían roto el pacto antiguo. También creen que Romanos 9:1-5 indica que los judíos estaban incluidos en el pacto aunque rechazaran las bendiciones que ofrecía. Aunque los judíos sigan en su incredulidad, llegará un momento en que reconocerán a Cristo como su Mesías, la nación de Israel llegará a ser el Israel espiritual y los judíos entrarán en las bendiciones del nuevo pacto (Ez. 28:25; 37:15-24; Is. 2:3; Ro. 11:25-27). Por tanto, las promesas de Dios a los judíos en el A.T. sobre un futuro reino no se cumplen solamente en la iglesia, sino también en el pueblo judío.

19. Henry Alford, *The Greek New Testament* (Chicago: Moody Press, 1968), tomo IV, p. 732.

## La naturaleza del reino

Al Mesías se le prometió un reino eterno (Is. 9:6-7; Dn. 2:44; 7:13-14; Ap. 11:15). Por tanto, el reino de Dios tiene que ver con la eternidad. Pero hay profecías que identifican el reino también con la tierra. Dios prometió a Abraham que haría de sus descendientes un gran *pueblo*. Luego, Dios dio una *tierra* a ese pueblo y unas instrucciones en cuanto al comportamiento de los *reyes* de ese futuro reino. Un reino consiste en un pueblo, una tierra y un rey. Si faltara uno de estos elementos, los dos que quedan no pueden constituirse en un reino. Cristo es el *Rey*. Aunque su reino es eterno (Is. 9:6-7; Dn. 2:44; 7:13-14; Ap. 11:15), se vincula con la tierra. Dios le prometió a Abraham que haría de sus descendientes a ese pueblo. Pero los judíos perdieron la soberanía de su tierra y fueron deportados a otras tierras en las cautividades de 722–721 a. C. (Asiria) y 586 a. C. (Babilonia). Además, cuando rechazaron al Rey del reino en los tiempos de los Evangelios, Dios ofreció a los gentiles la posibilidad de formar parte del pueblo del reino de Dios. En 1948 la Organización de las Naciones Unidas reconoció al estado de Israel en Palestina. Cabe la posibilidad de que ese evento fuera el comiezo del cumplimiento de las promesas sobre la vuelta de los judíos a la tierra que Dios les había dado. En este momento el grupo gentil del pueblo del reino está presente en la iglesia, pero falta el elemento judío. Por eso, todavía ha de ocurrir un avivamiento espiritual en el cual los judíos reconozcan a Cristo como su Mesías. Además, sigue faltando el rey. El milenio de Apocalipsis 20:1-6 ocurrirá cuando los tres elementos estén presentes a la vez. Ese momento llegará con la segunda venida de Cristo (Ap. 2:25-27).

## Las fuerzas y debilidades del premilenialismo

Durante la mayor parte del siglo XX los premilenialistas mostraban más interés y escribían más libros sobre la profecía que los postmilenialistas y amilenialistas, en parte porque su hermenéutica literal les daba la esperanza de poder entender la profecía. Y mientras que todas las posiciones tienen problemas para hacer que todas las piezas del rompecabezas profético encajen, el premilenialismo cuenta con menos dificultades exegéticas.

No obstante, cuenta con ciertas debilidades. Primero, los premilenialistas dispensacionalistas tienen la tendencia de dar un sabor judío al milenio, hasta el punto de que Israel prácticamente desplaza a la iglesia como el objeto primordial de la obra de Cristo, anulando así pasajes como Efesios 1:20-23. Algunos sugieren que su tendencia a interpretar el N.T. a la luz del A.T. anula el concepto de la revelación progresiva y la norma de interpretar el A.T. desde la revelación completa del N.T. Aunque los premilenialistas dispensacionalistas han refinado considerablemente su posición desde que Berkhof hizo su crítica de ella hace muchos años, no se puede descartar por completo su observación. En referencia a las siete dispensaciones que los premilenialistas dispensacionalistas creen ver en las Escrituras, Berkhof dice:

> Este principio de interpretación dispensacionalista ha tenido un efecto deplorable sobre el entendimiento de la verdad revelada en la Biblia. Tiende a oscurecer y hasta minar la unidad de la revelación redentora en cuanto al pacto de la gracia, además de la unidad de la Biblia. Su aplicación engendra un estudio de toda la Biblia a trozos o a fragmentos. Anima a una búsqueda de una verdad histórica en lugar de la verdad absoluta. Por tanto, limita y peligra en términos generales el carácter normativo de la Biblia. Es un principio divisorio que lleva a distinciones no justificadas como por ejemplo entre un libro del reino y un libro de la iglesia, dos pueblos de Dios, Israel y la iglesia, dos evangelios, el reino de Dios y el reino del cielo, una segunda venida de Cristo en dos etapas, tres o cuatro resurrecciones de los muertos y tres juicios después de la segunda venida de Cristo[20].

Segundo, algunos observan que Apocalipsis 20 es el único pasaje que habla de un reino de mil años. Aunque el reino de Dios era el tema principal de las parábolas de Cristo y de su discurso profético en Mateo 24–25, él nunca habló de un reino de mil años. Y aunque Pablo habló del reino de Dios, nunca hizo mención de un reino terrenal ni de un reino de mil años. Mientras que estas observaciones son ciertas, el premilenialista argumenta que Jesús y Pablo querían subrayar elementos del reino que eran más importantes que la duración de su reino. Y puesto que Apocalipsis es tan inspirado como los demás libros de la Biblia, no

---

20. Louis Berkhof, *The Kingdom of God* (Grand Rapids: Eerdmans, 1951), p. 138.

hace falta que este detalle profético sea citado por Jesús o un apóstol para que sea verídico.

A pesar de estas debilidades de la posición premilenialista, el autor de *Con precisión* está convencido de que una interpretación histórico-gramático-cultural de las Escrituras inevitablemente lleva al intérprete al premilenialismo por representar la posición que cuenta con menos problemas exegéticos.

## *Trabajo para realizar*

Explique la teoría de la recapitulación que emplean algunos amilenialistas y cómo afecta su interpretación de la atadura de Satanás y las dos resurrecciones mencionadas en Apocalipsis 20. ¿Cuál es la premisa fundamental del postmilenialismo? La cantidad de material y detalles que se tiene que dominar para distinguir entre las cuatro posiciones milenialistas puede marear al principiante. Sin embargo, se puede resumir de la siguiente forma. Repase este cuadro antes de pasar al capítulo siguiente[21].

21. La idea de este cuadro (pp. 326–327) y los nombres de algunos de los partidarios de las cuatro posiciones milenialistas son del excelente libro de Paul N. Benware, *Entienda la profecía de los últimos tiempos* (Grand Rapids: Portavoz, 2010), p. 133.

| | Amilenialismo | Postmilenialismo | Premilenialismo histórico | Premilenialismo dispensacionalista |
|---|---|---|---|---|
| **Israel y la iglesia** | No hay ninguna distinción entre los dos. Por tanto, las promesas de Dios a Israel se cumplen en la iglesia. | La misma posición que el amilenialismo. | Aunque hay una distinción entre los dos, están íntimamente relacionados. | Hay una distinción marcada entre los dos. Representan dos planes distintos para la salvación del hombre. |
| **Milenio** | Se ha identificado con la iglesia visible, la eternidad, el corazón de los creyentes vivos y el estado de bendición de los creyentes en el cielo. La última opción predomina. | Cristo reina en el corazón de las personas que se convierten. Llegará el momento en que prácticamente todo el mundo será cristianizado. | Un período de mil años en la tierra a partir de la segunda venida de Cristo. | La misma posición que el premilenialismo histórico. |
| **Gran Tribulación** | Se refiere a los sufrimientos de los creyentes en la actualidad. | Se refiere a los sufrimientos de los judíos entre la crucifixión de Cristo y la destrucción de Jerusalén en el año 70. | Un período de tres años y medio de paz seguido por tres años y medio de persecución de los judíos a escala mundial. La iglesia estará presente durante la G.T. | Un período de tres años y medio de paz seguido por tres años y medio de persecución de los judíos a escala mundial. La iglesia no estará presente por haber sido arrebatada. |
| **Segunda venida de Cristo** | No la precede ningún evento escatológico. | Ocurre después del milenio, que tiene lugar en este momento. | Ocurre después de la Gran Tribulación e introduce el reino de Cristo de mil años. | La misma posición que el premilenialismo histórico. |

| | **Amilenialismo** | **Postmilenialismo** | **Premilenialismo histórico** | **Premilenialismo dispensacionalista** |
|---|---|---|---|---|
| **Arrebatamiento** | Los creyentes resucitan y son arrebatados con la segunda venida de Cristo. | La misma posición que el amilenialismo. | Los creyentes de todas las épocas resucitan y son arrebatados en la segunda venida de Cristo. | Los miembros vivos y fallecidos de la Iglesia son arrebatados antes del comienzo de la Gran Tribulación. |
| **Resurrección** | La resurrección de los creyentes y no creyentes ocurre a la vez que la segunda venida de Cristo. | La misma posición que el amilenialismo. | Los creyentes de todas las épocas resucitan en la segunda venida de Cristo y los no creyentes al final del milenio. | Los miembros de la iglesia resucitan con el arrebatamiento antes de la Gran Tribulación, los creyentes judíos de todos los siglos en la segunda venida y los no creyentes al final del milenio. |
| **Partidarios** | Agustín, Martín Lutero, Juan Calvino, Philipp Melanchthon, B. B. Warfield[1], John Gresham Machen, Louis Berkhof, Anthony Hoekema, G. C. Berkhouwer, etc. | William Shedd, Augustus Strong, Charles Hodge, A. A. Hodge, Loraine Boettner, J. Marcellus Kik, etc. | George E. Ladd, Millard J. Erikson, Robert H. Gundry, Wayne Grudem, etc. | John Nelson Darby, Louis S. Chafer, Dwight Pentecost, Charles Ryrie, John Walvoord, etc. |

1. Algunos reclaman a Warfield como un postmilenialista.

# Sección IV
# La aplicación de las Escrituras

La meta del estudio e interpretación de las Escrituras no es que una persona se haga experta en temas bíblicos, sino que se conforme a la imagen de Cristo. Sin la aplicación de las Escrituras, el intérprete se queda a mitad de camino.


24. Textos que contienen expresiones culturales

25. La aplicación personal

24

# Textos que contienen expresiones culturales

En los capítulos anteriores tratamos la naturaleza divina y humana de las Escrituras y las normas de la hermenéutica que permiten al intérprete descubrir lo que los autores bíblicos pretendían comunicar a sus lectores originales. Pero si el intérprete se para aquí, habrá llegado solamente hasta la mitad del camino. Mientras que la exégesis tiene como meta descubrir el significado de un texto, la aplicación procura identificar la relevancia e implicaciones de ese significado para la vida del creyente.

## A. HISTORIA DE LA APLICACIÓN

En las generaciones anteriores la aplicación que se hacía de las Escrituras se limitaba más bien a textos del N.T. y hacía énfasis en la necesidad de hacer la voluntad de Dios y de glorificarlo mediante una vida santa. Pero llegó el momento en que los evangélicos se dieron cuenta de la necesidad de aplicar también el A.T., puesto que Pablo afirma que las experiencias del pueblo de Dios en el A.T. fueron incluidas en las Escrituras para instruir al creyente del N.T. (Ro. 15:4; 1 Co. 10:6, 11). Al tratar las aproximadamente 600 leyes encontradas desde Éxodo 20 hasta Deuteronomio 33, se enfrentaron no solamente con una gran cantidad de información, sino también con textos que no entendían porque tenían un trasfondo cultural que ellos desconocían. Para organizar en un conjunto coherente esa gran cantidad de textos, además de identificar aquellos textos que tenían una aplicación para el creyente actual, los dividieron en cuatro categorías de leyes: ceremoniales, dietéticas, morales y civiles.

## Categorías de leyes

*Leyes ceremoniales.* De las cuatro categorías, las leyes ceremoniales eran el grupo más grande. Estas leyes tenían que ver con los sacerdotes, los sacrificios, el templo, las fiestas y los demás elementos relacionados con el culto a Dios. Todos los evangélicos estaban de acuerdo en que esas leyes habían sido anuladas por la obra de Cristo en la cruz. Los millones de corderos que habían sido sacrificados en tiempos del A.T., los cuales eran un tipo, fueron sustituidos por el Cordero de Dios, el antitipo. Y el sistema sacerdotal fue desplazado por los creyentes, quienes eran un «real sacerdocio» (1 P. 2:9). Ahora cada creyente tenía acceso directo a Dios a través de Cristo (1 Ti. 2:5). Este es el gran mensaje de la Epístola a los Hebreos. Por este motivo, las leyes ceremoniales eran las más fáciles de resolver en cuanto a su aplicación; a saber, no tienen una aplicación *directa* para el creyente, sino indirecta al ilustrar el deseo de Dios de que su pueblo sea santo y le adore.

*Leyes dietéticas.* Las leyes dietéticas encontradas en pasajes como Deuteronomio 14:3-22 provocaban muchas interpretaciones. ¿Qué es lo que Dios pretendía al prohibir el consumo de ciertos animales? Puesto que la carne de los animales y aves mencionados era difícil de conservar en el desierto del Sinaí, algunos sugirieron que Dios quería proteger a los judíos de intoxicación alimenticia. Otros opinaron que era posible que dichos animales fueran empleados en los ritos paganos de los cananeos, y para que los judíos no los imitaran Dios prohibió su consumo. Todas estas sugerencias son posibles, puesto que Moisés introduce su lista de animales en Deuteronomio 14:3-22 con la declaración de que Dios quería que Israel fuera una nación única y santa (vv. 1-2), el mismo énfasis que hace en Levítico 20:25-26. Cada vez que un judío comía, recordaba que tenía la responsabilidad de ser santo. En el N.T. Dios no emplea leyes dietéticas como señal de la santidad.

Por eso, todas esas leyes fueron anuladas y no tienen ninguna aplicación para el creyente hoy (Hch. 10:9-16).

*Leyes morales.* Las leyes morales se encuentran en los diez mandamientos y en todo el resto de leyes que son una aplicación de estos. Los evangélicos creen que las leyes morales se pueden aplicar a todo creyente en cualquier siglo y cultura porque reflejan el carácter de Dios. Por eso, nueve de los diez mandamientos son repetidos de alguna forma en el N.T. El único que no se repite es el del día de reposo. Pero hasta ese mandamiento es repetido en cierto modo. En el A.T. el día de reposo estaba dedicado al culto a Dios y al descanso del trabajo de los otros seis días en conmemoración del séptimo día de la creación en el cual Dios dejó de trabajar. Pero los apóstoles y la iglesia naciente adoraban a Dios el primer día de la semana en conmemoración de la resurrección de Cristo. Aunque el N.T. no dice que el domingo sirva para el descanso físico, esa necesidad sigue vigente. Puesto que las leyes morales del A.T. reflejan el carácter de Dios, son absolutas, permanentes, normativas y tienen una aplicación para todo creyente en todo siglo y cultura.

*Leyes civiles.* Israel era una nación y, por tanto, necesitaba leyes civiles para mantener el orden público y resolver los típicos problemas de cualquier sociedad. Técnicamente hablando, las leyes civiles eran aplicables solo a los ciudadanos de Israel. No obstante, hay un consenso en que el principio que hay detrás de las leyes civiles es aplicable al creyente de hoy. Por ejemplo, el propietario de un buey que hiriera a alguien tenía la responsabilidad de hacer restitución a la persona perjudicada (Éx. 21:28-36). Aunque pocos lectores son propietarios de un buey, entienden que el principio detrás de esa ley los obliga a mantener en condiciones los frenos de su coche o motocicleta porque son responsables de cualquier daño que algo suyo haga a otra persona.

Aunque el sistema de categorías era un buen primer paso para la aplicación de las leyes del A.T., se quedaba corto. Algunas leyes no encajaban en ninguna de las cuatro categorías, como el mandamiento de hacer «flecos en las cuatro puntas de tu manto con que te cubres» (Dt. 22:12) o el mandamiento que prohibía arar con un buey y un asno en el mismo yugo (Dt. 22:10). Además, algunos insistían en que, teológicamente hablando, todas las leyes del A.T. son morales porque proceden de Dios. Por tanto, insistían en que el A.T. no hace ninguna distinción entre leyes ceremoniales, dietéticas, morales y civiles.

## Sistema de principios para los dos Testamentos

A mediados del siglo pasado los evangélicos empezaron a usar casi exclusivamente el sistema de principios para resolver las lagunas que se producían con el sistema de categorías de leyes. No era un planteamiento nuevo, puesto que ya lo habían utilizado con aquellos mandamientos del A.T. que contenían una expresión cultural. Con el sistema de principios, el intérprete procuraba (1) identificar el propósito de un mandamiento, (2) identificar el principio detrás de ese propósito y (3) determinar si la expresión cultural de ese mandamiento es vigente para el creyente hoy. Para entender el proceso que el intérprete seguía con esas tres tareas, servirá de ilustración el mandamiento que prohibía a los judíos guisar un cabrito en la leche de su madre (Éx. 23:19; 34:26; Dt. 14:21).

Para identificar el *propósito* de un mandamiento, el intérprete tiene que conocer el trasfondo cultural del mismo. Igual que las leyes de cualquier sociedad, las leyes bíblicas tienen el propósito de promover algún bien, atender alguna necesidad o prevenir algún mal. Cuando una de esas leyes tiene poco sentido para el lector moderno, por regla general se debe a que desconoce el trasfondo cultural de la misma. Un entendimiento del trasfondo cultural es imprescindible para que el intérprete pueda descubrir el propósito detrás de un mandamiento. Evidentemente, el conocimiento que tenemos del trasfondo cultural de la Biblia nunca será completo debido a los miles de años que nos separan de los tiempos bíblicos. Pero es precisamente aquí donde los descubrimientos de los arqueólogos juegan un papel tan importante.

Durante muchos años el propósito detrás de la prohibición de guisar un cabrito en la leche de su madre era una incógnita. El intérprete entendía lo que el mandamiento decía, pero no el propósito detrás de él. Sin embargo, en la década de los años 50 del siglo pasado los arqueólogos descubrieron unas tablas que indicaban que esta forma de preparar un cabrito formaba parte de un rito pagano de los ciudadanos de Ugarit, una ciudad de Siria[1].

Ahora el intérprete podía identificar el propósito de ese mandamiento; a saber, que Dios no quería que su pueblo imitara los ritos de

---

1. Aunque esta ciudad quedaba al norte de la tierra prometida, los eruditos concluyen que esta práctica fue adoptada por los cananeos.

la religión pagana de los cananeos. El *principio* detrás de este propósito es que Dios quería que su pueblo fuera santo. Por tanto, cada judío tenía la responsabilidad de abstenerse de «toda especie» (RVR60) o "clase" (NTV, NVI) de mal, de cada «forma» (LBLA) de pecado (1 Ts. 5:22). Como Pablo exhortó a los romanos: «No permitáis que se hable mal de lo que para vosotros es bueno» (Ro. 14:16, LBLA). No existe ninguna duda en cuanto a la vigencia de este principio para el creyente del siglo XXI.

Pero queda el tercer paso de *determinar si la expresión cultural de ese mandamiento es vigente para el creyente hoy.* Puesto que no existe en ningún país del siglo XXI la práctica de guisar un cabrito en la leche de su madre como parte de un rito pagano (hasta donde sabe el autor de *Con precisión*), el intérprete no tiene ninguna responsabilidad al respecto. Sin embargo, hay otras expresiones culturales de textos bíblicos, tanto en el N.T. como en el A.T., que no quedan tan claras en cuanto a su vigencia se refiere. El ejemplo clásico es la referencia de Pablo a «los que se bautizan por los muertos» (1 Co. 15:29), una frase que ha provocado unas treinta interpretaciones diferentes[2].

En las últimas décadas, los estudios realizados sobre la vigencia de las expresiones culturales se han centrado sobre textos encontrados en el N.T. Aunque han pasado dos mil años desde que fueron escritos, sus expresiones culturales no son tan antiguas, raras, ni tan imposibles de llevar a cabo como las del A.T. Además, el N.T. representa la última y máxima revelación de Dios al ser humano. Por tanto, interpretan los textos del N.T. que contienen una expresión cultural bajo la premisa de que tienen una aplicación más directa para el creyente que los del A.T.

La dificultad de determinar si una expresión es cultural en algunos textos del N.T. se debe, en algunos casos, al desconocimiento del trasfondo cultural de dichos textos. En otros casos se debe a una simple diferencia de interpretación por parte de los evangélicos, como se notará en algunos de los ejemplos a continuación. Todos los evangélicos aceptan como legítimas las primeras dos opciones de retener el principio y la expresión cultural de un texto bíblico, o retener el principio pero sustituir su expresión cultural. Pero existe mucho debate

2. Ver Haddon Robinson, «The Heresy of Application» en *Leadership* (otoño 1997), p. 23.

en cuanto a la tercera opción de descartar tanto el principio como la expresión cultural.

*1. Retener el principio y su expresión cultural.* El lavamiento de pies (Jn. 13:1-20) es el ejemplo clásico. En el primer siglo la mayoría de las calles de Palestina eran caminos de barro. La Pascua se celebraba en la época de lluvia. Así que las calles eran unos verdaderos lagos de barro y lodo. Para complicar aún más la situación, hacía un calor intenso en muchas partes de Palestina. Y puesto que todos se calzaban con sandalias, era inevitable que una persona llegara a su destino con los pies sudados, sucios y malolientes. Si la persona en cuestión volvía a su propia casa o llegaba a casa de alguien con pocos recursos, se quitaba las sandalias y se lavaba él mismo los pies. Pero si la casa era de alguien de cierta afluencia, le tocaba realizar esa labor tan desagradable a un esclavo o al siervo de menos estatus de la casa. Luego su anfitrión le daba un beso de bienvenida y lo ungía con aceite. Así que al asir una toalla y lavar los pies de sus discípulos, Jesús tomó el lugar de un esclavo o siervo. Al final de ese acto dijo a sus discípulos: «Pues si yo, el Señor y el Maestro, he lavado vuestros pies, vosotros también debéis lavaros los pies los unos a los otros» (Jn. 13:14).

El principio que hay detrás de este mandamiento es que cada creyente debe servir a sus hermanos hasta en sus necesidades más desagradables. Pero ¿debe el creyente del siglo XXI repetir la expresión cultural de este principio? Algunas denominaciones evangélicas practican el lavamiento de pies porque lo consideran una tercera ordenanza. Sin embargo, la mayoría de los evangélicos no comparten esa interpretación. Primero, porque en el primer siglo el lavamiento de pies atendía a una necesidad que no existe en el siglo XXI. Hoy en día una persona suele llegar aseada a cualquier lugar. Por tanto, tendría poco sentido lavarle los pies. Segundo, porque el lavamiento de pies no se repite en ningún otro texto del N.T., cosa que se esperaría de algo tan importante como una ordenanza. Por el contrario, las ordenanzas del bautismo y la Cena del Señor son repetidas en otros textos, y existe una evidencia amplia de que la iglesia naciente celebraba estas dos ordenanzas. Por lo que es muy sabio el consejo de Carson sobre aquellas expresiones culturales que son mencionadas solamente una vez en el N.T.

> Hemos de ser prudentes en cuanto a dar por absoluto lo que se dice o se ordena una sola vez. La razón no es que Dios tenga que decir

> las cosas más de una vez para que sean verídicas u obligatorias. La razón, más bien, es que lo que se dice únicamente una vez es fácilmente malinterpretado o se le da una aplicación errónea. Cuando algo se repite en varias ocasiones y en contextos ligeramente diferentes, los lectores disfrutarán de una mejor comprensión de lo que significa y lo que está en juego[3].

El hecho de que una sociedad considere una expresión cultural que aparece en la Biblia como una práctica extraña no es un criterio aceptable para descartarla, siempre y cuando esté claramente ordenada en las Escrituras. Es un gran error obligar a la Biblia a conformarse a lo que la sociedad moderna está dispuesta a aceptar. Los creyentes están llamados a actuar como sal de la tierra y agentes de cambio en sus respectivas sociedades para que estas se conformen a las Escrituras, no al revés. Así que cuando el intérprete ha de decidir si una expresión cultural del N.T. debe ser sustituida por otra más comprensible en su propia cultura, «el criterio [...] *no* debe ser si se conforma a las prácticas culturales modernas, sino si se expresa adecuada y exactamente el principio intencional dado por Dios»[4].

*2. Retener el principio pero sustituir su expresión cultural.* La Biblia no promueve ninguna cultura en particular porque los elementos básicos de cualquier cultura —los idiomas, las costumbres, etcétera— son amorales en sí. Además, muchas expresiones culturales no son transferibles de un país a otro en un mismo año, y mucho menos cuando hay muchos siglos por medio. Puede que una expresión en un país en el año presente no signifique nada en otro. Pero también existe la posibilidad de que signifique algo totalmente diferente y hasta escandaloso. Por tanto, sería aún más difícil importar al siglo XXI una expresión cultural del primer siglo. En estos casos el intérprete debe sustituir la expresión cultural bíblica por una que comunique mejor en su cultura el principio que hay detrás de esa expresión cultural[5].

---

3. Donald A. Carson, «¿Debo aprender a interpretar la Biblia?» en *Idea* (septiembre-diciembre 2008), p. 9.

4. Henry A. Virkler, *Hermenéutica: principios y procedimientos de interpretación bíblica* (Miami: Editorial Vida, 1994), p. 193.

5. A veces, el intérprete tiene que enfrentarse con lo que las leyes de su país permiten. La Ley del A.T. exigía que las personas que cometían incesto fueran

El ejemplo clásico de una expresión cultural que ha de ser sustituida es el «ósculo» con el cual las personas se saludaban en los países mediterráneos del primer siglo. El verdadero amor se expresa de forma física, sea entre padres e hijos, entre cónyuges y hasta entre los hermanos en la fe. No obstante, hay diferentes clases de besos. Por eso, en las cuatro ocasiones que Pablo exhorta a sus lectores a saludarse con un beso (Ro. 16:16; 1 Co. 16:20; 2 Co. 13:12; 1 Ts. 5:26), insiste en que sea un beso «santo». Por otro lado, Pedro hace énfasis en que tiene que ser un «ósculo de amor», una expresión de cariño sincero (1 P. 5:14). ¿Es transferible a otras culturas esta expresión tan típica de la cultura mediterránea? Aunque era totalmente aceptable y entendida en tiempos bíblicos, podría ser una cosa muy cuestionable según el país.

Hay otras expresiones culturales en el N.T. que no existen en el siglo XXI, pero el principio que hay detrás queda muy claro. Por ejemplo, en el primer siglo las carnicerías de Corinto vendían carne relacionada con los sacrificios a los ídolos[6]. Algunos creyentes querían comprar esa carne, quizás por ser de una calidad mejor o quizás porque costaba menos. Pero debido a su asociación con un rito pagano, querían saber si era lícito comprarla. Pablo les contestó que era lícito siempre y cuando su libertad de comprarla no fuera un «tropiezo para los débiles» que todavía no veían muy claro el asunto (1 Co. 8:9, NVI). Aunque el creyente del siglo XXI no encontrará ninguna carnicería que venda carne procedente de los sacrificios a los ídolos, tiene la responsabilidad de practicar el principio de no permitir que su libertad de participar en ciertas actividades legítimas anime a otro creyente a hacer lo mismo cuando aún sigue con dudas al respecto (1 Co. 8:9-13)[7].

---

apedreadas hasta la muerte (Lv. 20:11; ver también 18:7). Puesto que no se permitía esa clase de castigo en el Imperio romano, Pablo mandó a los corintios que excomulgaran de la iglesia a la madre y su hijo que cometían ese pecado (1 Co. 5:1-5).

6. No está claro si dicha carne sobraba al final del día o si ya se había ofrecido a los ídolos y se podía vender.

7. Este texto no tiene nada que ver con el legalista que prohíbe que otros participen en ciertas actividades en base a una aplicación extrema de un principio bíblico. El legalista no puede considerarse un hermano débil porque jamás haría lo que condena tan vehementemente. Su problema consiste en que encuentra cierta satisfacción en ofenderse por el comportamiento de otros creyentes. En muchos casos esta reacción es una forma de controlar a los demás y sentirse superior a ellos.

*3. Descartar tanto el principio como la expresión cultural.* A finales del siglo XIX nació el movimiento feminista con la meta de conseguir para la mujer el derecho a votar. Con el tiempo ese movimiento amplió sus metas al ámbito social y económico. Como muchos movimientos seculares que surgen para rectificar una injusticia de la sociedad, el movimiento feminista tenía metas nobles y más que justificadas. Pero sobre la marcha adoptó ciertas filosofías y metas antibíblicas. A mediados del siglo XX algunas de las implicaciones de ese movimiento comenzaban a notarse en las iglesias. Algunos que tenían un concepto bajo de la inspiración de las Escrituras acusaban a los que creían que la mujer debía someterse a su marido[8] de ser machistas y de reflejar el ambiente represor de la mujer que reinaba en el primer siglo.

Los evangélicos creen que la mujer fue creada igualmente a la imagen de Dios y que, por tanto, es igual en valor al hombre. No obstante, no existe un consenso sobre el papel y la autoridad de la mujer en la iglesia y el matrimonio. Algunos interpretan a partir de ciertos textos que Dios dio al varón la responsabilidad (no el derecho) de servir como la cabeza de su familia y que el varón debe desempeñar los principales puestos de liderazgo en la iglesia. Otros evangélicos que creen igualmente en la inspiración plena, verbal e inerrante de las Escrituras, interpretan esos mismos textos de otra forma. Por ejemplo, algunos argumentan que Pablo y Pedro no estaban en posición de cambiar la cultura que existía en el primer siglo con respecto a la mujer, aunque no estuviesen de acuerdo con ella. No era común que una mujer tuviera una responsabilidad principal en las sociedades de los países mediterráneos del primer siglo, ni que fuera la cabeza de su matrimonio, aunque ejerciera liderazgo en muchas áreas de su casa. Por tanto, los apóstoles adoptaron una posición pragmática para no crear escándalo y perjudicar el testimonio de los creyentes y las iglesias, y por ello mandaron a las esposas a someterse a sus maridos y nombraron a varones para ocupar los principales puestos de liderazgo en las iglesias. Pero estos evangélicos argumentan que la situación cultural del primer siglo no tiene ningún paralelo en muchos países del siglo XXI. Además, los creyentes están llamados a ser sal de la tierra y a desafiar y cambiar los

---

8. Una interpretación basada en textos como Efesios 5:22-33; Colosenses 3:18; Tito 2:4-5; 1 Pedro 3:1-2.

abusos que existen en sus respectivas sociedades. Por tanto, creen que la sumisión de la mujer en el matrimonio debe descartarse y que una mujer debe tener el derecho a ocupar cualquier posición de liderazgo en la iglesia. Como consecuencia, el tema del papel y la autoridad de la mujer en el matrimonio y en la iglesia se ha convertido en uno de los temas más debatidos en el momento actual.

Una vez más los eruditos bíblicos se encontraban con un sistema que hacía una buena aportación hasta donde llegaba, pero que se quedaba corto. Les faltaban criterios para determinar cuándo el principio subyacente a un mandamiento que tenía una expresión cultural debía retenerse y cuándo debía descartarse.

## B. CRITERIOS PARA IDENTIFICAR LO QUE ES NORMATIVO

En la búsqueda de unos criterios para determinar cuándo el principio detrás de un mandamiento que tenía una expresión cultural debía retenerse y cuándo debía descartarse, se inventó la palabra «contextualización». Originalmente, esta palabra se refería al acto de identificar y aceptar como vigente el principio que hay detrás de un mandamiento que tiene una expresión cultural, y entonces buscar la expresión cultural que mejor corresponda en el país del intérprete a esa expresión cultural del primer siglo. Aunque «contextualización» era una palabra nueva, el concepto que comunicaba era antiguo, puesto que a lo largo de la historia grandes exégetas de las Escrituras habían luchado con ese tema. Pero los teólogos liberales dieron otro significado a esa palabra. Por considerar el texto bíblico un reflejo de las costumbres, actitudes y formas de pensar anticuadas y pasadas de moda de los autores y pueblos mencionados en la Biblia, creían que era necesario actualizar el texto bíblico; o sea, «contextualizarlo» para que encajara con la forma de pensar del hombre moderno. En efecto, creían que el significado de un texto bíblico no se encuentra en la mente del autor bíblico, sino en lo que la sociedad moderna dicta. Por tanto, para ellos la Biblia no es la autoridad final en cuanto a lo que debemos creer; todo es relativo; no existe una teología que sirva para todas las personas, culturas y siglos.

La teología de la liberación es un ejemplo de la contextualización mal entendida. Los teólogos de la liberación «argumentan que el clima de opresión económica y depravación controla el proceso de la contextualización. Por tanto, el "pecado" es definido como la injusticia social y la "salvación" se convierte en la liberación de los pobres»[9]. En efecto, deciden de antemano lo que el texto bíblico tiene que significar y luego buscan textos que, en su opinión, apoyan la causa que quieren promocionar. El significado del texto bíblico no es determinado por los autores bíblicos, sino por el contexto contemporáneo y los eventos revolucionarios, los cuales se convierten en la «palabra de Dios». Para ellos «la Biblia es un mero ejemplo histórico de la forma en que Dios obró en un momento y lugar de la historia. La revelación de su voluntad proviene de los eventos que él está moldeando en el mundo hoy. Con este acercamiento de hacer que la Biblia sea culturalmente relevante, queda claro que la Biblia no es considerada como la autoridad final»[10].

Debido a abusos como este, que se han cometido en nombre de la «contextualización», algunos evangélicos tienden a evitar el uso de la contextualización bien entendida. Sin embargo, muchos de los textos problemáticos o difíciles de entender se resuelven una vez que el intérprete comprende el trasfondo cultural de los mismos. Por tanto, no es una cuestión de si *debemos* o no contextualizar dichos textos, sino de *cómo* hacerlo. Los evangélicos han establecido cinco criterios para identificar aquellos mandamientos y expresiones culturales que son absolutos, permanentes y normativos, y que tienen una aplicación para todo creyente en cualquier siglo y cultura, y los que no[11].

## Una similitud significativa entre los lectores originales y el creyente del siglo actual

De los cinco criterios, este es el más básico y fundamental. Tiene que haber una similitud entre la situación del lector original y la del

9. Grant R. Osborne, *The Hermeneutical Spiral* (Downers Grove: InterVarsity Press, 1991), p. 319.

10. J. Robertson McQuilken, «Problems of Normativeness in Scripture: Cultural Versus Permanent» en *Hermeneutics, Inerrancy, and the Bible* (Grand Rapids: Zondervan, 1984), pp. 222–223.

11. En esta sección el autor sigue el planteamiento de William J. Larkin, *Culture and Biblical Hermeneutics* (Grand Rapids: Baker, 1988), pp. 104–113.

creyente de hoy que sea significativa e importante. No puede ser un mero detalle. El mandamiento de Dios a Adán y Eva en Génesis 1:28 («Fructificad y multiplicaos; llenad la tierra...») es un ejemplo fácil de entender. Aunque este texto no conlleva ninguna expresión cultural, el mandamiento es claro. Pero ¿quiere decir que todos los matrimonios en el siglo XXI deben tener todos los hijos que puedan? Muchos evangélicos dirían que no porque no existe una similitud significativa. Adán y Eva eran los únicos seres humanos en toda la tierra. En muchos lugares del siglo XXI no hay comida suficiente porque la tierra no produce alimentos suficientes para todos, hay una mala distribución de la comida disponible o los oficiales gubernamentales son corruptos y roban lo que hay para su propio consumo e interés. Hasta en los países más desarrollados del mundo un matrimonio debe preguntarse si un hijo adicional perjudicará sus propios recursos para atender a las necesidades espirituales, económicas y educativas de los hijos que ya tienen. Además, ¿tendrán los fondos necesarios para alquilar o comprar una casa más grande para acomodar a un hijo más? A la luz de todas estas circunstancias, no sería legítimo aplicar Génesis 1:28 a los matrimonios del siglo XXI.

## La intención del autor

Las Epístolas del N.T. son documentos ocasionales en el sentido de que sus autores respondían a una situación, circunstancia, pregunta o necesidad de los lectores originales. Por tanto, antes de comenzar la exégesis de una epístola, el intérprete debe identificar la situación que motiva al autor a escribir su epístola. Si se trata de una cuestión local, algo que era peculiar y solamente de interés para la iglesia o persona que recibía esa epístola, entonces es probable que no tenga una aplicación para todos los creyentes de todas las culturas y siglos.

Pero se podría plantear este criterio desde el polo opuesto. ¿Por qué los autores bíblicos *no* trataron ciertos temas? Por ejemplo, ¿por qué no condenaron abierta y explícitamente la esclavitud? La esclavitud ha existido desde los tiempos más antiguos. En algunos casos los esclavos eran maltratados, como en el caso de los judíos en Egipto (Éx. 1:8-25). No obstante, cuando Israel se convirtió en estado retuvo la práctica de la esclavitud, aunque la Ley eliminó los aspectos más abusivos y denigrantes de ella[12]. Pero nadie que viva hoy día en un país con cierto trasfondo judeo-cristiano acepta la esclavitud. En 1 Timoteo 1:10 Pablo dice que la Ley condena a los «secuestradores» (RVR60, LBLA), o sea, «los traficantes de esclavos» (NVI, NTV). Pero los autores bíblicos dicen poco más. ¿Por qué?

Muchos eruditos creen que se debía a una decisión pragmática de los apóstoles. En tiempos del N.T. los creyentes eran pocos, estaban perseguidos y no tenían ningún poder ni influencia política. Además, la esclavitud era un mal tan arraigado en la cultura que habría requerido un levantamiento del pueblo, seguramente a precio de sangre, para erradicarla. ¿Qué sentido habría tenido dedicar los pocos esfuerzos e influencia que tenían en una batalla imposible de ganar? Además, el mandamiento de Jesús de ir a todo el mundo y predicar el evangelio representaba una clara prioridad. Los apóstoles no eran unos idealistas que estaban dispuestos a morir por un problema que no podían solucionar en aquel momento de la historia. Por tanto, eligieron ser pragmáticos y ganar cualquier batalla que pudieran. No es que aprobaran la esclavitud, sino que simplemente no tenían otra opción. Así que hacían lo que podían en aquellas circunstancias. Por ejemplo, Pablo afirmó que «ya no hay judío ni griego; no hay esclavo ni libre; no hay varón ni mujer; porque todos vosotros sois uno en Cristo Jesús» (Gá. 3:28), procurando eliminar así cualquier discriminación que existiera entre los creyentes. Esa era una batalla que los creyentes podían

---

12. Por ejemplo, exigía que los esclavos fueran tratados con dignidad como personas creadas a la imagen de Dios. La mayoría de los esclavos en Israel eran ciudadanos que se vendían a sí mismos como pago de una deuda (Lv. 25:39-42). No obstante, la Ley decía que «si se vendiere a ti tu hermano hebreo o hebrea, y te hubiere servido seis años, al séptimo le despedirás libre» (Dt. 15:12). Pero si quería, el esclavo podía quedarse como tal (15:16-17), porque en realidad era más bien un siervo con ciertos derechos. En tiempos del N.T. la esclavitud en el Imperio romano era similar a la de Israel en siglos anteriores. Aunque algunos esclavos eran el botín de las guerras ganadas, un ciudadano libre se convertía en esclavo por malhechor o como pago por sus deudas o las de su familia. Además, existía la figura del «cliente»: un hombre libre, cuya situación económica no era prometedora, que se ponía voluntariamente bajo la protección de un señor que lo proveía de comida y dinero a cambio de su lealtad y su voto. Igual que la ley de Moisés, la ley romana exigía que los esclavos fueran tratados de forma digna. Por eso, al andar por las calles de cualquier ciudad romana, era imposible distinguir entre un esclavo y un hombre libre de escasos recursos.

ganar. En cuanto al trabajo de los esclavos, los exhortó a obedecer a sus amos y a trabajar de forma responsable, recordando que su verdadero amo era el Señor (Ef. 6:5-8).

Aunque muchos creyentes del siglo XXI no tienen que enfrentarse directamente con la esclavitud, detrás de las exhortaciones de los autores bíblicos se encuentran unos principios que tienen una aplicación hoy. Por ejemplo, no debería haber ninguna discriminación ni menosprecio por parte del creyente hacia otras personas —sean creyentes o no— con base en su sexo, raza o país de origen.

## La confirmación de otros textos bíblicos

Este criterio se basa en la premisa de que el Espíritu Santo supervisó a los autores bíblicos de tal forma que no cometieron ningún error cuando pusieron por escrito las verdades espirituales que habían recibido de Dios por revelación especial. Por tanto, un texto no puede contradecir a otro texto. Los reformadores del siglo XVI hicieron mucho énfasis en este criterio, llamándolo *analogia scriptura*. Un mandamiento puede ser confirmado por otros textos bíblicos de cuatro maneras. (1) Cuando es repetido por otros textos bíblicos, indicando así que es normativo y autoritativo para todo creyente en todo siglo y cultura. (2) Cuando está de acuerdo con la enseñanza general de las Escrituras o su contenido específico está en armonía con otros textos que tratan el mismo tema. (3) Cuando un autor lo relaciona con los propósitos y la enseñanza del mismo libro en que dicho mandamiento aparece o con la enseñanza que ese autor incluye en otros libros suyos. (4) Cuando una revelación posterior (en el proceso de la revelación progresiva) no lo limite, modifique o anule.

## La naturaleza del contenido de un texto

Este criterio procura determinar si el contenido de un texto es intrínsecamente moral o amoral. Un *mandamiento* es moral por cuanto refleja la naturaleza de Dios o alguno de sus atributos. Por ese motivo un mandamiento es absoluto, permanente, normativo y aplicable a cualquier creyente en cualquier época y cultura. Un mandamiento no suele tener una expresión cultural. Por el contrario, lo que vamos a llamar una *directriz* es un texto cuyo contenido es amoral. Por ejemplo, 1 Corintios 11:5-6 dice que la mujer que profetiza debe cubrir su cabeza. La gran mayoría de los evangélicos creen que este texto no tiene que ver con una cuestión moral. Por tanto, lo que Pablo dice es una directriz que no es aplicable a las mujeres del siglo XXI, aunque el principio que hay detrás sí lo es. Las mujeres en Corinto tenían que obedecer esta directriz igual que cualquier mandamiento porque esta expresión cultural tenía sentido en la cultura del primer siglo.

## La base sobre la cual el autor fundamenta su mandamiento

Cuando los autores bíblicos explican una enseñanza o mandamiento, frecuentemente apelan a una de estas dos cosas. Primero, la naturaleza de Dios o algún atributo suyo. Puesto que la naturaleza y atributos de Dios son inmutables, cualquier mandamiento basado en ellos es aplicable a cualquier creyente en cualquier siglo y cultura. Segundo, las leyes, pautas y parámetros que Dios puso en marcha cuando creó al ser humano. Cuando el ser humano respeta esas leyes, su vida prospera; cuando las desobedece, ocurre lo contrario.

| **Criterios para identificar lo que es normativo** |
|---|
| 1. Una similitud significativa entre los lectores originales y el creyente del siglo actual.<br>2. La intención del autor.<br>3. La confirmación de otros textos bíblicos.<br>4. La naturaleza del contenido de un texto.<br>5. La base sobre la cual el autor fundamenta su mandamiento. |

Un día los fariseos preguntaron a Jesús si era lícito divorciarse «por cualquier causa» (Mt. 19:3) en referencia a Deuteronomio 24:1-4, uno de los pasajes más importantes sobre el divorcio en el A.T. Unas décadas antes el famoso rabino Hilel (c. 70 a. C.–10 d. C.) interpretó la frase «alguna cosa indecente» (v. 1) como «cualquier cosa». O sea, un hombre podía divorciarse de su esposa por el motivo que fuera. Pero el rabino Shamai (50 a. C.–30 d. C.) discrepaba con esa interpretación, insistiendo en que una «cosa indecente» se refería al adulterio. Lógicamente, el pueblo prefirió la interpretación de Hilel porque era más conveniente. Con el tiempo la frase «divorcio por cualquier causa» llegó a ser un término legal. Con esta interpretación en la mano, los judíos del primer siglo habían llegado hasta el extremo de divorciarse de sus esposas por quemar la cena. Cuando Jesús comenzó su ministerio, el «divorcio por cualquier causa» era la norma.

Antes de contestar la pregunta de los fariseos, Jesús hace referencia a tres pautas que Dios estableció cuando creó al ser humano. Primero, el matrimonio es la unión entre un hombre y una mujer, no entre dos personas del mismo sexo. Refiriéndose a Génesis 1:27 Jesús les pregunta: «¿No habéis leído que el que los hizo al principio, varón y hembra los hizo?» (Mt. 19:4). Este texto deshace el argumento de que Jesús nunca condenó la homosexualidad. Segundo, desde la creación el plan divino ha sido que el hombre tuviera un matrimonio monógamo. Todo acto sexual fuera del matrimonio es pecado. En el v. 5, Jesús apela una vez más al orden que Dios puso en marcha en la creación del hombre al citar Génesis 2:24: «Por tanto, dejará el hombre a su padre y a su madre, y se unirá a su mujer, y serán una sola carne». En 1 Corintios 6:16 Pablo identifica la frase «y serán una sola carne» como el acto sexual. Tercero, cuando Dios creó la institución del matrimonio, el divorcio no formaba parte de su plan. Por tanto, «lo que Dios juntó, no lo separe el hombre» (Mt. 19:6)[13]. Al apelar al orden que Dios estableció cuando creó al ser humano, estas tres verdades son absolutas, permanentes, normativas y aplicables a todo ser humano en todo siglo y cultura.

Entonces, Jesús contesta la pregunta de los fariseos afirmando que «alguna cosa indecente» (Dt. 24:1) no se refiere a cualquier causa, sino a la fornicación (Mt. 19:9). En el N.T. la palabra «fornicación» tiene dos significados. En su sentido estricto, se refiere al acto sexual por parte de una persona no casada. En su sentido más amplio, se refiere a un abanico de pecados sexuales, ya sean cometidos por un soltero o por una persona casada. Puesto que Deuteronomio 24 habla de una mujer casada que hace «alguna cosa indecente», Jesús interpreta esa frase para referirse al adulterio o cualquier otra perversión del acto sexual que una persona casada comete[14].

---

13. En este versículo Cristo está enseñando que Dios creó la institución del matrimonio, no que Dios casa a los cónyuges. Para una discusión de quién casa a los cónyuges ver el libro de Jaime Fasold, *Tu media naranja* (Grand Rapids: Portavoz, 1998), pp. 20–22.

14. Éxodo 21:7 describe cómo un padre vende a su hija como sierva. Luego, el v. 9 establece la forma en que esa hija debe ser tratada si el hijo del amo la toma como esposa. Como suele ocurrir en estos casos el marido favorece a la segunda esposa a expensas de la primera. Por eso, los vv. 10-11 hablan de la responsabilidad que

## *Trabajo para realizar*

1. Explique en sus propias palabras los cinco criterios que los evangélicos han establecido para determinar cuándo se debe retener, sustituir o descartar la expresión cultural de un texto o el principio que hay detrás de dicho texto.
2. Con base en los cinco criterios que los evangélicos han establecido para determinar cuándo es lícito retener, sustituir o descartar la expresión cultural de un texto o el principio que hay detrás, ellos afirman que los textos pertinentes a la homosexualidad no son una cuestión cultural, sino una clara condenación de los actos homosexuales. Lea «La contextualización y la homosexualidad» en el Apéndice H.

---

tiene el marido de proveer para su primera esposa alimento, ropa y «el deber conyugal», una frase que todos entienden como el acto sexual. Puesto que en muchos casos un abrazo significa más para una esposa que el acto sexual, algunos incluyen el afecto y el cariño en la frase «el deber conyugal». Aunque la primera esposa era una sierva que se convirtió en la esposa del hijo del amo, tiene el derecho a divorciarse de su marido si no la provee de alimento, ropa y el deber conyugal. Por tanto, pedir el divorcio no es un derecho exclusivo del marido como lo era en tiempos de Jesús. Mientras que Éxodo 21:10 identifica de forma clara tres causas legítimas para el divorcio (aparte del adulterio de Dt. 24:1), la aplicación de esas causas no es tan clara. Por ejemplo, ¿cuánta comida y de qué clase? ¿Cuánta ropa y de qué marca? ¿Y con qué frecuencia deberían celebrar los cónyuges el acto sexual? Los rabinos discutían estas preguntas. Aunque nos reímos de algunas de sus respuestas y rechazamos su legalismo en algunos casos, el hecho es que hicieron bien en intentar aplicar el principio de este texto a la vida diaria. De lo contrario, el principio queda como mera teoría. De la misma forma, si una esposa tiene derecho a divorciarse de su marido por no cumplir con estas tres obligaciones, ¿no tendrá también el marido derecho a divorciarse de ella si no cumple con sus responsabilidades dentro del matrimonio? Lo que queda claro es que los *dos* cónyuges tienen responsabilidades matrimoniales.

# 25

# La aplicación personal

Al comenzar este último capítulo de *Con precisión* conviene repasar lo que hemos visto hasta este punto. En la Sección I afirmamos que la interpretación de cualquier libro depende de su naturaleza. Y puesto que la Biblia es de origen y naturaleza divina, hacen falta normas espirituales para interpretarla correctamente y con precisión. Para que el no creyente entienda y acepte las verdades bíblicas como verídicas y se convierta a Cristo, tiene que ser humilde, tener el deseo de conocer la verdad y obedecerla y recibir la iluminación del Espíritu Santo. Después de convertirse, el Espíritu Santo lo seguirá iluminando para que vea y entienda otras verdades bíblicas que no podía entender antes de su conversión (1 Co. 2:6-16).

En la Sección II vimos que la Biblia también es un libro humano porque fue escrita por hombres que emplearon su propio vocabulario para comunicar las verdades que habían recibido por revelación especial de Dios. Y para asegurar que expresaran con precisión la revelación que habían recibido, el Espíritu Santo los supervisó en las palabras que emplearon. Puesto que la Biblia es también un libro humano, hacen falta leyes humanas para interpretarla correctamente y con precisión. Afirmamos que el método histórico-gramático-cultural es el método de interpretación que más consistentemente permite al intérprete identificar el significado de un texto bíblico. Seguidamente, tratamos las leyes que tradicionalmente han llevado el nombre de hermenéutica general.

En la Sección III repasamos los principios y normas requeridos para interpretar las formas especiales de la comunicación humana. Esta sección incluye también los tipos y la profecía, dos géneros literarios que se encuentran exclusivamente en la Biblia por cuanto solo Dios puede ver y controlar el futuro. Hasta aquí el autor de *Con precisión* ha subrayado los principios y normas requeridos para interpretar «con precisión» (2 Ti. 2:15, LBLA) la Palabra de Dios.

La Sección IV trata el tema de la aplicación de las Escrituras. En el primer capítulo de esta sección vimos cómo tratar los textos que contienen una expresión cultural. En este segundo capítulo planteamos una pregunta muy importante: ¿cuál es la finalidad, la meta, el propósito de interpretar correctamente y con precisión las Escrituras? ¿Es el mero hecho de conocer lo que la Biblia dice? Si el intérprete se detiene en este paso, habrá llegado solamente a la mitad del camino, porque las Escrituras se nos han dado «para enseñar, para reprender, para corregir, para instruir en justicia, a fin de que el hombre de Dios sea perfecto, equipado para toda buena obra» (2 Ti. 3:16-17, LBLA). O sea, una interpretación correcta de las Escrituras tiene como propósito hacer que el intérprete se parezca cada día más a Cristo.

> «No solo escuchen la palabra de Dios; tienen que ponerla en práctica. De lo contrario, solamente se engañan a sí mismos».
>
> **(Stg. 1:22, NTV)**

En el capítulo anterior se han subrayado las normas que el intérprete ha de utilizar para interpretar y aplicar a su vida aquellos textos que están adornados con una expresión cultural. Ese paso de la aplicación personal de las Escrituras es más bien técnico por naturaleza. Pero hace falta también una aplicación personal que toque el corazón, las emociones y la voluntad, sin dejar de usar el intelecto.

En las generaciones anteriores la exégesis y la aplicación personal solían mantenerse separadas porque la exégesis se consideraba una ciencia objetiva que era fácil de controlar, mientras que la aplicación personal se veía como algo muy subjetivo. Hay un elemento de verdad en esa observación. Por eso, La Sor opina que de las tres tareas principales del intérprete —elegir la traducción que mejor refleje el texto de los manuscritos originales, hacer una exégesis del texto y aplicar lo que descubre a su propia vida— la aplicación es «la más difícil y por lo visto la menos controlable»[1].

No obstante, cuando el creyente no toma la iniciativa de aplicar las enseñanzas bíblicas a su vida, no solamente pierde la bendición que Dios tiene preparada para él, sino que se convierte en un creyente estéril que entra en esa dinámica peligrosa en la cual pierde paulatinamente el conocimiento y entendimiento espiritual que ya había adquirido (Mt. 13:12)[2]. Para promover la aplicación de las Escrituras en su vida, muchos creyentes emplean lo que se llama «tiempo devocional», un tiempo diario en el cual leen la Biblia, meditan sobre el texto leído, alaban al Señor y piden que los guíe y sea glorificado a través de sus vidas durante ese día.

> «Hijo mío, presta atención a lo que te digo. Escucha atentamente mis palabras. No las pierdas de vista. Déjalas llegar hasta lo profundo de tu corazón, pues traen vida a quienes las encuentran y dan salud a todo el cuerpo».
>
> **(Pr. 4:20-22, NTV)**

> La coronación de todo estudio es el método devocional, por el cual las verdades descubiertas entran y se aplican a las necesidades del individuo. El estudio devocional no es tanto una técnica como un estudio espiritual. Es el espíritu de aventura que se arriesga a cumplir

1. William Sanford La Sor, «The *Sensus Plenior* and Biblical Interpretation» en *A Guide to Contemporary Hermeneutics* (Grand Rapids: Eerdmans, 1986), p. 48.

2. Por eso, en su libro *On the Preparation and Delivery of Sermons* (Nueva York: Harper and Brothers, 1944), p. 210, el gran maestro de la homilética John A. Broadus (1827–1895) dijo que «la aplicación en un sermón no es una mera posdata del discurso o una parte subordinada de este, sino la tarea principal que ha de realizar».

> lealmente la voluntad de Dios. Es el espíritu de adoración que quiere permanecer y permanece en la presencia de Dios[3].

Para que el tiempo devocional se convierta en un hábito que resulte en bendición en vez de ser una mera actividad en su horario diario, el creyente debe trabajar cuatro áreas de su vida o de su tiempo devocional.

## Trabajar un plan

Muchos creyentes tomaron en su momento la decisión de celebrar un tiempo devocional cada día. Pero esa decisión cayó en saco roto porque no tenían un plan para *comenzarlo* o, si lograron empezarlo, no tenían un plan para *realizarlo.* Para que un tiempo devocional llegue a ser un hábito que le sea de beneficio espiritual, el creyente ha de seguir dos pasos.

*1. Elegir el momento en que celebrará el tiempo devocional cada día.* Vivimos en un siglo en el cual todo se mueve a un ritmo cada día más veloz. ¡Hay tanto que hacer y tan poco tiempo para hacerlo! Por tanto, el creyente tendrá que tomar la iniciativa de identificar sus prioridades y apartar un tiempo específico para atender las actividades que considera realmente importantes. De cara a la vida tan ajetreada del siglo XXI, debe tener presente que lo importante raras veces tiene apariencia de urgente, y lo que se le presenta como urgente es raras veces importante. Y puesto que un tiempo devocional raras veces se le presentará como algo urgente, el creyente tendrá que tomar la iniciativa de identificar y apartar cada día ese momento en que celebrará su tiempo a solas con Dios. Si no lo hace, los quehaceres de la vida llenarán los huecos de su horario, animándolo a celebrar el tiempo devocional «más tarde». Pero ese «más tarde» nunca llega.

Es importante que el creyente no cambie el momento que ha elegido, a no ser que se dé cuenta de que hay otro momento mejor. El mayor obstáculo de un tiempo devocional es no tener un tiempo concreto para celebrarlo. Muchos eligen la mañana para celebrar su tiempo devocional, antes de comenzar todas las demás actividades y

3. Merrill C. Tenney, *Gálatas, la carta de la libertad cristiana* (Grand Rapids: Tell, sin fecha), pp. 221, 224.

responsabilidades del día. David tenía esa costumbre, aunque tenía muchas responsabilidades como rey (Sal. 5:3; 55:17; 59:16; 88:13).

*2. Determinar de antemano qué porción bíblica va a leer.* El hecho de no saber qué pasaje leer es el segundo obstáculo más grande del tiempo devocional. Esa incertidumbre es suficiente para disuadir a muchos creyentes de sentarse y leer la Biblia. Hay varios planes que el creyente puede adoptar.

- Leer un libro bíblico, un párrafo cada día. Limitarse a un solo párrafo dará al creyente más tiempo para meditar sobre el punto central del mismo.
- Seguir un plan para leer toda la Biblia en un año[4]. Por regla general, se puede leer en 10 o 15 minutos la porción que toca cada día. La ventaja de estos planes es que obliga al creyente a leer libros y pasajes que nunca habría elegido por su propia cuenta.
- Leer varias veces la vida de personajes bíblicos como Abraham, José, Moisés, David, etcétera.
- Meditar durante varios días sobre capítulos clave como 1 Reyes 8, 18; 2 Reyes 18–19; Salmo 1, 23, 119; Isaías 53; Lucas 2; Juan 15, 17; Hechos 2; Romanos 8; 1 Corintios 13, 15; Filipenses 2; Hebreos 11; 1 Juan 3; etcétera. La ventaja de este sistema es que permite al creyente meditar sobre pasajes que sabe que suplirán una necesidad espiritual que tiene en un momento determinado.

## Trabajar su mente

El Espíritu Santo transforma y renueva la mente del creyente con el propósito de que la use (Ro. 12:1; Ef. 4:23). Para hacer un buen uso de su mente, el creyente debe:

*1. Emplear los principios y leyes de la hermenéutica.* La exégesis y la aplicación personal tienen que andar de la mano. Desafortunadamente, en su afán por buscar la guía de Dios sobre un problema o

4. Muchos de estos planes pueden ser bajados de Internet con solo teclear «leer la Biblia en un año».

necesidad, hay quienes saltan directamente a la aplicación sin investigar primero lo que el texto significaba para los lectores originales. El mayor problema de ese procedimiento es que una aplicación correcta de un texto depende de una exégesis correcta del mismo. «Pero —argumentarán algunos— ¿qué importa si la aplicación incorrecta de *un* texto resulta ser la aplicación correcta de *otro* texto?». Hay dos argumentos que militan en contra de ese planteamiento. Primero, puede que una persona haga hoy una aplicación errónea de un texto que resulta ser la aplicación correcta de otro texto, pero no hay ninguna garantía de que mañana no hará una aplicación errónea de *un* texto que no sea la aplicación correcta de *ningún otro* texto. Segundo, los fines nunca justifican los medios. Por tanto, no es lícito buscar una bendición a expensas de la verdad. «Las aplicaciones prácticas de las Escrituras, si son basadas en una interpretación errónea, llegan a ser inválidas»[5].

> «Moisés reunió a todo el pueblo de Israel y dijo: "¡Escucha con atención, Israel! Oye los decretos y las ordenanzas que te entrego hoy, ¡para que los aprendas y los obedezcas!"».
>
> **(Dt. 5:1, NTV)**

*2. Meditar sobre el pasaje leído.* Una de las mayores tentaciones con la cual el creyente se enfrentará es la de leer el texto elegido a toda prisa, empujado por lo mucho que tiene que hacer ese día. Lo importante no es cuántos versículos lee durante su tiempo devocional, sino cuánto entiende y aprovecha de lo que lee. La meditación es un arte perdido que no admite prisas. Un carácter y unas actitudes bíblicas no se forjan con prisas, sino paulatinamente al tomar el tiempo para hacer varias preguntas:

- ¿Cuál es el tema principal de este pasaje?
- ¿Cuál es el versículo que mejor refleja ese tema?

---

5. El autor no ha podido localizar esta declaración de Milton S. Terry.

- ¿Quiénes son los personajes principales de este pasaje? ¿Ilustran con sus vidas un error a evitar o un ejemplo a seguir?
- ¿Contiene este pasaje una promesa para creer o una oración que hacer?
- ¿Cómo afecta a mi vida el pasaje que acabo de leer? ¿Qué es lo que debo corregir o desarrollar en mi vida?

Los salmistas tenían muy clara la necesidad de meditar sobre la Palabra de Dios. «Meditaré en todas tus obras» (77:12). «En tus mandamientos meditaré; consideraré tus caminos» (119:15). «Meditaré en tus estatutos» (119:48). «Mis ojos se anticipan a las vigilias de la noche, para meditar en tu palabra» (119:148, LBLA).

## Trabajar su corazón

Aunque el creyente debe emplear los principios y leyes de la hermenéutica, el tiempo devocional no es necesariamente un tiempo para hacer una investigación en toda regla del significado de una palabra griega. Tiene que haber un equilibrio porque Dios quiere hablar tanto a nuestro corazón como a nuestra mente. Por tanto, el creyente no debe menospreciar o descartar el elemento emocional del tiempo devocional.

> El combustible para una vida devocional inteligente debe sacarse de las conclusiones que cada uno se hace a sí mismo bajo la guía del Espíritu de Dios. El intelecto y el corazón deben participar juntamente en este esfuerzo. Un estudio poco intelectual de las Escrituras producirá un débil sentimentalismo y un tradicionalismo vacío, mientras que un estudio intelectual de la Biblia matará las facultades espirituales tanto del que enseña como del que recibe la enseñanza. En el estudio de la Biblia se necesitan tanto la luz como el calor[6].

Para que el tiempo devocional sea un tiempo equilibrado en el cual el creyente sea sensible a la voz de Dios tanto a un nivel emocional como intelectual, el creyente debe:

---

6. Tenney, ob. cit., pp. 221, 224.

> «Las enseñanzas del SEÑOR son perfectas, reavivan el alma. Los decretos del SEÑOR son confiables, hacen sabio al sencillo. Los mandamientos del SEÑOR son rectos; traen alegría al corazón. Los mandatos del SEÑOR son claros; dan buena percepción para vivir».
>
> **(Sal. 19:7-8, NTV)**

*1. Pedir en oración que Dios le dé amor por su Palabra.* De los 66 libros de la Biblia, el libro de los Salmos es quizás el más apreciado y leído por los creyentes en su tiempo devocional. Uno de los capítulos más conocidos es el 119. Lo que más destaca en ese capítulo es el amor que el autor tiene hacia la Palabra de Dios. «En mi corazón he atesorado tu palabra» (v. 11). «También tus testimonios son mi deleite; ellos son mis consejeros» (v. 24). «Me deleitaré en tus mandamientos, los cuales amo» (v. 47). «Mejor es para mí la ley de tu boca que millares de piezas de oro y de plata» (v. 72). «Tu ley es mi deleite» (v. 77)[7]. Todo creyente debe pedir que Dios le dé esta clase de amor hacia su Palabra.

*2. Confiar en la presencia de Dios, tanto si la siente como si no.* Sentir la presencia de Dios es una experiencia maravillosa. Pero suele ser una experiencia puntual; no ocurre tan frecuentemente como muchos quieren. Por eso, el creyente debe contar con la presencia de Dios tanto si la nota como si no. Muchos gigantes espirituales afirman en sus autobiografías que cuánto más maduraban en su vida cristiana, menos sentían emocionalmente la presencia de Dios, menos pruebas tangibles tenían de su presencia y de su guía, pero más creían en ellas. Habrá momentos en que las palabras saltarán de las páginas de la Biblia y otros momentos en que no. Algunos días el menú consistirá en pan y cebolla, y otros días en postre. Es cuestión de no preocuparse y volver sistemáticamente a la mesa para comer.

7. Todos estos textos son de la LBLA.

## Trabajar su voluntad

Aunque es muy importante que el creyente tenga un plan para celebrar un tiempo devocional y que trabaje su mente y su corazón, es precisamente en el área de su voluntad donde más se juega el propósito del tiempo devocional; a saber, que el creyente se conforme progresivamente a la imagen de Cristo, recuperando poco a poco esa santidad y vida completa que todos perdimos con la caída en Génesis 3. Porque hay demasiados ejemplos de creyentes que celebran asiduamente un tiempo devocional diario y hasta memorizan las Escrituras, pero nunca vencen los pecados que son más evidentes en sus vidas.

> «Asegúrense de obedecer todos los mandatos del Señor su Dios y de seguir sus instrucciones al pie de la letra. Manténganse en el camino que el Señor su Dios les ordenó que siguieran. Entonces tendrán una vida larga y les irá bien en la tierra donde están a punto de entrar y que van a poseer».
>
> **(Dt. 5:32-33, NTV)**

A veces el creyente reconoce que no tiene ganas de hacer lo que Dios está pidiendo de él a través del pasaje bíblico que acaba de leer. Pablo mandó a los filipenses que llevaran a cabo las obras propias de un hijo de Dios «porque Dios es quien obra en vosotros tanto el querer como el hacer» su voluntad (Flp. 2:13, LBLA). O sea, Dios provee no solamente el poder para cumplir con su voluntad, sino también el deseo de hacerlo. Evidentemente, Dios no se impone a nadie. Respeta nuestra voluntad. De ahí que a veces sea necesario que el creyente ore: «Señor, haz que esté dispuesto a obedecerte, porque en estos momentos reconozco que no quiero hacerlo».

Hace unos años un amigo del autor de *Con precisión* y de su esposa recibió un trasplante de corazón. El corazón que Larry recibió era de un joven que había fallecido en un accidente de automóvil. Después de un tiempo tuvo la oportunidad de conocer a la familia de ese joven. Resultó que los padres eran creyentes. Al saludar a la madre, esta le pidió permiso para abrazarlo. Puesto que Larry es más alto que ella, la cabeza de esa madre solo llegaba a la altura de su pecho.

A Larry le sorprendió que esa madre mantuviera el abrazo por más tiempo de lo que era normal. Al final ella exclamó con una alegría incontenible: «¡Eh! Oigo el latido del corazón de mi hijo». Cuando nuestro Padre celestial coloca su cabeza sobre nuestro pecho, ¿oye el latido del corazón de su Hijo? Eso es lo que espera oír. Para que Dios sea glorificado en su vida, el creyente debe interpretar «con precisión» la Palabra de Dios, pero después debe aplicar las enseñanzas bíblicas a su vida, dejando que el Espíritu Santo lo conforme cada día más a la imagen de Cristo.

## *Trabajo para realizar*

Si el lector no celebra un tiempo devocional, el autor de *Con precisión* lo anima a elegir un momento específico para realizar ese tiempo a solas con Dios cada día, a elegir la porción de las Escrituras que leerá durante ese tiempo y a comenzar cuanto antes. El autor sugiere que comience con el Salmo 119, escribiendo en una hoja las frases en las que David expresa su amor por la Palabra. Luego trabaje ese mismo amor en su propio ser para que la lectura del Salmo 119 sea una expresión de su propio corazón.

# Sección V
# Apéndices

A. La ley de la probabilidad
B. El papel de la fe y el intelecto
C. Crítica textual del A.T.
D. Crítica textual del N.T.
E. La historia de la crítica textual del N.T.
F. La relación entre una parábola y una alegoría
G. La cuestión del *sensus plenior*
H. La contextualización y la homosexualidad

# Apéndice A

## La ley de la probabilidad

Desde un punto de vista epistemológico (la ciencia del origen, naturaleza, métodos y límites del conocimiento humano), los seres humanos no somos capaces de probar nada en un sentido absoluto. Por eso la palabra «probar» siempre aparecerá a continuación entre comillas. Puede que una persona llegue a la convicción de que una idea es verídica. Pero nunca será con base en pruebas absolutas, tajantes y herméticas que no admitan discusión, sino siempre con base en la ley de la probabilidad.

Hay quienes creen que la revelación de Dios no necesita argumentos racionales para defenderse. Creen que usar nuestra inteligencia para sopesar la veracidad de los datos bíblicos es una afrenta al Espíritu Santo[1]. Sin embargo, la capacidad de razonar es parte de la imagen de Dios en el ser humano. Dios nos ha dado un intelecto porque necesitamos un sistema o mecanismo que nos permita evaluar las ideas[2].

No cabe duda de que las evidencias históricas del cristianismo solo nos permiten llegar a un nivel de seguridad que no va más allá de la probabilidad, porque la certidumbre absoluta solamente es posible en la lógica formal y las matemáticas. Pero no por eso carece de valor y utilidad la ley de la probabilidad. De hecho, cualquier decisión que los seres humanos toman está basada en esta ley. Aunque no es posible estar absolutamente seguro de si un acto histórico realmente

1. Quienes mantienen esta posición se llaman fideístas.
2. Quienes toman esta posición se llaman empiristas.

ocurrió, es relativamente fácil «probarlo» porque se trata de datos objetivos que pueden comprobarse. Por ejemplo, ¿cómo sabemos que Napoleón Bonaparte realmente vivió, gobernó Francia y realizó unas batallas militares famosas? ¿No es posible que todo sea un complot por parte del pueblo francés para embellecer su historia nacional? Todos aceptamos como un hecho «probado» que Napoleón vivió e hizo todo lo que leemos en los libros de historia porque hubo muchos testigos que presenciaron los eventos que rodearon su vida, fueron escritos muchos artículos en los periódicos de su época que confirman esos eventos y existen muchos artefactos de sus batallas. La probabilidad de que toda esta información sea verídica es tan alta que sería ridículo no creerlo. Es verdad que hemos de dar un salto de fe porque no estuvimos presentes para ver esos eventos con nuestros propios ojos, pero hay «pruebas» suficientes para convencernos de su veracidad.

De la misma forma podemos «probar» que Cristo murió en una cruz y que resucitó al tercer día en base a la ley de la probabilidad. Aunque tendremos que dar un salto de fe más largo por tratarse de un milagro, no representa un suicidio intelectual creer en su resurrección. Puesto que ocurrió en un contexto histórico, se puede investigar y evaluar de forma objetiva. Considere estos hechos: (1) Jesús predijo que resucitaría de la muerte. (2) Dijo que resucitaría al tercer día[3], un detalle que va mucho más allá de las profecías tan generales de algunos «profetas» modernos. (3) ¿Qué posibilidades tendrían los discípulos, hombres sin ninguna experiencia militar, de vencer a los soldados profesionales que guardaban la tumba, con tal de robar el cadáver de Jesús y declarar que había resucitado? (4) Si Cristo no resucitó, lo único que tenían que hacer los líderes religiosos de los judíos para desacreditar la noticia de que había resucitado era dirigirse a la tumba y mostrar su cadáver. ¿Por qué no lo hicieron? Si los discípulos no tenían el cadáver, ¿dónde estaba? (5) En el supuesto de que los discípulos hubieran sido capaces de robarlo, ¿cómo se explica su transformación de la noche a la mañana de hombres llenos de temor en personas valientes y dispuestas a jugarse la vida para predicar el mensaje de la resurrección de Jesús? ¿Quién está dispuesto a morir por una mentira? ¿Y cómo se

3. Los judíos contaban una parte de un día como si fuera un día entero. Por tanto, dos días parciales y un día entero cuentan como tres días enteros.

explica la vida de santidad que predicaban y vivían si sabían que lo que declaraban era una mentira? (6) Más de quinientas personas *a la vez* vieron a Jesús después de su resurrección (1 Co. 15:6).

«Probar» con la ley de la probabilidad que Cristo murió y resucitó es factible. Pero cuando la Biblia dice que Cristo murió *por nuestros pecados*, nos encontramos ante una clase de información que carece de datos objetivos que se puedan investigar y comprobar. La afirmación de que Cristo murió por nuestros pecados es una interpretación del *significado* de un evento histórico, no el evento en sí, el cual se podría investigar. Por tanto, las «pruebas» para demostrar que Cristo murió por nuestros pecados serán más indirectas que las que empleamos con la muerte y resurrección de Cristo. Jesús se enfrentó con ese mismo problema cuando los líderes religiosos de los judíos se negaron a creer sus afirmaciones de que era el Mesías (Jn. 10:24-25). Por eso Cristo apeló a una «prueba» indirecta al decir: «Aunque no me creáis a mí (o sea, mis afirmaciones), creed a *las obras*, para que conozcáis y creáis que el Padre está en mí, y yo en el Padre» (v. 38, énfasis añadido). Sus milagros y vida sin pecado eran «pruebas» indirectas de que era el Mesías.

De la misma forma, no podemos «probar» que la Biblia es de origen divino con evidencias objetivas como en el caso de un evento histórico. No obstante, existen evidencias indirectas de que sí lo es. (1) Los autores bíblicos declararon que sus palabras eran las palabras de Dios. Sería difícil creer que la Biblia es de origen divino si sus propios autores no lo hubieran dicho. (2) El gran número de profecías que se cumplieron en tiempos bíblicos, siendo la más importante el nacimiento de Cristo, el Mesías esperado. (3) La unidad y coherencia del mensaje de la Biblia, que cuenta con 66 libros escritos por más de treinta autores a lo largo de unos 1500 años. (4) El cambio tan positivo —en algunos casos un cambio radical— que la Biblia ha producido en la vida de tantas personas a lo largo de los siglos. (5) La superioridad de la Biblia sobre otros libros religiosos. (6) El hecho de que «las palas de miles de arqueólogos a lo largo de los siglos no han desacreditado la verdad de las Escrituras, ni toda la tierra que se ha puesto boca arriba ha demostrado que la Biblia sea falsa»[4]. Hay

4. Harold Lindsell, *The Battle for the Bible* (Grand Rapids: Zondervan,

muchos descubrimientos arqueológicos que apoyan las afirmaciones bíblicas en cuanto a eventos y personajes históricos, cultura, etcétera. (7) Pero la «prueba» indirecta más contundente de que la Biblia es de origen y naturaleza divina es que Jesús, quien declaró ser Dios y resucitó de la muerte para probarlo (Ro. 1:4), afirmó que las Escrituras son de origen divino.

No obstante, un no creyente puede ser consciente de todas estas «pruebas» en base a la ley de la probabilidad y las «pruebas» indirectas y todavía quedarse con dudas en cuanto a su veracidad. En el «Trabajo paro realizar» paso tres (p. 47), se planteará la cuestión de la relación entre la fe y el intelecto y nuestra aceptación de la veracidad de las declaraciones bíblicas.

---

1976), p. 30.

# Apéndice B

# El papel de la fe y el intelecto

Jesús y los apóstoles creían que las Escrituras son inspiradas e inerrantes en los manuscritos originales. Sin embargo, las «pruebas» citadas en el Apéndice A («La ley de la probabilidad») no son suficientes para convencer a todos los no creyentes de que la enseñanza bíblica es verídica, y de que tomen la decisión de arrepentirse y aceptar la salvación que Dios les ofrece en Cristo Jesús. ¿Qué es lo que falta? Aunque la caída de Adán no anuló la capacidad del ser humano de razonar, parece que este es incapaz de entender y aceptar dichas verdades de tal modo que se convierta a Cristo. Entonces, ¿es el entender y aceptar estas verdades una cuestión de fe o quizás una combinación del intelecto y la fe?

Los teólogos de siglos pasados lucharon con esta pregunta. Las cuatro respuestas que fueron propuestas siguen en líneas generales las posiciones de cuatro gigantes de la Iglesia.

*Tertuliano* (c. 160–c. 220) fue teólogo y apologeta. Su influencia fue tan grande que ha sido llamado «el padre del cristianismo latino» y «el fundador de la teología occidental». Creía que era un disparate exigir que el cristianismo tuviera sentido para el ser humano, por cuanto los pensamientos de un Dios infinito no caben en su mente finita. La única respuesta legítima del ser humano ante lo que Dios ha dicho es la fe, sin más.

En ese sentido la posición de Tertuliano se ha caracterizado por la frase: «Creo lo que es absurdo». A todos los efectos anula el papel del intelecto humano, las pruebas y las evidencias para evaluar la veracidad de una afirmación bíblica. Para apoyar su posición, Tertuliano acudió a textos como 1 Corintios 1:17-18, 22-23, 27; 2:2 y Colosenses 2:8-11. Pero hay al menos tres problemas con su posición. Primero, estos textos no dicen que el cristianismo *es* una locura, sino que *lo parece* porque el no creyente está cegado por sus pecados y prejuicios (1 Co. 2:14-16). Segundo, textos como Juan 20:30-31; Hechos 1:3 y 1 Pedro 3:15 afirman que hay razones legítimas para creer el mensaje cristiano, lo que claramente implica que el intelecto tiene un papel que jugar. Tercero, la posición de Tertuliano sustituye la fe por el intelecto, anulando así una capacidad que Dios ha dado al hombre como parte de su imagen. La posición de Tertuliano representa un subjetivismo puro y un salto de fe temerario.

*Orígenes* (185–254) fue un teólogo brillante[1]. Creía que el cristianismo es una filosofía intelectualmente racional. Recibió su educación en las escuelas griegas de filosofía y quería ganar a sus colegas para el cristianismo. Según Orígenes, el hombre debe creer lo que puede probar, porque creer sin tener pruebas es pura superstición. Nuestra fe debe poder justificarse al menos en principio. Puesto que Dios es racional y ha hecho al hombre a su imagen, es lógico que el hombre sea capaz de pensar, sopesar datos y llegar a la verdad mediante pruebas y evidencias tangibles. De la misma forma en que Tertuliano fue a un extremo, Orígenes fue al otro al insistir en que el hombre tenía que entender y justificar intelectualmente cada verdad espiritual antes de creerla. Al insistir en que existe una prueba intelectual para todo lo que creemos, su posición tiende a eliminar la necesidad de la fe y a engendrar orgullo intelectual.

1. Como otros teólogos de los primeros siglos, Orígenes mantuvo algunas posiciones totalmente heréticas. Era universalista, creyendo que todos se salvarían al final. Negó la deidad total de Cristo y su resurrección física, diciendo que tenía un cuerpo espiritual. Pero el legado principal de Orígenes fue la interpretación alegórica de las Escrituras en lugar de la interpretación literal. Su postura, sin embargo, es rechazada hoy en día.

*Tomás de Aquino* (c. 1225–1274) fue teólogo, filósofo y cura de la Iglesia Católica Romana. Apreciaba y abrazaba tanto la fe como el intelecto humano. Creía que las pruebas y evidencias nos ayudan a entender y aceptar la revelación de Dios como verdad y proveen una base neutral que permite que creyentes y no creyentes lleguen a un acuerdo en cuanto a la verdad. Este énfasis podría caracterizarse por la frase «entiendo para creer». Pero el error de Aquino es que separó la fe del intelecto humano. Por un lado, insistió en que la revelación de Dios ha de aceptarse como verídica con base en la autoridad divina, sin exigir razones, pruebas y evidencias. Pero, por otro lado, creía que el intelecto sirve para llevarnos a ideas que debemos aceptar solo cuando sean apoyadas por evidencias y pruebas que demuestren que sean verídicas. A primera vista parece que esta posición incluye los elementos positivos y evita los errores de las posiciones de Tertuliano y Orígenes; pero, en realidad, crea una dicotomía, una separación entre la fe y el intelecto, lo cual tiende a degenerar en un cristianismo dominguero.

| | |
|---|---|
| **Tertuliano** | «Creo lo que es absurdo». Una fe sin intelecto. |
| **Orígenes** | «Creo lo que puedo probar». El intelecto como criterio final. |
| **Tomás de Aquino** | «Entiendo para creer». Mejor que la posición de Orígenes, pero no relaciona adecuadamente el intelecto y la fe. |
| **Agustín de Hipona** | «Entiendo para creer y creo para entender». El intelecto y la fe están relacionados y se apoyan mutuamente. |

*Agustín de Hipona* (354–430) fue teólogo y es considerado uno de los cuatro padres más importantes de la iglesia latina[2]. Creía que tanto la fe como el intelecto humano jugaban un papel legítimo, pero que tenían que relacionarse de forma correcta. Igual que Tomás de Aquino, creía que el conocimiento nos lleva a la fe y al compromiso. O sea, «entiendo para creer». De lo contrario, la fe es totalmente ciega. El conocimiento nos permite saber qué es lo que hemos de creer. Este era su punto de partida. Pero creía también que la fe y el compromiso personal nos llevan al conocimiento. O sea, «creo para entender», un concepto enseñado en textos como Salmo

2. Los otros tres son Jerónimo, Gregorio y Ambrosio.

34:8; 36:9 y Juan 7:17. Dios no nos dará más luz hasta que hayamos aprovechado la luz que ya tenemos.

Agustín no ensalzó la fe hasta la exclusión del intelecto humano (como Tertuliano), pero tampoco permitió que el intelecto humano se colocara por encima de la fe (como Orígenes). No separó la fe del intelecto humano (como Aquino), sino que procuró relacionarlos de una forma correcta porque forman dos caras de la misma moneda. Tampoco descartó el papel del intelecto humano, las pruebas, los argumentos lógicos y las evidencias en la tarea de descubrir la verdad. Pero consideró que Dios tiene el derecho de interpretar sus propias palabras y que dicha interpretación es el único criterio fiable y seguro sobre el cual el ser humano puede fundamentar sus investigaciones, descubrimientos y conclusiones en cuanto a la verdad. La posición de Agustín valora el intelecto humano, pero solo en la medida en que este se subordine a la revelación divina.

Aunque el evangélico entiende que creer ciertas doctrinas bíblicas parece una locura, no está dispuesto a realizar un salto de fe tan ciego como requiere la posición de Tertuliano. A la vez aprecia el énfasis de Orígenes y Aquino sobre el papel del intelecto humano. No obstante, rechaza el extremo hasta donde algunos llegan de depender por completo del intelecto humano, diciendo: «Si la Biblia no me convence, no la creo». El evangélico no está dispuesto a subordinar la revelación divina al intelecto humano. Por eso, cree que la posición de Agustín coincide mejor con la enseñanza bíblica. Abraza el uso de la mente que Dios le ha dado y considera la alta crítica como legítima y necesaria para realizar una interpretación correcta de las Escrituras. También acepta cualquier descubrimiento científico, ya que es su Dios quien creó el universo y las leyes que lo controlan. Pero se niega a descartar *a priori* el origen divino de las Escrituras o cualquier otra enseñanza bíblica simplemente porque no encaje en el entendimiento humano.

Esta era la misma posición de B. B. Warfield (1851–1921), el gran erudito bíblico y profesor del Princeton Theological Seminary. Creía que la revelación general y la revelación especial se complementaban. La revelación especial dada por Dios en las Escrituras encaja con lo que se puede conocer de forma independiente por la mente humana. Las verdades enseñadas en la Biblia, las cuales están ancladas en la historia, pueden ser examinadas por el criterio normal de la historia, arqueología y demás ciencias pertinentes. Warfield creía que es posible profesar una fe en Dios en base a estas pruebas naturales sin la intervención del Espíritu Santo. Pero creía a la vez que la obra del Espíritu es absolutamente esencial para que la fe conseguida por el intelecto humano se convierta en un medio para la salvación.

Es precisamente en este punto donde la doctrina de la iluminación del Espíritu Santo juega un papel tan importante y definitivo, un tema que se trata en el capítulo 5.

# Apéndice C
# Crítica textual del A.T.

La doctrina de la inspiración tiene que ver con los manuscritos originales de los libros bíblicos, no con las copias y traducciones a otros idiomas que se hicieron de ellos a lo largo de los siglos. Esto plantea una pregunta: si no tenemos ni siquiera un trozo del manuscrito original de ninguno de los libros bíblicos, ¿de qué nos sirve esta doctrina y hasta qué punto podemos fiarnos de la Biblia que tenemos en nuestras manos? La respuesta es que, gracias a la ciencia de la crítica textual —la cual procura determinar el texto original de un documento antiguo en el caso de no tener el manuscrito original— se sabe con absoluta certeza lo que dice el texto original de la Biblia.

El hecho de que no tengamos ningún manuscrito original se debe a varios factores. Primero, en tiempos bíblicos se escribía sobre papiro y pergamino (piel de animales), materiales que se deterioran fácilmente con el uso y el tiempo. Segundo, la persecución de los judíos a lo largo de la historia produjo en algunas ocasiones la destrucción de ciudades enteras, incluyendo las sinagogas y los centros de investigación bíblica donde los judíos guardaban sus manuscritos del A.T. Tercero, los judíos estaban tan convencidos de que el A.T. era una revelación especial que Dios les había dado que destruyeron las copias deterioradas para evitar que alguien profanara un manuscrito que contenía el nombre sagrado de Dios[1]. Los rabinos guardaban esos manuscritos

1. Ver Ernst Würthwein, *The Text of the Old Testament* (Grand Rapids: Eerdmans, 1979), pp. 12–13.

en un almacén de la sinagoga hasta el momento en que había un número suficiente de ellos. Entonces, celebraban un rito litúrgico en el cual los enterraban bajo tierra, condenándolos así a desaparecer por completo con el tiempo[2]. Cuarto, durante los primeros tres siglos de la iglesia los cristianos fueron perseguidos y sus casas saqueadas. Puesto que celebraban sus cultos en casas particulares, cualquier manuscrito guardado en ellas fue destruido.

Este apéndice y el siguiente están dedicados a la crítica textual del A.T. y del N.T. respectivamente. Sin embargo, puesto que los mismos materiales fueron empleados para hacer las copias de los dos Testamentos, este tema solo se tratará en este apéndice.

## A. MATERIALES EMPLEADOS

Las inscripciones grabadas en piedra solían contener datos biográficos (lápidas) y leyes gubernamentales. Pero cuando se trataba de una información extensa y cotidiana, como en el caso de los libros bíblicos, se empleaban dos clases de material que eran más económicos, manipulables y transportables.

### Papiro

El papiro fue empleado durante muchos siglos en Egipto para documentos literarios y cotidianos (cartas, recibos, transacciones comerciales, etcétera). Era una planta que crecía de forma abundante en las orillas y en los pantanos del río Nilo, pero también en otros lugares del mundo mediterráneo. Consistía en un tallo triangular que crecía hasta una altura de 1,8 a 3,6 metros. Después de quitar la capa exterior, el interior esponjoso y fibroso se cortaba en tiras finas que se colocaban una al lado de otra. Luego, se superponía una segunda capa de tiras transversalmente sobre la primera. Después de golpear las dos capas para que se cohesionaran, se dejaban al aire libre para que se secaran.

2. Varios libros sobre crítica textual destacan que el único ambiente en que unos manuscritos de papiro podrían conservarse intactos durante muchos años es una arena muy árida y protegida, como fue el caso de los papiros encontrados cerca del mar Muerto.

Una vez secas, las hojas eran alisadas con un trozo de marfil o una concha de mar.

Las hojas se producían en dos medidas de aproximadamente 15,2 × 22,5 cm y 30,5 × 38 cm. Después se unían con pegamento y se vendían en rollos de veinte hojas. Por regla general, un rollo no excedía los 10,6 metros, puesto que un tamaño mayor lo haría prácticamente imposible de manipular. Aunque se hacían rollos de pergamino, es muy probable que los libros del N.T. fueran escritos sobre rollos de papiro. Una epístola corta como Filemón cabía en una sola hoja. El Evangelio de Lucas y su libro de Hechos son los dos libros más largos del N.T. Puesto que Lucas los dedicó a Teófilo (Lc. 1:3; Hch. 1:1), es posible que quisiera presentárselos en un solo rollo. Sin embargo, cada libro habría requerido un rollo de aproximadamente 9,4 a 9,7 metros, y la combinación de los dos habría superado el límite de 10,6 metros por rollo. Es posible que esta fuera la razón por la que sus dos libros (Lucas y Hechos) aparecen por separado en el N.T.[3]

La exportación de papiro era un negocio importante en Egipto, puesto que fue empleado en todos los países mediterráneos desde el siglo IV a. C. hasta el siglo VII d. C. Job, considerado el libro más antiguo del A.T., hace mención del papiro en 8:11. Aunque el papiro era la forma de papel más económica que existía, tenía la gran desventaja de ser altamente perecedero. Por eso existen tan pocos manuscritos de libros completos en papiro. Era solamente cuestión de tiempo que el pergamino se hiciera con el mercado de los materiales caligráficos para documentos importantes, aunque fuese más caro.

Han sobrevivido muchos fragmentos de papiro de contenido secular, pero solamente unos 120 fragmentos del N.T.[4] Los críticos textuales catalogan los manuscritos de papiro con una «*p*» seguida por un número. Los más antiguos encontrados hasta el momento son: (1) un fragmento con porciones de cuatro versículos de Juan 18. Se encuentra en la John Rylands University Library en Manchester, Inglaterra. Se conoce como el *p52* y data de c. 125. Es considerado el

---

3. Ver George E. Ladd, *Crítica del Nuevo Testamento* (El Paso: Editorial Mundo Hispano, 1990), p. 46.

4. Ver el sitio web https://en.wikipedia.org/wiki/List_of_New_Testament_papyri.

más antiguo de los manuscritos del N.T. que se conservan, habiendo sido copiado unos treinta años después de escribirse el manuscrito original. (2) Fragmentos de Mateo 21 (*p104*), Juan 18–19 (*p90*) y Apocalipsis (*p98*) que datan de c. 150–200. (3) Varios manuscritos que datan de c. 200 como el Magdalen (*p64, p67*) y Bodmer (*p66, p75*). (4) Una colección de tres manuscritos descubiertos y comprados en Egipto por Chester Beatty en 1931[5]. El *p45* contiene secciones de Romanos, Filipenses, Colosenses y 1 Tesalonicenses. El *p46* contiene la mayor parte de las Epístolas Paulinas y es el manuscrito más antiguo que contiene casi la totalidad de un libro del N.T. El *p47* consiste en diez hojas del libro de Apocalipsis. La colección de Beatty es el testigo más importante de la fiabilidad del texto del N.T., ya que muestra los escasos cambios que se han producido a pesar de las diversas copias realizadas a lo largo de los siglos.

## Pergamino

El pergamino, hecho de piel de animales (ternero, antílope, oveja y cabra), era empleado por los persas, hebreos y griegos desde tiempos antiguos, pero muy poco por los egipcios debido a la abundancia de papiro en su país. Los pergaminos más antiguos que se han encontrado datan de c. 1500 a. C.[6] Las bibliotecas de Orígenes (185–254) y Pánfilo de Cesarea (c. 263–c. 339) contenían rollos de papiro. Sin embargo, también existían manuscritos en la forma de libros, llamados «códices» (hojas de papiro o pergamino dobladas y cosidas juntas). En 2 Timoteo 4:13 Pablo pide a Timoteo que traiga sus «libros» (probablemente rollos de papiro) y «pergaminos», con toda probabilidad copias del A.T. Con el tiempo los libros se hicieron cada vez más

5. La colección de manuscritos que Beatty compró se encuentra en la Chester Beatty Library en Dublín, Irlanda.

6. Hay una anécdota interesante en cuanto al uso del papiro y el pergamino. En el siglo II a. C. Ptolomeo V Epífanes (210–181 a. C.), rey de Egipto, entró en una pugna con el rey de Pérgamo para ver quién tenía la mejor biblioteca de la época. Para dificultar la victoria de su contrincante, Epífanes decretó un embargo sobre la exportación de papiro. Por tanto, el rey de Pérgamo tuvo que buscar un material alternativo (de ahí salió el término *pergamino*).

populares. Aunque no se sabe cuándo los códices sustituyeron a los rollos de papiro, su uso era común en el siglo II[7].

El pergamino dominó el mercado de materiales caligráficos durante los siglos III al VII, cuando fue sustituido por el papel, que era menos costoso. Por eso, todos los manuscritos del N.T. encontrados hasta el momento que datan de los siglos II y III están escritos sobre papiro y, con pocas excepciones, todos los manuscritos a partir del siglo IV están escritos sobre pergamino. En 331 el emperador Constantino ordenó que se hicieran cincuenta copias de la Biblia en pergamino. Dos de ellas, el Códice Sinaítico y el Códice Vaticano, han sobrevivido y representan las dos copias más importantes que tenemos del N.T. El Códice Sinaítico contiene todo el N.T., una parte del A.T. y algunas obras cristianas. Se encuentra en el Museo Británico de Londres. El Códice Vaticano es probablemente el mejor manuscrito del N.T. Se ha guardado en la Biblioteca Vaticana de Roma desde 1481. Lamentablemente, las autoridades eclesiásticas no permitieron a los eruditos bíblicos de otras confesiones consultarlo hasta finales del siglo XIX. El Códice Vaticano contiene la mayor parte de los dos Testamentos. Faltan porciones de Hebreos, las Epístolas Pastorales y Apocalipsis.

## B. FUENTES PRINCIPALES DE INVESTIGACIÓN

La crítica textual del A.T. se enfrenta con unas circunstancias que son muy diferentes a las del N.T. Por eso, es necesario tratar los dos Testamentos por separado. De entrada, se requiere del crítico textual del A.T. una preparación y unos conocimientos mucho más amplios que los del crítico textual del N.T.

> Los eruditos del N.T. no tienen necesidad de moverse mucho más allá de un solo siglo (primer siglo d. C.), tienen solo cuatro idiomas que dominar (griego y latín de Europa; hebreo y arameo de Palestina) y solo dos culturas básicas que investigar (greco-romana

7. En su libro *Old Testament Textual Criticism* (Grand Rapids: Baker, 1994), p. 39, Brotzman dice que el códice fue empleado para copias privadas del A.T., pero que las sinagogas emplearon el rollo.

> y judía). Hacer justicia al A.T. requiere que el erudito domine un período de la historia que cubre un mínimo de dos mil años (tres mil para entender todo el fondo histórico) y tenga la habilidad de evaluar una cantidad inmensa y variada de documentos escritos en diez idiomas del Medio Oriente y un abanico de culturas[8].

Debido a su antigüedad, hay pocos manuscritos del A.T. en hebreo, mientras que existen gran cantidad del N.T. en griego. No obstante, mientras que el N.T. lleva una ventaja considerable en cuanto a la *cantidad* de material disponible, el A.T. queda más que compensado por la *calidad* de sus manuscritos. La caligrafía era común en tiempos de Esdras[9] puesto que había existido en el Cercano Oriente durante dos mil años. Además, Israel contaba con un gremio de escribas profesionales desde el tiempo de los jueces[10] que copiaban e interpretaban la ley de Moisés para el pueblo. Y, por creer que el A.T. fue recibido por revelación especial de Dios, se tomaron medidas para copiarlo con la mayor precisión posible.

La crítica textual del A.T. se basa en cuatro fuentes principales, siendo las últimas tres de mayor importancia y fiabilidad.

## El Pentateuco samaritano

Cuando Salomón falleció, c. 922 a. C., el reino se dividió porque su hijo Roboam insistió en cobrar impuestos excesivos. Las diez tribus del norte (Israel) siguieron a Jeroboam I como rey, y las dos del sur (Judá) a Roboam (1 R. 12:16). Nada más subir al trono, Jeroboam I designó a las ciudades de Dan y Betel como centros de culto para contrarrestar la

---

8. K. A. Kitchen, *On the Reliability of the Old Testament* (Grand Rapids: Eerdmans, 2003), p. xiii. El N.T. fue escrito en un período de aproximadamente cincuenta años, comenzando con Mateo (c. 50) y terminando con Apocalipsis (c. 95). El A.T. fue escrito a lo largo de mil años. Moisés escribió el Pentateuco c. 1400 a. C. y Malaquías su profecía entre el 435 y el 430 a. C.

9. Esdras llegó a Jerusalén con un segundo grupo de judíos de la cautividad babilónica c. 458 a. C.

10. En su libro *The Old Testament and Criticism* (Grand Rapids: Eerdmans, 1983), Armerding dice que la frase «los que tenían vara de mando» en Jueces 5:14 significa literalmente «los que manejan la vara del escriba» (p. 101).

influencia del templo en Jerusalén, asegurando así la lealtad del pueblo tanto en lo religioso como en lo político. Debido a su pecado, Israel fue llevado cautivo a Asiria en el 722 a. C. por el rey asirio Salmanasar V, quien creía que la mejor manera de apagar el fervor nacionalista de cualquier nación conquistada era deportar a su pueblo fuera de su tierra y poblar dicha tierra con asirios. No obstante, poco tiempo después permitió que algunos de los judíos volvieran a su tierra. Muchos de estos judíos se casaron con los colonos asirios. Los descendientes de estos matrimonios mixtos fueron llamados samaritanos.

En el 586 a. C. las dos tribus del sur sufrieron el mismo castigo, siendo deportadas a Babilonia. Pero los días del Imperio babilónico estaban contados, porque unos 47 años después (539 a. C.) el rey Ciro II de Persia conquistó Babilonia. Al año siguiente decretó que todos los judíos podían volver a su tierra. Los pocos de Judá que aprovecharon esta posibilidad volvieron a Jerusalén en tres grupos bajo el liderazgo de Zorobabel (538 a. C.), Esdras (c. 458 a. C.) y Nehemías (c. 444 a. C.). Comenzaron a reconstruir el templo bajo el ministerio de los profetas Hageo y Zacarías. Cuando los samaritanos se ofrecieron a ayudarles, los judíos rechazaron su oferta por considerarlos mestizos. Todo este trasfondo, conjuntamente con el hecho de que el ejército de Samaria formaba parte del grupo de enemigos que intentaron obstaculizar la reconstrucción de los muros de Jerusalén bajo el liderazgo de Nehemías (Neh. 4:2), convirtió a los samaritanos en los enemigos eternos de los judíos.

Los samaritanos aceptaban solamente el Pentateuco como su libro sagrado. Para defender y promover sus desvíos doctrinales, esta secta judía manipuló el texto. Por ejemplo, para justificar su decisión de designar el monte Gerizim como su centro de culto[11], combinaron los dos primeros de los Diez Mandamientos y añadieron un décimo que consistía en una combinación de frases sacadas de Deuteronomio 11:29-30; 27:2-3 y 28:4-7. También, en los 21 textos de

11. Cerca del año en que Nehemías llegó a Jerusalén los samaritanos decidieron construir su propio templo en el monte Gerizim, el lugar donde Dios mandó a Abraham que le ofreciera en sacrificio a su hijo Isaac. Con esta decisión, los samaritanos siguieron los pasos de Jeroboam I, quien designó a las ciudades de Betel y Dan como centros de culto. Por eso, hay quienes llaman a los samaritanos «neojerobomitas».

Deuteronomio donde Dios dice que «elegirá» en un futuro una ciudad que servirá como el centro de culto para su pueblo (una clara referencia a Jerusalén), los samaritanos cambiaron el texto para leer «eligió», afirmando así que Dios *ya había* elegido el monte Gerizim como el lugar de culto. Los eruditos opinan que la primera copia del Pentateuco samaritano fue redactada a finales del siglo II a. C. La copia más antigua que se conserva data del siglo XII, trece siglos más tarde. Los críticos textuales creen que el Pentateuco samaritano puede servir de cierta ayuda para determinar lo que decía el texto original. Pero no hace falta porque el Pentateuco es la parte del A.T. que menos problemas presenta al crítico textual.

## La Septuaginta (LXX)

Poco después de la época en que vivió Abraham (c. 2000 a. C.) los cananeos inventaron el hebreo. Igual que los demás idiomas de la época, todas sus letras eran consonantes. El hebreo no tenía vocales ni empleaba puntuaciones (comas, puntos finales, etcétera)[12]. Aunque cada idioma evoluciona con el tiempo, estas características perduraron durante los siguientes dos mil años. Es probable que los descendientes de Abraham aprendieran el hebreo, que se hablaba solamente en una parte de Palestina, en Canaán. En contraste, el arameo, que formaba parte de la misma familia de lenguas semíticas[13], existía mucho antes que el hebreo, habiendo aparecido a mediados de la Edad del Bronce (3600–1200 a. C.). Además, era el idioma franco de un territorio extenso que incluía el resto de Palestina, Mesopotamia (Irak en la actualidad) y Siria. Así que el hebreo estaba condenado a vivir a la sombra del arameo.

En tiempos de Moisés (c. 1400 a. C.) el hebreo seguía sin vocales. En algún momento desconocido después de Moisés, pero antes de que Malaquías escribiera el último libro del A.T. c. 435–430 a. C., se

12. Los eruditos del A.T. solían pensar que durante las primeras etapas del desarrollo del hebreo no existía una separación entre las palabras. Pero los rollos del mar Muerto demostraron que estaban equivocados. Para más información ver el cap. 2 del libro de Ellis Broztman, *Old Testament Textual Criticism* (Grand Rapids: Baker, 1994).

13. En honor a Sem, el progenitor de la raza hebrea (Gn. 10:21-31).

introdujo un sistema sencillo de señales que identificaban las vocales más importantes[14]. De hecho no hacía falta, porque los judíos que hablaban el hebreo cada día sabían qué vocales tenían que emplear. No obstante, ese sistema suplía una necesidad[15]. Cuando las diez tribus del norte y las dos del sur fueron desplazadas a Asiria y Babilonia respectivamente, tuvieron que aprender el arameo, la lengua franca de sus conquistadores. Con el tiempo el arameo fue desplazando al hebreo como la lengua franca de los judíos en el hogar, la calle y la sinagoga[16]. No es extraño, por tanto, que Daniel escribiera toda una sección de su profecía en arameo (2:4–7:28) y que Jeremías incluyera un texto en arameo (10:11). Unos cien años más tarde Esdras vuelve a Jerusalén con un grupo de exiliados. Había pasado toda su vida en Babilonia y hablaba el arameo. Por tanto, es lógico que Esdras 4:8–6:18 y 7:12-26 estén escritos en arameo. En Nehemías 8:1-2 Esdras lee la Ley a todos los habitantes de Jerusalén. Es muy probable que cuando los levitas y otras personas citadas en 8:7-8 «ponían el sentido, de modo que entendiesen la lectura», lo que hicieron fue traducir el texto hebreo al arameo, puesto que todos los presentes solo entendían el arameo.

Unos cien años después ocurrió un evento único y trascendental en la historia de los idiomas que supuso otro desafío para la supervivencia del hebreo. Cuando Alejandro Magno conquistó el Imperio persa (337 a. C.), el griego koiné se convirtió en la lengua franca de todos los países del mediterráneo oriental durante los siguientes mil años (siglos IV a. C.–VI d. C.)[17]. Aunque cada país seguía hablando su propia lengua y sus dialectos autóctonos, la koiné era el idioma común de los comerciantes y diplomáticos de cada nación. Como consecuencia, los judíos que nacieron en los países del mediterráneo oriental, pero fuera de Palestina, hablaban la koiné como su primer o único idioma. Los judíos que nacieron en Palestina hablaban el arameo, la koiné y posiblemente el hebreo, en ese orden de preferencia.

---

14. Ver R. Laird Harris, «How Reliable is the Old Testament Text?» en *Can I Trust The Bible?* (Chicago: Moody Press, 1968), p. 121.

15. En tiempos de Esdras se empleaba ese sistema libremente. El desarrollo definitivo de ese sistema se realizaría por los masoretas.

16. Los eruditos creen que la institución de la sinagoga fue creada durante la cautividad babilónica para suplir la necesidad de un lugar de culto.

17. La koiné es una forma simplificada del griego clásico.

En tiempos de Jesús, la lengua franca de los judíos de Palestina era el arameo. Aunque era el idioma principal de los discípulos, los que escribieron los libros del N.T. emplearon la koiné por ser el idioma que todo el mundo mediterráneo entendía. No obstante, de vez en cuando emplearon palabras arameas como *talitha qum* (Mc. 5:42), *ephphatha* (Mc. 7:34), *abba* (Mc. 14:36; Ro. 8:15), *eloi eloi lama sabachthani* (Mt. 27:46) y *maranatha* (1 Co. 16:22)[18].

Pero la mayor tragedia que estos eventos provocaron no fue la muerte lenta del hebreo, sino la incapacidad progresiva de los judíos de leer el A.T. Poco a poco el hebreo se convirtió en un idioma antiguo que solamente los miembros de la alta sociedad y la élite académica entendían. Pero pocos años después de la muerte de Alejandro Magno (323 a. C.) ocurrió un evento que tendría un valor incalculable; a saber, la traducción del A.T. al griego. Esa traducción, llamada la Septuaginta, ha sido considerada «la versión más importante para la crítica textual»[19] del A.T. La tradición dice que la LXX fue escrita durante el reinado de Ptolomeo II Filadelfo (285–246 a. C.), rey de Egipto, quien trajo a setenta ancianos judíos (de ahí LXX, las letras numéricas romanas para el número 70) desde Jerusalén a Alejandría porque quería tener una copia de la Ley judía para su biblioteca personal[20].

---

18. En su artículo «What Bible Version Did Jesus Read?» en *Christianity Today* (26 abril 1999), Craig Evans sugiere que «con toda probabilidad Jesús escuchara las Escrituras leídas (en las sinagogas) en hebreo y ocasionalmente en griego, y que luego fueran parafraseadas e interpretadas en arameo» (p. 98) porque el judío típico hablaba el arameo como su lengua habitual y no entendía el hebreo. Y cuando Jesús citaba textos del A.T., normalmente empleaba traducciones que estarían de acuerdo con los *targumim* en lugar de la versión hebrea del A.T. o la LXX. Un tárgum era una traducción (más bien una paráfrasis en lugar de una traducción literal) al arameo de textos del A.T. Puesto que el típico judío hablaba el arameo como su lengua habitual y no entendía el hebreo, las lecturas bíblicas en las sinagogas tenían que hacerse en arameo.

19. Bruce K. Waltke, «The Textual Criticism of the Old Testament» en *Biblical Criticism: Historical, Literary and Textual* (Grand Rapids: Zondervan, 1978), p. 4.

20. Puesto que esa tradición se basa en la *Carta de Aristeas*, un documento parcialmente ficticio que fue escrito en el primer siglo a. C. o un poco antes, los eruditos opinan que: (1) es mucho más probable que el proyecto de la LXX fuera motivado por las necesidades de la comunidad judía en lugar del capricho de un coleccionista pagano. (2) Algunas referencias históricas sugieren que participaron en el proyecto setenta y dos ancianos en lugar de setenta. No obstante, en su libro *The Language and Imagery*

La LXX es una traducción única y excepcional. Primero, en tiempos antiguos no era habitual que una obra literaria fuera traducida a otro idioma; y, en las pocas ocasiones en que se hacía, la traducción carecía de valor, ya que no reflejaba de forma fidedigna lo que decía el manuscrito original, todo lo contrario de lo que hicieron los eruditos judíos con la LXX. Segundo, fue la primera traducción que se hizo de una obra antigua larga[21]. La LXX es, además, la primera traducción del A.T. Tercero, la traducción de un libro implica que hubo un manuscrito original o copias del mismo anteriores a dicha traducción. En el caso de la LXX, se trataría de manuscritos que datan de antes del 250 a. C., los cuales son mucho más antiguos que los que tenemos a nuestra disposición hoy. Finalmente, la LXX es una traducción excepcional y un hecho insólito cuando tomamos en cuenta que se realizó sin la ayuda de léxicos, diccionarios, concordancias y libros de gramática[22].

Durante el primer siglo se convirtieron un gran número de gentiles. Puesto que no hablaban ni entendían el hebreo, la LXX se convirtió rápidamente en la Biblia de la Iglesia naciente y sirvió como la versión preferida de los cristianos durante los 300 años siguientes. Cuando los autores del N.T. incluían un texto del A.T. en su libro, de vez en cuando citaban una versión desconocida. En esos casos es posible que tradujeran directamente de manuscritos hebreos o que emplearan los

*of the Bible* (Filadelfia: Westminster Press, 1980), p. 123, Caird sugiere que «juzgando por la alta calidad de la traducción, el número de miembros que conformaba el comité de traducción tiene que haber sido considerablemente menos de setenta». (3) Originalmente, la palabra «Septuaginta» se refería al Pentateuco. Pero con el tiempo llegó a referirse a la traducción de todo el A.T. Los eruditos creen que el Pentateuco fue comenzado y posiblemente terminado c. 250 a. C. durante el reinado de Ptolomeo II Filadelfo, y que los demás libros del A.T. fueron traducidos no más allá de c. 150 a. C. No obstante, desde el descubrimiento de los rollos del mar Muerto, hay un consenso creciente de que la LXX data de c. 200 a. C. Para más información ver el libro de Laird Harris, *Inspiration and Canonicity of the Bible* (Grand Rapids: Zondervan, 1977), p. 99.

21. Ver G. B. Caird, *The Language and Imagery of the Bible* (Filadelfia: Westminster Press, 1980), p. 123.

22. Aunque la LXX fue escrita para los judíos que se encontraban en la diáspora que no hablaban ni entendían el hebreo, con el tiempo los judíos la rechazaron por ser adoptada por los cristianos en aquellas zonas donde la koiné era la lengua franca. No obstante, ese hecho no quita nada del valor de la LXX como una herramienta muy útil para la crítica textual del A.T.

textos encontrados en leccionarios, una colección de textos bíblicos que las iglesias empleaban en sus cultos. Pero en la mayoría de los casos sus citas son de la LXX. De las 93 veces que Pablo cita un texto del A.T., 51 de ellas son una copia exacta de la LXX[23].

## El texto masorético

El texto masorético es la más importante de las cuatro fuentes empleadas por los críticos textuales del A.T. El término «texto masorético» se usa en dos sentidos. En el sentido más estricto del término, se refiere al texto del Códice Cairo (c. 895) y del Códice Leningrado (c. 1008). Pero en su sentido más amplio se refiere a todas las copias del A.T. hechas por unos eruditos judíos llamados masoretas, los cuales destacaron por unas innovaciones que introdujeron en el texto hebreo. ¿En qué consistían esas innovaciones?

En el año 70 algunos rabinos tomaron la decisión de dedicarse a la conservación de los valores y literatura nacional de los judíos, tesoros que fácilmente podrían perderse con la nueva dispersión de los judíos provocada por la destrucción de Jerusalén. De hecho, muchos judíos de Palestina en esa época no entendían el hebreo. Por tanto, no podían leer el A.T., la obra literaria más importante del pueblo de Dios. Temiendo que la pronunciación correcta del hebreo se perdiera y que las ambigüedades y dudas se multiplicaran, estos judíos establecieron escuelas rabínicas en varios lugares. Aunque no es posible identificar una fecha para la aparición de los masoretas, estos rabinos en efecto eran sus precursores[24]. Para el año 500 los masoretas ya habían establecido sus dos escuelas más famosas en Babilonia (Irak en la actualidad) y Tiberias (en la orilla occidental del mar de Galilea). Estudiaban los manuscritos del A.T. que tenían a su alcance, realizaban los cambios que creían más acorde con el texto original y producían nuevas copias del texto del A.T.

---

23. Ver A. Berkeley Mickelsen, *Interpreting the Bible* (Grand Rapids: Eerdmans, 1963), p. 126.

24. Algunos sugieren que los masoretas surgieron en algún momento después de la destrucción de Jerusalén en el año 70. En su libro *Interpreting the Bible* (Grand Rapids: Eerdmans, 1963), p. 16, Mickelsen sugiere el siglo II.

Pero la innovación que distingue a los masoretas de otros eruditos de su tiempo es su codificación de la *masorah* (de ahí su nombre «masoretas»), las tradiciones que existían sobre la pronunciación e interpretación del texto original, y su diseño de un sistema de puntos y rayas colocados encima y debajo de las consonantes para indicar las vocales que se usaban en el pasado, pero sin cambiar ni tocar las consonantes[25]. También escribieron comentarios en los márgenes y debajo del texto sobre formas únicas de expresión en el texto, estadísticas sobre la forma de deletrear una palabra, variantes en los manuscritos que tenían a su disposición, la forma en que se leía litúrgicamente el texto, la sintaxis de las frases y una explicación de las formas arcaicas de palabras y frases que ellos habían modernizado.

Los masoretas eran muy conscientes de que solamente las consonantes eran inspiradas por Dios, no su sistema de vocales. Su propósito no era crear una nueva tradición, sino preservar las tradiciones antiguas que ya existían. Con su sistema de vocales, comentarios e instrucciones, lograron construir «un muro alrededor de la Ley... y ayudaron a los que copiaban las Escrituras a eliminar casi cada semblanza de error»[26]. Como una última línea de defensa contra la introducción de errores en las copias, colocaron al final de cada libro un «colofón[27] con el número total de consonantes en el texto, la identificación y el lugar de la consonante en el mismísimo centro del libro y otros mecanismos matemáticos que permitían a los copistas revisar una y otra vez su trabajo»[28]. Si un manuscrito contaba con más o menos palabras que el número correcto, era enterrado bajo tierra según la ley judía. Los historiadores creen que la

25. Debido al éxito del cristianismo en Palestina en el siglo II, muchos eruditos judíos que se dedicaban a la crítica textual del A.T. emigraron a Babilonia, donde fundaron varias escuelas. Pero la conquista de Palestina en el 638 por el Islam facilitó un resurgimiento de la crítica textual del A.T. por parte de los judíos en Tiberias. Fue el trabajo y sistema de vocalización de los masoretas de Tiberias el que eventualmente ganó prestigio y figuró en el texto masorético.

26. Carl E. Armerding, *The Old Testament and Criticism* (Grand Rapids: Eerdmans, 1983), p. 107.

27. Una especie de postdata.

28. Walter C. Kaiser, Jr., *The Old Testament Documents: Are They Reliable and Relevant?* (Downers Grove: InterVarsity Press, 2001), p. 43.

creación de este sistema de vocales fue iniciada en el siglo V o VI y que fue terminada en el siglo X por las escuelas rabínicas en Babilonia y Palestina[29]. Ese sistema goza de un gran valor por cuanto se basa en una información que data de antes del primer siglo.

Las dos obras más famosas y valiosas para la crítica textual del A.T. son el Códice Cairo y el Códice Leningrado. El Códice Cairo fue redactado por el masoreta Moses ben Asher c. 895 y contiene los libros proféticos. El Códice Leningrado, producido por el masoreta Samuel ben Jacob, data de c. 1008 y es la copia más antigua de *todo* el A.T. que existe en este momento[30]. Se ha guardado desde mediados del siglo XIX en la Biblioteca Nacional de Rusia en Leningrado. Es tan estimado por los eruditos bíblicos como un reflejo fidedigno del texto original que ha servido como la base del A.T. en todas las versiones de la Biblia que existen en la actualidad. La *Biblia Hebraica Stuttgartensia* contiene una selección de las notas encontradas en los márgenes del Códice Leningrado. Los estudiantes de hebreo de cualquier seminario emplean la *Biblia Hebraica Stuttgartensia* como libro de texto. Los Códices Cairo y Leningrado fueron confeccionados con base en miles de manuscritos que datan de la Edad Media (siglos V–XV). Lamentablemente, todos esos manuscritos fueron destruidos de acuerdo con la práctica de los judíos.

## Los rollos del mar Muerto

Debido a la práctica de los judíos de destruir los manuscritos deteriorados o cuyo texto era considerado inferior, las copias más antiguas del texto del A.T. encontradas habían sido: (1) unos amuletos de plata

---

29. Puesto que ya existía en tiempos de Esdras un sistema sencillo que introducía las innovaciones que más tarde fueron desarrolladas y sistematizadas por los masoretas, los eruditos se refieren a los textos que empleaban ese sistema sencillo como «protomasoréticos». Por eso, en su artículo «How Reliable is the Old Testament Text?» en *Can I Trust the Bible?* (Chicago: Moody Press, 1968), Harris habla de una clase de texto masorético que existía antes del 200 a. C.

30. El Códice de Alepo (Siria) data de la primera mitad del siglo X y, por tanto, representaba en su momento la copia completa del A.T. más antigua. Pero durante las manifestaciones antijudías en 1947 una cuarta parte de los folios fueron destruidos.

que contienen la bendición aarónica de Números 6:24-26, que datan de mediados del siglo VII a. C.; (2) un fragmento que data del siglo III a. C.; (3) unos 250.000 fragmentos descubiertos en 1897 en la genizá (almacén) de una sinagoga del Cairo, que datan de los siglos VI–VIII[31]; y (4) los Códices Cairo (c. 895) y Leningrado (c. 1008). Pero ese panorama cambió por completo en 1947 con el descubrimiento de los rollos del mar Muerto[32], unos 931 documentos que datan desde mediados del siglo III a. C. hasta el 40 d. C.[33] De repente la crítica textual del A.T. ganó unos ¡mil años! en cuanto a la antigüedad de los manuscritos que tenía a su disposición.

Este descubrimiento ocurrió de forma «accidental», igual que tantos otros descubrimientos significativos en el campo de la crítica textual de la Biblia. Un adolescente que pastoreaba las ovejas de su familia buscaba una oveja que se había descarriado. Al ver una cueva en la fachada de un precipicio, tiró una piedra dentro de ella con la esperanza de que la oveja estuviera allí y saliera asustada. Pero oyó cómo su piedra rompía una vasija. Al explorar esa cueva (designada por los arqueólogos como «cueva número 1») en busca de su oveja perdida, encontró varias tinajas, la mayoría de ellas rotas, que contenían rollos de pergamino envueltos en lino. Después, los arqueólogos encontraron en esta misma cueva siete rollos. Los más importantes fueron dos

---

31. Con base en el gran número de fragmentos encontrados en esta sinagoga, muchos creen que las genizás se empleaban para guardar las copias deterioradas o las que habían sido sustituidas por otras mejores.

32. Ha habido mucha discusión en cuanto al nombre que debe emplearse para describir el lugar de este descubrimiento. El sitio más cercano a la primera cueva y a otras diez en la zona inmediata que figura en el mapa son unas ruinas llamadas Khirbet Qumrán (donde vivían los esenios) y el Wadi Qumrán. De ahí el uso de la palabra Qumrán. La palabra *wadi* es de origen árabe y se refiere a un cauce fluvial que tiene agua solamente en tiempos de mucha lluvia. El mar Muerto queda a una milla (1,6 km) de distancia. Por tanto, el uso de la palabra *Qumrán* sería técnicamente más correcto. También se ha discutido si se debe hablar de los rollos o de los manuscritos del mar Muerto/Qumrán. Solamente una fracción de lo que se ha descubierto existe en forma de rollos. Pero como el mar Muerto es un sitio de conocimiento general para la mayoría de las personas interesadas en la Biblia, y como el público general se ha acostumbrado a hablar de rollos en lugar de fragmentos o manuscritos, usaremos el término «rollos del mar Muerto».

33. Ver *Why Trust the Bible?* (Torrence: Rose Publishing, 2008), p. 18.

copias del libro de Isaías[34], además de varios fragmentos de otros manuscritos. Pero fue en la cueva número 4 donde encontraron el mayor tesoro: aproximadamente 15.000 fragmentos que representaban unos 600 manuscritos. Cuando terminaron en 1956 la exploración de las más de 200 cuevas de la zona, veinticinco de ellas contenían rollos de pergamino, papiro y cobre, miles de fragmentos de papiro y objetos como monedas, cerámica, etcétera. En once de esas veinticinco cuevas encontraron fragmentos similares a los rollos de la primera, además de fragmentos de unos 600 libros, representando una extensa colección de literatura sectaria y obras apócrifas. Los historiadores creen que todo lo descubierto era la biblioteca de los esenios, una secta ascética del judaísmo que vivió en esa zona entre c. 150 a. C. y el 68–70. Se especula que estos documentos fueron enterrados precipitadamente sin ninguna clase de protección debido a la inminente invasión de los romanos en el 68, la cual acabó con la dcstrucción de Jerusalén en el año 70. Después de esa fecha los esenios desaparecieron. No se sabe si escaparon c. 68 o fueron destruidos por los romanos.

Una cuarta parte de los fragmentos encontrados son de textos bíblicos[35]. Algunos fueron encontrados en el suelo y son tan pequeños que contienen solamente una letra del alfabeto. Evidentemente, no tienen ningún valor para el crítico textual. Pero otros fragmentos contienen un par de palabras o un par de columnas de texto. Con una paciencia y perseverancia impresionantes, se ha podido identificar el texto del A.T. al cual pertenecen. Entre todos los rollos y fragmentos hallados en estas cuevas había porciones de todos los libros del A.T. (con la excepción de Ester), algunos de los cuales datan del 250 a. C. Juzgando por el número de manuscritos hallados de cada libro, es evidente que Deuteronomio, Salmos e Isaías eran los favoritos de los esenios, precisamente los mismos libros cuyos textos más citan los autores del N.T. Algunos libros cuentan con meros fragmentos (Crónicas cuenta con solamente seis líneas) mientras

34. El primero contenía todo el libro. El segundo estaba muy deteriorado y contenía solamente porciones de ciertos capítulos.

35. La «cueva 7» era única porque contenía los fragmentos de diecinueve manuscritos escritos en griego koiné, el idioma empleado por los autores del N.T.

que otros con porciones más extensas. Hay un manuscrito de todo el libro de Isaías (*copia a*) que data del 150 a. C. y otro (*copia b*) que contiene buena parte de los capítulos 38–66. La *copia b* data del primer siglo a. C. y se parece mucho al texto masorético. Aunque existen pequeñas diferencias entre los documentos del mar Muerto y el texto masorético, el acuerdo entre ellos es francamente sorprendente. Este hecho demuestra la precisión con la cual los judíos hicieron copias del A.T. a lo largo de los mil años siguientes.

## C. CONCLUSIONES

Hay tres conclusiones a las cuales podemos llegar en cuanto a las fuentes que los críticos textuales han tenido a su disposición y el resultado de su labor de identificar el texto que figuraba en los manuscritos originales del A.T.

*1. El Pentateuco samaritano tiene un valor limitado.* Los eruditos opinan que el Pentateuco samaritano fue escrito a finales del siglo II a. C. Aunque ese manuscrito original fue hecho con base en manuscritos anteriores a los que tenemos en este momento, la copia más antigua que existe del Pentateuco samaritano data del siglo XII; o sea, trece siglos después del manuscrito original. Además, sabiendo que los samaritanos cambiaron ciertos pasajes para defender sus doctrinas heréticas, el crítico textual no se fía mucho de esta fuente. Pero poco importa, porque los pasajes que han sido manipulados son más que evidentes. Además, el Pentateuco es la parte del A.T. que cuenta con menos variantes.

*2. El gran valor del texto masorético queda constatado.* Los masoretas copiaban las Escrituras con mucha más precisión que los esenios. No obstante, un poco más de la mitad de los rollos del mar Muerto, llamados protomasoréticos, los cuales datan del siglo II a. C. al primer siglo d. C., reflejan el mismo texto copiado por los masoretas Moses ben Asher c. 895 (Códice Cairo) y Samuel ben Jacob c. 1008 (Códice Leningrado). ¡Que la palabra de Dios haya sido preservada con tanta pureza durante tantos siglos es francamente espectacular! Los autores bíblicos escribieron sobre los eventos históricos de su época con una precisión que supera con creces las prácticas de los autores seculares de su día. Por ejemplo, no es fácil copiar correctamente los nombres de personas de otras culturas. Por eso, los nombres extranjeros son particularmente vulnerables al error. El A.T. hace referencia a unos veintiséis reyes de Egipto, Asiria, Babilonia, Moab y Persia. Sin embargo, la transliteración de esos nombres en el texto masorético coincide meticulosamente con los nombres de dichos reyes encontrados en documentos y monumentos seculares antiguos. Además, el tiempo histórico en el cual la Biblia coloca dichos reyes coincide con el tiempo que identifican esos documentos y monumentos.

*3. La LXX tiene un valor muy parecido, si no igual, al del texto masorético.* Aunque algunos eruditos opinan que el texto masorético es superior a la LXX, una comparación de los dos demuestra que en algunos textos la LXX es superior. Estas y otras consideraciones han llevado a Harris a afirmar:

> Debería decirse que el texto de la LXX está en armonía general con el texto masorético. No existen diferencias doctrinales. Aunque la LXX no es una traducción esclava de lo literal, se ve que está muy de acuerdo con el texto masorético. Pero aun con eso, las diferencias casi siempre se refieren a cuestiones pequeñas como las libertades propias de la labor de traducir, variaciones de estilo, errores menores cometidos al copiar el texto y la lucha con las dificultades del hebreo, los cuales son de interés para el erudito pero no representan ninguna diferencia significativa en el uso y significado del pasaje. El hecho es que, si dejáramos a un lado nuestras Biblias actuales, la LXX sería una copia muy satisfactoria del A.T., aunque sonaría algo extraña en ciertos pasajes. De hecho, durante los primeros tres siglos de la iglesia cristiana, cuando la mayoría de los creyentes hablaban el griego como su lengua franca, la LXX fue usada casi exclusivamente[36].

Debido a la gran precisión con que los judíos hicieron copias del A.T., los críticos textuales están absolutamente seguros en un 90 por ciento de lo que decían los manuscritos originales[37]. Y en cuanto al 10 por ciento restante, muchas de las variantes consisten en diferentes formas

36. Harris, «How Reliable is the Old Testament Text?», ob. cit., pp. 127–128.

37. Ver William Klein, Craig L. Blomberg y Robert L. Hubbard Jr., *Introduction to Biblical Interpretation* (Dallas: Word Publishing, 1993), p. 72.

de deletrear una palabra, el orden de aparición de las palabras, etcétera. Ese 10 por ciento irá reduciéndose en la medida en que se encuentren más manuscritos, puesto que la crítica textual del A.T. es una ciencia relativamente joven. Mientras tanto, las variantes no resueltas no afectan ninguna doctrina ni tambalean nuestra total confianza en la inspiración del A.T. y el texto que tenemos en nuestras Biblias.

# Apéndice D
# Crítica textual del N.T.

Mientras que los críticos textuales del A.T. cuentan con poco material pero de mucha calidad, sus colegas del N.T. están prácticamente inundados con manuscritos para investigar. Tanto es así que Harrington dice que «el mayor obstáculo con el cual el crítico textual del N.T. se enfrenta es la vergüenza que tanta riqueza provoca en él»[1]. Y aunque pueda parecer una desventaja que pocos de esos manuscritos sean iguales, la realidad es justo lo contrario. Cuantos más manuscritos tenga para comparar, más seguridad tendrá el crítico textual de poder identificar el texto original del N.T.

## A. FUENTES DE INVESTIGACIÓN

La cantidad de información que el crítico textual del N.T. tiene a su disposición es francamente espectacular. Se encuentra en cuatro fuentes principales.

*1. Cerca de 6000 manuscritos*[2]. Esta es la fuente más importante de la crítica textual del N.T. Muchos son fragmentos, y de los que no lo son, pocos abarcan todo un libro. Pero hay dos consideraciones

1. Daniel J. Harrington, *Interpreting the New Testament* (Wilmington: Michael Glazier, Inc., 1979), p. 16.

2. Según los datos que Plummer tenía a mano en 2013, dice en una nota a pie de página (p. 49) de su libro *Preguntas y respuestas sobre cómo interpretar la Biblia* (Grand Rapids: Portavoz, 2013) que «el recuento más reciente es de 5752 manuscritos».

que nos llevan a otorgarles un valor incalculable a estos manuscritos y fragmentos. Primera, la cantidad de material es tanta que «aun el libro menos representado del N.T., el libro de Apocalipsis, ha sido preservado en más de 300 manuscritos en griego, mientras que los Evangelios cuentan con miles de copias»[3]. Segunda, el número de años que ha transcurrido entre el manuscrito original y sus copias es marcadamente inferior al de los libros antiguos seculares.

*2. Unos 2000 leccionarios.* Los primeros cristianos seleccionaron textos bíblicos que consideraron apropiados para un día o evento especial en el calendario de sus iglesias y los colocaron en libros llamados leccionarios. Estos leccionarios servían también como un programa diario de lectura devocional para los miembros de las iglesias y representan la segunda fuente más importante para el crítico textual[4].

*3. Más de 10.000 traducciones al latín, siriaco, copto, armenio, árabe, persa, gótico, etcétera.* El valor de estas traducciones[5] consiste en que fueron hechas a partir de manuscritos más antiguos que los que tenemos a nuestra disposición hoy. Además, indican cómo los traductores entendían palabras griegas cuyo significado es difícil de identificar.

*4. Miles de citas bíblicas en los comentarios de los padres de la iglesia.* Con base en los muchos textos bíblicos que los padres citaron en sus comentarios, se podría reconstruir el texto original del N.T. sin los miles de manuscritos disponibles. La mayoría de estas citas fueron escritas en griego y latín, además de un número considerable en siriaco y en un par de idiomas más[6]. El valor de los leccionarios y de las citas de los padres es que fueron hechos a partir de manuscritos más antiguos que los que tenemos. Pero todos son copias porque ningún manuscrito original de un leccionario o comentario de un padre ha sobrevivido. Por tanto, antes de fiarse de cualquier manuscrito, el crítico textual ha

---

3. Gordon D. Fee, «The Textual Criticism of the New Testament» de *Biblical Criticism: Historical, Literary and Textual* (Grand Rapids: Zondervan, 1978), p. 129.

4. En 1978 Fee dijo que se habían descubierto hasta el momento 2193 manuscritos de leccionarios. Ver Fee, ob. cit., p. 132.

5. Estos manuscritos son llamados «versiones» por los críticos textuales.

6. Los escritos de Crisóstomo (347–407) son los más extensos de todos los padres de la iglesia. Era un predicador tan brillante que le dieron el apodo de «boca de oro».

de hacerse varias preguntas. Por ejemplo, cuando un padre citó un texto bíblico, ¿lo copió palabra por palabra de un manuscrito que tenía delante? ¿Lo citó de memoria (una práctica muy común)? ¿Hizo una referencia a este sin pretender citarlo palabra por palabra? ¿Introdujo las palabras de un pasaje paralelo que no aparecen en el texto bíblico que citó? Y, ¿es posible que la persona que hizo la copia de la obra de un padre alterara de alguna forma los textos bíblicos citados?

La cantidad de material encontrado en estas cuatro fuentes representa una ventaja significativa para el crítico textual del N.T., pero a la vez un gran desafío debido al gran número de errores[7] que existen en esas fuentes; unos 250.000 según algunos[8]. No obstante, la tarea de identificar el texto original del N.T. no es imposible ni tan formidable como parece.

> Aunque es verdad que no hay dos manuscritos que sean idénticos, es igualmente verdad que muchos manuscritos son tan parecidos que tienden a agruparse en tres (algunos críticos textuales piensan que en cuatro) familias principales de textos (clases de texto). Dichas clases de texto pueden identificarse en base (1) al porcentaje de acuerdos que ciertos manuscritos tienen entre sí en medio de sus respectivos desacuerdos y (2) la cantidad de veces que coinciden en variantes que sean peculiares a ellos[9].

## B. LA CAUSA DE LOS ERRORES EN LOS MANUSCRITOS

Durante más de 1500 años —hasta que Gutenberg inventó la imprenta tipográfica en 1450— todas las copias de la Biblia fueron hechas a mano por creyentes que simplemente querían una copia de un libro bíblico o por profesionales (escribas, copistas, monjes). En muchos casos los profesionales escribían al dictado en una sala, produciendo así muchas copias a la vez. Podemos clasificar los errores de estos profesionales en dos grupos.

---

7. Llamados «variantes» por los críticos textuales.
8. Ver *Biblia textual: Reina Valera* (Pembroke Pines, Florida: Sociedad Bíblica Iberoamericana, sin fecha), p. 3. Luis Riobueno sirvió como presidente de la Junta Directiva de esta revista.
9. Fee, ob. cit., pp. 134–135.

## Errores involuntarios

*1. Factores internos.* El cansancio y la monotonía que resultaban al copiar un manuscrito o escribir al dictado hora tras hora llevaron a muchos copistas a cometer errores sin querer. Puede que un monje escuchara bien una palabra, pero que la deletreara incorrectamente debido a su cansancio o a un simple desliz de su mano. Si era de edad avanzada y padecía de sordera o ceguera, era inevitable que introdujera aún más errores en el texto. Metzger añade otro factor que ni se nos ocurre en el siglo XXI.

> Aunque nos parece extraño hoy día, en tiempos antiguos no era costumbre sentarse a una mesa para escribir. Tanto las evidencias literarias como las artísticas sugieren que hasta la Edad Media era costumbre de los escribas estar de pie mientras hacían notas relativamente cortas o que se sentaran sobre un banco o taburete (o incluso en el suelo) mientras mantenían sus rollos o códices sobre sus rodillas. Evidentemente, dicha postura era más cansina que la de sentarse a una mesa, aunque esa última alternativa tenía que ser agotadora para los escribas que se dedicaban a esta tarea seis horas al día, mes tras mes[10].

*2. Factores externos.* Era fácil introducir un error en el texto al escribir al dictado en una sala donde no se oía muy bien, cuando la pronunciación de una palabra se parecía mucho a otra palabra, cuando un escriba resfriado tosía frecuentemente o cuando se producía otra clase de ruido. Si una persona hacía una copia a solas en su propio cuarto, y si la luz era insuficiente, era fácil que introdujera palabras en el texto que creía haber visto en el manuscrito que copiaba.

Pero había otro factor externo que produjo un número aún mayor de errores prácticamente imposibles de evitar. Hasta los comienzos del siglo IX se empleaba un tipo de escritura llamado «uncial», el cual consistía en letras mayúsculas sin ningún espacio entre las palabras. Por ejemplo, SINNINGÚNESPACIOENTRELASPALABRAS. A principios del siglo IX se creó otro tipo llamado «cursivo» (o «minúsculo»).

10. Bruce M. Metzger, *The Text of the New Testament* (Londres: Oxford University Press, 1964), pp. 16–17.

Igual que el tipo uncial, el cursivo no colocaba ningún espacio entre las letras. Por ejemplo, *nocolocabaningúnespacioentrelasletras.* Para finales del siglo X el cursivo había desplazado al uncial. Aproximadamente el 90 por ciento de los manuscritos griegos del N.T. encontrados hasta el momento provienen del período del cursivo[11]. Al leer las ilustraciones de estos dos estilos de escribir, el lector no ha tenido ningún problema en entenderlas porque la frase era corta y el autor acababa de decirla. Pero el escriba que copiaba a solas un manuscrito —en lugar de al dictado— se enfrentaba con la tendencia constante de saltar una palabra o frase entera, repetir una línea o escribir una palabra o línea dos veces debido a la falta de un espacio entre las palabras.

*3. Fallos de juicio.* Cuando las copias se hacían en grupo se les prohibía hablar a los escribas. Pero había quienes no podían contenerse y buscaban formas de comunicarse con su colega más cercano. A veces los copistas escribían mensajes cortos en el margen de la copia que hacían. A la vez, era común introducir en el margen una palabra que inadvertidamente habían dejado fuera del texto, corregir un error que habían cometido, sustituir una palabra difícil de entender por un sinónimo o incluir un comentario sobre el texto que copiaban. Años más tarde, cuando otro escriba hacía una copia de ese manuscrito, se enfrentaba con la necesidad de determinar si dichas palabras en el margen debían incluirse en el texto. En algunos casos era evidente que no. Por ejemplo, hay un caso en el que un escriba reprende a su colega por jugar con el texto, diciendo: «¡Tonto! ¿No puedes dejar el texto antiguo como estaba en vez de alterarlo?». En otro caso un escriba dice: «Qué frío hace hoy». Su colega responde: «Claro, estamos en invierno». O dice: «Esta lámpara da muy mala luz». Y su compañero le contesta: «Es hora de que nos pongamos a trabajar». Pero en otros casos no era tan evidente lo que se debía hacer. De ahí que un simple comentario a un colega pudiera incorporarse en el texto. Se ha estimado que un 95 por ciento de todos los errores son accidentales o involuntarios[12]. El 5 por ciento restantes fueron introducidos a propósito.

---

11. J. Harold Greenlee, *Introduction to New Testament Textual Criticism* (Grand Rapids: Eerdmans, 1970), p. 29.

12. Ver Robert L. Plummer, *Forty Questions About Interpreting the Bible* (Grand Rapids: Kregel, 2010), p. 52.

### Errores intencionales

*1. Correcciones.* Algunos escribas corregían lo que consideraban un error gramatical u ortográfico en el texto que copiaban. A veces cambiaban el orden de las palabras o eliminaban supuestas discrepancias o dificultades. En otras ocasiones añadían palabras que esperaban encontrar. Por ejemplo, si el texto decía «la Palabra», el copista añadía «de Dios». Aunque sus intenciones eran nobles, estas prácticas no hacían otra cosa que añadir un error más a los que ya existían.

*2. Aclaraciones.* A veces los escribas cambiaban el orden de las palabras, frases y párrafos con el deseo de producir un texto más coherente. Para lograr esa meta, algunos añadían palabras al texto[13].

*3. Armonización de pasajes paralelos.* Era costumbre de algunos escribas añadir las palabras de un texto paralelo para que el texto quedara más completo. Por ejemplo, Lucas 11:13 dice: «¿Cuánto más vuestro Padre celestial dará el Espíritu Santo a los que se lo pidan?». Puesto que el pasaje paralelo de Mateo 7:11 dice «buenas cosas», la copia que el escriba hacía de Lucas 11:13 podría leerse: «¿Cuánto más vuestro Padre celestial dará el Espíritu Santo *y buenas cosas* a los que se lo pidan?».

## C. LAS HERRAMIENTAS DE LA CRÍTICA TEXTUAL

A lo largo de los siglos muchos eruditos estudiaron los manuscritos que tenían a su alcance en un intento de identificar el texto de los manuscritos originales. Pero la crítica textual como ciencia formal no nació hasta el siglo XVIII con las investigaciones de eruditos en Inglaterra y el continente europeo. Los críticos textuales emplean varias herramientas para realizar su trabajo. La primera es la de fijarse en el material empleado para escribir y el estilo de escribir empleado por el

13. En su artículo «The Text of the New Testament and Modern Translations» en *Christianity Today* (22 junio 1973), p. 9, Gordon Fee opina que «se puede hacer demasiado hincapié en el concepto *deliberado.* La mayoría de estos cambios representaban un intento de ayudar al texto. Parece que los primeros escribas estuvieran más preocupados por el mensaje inspirado del texto que por las mismas palabras, porque frecuentemente hicieron que el mensaje fuera más claro al hacer que la gramática fuera más clara, añadieron sustantivos y pronombres donde podría haber ambigüedad, sustituyeron sinónimos comunes por palabras poco conocidas, clarificaron frases difíciles y confirmaron un pasaje con otro (especialmente en los Evangelios)».

copista, porque eso les permite establecer la fecha general en la cual dicho manuscrito fue producido. Pero quizás la herramienta más importante es la de determinar la familia a la cual pertenece el manuscrito.

## Familias de manuscritos

Al extenderse el cristianismo a los países del Mediterráneo y lugares más lejanos, cada iglesia quería tener una copia de los libros del N.T. que habían sido escritos hasta ese momento. Al hacer copias para suplir esa demanda, cada copista seguía las prácticas y costumbres de la zona en que vivía. El descubrimiento de este hecho no ocurrió hasta el siglo XVIII, pero el desarrollo de esta información no tomó lugar hasta la última mitad del siglo XIX. Aunque los críticos textuales siguen debatiendo el número de familias textuales que existen, muchos opinan que hay cuatro[14].

*1. Alejandrina*[15]. Puesto que los escribas de esta zona estudiaron y se prepararon en las tradiciones de los eruditos de Alejandría, sus manuscritos son muy precisos. Además, se caracterizan por la brevedad y austeridad. Puesto que el copista típico tenía la tendencia de ampliar el texto, los críticos textuales creen que el manuscrito más corto y con ciertas complicaciones gramaticales tiene más probabilidades de reflejar el manuscrito original que un manuscrito más largo y fácil de entender. Por estos motivos, los manuscritos alejandrinos y los que reúnen sus características son considerados los más fiables. El Códice Vaticano y el Códice Sinaítico del siglo IV son los representantes más importantes de esta familia de manuscritos.

*2. Occidental.* Esta zona incluía Italia, el norte de África, Europa occidental y las islas británicas (Gales, Irlanda, Inglaterra). Padres de la iglesia como Taciano (c. 120–c. 180), Ireneo (c. 130–c. 202), Tertuliano (c. 160–c. 220) y Cipriano (c. 200–258) citaban en sus escritos textos bíblicos que pertenecían a esta familia. El texto de esta familia es más largo que el texto de otras familias debido a las añadiduras de sus copistas. Además, faltan muchos textos. No obstante,

---

14. Además de estas cuatro familias principales, los críticos textuales han detectado que muchos manuscritos son de una procedencia mixta, de varias familias.

15. Llamada también *neutral* y *egipcia.*

hay indicaciones de que los manuscritos occidentales son tan antiguos como los de la familia alejandrina. Por eso, algunos críticos textuales consideran los textos de estas dos familias de igual valor. De hecho, hay poca diferencia entre sus respectivos textos[16].

*3. Cesarea.* No existe un consenso entre los críticos textuales en cuanto a la zona de donde proviene esta familia. Sus manuscritos reflejan una mezcla de textos occidentales y alejandrinos. Muchos críticos textuales creen que proceden de un lugar desconocido de Oriente. Por eso, colocan estos manuscritos en la familia bizantina (llamada también Imperio romano de Oriente).

*4. Bizantina.* Es posible que esta familia de manuscritos proceda de Antioquía (Siria). Los eruditos creen que un manuscrito hecho por esta familia fue llevado a Constantinopla y de allí fue distribuido por todo el Imperio bizantino. Durante su existencia el Imperio bizantino fue un baluarte del cristianismo. Los copistas de esta familia se esforzaron en hacer copias completas y lúcidas, puliendo cualquier expresión tosca y combinando textos paralelos de otros libros del N.T. Puesto que la población griega del Imperio bizantino necesitaba muchas copias del N.T., el texto bizantino fue el más difundido de todas las familias entre los siglos VI y XV. Un 80 por ciento de todos los manuscritos que se han descubierto proceden de esta familia. Como consecuencia, los manuscritos de esta familia fueron aceptados como los más autoritativos. No obstante, la mayoría de los eruditos creen que no representan el texto más antiguo ni el más fiable en cuanto a lo que decían los manuscritos originales.

## Principios y métodos de trabajo

Aunque la crítica textual es frecuentemente presentada como una ciencia exacta, no lo es. Por lo tanto, en lugar de aplicar unas leyes inflexibles que no admiten excepciones, el crítico textual ha de compaginar varios principios basados en el sentido común para llegar a una conclusión en cuanto al texto original de un libro del N.T.

Como paso previo a la aplicación de esos principios, el crítico

16. Ver R. Laird Harris, *Inspiration and Canonicity of the Bible* (Grand Rapids: Zondervan, 1977), pp. 92–93.

textual estudia todos los manuscritos que existen en el idioma original del N.T. con el propósito de identificar los textos donde se producen variantes. A continuación, consulta las citas bíblicas que los padres de la iglesia incluyeron en sus escritos y las traducciones a otros idiomas, porque en muchos casos han sido copiadas de manuscritos más antiguos. Estas traducciones, conjuntamente con otros manuscritos de obras seculares escritas en el primer siglo, ayudan al crítico textual a identificar el significado de ciertas palabras griegas que no son muy claras porque esos idiomas no se hablan desde hace dos mil años, o porque aparecen una sola vez en el N.T. y su contexto no aclara suficientemente su significado. Las traducciones indican cómo el traductor entendía esas palabras, mientras que las obras seculares proveen contextos y significados adicionales. Una vez que el crítico textual ha realizado estas tareas básicas, está en posición de aplicar unos principios basados en el sentido común. Por regla general, ninguno de ellos será capaz por sí solo de convencer al crítico textual de qué dice el manuscrito original. Por eso, ha de compaginar tantos de estos principios como pueda antes de tomar una determinación. Por ejemplo:

1. La *calidad* de un manuscrito pesa más que la *cantidad* de manuscritos que lo avalan. La tarea del crítico textual del N.T. no consiste en contar el número de manuscritos a favor de un texto, sino en sopesar la calidad de un manuscrito.

2. La copia más cercana en el tiempo al escrito original es la que con toda probabilidad mejor refleja ese texto original, ya que habrá experimentado menos copias con su correspondiente aumento de errores. El texto apoyado por los manuscritos y traducciones más antiguos, conjuntamente con las citas de los padres de la iglesia, suele ser idéntico al manuscrito original. Terry dice que «esta norma es tan obvia que no hace falta ningún comentario. Es un hecho interesante e importante que una gran parte del N.T. descanse sobre esta clase de evidencia que es tan decisiva. Aunque el número total de errores es de más de 100.000, la gran mayoría de ellos consisten en una mera diferencia de deletreo y otras diferencias ligeras debido a las costumbres peculiares de diferentes escribas»[17]. Desde que Terry hizo esta observa-

---

17. Milton S. Terry, *Biblical Hermeneutics* (Grand Rapids: Zondervan, 1969), p. 132.

ción en su libro clásico sobre la hermenéutica en 1883, se han descubierto muchos manuscritos más, aumentando el número de errores hasta 250.000 según la opinión de algunos. No obstante, sigue en pie la observación de Terry en cuanto a la naturaleza de los errores encontrados.

El pasaje sobre la mujer sorprendida en adulterio (Jn. 7:53–8:11) es el ejemplo clásico de este principio. Este texto figuraba en todas las versiones de la Biblia como una parte íntegra del texto del N.T., hasta que se descubrieron unos manuscritos muy antiguos que demostraron que fue introducido después del año 300. Ahora, aunque Juan 7:53–8:11 se encuentra en todas las versiones modernas del N.T., una nota de los editores advierte al lector de que no aparece en los manuscritos más antiguos.

3. El texto más corto y más difícil de entender tiene más probabilidades de reflejar el texto original puesto que los copistas tenían más tendencia a aumentar y cambiar las palabras de un texto para simplificar o clarificar frases difíciles de entender, que a recortar el texto o dejarlo tal y como estaba.

4. Sabiendo que algunos copistas se tomaron la libertad de combinar los detalles complementarios de pasajes paralelos, el texto que presente menos detalles tiene más probabilidades de reflejar el texto original.

## D. UN TEXTO FIABLE

Si tuviéramos en nuestro poder los manuscritos originales de los libros de la Biblia, no haría falta la ciencia de la crítica textual. Pero el hecho es que no tenemos ni un fragmento de un manuscrito original del A.T. ni del N.T. ¿Por qué no? La respuesta es sencilla y razonable. El papiro es un material demasiado frágil para sobrevivir tantos siglos. «Pero —alguien objetará— hay fragmentos de papiro del primer siglo de índole secular que sí han sobrevivido». La respuesta es sencilla y razonable; a saber, si se han requerido millones de comunicaciones seculares del primer siglo escritas en papiro para que sobrevivieran un par de fragmentos, ¿cuáles son las probabilidades matemáticas de que uno de los 27 manuscritos originales del N.T. haya sobrevivido? Y aún son mayores las probabilidades de que un manuscrito original de A.T. no sobreviviera debido a su mayor antigüedad.

Si aceptáramos como válida la premisa de que no podemos estar seguros de lo que decían los manuscritos originales de la Biblia porque no poseemos ni uno solo de ellos, eliminaríamos también buena parte de la historia secular, porque tampoco tenemos el manuscrito original de las obras de Platón, Aristóteles, Josefo, los autores griegos de tragedias y muchos otros autores antiguos. En algunos casos han sobrevivido solamente un par de copias de sus obras, algunas de las cuales datan de una fecha muy posterior a cuando se escribió el manuscrito original. Si aceptamos como fidedigno el texto de estas obras seculares, ¿cuánto más deberíamos hacer lo mismo con la Biblia, para la cual tenemos un promedio de mil veces más evidencia[18]?

Aunque no tenemos ningún manuscrito original de ningún libro de la Biblia, los críticos textuales de todas las tendencias teológicas y no teológicas afirman que saben lo que dicen los manuscritos originales en base a dos hechos. Primero, aunque nunca hemos visto un manuscrito original de un libro del N.T., otros sí los han visto. En el año 200, Tertuliano (c. 160–c. 220) dijo que los manuscritos originales se guardaban en las iglesias fundadas por los apóstoles donde podían ser inspeccionados. Por tanto, cualquier duda que había en cuanto a un supuesto error en una copia de un libro del N.T. podía ser despejada al compararla con el manuscrito original. Así que muchas de las primeras copias del N.T. reflejaban con absoluta precisión los manuscritos originales[19]. Segundo, aunque Dios no eligió conservar los manuscritos originales, la cantidad de manuscritos que tenemos del N.T. y la fiabilidad impresionante de los pocos manuscritos que tenemos del A.T. nos llevan a concluir que Dios en su providencia aseguró que el texto de su Palabra no se perdiera. Tanto es así que Bray dice:

> En cuanto al texto bíblico, a estas alturas no es de esperar que se hagan algunos descubrimientos nuevos dramáticos que lo alteren sustancialmente. Puede que haya un par de mejoras aquí y allá. Pero el texto griego ha sido acordado de forma demasiada amplia como para permitir un desafío serio por parte de un material

18. Ver Gordon Govier, «Sensation Before Scholarship» en *Christianity Today* (mayo 2012), pp. 12–13.

19. Ver Harris, ob. cit., p. 89.

nuevo. Esta impresión es igualmente verdad para el texto hebreo y arameo del A.T., el cual de todas formas nunca ha demostrado la misma variedad (entre los manuscritos)[20].

> «Las palabras de Jehová son palabras limpias, como plata refinada en horno de tierra, purificada siete veces. Tú, Jehová, los guardarás; de esta generación los preservarás para siempre». «Sécase la hierba; marchítase la flor; mas la palabra del Dios nuestro permanece para siempre».
>
> **(Sal. 12:6-7; Is. 40:8)**

Esta gran cantidad de manuscritos ha llevado a algunos eruditos a poner una cifra numérica para indicar el nivel de su convicción de que saben lo que decían los manuscritos originales. Los grandes críticos textuales B. F. Wescott (1825–1901) y F. J. A. Hort (1828–1892) vivieron hace más de cien años cuando aún no se habían encontrado muchos de los manuscritos que tenemos a nuestra disposición hoy. No obstante, en ese momento del desarrollo de la ciencia de la crítica textual, Hort declaró que si ignoráramos las trivialidades como el cambio del orden de las palabras, la inserción u omisión de un artículo definido delante de los nombres de personas, etcétera, el número de palabras que quedan en duda no supera la cifra de 1/1000 (una de cada mil) en todo el N.T.[21] D. A. Carson (1946– ), reconocido erudito evangélico del N.T., afirma que «casi todos los críticos textuales reconocen que un 96 por ciento y hasta un 97 por ciento del N.T. griego es seguro... No hay absolutamente ninguna duda al respecto»[22]. Algunos críticos textuales emplean la cifra de 99 por ciento.

---

20. Gerald Bray, *Biblical Interpretation Past and Present* (Downers Grove: InterVarsity Press, 1996), p. 585.

21. Citado por G. Kenyon en su libro *Handbook to the Textual Criticism of the New Testament* (Londres: Macmillan, 1912), p. 7.

22. D. A. Carson en el documental «Who is This Jesus? Is He Risen?», producido por D. James Kennedy y Jerry Newcombe (Fort Lauderdale, Florida: Coral Ridge Ministries, 2000).

Sea cual sea la cifra correcta, lo cierto es que estos eruditos están *absolutamente seguros* de la cifra que sugieren, saben exactamente dónde se encuentran los pasajes que están en duda, saben cuáles son las opciones que existen en cuanto a lo que decía el manuscrito original (en la mayoría de los casos esas opciones tienen que ver con cuestiones gramaticales insignificantes) y que no hay ninguna doctrina en juego. Por tanto, cuando hablamos de la inspiración verbal de las Escrituras en los manuscritos originales, no estamos hablando de algo abstracto o teórico, sino de una realidad hecha posible por la providencia de Dios al preservar su Palabra intacta para nuestra salvación y crecimiento espiritual.

# Apéndice E

# La historia de la crítica textual del N.T.

Muy lejos de sembrar dudas en la mente del creyente, el conocimiento de la historia de la crítica textual del N.T. refuerza su convicción de que la Biblia que tiene en sus manos realmente corresponde a lo que dice el texto original. Además, muchos de los hallazgos considerados accidentales y fortuitos de manuscritos clave para la identificación del texto original del N.T. dejan al creyente con la convicción de que han sido providenciales, de que Dios ha intervenido en dichos descubrimientos con el fin de preservar su Palabra. La historia de la crítica textual del N.T. puede dividirse en seis etapas.

## A. MUCHAS COPIAS Y ERRORES (hasta el año 405)

La gran mayoría de los errores que figuran en las copias que tenemos del N.T. fueron introducidos durante los primeros cuatro siglos del cristianismo por creyentes que simplemente querían tener una copia del N.T. para su uso personal. Puesto que no eran escribas profesionales y no existía ningún control sobre las copias que se hacían, era inevitable que se produjeran muchos errores.

Al extenderse la predicación del evangelio, surgió la necesidad de traducir los manuscritos griegos a otros idiomas. El latín era el más importante. Aunque los ciudadanos del Imperio romano hablaban la koiné en sus comunicaciones personales y comerciales, el latín era empleado en los círculos gubernamentales locales y por los diplomáticos de cada país, ya que era el idioma oficial del Imperio. Los historiadores no saben cuándo comenzaron a producirse las traducciones del N.T. al latín[1]. No obstante, lo claro es que eran toscas y contaban con muchas variantes. Tanto era así, que los judíos menospreciaban a los cristianos por la confusión que existía en sus libros sagrados. Hasta el filósofo pagano Celso acusó a los cristianos de cambiar a placer el texto de dichos libros. Respondiendo a esa acusación, Orígenes (185-254) tuvo que admitir que él también estaba frustrado con las muchas variantes que encontraba en los manuscritos que tenía a su disposición. Agustín (354–430) sugirió que el problema de fondo era que cada creyente que tenía cierto conocimiento de koiné y latín se creía capaz de traducir la copia que tenía al latín, aunque su entendimiento de estos idiomas fuese superficial.

Jerónimo (c. 340–420), un padre de la iglesia, fue uno de los eruditos más competentes de su época. Cuando se quejó al papa Dámaso I de que existían tantas traducciones al latín como manuscritos griegos, el papa le encomendó la tarea de revisar la Biblia latina y así proveer para la iglesia un texto autoritativo de cara a las nuevas herejías que surgieran. Jerónimo terminó su traducción del N.T. en 383–384 y del A.T. en 390–405. Esta obra monumental, llamada la Vulgata, se basó en unos manuscritos griegos antiguos y en las mejores traducciones en latín[2]. La Vulgata representó el final de una etapa de la crítica textual.

---

1. Llamadas también versiones antiguas latinas o Itala.

2. Aunque la Iglesia Católica no reconoció la Vulgata como la Biblia oficial hasta el Concilio de Trento (1546), sirvió como la Biblia de la iglesia de Europa occidental y del norte de África y como la fuente principal de muchas otras traducciones durante los mil años siguientes. Aunque Jerónimo era un escritor prolífico, que produjo comentarios bíblicos, traducciones y obras eclesiásticas, su mayor logro fue la Vulgata, llamada también la Biblia Latina, la Biblia de Gutenberg y la Biblia Mazarino. La Biblia Mazarino se refiere a la copia de la Vulgata que atrajo por primera vez la atención de los eruditos. Esa copia se encontraba en la biblioteca del cardenal Mazarino (1602–1661), un diplomático y político muy hábil que trabajaba al servicio del papa.

## B. COPIAS MÁS PRECISAS (405–1516)

Cuando el emperador Constantino se convirtió al cristianismo en 313, surgió la posibilidad de resolver el problema de la proliferación de tantos manuscritos inferiores como se habían producido durante la primera época. Ahora se podrían hacer muchas copias de una sola vez y más precisas mediante el sistema de tener un lector y unos escribas a los que se dictaba. Este sistema se empleaba principalmente en los monasterios por ser los centros académicos. Sin embargo, hubo dos factores que hicieron imposible aprovechar esta oportunidad al máximo. Primero, aunque la Vulgata de Jerónimo era una obra magnífica, algunos escribas en los siglos siguientes se tomaron la libertad de introducir en sus copias unas variantes encontradas en las versiones antiguas latinas que Jerónimo había descartado. Por eso, se encuentra una mezcla de varias familias de texto en los aproximadamente 8000 manuscritos de la Vulgata que existen. Tanto es así, que los críticos textuales han determinado que una gran parte de la Vulgata, tal y como la conocemos hoy, no es de Jerónimo[3]. Por ese motivo las copias de la Vulgata que tenemos en este momento son poco fiables a la hora de identificar el texto original del N.T. Segundo, no se hizo ninguna evaluación, clasificación, ni revisión del texto para eliminar las muchas variantes y errores que existían en los manuscritos ya hechos y en los que se hacían. Nadie se preocupaba por identificar lo que decían los manuscritos originales del N.T.

La imprenta tipográfica, inventada en 1450 por Johannes Gutenberg, puso fin a 1500 años de copiar las Escrituras a mano. Aunque muchos escribas no abandonaron sus plumas, ese sistema tenía sus días contados. Ahora era posible producir una copia de las Escrituras con un grado de precisión imposible en los siglos anteriores. En 1454 la imprenta de Fust & Gutenberg en Maguncia (Alemania) produjo

---

3. En 1496 el Concilio de Trento reconoció este problema y la necesidad de realizar una versión revisada. En 1592 el papa Clemente VIII preparó y publicó la versión clementina, la cual ha servido desde entonces como la versión latina de la Iglesia Católica. La *New American Bible* del 2011 es la primera traducción de toda la Biblia autorizada por la Iglesia católica en más de tres siglos y medio. Es también la primera Biblia autorizada por la iglesia que ha sido traducida al inglés directamente de los idiomas originales de la Biblia (hebreo, arameo, griego) en lugar de la Vulgata de Jerónimo.

el primer documento con una imprenta tipográfica. Se trató de una indulgencia de una sola hoja que la Iglesia Católica pretendía vender a sus feligreses. Dos años más tarde, Gutenberg imprimió una magnífica edición de la Vulgata[4].

Sin embargo, aparte de unas obras cortas y puntuales, el texto completo del N.T. *en griego* no fue publicado hasta 1516. Puesto que el latín era el idioma predominante en Occidente, la demanda para manuscritos griegos había desaparecido. En el siglo XV los eruditos bíblicos tenían poco interés en el texto griego del N.T. La Vulgata era su Biblia y no necesitaban otra en griego. Además de la dificultad y el costo de fabricar los tipos griegos, la publicación de un libro tan extenso como el N.T. hubiera subido el precio aún más. Pero el mayor obstáculo para la publicación del N.T. en su idioma original era la amenaza que representaba para el prestigio de la Vulgata. Cualquier erudito del griego podría cuestionarla, criticarla y corregirla.

## C. EDICIONES DEL N.T. GRIEGO (1516–1633)

El desarrollo de la ciencia de la crítica textual hizo un salto significativo en el siglo XVI debido a varios factores. Primero, la imprenta tipográfica permitió la publicación de libros con un alto grado de precisión, un factor que facilitaba la labor de constatar y comparar las variantes en los manuscritos. Segundo, hubo un creciente interés en Europa por los idiomas, las culturas y los textos antiguos. Tercero, los eruditos de la Reforma protestante y la Contrarreforma católica prestaron mucha atención al estudio de los manuscritos griegos y hebreos de la Biblia. Eruditos judíos como Elias Levita y Jacob ben Chayyim los ayudaron a entender el hebreo del A.T. La publicación en 1506 de una gramática y léxico en hebreo en un solo tomo, escrito por Johannes Reuchlin (1455–1522), fue uno de los resultados de esta colaboración entre judíos y cristianos. La publicación de la primera edición de un N.T. griego sería otro resultado de todos estos factores.

En 1502 el cardenal primado Francisco Jiménez de Cisneros (1436–1517) de Toledo (España) propuso publicar una edición de la

4. Quedan unas cuarenta copias de la Vulgata imprimida por Gutenberg.

Biblia en hebreo, arameo, griego y latín en cuatro columnas paralelas. Los editores que le ayudaban sugirieron que colocara el latín en el centro, «igual que Jesús se encontraba en la cruz entre dos ladrones»[5]. Para lograr esta meta Cisneros reclutó a eruditos protestantes y judíos de toda Europa. El N.T. fue terminado e imprimido en 1514, pero no fue publicado porque Cisneros quería terminar el A.T. y luego publicar los dos Testamentos juntos. El A.T. fue terminado en 1517, pero el papa no aprobó su publicación hasta 1520. Esta obra magnífica de Cisneros no fue publicada hasta 1522, y fue llamada la *Complutensian políglota* o *Biblia políglota complutense*[6]. Aunque Cisneros *imprimió* el primer N.T. griego en 1514, le correspondió a otro *publicar* el primero en 1516.

Desiderio Erasmo de Róterdam (1466–1536) fue un humanista, filólogo, filósofo y teólogo holandés que algunos consideran el erudito más destacado de su época. Su fama como humanista se debe principalmente a sus ataques contra los abusos y errores de la iglesia y el Estado. Cuando el suizo Johann Froben se enteró del interés de Erasmo por publicar un N.T. griego, le ofreció una remuneración económica que superaba lo que otros impresores podían darle. Pero para arrebatarle a Cisneros la ventaja comercial de ser el primero en publicar un N.T. griego, le pidió a Erasmo que terminara el proyecto cuanto antes. Aunque los historiadores no saben cuánto tiempo tardó en producir su *Novum Instrumentum omne*, coinciden en que su texto cuenta con problemas serios. A pesar de que empleó varios manuscritos para diferentes partes del N.T., Erasmo dependió casi exclusivamente de dos manuscritos que databan del c. siglo XII. Más tarde, estos manuscritos fueron reconocidos por los críticos textuales como muy inferiores por pertenecer a la familia bizantina, la familia de textos menos fiable de todas. Luego, para el libro de Apocalipsis empleó un manuscrito que

5. Ver J. Harold Greenlee, *Introduction to New Testament Textual Criticism* (Grand Rapids: Eerdmans, 1970), p. 69.

6. No se sabe mucho de los manuscritos que empleó, pero parece que fueron pocos en número y de una fecha tardía, aunque los editores dijeron que emplearon los manuscritos más antiguos disponibles. La palabra «políglota» («muchos idiomas») hace referencia a que el texto aparece en cuatro idiomas, y la palabra «Complutensian» se refiere a Alcalá (*Complutum* en latín), la ciudad universitaria donde fue imprimida.

estaba mutilado y en el cual faltaban varios pasajes, como por ejemplo los últimos seis versículos del libro. Para resolver este problema, Erasmo se dirigió a la Vulgata y tradujo estos versículos del latín al griego. Además de estos problemas, el texto contenía centenares de errores tipográficos. Tres años más tarde el propio Erasmo publicó una segunda edición y luego tres ediciones más. Pero consultó pocos manuscritos adicionales y corrigió pocos de los errores que figuraban en su primera edición. Estas cuatro ediciones fueron recibidas en ciertos círculos con sospecha y hasta hostilidad.

De todas las ediciones del N.T. griego que fueron publicadas en los años siguientes, hay tres que merecen nuestra atención. Robertus Stephanus (1503–1559)[7], un impresor real afincado en París, publicó cuatro ediciones del N.T. griego entre 1546 y 1551. En su tercera edición (1550) hizo uso de los textos de Erasmo, la *Complutense* y quince manuscritos. Incluyó en esta edición un aparato crítico, citando las variantes que encontraba en estas fuentes. Fue la primera vez que un aparato crítico fue incluido en una edición del N.T.[8]

Teodoro de Beza (1519–1605) fue un eminente erudito bíblico francés y sucedió a Juan Calvino en Ginebra. Publicó nueve ediciones del N.T. griego entre 1565 y 1604 y una décima póstuma (1611), las cuales en esencia eran los textos de Erasmo y Stephanus. Su reputación como erudito sirvió para popularizar lo que llegaría a llamarse el Textus Receptus.

Entre 1624 y 1652 los holandeses Bonaventure Elzevir (1583–1652) y Abraham Elzevir (1592–1652), tío y sobrino respectivamente, publicaron siete ediciones del N.T. griego, basadas en los textos de Erasmo y Beza. Su interés en un N.T. griego era más bien comercial. De ahí que afirmaran en el prefacio de su segunda edición de 1633: «Usted tiene en sus manos el texto (*textum*) que ahora es recibido (*receptum*) por todos, en el cual no le damos nada que sea alterado o corrompido». A causa de este prefacio puramente publicitario, el *Novum Instrumentum omne* de Erasmo, conjuntamente con las ediciones

7. A veces llamado por su nombre francés (Robert Estienne).

8. Otra novedad de esta edición era la división del texto en capítulos y versículos, la primera vez que se había hecho en un texto de la Biblia. Esta edición de Stephanus sirvió como base para la *King James Versión* (1611) de la Biblia en inglés.

publicadas por Stephanus, Beza y la familia Elzevir, llegaron a llamarse el Textus Receptus.

La publicación del *Novum Instrumentum omne* de Erasmo en 1516 fue sin lugar a dudas un logro monumental e histórico, subrayado por el hecho de que su texto sirvió como base para la mayoría de las traducciones que se hicieron a los idiomas vernáculos de los países europeos hasta 1881. Sin embargo, algunos eruditos no pudieron ignorar los problemas que observaban en el texto. Este hecho dio lugar a la siguiente etapa de la historia de la crítica textual, caracterizada por una búsqueda de los manuscritos más fiables para crear un texto más de acuerdo con los manuscritos originales. No fue una tarea fácil ni apreciada por todos. Bruce Metzger (1914–2007), un eminente crítico textual, describe los factores prácticos que hicieron tan difícil esa tarea.

> El texto de Erasmo es inferior al texto de la *Complutense* en cuanto a su valor crítico. Sin embargo, por el mero hecho de que fue el primero en llegar al mercado en una forma más económica y conveniente, adquirió una circulación mucho más amplia y ejerció una influencia mucho mayor que su rival, el cual había estado en preparación desde 1502 hasta 1514. Editores posteriores, aunque hicieron un número de alteraciones en el texto de Erasmo, en esencia reprodujeron esta forma degenerada del N.T. griego. Habiéndose asegurado una preeminencia que no merecía, lo que llegó a llamarse el Textus Receptus del N.T. resistió durante 400 años todos los esfuerzos de los eruditos de desplazarlo a favor de un texto más antiguo y preciso[9].

Aunque se han producido nuevas versiones de la Biblia desde 1881, hay algunos evangélicos que siguen defendiendo el Textus Receptus como el texto que mejor refleja lo que figura en los manuscritos originales y las traducciones de la Biblia al inglés, español, etcétera. que están basadas en este[10]. Rechazan las versiones modernas, las cuales se basan en las conclusiones de los críticos textuales.

---

9. Bruce M. Metzger, *The Text of the New Testament* (Londres: Oxford University Press, 1964), pp. 102–103.

10. Seguimos empleando la palabra «evangélico» para referirnos a quienes aceptan la inspiración plenaria, verbal e inerrante de las Escrituras en sus manuscritos originales.

Mientras que el autor de *Con precisión* respeta a estos hermanos suyos por su deseo y afán de proteger y promover el texto que figura en los manuscritos originales, un deseo y afán que él comparte, toma la siguiente posición. Primero, es verdad que muchos de los críticos textuales del pasado no eran evangélicos. Algunos de ellos eran simplemente filántropos, historiadores y personas que se interesaban por lo antiguo. Y hasta es posible —si no probable— que algunos de ellos intentaran manipular sus conclusiones en cuanto al texto para reflejar su propia doctrina. Sin embargo, en las últimas décadas ha aumentado el número de evangélicos que se dedican a la crítica textual porque las normas que la rigen son coherentes y favorecen la identificación del texto original. Por tanto, si un crítico textual no evangélico descubre algo que realmente refleja la verdad, el evangélico no tiene nada que temer. Segundo, en el pasado los críticos textuales —tanto los evangélicos como los que no lo son— se han equivocado en sus conclusiones por error humano involuntario o por no disponer de unos manuscritos mejores. Sin embargo, la colaboración que ha tenido lugar continuamente entre los eruditos ha permitido corregir la gran mayoría de esos errores. Tercero, las diferencias que existen entre las versiones basadas en el Textus Receptus y las basadas en otros manuscritos son de matices y énfasis no doctrinales ni fundamentales para la fe. Evidentemente, los detalles son importantes porque se trata de la Palabra de Dios, la cual es inspirada verbalmente. Pero, puesto que cada verdad se encuentra en varios pasajes, no es posible introducir un matiz en nuestras creencias doctrinales que contradiga la enseñanza de otros textos. Las palabras de Ladd sobre el papel de la crítica textual y la actitud que debe tener el erudito que se dedica a esta ciencia son muy apropiadas.

> La crítica textual no implica que el erudito se siente a juzgar la Palabra de Dios o a criticarla. Él solamente usa recursos críticos y científicos para establecer cuál es el texto. Significa también que cuando buscamos un buen texto, la piedad y la devoción nunca pueden tomar el lugar del conocimiento y del examen académico. No se puede solucionar un problema de variantes textuales divergentes mediante la oración o por la iluminación interna del Espíritu Santo, sino solo mediante el conocimiento amplio y la habilidad de la ciencia de la crítica textual[11].

11. George E. Ladd, *Crítica del Nuevo Testamento* (El Paso: Editorial Mundo Hispano, 1990), pp. 63–64.

## D. UNA BÚSQUEDA DE MÁS MANUSCRITOS (1633–1831)

La publicación del Textus Receptus en 1516 despertó tanto interés por el griego del N.T. que en el año 1633 ya existían un centenar de ediciones del N.T. griego. Y durante los dos siglos siguientes, varios eruditos bíblicos se lanzaron a la búsqueda de manuscritos griegos, obras de los padres y traducciones del N.T. a otros idiomas que se encontraban en bibliotecas, iglesias y museos de Europa y Medio Oriente. Igual que los eruditos de siglos anteriores, encontraron muchas variantes en el texto de esos manuscritos. Sin embargo, cuando llegó el momento de publicar toda esta nueva información, los editores no se atrevieron a apartarse del Textus Receptus. Por tanto, relegaron esa nueva información al aparato crítico o a los márgenes de las ediciones que publicaban. Debido a la reverencia casi supersticiosa que muchos mostraban hacia el Textus Receptus, cualquier erudito que se atrevía a publicar un texto diferente era ignorado o condenado.

No obstante, las dudas seguían aumentando. Hay siete eruditos que hicieron una contribución particularmente valiosa a la historia de la crítica textual durante esta época. En 1655–1657 Brian Walton (1600–1661) publicó en Londres una Biblia políglota de seis tomos que incluía la primera colección sistematizada de las variantes del texto.

John Mill (c. 1645–1707) fue el primero en hacer una colección sistemática de los textos bíblicos que los padres citaban en sus obras. Luego, hizo un excelente aparato crítico de las 30.000 variantes que encontró en los manuscritos a su disposición[12]. Finalmente, dedicó treinta años a la investigación antes de publicar su edición del N.T. griego en 1707. Era una obra monumental. Empleó el texto de la tercera edición de Stephanus porque le habría sido imposible publicar un texto que difiriera del Textus Receptus y que fuera aceptado. No obstante, en esa edición hizo uso de 79 manuscritos importantes e incluyó unas «notas en las cuales mostraba su preferencia hacia numerosos

12. Desafortunadamente, en lugar de enfrentarse con esta obra de forma honesta, hombres como Daniel Whitby clamaron que la autoridad de las Escrituras estaba siendo atacada y que la colección de dicha evidencia crítica representaba un intento de alterar o manipular el texto bíblico. Como vimos en el capítulo 23, Whitby popularizó el postmilenialismo.

textos que diferían del Textus Receptus»[13]. Como consecuencia, fue violentamente atacado.

Richard Bentley (1662–1742) fue un erudito en griego y latín. Continuó el trabajo de Mill, publicando el texto completo de todos los manuscritos descubiertos hasta ese momento. Defendió a Mill ante las personas que lo atacaban, insistiendo en que era imprescindible estudiar los manuscritos griegos más antiguos. Quiso publicar el texto que existía en el siglo IV del N.T. en griego y latín, pero encontró demasiada resistencia por parte de quienes consideraban el Textus Receptus, a todos los efectos, un texto sacrosanto e intocable. Aunque amasó una gran colección de manuscritos, su edad avanzada no le permitió realizar otros proyectos de interés para la crítica textual.

J. A. Bengel (1687–1752) publicó en 1734 una edición del N.T. griego que hizo uso del Textus Receptus. Los tiempos no eran propicios aún para reclamar cambios en el texto. No obstante, se atrevía a apartarse del Textus Receptus cuando encontraba una variante que en su opinión reflejaba mejor el manuscrito original, pero solo si otro autor ya había incluido esa variante en una publicación del N.T. griego. También introdujo en el margen una clasificación de las variantes que reflejaban mejor el texto original, los textos que eran de igual valor que el Textus Receptus y los textos que deberían ser rechazados. Sin embargo, su fe pietista en la inspiración verbal de las Escrituras fue perturbada por las 30.000 variantes que Mill había descubierto en los manuscritos que había consultado. Por tanto, Bengel se puso a estudiar el tema de la transmisión del texto del N.T. En ese proceso descubrió que el número de variantes serias era considerablemente menor de lo que parecía y que ninguna doctrina estaba en juego. Como resultado, su fe evangélica fue confirmada. Pero esa investigación que comenzó como un proyecto personal llevó a Bengel a realizar dos avances muy importantes en la ciencia de la crítica textual. (1) Fue el primero en reconocer y clasificar los manuscritos por familias. Identificó la africana y la asiática como dos de esas familias. (2) Estableció unos criterios para evaluar cualquier manuscrito, los cuales han sido aceptados desde entonces por todos los críticos textuales. Estas dos aportaciones

13. J. Harold Greenlee, *Introduction to New Testament Textual Criticism* (Grand Rapids: Eerdmans, 1970), p. 73.

de Bengel han llevado a muchos a considerarlo el padre de la crítica textual moderna. Lamentablemente, aunque su vida piadosa y posición doctrinal evangélica se encontraban más allá de cualquier duda, muchos lo trataron como un enemigo de la Palabra de Dios.

J. S. Semler (1725–1791) desarrolló el fundamento que Bengel había puesto sobre las familias de texto. Reconoció tres familias de texto (alejandrina, occidental y oriental).

J. J. Griesbach (1745–1812) estableció los fundamentos sobre los cuales la ciencia de la crítica textual se apoyaría durante los siglos siguientes. Propuso que había tres familias de texto (alejandrina, occidental y bizantina), una clasificación que sigue hasta el día de hoy. En 1774–1777 publicó un N.T. griego que no difirió mucho del Textus Receptus. Sin embargo, incluyó en él un excelente aparato crítico que definió los principios y normas de la crítica textual, los cuales retaron la validez del Textus Receptus. Su trabajo pionero preparó el camino para los cambios que vendrían en el futuro. En la opinión de Metzger, «la importancia de Griesbach para la crítica textual del N.T. es enorme. Por primera vez un erudito se atrevió a abandonar el Textus Receptus en algunos de sus pasajes y a publicar el texto del N.T. en la forma en que sus investigaciones indicaban. Aunque Griesbach se permitía a veces una preferencia demasiada mecánica cuando revisaba un texto, en líneas generales su labor textual se caracteriza por la cautela y la franqueza»[14].

J. M. A. Scholz (1794–1852) fue decano de la Universidad Mixta en Bonn (Alemania). Durante los últimos años del siglo XVIII muchos manuscritos habían sido coleccionados y publicados, pero toda esa labor fue frenada durante los primeros años del siglo XIX por las Guerras Napoleónicas. Cuando ese trabajo comenzó de nuevo en 1830, Scholz viajó mucho y examinó todos los manuscritos que pudo encontrar. Scholz es reconocido por su teoría sobre los orígenes de la familia occidental, su compilación de la primera lista exhaustiva de todos los manuscritos griegos en existencia y su énfasis sobre la importancia de descubrir el origen geográfico (familias de texto) de los manuscritos.

14. Metzger, ob. cit., p. 121.

## E. DESARROLLOS SIGNIFICATIVOS EN LA CRÍTICA TEXTUAL Y LA PUBLICACIÓN DE OTRAS VERSIONES DE LA BIBLIA (1831–1881)

A principios del siglo XIX se habían descubierto muchos manuscritos antiguos que diferían del Textus Receptus. Pero esta versión de la Biblia había sido aceptada de una forma tan absoluta por parte de tantas personas que aún representaba un acto temerario publicar una edición del N.T. griego que difiriera. No obstante, durante esta época se publicaron otras ediciones del N.T. griego basadas en el descubrimiento de otros manuscritos muy importantes y en el uso de los principios de la crítica textual iniciados por Griesbach y otros.

Karl Lachmann (1793–1851) fue un filólogo especializado en latín y griego antiguo. En 1831 publicó la primera edición del N.T. que rompía por completo con el Textus Receptus. En esa edición no pretendía duplicar el texto original del N.T. por considerarlo una meta imposible, sino publicar el texto que existía al final del siglo IV con base en los manuscritos más antiguos, las traducciones del N.T. a otros idiomas y las citas de los padres que tenía a su disposición. Sin embargo, puesto que no explicó sobre qué manuscritos había basado el texto de esta edición, fue duramente criticado. Al explicar en una segunda edición los principios que lo llevaron a redactar el texto, ganó partidarios a su posición y silenció a algunos críticos. El gran logro de Lachmann consistió en ser la primera persona en romper con el Textus Receptus y redactar un texto en base a los principios establecidos por la crítica textual. Su mayor fallo fue que eligió ignorar las familias de texto que sus predecesores habían identificado como las más fiables.

Samuel P. Tregelles (1813–1875) fue un erudito británico. Al observar cómo Scholz había abrazado el Textus Receptus, rechazando la evidencia que se encontraba en los muchos manuscritos que él mismo había descubierto, y cómo Griesbach quería quedarse entre dos aguas en cuanto al Textus Receptus, decidió hacer justo lo contrario. Pero al no saber que Lachmann se le había adelantado en ese propósito, Tregelles desarrolló algunos de los mismos principios de la crítica textual. Sin embargo, en lugar de publicar un N.T. griego en una sola edición, lo hizo en seis partes entre 1857 y 1875. En base a un examen sistemático de muchos de los manuscritos que existían en Europa, corrigió muchos errores que sus predecesores habían incluido en el texto de sus ediciones. Al abandonar por completo el Textus Receptus, Tregelles se convirtió en el hombre que más influencia tuvo sobre los ingleses en su decisión de abandonar su preferencia por el Textus Receptus, igual que Lachmann en el continente europeo.

Konstantin von Tishendorf (1815–1874) fue un lingüista y erudito bíblico alemán. En la opinión de muchos, Tishendorf hizo avanzar la crítica textual del N.T. más que cualquier otro hombre en la historia. Buscó, evaluó y publicó más ediciones críticas del N.T. griego que nadie. Durante sus primeros años como profesor en la Universidad de Leipzig, tenía un gran deseo de encontrar y utilizar los manuscritos más antiguos para recuperar el texto más antiguo del N.T. Para lograr esa meta, viajó por Europa y Medio Oriente, visitando museos, monasterios y otros lugares donde pudiera encontrarlos. Aunque hizo otras aportaciones importantes a la ciencia de la crítica textual, se le recuerda principalmente por descubrir el Códice Sinaítico. Este documento y el Códice Vaticano son considerados los testigos más antiguos y los que mejor reflejan los manuscritos originales del N.T. En 1844 visitó por primera vez el monasterio de Santa Catalina en el monte Sinaí. Durante su estancia vio una cesta de basura que contenía hojas de pergamino que unos monjes llevaban a una estufa para alimentar el fuego. Al examinarlas, encontró 43 hojas que eran los manuscritos más antiguos que había visto hasta ese momento. Resultaron ser las hojas de un códice antiguo de la LXX. Cuando se interesó por ellas, le dijeron que ¡ya habían echado dos cestas de hojas a la estufa! Antes de volver a Leipzig, Tishendorf vio otras 129 hojas en ese monasterio, pero solo le permitieron quedarse con las 43 hojas que había rescatado[15]. En 1846 Tishendorf publicó un facsímil de esas hojas del A.T. en griego sin divulgar dónde las había encontrado.

En 1853 volvió al monasterio de Santa Catalina con el propósito de encontrar las 129 hojas que había visto durante su primera visita. Sin embargo, no le permitieron verlas. Tishendorf volvió a Leipzig con la impresión de que habían sido vendidas a otro interesado. Hizo

15. Entregó estas hojas al rey Federico Augusto de Sajonia, quien había auspiciado su viaje a Medio Oriente. El rey las depositó en la biblioteca de la Universidad de Leipzig.

una tercera visita en 1859, pero en esta ocasión bajo los auspicios del gobierno de Rusia. De nuevo sus esperanzas fueron defraudadas. Pero la noche antes de marcharse, presentó al abad del monasterio una copia de la LXX que había publicado en base a las 43 hojas que recogió en su primera visita. Entonces, el abad le mostró 199 (¡no 129!) hojas que formaban parte del códice al que pertenecían esas 43 hojas. Escondiendo su entusiasmo, Tishendorf pidió permiso para estudiarlas esa noche en su cuarto. Descubrió que contenían la mayoría del A.T., todo el N.T. y dos obras cristianas del siglo II[16].

Reconociendo que esas hojas representaban la copia más antigua de la Biblia en griego que había visto en su vida, expresó su deseo de comprarlas. Pero su petición fue denegada. No obstante, al visitar un monasterio en El Cairo, solicitó al superior que pidiera al monasterio de Santa Catalina que enviara dichas hojas a El Cairo. Así que, con la colaboración de dos ayudantes, Tishendorf pudo copiar las 110.000 líneas de esas hojas durante los siguientes dos meses. Luego, persuadió a las autoridades del monasterio de Santa Catalina de que se ganarían el favor de Alejandro II, el zar de Rusia y protector de la iglesia griega, si le presentaban esas hojas como un obsequio. Así que lo que llegó a llamarse el Códice Sinaítico fue entregado a Tishendorf, quien publicó su texto y luego lo entregó al zar en nombre de los monjes[17].

Los Códices Sinaítico y Vaticano datan de la primera parte del siglo IV y son los manuscritos más fiables que existen en cuanto al texto original del N.T. El Códice Vaticano, llamado así porque fue hallado en la Biblioteca Vaticana de Roma, contiene la mayor parte de los dos Testamentos. Faltan porciones de Hebreos, las Epístolas Pastorales y Apocalipsis. Su existencia se dio a conocer por primera vez en 1481 cuando apareció en el catálogo de las posesiones de la Biblioteca Vaticana. Es muy probable que fuera traído a Roma por el papa Nicolás V

16. La Epístola de Bernabé, la cual se conocía solamente a través de una traducción muy pobre al latín, y el Pastor de Hermas, la cual se conocía solamente por su título.

17. Ciertos relatos de esta negociación dicen que Tishendorf compró el Códice Sinaítico por $6.750. En 1933 el gobierno ruso vendió el Códice Sinaítico al Museo Británico de Londres por $500.000.

en 1448 cuando la Biblioteca Vaticana fue fundada. Erasmo conocía su existencia en 1553.

Cuando Napoleón conquistó el Vaticano en 1809, el ejército francés llevó a París centenares de carruajes de libros y documentos (incluyendo el Códice Vaticano) de la Biblioteca Vaticana. Entre 1481 y 1809 los eruditos bíblicos no tuvieron mucho interés en estudiar ni consultar el Códice Vaticano. Después de ser devuelto a Roma todo este material en 1815, el Vaticano guardó celosamente todas sus posesiones de esa índole. Como resultado, eruditos de otras posiciones religiosas no tuvieron acceso al Códice Vaticano y otros documentos importantes. De vez en cuando el Vaticano permitió a eruditos reconocidos como Tishendorf y Tregelles estudiar el Códice Vaticano durante horas, pero sin el derecho a copiar el texto. En 1845 Tregelles consiguió permiso para estudiarlo durante varios días, pero sin tocarlo ni copiarlo. Al final de cada sesión era cacheado para comprobar que no llevaba encima ni pluma, ni tinta, ni papel. Sin embargo, durante ese tiempo memorizaba el texto y lo ponía por escrito durante la noche. Cuando el Vaticano se enteró de que Tregelles había adquirido el texto y que todo el mundo sabría del manuscrito tan histórico que tenían entre sus manos, el papa Pío IX ordenó que se publicara el texto. Sin embargo, las dos ediciones de 1857 y 1859 eran tan defectuosas y discrepaban entre sí en tantos pasajes que no sirvieron a los intereses de los eruditos. Sucedieron otras torpezas anecdóticas en cuanto a la política de guardar y divulgar el texto de Códice Vaticano, hasta que en 1889–1890 el papa León XIII autorizó a que se hiciera un facsímil fotográfico. Tishendorf y otros eruditos creían que los Códices Sinaítico y Vaticano eran dos de las cincuenta copias que el emperador Constantino encargó publicar después de convertirse al cristianismo.

Además de descubrir el Códice Sinaítico y otros manuscritos importantes, Tishendorf publicó ocho ediciones del N.T. griego. En su última edición (1872) incluyó un aparato crítico de todas las variantes que él y sus predecesores habían encontrado en los manuscritos escritos en unciales y cursivo, las traducciones del N.T. a otros idiomas y los textos bíblicos que los padres citaron. Tan importante fue esta obra que sigue siendo utilizada hoy por los críticos textuales como una herramienta indispensable. Además de esta edición, Tishendorf publicó 22 tomos de manuscritos de textos bíblicos.

B. F. Wescott (1825–1901) y F. J. A. Hort (1828–1892) fueron dos eruditos y amigos que impartían clases en la Universidad de Cambridge. La cumbre de esta época de la historia de la crítica textual fue afirmada por su labor en equipo, y compiten con Tishendorf por el honor de ser los hombres que más aportación hicieron a la ciencia de la crítica textual del N.T. Construyendo sobre todo el trabajo realizado por sus antecesores, sus aportaciones fueron espectaculares, reconocidas y permanentes. Nos limitamos a tres de ellas.

Primera, en 1881 publicaron *The New Testament in the Original Greek* [Nuevo Testamento en griego original], según Metzger «la edición crítica más importante jamás publicada por eruditos británicos del N.T. en griego»[18]. Esta edición, que representaba el trabajo de 28 años de investigación realizado por este equipo de eruditos, superó todas las demás ediciones publicadas hasta ese momento. Su propósito no era coleccionar manuscritos ni proveer un aparato crítico, sino utilizar las variantes descubiertas por otros para pulir la metodología de la crítica textual establecida por sus antecesores y aplicar esa metodología con todo rigor. En esta edición demostraron la necesidad de usar la crítica textual para un entendimiento del texto del N.T., definieron los principios y normas que deben usarse y explicaron cómo deben aplicarse esos principios. La erudición de esta edición fue tan completa y coherente que ha sido el punto de referencia de todas las ediciones publicadas desde entonces. De particular importancia es la evaluación que Hort hizo de la importancia *relativa* de las diferentes familias de texto. La crítica textual no se trata de unas leyes que se aplican de forma mecánica, sino de unos principios y normas que han de emplearse con mucho sentido común. En la opinión de Fee, «Wescott y Hort hicieron un trabajo tan completo y con una destreza tan excepcional, que todo el trabajo textual que se ha realizado desde entonces ha sido en reacción a, o como implementación del suyo»[19].

Segunda, establecieron la teoría de que existen cuatro principales familias de texto. Desde entonces, se han hecho ciertas

18. Metzger, ob. cit., p. 129.

19. Gordon D. Fee, «The Text of the New Testament and Modern Translations» en *Christianity Today* (22 junio 1973), p. 8.

modificaciones de las familias que propusieron. Con base en las características de estas familias, Wescott y Hort identificaron los Códices Sinaítico y Vaticano como miembros de la familia alejandrina y como los dos manuscritos que mejor reflejan el texto original del N.T. Además, demostraron que la familia bizantina es posterior a las demás familias y es la menos fiable de todas. Tercera, el trabajo de Hort y Wescott enterró para siempre el Textus Receptus para la gran mayoría de los eruditos al demostrar que se basaba en unos manuscritos más tardíos que se desviaban frecuentemente de los manuscritos originales del N.T.

## F. IDENTIFICACIÓN DEL TEXTO DEL N.T. (1881– Presente)

Esta época de la crítica textual se ha caracterizado por el descubrimiento de muchos manuscritos, la aplicación de los principios y normas de la crítica textual a esos manuscritos y la publicación de un gran número de ediciones del N.T. griego. Aunque hay aspectos de la crítica textual que son muy complejos, la gran mayoría de los eruditos de todas las tendencias teológicas afirman que ha servido para identificar el texto de los manuscritos originales de los dos Testamentos. En 1991 Osborne sugirió que la mejor edición del N.T. griego es la Nestle-Aland[20]. Después de dedicar sus primeros años al estudio del siriaco y la LXX, Eberhard Nestle decidió editar un texto crítico del griego del N.T. La primera edición, publicada en 1898, ha pasado por 25 revisiones, la última realizada por Erwin Nestle y Kurt Aland. Esa edición discrepa con la edición de Wescott y Hort en 558 textos.

Al darnos cuenta de los materiales tan perecederos que tenían a su disposición aquellos escribas profesionales y miembros de las iglesias que hicieron copias del N.T., las anécdotas de cómo fueron descubiertas algunas de esas copias y la historia de la ciencia de la crítica textual, es prácticamente imposible no quedarse con la convicción de que Dios ha intervenido en la historia para preservar su Palabra. Realmente es verdad la declaración del apóstol Pedro: «Toda carne es como

20. Ver Grant R. Osborne, *The Hermeneutical Spiral* (Downers Grove: InterVarsity Press, 1991), p. 46.

hierba, y toda la gloria del hombre como flor de la hierba. La hierba se seca, y la flor se cae; *mas la palabra del Señor permanece para siempre*» (1 P. 1:24-25, énfasis añadido)[21]. Podemos estar absolutamente seguros de que la Biblia que tenemos en nuestras manos es la Palabra de Dios. Y por eso, cada intérprete debe hacer todo lo posible para interpretarla «con precisión».

21. Parece que Pedro esté parafraseando Isaías 40:8: «Sécase la hierba, marchítase la flor; mas la palabra del Dios nuestro permanece para siempre».

# Apéndice F

# La relación entre una parábola y una alegoría

Estamos en deuda con muchos hombres de Dios del pasado por su aportación a nuestra comprensión de las enseñanzas y doctrinas bíblicas. No obstante, cabe decir también que uno de los errores más serios que muchos de ellos cometían era su uso de la alegorización como método de interpretación bíblica, en parte porque no tenían el privilegio de poseer la sabiduría colectiva de veinte siglos de estudio. Creían que existían algunas verdades más profundas detrás del texto bíblico que solamente la alegorización podía identificar.

## A. LA ALEGORIZACIÓN COMO MÉTODO DE INTERPRETACIÓN

Hay seis eruditos bíblicos que destacaron por su uso de la alegorización, por su papel en demostrar el error de ese sistema de interpretación o por su identificación de los principios que deben emplearse en la interpretación de una parábola.

### Orígenes (185–254)

La alegorización como método de interpretación se empleaba para la interpretación de obras seculares mucho antes de que los padres la adoptaran como un método de interpretación bíblica. Al observar que Jesús otorgó un significado a varios detalles en las parábolas del sembrador (Mc. 4:13-20) y del trigo y la cizaña (Mt. 13:36-43), creyeron que la alegorización les facilitaría la meta de identificar un supuesto significado más profundo. Aunque la alegorización era empleada por casi todos ellos, su mayor exponente fue Orígenes, un hombre cuya capacidad como teólogo y exégeta superaba a la de sus contemporáneos. Puesto que era un erudito tan competente y reconocido, la alegorización se convirtió en el principal método de la interpretación bíblica durante muchos siglos. Aunque los reformadores rechazaban la alegorización de forma categórica, algunos de ellos seguían alegorizando algunas parábolas. Por ejemplo, aunque Martín Lutero criticaba duramente el uso de la alegorización, la empleó en la parábola del buen samaritano. Juan Calvino, en cambio, era mucho más consistente en su oposición a la alegorización.

La interpretación que Orígenes hizo de la parábola del buen samaritano es quizás el ejemplo clásico de una interpretación alegórica[1]. Un intérprete de la ley pregunta a Jesús qué es lo que tiene que hacer para heredar la vida eterna (Lc. 10:25). Jesús, a su vez, le pregunta: «¿Qué está escrito en la ley?». El intérprete de la ley, citando Deuteronomio 6:5, contesta: «Amarás al Señor tu Dios con todo tu corazón, y con toda tu alma, y con todas tus fuerzas, y con toda tu mente; y a tu prójimo como a ti mismo» (v. 27). Pero sabiendo que su respuesta le ha atrapado, hace a Jesús una segunda pregunta: «¿Y quién es mi prójimo?» (v. 29). Aunque la parábola del buen samaritano debe interpretarse a la luz de esta pregunta, Orígenes la ignoró, como se ve en el gráfico. Su alegorización de esta parábola suscita dos preguntas serias: ¿de dónde sacó Orígenes esa interpretación? Y, ¿qué tiene que ver con la pregunta que hizo ese intérprete de la ley? La única respuesta es que la sacó de su gran creatividad e imaginación porque no tiene nada que ver con la pregunta del intérprete de la ley ni con la respuesta de Jesús mediante su parábola. Pero como veremos a continuación, hay otros problemas que surgen con la alegorización.

---

1. Casi todos los autores que escriben sobre el tema citan su interpretación de ella. A veces algún autor citará la de Agustín de Hipona (354–430) puesto que se parece mucho a la de Orígenes.

## Agustín de Hipona (354–430)

Igual que Orígenes, Agustín fue un gigante entre gigantes. Pero introdujo en su interpretación de la parábola del buen samaritano algunos detalles adicionales que ilustran otros tres problemas de la alegorización. Primero, puesto que Agustín ignora el contexto de esta parábola, no existe ningún criterio objetivo para determinar si su interpretación o la de Orígenes es la correcta. Si decimos que las dos interpretaciones son correctas, contradecimos el axioma del lenguaje de que una declaración tiene solamente un significado. Segundo, en raras ocasiones coinciden las interpretaciones de los que alegorizan un texto. Tercero, hay algunos detalles que los oyentes originales nunca podrían haber entendido. Por ejemplo, que el mesonero representa ¡al apóstol Pablo! A pesar de estos problemas, el intérprete del siglo XXI debe respetar a estos y otros gigantes de la fe que lucharon —aunque a veces de forma equivocada— a favor del reino de Dios. Como observa Snodgrass:

> Necesitamos ser muy cautelosos en nuestras evaluaciones de aquellos que alegorizaban, porque personas como Agustín no eran ignorantes. Aquellos que participaban en una interpretación alegórica daban por sentado que la vida tenía una relación con el texto bíblico y que el texto tenía el poder para dirigir sus vidas. No cabe duda de que dichos presupuestos eran muy nobles. Además, esos hombres no basaban sus posiciones doctrinales sobre una exégesis alegórica, sino que procuraban establecer controles para evitar los excesos al limitar el número de personas que podían participar en dichas interpretaciones y al establecer fronteras dentro de las cuales dichas interpretaciones tenían que tomar lugar[2].

---

2. Klyne R. Snodgrass, «From Allegorizing to Allegorizing: A History of the Interpretation of the Parables of Jesus» en *The Challenge of Jesus' Parables* (Grand Rapids: Eerdmans, 2000), p. 5.

| | **Orígenes** | **Agustín** |
|---|---|---|
| el viajero | Adán | |
| Jerusalén | el paraíso | |
| Jericó | el mundo | |
| ladrones | Satanás | |
| ataque de los ladrones | | le quitan al viajero su mortalidad |
| lo dejan herido | | lo incitan a pecar |
| lo dejan medio muerto | | medio muerto por su pecado y medio vivo por su conocimiento de Dios |
| heridas | desobediencia de Adán | |
| sacerdote | la Ley | el sacerdocio del A.T. |
| levita | los libros proféticos | el ministerio de los profetas |
| buen samaritano | Cristo | Cristo |
| el samaritano venda sus heridas | | detiene el pecado |
| aceite | | el consuelo de la esperanza |
| vino | | una exhortación a realizar buenas obras |
| cabalgadura | el cuerpo del Señor | |
| mesón | la Iglesia | |
| mesonero | | el apóstol Pablo |
| dos denarios | | el mandamiento de amar a Dios y al prójimo |
| el samaritano promete pagar lo que falte | la segunda venida de Cristo | la resurrección de Cristo |

## Richard C. Trench (1807–1886)

Trench fue un arzobispo anglicano irlandés. En 1850 escribió una obra monumental de 422 páginas titulada *Notes on the Parables of Our Lord*[3], la cual es considerada un referente para muchos autores evangélicos[4]. Casi todos los autores modernos que han escrito libros sobre las parábolas expresan su aprecio por él[5], Trench rechazaba la alegorización, recordando a sus lectores que Crisóstomo (347–407) advertía constantemente a sus contemporáneos que no deberían fijarse con demasiado afán en cada detalle de una parábola[6]. También les dijo que «las parábolas no deberían convertirse en un caballo a la caza de la controversia dogmática ni de la alegorización ingeniosa»[7].

Sin embargo, su rechazo de la alegorización era a medias porque seguía alegorizando las parábolas. Por un lado, advertía a sus contemporáneos del peligro de encontrar un significado en cada detalle. Pero por otro afirmaba que cuanto más se limita el intérprete a solamente algunos detalles de una parábola, «en esa medida desaparece la belleza particular de dicha parábola y el interés en ella se debilita»[8]. Por ejemplo, censuró a Calvino por no permitir que el aceite de las vasijas en la parábola de las diez vírgenes (Mt. 25:1-4) significara algo en particular. En su interpretación de la parábola del buen samaritano, Trench identifica el vino con la

---

3. Publicado en español como *Notas sobre las parábolas de nuestro Señor* (Grand Rapids: Subcomisión Literatura Cristiana de la Iglesia Cristiana Reformada, 1987).

4. Su introducción es particularmente útil. Desafortunadamente, la versión de este libro que Baker Book House publicó en 1965 no contiene todo lo que había en el original. Por ejemplo, falta una tercera parte de las notas bibliográficas que aparecieron en griego, latín, francés y alemán.

5. La única excepción que el autor de *Con precisión* ha encontrado es Blomberg, que en su libro *Interpreting the Parables* (Downers Grove: InterVarsity Press, 1990) dice que las obras de Trench, A. B. Bruce y G. Campbell Morgan «son obsoletas y su metodología es inadecuada en muchos respectos a pesar de contar con numerosas aportaciones devocionales» (p. 14).

6. Ver Richard Chenevix Trench, *Notes on the Parables of Our Lord* (Grand Rapids: Baker, 1965), pp. 32–33.

7. George A. Buttrick, *The Parables of Jesus* (Grand Rapids: Baker, 1979), p. xxv.

8. Trench, ob. cit., p. 36.

sangre de Cristo y el aceite con el ungimiento del Espíritu Santo. Aunque sus consejos eran muy acertados, no siempre era consecuente con ellos.

## Adolf Jülicher (1857–1938)

En 1888 Jülicher publicó el primero de dos voluminosos tomos sobre las parábolas[9]. En esta obra desacreditó y sepultó por completo y para siempre la alegorización de las parábolas, además de tener una gran influencia en reducir su uso en la interpretación de otros textos bíblicos. Aunque otros eruditos en siglos anteriores habían levantado su voz en contra de la alegorización, fue este teólogo liberal alemán quien le quitó el último aliento de vida. Por eso, es considerado por algunos el padre de los estudios modernos de las parábolas.

## Charles H. Dodd (1884–1973)

Dodd fue un galés que pastoreaba una iglesia congregacionalista. También fue profesor de Crítica y Exégesis del N.T. en las universidades de Manchester y Cambridge. Dodd es conocido por dos énfasis. Primero, su concepto de la «escatología realizada», basada en las declaraciones de Jesús de que el reino de Dios se trataba de una realidad actual y presente en lugar de un evento futuro[10]. Por eso, Dodd creía que cualquier estudio que ignorara el reino de Dios como el tema principal de *todas* las parábolas estaba condenado a fracasar. Segundo, Dodd hizo énfasis en la necesidad de interpretar las parábolas según el contexto histórico y cultural de la Palestina del primer siglo[11]. Hasta la publicación de su libro *The Parables of the Kingdom*[12] en 1936, los libros sobre

---

9. *Geschichte der Auslegung der Gleichnisreden Jesu* [Historia de la interpretación de las parábolas de Jesús]. Desafortunadamente, esta obra tan significativa nunca fue traducida a otros idiomas.

10. Dodd entendía que el reino de Dios ya había llegado debido a la presencia de Jesús. Por tanto, aquellas parábolas que parecen hablar de un reino futuro son un reflejo de las crisis que surgieron en el ministerio de Jesús.

11. Muchos eruditos que escriben sobre el contexto histórico y cultural del primer siglo emplean las palabras alemanas *sitz im leben*, cuya traducción sería «el contexto en el cual se encuentra».

12. Publicado en español como *Las parábolas del reino* (Madrid: Ediciones Cristiandad, 1974).

las parábolas solían centrarse en el significado y aplicación que tenían para la vida cotidiana del creyente del siglo XX. Dodd insistía en que el intérprete debía descubrir primero lo que las parábolas significaban para los judíos del primer siglo, y que ese significado tenía que coincidir con todas las demás enseñanzas de Jesús.

## Joachim Jeremias (1900–1979)

Jeremias era un teólogo alemán que recogió el testigo de Dodd sobre la necesidad de conocer el trasfondo histórico y cultural de la Palestina del primer siglo para entender las parábolas. En 1958 publicó *Las parábolas de Jesús*, la cual es considerada por muchos la obra más significativa del siglo XX sobre las parábolas. Con este libro, Jeremias culminó de una forma más erudita, sistemática y razonada lo que Dodd comenzó. Aunque Jeremias entendía su aportación como una continuación del trabajo de Dodd, lo criticó por centrarse casi exclusivamente en el tema de la «escatología realizada». O sea, la idea de que el reino de Dios se trataba de una realidad actual y presente en lugar de un evento futuro. Al contrario que Dodd, Jeremias creía que las parábolas sobre el reino de Dios tenían que ver con un reino futuro.

Puesto que Jeremias y Dodd abrazaban las premisas de la alta crítica, creían igual que Jülicher que los evangelistas habían retocado las parábolas de Jesús para reflejar la vida y el pensamiento de las iglesias del primer siglo con el propósito de atender sus necesidades[13]. Por tanto, intentaban identificar las palabras originales de Jesús con el propósito de entender las parábolas desde la perspectiva de Jesús y los primeros oyentes, además de suprimir las características alegóricas que los evangelistas habían introducido en ellas. En ese sentido Dodd y Jeremias seguían la tesis de Jülicher de que las parábolas no son alegorías. Sin embargo, aunque Dodd y Jeremias rechazaban la alegorización, es precisamente eso lo que hacían con las parábolas. «Dicha duplicidad llevó a Matthew Black a acusar a Dodd de correr con la liebre alegórica

13. Esto es muy diferente a la práctica de los evangelistas de *colocar* los eventos y las enseñanzas de Jesús en un orden que facilitara la posibilidad de hacer ciertos énfasis en sus Evangelios. Lo que Jeremias, Dodd y Jülicher proponían era que los evangelistas *cambiaron* a propósito las palabras de Jesús para facilitar el énfasis que querían hacer, lo cual se llama *crítica de redacción.*

mientras que cazaba con los perros de Jülicher»[14]. Aunque el enfoque de la alta crítica que Dodd y Jeremias empleaban en sus estudios de las parábolas no encaja con las doctrinas de la revelación, inspiración e inerrancia de las Escrituras, sus opiniones sobre la «escatología realizada» y la necesidad de entender el trasfondo histórico y cultural de la Palestina del primer siglo representan unas aportaciones muy valiosas.

## B. TRES PREGUNTAS CLAVE

A partir de la segunda mitad del siglo XX la alegorización fue rechazada y abandonada por todos los eruditos tanto a nivel intelectual como interpretativo. Como resultado, el debate que tenía lugar sobre las parábolas pudo centrarse en tres preguntas clave: ¿existen alegorías en la Biblia? ¿Son alegorías las parábolas? Y, ¿cuántos puntos centrales puede tener una parábola?

### ¿Existen alegorías en la Biblia?

Al rechazar la *alegorización* como método de interpretación bíblica, muchos rechazaban también la *alegoría* como una posible forma legítima de la comunicación figurativa en las Escrituras. Era una reacción comprensible después de tantos siglos de abusos a manos de la alegorización. Aunque son escasas, parece que la Biblia cuenta con alegorías entre sus páginas. Muchos creen que las palabras de Jesús sobre la vid, el labrador y los pámpanos en Juan 15:1-6 son una alegoría. Otros creen que la descripción de la viña del Señor en Isaías 5:1-7 es una alegoría. Mickelsen considera alegorías textos como Salmo 80:8-15; Proverbios 5:15-18; Eclesiastés 12:3-7; Ezequiel 13:8-16; 1 Corintios 3:10-15 y Efesios 6:11-17[15]. Pero el texto más claro es Gálatas 4:21-32, donde Pablo identifica sus palabras sobre Sara y Agar como una alegoría (v. 24)[16]. No obstante, en cualquier

---

14. Snodgrass, ob. cit., p. 10.

15. Ver A. Berkeley Mickelsen, *Interpreting the Bible* (Grand Rapids: Eerdmans, 1963), pp. 232, 234.

16. Algunos de los que no admiten la presencia de alegorías en las Escrituras sugieren que los gálatas habían aceptado las doctrinas erróneas de los falsos maestros al dejarse seducir por las alegorías que empleaban. Entonces, Pablo creó una alegoría no porque creyera en su uso en las Escrituras, sino para mostrar a los gálatas que se podía probar lo que fuera con una alegoría, tanto doctrinas falsas como verídicas.

estudio de estos textos, el intérprete debe tener en cuenta las observaciones de Mickelsen sobre las características de una alegoría.

> La alegoría, una forma muy legítima de enseñar una verdad, no debería confundirse con la alegorización, la cual emplea una narración que no pretendía enseñar ninguna verdad por identificación. Al hacer una comparación punto por punto, la alegorización obliga a la narración a comunicar ideas diferentes de las que el autor original pretendía. Por tanto, la alegorización es una manera arbitraria de interpretar cualquier narración. La alegoría de Pablo en Gálatas 4:21-31 es significativa porque esta clase de interpretación es muy rara en el N.T. La indicación explícita de Pablo de que alegorizaba indica que empleaba de forma consciente ese vehículo literario solamente en raras ocasiones. En este caso este procedimiento ilustra muy bien lo que Pablo procuraba comunicar. Sin embargo, la narración del A.T. que provee dicha ilustración no hablaba en ninguna manera de un Jerusalén terrenal y un Jerusalén celestial[17].

## ¿Son alegorías las parábolas?

La mayor aportación de Jülicher fue su rechazo bien razonado de la alegorización como método de interpretación de la Biblia en general y de las parábolas en particular. Pero propuso también otras dos tesis importantes. Primero, que cada parábola tiene solamente un punto central, un tema que se tratará en la pregunta siguiente. Segundo, que una alegoría y una parábola son completamente diferentes[18]. Jülicher hizo una distinción muy marcada entre un símil y una metáfora, y argumentaba que una parábola es un símil ampliado. O sea, cuando

---

17. A. Berkeley Mickelsen, *Interpreting the Bible* (Grand Rapids: Eerdmans, 1963), p. 231.

18. Jülicher insistía tanto en esta tesis que, de acuerdo con su teología liberal, culpaba a los evangelistas cada vez que encontraba una parábola con características alegóricas. Mantenía que los evangelistas no entendían ciertas parábolas. Pero sabiendo que Jesús las empleaba para esconder la verdad de algunas personas, tomaron la decisión de cambiar sus palabras y convertirlas en un misterio difícil de entender. Evidentemente, las personas que abrazan las doctrinas de la revelación, inspiración e inerrancia de las Escrituras rechazan esta posición de Jülicher.

se añade a un símil una segunda comparación, ese símil se convierte en una parábola. Es fácil entender un símil porque se parece mucho a la comunicación literal. Al emplear palabras como *semejante a, parecido a, como*, etcétera, todos entienden que el autor está haciendo una comparación. Pero para Jülicher, una alegoría es una *metáfora* ampliada, una forma del lenguaje figurado que no es tan fácil de entender o interpretar. Aunque la metáfora parece ser una declaración literal al decir que una cosa *es* otra, en efecto pretende comunicar una idea completamente diferente. Después de mucho debate durante las últimas décadas, la mayoría de los eruditos han aceptado la segunda premisa de Jülicher de que una parábola y una alegoría son distintas. Quienes discrepaban de esta tesis de Jülicher insistían en que una parábola es una *metáfora* ampliada. Algunos de sus argumentos gramaticales son difíciles de entender. Pero uno de sus mejores argumentos es que muchas parábolas tienen características alegóricas o son interpretadas de forma alegórica por Jesús. Tanto los evangélicos como los que mantienen otras tendencias teológicas han respondido a este argumento de tres formas. Algunos reconocen que ciertas parábolas contienen características alegóricas, pero no por eso creen que son alegorías. Otros creen que el número considerable de características alegóricas que contienen algunas parábolas los obliga a considerarlas como alegorías en lugar de parábolas[19]. Y otros creen que todas las parábolas son alegorías[20].

Era necesario que se produjera este debate para corregir la idea errónea de que las parábolas y las alegorías no tienen nada en común. No obstante, puesto que este debate se ha fijado tanto en lo que tienen en común se corre el riesgo de perder de vista las *diferencias* que existen. Por un lado, no debería sorprendernos que *todas las formas* de la comunicación figurativa que caben dentro de la palabra *mashal* tengan puntos en común. Todas comparten la misma naturaleza; a saber, son formas figurativas e ilustrativas del lenguaje. De ahí que

---

19. Las parábolas citadas más frecuentemente son las de los labradores malvados (Mt. 21:33-46; Mc. 12:1-12; Lc. 26:9-18), el sembrador (Mt. 13:3-8, 18-23; Mc. 4:3-9, 14-20; Lc. 8:5-8, 11-15), el trigo y la cizaña (Mt. 13:24-30, 36-43) y la fiesta de bodas (Mt. 22:1-14).

20. Craig Blomberg y Leland Ryken son los más representativos de esta posición en el campo evangélico.

a veces se solapen, haciendo que el intérprete tenga dudas en cuanto a la clase de lenguaje figurativo que tiene entre manos. Pero, por otro lado, sería ingenuo saltar de ahí a la conclusión de que las parábolas y las alegorías son iguales. Mientras que tienen puntos en común, también cuentan con características y matices que las hacen muy diferentes.

Hay al menos dos diferencias importantes. Primera, en una alegoría todos los detalles tienen un significado; no existen detalles que carezcan de importancia. Por eso, cada detalle tiene que ser interpretado. De ahí que una alegoría suela comunicar más de un concepto o idea. Pero una parábola tiene solamente un punto central, y solamente los detalles que apoyan o ilustran ese punto central tienen importancia. En una alegoría los detalles *son* el significado; en una parábola *ilustran* el punto central sin llegar a representar ningún significado adicional.

Segunda, en una alegoría el significado no brota de forma natural de los detalles, sino que tiene que ser impuesto arbitrariamente por el autor de la alegoría. Y, por tanto, es prácticamente obligatorio que el autor nos explique el significado de su alegoría. Quizás el mejor ejemplo de este hecho es la alegoría de Pablo en Gálatas 4:21-31, donde dice que Agar representa el pacto de la Ley (monte Sinaí, el Jerusalén terrenal) y Sara simboliza el pacto de la Gracia (Jerusalén celestial). Si Pablo no hubiera identificado esa conexión, a nosotros nunca se nos habría ocurrido hacerla. Puesto que las verdades comunicadas en una alegoría tienen poco o nada que ver con el contexto histórico en el cual se cuentan, el autor tiene que interpretarlas. Por el contrario, las comparaciones en una parábola suelen ser obvias y fáciles de entender, especialmente cuando el evangelista nos provee el contexto histórico en el cual Jesús la contó, como en el caso de Lucas 18:1 («También les refirió Jesús una parábola sobre la necesidad de orar siempre, y no desmayar»). Estos contextos históricos permiten al intérprete descubrir con facilidad y precisión lo que Jesús quería comunicar a los primeros oyentes. Cuando los evangelistas no identifican el contexto histórico de una parábola, el punto central de la parábola suele ser evidente.

## ¿Cuántos puntos centrales puede tener una parábola?

Además de afirmar que una parábola no es una alegoría, Jülicher insistía en que una parábola tiene solamente un punto central. Mientras que en una alegoría todos los detalles tienen un significado, en una parábola tienen importancia solamente aquellos detalles que apoyan y aportan algo al mensaje principal de la parábola. Los demás solo sirven como adorno para que Jesús pueda contar una historia con argumento. La mayoría de los teólogos evangélicos están de acuerdo con esta segunda tesis de Jülicher. No obstante, una minoría cree que Jülicher llegó a un extremo difícil de sostener porque algunas parábolas tienen, según ellos, más de un significado. Citan como ejemplo la parábola del hijo pródigo. En el contexto histórico (Lc. 15:1-2) los fariseos y escribas critican a Jesús porque «a los pecadores recibe, y con ellos come», una actividad que implicaba una amistad íntima en la cultura judía del primer siglo. Por tanto, esta parábola pretende contestar la pregunta: ¿por qué come Cristo con estos marginados de la sociedad? En la parábola (vv. 11-31) es evidente que el hijo pródigo *representa* a los publicanos y pecadores, el hijo mayor a los fariseos y escribas, y Jesús al padre. Pero eso es muy diferente a decir que hay *tres puntos centrales* o verdades distintas como si cada personaje tuviera un significado diferente[21].

Para identificar el punto central de esta parábola el intérprete debe contestar la pregunta: ¿por qué ese padre (Cristo) recibió a su hijo (publicanos y pecadores) con tanto cariño después de la vida tan vergonzosa que había llevado? Algunos dirán que fue porque su hijo se había arrepentido (vv. 17, 21). Pero no hay ninguna indicación de que los publicanos y pecadores que figuran en el contexto histórico de esta parábola se hubieran arrepentido. Otros dirán porque era hijo suyo. De ahí que algunos crean que esta parábola tenga que ver con el creyente que se aparta del Señor. Pero los publicanos y pecadores no eran creyentes. Por tanto, la parábola tiene que ver con los no creyentes. Hay solamente una respuesta que explica por qué Jesús (el padre)

21. Por ejemplo, en las pp. 68–69 de su libro *Interpreting the Parables* (Downers Grove: InterVarsity Press, 1990), Blomberg defiende la idea de que dieciocho parábolas comparan tres personajes principales y por tanto tienen tres puntos principales. Otras dieciséis parábolas hacen solamente una o dos comparaciones. Aunque Blomberg cree que puede haber más de un significado, no adopta una de las nuevas tendencias de la crítica literaria que promueve la «polivalencia» del texto bíblico, la cual afirma que una comunicación puede tener varios significados, cosa que contradice el axioma del lenguaje de que cada comunicación tiene solamente un significado.

recibía y comía con los publicanos y pecadores (hijo pródigo); a saber, porque los amaba. ¡Este es el punto central de la parábola! Las tres personas de la parábola no representan tres significados distintos, sino simplemente son detalles que apoyan el único punto central de que Jesús ama a los pecadores.

Cuando el hijo mayor se queja de que nunca se había celebrado una fiesta semejante en su honor, el padre le dice: «Tú siempre estás conmigo, y todas mis cosas son tuyas» (v. 31). No cabe duda de que Jesús incluyó este detalle en la parábola con el propósito de reprender a los fariseos y escribas por su actitud y dureza de corazón. Ellos tenían la Ley de Dios, la estudiaban y la guardaban. En ese sentido, siempre estaban en la presencia de Dios. Algunos eruditos consideran este detalle un segundo punto central; a saber, que todos debemos regocijarnos por la salvación de otras personas a pesar de la clase de vida que han llevado. Pero ese detalle es una *aplicación* del punto central en lugar de un significado totalmente ajeno a ello. En algunas parábolas Jesús hace una aplicación del punto central[22]. En esta parábola, el punto central es que Cristo ama a los pecadores, y la aplicación que hace de ese punto central es que los fariseos y escribas deberían regocijarse cuando un pecador entra en el reino de Dios.

Cabe destacar que la distinción que la mayoría de los evangélicos hacen entre un solo punto central y sus muchas aplicaciones posibles, y la posición de la minoría que cree que puede haber un segundo punto central es, al final de cuentas, una cuestión de semántica, una discusión sobre matices. De ahí que las dos posiciones interpreten la parábola del hijo pródigo de la misma forma sin caer en la alegorización tan típica de los siglos anteriores. La verdad de que Cristo ama a los pecadores, y el hecho de que debemos regocijarnos cuando uno de ellos entra en el reino de Dios, son dos conceptos muy relacionados,

22. Por ejemplo, en la parábola del sembrador (Mt. 13:3-8, 18-23) Jesús identifica cuatro clases de tierra en las que la semilla de la Palabra de Dios puede caer. Pero en lugar de representar cuatro significados completamente diferentes, las cuatro clases de tierra simplemente sirven para *explicar* o *aplicar* el punto central de esta parábola; a saber, que el éxito que tenga la predicación de la Palabra de Dios dependerá en gran parte de la disposición y receptividad de las personas que la escuchan.

no dos ideas totalmente distintas y ajenas al contexto histórico. Hasta Blomberg, que cree que todas las parábolas son alegorías, dice que «la erudición moderna ha hecho bien en rechazar la interpretación alegórica en favor de un acercamiento que entiende que cada parábola tiene tan solo un punto central»[23].

23. Craig L. Blomberg, *Interpreting the Parables* (Downers Grove: InterVarsity Press, 1990), p. 16. Otros prefieren decir que cada parábola *normalmente* tiene solamente un punto central. Pero en efecto están diciendo lo mismo.

# Apéndice G
# La cuestión del *sensus plenior*

El autor de *Con precisión* ha defendido desde el primer capítulo el axioma del lenguaje que afirma que cualquier comunicación solo puede tener un significado, el cual se encuentra en la mente del autor. También ha afirmado en el capítulo 21 que el autor del A.T. que describía una persona, evento, actividad, objeto o institución no sabía que tenía entre manos un tipo, algo que prefiguraba una verdad que sería revelada a los autores del N.T. Aún más difícil sería creer que esos autores del A.T. conocían la verdad que ese tipo prefiguraba.

El término *sensus plenior* fue creado en 1925[1] por el teólogo católico Andrés Fernández en un artículo que escribió sobre hermenéutica. Más adelante, ese término fue popularizado por el erudito católico R. E. Brown (1928–1998) en su disertación titulada *The* Sensus Plenior *of Sacred Scriptures* [El *sensus plenior* de las Sagradas Escrituras]. En ella definió el *sensus plenior* como «ese significado adicional y más profundo que Dios pretendió, pero que el autor humano no pretendió de forma clara, que se ve presente en las palabras del texto bíblico (o grupo de textos o la totalidad de un libro) cuando son estudiadas a la luz de

1. Algunos dicen 1927.

una revelación adicional o el desarrollo de nuestro entendimiento de dicha revelación»[2].

Según Brown, hay textos bíblicos que tienen un «significado adicional y más profundo» porque es algo «que Dios pretendió». O sea, si el autor de un texto del A.T. tenía en mente un significado para ese texto, pero un autor del N.T. lo identifica como un tipo, algo que el autor del A.T. no podía saber, entonces ese texto del A.T. tiene *dos* significados. En efecto, se anula el axioma del lenguaje de que una comunicación solamente puede tener *un* significado. Y volvemos a los primeros siglos de la iglesia cuando la alegorización era el método preferido de la interpretación bíblica con todos los errores que ese sistema produjo. Mientras que la gran mayoría de los evangélicos aceptan el concepto de que un texto podría tener un significado «más completo» o «más amplio» del que el autor humano percibía, rechazan la premisa de que un texto pueda tener dos significados diferentes. La diferencia entre estas dos posiciones es crítica.

Hay quienes afirman que 1 Pedro 1:10-12 demuestra que los autores del A.T. no entendían ciertos textos que ellos mismos escribían. Sin embargo, los profetas entendieron mucho de lo que escribieron sobre el Mesías. Por ejemplo, sus sufrimientos, su gloria, la secuencia en que esos eventos iban a suceder y el hecho de que sus escritos estaban destinados no solamente a las personas de su entorno inmediato, sino también a los creyentes de los siglos venideros. Lo que *no* entendían, y por tanto procuraban descubrir, era *el momento* («qué tiempo», v. 11) en que esos eventos sucederían. No obstante, es difícil creer que los autores de textos como Isaías 7:14; Jeremías 31:15 y Oseas 11:1 pudieran saber que describían un tipo como afirma Mateo (1:21-23; 2:15 y 2:16-18 respectivamente), y aún más difícil de aceptar que entendieran la verdad (antitipo) que prefiguraba[3].

---

2. R. E. Brown, *The* Sensus Plenior *of Sacred Scripture* (Baltimore: St. Mary's University, 1955), p. 92.

3. El hecho de que sea precisamente Mateo el autor del N.T. que identifica como tipos estos tres textos del A.T. tiene una explicación lógica. Mateo escribió su Evangelio con el propósito de convencer a los judíos de que Jesús era el Mesías prometido. Puesto que los judíos tenían una profunda convicción de que Dios era soberano, hasta el punto de poder ordenar y controlar los eventos de la historia, habrían entendido y aceptado fácilmente el concepto de un tipo.

Se ha escrito mucho sobre el *sensus plenior* porque es un tema complejo[4]. No obstante, hay varias observaciones que podemos hacer. Primera, es razonable entender que en muchos casos los autores del A.T. no se daban cuenta de que describían un tipo. En otros casos, cabe la posibilidad de que supieran que tenían entre manos la semilla de algo mucho más grande y significativo, lo cual se daría a conocer en el futuro. Segunda, el hecho de que un autor no entendiera que tenía un tipo entre manos, pero Dios sí, no significa que haya dos significados distintos, porque existe una relación real, auténtica y orgánica entre el tipo y el antitipo. El tipo es como una semilla que con el tiempo se convierte en un arbusto completamente crecido y desarrollado. Por tanto, en el caso del tipo y el antitipo no se trata de dos significados totalmente distintos. Tercera, un estudio gramático-histórico-cultural de las Escrituras no es capaz de identificar la enseñanza del antitipo solamente con base en el pasaje donde aparece el tipo. Hace falta que un autor del N.T. diga cuál es la enseñanza que el tipo prefiguraba.

---

4. Tres de las exposiciones más claras sobre el tema del *sensus plenior* se encuentran en: Roy B. Zuck, *Basic Bible Interpretation* (Colorado Springs: Victor, 1991), pp. 273–274; Dan McCartney y Charles Clayton, *Let the Reader Understand* (Wheaton: Victor Books, 1994), pp. 153–164; y Walter C. Kaiser, «The Single Intent of Scripture» en *Rightly Divided* (Grand Rapids: Kregel Publications, 1996), pp. 158–170.

# Apéndice H

# La contextualización y la homosexualidad

Los teólogos liberales, juntamente con algunos que se llaman «evangélicos», han empleado su particular definición de la «contextualización» para afirmar que la Biblia no condena la homosexualidad. En efecto, marchan al son de muchas sociedades del siglo XXI que consideran la homosexualidad una opción sexual legítima. En algunos de esos países hay leyes que obligan a los medios de comunicación a no solamente dejar de criticar la homosexualidad, sino también a promoverla.

Pero ¿qué dicen las Escrituras? Para determinar cuándo es lícito retener, sustituir o descartar una expresión cultural de un texto o el principio que hay detrás, los evangélicos creen que el intérprete debe tener en cuenta cinco criterios. A la luz de estos criterios, los evangélicos son unánimes en su posición de que la Biblia condena los actos homosexuales.

*1. Una similitud significativa entre los lectores originales y el creyente del siglo actual.* Quienes defienden la homosexualidad emplean varios argumentos. Consideraremos dos de ellos. Primero, dicen que la Biblia condena el acto homosexual en el contexto de los cultos a los ídolos. Segundo, dicen que la homosexualidad que el N.T. describe era abusiva y que no existía la opción de tener una relación homosexual caracterizada por el amor y el compromiso tan típico de muchas parejas homosexuales en el siglo XXI.

Sin embargo, estos argumentos no son sostenibles. En cuanto al primer argumento, es verdad que hay textos en el A.T. que condenan los actos homosexuales en el contexto de los cultos a los ídolos. Pero no solamente porque Dios condene la idolatría, sino porque también condena los actos homosexuales en otros contextos que no tienen nada que ver con la idolatría. Es precisamente por eso que los actos homosexuales aparecen en listas de pecados como 1 Corintios 6:9-10 y 1 Timoteo 1:9-10. Si la homosexualidad fuera una mera cuestión cultural, no aparecería en esas listas porque Dios no condena los elementos amorales de la cultura, sea del país que sea. En cuanto al segundo argumento, siempre ha habido relaciones homosexuales caracterizadas por la violencia y el abuso en todos las épocas y sociedades. Pero no se ha probado históricamente que en el primer siglo todas las relaciones homosexuales fueran abusivas. La relación homosexual que Pablo describe en Romanos 1:26-27 es consensual; no es abusiva ni impuesta. Por tanto, el hecho de que dos homosexuales, dos adúlteros, dos fornicarios o dos personas que cometen cualquier otra perversión del acto sexual se amen, no anula la condenación divina de esos pecados[1].

*2. La intención del autor.* En los pasajes narrativos de las Escrituras, el autor *describe* los actos buenos y malos de los personajes bíblicos, pero no suele *evaluar* de forma explícita si dichos actos merecen la condena o el elogio. Por ejemplo, en Génesis 19:4-8 Moisés describe las pretensiones homosexuales de los varones de Sodoma con los dos ángeles que visitaban a Lot. Para disuadirlos, Lot les ofrece sus dos hijas vírgenes para que satisfagan sus apetitos sexuales con ellas. Aunque Moisés no condena explícitamente lo que ocurre, el sentir del pasaje representa una condenación implícita de la homosexualidad. Es imposible leer la descripción de este evento sin quedarse con la clara impresión de que los actos homosexuales no reciben la aprobación divina. La destrucción de esta ciudad por Dios apoya esa conclusión. Jueces 19:16-30 describe un evento similar al de Sodoma. Aunque el autor no condena explícitamente la homosexualidad, dicha condenación está implícita en el texto. Es el mismo caso en textos como 1 Reyes 14:24; 15:12 y 22:46, los cuales describen cómo varios reyes

1. Para una consideración más amplia sobre la homosexualidad, ver el libro de Jaime Fasold, *Tu media naranja* (Grand Rapids: Portavoz, 1998), pp. 143–155.

eliminaron los templos donde los israelitas practicaban la homosexualidad, imitando las costumbres de los cananeos. Aunque el autor bíblico simplemente describe lo que hacían, estos textos en efecto representan una condenación de la homosexualidad.

*3. La confirmación de otros textos bíblicos.* Levítico 18:22 y 20:13 son los textos del A.T. que más explícita y claramente condenan la homosexualidad. Luego, Deuteronomio 23:17-18 prohíbe a los israelitas participar en los actos homosexuales, los cuales formaban parte de los ritos religiosos de los cananeos. Dios no condenó estos actos simplemente porque no quería que su pueblo imitara a los cananeos, sino porque los actos homosexuales son pecado.

Cuando llegamos al N.T. la homosexualidad es condenada no solamente por Jesús (Mt. 19:4-6), sino también por Pablo. En Romanos 1:26-27 el apóstol la condena, tanto la practicada por mujeres como por hombres, ya que no representa «el uso natural» del sexo según los propósitos de Dios cuando creó al ser humano. Lo natural y normal es que el ser humano practique la heterosexualidad. En 1 Corintios 6:9 Pablo dice que los injustos no heredarán el reino de Dios. Entonces, da una lista de pecadores entre los cuales se encuentran los *arsenokoitai*, traducido como «los que se echan con varones» (RVR60), «homosexuales» (LBLA), «los que [...] practican la homosexualidad» (NTV) y «sodomitas» (NVI)[2]. En 1 Timoteo 1:9 Pablo dice que la Ley no fue instituida para los justos, sino para los pecadores. Entonces, entre los diferentes pecadores mencionados en los vv. 9-10 se encuentran los *arsenokoitais* (v. 10), traducido como «sodomitas» (RVR60), «homosexuales» (LBLA, NVI) y «los que practican la homosexualidad» (NTV). El hecho de que la condenación de la homosexualidad en Levítico 18:22 y 20:13 sea repetida en otros textos bíblicos demuestra que son mandamientos en lugar de directrices de aplicación local y temporal. Por tanto, estos textos son aplicables a todo ser humano en cualquier época y cultura.

*4. La naturaleza del contenido de un texto.* Las cuestiones culturales no aparecen en las listas de pecados porque la expresión cultural de un principio a veces no es transferible a otro país o época. El hecho

2. Pablo no está diciendo que la persona que comete una o dos veces uno de estos pecados pierde la posibilidad de salvarse eternamente, sino que se refiere a quienes *practican* estos pecados, porque demuestran que no son creyentes. El creyente no *practica* el pecado (1 Jn. 3:8).

de que todos los textos que condenan explícitamente la homosexualidad se encuentren en listas de pecados demuestra que los actos homosexuales no son una cuestión cultural, sino actos pecaminosos.

*5. La base sobre la cual el autor fundamenta su mandamiento.* En Mateo 19:3-9 Jesús apela a Génesis 1:27 y 2:24, textos que aparecen en el contexto de la creación del ser humano, para defender el matrimonio como la unión entre un hombre y una mujer, no entre dos personas del mismo sexo, y para apoyar el hecho de que es pecado cualquier acto sexual fuera del marco del matrimonio. Y cuando Pablo dice en Romanos 1:26-27 que los actos homosexuales chocan con «el uso» (RVR60) natural del sexo o con «la forma natural de tener relaciones sexuales» (NTV), en efecto apela a los propósitos y pautas que Dios estableció cuando creó al ser humano. La homosexualidad atenta contra el orden que Dios estableció cuando creó al primer matrimonio como una unión «que es heterosexual, monógama, no incestuosa, socialmente visible y afirmada, física y permanente»[3]. Igual que otros pecados sexuales como el bestialismo, travestismo, incesto, etcétera, la homosexualidad «ofende un aspecto u otro de la naturaleza moral de Dios, sus atributos, su imagen en nosotros o su provisión y plan para la sexualidad, la familia y el matrimonio»[4].

---

3. C. J. H. Wright, «Learning to Love Leviticus» en *Christianity Today* (julio-agosto 2013), p. 33.

4. Walter C. Kaiser, «Legitimate Hermeneutics» en *Inerrancy* (Grand Rapids: Zondervan, 1980), p. 143.

# Guía de estudio

## CAPÍTULO 9: TEMA DEL LIBRO

En Efesios 1–3 se repiten las palabras «en Cristo Jesús/en Cristo» ocho veces (1:1, 3; 2:7, 10, 13; 3:6, 11, 21) y diez veces las palabras «en él» (1:4, 13; 3:12), «por medio de Jesucristo» (1:5), «en el Amado» (1:6), «en quien» (1:7; 2:21, 22; 3:12) y «en el Señor» (2:21), siendo todas ellas otra forma de decir «en Cristo». «En Cristo» es una expresión típica de Pablo que significa «en unión con Cristo». Quizás 2 Co. 5:17 sea el texto más conocido en el que se usa este término. «De modo que si alguno está *en Cristo*, nueva criatura es; las cosas viajas pasaron: he aquí todas son hechas nuevas»[1] (énfasis añadido).

En su contexto, es evidente que las palabras «con Cristo/con Cristo Jesús» (2:5-6), «con él» (2:6) y «por medio de él» (2:18) subrayan lo que el Padre ha hecho por el creyente debido a su unión con Cristo[2]. No hay ningún imperativo, ningún mandamiento en estos capítulos. El único imperativo es la palabra «acordaos» (2:11-12)[3]. Pero el con-

1. En 1:10, 20 «en Cristo» no se refiere a la unión que el creyente tiene con Cristo, sino a lo que el Padre hizo o hará a través de Cristo, obras que no tienen nada que ver directamente con el creyente. En 1:12 «en Cristo» se refiere a la fe que los creyentes depositaron en Cristo.

2. Las palabras «en sí mismo» de 1:9 y 2:15 se parecen a las otras frases, pero no tienen el mismo significado.

3. La LBLA indica que el imperativo «recordad» del v. 12 no aparece en el texto original. Los traductores lo han añadido para que la frase tenga sentido en español.

texto demuestra que Pablo está pidiendo que los efesios sigan el argumento que les está exponiendo. Les pide que recuerden la clase de vida que llevaban como gentiles antes de convertirse a Cristo. Por tanto, el imperativo «acordaos» es cualitativamente diferente al imperativo: «Sed, pues, imitadores de Dios» (5:1). En 3:13 Pablo hace la petición personal de que los efesios no desmayen a causa de sus tribulaciones (3:13). Pero no es un imperativo cargado de un elemento ético, sino simplemente una petición personal. Por tanto, el único «imperativo» en los capítulos 1–3 es 2:11-12. Por el contrario, los capítulos 4–6 están cargados de imperativos. Además, la palabra *andéis* se repite siete veces en 4:1, 17; 5:2, 8, 15.

Los capítulos 1–3 subrayan lo que el creyente tiene «en Cristo» o lo que el Padre ha hecho por él «por medio de» Jesucristo, mientras que los capítulos 4–6 hacen énfasis sobre la forma en que el creyente debe andar debido a todo lo que tiene «en Cristo». Primero la fe, después las obras. Dios no pide nada de nosotros hasta que él haya hecho todo por nosotros. El autor de *Con precisión* sugiere que el tema de Efesios es EN CRISTO JESÚS. Cuando lleguemos al capítulo siguiente, sugerirá que los capítulos 1–3 subrayan «Lo que tenemos en Cristo», mientras que los capítulos 4–6 hacen énfasis en «Cómo debemos andar en Cristo».

## CAPÍTULO 10: LA ORGANIZACIÓN DEL LIBRO (I)

### G. H. Lacy, *Comentario sobre la Epístola a los Efesios* (Casa Bautista de Publicaciones, 1946)

Saludo 1:1-2

I. LOS PROPÓSITOS DE LA GRACIA EN CRISTO JESÚS QUE DIOS TIENE PARA CON SU PUEBLO (1:3–3:21)

- A. La elección en Cristo (1:3-23)
    1. Los fines de la elección (1:3-6)
    2. Cristo, la suma y el fin de todas las cosas (1:7-12)
    3. El Espíritu como sello y garantía de la redención (1:13-14)
    4. La gratitud y oración de Pablo por sus lectores (1:15-19)
    5. La exaltación de Cristo sobre todas las cosas (1:20-23)

B. La nueva vida de los creyentes en Cristo (2:1-7)

1. Muertos en delitos y pecados (2:1-2)
2. El hombre carnal (2:3)
3. Dios, rico en misericordia (2:4-5)
4. Resucitados con Cristo para mostrar las riquezas de la gracia (2:6-7)

C. Por la gracia tanto judíos como gentiles son creados en Cristo, en quien hay paz y reconciliación con Dios el Padre (2:8-22)

1. Salvos por la fe y creados en Cristo para buenas obras (2:8-10)
2. Los que éramos extranjeros en Cristo hemos sido hechos cercanos (2:11-13)
3. Cristo es hecho paz y reconciliación (2:14-17)
4. En Cristo tenemos entrada como miembros de la familia de Dios (2:18-19)
5. Cristo, la piedra angular del edificio espiritual (2:20-22)

D. El misterio de la incorporación de los gentiles como coherederos y participantes de las promesas a Israel (3:1-7)

1. Pablo, el receptor de la dispensación de la gracia de Dios (3:1-2)
2. El misterio escondido en otras edades ha sido revelado a Pablo por el Espíritu (3:3-5)
3. Pablo, ministro del mensaje del misterio (3:6-7)

E. Pablo, predicador y maestro del evangelio a los gentiles para que por medio de la iglesia los ángeles vean la gracia y la sabiduría de Dios en Cristo (3:8-12)

1. La gracia de anunciar el evangelio a los gentiles (3:8)
2. El misterio escondido en Dios (3:9)
3. Los ángeles tienen conocimiento de la sabiduría de Dios por la iglesia (3:10)
4. El propósito está en Cristo, en quien tenemos libertad y entrada (3:11-12)

F. Oración para que los efesios reciban poder en el hombre interior para comprender la medida del amor de Cristo, que sobrepasa todo entendimiento (3:13-19)

1. Las tribulaciones del apóstol (3:13)
2. Oración a Cristo, de quien todo recibe su nombre (3:14-15)
3. Que sean confirmados por el Espíritu (3:16)
4. La presencia de Cristo en los corazones (3:17)

5. Las medidas del amor de Cristo (3:18)
6. El incomprensible amor de Cristo y la plenitud de Dios (3:19)

G. La doxología sugerida por la visión de las grandes verdades por las cuales había orado (3:20-21)

II. EL ESPÍRITU DE LOS CRISTIANOS Y SUS DEBERES (4:1–6:20)

A. Llamados a la unidad del Espíritu (4:1-6)
1. Que anden como dignos del Señor (4:1-2)
2. Virtudes que conducen hasta la unidad del Espíritu (4:2-3)
3. La unidad de la fe y la doctrina (4:4-6)

B. La diversidad de dones en la unidad de la fe (4:7-16)
1. Cristo glorificado (4:7-10)
2. Dones para nuestro perfeccionamiento (4:11-13)
3. La edificación del cuerpo en Cristo (4:14-16)

C. Como hombres nuevos despojados del hombre viejo, debemos andar en las virtudes de la nueva vida (4:17-32)
1. La vida de los paganos (4:17-19)
2. El despojamiento del hombre viejo según la verdad de Cristo (4:20-22)
3. El hombre nuevo y sus obras (4:23-32)

D. Deberes del cristiano en la vida práctica (5:1-21)

E. Deberes nacidos de las relaciones del matrimonio (5:22-33)
1. Deberes de las casadas comparados con los deberes de la iglesia para con Cristo (5:22-24)
2. Deberes de los casados comparados con los deberes de Cristo para con la iglesia (5:25-33)

F. Deberes de los hijos, padres, siervos y señores (6:1-9)
1. Deberes de los hijos (6:1-3)
2. Deberes de los padres (6:4)
3. Deberes de los siervos (6:5-8)
4. Deberes de los señores (6:9)

G. El soldado cristiano y su armadura (6:10-17)

H. El apóstol suplica que los efesios oren por él (6:18-20)

Conclusión: 6:21-24

### *Gray and Adams Bible Commentary* (Zondervan, 1903)

Saludo: 1:1-2

I. LA GLORIA DE LA IGLESIA (1:3–3:21)
  A. Fundamento y meta de la iglesia (1:3-23)
  B. Alcance y misión de la iglesia (2:1-22)
  C. Oficio y servicio de la iglesia (3:1-21)

II. EL MINISTERIO GUBERNAMENTAL DEL ESPÍRITU EN LA IGLESIA (4:1–6:20)
  A. Tema de esta sección (4:1-3)
  B. Motivos para la unidad (4:4-16)
  C. Deberes cristianos en general (4:17–5:21)
  D. Deberes cristianos específicos (5:22–6:9)
  E. Exhortación en conclusión (6:10-20)

Despedida: 6:21-24

### William Hendriksen, *Ephesians* (Baker, 1967)

I. ADORACIÓN DE LA IGLESIA GLORIOSA POR SU:
  A. Fundamento eterno «en Cristo» (Capítulo 1)
    1. Saludo (1:1-2)
    2. El resultado de «cada bendición espiritual» (1:3-14)
    3. Llevándonos a la gratitud y oración, pidiendo iluminación espiritual (1:15-23)
  B. Alcance universal: judío y no judío (Capítulo 2)
    1. Asegurado para ambos grupos (2:1-10)
    2. Mostrado por la reconciliación de los judíos y gentiles a través de la cruz (2:11-22)
  C. Meta alta (Capítulo 3)
    1. A fin de que la infinita sabiduría de Dios sea ahora dada a conocer... (3:1-13)
    2. Seáis capaces de comprender el amor de Cristo (3:14-21)

II. EXHORTACIÓN A LA IGLESIA GLORIOSA A QUE TENGA:
  A. Unidad orgánica (4:1-16)

B. Renovación gloriosa (4:17–6:9)
1. Para todos (4:17–5:21)
2. Para grupos especiales (5:22–6:9)
C. Armadura eficaz (6:10-20)

Conclusión: 6:21-24

**Hoke Smith, *Efesios: El propósito eterno de Dios* (Casa Bautista de Publicaciones, 1976)**

Saludo: 1:1-2

I. DOCTRINA: LA DECLARACIÓN DEL PROPÓSITO ETERNO DE DIOS (1:3–3:21)
«Reunir todas las cosas en Cristo»
A. Su gloria esencial (1:1-14)
B. Su poder efectivo (1:15-23)
C. Su bendición individual (2:1-10)
D. Su alcance universal (2:11-22)
E. Su comunicación apostólica (3:1-13)
F. Su realización final (3:14-21)

II. ÉTICA: EL DESARROLLO DEL PROPÓSITO ETERNO DE DIOS (4:1–6:20)
«Que andéis como es digno de la vocación»
A. En la iglesia (4:1-16)
B. En la vida moral (4:17–5:20)
C. En el hogar (5:21–6:9)
D. En la conquista espiritual (6:10-20)

Conclusión: 6:21-24

### Walter Dunnett, *An Outline of New Testament Survey* (Moody, 1960)

Saludo: 1:1-2

I. LA IGLESIA EN EL PROPÓSITO DE DIOS (1:3-14)
  A. Obra del Padre (1:3-6)
  B. Obra del Hijo (1:6-12)
  C. Obra del Espíritu Santo (1:13-14)

II. LA IGLESIA Y EL PODER DE DIOS (1:15–2:10)
  A. Ilustrado en la resurrección de Cristo (1:15-23)
  B. Llevado a cabo en el avivamiento de pecadores (2:1-10)

III. LA IGLESIA COMO MORADA Y CASA DE DIOS (2:11-22)

IV. LA IGLESIA COMO LA REVELACIÓN DE DIOS (3:1-13)
  A. El misterio de Cristo (3:1-9)
  B. La sabiduría de Dios (3:10-13)

V. LA IGLESIA Y LA PLENITUD DE DIOS (3:14-21)

VI. LA IGLESIA Y LAS NORMAS
  A. El ruego por la unidad espiritual (4:1-16)
  B. La demanda de pureza moral (4:17–5:21)
  C. Las obligaciones en los deberes domésticos (5:22–6:9)

VII. LA IGLESIA Y LA ARMADURA DE DIOS (6:10-20)
  A. La exhortación (6:10-11)
  B. El enemigo (6:12-13)
  C. La armadura (6:14-20)

Conclusión: 6:21-14

### John H. Gerstner, *The Epistle to the Ephesians* (Baker, 1958)

Introducción: 1:1-2

I. DOCTRINAS (1:3–4:16)
- A. Elección (1:3-6)
- B. Redención (1:7–2:10)
  - 1. Aspecto objetivo: la sangre de Cristo (1:7-12)
  - 2. Aspecto subjetivo (1:13–2:10)
    - a. Fe (1:13)
    - b. Sello (1:14)
    - *Primera oración de Pablo (1:15-23)*
    - c. Regeneración (2:1-10)
- C. La iglesia (2:11–4:16)
  - 1. Su unidad (2:11-22)
    - a. De judíos y gentiles (2:11-19)
    - b. De Cristo y creyentes (2:20-22)
  - 2. Su misterio (3:1-13)
    - *Segunda oración de Pablo (3:14-21)*
  - 3. Sus miembros (4:1-16)
    - a. Unidos (4:1-6)
    - b. Diversos (4:7-11)
    - c. Edificados (4:12-16)

II. DEBERES (4:17–6:24)
- A. Principios generales (4:17–24)
  - 1. Negativos (4:17-22)
  - 2. Positivos (4:23-24)
- B. Aplicación a asuntos específicos (4:25–6:9)
  - 1. Varios (4:25-30)
    - a. Honradez (4:25)
    - b. Ira (4:26-27)
    - c. Robar (4:28)
    - d. Conversación (4:29-30)
  - 2. Contrastes (4:31–5:20)
    - a. Amor vs. concupiscencia (4:31–5:7)
    - b. Luz vs. oscuridad (5:8-17)
    - c. Espíritu Santo vs. vino (5:18-20)

3. Relaciones humanas (5:21–6:9)
   a. Principio en general (5:21)
   b. Esposos (5:22-33)
   c. Padres e hijos (6:1-4)
   d. Amos y siervos (6:5-9)

C. Resumen de exhortación y bendición (6:10-24)

### Merrill C. Tenney, *New Testament Survey* (Eerdmans, 1961)

Introducción: 1:1-2

I. EL ESTABLECIMIENTO (*constitution*) DE LA IGLESIA (1:3-14)
   A. Por el Padre (1:3-6)
   B. En el Hijo (1:6-12)
   C. A través del Espíritu Santo (1:13-14)

II. EL CONOCIMIENTO (*consciousness*) DE LA IGLESIA; UNA ORACIÓN (1:15-23)

III. LA CREACIÓN (*creation*) DE LA IGLESIA (2:1-10)

IV. EL ACUERDO (*concord*) DE LA IGLESIA (2:11-22)

V. LA VOCACIÓN (*calling*) DE LA IGLESIA (3:1-21)
   A. Revelar la sabiduría de Dios (3:1-13)
   B. Experimentar la plenitud de Dios; una oración (3:14-21)

VI. LA CONDUCTA (*conduct*) DE LA IGLESIA (4:1–6:9)
   A. Su ministerio: diversidad y unidad (4:1-16)
   B. Sus normas morales (4:17–5:14)
   C. Su conducta como iglesia ante el mundo (5:15-21)
   D. Sus normas domésticas (5:22–6:9)

VII. EL CONFLICTO (*conflict*) DE LA IGLESIA (6:10-20)

Conclusión: 6:21-24

### John Phillips, *Exploring the Scriptures* (Moody, 1965)

Introducción: 1:1-2

I. CONTEMPLANDO (*considering*) LAS CUMBRES (1:3-14)
- A. Las misericordias de Dios el Padre (1:3-6)
- B. La meditación de Dios el Hijo (1:7-12)
- C. El ministerio de Dios el Espíritu Santo (1:13-14)

II. ESCALANDO (*climbing*) LAS CUMBRES (1:15-23)

III. COMPRENDIENDO (*comprehending*) LAS CUMBRES (cap. 2–3)
- A. Redención (*redemption*) (2:1-10)
- B. Relaciones (*relationship*) (2:11-14)
- C. Reconciliación (*reconciliation*) (2:15-18)
- D. Reconstrucción (*reconstruction*) (2:19-22)
- E. Revelación (*revelation*) (3:1-6)
- F. Responsabilidad (*responsibility*) (3:7-13)
- G. Recursos (*resources*) (3:14-21)

IV. RECLAMANDO (*claiming*) LAS CUMBRES (4:1–6:9)
- A. La vitalidad del cuerpo de Cristo (4:1-16)
  1. Su grandeza (*greatness*) (4:1-6)
  2. Sus dones (*gifts*) (4:7-16)
- B. La victoria del creyente en Cristo (4:17–6:9)
  1. El creyente y él mismo (*self*) (4:17-24)
  2. El creyente y Satanás (*Satan*) (4:25-27)
  3. El creyente y el pecado (*sin*) (4:28–5:4)
  4. El creyente y la salvación (*salvation*) (5:5-14)
  5. El creyente y el servicio (*service*) (5:15-21)
  6. El creyente y la sociedad (*society*) (5:22–6:9)

V. CONQUISTANDO (*conquering*) LAS CUMBRES (6:10-20)
- A. Los adversarios (6:10-12)
- B. La armadura (6:13-17)
- C. El ataque (6:18-20)

Conclusión: 6:21-24

## NOTA DEL AUTOR

Antes de que el lector siga con el trabajo de redactar su bosquejo de Efesios 1–3, el autor cree conveniente hacer una evaluación de los bosquejos dados arriba. Ha incluido los capítulos 4–6 para que el bosquejo de cada autor sea completo.

1. El bosquejo de Lacy es excesivamente detallado. El título que aparece en el apartado I. A. incluye solamente la obra de Cristo e ignora la obra de las otras dos personas de la Trinidad.

2. Como contraste, el bosquejo de Gray y Adams es demasiado corto. Además, raras veces encaja el bosquejo de un libro de forma exacta con la división de los capítulos como Gray y Adams lo hacen en el apartado I. A-C.

3. En el bosquejo de William Hendriksen, el saludo no suele formar parte del bosquejo porque no suele aportar nada significativo. Igual que el bosquejo de Gray y Adams, raras veces encajan los capítulos de forma exacta con el bosquejo como lo hace en el apartado I. A-C.

4. El bosquejo de Hoke Smith es aceptable. Pero en lugar de títulos de resumen tan confusos, sería mejor decir en qué consiste «su gloria esencial» (I. A.) y «su alcance universal» (I. D.).

5. El bosquejo de Walter Dunnett es muy aceptable. Es evidente que cree que el tema de Efesios es «la iglesia», probablemente porque 2:11–3:13 representa la mención plena de la Iglesia. No obstante, el hecho de que un libro contenga la mención plena de una doctrina no la convierte en el tema del mismo. Primera de Corintios 15 es la mención plena de la resurrección y Filipenses 2:1-11 la de la encarnación de Cristo. Sin embargo, el tema principal de 1 Corintios no es la resurrección, ni es la encarnación de Cristo el tema principal de Filipenses.

6. Además de captar muy bien el énfasis doctrinal de los capítulos 1–3 y el énfasis práctico de los capítulos 4–6, el bosquejo de John H. Gerstner es claro y conciso. Sin embargo, ¿es posible que el texto sea tan sencillo como indican los títulos que aparecen en los apartados I. A-C. y I. B.? Su bosquejo en el apartado I. C. 3. es muy acertado.

7. Igual que Dunnett, Merrill C. Tenney cree que el tema principal de Efesios es «la iglesia». Pero su bosquejo aparece en forma de aliteración. O sea, la palabra clave de cada título comienza con la letra «c» en inglés (el autor ha incluido las palabras inglesas en paréntesis).

El mayor problema de las aliteraciones, especialmente cuando hay muchos elementos, es que tarde o temprano el intérprete se enfrentará con el problema de que no existe una palabra en su idioma que capte con precisión el significado del texto bíblico y que comience con la letra que el autor ha elegido para su aliteración. Entonces, tendrá que abandonar el formato de la aliteración o emplear una palabra que no corresponda al significado del texto, sacrificando así su significado.

8. John Phillips sigue el mismo sistema de aliteración que Tenney, pero en la opinión del autor de *Con precisión* se ha excedido. Phillips cree que el tema de Efesios es «en los lugares celestiales», una frase que aparece solamente en Efesios (1:3, 20; 2:6; 3:10 y 6:12). Por tanto, el bosquejo de Tenney es mejor que el de Phillips.

## CAPÍTULO 10: LA ORGANIZACIÓN DEL LIBRO (II)

A continuación, el autor de *Con precisión* presenta su bosquejo de Efesios, seguido por un resumen de cómo interpreta los primeros tres capítulos en base al mismo.

Saludo: 1:1-2

I. LO QUE TENEMOS «en Cristo» (1:3–3:21)
  A. Nos bendijo con toda bendición espiritual (1:3-14)
    1. El Padre nos escogió (1:3-6)
    2. El Hijo nos redimió (1:7-12)
    3. El Espíritu Santo nos selló (1:13-14)
    Oración por iluminación espiritual para que el creyente se dé cuenta de: (1:15-23)
    1. Su esperanza (v.18)
    2. La herencia que tiene Dios (v. 18)
    3. La supereminente grandeza del poder de Dios (v. 19)
  B. Nos dio vida (2:1-10)
    1. Lo que éramos en el pasado: muertos (2:1-3)
    2. Lo que somos ahora: vivos (2:4-6)
    3. Lo que seremos: mostradores, escaparates de la gracia de Dios (2:7-10)
  C. Hemos sido hechos cercanos (2:11–3:13)

1. Condición anterior de los gentiles: el problema (2:11-12)
2. La obra de Cristo en la cruz: la solución (2:13-22)
3. La responsabilidad de Pablo de predicar esta verdad: la misión (3:1-13)
   Oración dc Pablo para que: (3:14-21)
   1. Los efesios sean fortalecidos en el hombre interior (v. 16)
   2. Habite Cristo en su corazón por la fe (v. 17)
   3. Los efesios comprendan el amor de Cristo (vv. 18-19)

II. CÓMO DEBEMOS ANDAR «en Cristo» (4:1–6:20)
- A. Dignos de nuestra vocación (4:1-16)
- B. No como los otros gentiles (4:17-32)
  1. En general/términos teológicos (4:17-24)
  2. En específico/términos prácticos (4:25-32)
- C. En amor (5:1-2)
- D. Como hijos de luz (5:3-14)
- E. Como sabios (5:15–6:9)
  1. Aprovechando bien el tiempo (5:16)
  2. Entended cuál es la voluntad de Dios (5:17)
  3. Sed llenos del Espíritu Santo (5:18)
     a. Cantando (5:19)
     b. Dando siempre gracias (5:20)
     c. Sometiéndonos (5:21)
        - Esposas a esposos (5:22-33)
        - Hijos a padres (6:1-4)
        - Siervos a amos (6:5-9)
- F. El andar cristiano es como una guerra (6:10-20)

Últimas explicaciones y bendiciones (6:21-24)

## Comentario

Por regla general, el saludo de una Epístola no se incluye en el bosquejo. El tema de Efesios es «en Cristo». Los capítulos 1–3 subrayan lo que el creyente tiene gracias a su unión con Cristo y lo que Dios ha hecho por él «en Cristo», mientras que los capítulos 4–6 hacen énfasis en cómo debe andar. En los capítulos 1–3 Pablo cita solamente tres de las muchas cosas que Dios ha hecho por el creyente.

*1. Nos bendijo con toda bendición espiritual (1:3-14).* El verbo «ha bendecido» (1:3, LBLA) indica que Pablo se refiere a algo que Dios ya ha hecho. Aunque cada persona de la Trinidad ha realizado varias obras en el creyente, el apóstol cita solamente una por persona. Al final de cada subpunto que subraya la obra que ha realizado cada persona de la Trinidad, Pablo declara que Dios lo ha hecho «para alabanza [...] de su gracia, [...] de su gloria» (vv. 6, 14).

Antes de pasar a la segunda cosa que Dios ha hecho por cada creyente debido a su unión con Cristo, Pablo introduce en 1:15-23 una oración que representa una especie de paréntesis. Normalmente no se emplea un paréntesis en un bosquejo, pero es una forma muy gráfica de mostrar que este pasaje es precisamente eso. Una oración es muy personal en contraste con un pasaje didáctico, que suele presentar una enseñanza de forma muy organizada. Por eso, 1:15-23 es difícil de bosquejar. No obstante, lo que queda claro es que Pablo pide que Dios abra los ojos del entendimiento de los efesios para que vean y aprovechen todas las bendiciones que *ya son* suyas. De lo contrario serán como la persona que se dirige a un gran almacén de alimentos para comprar algo para la cena, pero en lugar de escoger la carne más sabrosa y cara escoge unas manzanas porque ignora que es ¡el propietario de dicho almacén!

Pablo pide en oración que los efesios vean con los ojos de su entendimiento la esperanza a la que Dios los ha llamado, «las riquezas de la gloria de *su* herencia en los santos» (énfasis añadido) y el gran poder de Dios «para con nosotros los que creemos». La primera y tercera petición se refieren a algo que los creyentes tienen a su disposición, pero la segunda tiene que ver con una persona. ¿Quién es la persona a la que se refiere la palabra «su» en el v. 18? Si Pablo hubiera querido referirse a los efesios, habría usado la palabra «vuestra». Es evidente que «su» se refiere a la persona identificada pocas palabras antes como «él»; o sea, Cristo mismo. El creyente tiene una herencia que le espera (1:11). Pero Cristo también tiene una herencia. La frase «en los santos» significa que los creyentes somos la herencia de Cristo. Con la frase «las riquezas de la gloria» parece que Pablo está luchando por encontrar las palabras adecuadas para describir cuánto nos valora Dios. Se habla mucho en círculos psicológicos de personas que tienen una autoestima baja. El remedio es que el creyente se dé cuenta de cuánto vale para Dios. Nuestro valor como creyentes estriba en cuánto Dios nos valora, no en lo que piensan los demás de nosotros ni en lo que pensamos nosotros.

*2. Nos dio vida (2:1-10).* El tiempo de los verbos en este párrafo representa la clave del bosquejo. O sea, lo que éramos antes de conocer a Cristo, lo que somos ahora que lo conocemos y lo que seremos en los siglos venideros (2:7). ¿A qué tiempo se refieren esos «siglos venideros»? ¿Los siglos en que han vivido los creyentes desde el primer siglo? Evidentemente, el creyente debe caracterizarse por buenas obras, las cuales servirán para que los no creyentes sean atraídos a Dios (Mt. 5:16). Sin embargo, parece que Pablo se refiere a lo que haremos en el cielo. Todos seremos como escaparates o aparadores de la gracia de Dios en nuestras vidas. Me pregunto si mucho del «tiempo» que pasaremos en el cielo no estará ocupado con el gran privilegio de contar a otros los detalles de todo lo que Dios hizo por nosotros en la tierra. Hay muchas historias absolutamente impresionantes.

*3. Hemos sido hechos cercanos (2:11–3:13).* El hecho de que Pablo dirija estos versículos a «vosotros, los gentiles» (2:11), además de la presencia de otras referencias a los gentiles en esta Epístola, demuestran que la iglesia en Éfeso estaba compuesta mayoritariamente por gentiles. Esta sección representa la mención plena de la doctrina de la iglesia. En el día de hoy el creyente tiene más que asumido que la iglesia está compuesta por miembros de todos los pueblos y grupos étnicos. Pero esta verdad no era tan evidente para los primeros creyentes, muchos de los cuales eran judíos (2:11-12).

Los primeros tres capítulos de Efesios terminan con otra oración en 3:14-21. De nuevo, sugerimos que es difícil bosquejar una oración por ser tan personal. En contraste con la oración de 1:15-23, es complicado encontrar un título que englobe de forma clara las tres peticiones tan diferentes que Pablo hace a Dios por los efesios. Finalmente, ¿qué relación guarda esta oración con el párrafo que la antecede (2:11–3:13)?

Este trabajo no ha requerido que el lector realice un bosquejo de los capítulos 4–6. No obstante, en el capítulo 13 tiene la oportunidad de ver cómo la gramática juega un papel muy importante en el bosquejo del autor para esos capítulos.

# CAPÍTULO 12: PALABRAS

## 2 Corintios 1:22

En el v. 20 Pablo hace referencia a Dios, que en el N.T. casi siempre se refiere al Padre para distinguirle de las otras dos personas de la Trinidad. El v. 21 indica que el Padre nos confirma y nos unge. El v. 22 completa la frase diciendo que es el Padre quien sella al creyente, no el Espíritu Santo. Aunque los otros dos textos lo dirán de forma más clara, el hecho es que el Espíritu *es* el sello con el cual el Padre sella al creyente. El Espíritu actúa como unas arras, un pago y señal, una garantía. Pero este texto no nos dice de qué es garantía. A la luz de estas observaciones, los mejores candidatos para el significado de «sellado» son los de una garantía de entrega segura *ahora* y de un pago y señal de *cara al futuro.*

La RVR60 dice que el Espíritu es como unas arras. La LBLA emplea la palabra «garantía». Sin embargo, en el margen dice «O, *arras*», indicando que una minoría numerosa de los miembros del comité que redactaron el texto creían que «arras» era la palabra más apropiada. Evidentemente, «arras» se presta al concepto de garantía. Pero los traductores de la NTV («nos identificó como suyos») y la NVI («como propiedad suya») en efecto dan su opinión sobre cuál de los cuatro significados de «sellar» había en la mente de Pablo. El lector que desconoce este hecho da por sentado que el texto original dice que el acto divino de sellar al creyente tiene que ver con su pertenencia a Dios. Evidentemente 1 Corintios 6:19 enseña que el creyente es propiedad de Dios («no sois vuestros»), igual que hay textos que afirman la verdad expresada por los otros tres significados de la palabra «sellado» (señal de transacción terminada; garantía de que lo que se entrega ahora es completo; pago y señal). Pero ¿es eso lo que significa la palabra «sellado» en el v. 22? Para contestar esa pregunta el intérprete tiene que estudiar el contexto inmediato de cada uno de los tres textos.

## Efesios 4:30

Al decir que el creyente ha sido sellado «con» el Espíritu Santo, enviándolo a morar en cada creyente (2 Co. 1:22), Pablo indica de nuevo que el Espíritu es el sello con el cual el Padre sella al creyente. Ha realizado esta obra «para el día de la redención». Puesto que Pablo está hablando de algo que ocurrirá en el futuro, no se refiere a la obra de Cristo en la cruz o al momento en que cada creyente se convirtió a Cristo. Por tanto, la única opción que queda es el día en que el creyente verá a Jesús cara a cara y participará de todos aquellos aspectos de la salvación que son suyos en Cristo pero de los cuales no disfruta en este momento (un cuerpo glorificado, la liberación total y definitiva del pecado, ocupar el hogar que Cristo le ha preparado en el cielo, etcétera).

### Efesios 1:13-14

Según el v. 13, el creyente fue sellado con el Espíritu Santo cuando recibió la salvación. La tercera persona de la Trinidad se describe como «el Espíritu Santo de la promesa» porque Cristo prometió que el Espíritu se daría a cada creyente (Jn. 7:37-39). En el v. 14 el Espíritu se describe como las «arras de nuestra herencia», como la garantía o pago y señal de que el creyente recibirá en el futuro esa parte de la gran salvación que tiene en Cristo pero de la cual no disfruta en este momento. ¿Qué garantía tiene el creyente de que no llegará a la eternidad solamente para descubrir que debería haber depositado su fe en Mahoma en lugar de Cristo, cuando ya no le queda tiempo para cambiar de bando? La presencia del Espíritu en su vida aquí y ahora es la garantía de que no se ha equivocado y de que recibirá la herencia que Cristo ha adquirido para él con su sangre. El hombre enamorado de una mujer le entrega un anillo (arras) como pago y señal, como garantía de que su novio se convertirá en su esposo el día de su boda. De igual forma, el Espíritu Santo es el anillo que Dios ha dado al creyente como garantía de que recibirá la mejor y mayor parte de su salvación cuando lo vea cara a cara.

## CAPÍTULO 16: LENGUAJE FIGURADO

En el primer grupo de textos citados a continuación es evidente la clase de lenguaje figurado que el autor bíblico emplea. Pero dadas las dificultades de los textos indicados con un (+) o asterisco (*), el autor de *Con precisión* explica a continuación cómo ha llegado a su conclusión en cuanto a la clase de lenguaje figurado que el autor bíblico emplea.

Gn. 49:17 – metáfora
Nm. 16:32 – personificación
1 S. 17:7 – símil
1 R. 18:27 – ironía
Sal. 18:1 – metáfora
Sal. 84:11 – metáfora
Sal. 90:1- metáfora
Sal. 114:3 – personificación
Pr. 25:25 – símil
Cnt. 2:2 – símil
Cnt. 2:9 – símil
Os. 13:3 – símil
Os. 13:7 – símil
Am. 2:13 – símil
Am. 4:4 – ironía
Hab. 3:10 – personificación
Lc. 13:32 – metonimia
Jn. 6:48 – metáfora
Jn. 10:7 – metáfora
Jn. 14:6 – metáfora
Jn. 15:1 – metáfora
Jn. 21:25 – hipérbole
1 Co. 4:8 – ironía
1 Co. 13:1 – símil
2 Co. 12:13 – ironía
Gá. 2:9 – símil

**Job 12:2+** Con la frase «Ciertamente vosotros sois el pueblo» Job emplea la ironía. Sus amigos se creen los portavoces de lo que piensan todos los demás. Como no era verdad, Job les echa en cara su prepotencia y arrogancia. Con la frase «Y con vosotros morirá la sabiduría» sigue con su ironía, pero atribuye a la sabiduría una característica del ser humano; a saber, la muerte. En este caso emplea la personificación.

**Salmo 23:4+** Con la tercera frase de este versículo David dice que la vara y el cayado que Dios emplea le infunden aliento, una clara personificación puesto que se atribuye a esas dos herramientas una característica humana. A la vez cabe la posibilidad de que esas herramientas representen una metonimia, porque Dios no las tiene ni las emplea. Al mencionar la vara y el cayado, cualquier judío sabía que los pastores las usaban para dirigir a una oveja o para rescatarla cuando se encontraba en un lugar de difícil acceso.

**Salmo 119:105+** David compara la Palabra de Dios con una lámpara o lumbrera usando solo el verbo «ser». Por tanto, emplea una metáfora. Pero al referirse a los pies del creyente, emplea la sinécdoque, en este caso la parte por la totalidad, porque Dios guía no solamente los pies del creyente, sino también todo su ser. Evidentemente, David hace mención de los pies porque son los miembros del cuerpo humano que más se asocia con andar por un camino.

**Isaías 1:8+** El profeta compara la «hija de Sion» con una «enramada en viña», una «cabaña en melonar» y una «ciudad asolada». O sea, tres símiles. Pero ¿qué es Sion? Sion era el nombre de la fortaleza de los jebuseos que David conquistó en 2 S. 5:7. A partir de ese momento se llamó la Ciudad de David (1 R. 8:1). Por tanto, Isaías dirige su profecía a Judá con su capital en Jerusalén (ver 1:1). Pero ¿«hija»? En momentos de crisis y de guerra, las mujeres y los niños son los más indefensos y perjudicados. Así era el pueblo de Israel. En este caso, la palabra «hija» actúa como una metonimia, trayendo a nuestra mente un concepto.

**Oseas 7:8+** Como en otras ocasiones en los libros proféticos, la tribu de Efraín sirve como el representante de todas las diez tribus del reino del norte. En este caso el profeta emplea una sinécdoque. Pero en la segunda parte del versículo compara a Israel con una «torta no volteada». Al usar solamente el verbo «ser» es una metáfora.

**Oseas 14:5+** Hablando del día en que los judíos reconocerán a Cristo como su Mesías y Dios los restaurará, Oseas comienza este versículo con dos símiles en los que compara a Dios con el rocío y al pueblo de Dios con un lirio. Será un día en que el pueblo de Dios prosperará como nunca, llegando al punto de extender «sus raíces». Evidentemente, el profeta no está hablando de raíces literales. Cuando una planta o un árbol está sano extiende sus raíces. Por tanto, el profeta emplea una metonimia.

**Habacuc 3:19+** Primero el profeta compara a Dios con una fortaleza, empleando una metáfora al usar solamente el verbo «ser». Luego, emplea un símil al decir que Dios hace que sus pies sean «como» los de las ciervas. ¿«Pies»? No está hablando de pies literales, sino de aquellos miembros del cuerpo humano con los cuales se asocia el andar. O sea, una sinécdoque.

**Mateo 7:15+** Jesús advierte a sus seguidores de que en el futuro vendrán falsos profetas. Se vestirán «de ovejas». Desde luego, no es una referencia a una ropa hecha de lana, sino que la palabra «oveja» nos trae a la mente un animal que no es agresivo ni peligroso. O sea, una metonimia. Así serán los falsos profetas. Serán amables y se mostrarán amigos de todos, pero «por dentro son lobos rapaces». O sea, una metáfora.

**1 Corintios 10:21*** Cuando Jacobo y Juan pidieron a Jesús que los dejara sentarse a su derecha e izquierda cuando viniera su reino, Jesús les preguntó: «¿Podéis beber la copa que yo bebo?». En este caso empleó la palabra «copa» como una metonimia (el recipiente por el contenido) del trago amargo que tendrían que beber, del sufrimiento que tendrían que padecer poco después (Mc. 10:38, LBLA). A primera vista la frase de 1 Corintios 10:21 («No podéis beber la copa del Señor, y la copa de los demonios») podría considerarse una sinécdoque en la cual Pablo cita solamente uno de los dos elementos empleados en la celebración de la Cena del Señor puesto que el contexto inmediato (vv. 16-17) habla de ella. Por otra parte, podría ser una metonimia (el contenido de un recipiente); o sea, no es posible participar en las bendiciones de pertenecer a Cristo y a la vez participar en los «deleites temporales del pecado» (Heb. 11:25) que Satanás ofrece.

## CAPÍTULO 19: PARÁBOLAS (II)

En Mateo 22:2-14 Jesús cuenta la parábola de la fiesta de bodas. Su contexto histórico (v. 1) indica que Jesús la contó en respuesta a una pregunta, pero no identifica la pregunta. Al mirar los versículos anteriores (21:45-44), Mateo nos informa de que los principales sacerdotes y fariseos quisieron «echarle mano» a Jesús porque entendían que la parábola que acababa de contarles (los labradores malvados en 21:33-44) iba dirigida a ellos. Pero 21:45-46 tampoco nos dice cuál era la pregunta que Jesús contestaba con esta parábola. Al buscar más atrás encontramos la parábola de los dos hijos y la viña (21:28-32), la cual tampoco indica la pregunta que Jesús contestaba con la parábola de la fiesta de bodas.

Volviendo aún más atrás encontramos un contexto histórico en 21:23-27 donde los principales sacerdotes y ancianos del pueblo preguntan a Jesús: «¿Con qué autoridad haces estas cosas, y quién te dio esta autoridad?» (v. 23, LBLA). Esta es la pregunta a la que se refiere 22:1. Pero para entender la conversación que Jesús tuvo con ellos a continuación (vv. 24-27) hemos de averiguar a qué se refieren «estas cosas» (v. 23), porque nada más terminar su conversación con los sacerdotes y ancianos, Jesús cuenta las tres parábolas de los dos hijos (21:28-32), los labradores malvados (21:33-44) y la fiesta de bodas (22:2-14).

Yendo más atrás todavía nos encontramos con el episodio de la higuera que Jesús vio a lo lejos (21:18-22). Cuando se acercó a ella y no encontró el fruto que esperaba, la maldijo. (Comentaremos más abajo este evento tan extraño en el ministerio de Jesús.) Al retroceder aún más, por fin encontramos en 21:1-3 el contexto histórico que necesitamos para entender la pregunta que Jesús contesta en 22:1. Al acercarse a Jerusalén, Jesús envía a sus discípulos a buscar una asna en una aldea cercana a la capital. Mateo dice que este acto es el cumplimiento de la profecía de Zacarías 9:9 («He aquí, tu Rey viene a ti, manso, y sentado sobre una asna...», 21:5). Mateo cita esta profecía porque dirige su Evangelio a los judíos con el propósito de convencerlos de que Jesús es el Mesías tan esperado, el Rey que establecerá un reino caracterizado por la justicia y la paz. Entonces, Jesús entra en Jerusalén y la multitud lo aclama, diciendo: «¡Hosanna al Hijo de David! ¡Bendito el que viene en el nombre del Señor!» (v. 9). Nada más llegar al templo, vuelca las mesas de los cambistas y las sillas de los que vendían palomas (21:12-13). Evidentemente, los principales sacerdotes y escribas se indignaron (v. 15).

Terminado este episodio en el templo, Jesús se retira a Betania y pasa allí la noche (v. 17), con toda probabilidad en casa de Lázaro y sus hermanas María y Marta. Por la mañana se dirige a Jerusalén de nuevo. Antes de llegar a la capital, maldice la higuera que no tiene fruto. Cuando llega al templo, los principales sacerdotes y los ancianos del pueblo le preguntan: «¿Con qué autoridad haces estas cosas, y quién te dio esta autoridad?» (v. 23, LBLA). O sea, ¿con qué derecho hizo Jesús tantos destrozos en el templo? ¿Quién lo nombró juez y jurado? *Este es el contexto histórico que estamos buscando, la pregunta que Jesús contesta en 22:1.* Pero en lugar de contestar la pregunta de los sacerdotes y ancianos, Jesús les hace otra pregunta: «El bautismo de Juan, ¿de dónde era? ¿Del cielo, o de los hombres?». Reconociendo que Jesús les ha tendido una trampa, responden que no conocen la respuesta. Entonces, Jesús se niega a decirles con qué autoridad limpió el templo de los cambistas y vendedores de animales para los sacrificios. Y aunque no contesta esa pregunta, Jesús trata el problema que hay detrás de esa pregunta de los sacerdotes y ancianos a través de las tres parábolas; a saber, el rechazo de los judíos a Jesús como el Mesías.

En la parábola de los dos hijos (21:28-32), el punto central se encuentra en los vv. 31-32 donde Jesús afirma que los publicanos y prostitutas entran en el reino de Dios por delante de los líderes religiosos.

Entonces, Jesús cuenta la parábola de los labradores malvados (21:33-44). Puesto que los labradores (judíos) rechazaron al hijo (Cristo) del padre de familia (Dios el Padre), además de a sus siervos (los profetas y otros siervos de Dios), el punto central de esta parábola es que el reino será quitado de los judíos y entregado «a gente que produzca los frutos de él» (21:43). Puesto que Jesús se encontraba en la última semana de su vida, es muy probable que el episodio con la higuera fuera un acto simbólico de lo que Dios iba a hacer dentro de pocas semanas con los judíos; a saber, rechazarlos como su canal de la redención y entregar esa responsabilidad a la Iglesia.

Cuando Jesús terminó de contarles la parábola de los labradores malvados, los principales sacerdotes y los fariseos querían echarle mano porque entendían que hablaba de ellos (21:45-46). Pero temían prenderlo porque el pueblo lo consideraba un profeta. Entonces, «respondiendo Jesús, les volvió a hablar en parábolas...». Y ahora llegamos a la parábola de la fiesta de bodas. Un rey invita a varias personas a la boda de su hijo. En Medio Oriente se extendían dos convocatorias para fiestas importantes. En la primera se invitaba a la gente con el fin de confirmar quién iba a asistir a la fiesta. La segunda convocatoria se extendía cuando todos los preparativos estaban hechos. De acuerdo con las costumbres de Medio Oriente, los invitados dejaban lo que hacían y acudían enseguida a la fiesta. Pero en este caso se negaron a ir, rompiendo así con su compromiso previo. Hasta mataron a algunos de los siervos que el rey les había enviado para animarlos a rectificar su decisión de no ir a la fiesta. Por tanto, el rey los mató y envió a sus siervos a invitar a cuantos hallaran en la calle. Puesto que no eran del mismo nivel social del rey, y de acuerdo con la costumbre en estos casos, se les proveyó a la entrada de la boda de una especie de poncho para cubrir su ropa sencilla y pobre. Sin embargo, hubo un invitado que logró entrar sin poncho.

Es evidente que el rey de la parábola es Dios el Padre, su hijo es Cristo, los primeros invitados son los judíos, y los siervos son los profetas y otros siervos que Dios había enviado y a los cuales los primeros invitados (los judíos) maltrataron y mataron. Pero ¿quiénes son las personas encontradas en la calle y quién es el hombre que entró sin la indumentaria adecuada? Aunque el punto central de cada una de las tres parábolas de Mateo 21 y 22 es diferente, están íntimamente relacionados. El punto central de la parábola de los dos hijos es que los publicanos y prostitutas entran en el reino de Dios por delante de los líderes religiosos. El punto central de los labradores malvados es que el reino será quitado de los judíos y entregado a otra gente que producirá el fruto que Dios quiere. Entonces, por lógica, el foco de la fiesta de bodas tiene que centrarse en ese nuevo pueblo.

Sabemos que los primeros miembros de la iglesia eran judíos. Pero con el tiempo la gran mayoría de los miembros fueron gentiles. Por tanto, la parábola de la fiesta de bodas ilustra cómo Dios invita a todos los gentiles a entrar en su reino. Evidentemente, solamente algunos aceptarán su invitación. Y siempre habrá quienes intenten entrar en el reino de Dios a su manera, sin la «indumentaria adecuada». Estos serán echados «en las tinieblas de afuera; allí será el lloro y el crujir de dientes. Porque muchos son llamados, y pocos escogidos» (Mt. 22:13-14). Romanos 11:11-21 es el texto didáctico que más ampliamente describe la caída en desgracia de los judíos por haber rechazado a Cristo como su Mesías, la bendición que ese rechazo ha representado para los gentiles y la eventual restauración del pueblo judío.

# Índice de textos bíblicos

Este Índice no incluye los textos citados en los bosquejos de las páginas 446–454 y 456–457 ni los textos que aparecen en el «Trabajo para realizar» al final de algunos capítulos.


**Génesis**

cap. 1 *94*
cap. 1–2 *92*
1:1–2:3 *92*
1:11-12 *94*
1:18 *342*
1:21 *94*
1:25 *94*
1:27 *94, 346, 444*
1:28 *342*
2:2-3 *272, 285*
2:24 *50, 346, 444*
cap. 3 *193, 357*
3:15 *125*
4:8 *55*
4:23 *227*
7:4 *272*
9:6 *40*
10:21-31 *378*
12:1-7 *299*
15:6 *209*
16:11 *271*
16:14 *271*
17:5 *271*
19:4-8 *130, 442*
cap. 22 *283*
24:14 *297*
24:16 *297*
24:43 *297*
29:18 *272*
30:11 *209*
30:13 *209*
41:2 *272*
41:18 *272*
46:16-18 *209*
49:17 *462*
49:28 *272*
50:10 *272*
50:20 *118*

**Éxodo**

1:5 *209*
1:8-25 *342*
2:8 *297*
3:6 *60*
4:10-16 *218*
4:21 *241*
7:3 *241*
7:7 *218*
7:13-14 *241*
7:22 *241*
8:15 *241*
8:19 *241*
8:32 *241*

9:7 *241*
9:12 *241*
9:34 *241*
9:35 *241*
10:1 *241*
10:20 *241*
10:27 *241*
11:10 *241*
cap. 12 *285*
12:15 272
12:36 *118*
14:8 *241*
17:2 *297*
17:6 *285*
cap. 20–Dt. 33 *331*
21:7 *346*
21:10 *347*
21:10-11 *346*
21:28-36 *333*
23:19 *334*
24:18 *272*
25:10-11 *270*
25:17 *270*
25:17-21 *268*
25:18 *270*
25:18-22 *268*
25:21 *270*
25:23-24 *270*
25:28-29 *270*
25:31 *270*
28:1-4 *218*
28:15-21 *271*
28:21 *272*
32:16 *50*
34:26 *334*

**Levítico**

8:2 *281*
8:3 *281*
8:12 *218*
18:6 *223*
18:7 *338*
18:7-16 *223*
18:22 *443*
19:32 *219*
20:11 *338*
20:13 *443*
20:25-26 *332*
25:39-42 *343*

**Números**

6:24-26 *384*
6:24-27 *272*
14:34 *272*
16:32 *462*
21:4-9 *285, 286*
23:19 *62*
32:13 *272*

**Deuteronomio**

4:1-2 *332*
5:1 *354*
5:32-33 *357*
5:33 *357*
6:5 *424*
6:16 *297*
8:1-5 *272*
11:29-30 *377*
14:3-22 *332*
14:21 *334*
15:12 *343*
15:12-18 *208*
15:16-17 *343*
15:17 *208*
17:14-20 *299*
22:10 *333*
22:12 *333*
22:24 *297*
23:17-18 *443*
cap. 24 *346*
24:1 *346, 347*
24:1-4 *345*
27:2-3 *377*
28:4-7 *377*
28:62-63 *299*
28:63-68 *299*
32:43 *61*

**Josué**

4:9 *272*
cap. 6 *137*
6:4 *272*
10:13 *58*

**Jueces**

5:14 *376*
9:7-20 *246*
19:16-30 *442*

**1 Samuel**

4:4 *268*
12:17 *144*
17:7 *462*
24:3 *223*

**2 Samuel**

1:1-18 *58*
5:7 *218, 463*
6:2 *268*
7:11-15 *300*
7:12-17 *285*
7:16 *300*
12:1-13 *237*
12:7 *237*
12:13 *237*

15:7-17 *143*
22:50 *61*
23:2-3 *227*

**1 Reyes**

cap. 8 *353*
8:1 *218, 463*
8:18 *353*
11:41 *58*
12:16 *376*
14:24 *442*
15:12 *442*
cap. 18 353
18:27 *222, 462*
22:46 *442*

**2 Reyes**

8:18 *209*
8:26 *209*
9:2 *209*
9:20 *209*
10:1-28 *266*
10:15-16 *266*
10:23 *266*
14:9 *246*
14:22 *142*
15:1-2 *142*
15:3 *142*
15:4 *142*
17:6 *297*
cap. 18–19 *353*
18:1–20:21 *56*
19:15 *268*
24:8 *89*
24:15 *90*

**1 Crónicas**

2:55 *266*
29:29 *58*

**2 Crónicas**

9:29 *58*
12:15 *58*
18:33 *56*
20:34 *58*
24:21 *55*
24:27 *58*
cap. 25 *58*
25:6 *270*
25:26 *58*
26:2 *142*
26:5 *142*
26:7 *142*
26:8 *142*
26:10 *142*
26:15-16 *142*
26:16-18 *142*
26:22 *58, 59, 142*
cap. 28 *58*
28:13 *297*
28:14 *297*
28:16-20 *297*
28:26 *58*
31:10 *254*
32:32 *58*
36:9 *89*

**Esdras**

4:8–6:18 *379*
7:11-26 *58*
7:12-26 *379*

**Nehemías**

4:2 *377*
8:1-2 *379*
8:7-8 *379*

**Job**

1:1-20 *225*
2:1-13 *225*
8:11 *373*
12:2 *462*
19:25-26 *44*
32:1-5 *225*
42:7-16 *225*

**Salmos**

cap. 1 *353*
1:1 *228, 229*
1:2 *228, 229*
3:5 *143*
cap. 5 *232*
5:3 *353*
cap. 10 *232*
12:6-7 *402*
cap. 17 *232*
18:1 *462*
18:20 *170*
18:49 *61*
19:1-6 *40*
19:4 *90*
19:6 *90*
19:7-8 *356*
22:1 *285*
cap. 23 *353*
23:4 *462*
25:2 *231*
34:8 *367*
34:15 *223*
cap. 35 *232*
36:9 *368*
cap. 47 *311*
51:11 *162*
55:4 *231*
55:12-13 *231*
55:17 *353*
56:3 *231*
56:11 *231*

cap. 58–59 *232*
59:16 *353*
62:5 *231*
68:28 *297*
cap. 69–70 *232*
71:9 *231*
cap. 72 *311*
73:3 *231*
77:12 *355*
cap. 79 *232*
80:8-15 *430*
cap. 83 *232*
84:11 *462*
88:13 *353*
90:1 *462*
cap. 109 *232*
109:6-11 *231*
109:13 *232*
cap. 110 *311*
110:1 *311*
114:3 *462*
117:1 *61*
cap. 119 *353, 356*
119:11 *356*
119:15 *355*
119:18 *110*
119:24 *356*
119:47 *356*
119:48 *355*
119:72 *356*
119:77 *356*
119:105 *161, 462*
119:148 *355*
119:162 *231*
119:164 *272*
120:1 *231*
cap. 129 *232*
133:1-3 *217*
cap. 137 *232*
cap. 140 *232*

**Proverbios**

1:20-21 *222*
1:20-33 *232*
3:9-10 *164*
3:13 *232*
3:16 *232*
4:20-22 *351*
cap. 5 *232*
5:15-18 *430*
6:2 *227, 227*
8:1-2 *222*
8:10 *210*
9:1-2 *222*
11:24-25 *164*
14:24 *228*
14:34 *228*
15:1-2 *228*
22:6 *233*
24:16 *272*
25:25 *462*
30:19 *297*

**Eclesiastés**

1:5 *90*
12:3-7 *430*

**Cantar de los Cantares**

1:3 *297*
2:2 *462*
2:9 *462*
6:8 *297*

**Isaías**

1:1 *58, 118, 129, 142, 233, 463*
1:8 *463*
1:18 *129, 216, 269*
2:3 *322*
5:1-7 *129, 430*
6:1 *58*
6:3 *129, 272*
6:9 *111*
6:9-10 *107*
6:9-13 *242*
7:1 *58*
7:4 *297*
7:8 *297*
7:12 *297*
7:14 *292, 296, 297, 438*
8:1-4 *271*
9:6-7 *295, 300, 323*
9:7 *295*
9:9-10 *242*
10:5-6 *118*
10:13 *41, 44*
11:1 *292*
11:10 *61*
cap. 24–27 *293*
24:1 *191*
25:1 *301*
32:8 *129*
37:16 *268*
37:26 *291*
40:8 *402, 422*
40:18-26 *41*
45:22-25 *311*
cap. 53 *353*
53:6 *215*
53:7 *129*
58:10-11 *164*
61:1-3 *296*
66:1 *50*

**Jeremías**

1:2 *50*

1:11-12 *265*
1:13-16 *265*
2:13 *216*
7:1 *210*
7:13 *266*
7:22-23 *211*
7:25 *266*
10:11 *379*
13:1-11 *266*
13:9 *266*
18:1-11 *265*
cap. 19 *266*
19:11 *266*
23:7-8 *300*
cap. 24 *265*
24:1 *274*
24:4-10 *274*
25:1 *90*
26:5 *266*
cap. 27 *266*
27:6 *266*
28:12-17 *267*
28:15-16 *267*
29:19 *266*
30:7 *197*
31:1 *200*
31:15 *281, 285, 438*
31:19 *220*
31:20 *220*
31:27 *296*
31:27-40 *296, 311*
31:31-33 *322*
31:31-34 *200*
32:1-15 *267*
32:15 *267*
32:36-41 *300*
cap. 35 *266, 267*
35:2-6 *266*
35:14-15 *266*
35:18-19 *266*
43:8-13 *267*
43:10-11 *267*
44:4 *266*
51:59-64 *267*
51:64 *267*

**Lamentaciones**

1:16 *273*
3:22-23 *164*

**Ezequiel**

1:1 *50*
13:8-16 *430*
cap. 17 *246*
20:33-38 *315*
28:25 *322*
28:25-26 *300*
32:5 *221*
37:1-14 *275*
37:15-24 *322*
37:15-28 *300*
cap. 38–39 *293*
cap. 40–48 *294*
40:1–44:3 *295*
40:46 *254*
44:4–45:17 *295*
44:5 *171*
44:6 *171*
44:15 *254*
45:18–46:24 *295*
cap. 47–48 *295*
48:11 *254*

**Daniel**

1:1 *90*
2:4-7:28 *379*
2:19-21 *41, 44*
2:21 *118*
2:44 *300, 323*
cap. 2 *270*
cap. 7–12 *293*
7:1-14 *300*
7:9 *269*
7:13-14 *300, 323*
10:5 *265*
12:1-2 *44, 321*
12:2 *296*

**Oseas**

1:1 *51, 142*
1:2 *219*
1:4 *178*
1:10-11 *300*
2:23 *311*
7:8 *463*
7:13-14 *300*
11:1 *281, 285, 292, 438*
11:8 *227*
13:3 *462*
13:7 *462*
14:5 *463*

**Joel**

1:1 *51*
1:8 *297*
2:28-32 *200*

**Amós**

1:1 *142*
1:3 *51*
2:13 *462*
4:4 *462*

**Abdías**

1:1 *51*

**Jonás**

1:1 *51*

**Miqueas**

1:1 *51*
4:3 *220*
5:2 *292*

**Habacuc**

3:10 *462*
3:19 *463*

**Sofonías**

1:1 *51*

**Hageo**

1:1 *51*

**Zacarías**

cap. 1–6 *293*
1:1 *51*
3:8 *273*
4:2 *272*
cap. 9–14 *293*
9:9 *292, 465*
10:6-10 *300*

**Malaquías**

1:1 *51*
3:10 *164*
4:5 *298, 299*
4:5-6 *285*

**Mateo**

1:1-16 *59*
1:21 *179*
1:21-23 *438*
1:22-23 *292*
2:5-12 *292*
2:15 *281, 285, 438*
2:16-18 *438*
2:17 *281*
2:17-18 *285*
2:23 *292*
3:9 *322*
4:1-11 *96*
4:2 *272*
4:17 *300*
5:13 *312*
5:16 *459*
5:17-18 *60*
5:18 *61*
5:21-22 *84, 236*
5:27-28 *84, 236*
5:31-32 *84, 236*
5:33-34 *84, 236*
5:38-39 *84, 236*
5:43-44 *84, 236*
5:45 *209*
5:46 *209*
6:24 *226*
7:7-11 *97*
7:11 *97, 396*
7:15 *463*
7:24-27 *251*
7:29 *238*
8:28 *96*
9:16-17 *250*
9:24 *223*
10:1 *272*
10:15 *55*
10:19-20 *52*
11:3 *104*
11:10-14 *298*
11:20-24 *104*
11:20-26 *104*
11:23-24 *55*
11:25 *105, 110*
11:25-26 *104*
11:25-30 *104*
11:27 *110*
12:22-32 *209*
12:25-29 *306*
12:27 *209*
12:39-41 *55*
12:40 *81, 211, 285*
12:45 *272*
cap. 13 *245, 310*
13:1-2 *106*
13:1-23 *238*
13:3 *106, 245*
13:3-8 *250, 257, 432, 435*
13:5-6 *111*
13:9 *111*
13:10 *106, 239, 245*
13:10-17 *105, 106, 123*
13:11 *106, 240*
13:11-12 *239*
13:12 *106, 107, 108, 113, 351*
13:13 *107, 111, 239, 245*
13:13-15 *106, 240*
13:14 *108, 111*
13:14-15 *240, 242*
13:15 *107*
13:18-23 *250, 257, 435*
13:24-30 *250, 257, 312, 310, 432*
13:31 *243*
13:31-32 *244, 250, 310*
13:32 *92*

13:33 *244, 250, 310*
13:34 *243*
13:36-43 *250, 257, 424, 432*
13:44 *245, 250*
13:45-46 *245, 250*
13:47-48 *245*
13:47-50 *250, 310*
13:51-53 *251*
15:2-6 *255*
15:4 *50*
15:13 *244*
15:15 *244*
16:5-6 *264*
16:6 *214*
16:6-7 *125*
16:13 *103*
16:16 *103*
16:17 *42, 104, 110*
16:19 *219*
17:1-13 *298*
17:2 *269*
17:10 *285*
17:11 *298*
17:12 *298*
17:13 *298*
18:1 *253*
18:12-14 *249, 253*
18:17 *256*
18:23-35 *250, 254*
19:3 *345*
19:3-9 *444*
19:4 *346*
19:4-6 *50, 443*
19:5 *346*
19:6 *346*
19:9 *346*
20:1-16 *250*
cap. 21 *374, 466*
21:1-3 *465*
21:1-5 *292*
21:9 *465*
21:12-13 *465*
21:15 *465*
21:17 *465*
21:18-22 *464*
21:23 *464, 465*
21:23-27 *464*
21:24-27 *464*
21:31-32 *465*
21:33-34 *464, 466*
21:33-44 *242*
21:33-46 *249, 432, 464*
21:38-32 *249, 464, 466*
21:43 *466*
21:45 *243*
21:45-46 *464, 466*
21:46 *242*
cap. 22 *466*
22:1 *464, 465*
22:1-14 *249, 253, 432, 464*
22:13-14 *467*
22:15-22 *256*
22:23-32 *60*
22:32 *60*
23:12 *226*
23:13-16 *238*
23:30-31 *55*
23:35 *55*
cap. 24–25 *324*
24:9-14 *312*
24:14 *311*
24:32 *244*
24:37-39 *55*
25:1-4 *427*
25:1-13 *250*
25:14-30 *250*
25:31-46 *251, 315*
26:26 *216, 264*
26:26-28 *264, 268*
27:12 *129*
27:37 *96*
27:46 *285, 380*
28:3 *269*
28:18-20 *311*
28:19 *272*
28:19-20 *52*

**Marcos**

1:5 *136*
1:10 *272*
1:15 *300*
1:21 *238*
2:1 *238*
2:16 *238*
2:18 *238*
2:21-22 *250*
3:17 *208*
3:23-27 *245*
4:1-2 *238*
4:1-20 *238*
4:3-8 *250*
4:3-9 *432*
4:10 *239*
4:11 *240*
4:12 *240*
4:13 *243*
4:13-20 *424*
4:14-20 *250, 432*
4:21-25 *250*
4:26-29 *250*
4:30 *243*
4:33-34 *238*
5:2 *96*

5:39 *223*
5:41 *136*
5:42 *380*
7:1-5 *136*
7:1-13 *238, 255*
7:2-4 *136*
7:10 *50*
7:11 *136*
7:17 *244*
7:34 *136, 380*
8:35 *226*
10:38 *224, 464*
12:1-12 *249, 432*
12:12 *243*
12:18-27 *238*
12:42 *136*
13:3 *136*
13:11 *52*
14:12 *136*
14:36 *380*
15:22 *136*
15:26 *96*
15:34 *136*
15:42 *136*
16:16-20 *52*

**Lucas**

1:1-3 *59*
1:1-4 *147*
1:3 *373*
1:17 *298*
1:32-33 *300*
1:46-55 *225*
1:68-79 *225*
cap. 2 *353*
2:1-4 *256*
2:29-32 *225*
4:13 *96*
4:16-21 *296*
4:32 *238*
4:36 *238*
5:1-2 *257*
5:11-32 *257*
5:17 *238*
5:20 *104*
5:30 *257*
5:36-39 *245, 250*
6:39 *245*
6:48-49 *251*
7:35 *208*
7:41-43 *250*
8:4-15 *238*
8:5-8 *250, 432*
8:10 *240*
8:11-15 *250, 432*
8:16-18 *250*
8:27 *96*
10:6 *208*
10:22 *42*
10:25 *424*
10:29 *424*
10:30-37 *250, 254*
10:34 *217*
11:1 *237*
11:2-4 *237*
11:5-7 *257*
11:5-13 *97, 237, 249*
11:13 *97, 396*
11:29-32 *55*
11:30 *285*
12:16-21 *250*
12:35-40 *250*
12:41-48 *251*
13:6-9 *250*
13:18-19 *250*
13:20-21 *250*
13:23-40 *251*
13:32 *462*
14:7-8 *244, 245*
14:7-15 *250*
14:12-13 *210*
14:14 *321*
14:16-24 *250, 253*
14:26 *221*
14:28-30 *251*
14:31-32 *251*
cap. 15 *252*
15:1-2 *252, 434*
15:1-7 *253*
15:3-7 *249, 252*
15:8 *252*
15:8-10 *249, 252*
15:11-31 *434*
15:11-32 *249, 251*
15:17 *434*
15:21 *434*
15:31 *435*
16:1-13 *250*
16:14-15 *239*
16:17 *60*
16:19-31 *107, 249*
16:20 *107*
16:29 *220*
16:30-31 *107*
17:7-10 *250*
17:20-21 *300*
17:26-27 *55*
18:1 *433*
18:1-8 *250*
18:9-14 *250, 255*
18:11 *256*
19:11-27 *250*
20:9-18 *249*
20:19 *243*
20:33 *320*
30:34-35 *320*

20:35 *320*
20:42-43 *311*
23:9 *129*
23:38 *96*
24:25 *55, 283*
24:27 *283*
26:9-18 *432*

**Juan**

1:14 *42*
1:29 *272, 285*
3:3 *108*
3:14 *285, 287*
3:14-15 *277, 283, 286*
3:15 *287*
3:16 *184, 232*
4:14 *214*
4:25-30 *104*
4:39-42 *104*
5:39 *66, 283*
6:30-42 *104*
6:44 *241*
6:48 *462*
6:53 *121*
6:54 *214*
6:63 *60*
7:3 *105*
7:12 *106*
7:17 *105, 106, 123, 368*
7:37-39 *461*
7:53–8:11 *400*
8:35 *208*
10:6 *243*
10:7 *462*
10:9 *216*
10:19 *96*
10:24-25 *363*
10:29 *223*
10:35 *61*
10:38 *363*
11:11 *223*
12:37-40 *42*
13:1-17 *217*
13:1-20 *336*
13:14 *336*
13:34 *32*
13:35 *151*
14:6 *462*
14:9 *42*
14:26 *52, 53*
cap. 15 *353*
15:1 *462*
15:1-6 *430*
15:16 *52*
16:13 *52, 53*
16:25 *243*
16:29 *23, 243*
cap. 17 *353*
17:12 *209*
caps. 18–19 *374*
20:25 *278*
20:30-31 *366*
20:31 *147,148*
21:22-23 *125*
21:25 *96, 462*

**Hechos**

cap. 1–12 *139*
1:1 *147, 373*
1:3 *366*
1:10 *269*
cap. 2 *131, 162, 196, 197, 199, 219, 353*
2:16-21 *200*
2:34-35 *311*
2:42 *220*
2:44-45 *131*
3:1-6 *162*
4:36 *208*
5:9 *220*
cap. 6 *177*
6:2 *177*
6:3 *272*
7:29-30 *272*
7:43 *278*
7:44 *278*
cap. 10 *219*
10:9-16 *333*
14:12 *23*
14:15-17 *40*
14:17 *40*
17:22-29 *40*
17:23-24 *40*
17:24-25 *40*
17:25-26 *40*
17:26 *118*
17:28 *40*
18:1-6 *132*
18:9-10 *133, 134*
18:24 *63*
20:7 *132, 220*
21:27-29 *142*
22:3 *63*
23:25 *278*
24:14 *55*

**Romanos**

1:1-7 *188, 189*
1:4 *364*
1:17-32 *242*
1:18-21 *40*
1:20 *40, 41, 44*
1:20-21 *41*
1:21, 23 *41*

1:24 *242*
1:26 *242*
1:26-27 *442, 443, 444*
1:28 *242*
1:32 *41*
2:1 *41*
2:5 *42*
2:12-16 *40*
2:14-16 *107*
2:28-29 *322*
3:2 *66*
cap. 4–5 *56*
4:5 *163*
5:12-21 *285*
5:14 *278*
5:17 *170*
6:1-4 *268*
6:4 *321*
6:17 *278*
7:18-19 *252*
cap. 8 *353*
8:1 *186*
8:15 *380*
8:18 *42*
cap. 9 *200*
9:1-5 *322*
9:6-8 *322*
11:1 *200*
11:11-21 *467*
11:13 *200*
11:16-24 *199*
11:17 *200*
11:19 *200*
11:23-24 *200*
11:25 *311*
11:25-26 *300*
11:25-27 *322*
12:1 *353*
12:2 *40*
12:9-21 *161*
15:4 *130, 331*
15:8-12 *61*
15:9 *61*
15:10 *61*
15:11 *61*
15:12 *61*
16:14 *335*
16:16 *32, 338*
16:22 *64*
16:25 *43*

**1 Corintios**

1:17-18 *366*
1:18 *108*
1:22-23 *366*
1:23 *108*
1:27 *366*
2:2 *366*
2:3 *109*
2:4-5 *109*
2:6-16 *109, 110, 349*
2:9 *110*
2:9-10 *42*
2:10 *110*
2:11 *110*
2:11-12 *110*
2:13 *53, 61*
2:14 *108*
2:14-15 *110, 171*
2:14-16 *366*
2:16 *110*
3:1 *171*
3:1-2 *123*
3:10-15 *430*
3:19 *108*
4:8 *222, 462*
5:1-5 *338*
5:6-8 *287*
5:7 *285, 287*
5:9 *68, 287*
6:9 *443*
6:9-10 *442*
6:16 *346*
6:19 *460*
8:1 *111*
8:9 *338*
8:9-13 *338*
9:17 *195*
10:3 *285*
10:4 *285*
10:6 *278, 331*
10:6-10 *130*
10:11 *130, 278, 331*
10:16-17 *464*
10:21 *224, 463, 464*
11:5-6 *344*
11:23-26 *268*
11:25 *200*
11:26 *140*
cap. 13 *353*
13:1 *462*
13:5 *179*
14:37 *53, 54*
cap. 15 *44, 353, 455*
15:6 *363*
15:12 *154*
15:20 *321*
15:20-26 *320, 321*
15:23 *321*
15:29 *335*
15:45 *285*
16:1-2 *132*
16:20 *338*
16:21 *64*
16:22 *380*

**2 Corintios**

1:20 *460*
1:21 *460*
1:22 *174, 460*
3:13-16 *285*
4:3-4 *108*
4:12 *108*
4:14 *108*
4:34 *108*
5:9-11 *315*
5:17 *445*
7:1 *154*
7:8 *68*
9:6 *164*
9:9 *208*
10:10 *109*
11:3-4 *320*
11:6 *109*
11:13-15 *320*
11:27-28 *143*
12:1 *43*
12:7 *43, 65*
12:13 *462*
13:3 *53*
13:12 *338*
13:14 *272*

**Gálatas**

1:1, 12 *53*
1:11-12 *43*
1:15-16 *42*
2:1-2 *42*
2:9 *462*
cap. 3 *200*
3:7 *209, 322*
3:16 *61*
3:28 *343*
4:1 *154*
4:21-31 *431, 433*
4:21-32 *430*
4:24 *430*
6:11 *64*
6:16 *322*

**Efesios**

cap. 1–3 *445, 446, 455, 457*
1:1 *445*
1:3 *187, 445, 456, 458*
1:3-14 *163, 164, 170, 458*
1:4 *445*
1:5 *445*
1:6 *445*
1:7 *445*
1:9 *445*
1:9-10 *281*
1:10 *195, 445*
1:11 *458*
1:12 *445*
1:13 *172, 174, 181, 445, 461*
1:13-14 *458, 461*
1:14 *461*
1:15-23 *163, 164, 458, 459*
1:17-19 *42*
1:18 *103, 109, 110, 163, 458*
1:20 *445, 456*
1:20-23 323
2:1 *307, 321*
2:1-10 *459*
2:2 *208*
2:4 *208*
2:5 *445*
2:6 *307, 321, 456*
2:7 *459*
2:10 *445*
2:11 *459*
2:11-12 *164, 446, 459*
2:11-22 *445*
2:11–3:13 *455, 459*
2:12 *445*
2:13 *445*
2:15 *445*
2:15-23 *458*
2:18 *445*
2:20 *54*
2:21 *445*
2:22 *445*
3:1 *142, 154*
3:2 *195*
3:3 *43*
3:5 *43*
3:6 *445*
3:9 *195*
3:10 *456*
3:11 *445*
3:12 *445*
3:13 *142, 446*
3:14-21 *164, 459*
3:16-19 *164*
3:21 *445*
cap. 4–6 *446, 455, 457, 459*
4:1 *142, 446*
4:2 *32*
4:13 *112*
4:17 *155, 446*
4:17-24 *155*
4:17-32 *174*
4:23 *40, 353*
4:25 *155*
4:25-32 *155*

4:28 *32, 132*
4:30 *162, 174, 460*
4:32 *155*
5:1 *446*
5:8 *208, 446*
5:14 *225*
5:15 *446*
5:18 *186*
5:19 *186*
5:20 *186*
5:21 *186*
5:21–6:9 *166*
5:22-24 *73*
5:22-33 *339*
5:33 *73*
6:5-8 *344*
6:11-17 *430*
6:12 *456*
6:18-19 *32*

**Filipenses**

1:1 *149*
1:4 *149*
1:4-5 *149*
1:7-8 *149*
1:18 *149*
1:25 *149*
1:27 *149*
cap. 2 *44, 353*
2:1 *154*
2:1-11 *149, 455*
2:2 *149*
2:5 *149*
2:11–3:13 *164*
2:12 *154*
2:13 *357*
2:17 *149*
2:17-18 *149*
2:26 *149*
2:28-29 *149*
3:3 *322*
3:15 *42, 112*
3:15-16 *149*
3:17 *278*
4:1 *149*
4:2 *149*
4:4 *149*
4:10 *149*
4:10-18 *164*
4:10-19 *149*
4:11-12 *165*
4:12-13 *162*
4:13 *165*
4:19 *164*

**Colosenses**

1:9-10 *112*
1:9-20 *187*
1:16 *93*
1:18 *42*
1:25 *195*
2:6 *150*
2:8-11 *366*
2:12 *321*
2:15 *306*
2:16-17 *283*
2:17 *278*
3:18 *73, 339*
3:18–4:1 *166*
4:16 *54*
4:18 *64*

**1 Tesalonicenses**

1:5 *108*
1:7 *278*
1:9 *62*
2:13 *53, 154*
3:1 *154*
4:13 *223*
4:17 *208*
4:23 *223*
5:5 *209*
5:22 *335*
5:26 *338*
5:27 *54*

**2 Tesalonicenses**

1:6-8 *118*
3:9 *278*
3:17 *64*

**1 Timoteo**

1:4 *246*
1:9 *443*
1:9-10 *442, 443*
1:10 *343, 443*
2:4 *191, 201*
2:5 *332*
3:8 *177*
3:16 *225*
4:2 *44*
4:7 *246*
4:12 *278*
5:17 *178*

**2 Timoteo**

1:16 *65*
2:1 *154*
2:7 *111*
2:14 *273*
2:15 *19, 25, 111, 350*
3:15 *19, 66, 83*
3:15-16 *83*
3:16 *49, 51, 55, 57, 62, 79, 83*
3:16-17 *350*

3:17 *171*
4:2 *170*
4:13 *56, 374*
4:22 *54*

**Tito**

1:2 *62*
1:14 *246*
2:4-5 *73, 339*
2:7 *278*

**Filemón**

1:8 *154*

**Hebreos**

1:5 *285*
2:3-4 *52*
3:1-6 *285*
3:7-11 *285*
4:4-11 *285*
5:4-5 *285*
5:11-14 *113*
6:18 *62*
7:1-17 *285*
8:1-4 *279*
8:1-5 *279*
8:5 *278, 285*
8:7-13 *296*
9:1–10:18 *285*
9:6-12 *280*
9:9 *278*
9:24 *279, 285*
10:1 *277, 278*
10:11-22 *285*
10:15-17 *296*
cap. 11 *353*
11:3 *93*
11:17-19 *283*
11:25 *464*
12:1 *154*
13:7 *178*
13:17 *178*
13:24 *178*

**Santiago**

1:22 *350*
2:17 *163*
2:24 *163*

**1 Pedro**

1:10-12 *125, 438*
1:11 *438*
1:12 *42*
1:13 *154*
1:24-25 *422*
1:25 *208*
2:2 *123*
2:9 *332*
3:1-2 *73, 339*
3:3 *211*
3:15 *366*
3:20-21 *285*
3:21 *279*
4:1 *154*
4:13 *42*
5:1 *42*
5:3 *278*
5:12 *64*
5:14 *338*

**2 Pedro**

1:12 *154*
1:16 *246*
1:20-21 *51, 55*
1:21 *51, 57, 58*
2:4 *315*
2:22 *243*
3:14 *154*
3:16 *54*

**1 Juan**

1:4 *147, 150*
2:1 *147, 150*
2:3 *150*
2:3-5 *150*
2:4 *150*
2:5 *149, 150*
2:10 *149*
2:11 *150*
2:13-14 *150*
2:15 *149*
2:18 *150, 320*
2:18-19 *151*
2:20 *150*
2:21 *150*
2:26 *320*
2:29 *150*
cap. 3 *353*
3:1 *149*
3:2 *150*
3:5 *150*
3:6 *150*
3:8 *443*
3:8-10 *150*
3:10 *149*
3:11 *149*
3:13-15 *151*
3:14 *150*
3:14-18 *149*
3:19 *150*
3:20 *150*
3:21 *150*
3:23 *149*
3:24 *150*
4:2 *150*
4:6 *150*

4:7 *150*
4:7-12 *149*
4:8 *150*
4:13 *150*
4:16 *150*
4:16-21 *149*
4:17 *150*
5:1-3 *149*
5:2 *150*
5:4-5 *151*
5:13 *147, 150*
5:14 *150*
5:15 *150*
5:18 *150*
5:19 *150*
5:20 *62, 150*

**Apocalipsis**

1:1 *43*
1:1-2 *53*
1:4 *272*
1:11 *53*
1:12 *264, 272*
1:14 *269*
1:16 *274*
1:19 *53*
2:25-27 *323*
3:17-18 *144*
cap. 4–7 *306, 308*
cap. 4–18 *316*
cap. 4–22 *293*
4:1-4 *267*
4:4 *269*
4:5 *267, 272*
4:6 *267*
4:8 *225, 272*
4:11 *225*
5:1 *272*
5:6 *272*
5:9-10 *225*
5:12-13 *225*
6:11 *269*
7:1 *308*
7:5-8 *308*
7:9 *269*
7:13-14 *269*
cap. 8–11 *306*
8:1 *272*
8:6 *308*
11:3 *308*
11:8 *272*
11:15 *301, 323*
cap. 12 *319*
cap. 12–14 *306*
cap. 12–20 *319*
12:7-9 *306*
cap. 13 *319*
13:18 *264*
cap. 14–16 *319*
14:8 *272*
cap. 15–16 *306*
15:1 *272*
16:1 *272*
16:19 *272*
cap. 17 *319*
cap. 17–19 *306*
cap. 18 *319*
18:2 *272*
cap. 19 *316*
19:11 *319*
19:14 *269, 319*
19:18-19 *319*
19:20 *319*
19:21 *319*
cap. 20 *306, 312, 316, 319, 321, 324*
cap. 20–22 *306*
20:1 *319*
20:1-2 *319*
20:1-3 *306*
20:1-6 *301, 303, 306, 323*
20:1-10 *306*
20:2-3 *319*
20:4 *302, 304, 319, 320*
20:4-5 *321*
20:4-6 *307, 315, 317, 320*
20:5 *320, 321*
20:5-6 *319*
20:6 *302*
20:7-8 *319*
20:9 *319*
20:10 *315, 319*
20:11 *269, 319*
cap. 21–22 *316*
21:1 *201*
21:2 *271*
21:12 *272*
21:12-14 *271*
21:14 *272*
22:18-19 *53*

# Índice temático


Adams, George M. *449, 455*
Agustín de Hipona *87, 196, 304–305, 314, 367–368, 406, 424–426*
Aland, Kurt *421*
Alegoría, interpretación alegórica *121, 279, 281–282, 303–304, 423–436*
Alejando II, zar de Rusia *418*
Alejandro Magno *379–380*
Ambrosio *367*
Amilenialismo *303–327*
Antropomorfismo *223*
Aplicación
  textos con expresiones culturales *331–347*
  historia de su interpretación *331–340*
  criterios para identificar lo que es normativo *340–346*
  aplicación personal *349–358*
Aristóteles *401*
Arthur, Kay *185*
Armerding, Carl F. *314, 376, 383*
Arqueología *136–141*
Asher, la familia ben *153*
Asher, Moses *384, 387*
Ast, Fredrich *31*
Atanasio *67*
Bailey, Kenneth *236*
Baillie, John *45*
Barth, Karl *45–46, 76*
Bauer, Walter *176*
Baur, Ferdinand C. *73*
Beatty, Chester *374*
Bengel, J. A. *414–415*
Bentley, Richard *414*
Berkhof, Louis *173–174, 204, 214, 295, 306, 308, 324*
Beza, Teodoro de *410*
Biblia de Gutenberg *406*
Biblia latina *406*
Biblia Mazarino *406*
Biblia políglota complutense *409*
Biblioteca Nacional de Rusia en Leningrado *384*
Biblioteca Vaticana *375, 418–419*
Black, Matthew *429*
Blaiklock, E. M. *138*
Blaising, Craig A. *195, 201*
Blomberg, Craig L. *388, 427, 432, 434, 436*

Bock, Darrell L. *195, 201*
Bodmer *374*
Boettner, Loraine *307, 312, 317*
Bray, Gerald *402*
Briggs, Charles A. *74, 128*
Broadus, John A. *351*
Bromiley, Geoffrey W. *72, 173*
Broomall, Wick *89*
Brotzman, Ellis B. *375, 378*
Brown, R. E. *437–438*
Bruce, A. B. *427*
Brunner, Emil *45*
Buttrick, George A. *246, 427*
Caird, G. B. *380–381*
Calvino, Juan *30, 72, 305–307, 410, 424, 427*
Carnell, Edward *76*
Carson, Donald A. *178, 185, 203, 336–337, 402*
Carta de Aristeas *380*
Celso *406*
Chayyim, Jacob ben *408*
Chicago Statement on Inerrancy, The *78–79*
Cipriano *397*
Cisneros, Francisco Jiménez de *408–409*
Clark, Gordon H. *108*
Clayton, Charles *221, 439*
Clemente de Roma *177, 282*
Clemente VIII, el papa *407*
Cocceius, Johannes. *193, 201*
Códice de Alepo *384*
Códice Cairo *382, 384–385, 387*
Códice Leningrado *382, 384–385, 387*
Códice Sinaítico *375, 397, 417–419, 421*
Códice Vaticano *375, 397, 417–419, 421*
Complutensian políglota *409*
Concilio de Trent *406*
Constantino *305, 375, 407, 419*
Contexto
  definición *161–162*
  siete clases de contexto *162–166*
Contextualizacion *340–341, 441–444*
Couch, Mel *289*
Crisóstomo *392, 427*
Crítica, baja y alta
  definición 33
  baja crítica *33–34, 73*
  alta crítica *34, 72–74, 88*
Crítica textual (crítica baja)
  del A.T. *371–389*
  del N.T. *391–403*
  historia de la crítica textual del N.T. *405–422*
Cursivo *394–395*
Dámaso I, el papa *406*
Dana, H. E. *282*
Darby, John Nelson *194–196, 201, 316–318*
Denyer, C. P. *243*
Dispensacionalismo *193–198, 199–201, 293, 296, 298*
Dodd, Charles H. *45, 251, 428–429*
Dods, Marcus *98*
Domiciano *293*
Donatistas *304*
Doriani, Daniel M. *130*
Dunnett, Walter *451, 455*
Duvall, J. Scott *66, 128*

Eclecticismo *193–194, 198–201, 293, 296, 298*
Elzevir, Abraham *410*
Elzevir, Bonaventure *410*
Empirista, una definición de *361*
Enns, Peter *78*
Epístola de Bernabé *418*
Erasmo, Desiderio *409–411*
Erikson, Millard J. *307*
Esquematizar un párrafo *187–189*
Estienne, Robert *410*
Etimología *177–180*
Eufemismo *223*
Eusebio, Obispo de Cesarea *68*
Evangelical Theological Society *78*
Evangélico, definición de *33*
Evans, Craig *380*
Exégesis *30–31, 202*
Fe vs. intelecto *365–369*
Fábula *246*
Familias de manuscritos (ver Manuscritos, familias de)
Fee, Gordon D. *139–140, 392–393, 396, 420*
Fideísta, definición de *361*
Fields, Leslie Leland *130*
Filón de Alexandría *64, 72*
Friedrich, Gerhard *173*
Froben, Johann *409*
Fuller, Daniel *81, 83–85*
Fuller Theological Seminary *76–77*
Fundamentalista, el movimiento *75–76*
Gaffin Jr., Richard B. *68*
Garstang, John *137*
Gasque, W. Ward *314*
Geisler, Norman L. *24, 78*
Gematría *273*
Géneros literarios
  descripción general *127–130*
  narración *130–134*
Gerstner, John H. *71, 452*
Giese, Ronald *128*
Girdlestone, R. B. *176*
Gnosticismo *150*
Govier, Gordon *401*
Graham, Billy *76*
Gramática *183–189*
Gray, James C. *449, 455*
Greenlee, J. Harold *395, 409, 414*
Gregorio *367*
Grenz, Stanley *78*
Griesbach, J. J. *415–416*
Grimstead, Jay *77*
Grudem, Wayne *99, 318*
Gundry, Robert H. *198, 318*
Guttenberg, Johannes 393, 406, 408
Harrington, Daniel J. *391*
Harris, R. Laird *56, 63, 89–90, 97–99, 379, 381, 384, 388, 398, 401*
Hartill, J. Edwin *272*
Hayes, Daniel *66, 128*
Hendriksen, William *449, 455*
Henry, Carl F. H. *46, 76*
Hermenéutica *23–24*
Hilel *345*
Hipérbole *221*
Hipólito de Roma *313*
Hirsch, E. D. *29*
Histórico-gramático-cultural, el método *117–125, 135–145*
Hitita, Imperio *88*
Hodge, A. A. *74, 312*
Hodge, Charles *74, 196, 310, 312*
Hoekema, Anthony A. *201, 308*
Hoerth, Alfred J. *138*

Homosexualidad *141, 441–444*
Hort, F. J. A. *402, 420–421*
Hubbard, David A. *81, 84–85*
Hubbard, Robert L. *388*
Iglesia e Israel, la relación entre *192–203*
Ignacio de Antioquía *177*
Iluminación *103–114*
Inductivo, el método *121–123*
Inerrancia
  definición *71–72*
  el trasfondo histórico del debate *72–74*
  las tres etapas del debate *74–79*
  tres posiciones sobre la inerrancia *79–85*
  ¿supuestos errores o reales? *87–99*
  ¿qué hay en juego? *99–100*
Inspiración
  de origen divino *49–54*
  toda Escritura *54–59*
  cada palabra en los manuscritos originales *59–65*
  no hay omisiones *65–69*
International Council on Biblical Inerrancy *77*
Ireneo *67, 313–314, 397*
Ironía *222*
Irving, Eduardo *316*
Israel y la iglesia, la relación entre *192–203*
Jacob, Samuel ben *384, 387*
Jeremias, Joachim *251, 429–430*
Jerónimo *87, 176, 282, 367, 406–407*
John Rylands University Library *373*
Johnson, Elliott *107*
Johnston, Robert K. *79, 81*
Josefo *67, 72, 401*
Jowett, Benjamín *73*
Jülicher, Adolf *428–429, 431–434*
Kaiser Jr., Walter C. *63, 89, 120, 183, 383, 439, 444*
Kantzer, Kenneth S. *46, 76, 91*
Keil, Karl A. G. *120*
Kennedy, James *402*
Kenyon, Frederic G. *98, 402*
Kik, J. Marcellus *312*
Kirbit Qumrán *385*
Kittel, Gerhard *173*
Kitchen, Kenneth A. *89, 376*
Klein, William *388*
Köstenberger, Andreas *65, 293*
Lachmann, Karl *416, 417*
La Sor, William Sanford *351*
Lactancio *313*
Lacy, G. H. *446, 455*
Ladd, George E. *34, 63, 74, 318, 373, 412*
Langton, Stephen *153–154*
Larkin, William J. *341*
Leccionarios *392*
Lenguaje figurado *213–223*
León XIII, el papa *419*
Levita, Elías *408*
Léxicos, lexicografía *173–174, 176–177, 183*
Liberación, teología de la *340*
Lindsell, Harold *72, 76–77, 100, 363*
Locke, John *72*
Lockhart, Clinton *275*
Long, V. Phillips *138*
Lowth, Robert *128, 226*

Lutero, Martín *40, 60, 163, 183, 307, 424*
Machen, J. Gresham *75, 307*
Magdalen *374*
Manuscritos, familias de
  alejandrina *397, 415, 421*
  bizantina *398, 409, 415, 421*
  cesarea *398*
  egipcia *387*
  neutral *397*
  occidental *397–398, 415*
Mari *88, 137*
Marshall, I. Howard *117*
Martínez, José María *113*
Mártir, Justino *313, 314*
Masorah *383*
Masorético, el texto *382–384, 387, 388*
Mayer, Herbert *43*
Mazarino, el cardinal *406*
McCartney, Dan *221, 439*
McGowan, Andrew *78*
McLaren, Brian *78*
McQuilken, J. Robertson *341*
Melanchthon, Philipp *183, 307*
Melitón *67*
Metáfora *216–219*
Metonimia *219–220*
Metzger, Bruce M. *394, 411, 415, 420*
Mickelsen, A. Berkeley *175, 230, 232, 246, 268, 278, 279, 382, 430, 431*
Mill, John *413, 414*
Minúsculo *394, 395*
Modernista, el movimiento *76*
Modismos hebreos *207–212*
Moody, Dwight L. *318*
Morfología *184*
Morgan, G. Campbell *147–148, 240, 245, 427*
Museo Británico de Londres *375, 418*
Nabucodonosor *89–90*
Nag Hammadi *66*
Neoortodoxia *76*
Nestle, Eberhard *421*
Nestle, Erwin *421*
Newcombe, Jerry *402*
Newton, B. W. *316*
Newton, Isaac *72*
Nicolás V, el papa *418*
Ockenga, Harold *76*
Orígenes *67, 282, 366–368, 374, 406, 423–425*
Ortíz, Pedro *172*
Osborne, Grant R. 31, 65, 155, 164, 177, 184, 227, 259, 341, 421
Owen, John *29*
Pache, René *50, 59–60, 99, 113*
Packer, J. I. *112*
Padres apostólicos *176–177*
Padres de la Iglesia *32–33, 64, 71, 293, 367, 392, 413*
Palabras
  características de *169–170*
  ¿dónde se encuentra su significado? *170–180*
Pánfilo de Cesarea *374*
Papiro *371, 372–375, 386*
Parábolas
  el propósito de Jesús al emplearlas *236–243*
  definición *243–246*
  parábolas en los Evangelios sinópticos *249–251*
  normas de interpretación *251–261*

el uso y rechazo de la alegorización en su interpretación *423–436*
Paralelismo hebreo *175*
Pastor de Hermes *418*
Pate, C. Marvin *201*
Patterson, Richard *65, 293*
Pentateuco samaritano *376–378, 387*
Pergamino *373, 374–375, 385–386*
Pérgamo, rey de *374*
Personificación *222*
Phillips, John *454, 456*
Pinnock, Clark, *78, 81–83, 85*
Pío IX, el papa *419*
Platón *401*
Plummer, Robert L. *153–154, 391, 395*
Poesía hebrea *225–234*
Policarpo de Esmirna *177*
Postmilenlialismo *294, 309–327*
Poythress, Vern S. *195*
Premilenialismo *313–327*
Princeton Theological Seminary *74–75, 318, 368*
Probabilidad, la ley de la *361–364*
Profecía *291–327*
Ptolomeo II Filadelfo *380*
Ptolomeo V Epífanes *374*
Qumrán *385* (ver también Rollos del Mar Muerto)
Ramm, Bernard *58, 92–93, 98–99, 120, 202, 259, 276, 280, 288, 299*
Ramsay, W. M. *139*
Reforma, reformadores *28, 30, 43, 63, 71, 74, 121, 183, 193, 305, 314, 317, 344, 408, 424*
Reino de Dios *299–302, 429*
Reuchlin, Johannes *408*
Revelación *39–46*
Revelación progresiva *43–44, 197, 299*
Riobueno, Luis *393*
Roach, William C. *24, 78*
Robinson, Haddon *335*
Rollos del Mar Muerto *381, 384–387*
Ryken, Leland *432*
Ryrie, Charles C. *201, 204*
Sandy, Brent *128*
Santa Catalina, Monasterio de *417–418*
Sarcasmo *222*
Schaff, Phillip *75*
Schleiermacher, Friedrich *31*
Scholz, J. M. A. *415*
Scofield, C. I. *201, 318*
Semler, J. S. *415*
Sensus plenior *437–439*
Septuaginta (LXX) *176, 243–244, 249, 297, 378–382, 388, 417, 421*
Shamai *345*
Significado
definición *24–25*
axiomas del lenguaje *25–29*
¿dónde se encuentra el significado de una palabra? *171–180*
Silva, Moisés *178*
Silvano *64–65*
Símbolos *263–276*
Símil *216*
Sinécdoque *220*
Sinónimos, palabras y libros de *175–175*

Sintaxis *184*
Smith, Hoke *450, 455*
Snodgrass, Klyne *259, 425, 430,*
Soares, Sidney *289*
Soulen, Richard N. *24*
Southern Baptist Convention *78*
Sparks, Kenton *78*
Spinoza, Baruc *72*
Sproul, R. C. *43*
Stein, Robert H. 178, 226, 228, 231
Stephanus, Robertus *154, 410, 413*
Sterret, T. Norman *288*
Strauss, David F. *73*
Strong, James *172, 243*
Taciano *397*
Tenney, Merrill C. *352, 355, 453, 456*
Teología del pacto *193, 194, 199, 201, 293, 296*
Tercio *64*
Terry, Milton S. *29, 216, 243, 270, 271, 274, 399, 400*
Tertuliano *64, 195, 365, 366–368, 397, 401*
Textus Receptus *410–411, 413–417, 421*
Thiselton, Anthony C. *30*
Ticonio *304*
Tillich, Paul *45, 46*
Tipos *28, 277–289*
Tishendorf, Konstantin von *417, 418, 419, 420*
Tomás de Aquino *367, 368*
Trasfondo histórico y cultural *135–145*
Tregelles, Samuel P. *416, 417, 419*
Trench, R. C. *176, 260, 427–428*
Trent, Concilio de *407*
Tubinga, Escuela de *73*
Ugarit *88, 137, 138*
Uncial *394, 395*
Union Theological Seminary *74, 128*
Ur de los Caldeos *137*
Vanhoozer, Kevin *78*
Virkler, Henry A. *173, 199, 258, 259, 337*
Voltaire *72*
Vulgata *154, 176, 406, 407, 408, 410*
Wadi Qumrán *385*
Wallace, David H. *253*
Waltke, Bruce K. *380*
Walton, Brian *413*
Warfield, Benjamín B. *58, 74, 75, 82, 307, 368, 369*
Wellhausen, Julius *73*
Wenham, David *259*
Wescott, B. F. *402, 420–421*
Westminster Theological Seminary *75*
Whitby, Daniel *312, 413*
White, James Emery *56*
Witsius, Herman *193, 201*
Woodward, Stephen B. *177*
Wright, C. J. H. *444*
Würthwein, Ernst *371*
Yamauchi, Edwin M. *145*
Young, Edward J. *90, 94–95*
Zuck, Roy B. *269, 284, 308, 439*

# Bibliografía

## OBRAS GENERALES


Alexander, T. Desmond y David W. Baker, eds. *Dictionary of the Old Testament: Pentateuch.* Downers Grove: InterVarsity Press, 2003.

Alford, Henry. *The Greek New Testament.* Chicago: Moody Press, 1968.

*Anderson, Marvin W. «La Reforma y la interpretación» en *Diccionario de la teología práctica: hermenéutica*, ed. Rodolfo G. Turnbull. Grand Rapids: Subcomisión Literatura Cristiana de la Iglesia Cristiana Reformada, 1984, pp. 52–59.

*Arthur, Kay. *Cómo estudiar tu Biblia.* Chattanooga: Ministerios Precepto Internacional, 2002.

Barackman, F. *How to Interpret the Bible.* Grand Rapids: Kregel, 1991.

Barton, John. *Reading the Old Testament: Method in Bible Study.* Filadelfia: Westminster Press, 1984.

__________. «Historical-Critical Approaches» en *The Cambridge Companion to Biblical Interpretation*, ed. John Barton. Cambridge: Cambridge University Press, 1998, pp. 9–20.

__________, ed. *The Cambridge Companion to Biblical Interpretation.* Cambridge: Cambridge University Press, 1998.


---

**Libros y artículos en español*

Bauer, Walter, William F. Arndt y F. Wilbur Gingrich. *A Greek-English Lexicon of the New Testament and Other Early Christian Literature.* Chicago: University of Chicago Press, 1952.

Baxter, J. Sidlow. *Studies in Problem Texts.* Grand Rapids: Zondervan, 1971.

__________. *The Strategic Grasp of the Bible.* Grand Rapids: Kregel, 1991.

*Becker, Siebgert. «El método histórico-crítico de la interpretación de la Biblia» en *Wisconsin Lutheran Quarterly*, vol. 74, enero (pp. 13–55) y abril (pp. 132–156) de 1977. Este artículo puede encontrarse en Internet.

*Berg, Miguel. *El placer de estudiar la Biblia.* San José: Caribe, 1973.

*Berkhof, Louis. *Principios de interpretación bíblica.* Tarrasa: CLIE, 1973.

*__________. *Teología sistemática.* Grand Rapids: Tell, 1976.

Blackman, E. C. *Biblical Interpretation.* Filadelfia: Westminster Press, 1957.

Blomberg, Craig L. «Historical Criticism of the New Testament» en *Foundations for Biblical Interpretation*, eds. David S. Dockery, Kenneth A. Mathews y Robert B. Sloan. Nashville: Broadman & Holman, 1994, pp. 414–433.

__________. «The Legitimacy and Limits of Harmonization» en *Hermeneutics, Authority, and Canon*, eds. Donald A. Carson y John D. Woodbridge. Grand Rapids: Zondervan, 1986, pp. 139–174.

Braatan, Carl E. y Robert W. Jenson, eds. *Reclaiming the Bible for the Church.* Edimburgo: T & T Clark, 1996.

Braga, James. *How to Study the Bible.* Portland: Multnomah Press, 1982. Ha sido publicado con el título de *Cómo estudiar la Biblia* (Miami: Editorial Vida).

Briggs, Charles Augustus. *General Introduction to the Study of the Holy Scripture.* Grand Rapids: Baker, 1970.

*Carson, Donald A. *Falacias exegéticas.* Viladecavalls: CLIE, 1996.

*__________. «¿Debo aprender a interpretar la Biblia?» en *Idea,* septiembre–diciembre 2008, pp. 8–16.

__________, ed. *Biblical Interpretation and the Church.* Carlisle: Paternoster Press, 1984.

*Chafer, Lewis Sperry. *Teología sistemática.* Dalton: Publicaciones Españolas, 1974.

Chafer, Rollin Thomas. *The Science of Biblical Hermeneutics.* Dallas: Biblioteca Sacra, 1939.

Corley, Bruce, Steve Lemke y Grant Lovejoy (eds.). *Biblical Hermeneutics.* Nashville: Broadman & Holman, 1996.

Couch, Mel. *An Introduction to Classical Evangelical Hermeneutics.* Grand Rapids: Kregel, 2000.

*De Wit, Hans. *En la dispersión el texto es patria.* San José, Costa Rica: Universidad Bíblica Latinoamericana, 2002.

Dockery, David S. «Study and Interpretation of the Bible» en *Foundations for Biblical Interpretation*, eds. David S. Dockery, Kenneth A. Mathews y Robert B. Sloan. Nashville: Broadman & Holman, 1994, pp. 36–54.

Dockery, David S., ed. Kenneth A. Mathews y Robert B. Sloan. *Foundations for Biblical Interpretation.* Nashville: Broadman & Holman, 1994.

*Dockery, David S. y George H. Guthrie. *Interpretación bíblica.* Nashville: Broadman y Holman, 2004.

Donfried, Karl P. «Alien Hermeneutics and the Misappropriation of Scripture» en *Reclaiming the Bible for the Church*, eds. Carl E. Braaten y Robert W. Jenson. Edimburgo: T & T Clark, 1996, pp. 19–45.

Duce, Philip y Daniel Strange. *Encountering God's Word.* Leicester: Apollos (InterVarsity Press), 2003.

Dunn, James D. G. «Demythologizing: The Problem of Myth in the New Testament» en *New Testament Interpretation: Essays on Principles and Methods*, ed. Howard I. Marshall. Eugene, Oregón: Wipf & Stock Publishers, 2006, pp. 285–301.

Dunnet, Walter M. *The Interpretation of Holy Scripture.* Nashville: Thomas Nelson, 1984.

*Duvall, J. Scott y Daniel J. Hays. *Hermenéutica: entendiendo la Palabra de Dios.* Viladecavalls: CLIE, 2008.

*Eco, Umberto. *Interpretación y sobreinterpretación.* Cambridge: Cambridge University Press, 1992.

Erickson, Millar J. *Evangelical Interpretation.* Grand Rapids: Baker, 1993.

*Espinoza Treviño, Héctor. *Cómo estudiar la Biblia.* México (D. F.): Editorial El Camino, 1974.

Fee, Gordon D. *Listening to the Spirit in the Text.* Grand Rapids: Eerdmans, 2000.

__________. *Gospel and Spirit: Issues in New Testament Hermeneutics.* Peabody: Hendrickson Publishers, 1991.

__________. *New Testament Exegesis.* Louisville: Westminster/John Knox Press, 1993. Ha sido publicado con el título de *Exégesis del Nuevo Testamento: manual para estudiantes y pastores* (Deerfield: Editorial Vida, 1992).

Ferguson, Duncan S. *Biblical Hermeneutics.* Atlanta: John Knox Press, 1986.

Finzel, Hans. *Unlocking the Scriptures.* Colorado Springs: Victor, 2003.

*Fountain, Thomas. *Claves de interpretación bíblica.* Casa Bautista, 1971. Algunas ediciones posteriores traducen el apellido del autor al español: «De la Fuente».

Fuller, Daniel P. *The Unity of the Bible.* Grand Rapids: Zondervan, 1992.

Goldingay, John. *Approaches to Old Testament Interpretation.* Leicester: Apollos (InterVarsity Press), 1990.

__________. *Models for Interpretation of Scripture.* Grand Rapids: Eerdmans, 1995.

Goldsworthy, Graeme. *Gospel-Centered Hermeneutics.* Nottingham: Apollos (InterVarsity Press), 2006.

*Grudem, Wayne. *Teología sistemática.* Miami: Editorial Vida, 2009.

Harrison, Everett F., Geoffrey W. Bromiley y Carl F. H. Henry, eds. *Baker's Dictionary of Theology.* Grand Rapids: Baker, 1966.

*Hartill, J. Edwin. *Manual de interpretación bíblica.* Puebla: Publicaciones Las Américas, 1968.

*Haskell, Rob. *Hermenéutica: interpretación eficaz hoy.* Viladecavalls: CLIE, 2009.

Hatch, James M. Notas de clase de la asignatura de Hermenéutica en la Columbia International University c. 1962.

Hayes, John H. y Carl R. Holladay. *Biblical Exegesis: A Beginner's Handbook.* Atlanta: John Knox Press, 1982.

*Henrichsen, Walter A. *Entendamos: 24 principios básicos para interpretar la Biblia.* Miami: Editorial Caribe, 1978.

Hendricks, Howard G. y William D. Hendricks. *Living by the Book.* Chicago: Moody Press, 1991. Este libro ha sido publicado con el título *Interpretación bíblica, una introducción.* Weston: Patmos.

Hirsch, E. D. *Validity in Interpretation.* New Haven: Yale University Press, 1967.

Hodge, Charles. *Systematic Theology.* Peabody: Hendrickson Publishers, 2003. Ha sido publicado con el título *Teología sistemática.* Viladecavalls: CLIE.

Jasper, David. *A Short Introduction to Hermeneutics.* Londres: Westminster/John Knox Press, 2004.

Jensen, Irving L. *Independent Bible Study.* Chicago: Moody Press, 1963.

Johnson, Elliott E. *Expository Hermeneutics: An Introduction.* Grand Rapids: Zondervan, 1990.

Johnson, Sharon. «Issues in Contemporary Hermeneutics» en *Rightly Divided,* ed. Roy B. Zuck. Grand Rapids: Kregel, 1996, pp. 46–52.

*Juan Pablo II. *La interpretación de la Biblia en la Iglesia.* Madrid: PPC, 2007.

Kaiser Jr., Walter C. *Toward an Exegetical Theology.* Grand Rapids: Baker, 1981.

__________. *The Uses of the Old Testament in the New.* Chicago: Moody Press, 1985.

__________ y Silva, Moisés. *An Introduction to Biblical Hermeneutics.* Grand Rapids: Zondervan, 1994.

__________ *et al. Hard Sayings of the Bible.* Downers Grove: InterVarsity Press, 1996.

Klein, William W., Craig L. Blomberg y Robert L. Hubbard Jr. *Introduction to Biblical Interpretation.* Dallas: Word Publishing, 1993.

Köstenberger, Andreas y Richard Patterson. *Invitation to Biblical Interpretation.* Grand Rapids: Kregel, 2011.

Lockhart, Clinton. *Principles of Interpretation.* Fort Worth: S. H. Taylor, 1915.

Longenecker, Richard N. Notas de clase de la asignatura de Hermenéutica en la Trinity Evangelical Divinity School, 1965.

*Lund, E. *Hermenéutica: reglas de interpretación de las Sagradas Escrituras.* Miami: Editorial Vida, 1970.

Lund, E., P. C. Nelson y Alice E. Luce. *Hermenéutica: introducción bíblica.* Miami: Editorial Vida, 1977.

Lundin, Roger. *Disciplining Hermeneutics.* Grand Rapids: Eerdmans, 1997.

Lundin, Roger, Anthony C. Thiselton y Clarence Walhout. *The Responsibility of Hermeneutics.* Grand Rapids: Eerdmans, 1985.

Maier, Gerhard. *Biblical Hermeneutics.* Wheaton: Crossway Books, 1994.

Marsh, F. E. *The Structural Principles of the Bible or How to Study the Word of God.* Grand Rapids: Kregel, 1973.

Marshall, I. Howard. *Beyond the Bible, Moving from Scripture to Theology.* Grand Rapids: Baker, 2004.

__________. «The Holy Spirit and the Interpretation of Scripture» en *Rightly Divided,* ed. Roy B. Zuck. Grand Rapids: Kregel,1996, pp. 66–74.

__________, ed. *New Testament Interpretation: Essays on Principles and Methods.* Eugene, Oregón: Wipf & Stock Publishers, 2006.

*Martin, James P. «Instrumentos del intérprete» en *Diccionario de la teología práctica: hermenéutica,* ed. Rodolfo G. Turnbull. Grand Rapids: Subcomisión Literatura Cristiana de la Iglesia Cristiana Reformada, 1984, pp. 89–96.

*Martínez, José María. *Hermenéutica bíblica.* Tarrasa: CLIE, 1984.

*Mayer, Herbert T. *Cómo interpretar las Escrituras.* Saint Louis: Editorial Concordia, 2007.

*Mayhue, Richard. *Cómo interpretar la Biblia uno mismo.* Grand Rapids: Portavoz, 1994.

McCartney, Dan y Charles Clayton. *Let the Reader Understand.* Wheaton: Victor Books, 1994.

*McDowell, Josh. *Guía para entender la Biblia.* Tarrasa: CLIE, 1988.

McKim, Donald K., ed. *A Guide to Contemporary Hermeneutics.* Grand Rapids: Eerdmans, 1986.

Mickelsen, A. Berkeley. *Interpreting the Bible.* Grand Rapids: Eerdmans, 1963.

*Mock, Dennis J. *Métodos de estudio bíblico* y *reglas de interpretación.* Atlanta: Dennis Mock, 1990.

Muller, Richard A. «The Study of Theology» en *Foundations of Contemporary Interpretation,* ed. Moisés Silva. Grand Rapids: Zondervan, 1996, pp. 533–566.

Newport, John P. «Contemporary Philosophical, Literary, and Sociological Hermeneutics» en *Biblical Hermeneutics,* ed. Bruce Corley,

Steve Lemke y Grant Lovejoy. Nashville: Broadman & Holman, 1996, pp. 133–144.

Orr, James. *Progress of Dogma.* Cambridge: James Clark & Co., 1901.

Osborne, Grant R. *The Hermeneutical Spiral.* Downers Grove: InterVarsity Press, 1991.

__________ y Stephen B. Woodward. *Handbook for Bible Study.* Grand Rapids: Baker, 1983.

Packer, J. I. «Is Systematic Theology a Miracle? An Introductory Discussion» en *Doing Theology in Today's World,* ed. John D. Woodbridge y Thomas E. McComiskey. Grand Rapids: Zondervan, 1991, pp. 17–38.

Perry, Lloyd M. y Robert D. Culver. *How to Search the Scriptures.* Grand Rapids: Baker, 1971.

*Phillips, John. *Cómo entender e interpretar la Biblia: una introducción a la hermenéutica.* Grand Rapids: Portavoz, 2008.

Pieper, Francis. *Christian Dogmatics,* vol. 1. St. Louis: Concordia, 1959.

Pink, Arthur W. *Interpretation of the Scriptures.* Grand Rapids: Baker, 1972.

*Plummer, Robert L. *Preguntas y respuestas sobre cómo interpretar la Biblia.* Grand Rapids: Portavoz, 2013.

Ramm, Bernard. *Protestant Biblical Interpretation.* Grand Rapids: Baker, 1978.

__________. *Varieties of Christian Apologetics.* Grand Rapids: Baker, 1982.

*__________. «Interpretación bíblica» en *Diccionario de la teología práctica: hermenéutica,* ed. Rodolfo G. Turnbull. Grand Rapids: Subcomisión Literatura Cristiana de la Iglesia Cristiana Reformada, 1984, pp. 5–19.

*__________. «La nueva hermenéutica» en *Diccionario de la teología práctica: hermenéutica,* ed. Rodolfo G. Turnbull. Grand Rapids: Subcomisión Literatura Cristiana de la Iglesia Cristiana Reformada, 1984, pp. 83–88.

__________. «Biblical Interpretation» en *Hermeneutics,* eds. Bernard Ramm *et al.* Grand Rapids: Baker, 1972.

__________, *et al. Hermeneutics.* Grand Rapids: Baker, 1972.

*Schökel, L. Alonso. *Hermenéutica de la Palabra: hermenéutica bíblica,* vol. I. Madrid: Ediciones Cristiandad, 1986.

*Schreiner, Josef. *Introducción a los métodos de la exégesis bíblica.* Barcelona: Herder, 1974.

Schultz, Samuel J. y Morris A. Inch, eds. *Interpreting the Word of God.* Chicago: Moody Press, 1970.

Silva, Moisés. «Has the Church Misread the Bible?» en *Foundations of Contemporary Interpretation*, ed. Moisés Silva. Grand Rapids: Zondervan, 1996, pp. 15–90.

__________, ed. *Foundations of Contemporary Interpretation.* Grand Rapids: Zondervan, 1996.

Smith, Wilbur M. *Profitable Bible Study.* Boston: W. A. Wilde Company, 1939.

Soulen, Richard N. *Handbook of Biblical Criticism.* Atlanta: John Knox Press, 1981.

*Sproul, R. C. *Cómo estudiar e interpretar la Biblia.* Miami: Logoi/FLET, 1996.

Stein, Robert H. *The Method and Message of Jesus' Teachings.* Louisville: Westminster/John Knox Press, 1994.

__________. *A Basic Guide to Interpreting the Bible.* Grand Rapids: Baker, 1994.

*Stenger, Werner. *Los métodos de la exégesis bíblica.* Barcelona: Herder, 1990.

Sterrett, T. Norton. *How to Understand our Bible.* Downers Grove: InterVarsity Press, 1974.

Strong, Augustus Hopkins. *Systematic Theology.* Valley Forge, Pensilvania: Judson Press, 1963.

*Tenney, Merrill C. *Gálatas, la carta de la libertad cristiana.* Grand Rapids: Tell, sin fecha. Este libro ha sido publicado con el título de *Hermenéutica aplicada.* Viladecavalls: CLIE, 1973.

Terry, Milton S. *Biblical Hermeneutics.* Grand Rapids: Zondervan, 1969. Este libro ha sido publicado con el título *Hermenéutica* en 1928 (Buenos Aires: Editorial La Aurora) y luego en una fecha desconocida. Tarrasa: CLIE.

Thayer, Joseph Henry. *A Greek-English Lexicon of the New Testament.* Nueva York: American Bible Society, sin fecha.

Thiselton, Anthony C. *The Two Horizons: New Testament Description with Special Reference to Heidegger, Bultmann, Gadamar, and Wittgenstein.* Exeter: Paternoster Press, 1980.

__________. *New Horizons in Hermeneutics.* Grand Rapids: Zondervan, 1992.

__________. «The New Hermeneutic» en *A Guide to Contemporary Hermeneutics*, ed. Donald K. McKim. Grand Rapids: Eerdmans, 1986, pp. 78–107.

Thomas, Robert L. *Evangelical Hermeneutics.* Grand Rapids: Kregel, 2002.

*Traina, Robert A. *Método para el estudio de la Biblia.* Miami: Logoi, 1981.

*Trenchard, Ernesto. *Normas para la recta interpretación de las Sagradas Escrituras.* Chicago: Moody, sin fecha.

*Turnbull, Rodolfo G., ed. *Diccionario de la teología práctica: hermenéutica.* Grand Rapids: Subcomisión Literatura Cristiana de la Iglesia Cristiana Reformada, 1984.

Verkruyse, Peter. *Building Blocks for Bible Study.* Joplin: College Press Publishing Company, 1997.

Virkler, Henry A. *Hermenéutica: principios y procedimientos de interpretación bíblica.* Miami: Editorial Vida, 1994.

Vos, Howard F. *Effective Bible Study.* Grand Rapids: Zondervan, 1956.

*Warren, Rick. *Métodos de estudio bíblico personal.* Miami: Editorial Vida, 2005.

Wilkinson, John T. *Interpretation and Community.* Londres: MacMillan & Co. Ltd., 1963.

__________. *Principles of Biblical Interpretation.* Londres: The Epworth Press, 1960.

Woodbridge, John D. y Thomas E. McComiskey, eds. *Doing Theology in Today's World.* Grand Rapids: Zondervan, 1991.

Young, Edward J. *An Introduction to the Old Testament.* Grand Rapids: Eerdmans, 1952. Ha sido publicado con el título *Una introducción al Antiguo Testamento.* Grand Rapids: T.E.L.L.

Zuck, Roy B. *Basic Bible Interpretation.* Colorado Springs: Victor, 1991. Ha sido publicado con el título *La interpretación básica de la Biblia.* Morelia, México: Berea Publishing Co.

__________, ed. *Rightly Divided.* Grand Rapids: Kregel, 1996.

__________, ed. *Vital Biblical Issues.* Grand Rapids: Kregel, 1994.

## SIGNIFICADO

Geisler, Norman L. «The Relation of Purpose and Meaning» en *Rightly Divided*, ed. Roy B. Zuck. Grand Rapids: Kregel, 1996, pp. 229–245.

Harris, R. Laird. «The Problem of Communication» en *The Bible: The Living Word of Revelation*, ed. C. Merrill Tenney. Grand Rapids: Zondervan, 1977, pp. 83–100.

Johnson, Alan F. «A Response to Problems of Normativeness in Scripture: Cultural Versus Permanent» en *Hermeneutics, Inerrancy, and the Bible*, ed. Earl D. Radmacher y Robert D. Preus. Grand Rapids: Zondervan, 1984, pp. 257–282.

__________. «History and Culture in New Testament Interpretation» en *Interpreting the Word of God*, ed. Samuel J. Schultz y Morris A. Inch. Chicago: Moody Press, 1970, pp. 128–161.

Johnson, Elliott. «Author's Intention and Biblical Interpretation» en *Hermeneutics, Inerrancy, and the Bible*, ed. Earl D. Radmacher y Robert D. Preus. Grand Rapids: Zondervan, 1984, pp. 409–429.

__________. «Dual Authorship and the Single Intended Meaning of Scripture» en *Rightly Divided*, ed. Roy B. Zuck. Grand Rapids: Kregel, 1996, pp. 171–179.

Johnson, Sharon. «The Single Intent of Scripture» en *Rightly Divided*, ed. Roy B. Zuck. Grand Rapids: Kregel Publications, 1996, pp. 158–170.

McQuilkin, Robertson J. «Problems of Normativeness in Scripture: Cultural Versus Permanent» en *Hermeneutics, Inerrancy, and the Bible*, ed. Earl D. Radmacher y Robert D. Preus. Grand Rapids: Zondervan, 1984, pp. 210–240.

*Ricoeur, Paul. *Hermenéutica y estructuralismo.* Buenos Aires: Ediciones Megápolis, 1975.

Silva, Moisés. «God, Language and Scriptures» en *Foundations of Contemporary Interpretation*, ed. Moisés Silva. Grand Rapids: Zondervan, 1996, pp. 193–280.

*Stam B., Juan. «Ciencias del lenguaje y hermenéutica evangélica» en *Boletín teológico de la fraternidad teológica latinoamericana,* año 27, núm. 58, junio 1995, pp. 63–68.

Vanhoozer, Kevin J. *Is There Meaning in This Text?* Grand Rapids: Zondervan, 1998.

## ALTA CRÍTICA

Armerding, Carl E. *The Old Testament and Criticism.* Grand Rapids: Eerdmans, 1983.

Broomall, Wick. *Biblical Criticism.* Grand Rapids: Zondervan, 1957.

Harrison, R. K. «The Historical and Literary Criticism of the Old Testament» en *Biblical Criticism: Historical, Literary and Textual*, eds. R. K. Harrison *et al.* Grand Rapids: Zondervan, 1978, pp. 3–44.

Kitchen, K. A. *On the Reliability of the Old Testament.* Grand Rapids: Eerdmans, 2003.

*Ladd, George Eldon. *Crítica del Nuevo Testamento.* El Paso: Editorial Mundo Hispano, 1990.

Linnemann, Eta. *Biblical Criticism on Trial.* Grand Rapids: Kregel, 2001.

__________. *Historical Criticism of the Bible. Methodology or Ideology? Reflections of a Bultmannian Turned Evangelical.* Grand Rapids: Baker, 1995.

## REVELACIÓN, INSPIRACIÓN, INERRANCIA

Archer, Gleason L. «Alleged Errors and Discrepancies in the Original Manuscripts of the Bible» en *Inerrancy*, ed. Norman L. Geisler. Grand Rapids: Zondervan, 1980, pp. 57–82.

__________. «The Witness of the Bible to its Own Inerrancy» en *The Foundation of Biblical Authority*, ed. James Montgomery Boice. Grand Rapids: Zondervan, 1978, pp. 85–99.

Bahnsen, Greg L. «The Inerrancy of the Autographa» en Inerrancy, ed. Norman L. Geisler. Grand Rapids: Zondervan, 1980, pp. 151–193.

Baillie, John. *The Idea of Revelation in Recent Thought.* Nueva York: Columbia University Press, 1956.

Bartsch, Hans Werner y H. Fuller. *Kerygma and Myth,* vol. 1. Londres: S.P.C.K., 1954.

Bock, Darrell L. «Evangelicals and the Use of the Old Testament in the New – Part One» en *Rightly Divided*, ed. Roy B. Zuck. Grand Rapids: Kregel, 1996, pp. 206–217.

__________. «Evangelicals and the Use of the Old Testament in the New – Part Two» en *Rightly Divided*, ed. Roy B. Zuck. Grand Rapids: Kregel, 1996, pp. 218–227.

Bogue Jr., Carl W. «Berkouwer and the Battle for the Bible» en *Inerrancy and the Church*, ed. John D. Hannah. Chicago: Moody Press, 1984, pp. 381–411.

Boice, James Montgomery, ed. *The Foundation of Biblical Authority.* Grand Rapids: Zondervan, 1978.

Bromiley, Geoffrey W. «The Church Fathers and the Holy Scripture» en *Scripture and Truth*, ed. Donald A. Carson y John D. Woodbridge. Grand Rapids: Baker, 1992, pp. 195–220.

__________. «The Authority of Scripture in Karl Barth» en *Hermeneutics, Authority, and Canon*, ed. Donald A. Carson y John D. Woodbridge. Grand Rapids: Zondervan, 1986, pp. 275–294.

Bultmann, Rudolf. *Jesus Christ and Mythology.* Nueva York: Charles Scribner's Sons, 1958.

Busch, Eberhard. *Karl Barth: His Life from Letters and Autobiographical Texts.* Grand Rapids: Eerdmans, 1994.

Carson, Donald A. «Recent Developments in the Doctrine of Scripture» en *Hermeneutics, Authority, and Canon*, ed. Donald A. Carson y John D. Woodbridge. Grand Rapids: Zondervan, 1986, pp. 5–48.

Carson, Donald A. y John Woodbridge, ed. *Scripture and Truth.* Grand Rapids: Baker, 1992.

__________. *Hermeneutics, Authority, and Canon.* Grand Rapids: Zondervan, 1986.

Clark, Gordon H. «How May I Know the Bible is Inspired?» en *Can I Trust the Bible?*, ed. Howard F. Vos. Chicago: Moody Press, 1968, pp. 9–31.

Dunbar, David G. «Why the Canon Still Rumbles». *Christianity Today,* 5 febrero 1988, pp. 35–37.

Ellis, E. Earle. *The Old Testament in Early Christianity.* Grand Rapids: Baker, 1991.

__________. *Paul's Use of the Old Testament.* Grand Rapids: Baker, 1957.

Erickson, Millar J. «Revelation» en *Foundations for Biblical Interpretation*, ed. David S. Dockery, Kenneth A. Mathews y Robert B. Sloan. Nashville: Broadman & Holman, 1994, pp. 3–18.

Feinberg, Paul D. «The Meaning of Inerrancy» en *Inerrancy*, ed. Norman L. Geisler. Grand Rapids: Zondervan, 1980, pp. 267–304.

Foos, Harold. «The Word of God: Why Inerrancy is Paramount». *Moody Monthly*, enero 1978, pp. 35–37.

Geisler, Normal L. *Decide For Yourself.* Grand Rapids: Zondervan, 1982.

__________. «Una evaluación del libro *Biblical Authority*» (Word, 1977) en *Christianity Today*, 24 febrero 1978, pp. 34–36.

__________, ed. *Inerrancy.* Grand Rapids: Zondervan, 1980.

Geisler, Norman L. y Thomas Howe. *When Critics Ask.* Grand Rapids: Baker, 1992.

Geisler, Norman L. y William C. Roach. *Defending Inerrancy.* Grand Rapids: Baker, 2011.

Gerstner, John H. *A Bible Inerrancy Primer.* Grand Rapids: Baker, 1965.

__________. «The Church's Doctrine of Biblical Inspiration» en *The Foundation of Biblical Authority*, ed. James Montgomery Boice. Grand Rapids: Zondervan, 1978, pp. 23–58.

__________. «Warfield's Case for Biblical Interrancy» en *God's Inerrant Word*, ed. John Warwick Montgomery. Minneapolis: Bethany Fellowship, 1974, pp. 115–142.

Gregory, C. R. *Canon and Text of the New Testament.* Edimburgo: T&T Clark, 1907.

Grimstead, Jay. «How the International Council on Biblical Inerrancy Began». Este artículo se encuentra en Internet.

Gundry, Stanley N. «John Owen on Authority and Scripture» en *Inerrancy and the Church*, ed. John D. Hannah. Chicago: Moody Press, 1984, pp. 189–221.

Hannah, John D., ed. *Inerrancia and the Church.* Chicago: Moody Press, 1984.

Harris, R. Laird. *Inspiration and Canonicity of the Bible.* Grand Rapids: Zondervan, 1977.

Henry, Carl F. H. *God, Revelation and Authority: God Who Speaks and Shows,* Tomo I. Waco: Word Books, 1977.

__________. *God, Revelation and Authority: God Who Speaks and Shows,* Tomo II. Waco: Word Books, 1976.

Jewett, Paul King. «Emil Brunner's Doctrine of Scripture» en *Inspiration and Interpretation*, ed. John F. Walvoord. Grand Rapids: Eerdmans, 1957, pp. 210–238.

Johnson, Sharon. «Legitimate Hermeneutics» en *Inerrancy*, ed. Norman L. Geisler. Grand Rapids: Zondervan, 1980, pp. 117–147.

__________. «Why Doesn't the New Testament Always Quote the Old Testament Accurately?» en *Hard Sayings of the Bible.* Downers Grove: InterVarsity Press, 1996, pp. 76–78.

Johnston, Robert K. *Evangelicals at an Impasse.* Atlanta: John Knox Press, 1984.

Kantzer, Kenneth S. «What's Wrong with the Neo-Orthodox View of Scripture?» en *Moody Monthly*, mayo 1969, p. 28 y ss.

__________. «Evangelicals and the Doctrine of Inerrancy» en *The Foundation of Biblical Authority*, ed. James Montgomery Boice. Grand Rapids: Zondervan, 1978, pp. 147–156.

__________. «Evangelicals and the Inerrancy Question» en *Christianity Today*, 21 abril 1978, pp. 16–21.

__________. «The Communication of Revelation» en *The Bible: The Living Word of Revelation*, ed. C. Merrill Tenney. Grand Rapids: Zondervan, 1977, pp. 53–80.

__________. Notas de clase de la asignatura de Teología sistemática: revelación e inspiración en la Trinity Evangelical Divinity School, 1964–65.

__________. «Why I Still Believe the Bible is True» en *Christianity Today*, 7 octubre 1988, pp. 22–25.

__________. «The Christ-Revelation as Act and Interpretation» en *Jesus of Nazareth: Saviour and Lord.* Londres: Tyndale Press, 1966, pp. 243–264.

Kline, Meredith G. «Is the History of the Old Testament Accurate?» en *Can I Trust the Bible?*, ed. Howard F. Vos. Chicago: Moody Press, 1968, pp. 135–151.

Lindsell, Harold. *The Battle for the Bible.* Grand Rapids: Zondervan, 1976.

__________. *The Bible in the Balance.* Grand Rapids: Zondervan, 1979.

__________. «The Infallible Word» en *Christianity Today*, 25 agosto 1972, pp. 7–12.

Marshall, I. Howard. *Biblical Inspiration.* Grand Rapids: Eerdmans, 1985.

Montgomery, John Warwick, ed. *God's Inerrant Word.* Minneapolis: Bethany Fellowship, 1974.

__________. «Biblical Inerrancy: What is at Stake?» en *God's Inerrant Word*, ed. John Warwick Montgomery. Minneapolis: Bethany Fellowship, 1974, pp. 15–42.

__________. «Whither Biblical Inerrancy?» en *Christianity Today*, 29 julio 1977, pp. 38, 42.

Moo, Douglas J. «The Problem of *Sensus Plenior*» en *Hermeneutics, Authority, and Canon*, ed. Donald A. Carson y John D. Woodbridge. Grand Rapids: Zondervan, 1986, pp. 179–211.

Mounce, Robert H. «Is the New Testament Historically Accurate?» en *Can I Trust the Bible?*, ed. Howard F. Vos. Chicago: Moody Press, 1968, pp. 173–190.

Nicole, Roger. «New Testament Use of the Old Testament» en *Revelation and the Bible*, ed. Carl Henry. Grand Rapids: Baker, 1958.

*__________. «Citas del Antiguo Testamento en el Nuevo Testamento» en *Diccionario de la teología práctica: hermenéutica*, ed. Rodolfo G. Turnbull. Grand Rapids: Subcomisión Literatura Cristiana de la Iglesia Cristiana Reformada, 1984, pp. 27–34.

Pache, René. *The Inspiration and Authority of Scripture.* Chicago: Moody Press, 1978.

Packer, J. I. *«Fundamentalism» and the Word of God.* Grand Rapids: Eerdmans, 1977.

__________. *Honouring the Written Word of God.* Carlisle: Paternoster Press, 1999.

__________. «Infallible Scripture and the Role of Hermeneutics» en *Scripture and Truth*, ed. Donald A. Carson y John D. Woodbridge. Grand Rapids: Baker, 1992, pp. 320–356.

__________. «A Lamp in a Dark Place» en *Can We Trust the Bible?*, ed. Earl D. Radmacher. Wheaton: Tyndale House, 1979, pp. 15–30.

__________. «The Necessity of the Revealed Word» en *The Bible: The Living Word of Revelation*, ed. C. Merrill Tenney. Grand Rapids: Zondervan, 1977, pp. 31–49.

__________. «Encountering Present-Day Views of Scripture» en *The Foundation of Biblical Authority*, ed. James Montgomery Boice. Grand Rapids: Zondervan, 1978, pp. 61–82.

__________. «Text Criticism and Inerrancy» en *Christianity Today*, 7 octubre 2002, p. 102.

Payne, J. Barton. «Higher Criticism and Biblical Inerrancy» en *Inerrancy*, ed. Norman L. Geisler. Grand Rapids: Zondervan, 1980, pp. 83–113.

Peck, Edson R. «Does Science Contradict the Bible?» en *Can I Trust the Bible?*, ed. Howard F. Vos. Chicago: Moody Press, 1968, pp. 49–63.

Pinnock, Clark H. *Biblical Revelation.* Chicago: Moody Press, 1971.

__________. «The Inspiration of the New Testament» en *The Bible: The Living Word of Revelation*, ed. C. Merrill Tenney. Grand Rapids: Zondervan, 1977, pp. 143–161.

__________. «Limited Inerrancy: A Critical Appraisal and Constructive Alternative» en *God's Inerrant Word*, ed. John Warwick Montgomery. Minneapolis: Bethany Fellowship, 1974, pp. 143–158.

__________. «The Inspiration of Scripture and the Authority of Jesus Christ» en *God's Inerrant Word*, ed. John Warwick Montgomery. Minneapolis: Bethany Fellowship, 1974, pp. 201–218.

Poythress, Vern. S. «Science and Hermeneutics» en *Foundations of Contemporary Interpretation*, ed. Moisés Silva. Grand Rapids: Zondervan, 1996, pp. 431–531.

Preus, Robert C. «Scripture: God's Word and God's Power» en *Can We Trust the Bible?*, ed. Earl D. Radmacher. Wheaton: Tyndale House, 1979, pp. 57–71.

Radmacher, Earl D., ed. *Can We Trust the Bible?* Wheaton: Tyndale House, 1979.

Radmacher, Earl D. y Robert D. Preus, eds. *Hermeneutics, Inerrancy, and the Bible.* Grand Rapids: Zondervan, 1984.

Ramm, Bernard. *Special Revelation and the Word of God.* Grand Rapids: Eerdmans, 1961. Este libro ha sido publicado con el título *La revelación especial y la Palabra de Dios.* Buenos Aires: La Aurora, 1967.

Ryrie, Charles C. «The Bible: Truth Without Error» en *Voice,* noviembre–diciembre 1977, pp. 7–9.

Schaeffer, Francis A. *The Church at the End of the Twentieth Century.* Londres: The Norfolk Press, 1970.

Souter, Alexander. *The Text and Canon of the New Testament.* Londres: Duckworth, 1913.

Sproul, R. C. «The Internal Testimony of the Holy Spirit» en *Inerrancy*, ed. Norman L. Geisler. Grand Rapids: Zondervan, 1980, pp. 337–354.

__________. «Sola Scriptura: Crucial to Evangelicalism» en *The Foundation of Biblical Authority*, ed. James Montgomery Boice. Grand Rapids: Zondervan, 1978, pp. 103–119.

__________. «The Case for Inerrancy: A Methodological Analysis» en *God's Inerrant Word*, ed. John Warwick Montgomery. Minneapolis: Bethany Fellowship, 1974, pp. 242–261.

Taylor, G. Aiken. «Is God as Good as His Word?» en *Christianity Today*, 4 febrero 1977, pp. 22–25.

Tenney, Merrill C., ed. *The Bible: The Living Word of Revelation.* Grand Rapids: Zondervan, 1977.

Tinder, Donald. «Proinerrancy Forces Draft Their Platform» en *Christianity Today*, 17 noviembre 1978.

Van Til, Cornelius. *Christianity and Barthianism.* Filadelfia: The Presbyterian and Reformed Publishing Company, 1962.

Walvoord, John F., ed. *Inspiration and Interpretation.* Grand Rapids: Eerdmans, 1957.

Warfield, B. B. *The Inspiration and Authority of the Bible.* Filadelfia: Presbyterian and Reformed Publishing Co., 1964.

__________. *Revelation and Inspiration.* Grand Rapids: Baker, 1981.

Wenzel, Charles. Notas de clase de la asignatura de Inspiración y revelación en la Columbia Internacional University c. 1963.

White, James Emery. «Inspiration and Authority of Scripture» en *Foundations for Biblical Interpretation*, ed. David S. Dockery, Kenneth A. Mathews y Robert B. Sloan. Nashville: Broadman & Holman, 1994, pp. 19–35.

Witherington III, Ben. «Why the "Lost Gospels" Lost Out» en *Christianity Today*, junio 2004, pp. 26–32.

Woodbridge, John y Wendy Murray Zoba. «Standing on the Promises» en *Christianity Today*, 16 septiembre 1996.

Woudstra, Marten H. «The Inspiration of the Old Testament» en *The Bible: The Living Word of Revelation*, ed. C. Merrill Tenney. Grand Rapids: Zondervan, 1977, pp. 123–140.

Young, Edward J. «Are the Scriptures Inerrant?» en *The Bible: The Living Word of Revelation*, ed. C. Merrill Tenney. Grand Rapids: Zondervan, 1977, pp. 103–119.

Youngblood, Ronald F. «Old Testament Quotations in the New Testament» en *Rightly Divided*, ed. Roy B. Zuck. Grand Rapids: Kregel, 1996, pp. 199–205.

## BAJA CRÍTICA/CRÍTICA TEXTUAL

Aland, Kurt (ed.). *Synopsis of the Four Gospels*. Stuttgart: Biblia-Druck, 1993.

Barker, Kenneth. «An Insider Talks About the NIV» en *Kindred Spirit*, otoño 1978, pp. 7–9.

Brotzman, Ellis B. *Old Testament Textual Criticism*. Grand Rapids: Baker, 1994.

Brunn, David. «Translation Truth» en *Christianity Today*, junio 2013, p. 71.

*Chávez, Moisés. *Hermenéutica: el arte de la paráfrasis libre*. Miami: Editorial Caribe, 1979.

Danker, Frederick W. *Multipurpose Tools for Bible Study*. Saint Louis: Concordia Publishing House, 1960.

Evans, Craig A. «What Bible Version Did Jesus Read?» en *Christianity Today*, 26 abril 1999, p. 98.

Fee, Gordon D. «The Textual Criticism of the New Testament» en *Biblical Criticism: Historical, Literary and Textual*, ed. R. K. Harrison *et al.* Grand Rapids: Zondervan, 1978, pp. 127–155.

__________. «The Text of the New Testament and Modern Translations» en *Christianity Today*, 22 junio 1973, pp. 6–11.

Greenlee, J. Harold. *Introduction to New Testament Textual Criticism*. Grand Rapids: Eerdmans, 1970.

Grudem, Wayne. «Do Inclusive-Language Bibles Distort Scripture? Yes» en *Christianity Today*, 27 octubre 1997, pp. 27–32.

Gundry, Stanley N. «Which Version is Best?» en *Moody Monthly*, enero 1979, pp. 40–42.

Harris, R. Laird. «How Reliable is the Old Testament Text?» en *Can I Trust the Bible?*, ed. Howard F. Vos. Chicago: Moody Press, 1968, pp. 119–132.

Harrison, R. K. *et al. Biblical Criticism: Historical, Literary, and Textual*. Grand Rapids: Zondervan, 1978.

Hoerth, Alfred J. «Archaeology and the Christian Mind» en *Interpreting the Word of God*, ed. Samuel J. Schultz y Morris A. Inch. Chicago: Moody Press, 1970, pp. 31–45.

Kaiser Jr., Walter C. *The Old Testament Documents: Are They Reliable and Relevant?* Downers Grove: InterVarsity Press, 2001.

Kent Jr., Jomer A. «How We Got Our New Testament» en *Moody Monthly*, febrero 1966, pp. 23–26, 40.

Kenyon, Frederic G. *Handbook to the Textual Criticism of the New Testament.* Londres: Macmillan, 1912.

__________. *The Text of the Greek Bible.* Londres: Gerald Duckworth and Company, 1937.

__________. *Textual Criticism of the New Testament.* Londres: Macmillan and Co., 1912.

La Sor, William Sanford. *The Dead Sea Scrolls and the Christian Faith.* Chicago: Moody Press, 1977.

*Lacueva, Francisco. *Biblia textual: Reina Valera.* Sociedad Bíblica Iberoamericana, sin fecha.

*Laurin, Robert B. «Los pergaminos del Mar Muerto y la interpretación» en *Diccionario de la teología práctica: hermenéutica*, ed. Rodolfo G. Turnbull. Grand Rapids: Subcomisión Literatura Cristiana de la Iglesia Cristiana Reformada, 1984, pp. 43–51.

Metzger, Bruce M. *The Text of the New Testament.* Londres: Oxford University Press, 1964.

Miller, H. S. *General Biblical Introduction.* Houghton: The Word-Bearer Press, 1959.

Neff, David. «A Translation Fit for a King» en *Christianity Today*, 22 octubre 2001, pp. 37–75.

__________. «The Great Translation Debate» en *Christianity Today,* 27 octubre 1997, pp. 16–17.

Nestle, Eberhard. *Novum Testamentum Graece.* Nueva York: American Bible Society, 1960.

Osborne, Grant R. «Do Inclusive-Language Bibles Distort Scripture? No» en *Christianity Today,* 27 octubre 1997, pp. 33–38.

*Riobueno, Luis. *Biblia textual: Reina Valera.* Pembroke Pines: Sociedad Bíblica Iberoamericana, sin fecha.

Robertson, A. T. *An Introduction to the Textual Criticism of the New Testament.* Nashville: Broadman Press, 1925.

Twilley, L. D. *The Origin and Transmission of the New Testament.* Grand Rapids: Eerdmans, 1959.

Van Leeuwen, Raymond C. «We Really Do Need Another Translation» en *Christianity Today*, 22 octubre 2001, pp. 28–35.

Vos, Howard F., ed. *Can I Trust the Bible?* Chicago: Moody Press, 1968.

Waltke, Bruce K. «The Textual Criticism of the Old Testament» en *Biblical Criticism: Historical, Literary and Textual*, ed. R. K. Harrison *et. al.* Grand Rapids: Zondervan, 1978, pp. 47–82.

Watson, Douglas. Notas de clase dadas en la asignatura de Introducción bíblica en la Columbia International University c. 1962.

Williams, Peter J. «Textual Criticism» en *Dictionary of the Old Testament: Pentateuch*, ed. T. Desmond Alexander y David W. Baker. Downers Grove: InterVarsity Press, 2003, pp. 834–841.

Würhwein, Ernst. *The Text of the Old Testament.* Grand Rapids: Eerdmans, 1979.

Youngblood, Ronald F. «The Process: How We Got Our Bible» en *Christianity Today*, 5 febrero 1988, pp. 24–28.

## EL MÉTODO HISTÓRICO-GRAMÁTICO-CULTURAL

Tolar, William. B. «The Grammatical-Historical Method» en *Biblical Hermeneutics*, ed. Bruce Corley, Steve Lemke y Grant Lovejoy. Nashville: Broadman & Holman, 1996, pp. 218–234.

Waltke, Bruce K. «Historical Grammatical Problems» en *Hermeneutics, Inerrancy, and the Bible*, ed. Earl D. Radmacher y Robert D. Preus. Grand Rapids: Zondervan, 1984, pp. 69–129.

## GÉNEROS LITERARIOS

Alter, Robert. «The Poetic and Wisdom Books» en *The Cambridge Companion to Biblical Interpretation*, ed. John Barton. Cambridge: Cambridge University Press, 1998, pp. 226–240.

Fee, Gordon D. «The Genre of New Testament Literature and Biblical Hermeneutics» en *Interpreting the Word of God*, ed. Samuel J. Schultz y Morris A. Inch. Chicago: Moody Press, 1970, pp. 105–127.

*Fee, Gordon D. y Stuart, Douglas. *La lectura eficaz de la Biblia*. Miami: Editorial Vida, 1985.

Feinberg, John S. «Literary Forms and Inspiration» en *Cracking Old Testament Codes*, ed. Brent Sandy y Ronald Giese. Nashville: Broadman & Holman, 1995, pp. 45–67.

Fields, Leslie Leyland. «Gospel is More Than Story» en *Christianity Today*, julio-agosto 2012, pp. 39–43.

Giese, Ronald L. «Literary Forms of the Old Testament» en *Cracking Old Testament Codes*, ed. Brent Sandy y Ronald Giese. Nashville: Broadman & Holman, 1995, pp. 5–67.

Kaiser, Walter C. «Narrative» en *Cracking Old Testament Codes*, ed. Brent Sandy y Ronald Giese. Nashville: Broadman & Holman, 1995, pp. 69–88.

Longman III, Tremper. *Literary Approaches to Biblical Interpretation*, vol. 3. Grand Rapids: Zondervan, 1987.

__________. «Biblical Narrative» en *A Complete Literary Guide to the Bible*, ed. Leland Ryken y Tremper Longman III. Grand Rapids: Zondervan, 1993, pp. 69–79.

__________. «Biblical Poetry» en *A Complete Literary Guide to the Bible*, ed. Leland Ryken y Tremper Longman III. Grand Rapids: Zondervan, 1993, pp. 80–94.

Pratt Jr., Richard L. *He Gave Us Stories*. Phillipsburg: Presbyterian and Reformed Publishing Company, 1993.

Ryken, Leland. *Words of Delight: A Literary Introduction to the Bible*. Grand Rapids: Baker, 2003.

__________. «The Bible as Literature: A Brief History» en *A Complete Literary Guide to the Bible*, ed. Leland Ryken y Tremper Longman III. Grand Rapids: Zondervan, 1993, pp. 49–68.

__________. «Bible as Literature» en *Foundations for Biblical Interpretation*, ed. David S. Dockery, Kenneth A. Mathews y Robert B. Sloan. Nashville: Broadman & Holman, 1994, pp. 55–72.

Ryken, Leland y Tremper Longman III, eds. *A Complete Literary Guide to the Bible*. Grand Rapids: Zondervan, 1993.

Sandy, Brent y Ronald Griese, eds. *Cracking the Old Testament Codes*. Nashville: Broadman & Holman 1995.

*Schökel, L. Alonso. *Hermenéutica de la Palabra: interpretación literaria de textos bíblicos*, vol. II. Madrid: Ediciones Cristiandad, 1987.

Stein, Robert H. *A Basic Guide to Interpreting the Bible.* Grand Rapids: Baker, 1994.

Woodard, Branson y Michael E. Travers. «Literary Forms and Interpretation» en *Cracking Old Testament Codes*, ed. Brent Sandy y Ronald Giese. Nashville: Broadman & Holman, 1995, pp. 29–43.

## TRASFONDO HISTÓRICO-CULTURAL

Blaicklock, E. M. «The Use of Archaeology in Interpretation» en *Hermeneutics*, eds. Bernard Ramm *et al.* Grand Rapids: Baker, 1972, pp. 54–66.

Govier, Gordon. «Bible in One Hand, Spade in the Other» en *Christianity Today*, noviembre 2011, pp. 49–52.

Jennings, J. E. «Ancient Near Eastern Religion and Biblical Interpretation» en *Interpreting the Word of God*, ed. Samuel J. Schultz y Morris A. Inch. Chicago: Moody Press, 1970, pp. 11–30.

Keener, Craig S. *The IVP Bible Background Commentary: New Testament.* Downers Grove: InterVarsity Press, 1993.

Walton, John H. «Cultural Background of the Old Testament» en *Foundations for Biblical Interpretation*, ed. David S. Dockery, Kenneth A. Mathews y Robert B. Sloan. Nashville: Broadman & Holman, 1994, pp. 255–273.

Yamauchi, Edwin M. *The Stones and the Scriptures.* Filadelfia: Lippincott, 1972.

## EL PROPÓSITO Y PLAN DIVINO

Bass, Clarence B. *Backgrounds to Dispensationalism.* Grand Rapids: Baker, 1960.

Blaising, Craig A. y Darrell L. Bock. *Progressive Dispensationalism.* Grand Rapids: Baker, 1993.

Poythress, Vern S. *Understanding Dispensationalists.* Phillipsburg: R & R Publishing, 1994.

*Ryrie, Charles R. *Dispensacionalismo hoy.* Barcelona: Portavoz Evangélico, 1974.

## LENGUAJE FIGURADO

Caird, G. B. *The Language and Imagery of the Bible.* Filadelfia: Westminster Press, 1980.

## PARÁBOLAS

Arnot, William. *Parables of our Lord.* Grand Rapids: Kregel, 1981.
__________. *The Lesser Parables of our Lord.* Grand Rapids: Kregel, 1981.
*Bailey, Kenneth E. *Las parábolas de Lucas.* Miami: Editorial Vida, 2009.
__________. *Poet and Peasant: A Literary Cultural Approach to the Parables in Luke.* Grand Rapids: Eerdmans, 1976.
Blomberg, Craig L. *Interpreting the Parables.* Downers Grove: InterVarsity Press, 1990.
Bruce, Alexander B. *The Parabolic Teaching of Christ.* Nueva York: George H. Doran Company, 1884.
Buttrick, David. *Speaking Parables.* Louisville: Westminster/John Knox Press, 2000.
Buttrick, George A. *The Parables of Jesus.* Grand Rapids: Baker, 1979.
Calderwood, Henry. *The Parables of Our Lord.* Londres: Macmillan, 1880.
*Cruz, Antonio. *Parábolas de Jesús en el mundo postmoderno.* Tarrasa: CLIE, 1998.
Dodd, C. H. *The Parables of the Kingdom.* Londres: The Religious Book Club, 1942. Ha sido publicado con el título *Las parábolas del reino.* Madrid: Ediciones Cristiandad.
Dods, Marcus. *The Parables of Our Lord (The Parables Recorded by St. Matthew).* Londres: Hodder and Stoughton, 1908.
Findlay, J. Alexander. *Jesus and His Parables.* Londres: The Epworth Press, 1950.
*Fricke S., Roberto. *Las parábolas de Jesús.* El Paso: Editorial Mundo Hispano, 2005.
*Guerra, Eduardo. *La parábola del buen samaritano.* Tarrasa: CLIE, 1999.
Habershon, Ada R. *The Study of the Parables.* Grand Rapids: Kregel, 1975.

Hanko, Herman C. *The Mysteries of the Kingdom: An Exposition of the Parables.* Grand Rapids: Reformed Free Publishing Associaton, 1991.

Hendrickx, Herman. *The Parables of Jesus.* San Francisco: Harper & Row, 1986.

Hultgren, Arland J. *The Parables of Jesus.* Grand Rapids: Eerdmans, 2000.

*Jeremias, Joachim. *Las parábolas de Jesús.* Estella: Verbo Divino, 1981.

Keach, Benjamin. *Exposition of the Parables.* Grand Rapids: Kregel, 1974.

Kendall, R. T. *The Complete Guide to the Parables.* Grand Rapids: Chosen Book (Baker), 2004.

Lang, G. H. *The Parabolic Teaching of Scripture.* Grand Rapids: Eerdmans, 1956.

Lockyer, Herbert. *All the Parables of the Bible.* Grand Rapids: Zondervan, 1969. Ha sido publicado con el título *Todas las parábolas de la Biblia.* Miami: Editorial Vida.

Longenecker, Richard N., ed. *The Challenge of Jesus' Parables.* Grand Rapids: Eerdmans, 2000.

McFadyen, J. F. *The Message of the Parables.* Londres: James Clarke & Company, sin fecha.

*McQuilkin, Robert C. *«Explícanos...»: estudios en las parábolas del Señor.* San José: Editorial Caribe, 1966, segunda serie. La primera serie introduce el tema del estudio de las parábolas y comenta unas parábolas no tratadas en la segunda.

Morgan, G. Campbell. *The Parables and Metaphors of our Lord.* Londres: Marshall, Morgan & Scott Ltd., 1944.

__________. *The Parables of the Kingdom.* Londres: Hodder and Stoughton, 1907.

*Neal, C. L. *Parábolas del evangelio.* El Paso: Casa Bautista, 1986.

Seagren, Dan. *The Parables.* Wheaton: Tyndale House, 1979.

*Sider, John W. *Interpretar las parábolas.* Madrid: San Pablo, 1997.

Snodgrass, Klyne. *Stories with Intent: A Comprehensive Guide to the Parables of Jesus.* Grand Rapids: Eerdmans, 2008.

__________. «From Allegorizing to Allegorizing: A History of the Interpretation of the Parables of Jesus» en *The Challenge of Jesus' Parables*, ed. Richard N. Longenecker. Grand Rapids: Eerdmans, 2000, pp. 3–29.

Stein, Robert H. *An Introduction to the Parables of Jesus.* Filadelfia: Westminster Press, 1981.

__________. «The Genre of the Parables» en *The Challenge of Jesus' Parables*, ed. Richard N. Longenecker. Grand Rapids: Eerdmans, 2000, pp. 30–50.

Taylor, William M. *The Parables of Our Saviour.* Grand Rapids: Kregel, 1975.

Trench, Richard Chenevix. *Notes on the Parables of Our Lord.* Nueva York: D. Appleton & Company, 1850. En 1965 Baker Book House (Grand Rapids) publicó esta obra de Trench en forma reducida, eliminando varios elementos del original, como la tercera parte de las notas bibliográficas que aparecían en griego, latín, francés y alemán.

*Wallace, David H. «Interpretación de parábolas» en *Diccionario de la teología práctica: hermenéutica*, ed. Rodolfo G. Turnbull. Grand Rapids: Subcomisión Literatura Cristiana de la Iglesia Cristiana Reformada, 1984, pp. 20–26.

## SÍMBOLOS

*Bullinger, Ethelbert W. *Cómo entender y explicar los números de la Biblia.* Tarrasa: CLIE, 1990.

Witherington III, Ben. «A Cracked Code» en *Christianity Today*, 12 julio 1999, p. 60.

## TIPOS

Fairbairn, Patrick. *The Typology of Scripture*, Tomo I. Nueva York: Fund & Wagnallis, 1900.

Goppelt, Leonhard. *Types.* Grand Rapids: Eerdmans, 1982.

La Sor, William Sanford. «The *Sensus Plenior* and Biblical Interpretation» en *A Guide to Contemporary Hermeneutics*, ed. Donald K. McKim. Grand Rapids: Eerdmans, 1986, pp. 47–64.

*Laurin, Robert B. «Interpretación tipológica del Antiguo Testamento» en *Diccionario de la teología práctica: hermenéutica*, ed. Rodolfo G. Turnbull. Grand Rapids: Subcomisión Literatura Cristiana de la Iglesia Cristiana Reformada, 1984, pp. 75–82.

__________. «Typological Interpretation of the Old Testament» en *Hermeneutics*, eds. Bernard Ramm *et al.* Grand Rapids: Baker, 1972.

Poythess, Vern S. *The Shadow of Christ in the Law of Moses.* Phillipsburg: P & R Publishing, 1991.

Rad, Gerhard von. «Typological Interpretation of the Old Testament» en *A Guide to Contemporary Hermeneutics*, ed. Donald K. McKim. Grand Rapids: Eerdmans, 1986, pp. 28–46.

Woollcombe, K. J. «The Biblical Origins and Patristic Development of Typology» en *Essays on Typology.* Naperville: Alec R. Allenson, Inc., 1957, pp. 39–75.

## PROFECÍA

*Andreu, Ginés y Santiago Giordano, eds. «Carta abierta a los ancianos y estudiosos de la Biblia». Los editores eran ancianos de Asambleas de Hermanos en Barcelona cuando publicaron este librito, el cual contiene artículos por John Sanderson, Ernesto Trenchard y unas breves observaciones por Andreu y Giordano.

Armerding, Carl E. y W. Ward Gasque, eds. *Dreams, Visions, and Oracles.* Grand Rapids: Baker, 1977.

*Benware, Paul N. *Entienda la profecía de los últimos tiempos.* Grand Rapids: Portavoz, 2010.

Berkhof, Louis. *The Kingdom of God.* Grand Rapids: Eerdmans, 1951.

Blackstone, W. E. *Jesus Is Coming*. Chicago: Fleming H. Revell, 1908.

Culver, Robert D. «The Difficulty of Interpreting Old Testament Prophecy». Este artículo fue publicado originalmente en *Biblioteca Sacra* en julio de 1957 y luego distribuido a los estudiantes de la asignatura de Escatología en la Trinity Evangelical Divinity School c. 1966.

Erickson, Millard J. *Contemporary Options in Eschatology: A Study of the Millennium.* Grand Rapids: Baker, 1977.

Grenz, Stanley J. «The 1,000-Year Question» en *Christianity Today*, 8 marzo 1993, pp. 32–34.

Gundry, Robert H. *The Church and the Tribulation.* Grand Rapids: Zondervan, 1973.

Howard, Tracy L. «The Use of Hosea 11:1 in Matthew 2:15» en *Vital Biblical Issues*, ed. Roy B. Zuck. Grand Rapids: Kregel, 1994, pp. 86–87.

*La Sor, William Sanford. «Interpretación de profecías» en *Diccionario de la teología práctica: hermenéutica*, ed. Rodolfo G. Turnbull. Grand Rapids: Subcomisión Literatura Cristiana de la Iglesia Cristiana Reformada, 1984, pp. 60–74.

Ladd, George Eldon. *The Blessed Hope*. Grand Rapids: Eerdmans, 1966.

MacPherson, David. *The Incredible Cover-Up*. Plainfield, NJ: Logos International, 1975.

Pate, C. Marvin, ed. *Four Views on the Book of Revelation*. Grand Rapids: Zondervan, 1998.

*Pentecost, J. Dwight. *Eventos del porvenir*. Venezuela: Editorial Libertador, 1977.

Walvoord, John F. *The Rapture Question*. Findlay, OH: Dunham Publishing Co., 1957.

## LA APLICACIÓN DE LAS ESCRITURAS

Branson, Mark y C. René Padilla, eds. *Conflict and Context, Hermeneutics in the Americas*. Grand Rapids: Eerdmans, 1986.

Carson, Donald A. (ed.). «A Sketch of the Factors Determining Current Hermeneutical Debate in Cross-Cultural Contexts» en *Biblical Interpretation and the Church*. Carlisle: Paternoster Press, 1984, pp. 11–29.

Doriani, Daniel M. *Getting the Message: A Plan for Interpreting and Applying the Bible*. Phillipsburg: R & R Publishing, 1996.

__________. *Putting the Truth to Work: The Theory and Practice of Biblical Application*. Phillipsburg: R & R Publishing, 2001.

*García Ruiz, Máximo. «Teología de la liberación». Estudio inédito en España de 13 páginas.

*Grau, José. «Teología de la liberación». Estudio inédito en España de 16 páginas.

Harrisville, Roy y Walter Sundberg. *The Bible in Modern Culture*. Grand Rapids: Eerdmans, 1995.

Hitt, Russell T. «The Latin America Experience» en *Eternity*, noviembre 1975, pp. 14–17.

Keener, Craig S. «Veils, Kisses, and Biblical Commands» en *Christianity Today*, 26 octubre 1998, p. 90.

Kuhatschek, Jack. *Taking the Guesswork out of Applying the Bible.* Downers Grove: InterVarsity Press, 1990.

Kuhn, Harold B. «More on Libertation Theology» en *Christianity Today*, 4 noviembre 1977, pp. 66–67.

Larkin, William J. *Culture and Biblical Hermeneutics.* Grand Rapids: Baker, 1988.

Leggett, Paul y Juan Stam. «Listening to Latin America – Communication Across Cultures» en *Christianity Today*, 24 septiembre 1976, pp. 14–16.

McQuilkin, Robertson. *Understanding and Applying the Bible.* Chicago: Moody Press, 1992.

__________. «Problems of Normativeness in Scripture: Cultural Versus Permanent» en *Hermeneutics, Inerrancy, and the Bible*, ed. Earl D. Radmacher y Robert D. Preus. Grand Rapids: Zondervan, 1984, pp. 210–240.

Nuñez, Emilio A. «The Church in the Liberation Theology of Gutiérrez: Description and Hermeneutical Analysis» en *Biblical Interpretation and the Church*, ed. Donald A. Carson. Carlisle: Paternoster Press, 1984, pp. 166–194.

Padilla, C. René. «The Interpreted Word: Reflections on Contextual Hermeneutics» en *A Guide to Contemporary Hermeneutics*, ed. Donald K. McKim. Grand Rapids: Eerdmans, 1986, pp. 297–308.

Pinnock, Clark H. «Our Audience: Atheist or Alienated?» en *Conflict and Context, Hermeneutics in the Americas*, eds. Mark Branson y C. René Padilla. Grand Rapids: Eerdmans, 1986, pp. 37–51.

__________. «Liberation Theology: The Gains, the Gaps» en *Christianity Today*, 16 enero 1976, pp. 13–15.

Roberts, W. Dayton. «Where Has Liberation Theology Gone Wrong?» en *Christianity Today*, 19 octubre 1979, pp. 26–27.

Robinson, Haddon. «The Heresy of Application» en *Leadership*, otoño 1997, pp. 21–27.

Veenker, Judy. «Culture Clash» en *Christianity Today*, 10 julio 2000, pp. 19–20.

Webb, William J. *Slaves, Women and Homosexuals: Exploring the Hermeneutics of Cultural Analysis.* Downers Grove: InterVarsity Press, 2001.

Wright, C. J. H. «Learning to Love Leviticus» en *Christianity Today*, julio–agosto 2013.

Zuck, Roy B. «Application in Biblical Hermeneutics and Exposition» en *Rightly Divided*, ed. Rob B. Zuck. Grand Rapids: Kregel, 1996, pp. 278–296.